501

Introduction to Psychotherapy

SECOND EDITION

Introduction to Psychotherapy

Common Clinical Wisdom

Randolph B. Pipes
Auburn University

Donna S. Davenport
Texas A&M University

Allyn and Bacon

Boston ▪ London ▪ Toronto ▪ Sydney ▪ Tokyo ▪ Singapore

Series Editorial Assistant: Susan Hutchinson
Manufacturing Buyer: Suzanne Lareau
Editorial-Production Service: Omegatype Typography, Inc.

Library of Congress Cataloging-in-Publication Data

Pipes, Randolph Berlin.
    Introduction to psychotherapy : common clinical wisdom / Randolph
B. Pipes and Donna S. Davenport. — 2nd ed.
        p.   cm.
    Includes bibliographical references and index.
    ISBN 0-205-29252-6
    1. Psychotherapy.   I. Davenport, Donna S.   II. Title.
    [DNLM: 1. Psychotherapy.   2. Physician-Patient Relations.   WM 420
P665i 1999]
RC480.P48   1999
616.89′14—dc21
DNLM/DLC
for Library of Congress   98-22426
                                                                              CIP

Printed in the United States of America

10   9   8   7   6   5   4   3   03   02   01

DEDICATION

To Anne, Greg, Velma, and Bebe, and to the memory of RB and Walter

—RBP

To Unkie Led, who is always there.

—DSD

CONTENTS

7 The Therapeutic Stance   196

8 Listening   213

9 Mistakes That Therapists Make   232

√
2-16

PREFACE

Much of what we said in the preface to the first edition remains applicable to the second edition. The primary emphasis remains on what we continue to call "common clinical wisdom"—ideas that are typically endorsed by a diversity of experienced counselors and psychotherapists. By using the phrase in the title of the book, we have obviously underscored our belief that there *is* such a thing as "common clinical wisdom." We have stated throughout the text, and we underscore here, our understanding that what we see as wisdom, others may see as misinformation or even folly. On the other hand, the feedback we received on the first edition suggested that readers by and large agreed with this idea of "common clinical wisdom."

Perhaps the major change in this edition is the increased emphasis in the text on cultural factors. In the eight years since we first published the book, there has been a virtual explosion of interest and research in cultural factors in psychotherapy. The Diagnostic and Statistical Manual (4th ed.; DSM-IV), places increased emphasis on cultural factors and, in general, the field is much more aware of, and interested in, placing human behavior in a cultural context (e.g., Alvidrez, Azocar, & Miranda, 1996). We have added a chapter on multicultural counseling and have throughout the text emphasized the role of culture in understanding human behavior. The text retains a broadly interpersonal and existential flavor—a perspective that, in our view, is, despite some exceptions, generally compatible with an emphasis on culture.

Because training agencies are increasingly emphasizing brief therapy, in a final chapter we very briefly summarize a few of the tenets of that orientation to psychotherapy. In several places throughout the book we have noted how issues under discussion may be impacted by the constraints of brief therapy. We encourage students (and practitioners and professors who haven't done so already) to read some literature in the area of brief therapy. Whatever your theoretical orientation, and wherever you work, it is highly likely that you will be influenced by pressures to make therapy efficient, if not efficient *and* brief.

Other changes to the text include expansion of the ethics chapter, adding discussion questions at the end of each chapter, substantially updating the references, and reformatting the chapters in response to feedback. Additionally, we have elaborated and clarified many points of discussion, included new examples, and "cleaned up" outdated language.

The book is about individual counseling and psychotherapy. We make no attempt to discuss other models such as group therapy or family therapy, although much of what we say is applicable to those areas also. In fact, the literature on group therapy has long emphasized the role of common curative factors in psychotherapy.

We do not attempt to discuss theory at great length; we assume some familiarity with theories of counseling and psychotherapy. We do make some theoretical assumptions (discussed in the Introduction), but perhaps our first assumption is that psychotherapy generally does produce positive change. In the first edition, we noted research supporting this conclusion (e.g., Howard, Kopta, Krause, & Orlinsky, 1986; Shapiro & Shapiro, 1982; Smith, Glass, & Miller, 1980). Influential writing since that time (e.g., Lambert & Bergin, 1994; Seligman, 1995; Wampold, Mondin, Moody, Stich, Benson, & Ahn, 1997) continues to justify this conclusion.

A number of chapters in this book are developed around issues traditional to the introductory text—for example, Listening, Resistance, and Termination. We have also added other material not generally found in introductory texts. After the Introduction, we begin with a lengthy chapter that attempts to address in practical and straightforward terms many of the questions beginning therapists ask. For the second edition, we have added several questions and refined answers to old ones based on new literature and feedback from colleagues and students. Late in the text, we include two chapters, Responsibility and Relationships, which we hope will give students an example of how experienced therapists think about broad therapeutic issues. (Like other chapters in the book, these two take an interpersonal and existential perspective, broadly speaking.) Chapters on Client Fears, Therapist Fears, and Mistakes Therapists Make are also included. Typically, book chapters have not been devoted to these important areas.

We have tried to write the book the way we do supervision. In part, this means that some issues are emphasized in more than one chapter. Our experience has been that ideas used in the supervision of psychotherapy are closely intertwined and are not easily compartmentalized—as if there were predetermined fault lines. Also consistent with our supervisory style, we attempt to have an ongoing, informal mix of specific practical ideas and somewhat eclectic conceptualization having primary roots in interpersonal and existential theory.

There is debate, much of it cultural and political in our view, as to the difference (if there is one) between counseling and psychotherapy. We use the terms more or less interchangeably.

The examples we give are a mixture of actual cases and constructed ones. They include examples that are mixtures of several different cases, as well as ones completely fabricated to illustrate a point. Any actual cases involving sensitive, identifiable elements have been altered to ensure anonymity.

It has been our goal to avoid discriminatory language—words do make a difference. We have included a few quotes that contain sexist language, but we have alerted the reader to the problematic nature of the terminology.

In the preface to the first edition, we suggested that in our writing we had tried to be clear when something was our opinion—rather than fact—and that we had tried to include opinions differing from, and evidence raising questions about, our positions. Reexamination of the text suggests that we were perhaps not altogether successful in doing this. Perhaps it would be a little more accurate to say that we have tried to indicate when there are varying positions, but we make no pretense at having identified all areas of controversy. Had we wanted to do this, and been successful at it, this would have produced a book much too long. Similarly, not all points of view have been equally explored and defended.

Acknowledgments

Our thanks to the following reviewers for their helpful comments: Rodney Good-year, Russ Allison, and Patricia Sakai of the University of Southern California; Arthur Horne, University of Georgia; and Cynthia Kalodner, West Virginia University. Thanks to Sean Wakely and Susan Hutchinson at Allyn and Bacon; also, to Elydia Davis at Solar Script, Inc., and Susan Krusemark at Omegatype for editorial services in the production of this second edition.

DSD: I would especially like to thank Earl Koile. My contact with him over the last 25 years has continued to be as stimulating and supportive as it was when I entered the University of Texas doctoral program and met him for my first counseling course. He has served as an invaluable mentor as I have grown professionally and taken on various roles, and I count on his continued availability until I retire!

Several of the students I have worked with over the years have enriched my life both personally and professionally, particularly Shelly Merkle and Tammi Vacha-Haase. In addition, a number of colleagues at Texas A&M have provided support and challenge that has contributed to my professional growth.

And finally, thanks to my family members—especially my mother and my son—and my friend Maree. Your support and encouragement through all the years has been my haven.

RBP: My thanks to those colleagues and students whose ideas have crept into this book without my knowledge, to Holly Stadler for the administrative support she has provided, and to Becky Liddle for helpful feedback which influenced some of our comments in Chapter 2. Thanks also to a number of people who in one way or another have influenced me and my thinking about how life should be lived and how psychotherapy should be conducted: Ollie Bown, Collie and Jane Conoley, Lucia Gilbert, Earl Higgins, Earl Koile, Mark Kunkel, Phil Lewis, Marylu McEwen, Gene Meadows, Frank Richardson, and John Westefeld.

Having good parents is the best foundation for any project, including writing a book—my thanks to my parents for getting me started. To Greg: Thanks for your help on the book. You have a terrific sense of humor and a very kind heart. For all that you are, and for our relationship, I am thankful. Finally, my love, appreciation, and deepest thanks to Anne. Her ideas, her support, her time, and her love have made writing both editions possible. For the shortcomings in what I have written, I am responsible; for all else, Anne shares the credit.

REFERENCES

Alvidrez, J., Azocar, F., & Miranda, J. (1996). Demystifying the concept of ethnicity for psychotherapy researchers. *Journal of Consulting and Clinical Psychology, 64,* 903–908.

Howard, K. I., Kopta, S. M., Krause, M. S., & Orlinsky, D. E. (1986). The dose-effect relationship in psychotherapy. *American Psychologist, 41,* 159–164.

Lambert, M. J., & Bergin, A. E. (1994). The effectiveness of psychotherapy. In A. E. Bergin & S. L. Garfield (Eds.), *Handbook of psychotherapy and behavior change* (4th ed., pp. 143–189). New York: Wiley.

Seligman, M. E. P. (1995). The effectiveness of psychotherapy: The *Consumer Reports* study. *American Psychologist, 50,* 965–974.

Shapiro, D. A., & Shapiro, D. (1982). Meta-analysis of comparative outcome studies: A replication and refinement. *Psychological Bulletin, 92,* 581–604.

Smith, N. L., Glass, G. V., & Miller, T. I. (1980). *Benefits of psychotherapy.* Baltimore: Johns Hopkins University Press.

Wampold, B., Mondin, G. W., Moody, M., Stich, F., Benson, K., & Ahn, H. (1997). A meta-analysis of outcome studies comparing bonafide psychotherapies: Empirically, "all must have prizes." *Psychological Bulletin, 122,* 203–215.

1 Introduction: A View of Psychotherapy

Owing to an egg's shape, a beast banging on it from the outside will have great trouble breaking it open. But the slightest tap from inside the shell can shatter it; when the chick is ready it can pop out and get started. Nature in its selective wisdom thus favors the new generation—for instance, the unborn ostrich over a pride of lions, who can slam an egg halfway across the Serengeti without being able to open it. Nearly all the leverage is from within.

By the same token, a patient, any *patient, tapping even lightly, can accomplish more personality change than even the best therapist working alone from the outside.*

…Beyond our offering warmth and insights, we must find places where each patient can tap, even gently, against the surface of [the] container. We encourage effort. But only by the patient's own exertions of will, by his or her acts, can real change be produced.

—George Weinberg

Everyone has won and all must have prizes.

—the Dodo, from *Alice in Wonderland*

Dolly T. was a 46-year-old music teacher whose personal traumas were substantial. In the process of our work together, she gradually reconstructed memories of having been physically and sexually abused by her father. Months later, it also became apparent to her that her mother had colluded in her abuse, at first by not protecting her from her father and later by sexually abusing her herself. Dolly's pain was excruciating. She struggled with suicidal depression and feelings of hopelessness for a long time. I struggled along with her, not knowing what I could do to ease her pain or to accelerate her psychological movement. In the course of all of this, Dolly became increasingly interested in spiritual works on the phenomenon of reincarnation. Over many months, her own spirits began to lift as she developed an elaborate scaffolding of past lives in which she believed that she had been both the victim and perpetrator of abuses. She consulted a mystic, who encouraged her dawning awareness.

Meanwhile, I changed my academic home. Accepting an offer from another university forced me to inform Dolly that our work together would have to end. I explored possibilities for her referral and eventually recommended a local counselor who was relatively liberal in the realm of religious and spiritual scaffolding. Dolly was not happy that I was leaving, but she later reported very positive results from her work with this transpersonal counselor.

I was, to say the least, relieved. At the same time, however, I was challenged. If the circumstances had been different, and I had remained her counselor, what could or should I have done? Given the limitations of my own spiritual education and personal experience, I was not prepared to openly accept or affirm her constructions about reincarnation and karma. At the same time, however, I had developed enough self-awareness and epistemological conscience to realize that I could not claim any guaranteed (authorized) warrant for rejecting or discouraging her conceptual scaffolding. Who was I to tell her that her mystical explorations were not acceptable or healthy in her attempts to organize the experience of having been abused by both of her parents? (from Mahoney, 1995, pp. 393–394)

This brief summary raises profound questions about psychotherapy. What is the effect of early trauma on subsequent personality development? How are we to make sense of "recovered" or "delayed" memories? What is it that therapists do to facilitate the healing process? To what extent can individuals who suffer early or serious trauma expect to transcend the influence of such trauma? Can successful accommodation to environmentally imposed stress include the adoption of religious practices that are quite dissimilar to the client's cultural background? By what standards should we judge the outcome of psychotherapy? What does healthy behavior look like? What is the relationship between spiritual matters and psychotherapy? To what extent do, and in what way should, the values of the psychotherapist influence the values and the life of the client?

It is in part questions such as these that make psychotherapy an exciting, complicated, and challenging endeavor. Although this book is not intended to answer the above questions, we do intend that the book serve as a stimulus for you to consider questions of this type, as well as to consider more practical ones, such as (for the opening vignette): What was the therapist's responsibility when he learned that he was leaving? How should one go about identifying a person to whom the client could be referred? How likely is it that the client will be very upset to learn that her or his therapist will be moving?

A part of the complexity of psychotherapy is that whether it is to last 1 session or 600, its finest interventions cannot be scripted. The therapist has to know what to do, but perhaps even more importantly, the therapist has to know *when* to do it. An example from Irving Yalom's (1989) book, *Love's Executioner,* is a powerful reminder of the difficulty of writing a manual for psychotherapy:

Alongside her [the client's] love for her father, she also had negative feelings; she felt ashamed of him, of his appearance (he was extremely obese), of his lack of ambition and education, of his ignorance of social amenities. As she said this, Betty broke down and sobbed. It was so hard to talk about this, she said, because she was so ashamed of being ashamed of her own father.

As I searched for a reply, I remembered something my first analyst, Olive Smith, said to me over thirty years before. (I remember it well, I think, because it was the only remotely personal—and the most helpful—thing she said in my six hundred hours with her.) I had been badly shaken by having expressed some monstrous feelings about my mother, and Olive Smith leaned over the couch and said gently, "That just seems to be the way we're built." (pp. 112–113)

Yalom's analyst was not exactly being empathic and she was not offering an interpretation. Instead, she was offering a kind of forgiveness transmitted by stating her understanding of a psychological fact. What made that intervention so powerful for Yalom perhaps cannot be completely specified, but in part it was powerful because it was said at exactly the right time.

This issue of how the therapist is to know the *right* moment is an example of why psychotherapy—particularly if it is to last more than a few sessions—resists being manualized. The difficulty lies in specifying what the therapist is to do, at what time, in a complex and dynamic interpersonal relationship whose goal includes struggling with terrifying feelings and tangled motivations. This does not mean that research is not helpful. Although psychotherapists most certainly share some common ground with witch doctors, we believe that the scientist–practitioner model (e.g., Bernstein & Kerr, 1993; Beutler, Williams, & Wakefield, 1995; Davison, 1998; Howard, 1986) is better than the witch doctor model of helping. We believe that research does indeed produce ideas that can be used by practitioners. Unfortunately, this process can be agonizingly slow.

In J. R. R. Tolkien's *Lord of the Rings* (1965), the following interchange takes place:

Frodo: "Now I am wondering what can have happened. Should I wait for him?"

Gildor was silent for a moment. "I do not like this news," he said at last.... "The choice is yours: to go or wait."

"And it is also said," answered Frodo, "go not to the Elves for counsel, for they will answer both no and yes."

"Is it indeed," laughed Gildor. "Elves seldom give unguarded advice, for advice is a dangerous gift, even from the wise to the wise, and all courses may run ill. But what would you? You have not told me all concerning yourself; and how then shall I choose better than you?" (p. 123)

Tolkien understood one of the central dialectics that runs through Western psychotherapy. On the one hand is the urge to instruct clients in some better way of living their lives, the inclination to point out how clients can better fit some external reality, and/or improve their rationality. On the other hand is a set of more ambiguous inclinations centered around some sort of trust in the client to achieve satisfaction within a reality created by the client and nurtured by the therapist (e.g., Neimeyer & Mahoney, 1996). Most typically in this view, clients are fundamentally seen as participating in and profiting from an interpersonal experience more than from receiving information or being persuaded about something.

In his imperfect way, Gildor may be said to represent therapists who are reluctant to use "absolute reality" as a frame for all clients. Gildor is reluctant to point out pitfalls or issue warnings right away. Despite the potential drawbacks of his position, the view of psychotherapy endorsed in this book, although integrative, is quite sympathetic to the philosophy expressed by Gildor.

As we said in the preface, this is not a psychotherapy theories book. We are not trying to build a theory. However, as we briefly describe below, and so the reader can understand our biases, we suggest that we are influenced by a variety of theorists, with perhaps slightly more emphasis on the interpersonal school of psychotherapy. Like many other therapists, we are integrative and eclectic in our approach, although we make no attempt to develop formally an eclectic framework (Beutler, Consoli, & Williams, 1995).

Focus of Therapy: The Person or the Environment

Presumably, one of the characteristics of all human cultures is that within the culture, there are certain people, at certain times, who exhibit and/or report an undesirable (to them) state of affairs in terms of their perceptions, thoughts, behavior, or emotions, or some combination thereof. These may or may not be undesirable to others. Presumably, it is also a characteristic of each culture that certain processes, procedures, and structures are both made available to and at times imposed upon the individual in order to deal with these perceived problems. This book is about one such process—we call it psychotherapy or counseling.

Although there are various ways by which people may achieve satisfaction with regard to these perceptions, thoughts, feelings, and behavior, one can identify two more or less inclusive broad paths: (a) individuals can make changes in themselves, or (b) individuals can alter their environment. As we see it, psychotherapy is concerned with each of these categories both individually and in interaction. In practice, psychotherapy is almost always some interaction between these two categories, chiefly for three reasons: (a) In outpatient psychotherapy, the therapist has access to the client's environment only through the client (an obvious exception is the client–therapist relationship itself, with the therapist *being* a part of the environment in that case); (b) We assume that individuals and their environments reciprocally influence each other; and (c) Complex problems typically require intervention at more than one level.

The psychotherapy we describe in this book is aimed first and foremost at enabling individuals to change themselves. This does not mean that we hold the environment to be of little consequence in terms of people's "good mental health." For example, if individuals are harassed at the office where they work because of their sexual orientation, their gender, or their race, we would scarcely be surprised when they begin to suffer psychological consequences. Obviously, such examples underscore the role the environment may play in pathology. Furthermore, from an interpersonal perspective, it is the interpersonal environment which is often responsible for the creation and/or maintenance of psychological difficulties. Thus, at one level, the book emphasizes the role of the environment. We also believe, however, that many individuals who come for therapy cannot initially make the kinds of changes that would be needed in their environment to facilitate maximally their mental health without first making some changes in how they view and experience themselves in relationship to their world.

Limits of Psychotherapy

Linda, a 38-year-old woman, sought help at a local community mental health center. She had no job, and had not graduated from high school. She currently lived with her physically and emotionally abusive husband, with whom she argued frequently. Linda reported that he would not let her work outside their home and that he was quite demanding of her. Linda had come to the center at the insistence of her mother, and her chief complaint at intake was her mother's lack of respect for her husband. She reported that her mother had been divorced three times and that she herself intended to make her own marriage work. The client's commitment to her marriage was rooted both in her personal vow to achieve what her mother had not (a marriage with no divorce), as well as in her strong religious commitment to avoid divorce. She believed that her husband would treat her much better once she was able to figure out his "moods." Linda's therapist was experienced and had an excellent reputation for establishing a strong therapeutic relationship with her clients. Following intake, Linda returned for two sessions of therapy, but she showed little insight into her relationship with her abusive husband and she evidenced little motivation to change her living situation. At the end of the third session, she announced that she no longer had time to come to therapy and that her mother had, at least temporarily, stopped pressuring her. Linda thanked the therapist for her kindness and did not return to therapy.

John, an 18-year-old college freshman sought therapy at the university counseling center in the small university town where he attended college and lived with his parents. He reported that he had little social life and on occasion he called himself a "dork." He said that he felt alienated from his parents, although he knew they loved him very much. He was in his second semester and had been placed on academic probation for his poor grades in the fall semester. John indicated that he was concerned that he might not do well this semester and he feared that he would subsequently be expelled from college. He reported that he felt as if life were passing him by. He said that he had been unhappy throughout much of high school and that this had continued into college. Psychological tests administered at intake suggested that he was very depressed, with some risk of suicide. Although the therapist could tell that the student was very distressed, it seemed impossible to identify any central problems. John was referred to a psychiatrist and was placed on an antidepressant. His mood briefly elevated following his going on medication, but just as quickly, he became depressed again. He was seen for the 10-session limit at the counseling center and was given a referral, although he indicated that he would likely not follow up for financial reasons. In his 10th and last session, John asked repeatedly about confidentiality and then revealed that he was quite certain that he was gay; he believed that his parents would be "crushed" if they knew his sexual orientation. He told the therapist that he had resigned himself to living "a lie" for at least the next four years (while he lived at home and attended college). The therapist suggested that he might be able to see him for a few more sessions to work on this new development in therapy. The client refused the offer, saying that he would never "betray" his parents and that he would just "live with the situation" at least until he had graduated. A little over one year later, the therapist was attending a local AIDS benefit during a holiday and happened to notice the same young man. John came over and spoke to the therapist, telling the therapist that he remembered being in therapy and wanted to say hello. The therapist asked him how he was doing and John said that he was doing "great." John had transferred to another college, had decided that his parents would survive knowing that he was gay, and had become active in an AIDS prevention program at his new university. He reported a sense of relief following "coming out," and his description of his new life suggested that he felt good about himself and found rewards in being invested in the gay community. John volunteered that, a few months after being in therapy, he saw a talk show on "coming out" and had been particularly impressed with the courage of several of the men. He had vowed to himself that he would no longer be, in his words, "a coward." Shortly thereafter he told his parents and, despite their acceptance of him and his sexual orientation, he chose to move out and transfer to another university. He apparently had good memories of his time in therapy, but he clearly attributed his decision and new behavior to the television program and the effects of seeing how other people who were gay were living their lives.

In each of the above examples, the client suffered in her or his life, yet psychotherapy, even though it was being conducted by a competent professional, did not seem to solve the problem. In Linda's case, psychotherapy reached its limits because the client had been pressured into coming to sessions and because she did not consider abuse to be a problem. In John's case, psychotherapy may or may not have been partially causal for the change, but it was not considered as such by the client.

One of the first lessons clients teach new psychotherapists is that when clients come to psychotherapy, they have reasons that make them want to keep doing what they are doing. At times, those reasons may be apparent to both therapist and client; at other times they are more hidden. In most cases these reasons include some direct or indirect "payoff" (sometimes great, often tragically small by more objective standards) for continuing life as is, as well as a fear of what will be if change is made. The client's understanding of her or his problem is likely to contain conscious and unconscious elements of pure fiction, mixed with absolutely correct assessments of the costs and benefits involved in changing or not changing.

There are many problems for which our tool for helping people change, psychotherapy, is simply not up to the task of contending with payoffs (often unconscious) that keep coming as long as there is no change and as long as there is fear of what will happen if there are changes. The problem of "payoffs and fears" is exacerbated by myriad other environmental, biological, and social impediments. After seeing a few "difficult" clients, psychotherapists usually come to appreciate the forces that are arrayed against them (and the client) in the pursuit of behavior change. These forces often seem powerful enough to prevent change despite clients' suffering so greatly and wanting so badly to have a different life. Somehow these persons, despite their struggle, may not be able to use psychotherapy to help themselves break free of their constricting and tormenting problems. One is reminded of the words attributed to Karl Menninger; he uses a beautifully simple, yet powerful metaphor, and we quote him here despite being unable to find the original source (and despite his use of the outdated pronoun "he" to mean both genders):

> When a trout, rising to a fly, gets hooked on a line and finds himself unable to swim about freely, he begins with a fight which results in struggles and splashes and sometimes an escape. Often, of course, the situation is too tough for him. In the same way the human being struggles with his environment and with the hooks that catch him. Sometimes he masters his difficulties; sometimes they are too much for him. His struggles are all that the world sees and it naturally misunderstands them. It is hard for a free fish to understand what is happening to a hooked one.

Psychotherapy is limited in a number of ways: by the fact that it seems to need cultural sanction, by biological factors such as pharmacological effects of drugs and clients' genetic endowment, by clients' childhood experiences, by the current environment in which they live, by our own expertise, by the small amount of actual time spent with the therapist, by the sheer complexity of some problems, and by chance. When we say that psychotherapy has limits, we are echoing the ideas of a diverse group of psychotherapists. In fact, the idea that psychotherapy has limits is a good example of common clinical wisdom. For example, Freud clearly recognized some of these limitations when he said that psychoanalysis was designed to turn neurosis into ordinary misery. The existential psychotherapists have also recognized the limits of psychotherapy by emphasizing the centrality of experiences that have powerful influences on us but which we cannot escape (e.g., death and freedom).

In our view, it is important to remember that change may be activated or enhanced by unpredictable and uncontrollable events (Miller, Hubble, & Duncan, 1995). For example, one's new supervisor may turn out to be a racist who discriminates against individuals of the client's ethnicity; one's child may contract a terminal illness; a lucrative position may become available just as one begins searching for a job; a tennis game between strangers may lead to a lasting friendship; or an individual may have the good fortune to be referred to an excellent psychotherapist. Such events obviously have profound effects upon people. Against the backdrop of the unpredictability of life, we should promise neither our clients nor ourselves more than may be possible. We must accept, not with resignation but with humility, that chance, more so than our own contributions, may play a part in our clients' lives.

Assumptions of the Book

We make a number of assumptions in this book. Implicit, though not discussed, are the following two: (a) Human beings are to some extent free and their behavior is not determined; and (b) Development is a life-long process that alters some, but not all, basic personality structures. We will also comment briefly on a number of other assumptions, including: (a) There is such a thing as common clinical wisdom; (b) Integrative and eclectic approaches to psychotherapy are increasingly the choice among practitioners; (c) There are common curative factors in all psychotherapies; (d) The interpersonal aspect of psychotherapy is one key to its power; (e) Culture and the family play a central role in mental health or the lack thereof; (f) Affect frequently plays a central role in psychotherapy; (g) The construct of the self is an important one in psychotherapy; (h) Early experience has a profound and lasting impact on personality development; (i) Toxic interpersonal experiences, although not always causal, often contribute significantly to psychopathology.

Common Clinical Wisdom

Perhaps the most important assumption in the book is that there is such a thing as common clinical wisdom. As we will say in more than one place, certainly one's theoretical orientation determines to some extent what one does, what one sees as important, and what one sees as mistakes. Despite this, we believe that good psychotherapists, whatever their theoretical orientation, use many of the same techniques and even conceptualizations. These range from almost universally accepted perceptions (for example, the idea that individuals tend to make progress in psychotherapy if they take appropriate responsibility for factors in their lives over which they have, or should have, some control) to principles of intervention (such as noting that allowing clients to talk mainly about others rather than about themselves rarely leads to behavior change). Other ideas expressed through common clinical wisdom include the advisability of encouraging some modicum of hope in the client, and the principle of avoiding punitiveness, rigidity, and judgmentalness in one's role as a psychotherapist. Beutler, Machado, and Neufeldt (1994) concluded that, "Among the therapist's subjective traits and states, consistent evidence exists to support the assertion (now nearly a "truism") that a warm and supportive therapeutic relationship facilitates therapeutic success…" (p. 259). Strupp (1996) has well expressed several ideas based on many years of conducting and researching psychotherapy. These included, but were not limited to:

> (a) Stimulate the patient's *curiosity* about him/herself and his/her interest in collaborating with you; (b) Listen for the *theme* or *themes* of the hour; (c) Be patient! *Patience* is the hallmark of a good therapist (especially when your patience is being tried!); (d) Pay close attention to your own feelings and reactions to the patient's communications; (e) Be aware of your own *limitations*; and (f) *Assiduously avoid criticisms and pejorative communications.* (italics in original; p. 137)

The sorts of ideas expressed by Strupp are ones accepted by a great many psychotherapists. Thus, they are a part of "common clinical wisdom." Although other therapists certainly emphasize somewhat different "lifetime lessons," surveying the comments of six well-known psychotherapists (including Strupp), Norcross (1996) concluded that "If there is an overarching commonality or super-ordinate theme to these six diverse articles it might be this: be flexible and integrative in clinical pursuits" (p. 130).

An idea related to common clinical wisdom is that psychotherapists *as a group* struggle with common problems or dilemmas. These include questions such as "To what extent should my values impact my clients' values (Beutler, Machado, & Neufeldt, 1994)?" "What should I do about a client who keeps coming to therapy but seems to be making no progress?" "When (if ever) should I allow my clients' problems to take serious precedence over my personal life?" "What action (if any) should I take if I know that my adult client is being physically abused?" Although one's answers to questions such as these are driven in part by theoretical considerations, we would argue that cultural values, logical thinking, common sense, and an overarching commitment to decency frequently determine our responses to our clients. In this book we attempt to grapple with some of the issues that seem to arise inevitably for psychotherapists.

Integrative and Eclectic Approaches

It now seems to be clear that of all theoretical orientations, the largest percentage of psychologists identify themselves as eclectic or integrative, and there appears to be increasing interest among psychologists in crossing theoretical boundaries when conceptualizing, practicing, and doing research in psychotherapy (Garfield & Bergin, 1994; Goldfried & Norcross, 1995; Norcross, 1997). To the extent that psychotherapy process is transtheoretical (in intent if not in label), the process-outcome research literature (e.g., Orlinsky, Grawe, & Parks, 1994) may be viewed as a kind of common factors (see below) approach to psychotherapy. Even though there are some important theoretical distinctions between approaches to psychotherapy identified as common factors, integrative, technical eclecticism, and eclecticism (Beutler, Consoli, & Williams, 1995), in this book we are not emphasizing those differences. By using these terms, we imply that many therapists draw on more than one theory, that they use techniques popularized by more than one theory, and they frequently agree with Beutler, Consoli, and Williams: "therapeutic procedures can be applied independently of the theories from which they were derived" (p. 275). In fact, well-known psychotherapists who are closely identified with a particular theory often describe what they actually did in a session from a perspective that is quite different from the one with which they are identified. For example, Yalom (1989), who has written extensively as an existential therapist, summarized a part of his work with one client this way:

> I used a rational approach to her guilt and her tenacious clinging to the memory of her daughter: I confronted her with the incongruity between her reincarnation beliefs and her behavior. While often such an appeal to reason is ineffective, Penny was fundamentally a well-integrated and resourceful person who was responsive to persuasive rhetoric. (p. 141)

Is it in any way far-fetched to think that Arron Beck or Albert Ellis might have written much the same thing about a similar client?

A second example that illustrates how therapists of a given theoretical persuasion (in this case, psychodynamic) may intervene in ways barely, if at all, anticipated by their primary theory is found in Hammer (1990). Hammer described a client, a man 17 years of age when he first came for therapy, who was "overconceptualized, constricted, joyless." The session described below took place when the client was a freshman in college and had been in therapy for approximately two and one-half years:

> [During this time period, the client had been engaged in] continual obsessing about a decision he simply could not make. Writhing in indecisiveness, he agonized: Should he go to summer school, or should he go to summer camp (for the first time and as a counselor)? He kept insisting that summer school (which he did not need for reasons of repairing deficient grades, for he was close to being a straight A student) was in the interest of "advancing"—translatable as responsibility, duty, conscientiousness, obeisance to his superego—and that camp was in the interest of "fun." Transparent in my "neutral" role, I think it was discernible which side I was on.
>
> Session after session he lay on the couch, obsessing: Should he go to summer school, should he go to camp, should he go to school, and round and round. We did analytic work on his need to obsess, and to obsess on this particular conflict, but still he stayed on the fence. Finally, in utter frustration with himself, he one day revealed a preference and implored me, "Help me go to camp."
>
> What I did in response to his decision, his distress, his pleas, and the obsessional atmosphere that had by now so tied us up, was to get out of my chair, come around in front of him on the couch, and pumping my arms like a cheerleader, chant, "Go *to* camp! Go *to* camp! Go *to* camp!" He giggled. His giggling built, and burst forth in the first laugh in treatment.... He went to camp, and he profited from the experience. (pp. 118–119)

Although the process underlying the intervention—movement toward a less restrictive and less punitive superego—can be nicely described by psychoanalytic theory, the intervention itself is scarcely what one would anticipate from a therapist who has his clients lie on a couch. However, the idea that therapists of diverse theoretical orientations are sometimes "cheerleaders" for their clients is quite consistent with an integrative perspective on psychotherapy.

Common Elements of Psychotherapy

Reviews of the psychotherapy outcome literature seem to conclude that psychotherapy is effective for many people, that its outcomes are superior to those of no psychotherapy, as well as to those of placebo interventions, and that with perhaps a few limited exceptions, one form of psychotherapy has not been demonstrated superior to another (Lambert & Bergin, 1994; Seligman, 1995; Wampold, Mondin, Moody, Stich, Benson, & Ahn, 1997). Generally speaking, research seems to suggest that differential effectiveness, while at times claimed by some schools of theory, has yet to be established. However, it should be noted that some questions have been raised as to whether the outcome studies, by focusing on main effects, have obscured the possibility that different types of clients may respond differentially to various types of psychotherapy (Beutler, 1991; Beutler & Hodgson, 1993). Furthermore, in part due to the immense complexity of these issues, methodological questions are typically raised when psychotherapy outcome studies or meta-analyses are conducted (Crits-Christoph, 1997; Howard, Krause, Saunders, & Kopta, 1997; Wampold, Mondin, Moody, & Ahn, 1997). Nonetheless, for now we have some degree of confidence that psychotherapy frequently works, and it has been very difficult to establish that one treatment is superior to another. Wampold, Mondin, Moody, and Ahn (1997) have well expressed the idea of uniform efficacy:

> We would cherish the day that a treatment is developed that is dramatically more effective than the ones we use today. But until that day comes, the existing data suggest that whatever differences in treatment efficacy exist, they appear to be extremely small, at best. Although uniform efficacy may not be a popular finding for some, this empirical result should guide, rather than obstruct, research and practice. (p. 230)

One of the explanations offered for the similarity in psychotherapy outcome (frequently labeled the "Dodo bird effect") is that all psychotherapies contain "common elements." This idea was first proposed by Rosenzweig (1936) and a number of authors (e.g., Frank & Frank, 1991; Garfield, 1980; Goldfried, 1980; Grencavage & Norcross, 1990; Hobbs, 1962; Weinberger, 1995) have speculated about these factors and have often suggested what these common elements might be. For example, Pennebaker (1997) suggested:

> A process common to most therapies is labeling the problem and discussing its causes and consequences. Further, participating in therapy presupposes that the individual acknowledges the existence of a problem and openly discusses it with another person...The mere act of disclosure is a powerful therapeutic agent that may account for a substantial percentage of the variance in the healing process. (p. 162)

Grencavage and Norcross (1990) suggested that while it may be easy to agree with the idea of common factors, achieving consensus on what they are is perhaps a somewhat more difficult task. We are in agreement with the basic idea that common elements are important. Following several of the writers just mentioned, we suggest the existence of four such elements:

1. An emotionally charged relationship—which by providing an optimum balance of challenge, support, and involvement, offers an opportunity for development and restoration of the self in a more or less healthy interpersonal environment

2. A new way of looking at the problem (including a rationale for it) and potential solutions in relationship to the self
3. Encouragement to try new and more adaptive behavior
4. An influential person (the therapist) who models and encourages self-acceptance and courage

These four processes frequently overlap and complement each other. Obviously, however, different client problems draw differentially on these common elements. For example, individuals with a personality disorder are perhaps more heavily influenced by the first process; a client whose spouse has died may be heavily influenced by the second process; clients with phobias probably chiefly respond to the third element; and people who feel guilty about something may be heavily influenced by the fourth process.

Importance of the Therapeutic Relationship

Beutler, Machado, & Neufeldt (1994) stated: "Researchers and clinicians alike have been unyielding in their belief that characteristics of therapists are associated with or predictive of psychotherapy outcome" (p. 229). We assume that the relationship between the client and therapist is of critical importance in whether the client will make good progress in psychotherapy (e.g., Horvath & Greenberg, 1994). Although writers have used the term "therapeutic alliance" in several different ways, we believe that this term captures the essence of a key ingredient in therapy—the idea that the client and therapist work together in *alliance* toward solving a common goal, which is typically the reduction of psychological suffering, the restoration of hope, and an enhanced sense of meaning and satisfaction in life for the client. Like any alliance, the therapeutic one is subject to the vicissitudes of human emotion—both of the client and of the therapist. Certainly, clients may become angry with therapists and vice versa, either or both parties may at times retreat from the relationship, and so forth. But the fundamental stance taken by the therapist is that the client is to be supported and understood, and that the therapist will not turn mean or demanding if the client is having trouble in the relationship. If we can do this as therapists, if we can be consistently empathic, and if we can, for the most part, avoid using the client for our own neurotic needs, we have thereby laid the foundation for change. Put another way, clients' perceptions of our having their best interests as an unambiguous goal to which we are actively committed, coupled with our capacity to communicate to clients, on an ongoing basis, our deep understanding of what it is like to be them, is probably enough to ensure psychotherapeutic gain for many individuals. Additionally, it forms the basis for therapeutic gain in other cases, which may call on additional skills and activities of the therapist.

In our view, if progress is not seen in psychotherapy, the first "suspect" is the relationship between client and therapist. Even if there are other issues involved

progress again!

PPCA P-32

(for example, the personality structure of the client, or the environment), these other issues often interact with aspects of the relationship to retard progress. So we urge the therapist to keep as a central and ongoing focus the question of, "What kind of relationship am I offering the client and how is the relationship affecting the client's progress or lack thereof?"

Impact of Culture and the Social Environment

We believe that the client's environment often plays a central role in causing and maintaining the client's difficulties. Behavior therapists, family therapists, feminist therapists, and cross-cultural researchers have all made contributions to our understanding of how the environment affects the individual. Many of these contributions are consistent with the "common clinical wisdom" perspective that we take in this book. For example, we are in full agreement with feminist psychotherapists (e.g., Brown, 1994; Worell & Remer, 1992) who have argued that the sexist nature of society places women at greater risk for abuse, conflicts, and psychological "difficulties." This idea is not just some abstract political theory, but rather has immediate and real consequences for how we as therapists view the difficulties of our clients. For example, when a woman reports being upset due to sexual harassment at the office, most therapists (we hope) are likely to start with the assumption that office environments often do include sexual harassment, that such processes are damaging to women's mental health, and that this damage occurs at least in part because the woman is a human being and not, for example, because she is afraid of her sexuality, is lacking in maturity, or is suffering from some other personality deficit. Similarly, ethnicity and racism—and related constructs such as racial identity and acculturation—are important in understanding the etiology and maintenance of behavior pathology, and they have important implications for treatment (e.g., Kiselica, 1998; Pope-Davis & Coleman, 1997; Sue, 1998). For example, the African American college student who often sees racist graffiti in the bathroom is being subjected to a stressful environment that almost certainly will exacerbate any existing or developing psychological problems.

As we said earlier, we do not emphasize an analysis of the environment herein. In our view, strong conceptualizations of the environment that do justice to the complex relationship between external reality and internal perception have yet to be developed. This is particularly true when one confronts the dilemma of the extent to which one does or does not choose one's environments.

Although therapeutic orientations vary widely in terms of the importance attached to the environment as an ongoing cause of behavioral and emotional difficulties, and although current conceptualizations of the environment seem incomplete, common clinical wisdom would suggest that therapists should routinely remind themselves that clients live in a social, cultural, and family context that exerts an ever-present, powerful influence on their lives. All the observations and suggestions we make in this book are intended to be consistent with, and supportive of, this idea.

Existentialists may not be concerned with etiology

The Role of Affect

We believe that affect is something to be focused on in psychotherapy and that it plays a number of key roles in the therapeutic process. It can help motivate clients to seek and make changes; it helps clients signal to their therapist when they are overwhelmed; it can help clients and therapists better identify what is of central importance to the client; it helps clients and therapists identify areas in need of development and change; and it helps give access to clients' self system—their deepest beliefs, assumptions, perceptions, and the like, thereby making change more likely. Its expression, in appropriate form, is seen as part of being mentally healthy. In many cases, catharsis—especially if accompanied by insight—seems to provide some relief for clients. (Of course we do not really know whether such emotional expression actually has healing properties or only signals an important change in the self system.) Cognitive therapies, by focusing on and attributing a causal role to cognitions in the formation and maintenance of psychological difficulties, have greatly influenced psychotherapy in the United States. Far fewer attempts have been made to conceptualize affect (e.g., Greenberg & Safran, 1989). Even if it seems a bit simplistic, we think it important to underscore that a problem with affect is the reason, in the eyes of most clients, they come seeking psychotherapy.

Centrality of the Self

The self is seen as having or lacking such key properties as attachment, autonomy, sense of efficacy, and openness to immediate experience. We find especially helpful many of the ideas of Kohut (e.g., 1977, 1984), who focused on the "self" and the relationship between the self and the therapist. Thus, the reader will find us using the word "self" in this book, suggesting its heuristic value for conceptualizing disturbance. Mahoney (1985) has described well the idea that symptoms are less something to be altered than an expression of a self configuration:

> My own experiences as a therapist have led me to agree cautiously that a vast amount of personal energy seems to be chambered into the avoidance of certain changes. For example, several of my clients seemed to have identified with their problems to the point that symptomatic improvements were frightening assaults on identity. When I asked one chronically depressed man what he thought it would take for him to change, he answered, "I guess I would have to be somebody else." (p. 33)

Importance of Early Interpersonal Experiences

We assume that many of the experiences of central importance to a client's current functioning are those occurring in the long dependency (roughly 15 years) of childhood common to each of us. That is to say, the difficult problems that bring clients to therapy most often involve contributing factors from childhood or adolescence. There are two reasons why we believe that this assumption makes sense.

The first is that the tens of thousands of interactions between parent and child provide the ideal setting for learning. Second, the inherent and powerful attachment/ dependency structure of the learning environment is believed to result in beliefs, assumptions, and expectations that are highly resistant to change. Such belief are fully integrated into a self system that uses them not so much as appendages as fundamental building blocks of identity and as core assumptions about the trustworthiness of others (Lopez, Melendez, Sauer, Berger, & Wyssmann, 1998).

Some readers may object that all problems do not originate in childhood; others will argue that even if they do there is no practical implication. We are not proposing a trauma theory of neuroses. That is, we believe that only a very small percentage of clients come to therapy primarily because of one traumatic event in their childhood. Even Freud abandoned this position as too simplistic early in his work. On the other hand, we do believe that severe disturbances in personality are most often the result of the repeated failure of the environment to provide an optimum balance of consistent and safe structure and empathy for the child.

We also realize that there are certain developmental (for example, the aging process) and situational (for example, death of a spouse) problems that bring clients to therapy and perhaps which do not have childhood experiences as their linchpin. In our view, these types of problems, if they do not involve the self system developed during childhood and adolescence, will prove to be very responsive to psychotherapy. This is not to suggest that such problems are simple or that they will be easily resolved. For example, being raped or having one's spouse die may require many months or years of painful adjustment. On the other hand, when progress is not forthcoming (and assuming that the therapist is reasonably skilled and is providing a warm, caring environment), there is an increased possibility that long-standing behavior patterns are contributing to the delay in adjustment. We believe that in actuality it would be rather puzzling for the sense of self developed in our first 15 years *not* to impact how we cope and struggle with the problems we now face. Certainly, many have in a sense transformed the self they were, but the deep structures created in the powerful early learning environment are never destroyed; as a minimum they affect the type of transformation that has taken place. Guidano and Liotti (1985) expressed this idea well:

> Moreover, from the beginning the gradual structuring of self-knowledge is constantly biasing—within the possibilities of slow cognitive growth—the child's ongoing perception of incoming information through the selection of specific domains of exchange in his [sic] interaction with experience. (p. 109)

Guidano and Liotti tie who we are directly to childhood and interpersonal experience:

> As a logical consequence of the assumption that human knowledge is imbued with interactive–reflective properties, a crucial role is attributed to interpersonal and relational domains in the development of self-knowledge. (pp. 108–109)

Those readers unfamiliar with Guidano and Liotti may be surprised to learn that the material quoted above comes from a book neither on neoanalytic psychotherapy nor developmental psychology, but rather from a book entitled *Cognition and Psychotherapy* (Mahoney & Freeman, 1985). Thus, we believe that our broad theoretical perspective, which for want of perhaps a better term we label "interpersonal," shares common assumptions with other perspectives, such as some cognitive ones. Furthermore, we assume that some focus on the childhood learning environment provides the therapist with a potentially emotionally charged, workable route to the sense of self identity that shapes and controls our reactions to the environment and other purposeful activity.

Poor Interpersonal Relationships and Pathology

As noted earlier, it is extremely difficult to sort out the causal factors in the tangled web of pathology. Nonetheless, we believe that many client problems are related in some way to interpersonal experiences. This is in no way to diminish the importance of biological and environmental factors, but we are particularly influenced by writers of the "interpersonal" school such as Kiesler (1996) who drew on the work of Harry Stack Sullivan, and by the Stone Center's "self in relation" theory (e.g., Surrey, 1985). Thus, the general orientation of this book is "interpersonal," with less emphasis on drive theory, conflict theory, behavioral theory, or cognitive theory. As we will say repeatedly, however, many therapeutic situations, in our opinion, seem to be addressed similarly by divergent theory systems. For example, many therapists working with clients who have set impossibly high standards for themselves most likely spend some therapy time focusing on what happens when clients do not meet their standards and also help clients reexamine the issue of whether these standards are in fact ones they now want to follow. Or, when clients come seeking therapy following the death of someone they loved, therapists often help such persons better express their feelings about the loss and the person who died and help them identify how their life has been changed. Therapists also help clients both accept what has happened and, as time passes, perhaps spend some therapy time focusing on how the client wants to move forward with his or her life. Surely, when clients are grappling with the limits of their lives and their resources, there must be some common things that many therapists do.

Summary

Psychotherapy is a form of help that shares the "helping stage" with other cultural structures and other formal and informal helping professions. Like other forms of helping, psychotherapy has its limits. A key assumption here is that many psychotherapists share similar ideas about what is good therapeutic practice in a wide variety of situations. Research suggests that psychotherapy helps the majority of people who seek it, but there is little evidence that one form is better than another.

There are assumed to be common elements (e.g., a rationale for what has caused the problem) in the various schools of psychotherapy.

This book is written from what might be called an "interpersonal perspective" (e.g., Teyber, 1997), which emphasizes the importance of interpersonal relationships in the development of both psychological suffering and psychological health. Psychotherapy should include a focus on affect in general, and in particular on the affect associated with interpersonal relationships, including the therapeutic one.

We view childhood and adolescent experiences as frequently being important in the development of psychological difficulties; however, psychotherapy is not typically the search for some childhood trauma. The sense of "self in relationship to the world" developed by repeated experience in our interpersonal family environment has a lasting influence on how we process experience, feel about ourselves, select environments, and react to current interpersonal relationships.

As already indicated, we strongly emphasize the importance of the relationship between client and therapist. We emphasize the therapeutic relationship for at least three reasons. First, clients are not likely to be influenced in a strongly positive way by therapists with whom they have a poor relationship. Second, past and present relationships have such an impact on how people feel about themselves, it seems reasonable to assume that the relationship between client and therapist is an important variable in the therapeutic process. We assume that clients frequently (although certainly not always) seek therapy as a direct or indirect result of the deleterious effect of one or more past or present poor relationships. The therapeutic relationship thus offers the client the opportunity to develop or restore an appropriately positive sense of self, as well as to develop the interpersonal skills needed to negotiate the environment. Third, conclusions from research seem to be unequivocal: the therapeutic relationship is a very important part of therapy outcome.

Despite our "interpersonal" orientation, however, our chief aim is to identify and present ideas, techniques, and clinical wisdom cutting across many theoretical lines. For example, some client difficulties are seen by us and many other therapists as greatly exacerbated (or even primarily caused) by environmental forces. As a second example, many therapists, whatever they call it, and whether they do it to a greater or lesser extent, probably try in part to help clients see problems from a different perspective.

By citing research studies in this book, we signal our belief that psychotherapy can be informed by empirical studies (Beutler, 1998; Chambless & Hollon, 1998). As one example, the prohibition against sexual intimacies between therapists and their clients evolved in part because of data collected on the deleterious effects of such relationships. A second example is that of limited phobias, which seem to respond very well to behavioral interventions such as exposure or desensitization. These are examples of science and practice working together.

Although we believe that research will and should continue to support and direct our evolving understanding of psychotherapy, we also believe that psychotherapy as practiced by many psychologists and counselors will always contain art as well as science, wisdom as well as research. The pursuit of empirically supported treatments (Kendall & Chambless, 1998; Nathan & Gorman, 1997; Woody & Sanderson, 1998) will likely produce interventions that for some populations are differentially effective; however, science is still a long way from being able to teach us when to say, like Yalom's analyst, "That just seems to be the way we're built."

DISCUSSION QUESTIONS

- Are you more persuaded that psychotherapy heals through common factors or through ingredients specific to each approach?

- Is the theoretical orientation you use to conceptualize clients the same one that you would seek out in a psychotherapist for yourself?

- Would the theoretical orientation of the psychotherapist you would seek for yourself depend on the problem that was bothering you?

- What are some specific interventions you will use as a counselor or psychotherapist that are based on empirical evidence of efficacy?

- Are there generalizations we can make about the efficacy of particular types of psychotherapy irrespective of the client's gender and ethnicity. What are the implications of your answer?

- In one of the examples given in this chapter, the therapist told the client, "Go to camp!" What are your reactions to this intervention?

- What kinds of questions about psychotherapy do practitioners want researchers to answer that the researchers have some reasonable chance of answering?

BIBLIOGRAPHY

Bernstein, B. L., & Kerr, B. (1993). Counseling psychology and the scientist–practitioner model: Implementation and implications. *The Counseling Psychologist, 21,* 136–151.

Beutler, L. E. (1991). Have all won and must all have prizes? revisiting Luborsky et al.'s verdict. *Journal of Consulting and Clinical Psychology, 59,* 226–232.

Beutler, L. E. (1998). Identifying empirically supported treatments: What if we didn't? *Journal of Consulting and Clinical Psychology, 66,* 113–120.

Beutler, L. E., Consoli, A. J., & Williams, R. E. (1995). Integrative and eclectic therapies in practice. In B. Bongar & L. E. Beutler (Eds.), *Comprehensive textbook of psychotherapy* (pp. 274–292). New York: Oxford.

Beutler, L. E., & Hodgson, A. B. (1993). Prescriptive psychotherapy. In G. Stricker & J. R. Gold (Eds.), *Comprehensive handbook of psychotherapy* (pp. 151–163). New York: Plenum.

Beutler, L. E., Machado, P. P. P., & Neufeldt, S. A. (1994). Therapist variables. In A. E. Bergin & S. L. Garfield (Eds.), *Handbook of psychotherapy and behavior change* (4th ed., pp. 229–269). New York: Wiley.

Beutler, L. E., Williams, R. E., Wakefield, P. J., & Entwistle, S. R. (1995). Bridging scientist and practitioner perspectives in clinical psychology. *American Psychologist, 50,* 984–994.

Brown, L. (1994). *Subversive dialogues: Theory in feminist therapy.* New York: Basic.

Chambless, D. L., & Hollon, S. D. (1998) . Defining empirically supported therapies. *Journal of Consulting and Clinical Psychology, 66,* 7–18.

Crits-Christoph, P. (1997). Limitations of the "Dodo bird" verdict and the role of clinical trials in psychotherapy research: Comment on Wampold et al. (1997). *Psychological Bulletin, 122,* 216–220.

Davison, G. C. (1998). Being boulder with the Boulder Model: The challenge of education and training in empirically supported treatments. *Journal of Consulting and Clinical Psychology, 66,* 163–167.

Duncan, B. L., Hubble, M. A., Miller, S. D. (1997). *Psychotherapy with "impossible" cases: The efficient treatment of therapy veterans.* New York: Norton.

Frank, J. D., & Frank, J. B. (1991). *Persuasion and healing* (3rd ed.). Baltimore: The Johns Hopkins University Press.

Garfield, S. L. (1980). *Psychotherapy: An eclectic approach.* New York: Wiley.

Garfield, S. L., & Bergin, A. E. (1994). Introduction and historical overview. In A. E. Bergin & S. L. Garfield (Eds.), *Handbook of psychotherapy and behavior change* (4th ed., pp. 3–18). New York: Wiley.

Goldfried, M. R. (1980). Toward the delineation of therapeutic change principles. *American Psychologist, 35,* 991–999.

Goldfried, M. R., & Norcross, J. C. (1995). Integrative and eclectic therapies in historical perspective. In B. Bongar & L. E. Beutler (Eds.), *Comprehensive textbook of psychotherapy* (pp. 254–273). New York: Oxford.

Greenberg, L. S., Rice, L. N., & Elliott, R. (1993). *Facilitating emotional change: The moment-by-moment process.* New York: Guilford.

Greenberg, L. S., & Safran, J. D. (1989). Emotion in psychotherapy. *American Psychologist, 44,* 19–29.

Grencavage, L. M., & Norcross, J. C. (1990). Where are the common factors? *Professional Psychology: Research and Practice, 21,* 372–378.

Guidano, V. F., & Liotti, G. (1985). A constructivistic foundation for cognitive therapy. In M. J. Mahoney and A. Freeman (Eds.), *Cognition and psychotherapy* (pp. 101–142). New York: Plenum.

Gurman, A. S., & Messer, S. B. (Eds). (1996). *Essential psychotherapies: Theory and practice.* New York: Guilford.

Hammer, E. (1990). *Reaching the affect: Style in the psychodynamic therapies.* Northvale, NJ: Jason Aronson.

Hobbs, N. (1962). Sources of gain in psychotherapy. *American Psychologist, 17,* 741–747.

Horvath, A. O., & Greenberg, L. S. (1994). *The working alliance: Theory, research, and practice.* New York: Wiley.

Howard, G. S. (1986). The scientist–practitioner in counseling psychology: Toward a deeper integration of theory, research, and practice. *The Counseling Psychologist, 14,* 61–106.

Howard, K. I., Krause, M. S., Saunders, S. M., & Kopta, S. M. (1997). Trials and tribulations in the meta-analysis of treatment differences. Comment on Wampold et al. (1997). *Psychological Bulletin, 122,* 221–225.

Kendall, P. C., & Chambless, D. L. (Eds.). (1998). Empirically supported psychological therapies [Special Section]. *Journal of Consulting and Clinical Psychology, 66,* 3–167.

Kiesler, D. J. (1996). *Contemporary interpersonal theory and research: Personality, psychopathology, and psychotherapy.* New York: Wiley.

Kiselica, M. S. (1998). Preparing Anglos for the challenges and joys of multiculturalism. *The Counseling Psychologist, 26,* 5–21.

Kohut, H. (1977). *The restoration of the self.* New York: International Universities Press.

Kohut, H. (1984). *How does analysis cure?* Chicago: University of Chicago Press.

Lambert, M. J., & Bergin, A. E. (1994). The effectiveness of psychotherapy. In A. E. Bergin & S. L. Garfield (Eds.), *Handbook of psychotherapy and behavior change* (4th ed., pp. 143–189). New York: Wiley.

Lewis, M. (1997). *Altering fate: Why the past does not predict the future.* New York: Guilford.

Lopez, F. G., Melendez, M. C., Sauer, E. M., Berger, E., Wyssmann, J. (1998). Internal working models, self-reported problems, and help-seeking attitudes among college students. *Journal of Counseling Psychology, 45,* 79–83.

Mahoney, M. J. (1985). Psychotherapy and human change processes. In M. J. Mahoney & A. Freeman (Eds.). *Cognition and psychotherapy* (pp. 3–48). New York: Plenum.

Mahoney, M. J. (1995). The psychological demands of being a constructive psychotherapist. In R. A. Neimeyer & M. J. Mahoney (Eds.), *Constructivism in psychotherapy* (pp. 385–399). Washington, DC: American Psychological Association.

Mahoney, M. J., & Freeman, A. (Eds.). (1985). *Cognition and psychotherapy.* New York: Plenum.

Miller, S., Hubble, M., & Duncan, B. (1995, March/April). No more bells and whistles. *The Family Therapy Networker,* pp. 52–58, 62–63.

Nathan, P. E., & Gorman, J. M. (Eds.). (1997). *A guide to treatments that work.* New York: Oxford University Press.

Neimeyer, R. A., & Mahoney, M. J. (Eds.). (1996). *Constructivism in psychotherapy.* Washington, DC: American Psychological Association.

Norcross, J. C. (1996). The lifetime lessons of six psychologists: An introduction. *Psychotherapy, 33,* 129–130.

Norcross, J. C. (1997). Emerging breakthroughs in psychotherapy: Three predictions and one fantasy. *Psychotherapy, 34,* 86–90.

Orlinsky, D. E., Grawe, K., & Parks, B. K. (1994). Process and outcome in psychotherapy—noch einmal. In A. E. Bergin & S. L. Garfield (Eds.), *Handbook of psychotherapy and behavior change* (4th ed., pp. 270–376). New York: Wiley.

Pennebaker, J. W. (1997). Writing about emotional experiences as a therapeutic process. *Psychological Science, 8,* 162–166.

Pope-Davis, D. B., Coleman, H. L. K. (Eds.). (1997). *Multicultural counseling competencies: Assessment, education and training, and supervision.* Thousand Oaks, CA: Sage.

Rosenzweig, S. (1936). Some implicit common factors in diverse methods of psychotherapy. *American Journal of Orthopsychiatry, 6,* 422–425.

Seligman, M. E. P. (1995). The effectiveness of psychotherapy: The *Consumer Reports* study. *American Psychologist, 50,* 965–974.

Strupp, H. H. (1996). Some salient lessons from research and practice. *Psychotherapy, 33,* 135–138.

Sue, S. (1998). In search of cultural competence in psychotherapy and counseling. *American Psychologist, 53,* 440–448.

Surrey, J. (1985). The "self-in-relation": A theory of women's development. *Work in progress (No. 13).* Wellesley, MA: Stone Center for Developmental Services and Studies.

Teyber, E. (1997). *Interpersonal process in psychotherapy: A relational approach* (3rd ed.). Pacific Grove, CA: Brooks/Cole.

Tolkien, J. R. R. (1965). *The lord of the rings: Part 1. The fellowship of the ring.* New York: Ballantine Books.

Vaughan, S. C. (1997). *The talking cure.* New York: G. P. Putnam's Sons.

Wachtel, P. L. (1997). *Psychoanalysis, behavior therapy, and the relational world.* Washington, DC: American Psychological Association.

Wachtel, P. L., & Messer, S. B. (Eds.). (1997). *Theories of psychotherapy: Origins and evolution.* Washington, DC: American Psychological Association.

Wampold, B., Mondin, G. W., Moody, M., & Ahn, H. (1997). The flat earth as a metaphor for the evidence for uniform efficacy of bonafide psychotherapies: Reply to Crits-Christoph (1997) and Howard et al. (1997). *Psychological Bulletin, 122,* 226–230.

Wampold, B., Mondin, G. W., Moody, M., Stich, F., Benson, K., & Ahn, H. (1997). A meta-analysis of outcome studies comparing bona fide psychotherapies: Empirically, "all must have prizes." (1997). *Psychological Bulletin, 122,* 203–215.

Weinberger, J. (1995). Common factors aren't so common: The common factors dilemma. *Clinical Psychology: Science and Practice, 2,* 45–69.

Woody, S. R., & Sanderson, W. C. (Eds.). (1998). *Manuals for empirically supported treatments: 1998 update.* (Available from Division 12 Central Office, P.O. Box 1082, Niwot, CO 80544)

Worell, J., & Remer, P. (1992). *Feminist perspectives in therapy.* New York: Wiley.

Yalom, I. D. (1989). *Love's executioner.* New York: Basic Books.

2 Questions That Beginning Therapists Ask

In the great crises of life, in the supreme moments when to be or not to be is the question, little tricks of suggestion do not help. Then the doctor's whole being is challenged.

—C. G. Jung

The only interesting answers are those which destroy the questions.

—Susan Sontag

The purpose of this chapter is to reduce some of your anxiety and stir up some discussion. First, a caveat: If you view what we write as providing definitive answers to the questions we pose, we will have failed in our purpose. In most cases the questions are difficult to answer outside of a specific context, and any given question reflects various concerns depending on who has asked it. We cannot emphasize too strongly the limitations of addressing complex questions in a brief fashion. We also know, however, that when you are just starting out to be a therapist there are a great many unknowns and many things about which to be worried. Because we believe that therapy is seldom effective when the therapist is being overwhelmed by anxiety, and because we believe that having at least a little information about unknown areas reduces anxiety, we will in this chapter pose and address a number of questions that, over the years, our students have raised.

We will discuss each question briefly, outlining some ideas we have about the issue being addressed. In many cases we will tell you what we might do. As we have stated, we do not think of our comments as being definitive answers, but rather as the starting point for you to provide your own answers with the help of your supervisor.

We emphasize strongly that when we place possible therapists' responses in quotes, we are *not* telling you to say those exact words (in fact we would seldom say those exact words ourselves), but are giving you some ideas about ways to approach the problem. At times you may believe that our suggestions are "off base"; certainly there will be times when your supervisor will disagree with our suggestions. This is a part of what we meant when we said that our purpose included stirring up some discussion. We hope you will think critically about how our ideas are different from yours. Our greatest hope is that these questions will be used by you individually and in supervision or class in such a way as to stimulate your thinking on the subject.

We caution that there is tremendous variation among agencies in terms of their policies about some of these issues and that the answers to some questions will vary according to local norms and client ethnicity. Furthermore, different supervisors will answer the questions in different ways, and you are particularly encouraged to discuss with your supervisor any comments that trouble you. Despite these cautions, we hope and believe that you will find a number of specific suggestions that will be helpful to you. We also hope that this chapter will be a kind of second "introduction" to the book by giving you a flavor for how we think about some of the challenges faced by counselors and psychotherapists. See the appendix to this chapter for a complete list of the questions discussed in the chapter. For organizational purposes, we have divided the questions into four categories: Boundary/Management Issues, Personal Inquiries and Emotional Issues, General Therapeutic Issues, and Supervisory Issues. For an additional list of questions (with comments), see Chapter 62 of Lewis Wolberg's *The Technique of Psychotherapy* (1988).

Boundary/Management Issues

Psychotherapy involves a set of implicit rules about where it should be practiced, what form it should take, when and where it should be conducted, the kinds of behaviors required of therapist and client, and the like. Taken together, these issues are often referred to as "boundary conditions," or the "therapeutic frame." Before addressing questions about therapeutic boundaries, we emphasize that there is some degree of debate among psychotherapists about how rigidly the "boundary conditions" of psychotherapy should be maintained (e.g., Lazarus, 1994; Williams, 1997). Depending on the therapist's theoretical orientation (and perhaps personal value system), these boundaries are viewed as protecting clients from exploitation, promoting clients' sense of safety, and providing for clients a structure that may be curative in itself in terms of self-esteem enhancement, development of autonomy, and so forth (Bennett, Bricklin, & VandeCreek, 1994; Borys, 1994). As you read through our comments on boundary issues, it is important to remember that there are some serious differences of opinion among therapists in terms of both what they believe to be effective psychotherapy and of how they understand their responsibility as an ethical psychotherapist.

1. *How should I introduce myself?* Some settings, especially hospitals, have a norm that suggests using forms of addresses (Mr., Ms., Dr.). The authors prefer the use of the given and last name without titles if there is no specific norm. Even when there is a norm, there are usually a few intrepid souls who use whatever form they find most comfortable. Some inpatient facilities may want you to use a specific form of address in order to help maintain boundary conditions. Except under such circumstances, we encourage you to introduce yourself the way you feel most comfortable. If you are seeing clients in a clinic where there is a waiting room, in order to help ensure confidentiality to the extent possible, avoid calling out the client's full name in public.

2. *If I am a student in training, should I inform clients of this fact?* Yes, if the clients have not already been so informed. The *Ethics Code* of the American Psychological Association (APA, 1992) requires that you do this. Clients have a right to know that you are delivering services as a part of a class, or as part of your responsibility as a practicum student.

3. *How should I bring up the issue of audio or video recording?* Most training programs require that you audio or video record your counseling sessions; furthermore, the vast majority of agencies require that you obtain written permission to do so. Certainly, you should never record a session without the client's being aware of the recording. If you are required to record the session, tell the client that in the shortest, most straightforward way. If recording is not an absolute requirement, perhaps the easiest way to handle this issue is, following introductions, to say something like this: "Before we get started, I'd like to mention a couple of things. I'm a student in the graduate program at _____ university, and as a matter of routine I tape-record my sessions. This is helpful to me since I, and at times my supervisor, can go back over the tape to listen for how I might have been more helpful to you. So, if it's okay with you, I'd like to ask you to sign the form that we ask everyone to sign, and then I'll record the session." We strongly advise against long explanations. If you present taping in a short, straightforward and positive manner, you will find that the vast majority of your clients will readily agree to this procedure. If you are not required to record and the client expresses reservations, you might say something like this: "Of course, the choice is yours. Since recording the sessions is so helpful to me, I wonder if we could just give it a try, and then if you feel too anxious, we can always cut it off. How does that sound?" If the client still refuses to be taped, we recommend that you discontinue, for the time being, the discussion. Of course, refusal on the part of the client is almost always very diagnostic. Sometimes you will find that clients have a very simple question about taping that, once answered, resolves the problem. For example, they may want to know when the tapes will be erased (a good release form should contain this information anyway) or whether certain people (for example, their instructors if they are college students) will have access to the tape. The issue of taping cannot be separated from the issue of confidentiality (see next question).

4. *What should I tell clients about confidentiality?* You should know that experienced therapists differ widely among themselves in how they address with clients the issue of confidentiality. Although it is likely that many therapists have always provided such information, since 1992, the APA *Ethics Code* has specifically required that clients be told about confidentiality (Standards 4.01 and 5.01). This information should be provided as soon as feasible—generally in the first session.

Legally, you may find yourself in trouble if you do not break confidentiality under certain circumstances. These circumstances vary from state to state but

Confidentiality
Required
Permitted

usually include situations in which the client is a danger to self or others, or in the case of child abuse. Depending on the state, possible elder abuse or other offenses may also be reportable. State laws also vary greatly as to whether the therapist is *required* to break confidentiality versus whether the therapist is *permitted* to break confidentiality. The law may also require you to report other criminal acts (whether they were committed in the past or have been threatened) in which the client is involved. Similarly, you may be compelled, under threat of contempt of court, to testify or release information about your client. In fact, if you are a student (or are otherwise not licensed) you may be especially vulnerable to such court orders since what is called "privileged communication" often extends only to licensed professionals.

Probably you will find that one of the forms used by the agency where you are working gives the client some information about confidentiality. If for some reason the printed material provided to clients at your practicum site does not include such information, you will need to describe confidentiality and privileged communication in the first session. More discussion may be necessary if the client is particularly concerned about the issue. If you believe that confidentiality must be broken, you should, of course, first consult with your supervisor. Alternatives to breaking confidentiality should be explored fully. Furthermore, the client should be informed of your impending actions. If possible, the client should be an active participant in the process. For example, an alternative to your breaking confidentiality may be to have the client make a telephone call from your office to the person or agency who may need to be contacted. Or, if the client is in your office, you may make the telephone call in her or his presence so that it will be clear exactly what you have told the other person. The entire process should be used to benefit the client in every way possible, so that the client retains as much autonomy as possible and so that the therapeutic relationship can suffer as little damage as is possible.

We recommend that you use a written form of some sort to convey information about confidentiality and that you ask clients to sign the form acknowledging their awareness of the issues involved. If the client asks about what "all this means" or if you prefer to make a comment without the client's asking, you are encouraged to be somewhat brief and nonapologetic. For example, you might say something like, "There are a few extreme instances in which I might have to tell someone what you've said—for example, when you are a danger to yourself. In fact, this type of situation rarely occurs." If the client requests an explanation, it is very important that you provide the client an opportunity to ask questions and express feelings.

You will find additional discussion concerning this issue in Chapter 3, Client Fears, and in Chapter 5, Ethical and Legal Issues.

5. *What should I tell clients about psychotherapy?* It is an ethical requirement that you describe the nature of psychotherapy to the client (APA *Ethics Code*, 1992); however, the way in which this is done varies widely from therapist to therapist, and perhaps from client to client for any given therapist. Particularly in a managed-care, short-term therapy environment, one may not have the luxury of allowing the client to "experience" therapy, rather than receive an explanation.

Because there are so many theoretical orientations to psychotherapy, and so many different clients in terms of psychological awareness, presenting complaints, personality structure, and the like, it is very difficult to answer this question without getting into controversy. Nonetheless, consider something like this as a start: "Psychotherapy involves our working together to help you solve your problems. This is a place where you can talk about feelings and thoughts you've had that you can't talk about with other people. Together, we will try to figure out how you might change the thoughts, or feelings, or behaviors that are giving you trouble. I will ask you to be honest with me, and with yourself. In turn, I will try to help you as you struggle to change yourself and accept yourself."

Of course you will need to have clients give their reaction to what you say and you will also need to provide more information, especially about confidentiality (see Question 4). As we have said, what you say depends on your theoretical orientation and the client's personality and overall knowledge of psychotherapy. Furthermore, cultural and social-class variables associated with the client will affect how one answers this question. One point we want to emphasize is that when clients ask, "What is psychotherapy?" don't try to "interpret" the question. Sarason (1985) gives an excellent example of a student therapist who, when asked this question by a client, responded with, "Why do you ask that question?"

> In supervision, the supervisor asked the student, "What would you have done if in this hour, during which you felt that he was quite anxious, he [the client] had asked you where the toilet is? Would you have refused to tell him because you were convinced that he wanted time out from you?" (p. 153)

Although this is a humorous example, it clearly points out the danger in trying to "overinterpret" the questions our clients ask us. In general, the literature suggests that disclosure of pretherapy information is helpful to the therapeutic process (Dauser, Hedstrom, & Croteau, 1995; Sullivan, Martin, & Handelsman, 1993). Additional discussion of what to tell clients about psychotherapy may be found in Chapter 5, Ethical and Legal Issues.

6. *Should I give clients my home phone number?* In most cases there is little reason to do this. There are several reasons not to give out your telephone number including: (a) it may encourage excessive dependency on the part of the client; (b) it may confuse the client about boundaries; or (c) it may create a perilous situation for the therapist if the client is dangerous. Similarly, clients who use "Caller ID" may be able to learn your telephone number if you even place a call to them from your home. Furthermore, if you have an answering machine at home and the client leaves you a message there, the client's confidentiality may be compromised if you live with another person. Many agencies discourage or even forbid therapists from giving out their home telephone numbers; be sure to check with the agency where you work to find out its policy on this matter. Furthermore, the policies of different academic training programs vary in this regard, so you should check with your training director, faculty clinical supervisor, or other responsible person on the faculty, in addition to talking with the agency where you work.

Arguments cited to support giving out a phone number include: (a) the client feels cared for; (b) you may be legally responsible if you don't make provision for emergencies; and (c) you may want clients to call if they are "desperate." If your phone number is listed, clients can, of course, call you even if you don't give it to them. Nonetheless, giving your phone number is, of course, much more than merely providing information. Our policy is to give our telephone number to clients who are suicidal or who are in acute distress. When the "privilege" is abused, this development is processed in therapy. However, you will find that most clients will not abuse the privilege of calling you in a crisis. We believe that most want to be independent. If you are getting, from several clients, what you consider to be too many calls, consider the possibility that you may actually want clients to be dependent on you in this way. As a practical matter, if clients need your phone number, they most certainly need the number for the local crisis center. After all, you are not at home 24 hours of each day.

7. *Do I need liability insurance?* Increasingly, the answer to this question is, "Yes." You may or not be required by your training program to carry such insurance. Professional organizations such as the American Psychological Association and the American Counseling Association offer student policies, as do several private companies. If you take out a policy, it is a good idea to get one that protects you from any legal suit arising from having seen a client while the policy was in force, even if the suit was brought after the policy expired.

8. *Should I keep personal notes regarding my clients?* At times it may be helpful to keep brief, unofficial notes on clients. The critical point is that such notes be safeguarded and written in such a way so that loss will not compromise confidentiality. We should point out that some agencies may have policies forbidding the keeping of personal notes. One problem with such notes is that if there is a crisis and you are not available, the official notes, not your personal ones, will of course be the basis of treatment. Make sure that important relevant information is in the official notes. Remember that personal notes may also be subpoenaed. Additional comments concerning record keeping are found in the chapter Ethical and Legal Issues, as well as in subsequent questions in this chapter.

9. *Should I take notes during therapy sessions?* We believe that it is best not to take notes during the session, perhaps excepting intake interviews. We believe that many clients are "put off" by note taking, and, in our view, the process seems to put a barrier between client and therapist. However, it is also true that many therapists *do* take notes. Your supervisor (either at the university or at the agency) may be of the opinion that you should keep notes, and in such cases you should follow the advice of your supervisor. Certainly, if you have trouble remembering significant events during the therapy hour, you should take notes. In any event, allow yourself a little time after each session so that you can make notes in the chart and/or for your personal records.

10. *What should I write in progress notes?* Psychology's increasing awareness of legal issues, coupled with the consumer rights movement, has made the issue of progress notes a potential battleground in the ethical and legal arena. For example, the rights family members may have to review the records of clients suffering from a mental illness (Haas & Malouf, 1995) is but one example of the kinds of questions arising in practice settings. Most agencies have a required format for use in progress notes. The most widely used (or some variant thereof) is the Subjective-Observed-Assessment-Plan (SOAP) system. (SOAP is actually a part of a comprehensive system labeled Problem Oriented Medical Record in Weed, 1968.) *Subjective* refers to the client's self-report—for example, "I feel depressed," or "I have been shouting at my wife lately." *Observed* refers to what the therapist actually sees during therapy—for example, "Client was dressed shabbily," or "Client cried throughout the session." *Assessment* refers to your analysis of what produced the client's current symptoms—for example, "The client's inability to express his feelings toward his wife has resulted in depression," or "The client's anger appears to be a result of his low self-esteem." Assessment may also include a classification from the Diagnostic and Statistical Manual, Fourth Edition (DSM-IV; American Psychiatric Association, 1994) or a change in the client's condition (e.g., less depressed, more anxious, etc.). *Plan* refers to the action that the therapist and client anticipate taking to alleviate symptoms, for example, "Will continue desensitization," or "Will continue discussing the client's feelings of insecurity." As you can see, the SOAP system is somewhat behavioral in its philosophical underpinnings. Agencies receiving state or federal money tend to use this or a similar system. Other agencies (for example, many university counseling centers) may require only a brief summary of the session.

One thing to keep in mind is that increasingly the consumer rights movement has resulted in the rights of clients to greater access to, and to appeal or complain about, what is written in their files (Penney, personal communication, 1997). Some agencies tell therapists not to write *anything* in the therapy record that they do not want read by the client. This means that there must be greater collaboration between client and therapist and that therapists will "stick closer" to observed or reported behavior rather than interpreting it. As one example (from a mental health center), an overweight client became incensed when she read the words "overweight" in her chart. In this case, the therapist should have written, "Client was 5 feet, 2 inches tall, and weighed 260 pounds."

From a legal standpoint, you should always record any threat to self or others, together with action taken as a result. For example: "Client threatened suicide. Made assessment of danger; no specific plan, no immediate means, good family support. Discussed with Drs. Lopez and Jones. Joint decision—no immediate threat. Gave client my phone number and number of crisis center." In general, if there is a legal issue involved, you should make entries in the record that will help protect you from a suit. It is unfortunate that progress notes have become a legal battleground, but the fact is that they have. Twenty years ago it might have been fine to just do your best; today you must do your best *and* record *how* you have done your best (Jobes & Berman, 1993; Sommers-Flanagan & Sommers-Flanagan, 1995).

In general, labels should be avoided when writing in progress notes. For example, because of the prejudice against individuals who are bisexual, gay, or lesbian, many therapists, including the authors, are reluctant to use words such as "gay" in progress notes and prefer instead to talk about "sexual orientation issues." Naturally, if the client is gay but does not present with this issue, no entry about sexual orientation would be made. Additional comments concerning record keeping may be found in Chapter 5, Ethical and Legal Issues, and in Chapter 6, Intake Interviewing.

11. *When should I deviate from the usual session frequency?* For many outpatient agencies, clients are seen once a week; however, the increasing emphasis on brief and time-effective psychotherapy (e.g., Friedman, 1997) has raised questions about the traditional view. Despite the evolution of this issue of frequency, we believe that the most common model is probably once per week. Therapists frequently follow this model unless there is an unusual circumstance. One such unusual circumstance would be clients in acute crisis who are often seen twice each week (or more if necessary). Special forms of therapy (e.g., biofeedback, relaxation, desensitization) are exceptions to the rule, and you should obtain specific supervision on such techniques. Orthodox psychoanalysis, of course, involves having more than one contact per week since the client's defenses are assumed to solidify too easily over the period of an entire week.

For a variety of reasons, some clients may ask to be seen every other week or once a month. This is especially true in rural areas and in cases involving follow-up at psychiatric hospitals. Our inclination is to allow clients to be seen at the interval they request. Obviously, clients who want to be seen only once per month are making a statement about the level of involvement they want in this enterprise of psychotherapy. Moreover, clients who are terminating may, toward the very end of therapy, be seen every two weeks, and then even this length of time might be extended to once a month. Do not encourage "dropping by" or the setting of extra appointments. Naturally there will be times when clients are in a crisis, will come by, and will need to be seen, or they may call while in crisis and request an extra appointment. When this happens, you should agree to see them if there seems to be a pressing concern of a critical nature. Alternatively, talking with them at the time for a few minutes on the phone may be intervention enough until their regularly scheduled appointment. Another option would be to ask them to call you at the office at a specific time prior to their next appointment. Or you might simply leave open the option of their calling again should the need arise. Often just knowing that you *would* be available in a crisis helps to prevent it. The decision as to which of these alternatives is most appropriate should be made jointly with the client.

Finally, we underscore that cultural variables, as well as socioeconomic status, may impact how often a client can come to therapy. The client who has a minimum-wage job and who has to ride a bus to get to a therapy appointment faces real challenges that we must understand and be tolerant of, rather than labeling the behavior as resistance.

12. *Should I allow clients to switch appointment times?* Generally speaking, we encourage you to find a time that is workable for you and the client and then try to meet consistently at that time if possible; however, you should use common sense and a reasonable degree of flexibility if there is a problem. If you start moving appointment times around, you will find that clients often have more and more special circumstances requiring them to make changes. That is, if you reinforce behavior, do not be surprised when it increases in frequency. In our view, clients often need the stability and reassurance that comes with having a specific time for therapy. For example, if the two of you have agreed to meet on Thursdays at 10:00 A.M., try to stick to this schedule rather than allowing little problems to dictate meeting at 9:00 A.M. one week, 1:00 P.M. the next, and back to 10:00 A.M. the following week. One of the ways in which the client values therapy is to make a commitment about the time. If minor problems keep arising that seem to call for rescheduling the meeting time, you should rightly wonder how serious the client is about therapy. These comments do not apply if you work in an agency where clients do not receive an unchanging time slot. Furthermore, although a stable "time slot" for a client is desirable, this goal does not mean that the therapist should be rigid or unreasonable. There are actually wide differences among therapists on this issue, although our impression is that therapists, whether for financial or philosophical reasons, are somewhat more flexible about appointment times than they once were. In any event, we recommend that you make sure that *you* do not find yourself frequently needing to change clients' appointment times. Under such a circumstance, they may wonder about your commitment to them and the degree to which you see them as important.

13. *Should I allow clients to start early if they are in the waiting room and I am available?* In the previous question we discussed the issue of stability of appointment times. The same principle applies to starting early. Clients may show up early and ask if you are free. The answer is "no" unless there is a crisis.

14. *What should I say if a client wants to tape-record the session?* Therapists differ widely as to whether they object to the client's recording of the session. Some therapists encourage their clients to do so; other therapists believe that such a procedure tends to dilute therapy or foster intellectualizing. Our advice is to be cautious about permitting this but not to arbitrarily rule it out. The most important question is not whether you should or should not, but rather in what way the request is related to the client's dynamics. For example, individuals who are extremely paranoid should not be encouraged to record the sessions, nor should individuals who are in legal difficulty. Before you say, "Yes," to this request, remember that clients are not bound by confidentiality and that they may allow other people to listen to the tape. Our comments concerning this question also apply if the client asks to borrow *your* recording of the session.

15. *What should I say if a client wants to bring a friend or parent to meet me?* We discourage this practice except near the end of therapy. In any case, it is most important to try to understand why clients want to do it. At times, they may have been maneuvered into suggesting it by an individual who feels threatened by what is happening in therapy and wants to "check you out." Other times, they may be motivated to show you off—"This is the person who has helped me so much." In such instances, dependency is a prime candidate for the motivating dynamic. Near the end of the therapy, however, clients may be using the introduction as one of their ways to end the therapy experience. In such cases, it may be part of a positive termination. We say this realizing that when the client introduces the therapist to a friend or relative during the termination phase of therapy, there may be a fantasy that the therapist will be reborn in the person with whom the client *will* have an ongoing relationship.

It is also important to consider the cultural group from which the client comes when making decisions about this issue. For example, in some American Indian cultures it would not be uncommon for family members to accompany the client to therapy. Similarly, in Latino/Latina cultures and with some Asian Americans or Pacific Islanders the family tends to play a key role in therapy. Thus, in some cultures, it would be an affront to the client and the family for the therapist to refuse to meet with them. Under such circumstances, we strongly recommend that you use good common sense and sensitivity to cultural variables.

16. *What kind of clothes should I wear as a therapist?* Naturally, it depends on the agency. Ties are usually not required for males nor are dresses for females. Shorts and cutoffs are generally not appropriate. If you are a student, when you go for an interview it is appropriate to ask about the clothes typically worn by therapists at that particular agency. A good example of a personal appearance issue is that of dying one's hair an unusual color. In some agencies you are quite free to express yourself in this way; but in others, directors may be hesitant about allowing such a procedure if the client population is extremely conservative. In general, your appearance, whether it concerns clothes, hair, earrings, or whatever, should not do violence to the cultural norms and expectations of the population with which you will be working. Strong (1968) articulated a model of counseling that gives theoretical reasons for the therapist to be considered an "expert," "trustworthy," and "socially attractive" by the client. If the client is uncomfortable with your appearance, any or all of these variables may be affected.

17. *What should I do when clients call me at home when they are in crisis?* Earlier we discussed the issue of whether you should or should not give your telephone number to clients. We also noted that unless you have an unlisted number, clients can still call even if you do not give them your number. So, let us assume that however your number was obtained, the client does call you. First, agencies frequently have guidelines to assist you in such a situation, so be sure to check to see if this is true in your case. Outcomes to this sort of crisis fall into three categories. One possibility is that the client, after talking with you for a few minutes, will decide that he or she can make it until the next appointment, or at least until you can meet the next day on an emergency basis. A second possibility is that some arrangement for family or friends may be made to assist in the crisis. Such arrangements must be made with the cooperation of the client, since in some circumstances the *worst* thing to do would be to involve family or friends. As a third possibility, if you believe, on the basis of the telephone conversation and your previous contact with the client, that the client is an imminent danger to self or others, you will need to make arrangements for hospitalization. Do not go to the client's house—and especially not alone. Under most circumstances, the first choice is to have clients go to the emergency room (either driving themselves or having a friend drive them). Depending on the situation, you or another on-call therapist may meet them there to assist them in being admitted. Depending on the agency you work for and the rules of the local hospital, you will need a staff psychologist, a consulting psychiatrist, or another medical doctor to approve the admission. This can usually be accomplished by your calling the person with authority to admit, explaining the situation, and asking him or her to call the hospital. In an extreme emergency, clients can go to any hospital emergency room, but the treatment received at such facilities varies widely and will be much better if a mental health professional has at least called to explain the situation. Be sure to talk with your on-site supervisor about this issue. If you know what to do before the problem arises, it will be much less difficult to handle.

18. *Should I visit a client who has been admitted to the hospital?* If your client has been admitted to a local psychiatric hospital, the answer is frequently, "Yes." The form of treatment you should be delivering, how often you should go, and the like will need to be discussed between you, your supervisor, and the psychologist or psychiatrist who is supervising the client's case in the hospital. If your client will be hospitalized for only a day or two, a visit may not be necessary. Remember that, except in emergencies, a "release of information" from the client is needed before you can talk to the hospital staff about your client. Although you may not need a release from the client to write in the hospital progress notes, you should use good judgment in deciding what to document there. (You may not be *permitted* to write in the notes; that depends on the hospital.) It is generally advisable to talk with your client and the hospital's supervising psychologist expeditiously to ensure that the client is receiving what you view as appropriate treatment. Moreover, if your client is to be discharged into the care of parents, or will be leaving the city upon discharge, it is very important that you help ensure continuity of treatment.

If your client is being admitted to an inpatient drug or alcohol treatment program, you will not generally be able to visit, because these sorts of programs often do not allow visitors of any sort for a while. However, there may be exceptions to this rule if, for example, you have seen the client over a long period of time.

If clients have been admitted to a hospital for medical reasons, we generally do not visit them. The general guideline is to visit clients only when you are seeing them as a part of your professional relationship. This is not to say that if one of your clients is in a serious accident you should never visit her or him in the hospital. The point is that when you are inclined to deviate from the typical therapy session contact, you should be very clear on why you are deviating and the possible drawbacks for changing the usual rules. In all cases, your supervisor should be contacted before you visit a client in the hospital. It is important to remember that some agencies have a very strict policy about seeing clients away from the office (see below).

19. *Is it all right to schedule a therapy session away from the office?* There are, of course, some behavioral treatment programs that utilize such procedures as a central part of the treatment. If you have taken appropriate precautions and cleared the procedure with your supervisor, there should be no problem in such instances. In more traditional forms of psychotherapy, you should be very cautious about seeing clients outside the office setting. For example, clients with a borderline personality disorder may be very confused about this sort of "boundary violation." Clients who are attracted to you may misread your intentions. If a client were to be injured during the session, there would be the question of liability, and of course confidentiality is much harder to ensure outside an office setting. Furthermore, as we have said, some agencies place severe limitations on the circumstances under which a client can be seen away from the office. For example, under no circumstances should you invite a client to your home for therapy, or try to conduct therapy in restaurants.

Therapists differ about whether it is ever permissible to have a session "over coffee." We do not believe that it is appropriate even under very favorable conditions. There are probably some therapists who, toward the end of therapy with a few clients, are willing to "have coffee" as a part of the process of ending therapy. However, we believe that the risks inherent in such a process far outweigh potential gains.

On the other hand, we believe that hospitalized clients—especially adolescents—at times may benefit from walking on the hospital grounds with you during a therapy session. Some therapists would advise strongly against this procedure. At a minimum, such a visit in a hospital setting should be discussed with the treatment team.

20. *What should I do if a client invites me to a social occasion such as a graduation?* The answer to this question depends greatly on several issues, three of which are: (a) your theoretical orientation; (b) the client's diagnosis; and (c) how long you have seen the client. Psychoanalysts, and persons of similar theoretical orientations, are unlikely to attend social events to which they have been invited because such attendance would most typically be seen as a violation of the treatment frame. The client's diagnosis is obviously critical. We have made some related comments, so here we will merely emphasize that for clients who have had previous difficulty in respecting boundaries in therapy, you should be extremely cautious about attending their social functions. Furthermore, you should be very cautious when a client who seems to be attracted to you extends an invitation. Similarly, clients who are prone to serious interpersonal distortions are at risk under these conditions, as are clients who are labile in their feelings toward the therapist.

In our own view, you should never attend a social occasion to which you have been invited by the client if you have not already seen the client for quite a number of sessions. This is true for two reasons. First, our rationale is that breaking the therapeutic frame requires that there be a therapeutic relationship established that makes such attendance *meaningful* from a "reasonable person" perspective. In other words, the client should be able, on some more or less realistic criteria, to integrate the event *into* an established relationship. Second, if you have seen the client only two or three times, you really have very little data to rule out the possibility that the client might distort the occasion and your attendance.

Perhaps the best advice we can give on this matter is to try not to let yourself be trapped into responding quickly to a client's invitation. So if the client says, "Can you come to my graduation next month?" you might respond, "Let me think about that. I know that is a big occasion for you. Let's discuss it next week." To be realistic, however, we know that sometimes clients will give you very little warning. They might say, for example, "Tomorrow I'm receiving a big award at the Rotary Club. Could you come?" Obviously if you have another commitment you can truthfully say, "I'm sorry. I'm already committed at that time." (Of course that would not be the end of the discussion, because the invitation is of interest by itself.) If you do not have a commitment, you may have to make a very quick decision about whether it is best for the client for you to attend. In such a case (clients waiting until the last moment to invite you), the chances are very good that the client is extremely ambivalent about the entire issue. Our own philosophy is to be *very* cautious about attending events outside the therapy hour. We do not rule it out completely, but it is the exception. An example might be a person you had seen for several months who had struggled in therapy with the idea of commitment to an intimate relationship, who finally was able, with your help, to "turn the corner," and who then invited you to a commitment ceremony or marriage. If the client was basically mentally healthy, it might be permissible for you to attend the ceremony. Obviously, you should discuss such issues with your supervisor, and you must take into consideration cultural values (e.g., ethnicity, rural versus urban environment, etc.) that might be operating.

Personal Inquiries and Emotional Issues

From time to time, clients ask their therapists questions. These range from the quite reasonable (e.g., "What is your fee?"), to ones that may be in a "gray area," (e.g., "Are you married?"), to extremely personal and inappropriate ones (e.g., "What is your deepest fear?"). Glickauf-Hughes and Chance (1995) have discussed client questions and have developed a system to categorize them: (a) genuine requests for information; (b) indirect requests for some type of gratification from the therapist; (c) questions that are really statements; (d) questions that are tests; and (e) questions that push the therapist's boundaries. Glickauf-Hughes and Chance caution that a middle ground must be sought, in which clients are not permitted to violate the personal boundaries of the therapist, while they are also given the information they need. Wachtel (1993) points out that refusal to answer reasonable questions may result in a power struggle between the client and therapist. In this section, we will address a few of the more common questions that beginning therapists are worried about being asked (hence producing questions for supervisors). We will also discuss a few other questions raised by supervisees that have to do with emotional or "touchy" areas. A general area that is related to these issues is therapist self-disclosure (e.g., Knox, Hess, Petersen, & Hill, 1997; Stricker & Fisher, 1990).

 21. *What should I do when clients make racist or sexist comments?* This is a very difficult question to answer because it depends so heavily on the client's pathology, as well as on the therapist's values. There is also the issue of whether the comment applies to the therapist. For example, if the therapist is an African American and the client makes what sounds like (or is) a racist remark, that is quite different than if the client and therapist are of the same ethnicity. Here are a few ideas to consider. First, outrageous comments should not go unprocessed. If the client has said something that is (or seems to be) insulting, the therapist should process this material. Your goal is not to "outdo" clients, or put them in their place, but rather to use the incident in a therapeutic fashion. For example, suppose that an African American therapist is seeing a Caucasian client when the client says something like the following, "Now, I don't want to offend you and I'm no racist, but there sure are a lot of blacks on welfare and they don't want to work. They would just rather draw a check for doing nothing." In this sort of case, we are interested in two things primarily. First, the therapist should use this opportunity to ask the client what it is like having a black person be his therapist. That is to say, the racist remark should be used as a catalyst to discuss the client–therapist relationship. Second, the *self* feelings expressed in the comment should be explored. For example, an actual case similar to this involved a client who had had a very hard life; he held down a job with no car (in a rural environment) and lived in substandard housing. His childhood had been traumatic and he bore the emotional scars from those years. Thus, in this case, the statement about "lazy people" leads to a discussion of what it is like to grow up feeling as if you have to fight just to stay alive. Clearly, emotional scars do not provide justification for racist remarks; however, the scars can lead us to an understanding of how we might use the feelings being expressed in the service of broad psychotherapeutic issues. There are other times when it may be advisable to confront directly the racist or sexist remarks. For example, if a client with a personality disorder makes a disparaging remark about people of the therapist's gender or race, it may be quite appropriate to confront the issue directly and explore the client's beliefs about the impact such comments have on others. Similarly, if the client and therapist are of the same ethnicity or gender, and the client makes sexist or racist comments about other people, these also may be explored. Additionally, it may be appropriate for the therapist to give her or his own personal reaction to such statements. In any event, the therapist must constantly remember that the client is to be served by our comments. Although we may, in some sense, "pass judgment" on certain client values, we are still there to help clients, not to punish them or persuade them to agree with all of our values. When clients say something with which you disagree, one option is to say in a very nondefensive, straightforward way, "I don't agree with you on that, but I'd be interested in knowing what experiences you have had that led you to that conclusion."

22. *Should I tell clients if they make me angry?* Therapists do become angry with their clients (Pope & Tabachnick, 1993). The broader question here is the extent to which it is advisable to tell your client what you are feeling. Each of the authors has occasionally found it helpful to share with clients our reaction to them. In general, however, we believe that the special relationship between therapist and client rules out the advisability of routinely communicating your feelings. Whether you like it or not, the relationship is not an equal one, has certain limits set on it, and in the vast majority of cases does not last across time as does a friendship. Furthermore, it seems to us that clients should be able to expect that the purpose for the relationship is for them to feel better. If you become angry at a client and express your anger, how can you be sure that the results will be therapeutic? The minimum conditions for expressing anger toward the client are: (a) you have a sound reason for believing that it will be therapeutic; and (b) your anger does not appear to be related to countertransference issues. Some therapists take the position that any strong feeling toward the client does represent countertransference, but we do not completely agree with this position. For example, if you negotiate with a client, at his request, for an extra session after normal working hours and he fails to show up because he decided to go to a movie instead, we would not view a degree of anger as countertransference. In such a case, it *may* be therapeutic to share some of your reactions with the client. We emphasize, however, that what separates the therapeutic relationship from other relationships is that the purpose is to help the client. In the above example, if you were to express some degree of anger, it should be only a small part of the processing done with the client. Ultimately, the processing must focus not on your being upset, but rather on the fear, anger, or whatever, felt by the client and carried out in the behavioral outcome. Furthermore, if you do express anger, it is vitally important that you not reject clients or implicitly threaten abandonment and that you use your anger to help clients focus on *their* feelings.

On the whole, we believe that being angry with, and expressing anger toward clients is not particularly helpful to them. Usually, when you find yourself angry with a client it is time to: (a) ask yourself what pain the client seeks to avoid by doing something to make you angry (asking such a question will make it easier for you to identify with clients and make it more likely that you can intervene based on their needs, not yours); (b) question what gain the client may be anticipating by making you angry; (c) ask yourself what you can learn about the client's personality organization and interpersonal style by considering the context in, and process by, which you were provoked; and (d) seek supervision so as to understand better the extent to which your dynamics are being tapped by the client (with resulting anger on your part). One of the purposes of supervision is to help you better and more quickly identify situations that spark responses from you that are founded less on client needs than on your own "trouble spots."

23. *What should I say to a client who wants "personal" information about me?* Clients ask these sorts of questions for many reasons, including wanting to gain power and wanting to shift the focus of attention. Questions may include those about age (they may fear that you are too inexperienced to help them), children (they may wonder how you can help them with their parenting problems if you are not a parent yourself), or religion (they may wonder if you share their values). You should not make the mistake of assuming you know why a question about you was asked. For example, there may be cultural factors influencing such questions, or the person may lack certain social skills or may be simply trying to get to know you a little better in the best way he or she knows how. Our usual procedure is to answer demographic questions straightforwardly with no further comment or question *at that time.* We would, of course, make a mental note in the event the theme arises later. An alternative is to say, "Well, I'm certainly willing to answer that question, but I'm wondering why you asked." Some therapists prefer this latter approach.

In addition to demographic issues, you may also be asked things such as, "Where do you live? What do you like to read? How do you like living in _____? How long have you been married?" In such cases, our general rule would be, "Let common sense prevail." If the client has been making sexual advances toward you and then asks, "Where do you live?" you should probably answer by saying something like, "I'm not sure how knowing where I live is going to help you; maybe this would be a good time for us to review what you want from therapy." Later you may want to more directly process the client's attempt to cross the client–therapist boundary. On the other hand, if you are nearing the end of therapy with a couple and they ask how long have you been married or lived with someone, there is probably little reason not to answer the question. In any instance of the client's asking for information about you, the client's dynamics, the context of the question, and recent developments in therapy all must be taken into consideration when considering whether to provide an answer. Like any question from the client, questions about you are grist for the therapeutic mill. (Also, see comments below addressing the issue of clients' asking about your sexual orientation.).

24. *What should I say to clients who ask me about my sexual orientation?* There are substantial differences among therapists as to what to do when clients ask such questions. Many therapists believe that boundary constraints require you not to answer personal questions of this nature. However, other therapists may believe that this is the sort of information to which clients are fully entitled should they ask. Our own view of this matter is that it is generally permissible, if you are asked, to disclose your sexual orientation. We understand that many psychotherapists disagree with this position; however, we believe that this question is posed most often in a spirit of, "Are you like me?" or "Can you understand what I am like?" Answering the question directly at least "gets the ball rolling" about those issues. If you are gay, lesbian, or bisexual and prefer that clients not know this because you fear consequences to yourself, obviously that will influence your own thinking on this matter. Moreover, if, in your judgment, the client appears to be very impressionable or dependent or suffers from a serious personality disorder, the therapist should give a little more consideration before answering such a personal question.

Irrespective of feelings of personal threat, if you tend to be somewhat conservative in this matter (e.g., if you have been heavily influenced by psychoanalytic models of therapy), you may face a particularly difficult choice if your sexual orientation places you in a "minority" population and the client is also a member of that minority. If, for example, the client has some intuition (or might even have more direct information, as is possible in minority communities) that you share the same sexual orientation, you may prefer to maintain the boundary conditions, but if you do, there may be a price to pay. That is, if you refuse to answer the question, the client may feel discouraged and believe that this is just another case of someone who is gay, lesbian, or bisexual agreeing to be invisible. Other possibilities include clients' losing trust in their intuition, or devaluing their sexual orientation if you won't admit to yours. Conversely, a client who is heterosexual may ask the therapist about sexual orientation because the client is "nervous" around people who do not have the same sexual orientation. In such a case, if you are not heterosexual, you may face the choice of not answering the question or risking the client's leaving therapy. Because there can be legitimate reasons for a client to request to see a gay therapist, it is important that some therapists who are not heterosexual be "out" and willing to indicate that to clients. Furthermore, if you are heterosexual and refuse to answer a question about your sexual orientation, do not be surprised when individuals who are gay (or who think they might be gay) decline to see you in therapy.

There are many times when we believe that a straightforward answer is clearly the best one. Assume, for example, that the client says, shortly after he introduces himself, "I want you to know that I am bisexual, because some therapists have a hangup about that, and if you do, I'd like to get another therapist. As long as you accept who I am, I don't really care what your orientation is, but I'd like to know it just so I know where you're coming from." In this case, our belief is that it would probably be best to answer the question directly, although, as we have noted, your own feelings about others knowing your sexual orientation will obviously play a role in your decision.

Again, we emphasize that this general issue tends to be surrounded by differences of opinion among therapists. Stated slightly more forcefully, some therapists cringe at the thought of revealing this kind of information and believe that to do so would be a serious violation of one's professional responsibility; others believe that it borders on the unethical *not* to answer the question. Your stance on this issue should reflect your theoretical commitments and your personal values. In any event, it is an issue to which you should give some thought. You should also discuss it with your peers and supervisor, since when the question is asked, you will find it a little awkward to say, "I need to talk to my supervisor before I answer that question."

25. *What should I say if a client asks me about my religious beliefs?* Religion and spiritual matters have always been important to many people, and they are being given increasing attention by psychologists (e.g., Cornett, 1998; Richards & Bergin, 1997; Shafranske, 1996). Many clients are interested in religion, whether or not they introduce the topic in a discussion. Thus, it is not uncommon for devoutly religious persons to be concerned about the religion of their therapist. In part this is because religion and psychotherapy share an interest in "the human condition" as well as an interest in transformation (or development), meaning, and purpose. Put another way, many of the questions and concerns that bring people to psychotherapy often have what some philosophers and psychotherapists might call a spiritual component. We mean this not to invoke the supernatural, but rather to emphasize that therapy is often about valuing, about what is of central importance to the "real self." In addition to their personal concerns about the issue, individuals with deep religious beliefs are at times influenced by other religious individuals who have criticized psychotherapy for being too "humanistic."

Generally speaking, we advise against your describing to your clients your religious beliefs (or lack thereof) in detail. Especially in the first session or two you need to develop a sense of what the client is looking for, what anxieties are operating around this issue. Worthington (1986) concluded:

> Generally, religious clients prefer counselors who share their values. This is true before or just after counseling begins. Usually by the end of one session, clients do not distinguish between religious and secular counseling unless some issue arises that dramatizes religious values, beliefs, or practices. (p. 429)

A client's asking about religion presents a sensitive area in that it involves deeply held values. Our own practice is to say something like, "Religion to me is a very personal thing; do you have a particular question or concern about that?" Many clients answer, "No, I just wanted to know a little about you." Others may be looking for, and express that they are looking for, a therapist who professes to be "a Christian," or "born-again," or "a devout Catholic," or "of the Jewish faith." If you do not fall within the group in which the client expresses an interest, this issue should be addressed as directly as possible while still giving clients an easy way to change their mind or at least to defer judgment about whether they will or will not continue to see you. For example, if a client says, "I am looking for a Christian counselor," and you do not describe yourself in that way, consider a response of this nature: "I can see that the issue is important to you. I want to be straightforward and tell you that I do not consider myself to be a Christian counselor. On the other hand, I do share many of the values that Christianity emphasizes, and I've certainly had as clients individuals who spoke of being Christians. In those cases my clients have seen, as we worked together, that I would respect their values. However, I certainly will be glad to refer you to someone else if you prefer. (Pause) What are your reactions to what I just said?" The typical scenario at this point is for a discussion to ensue, the decision is put off until the end of the first session, and in the end the client elects not to be referred. If the question is asked after the first session, then we would typically not offer referral (although we would, of course, be *willing* to make a referral) since the client is generally not asking for that after the first session.

If, for example, you consider yourself to be a "born-again Christian" and the client initially states a preference for such a counselor, in our view, it would perhaps be permissible, although not necessarily advisable, to indicate that you are indeed "a born-again Christian." (Some experienced therapists would say that you should *never* disclose your religious beliefs to a client, so it is a good topic to discuss with your supervisor.) On the other hand, it is important for you to indicate that you are, for example, more than a *Christian* counselor or therapist. With regard to this particular phrase, the words have come to suggest a reliance exclusively on what are called Biblical principles. This is not what you are in graduate school training to learn and it is important that clients not be confused by your saying that you are a born-again Christian counselor. Obviously you do not want to say something that will have the effect of confusing the client, or limiting the kinds of interventions you can make or both. Thus, you should emphasize that you deal with the total person and not just with "matters of faith." For example, one therapist we know who is devoutly religious is from time to time asked, "Are you a Christian counselor?" He answers this question by saying something to the effect of, "I am a Christian but I am not a Christian counselor. I do not rely exclusively on the Bible to understand people."

A somewhat related issue involves very religious people and whether it is ever advisable to quote the Hebrew Scripture, the Christian Bible, the Koran, or another religious book to them. Many therapists do know some religious stories or verses and may be inclined to quote one of them to a religious client who, for example, keeps talking about "sin" but never about "love" or "forgiveness." In general, we are not inclined to quote religious books because the client may easily confuse your role as therapist with that of spiritual advisor. On the other hand, these books do contain some very powerful stories that may on occasion be used effectively. The important things to remember are that you should not confuse the client about your role and you should not allow yourself to become an interpreter of religion for the client. It can be quite easy to allow yourself to be put in the role of moral authority. Clients can view you this way no matter what you do, and they certainly do not need your assistance. Worthington (1988) has outlined a model designed to help psychotherapists understand the religious client. It is helpful to know therapists in your area who are of several religious persuasions, since you will certainly be asked to make referrals on this basis from time to time. If you work for a public agency, clients generally assume, or are told if they call and ask, that religious counseling is not done at the agency. Hawkins and Bullock (1995) have suggested that one way to deal with the issue of religion and religious values is through informed consent. They emphasize that the therapist should not try to hide behind neutrality.

26. *What should I say if the client says, "You don't really care—this is just your job"?* Clients make this statement on occasion. Perhaps it is most frequently made in intake sessions when a client is suicidal. It may also be made later in therapy when the client feels misunderstood. Even though its absolute frequency is not great, when said to a beginning therapist it may be very disconcerting. If you have just started with the client and the client is in crisis, perhaps the most important things to remember are not to get into a power struggle, and not to imply that there is a deep relationship between the two of you. There obviously is little relationship yet, and in our view, you do your clients a disservice in trying to convince them otherwise. Avoid the trap of saying something like, "Life is very important to me—so are you." Such a response is overly abstract ("life is important to me") as well as being presumptuous ("so are you"). A very positive part of what the client has said ("You don't care") is that there is an implied challenge in it—"Prove me wrong." Thus, although the statement is indeed somewhat hostile, it also has the quality of approaching you, and implicitly, of asking you for help. This positive but hostile approach usually means that something more than just reflecting feelings will be required from you, although acknowledging feelings will certainly be a part of any good response. After saying such a thing, the client expects to be told, "You are wrong." It is helpful to say in essence, "You are right," thereby disarming a part of the hostility. How do you do this? One way is to say something like this: "Well, you are right. Sitting down with people who are searching for a better life—maybe even a reason to live, is my job. It's a job I've chosen because I like being able to invest myself with other people as they struggle for something better. I like the relationships that come out of that. I know that right now you are wondering if you should invest with me—you're not sure how it will turn out, and I surely don't blame you for being skeptical when others have let you down."

Certainly we are not suggesting that you repeat verbatim what we have written. Nothing could be worse than memorizing a line to deliver at such a critical point in therapy. Your greatest asset as a therapist is your humanness—your ability to make real contact with persons who, for whatever reason, have had great difficulty in doing that with others. We are emphasizing that when clients say, in essence, you are a "hired gun," you might as well acknowledge that you do, indeed, get paid for it. Once clients realize that you are not interested in defending yourself, that you have no reason to argue with them, they will be able to listen to you. They will be able to hear that you have some understanding of their conflicted feelings, their fears, and the felt constraints under which they labor. They will be able to hear that you are reaching out and that you recognize their reaching out. In the client's eyes, the odds now shift, if only slightly, toward an outcome in which the two of you can meet and she or he can be cared for. This was what the question was about. If the question occurs later in therapy, it may either signal a failure on the part of the therapist to make the client feel understood or it may reflect client dynamics; for example, "no one can love me," or "the good mother should be perfect," or even "I (the client) need to abandon you (the therapist) before you abandon me."

A good supervisor can help you understand whether the sentence arises primarily from a shortcoming on your part or from transference issues on the part of the client. Certainly, you should look very carefully at your own feelings about clients in such circumstances. For example, do you dislike in particular some things about them? Do they remind you of yourself? Have you been subtly withdrawing from the client? The general rule is to consider first your own role in blocking client progress and then to look at client dynamics. Otherwise, it is all too easy to "blame the client" for lack of progress, and you thereby risk losing important insights about yourself—insights that will help make you a better therapist.

27. *What should I say if a client wants to know my credentials or training?* Of course, a question about training may be an attempt to undercut your power, may be indicative of the client's inability to trust, may reflect the client's ambivalence about being in therapy, or some combination of the above. Psychotherapists are, however, increasingly cognizant of the client's rights as a consumer. Furthermore, the growing number of different types of help-giving specialties inevitably leads to some confusion on the part of clients. The media has also played a part in disseminating information about what therapists do. For example, there are books for the general population describing the differences between approaches such as Gestalt, Psychoanalytic, and Behavioral psychotherapies. Therefore, you can scarcely blame clients for asking about some of these issues—even though we also may get a glimpse of their personalities when they ask such questions, especially if the point is belabored.

If you are sympathetic to the idea that questions about credentials should be handled straightforwardly, you will find an ally in Arnold Lazarus, who, in his book *Behavior Therapy and Beyond* (1971), describes an incident in which a client responded well to his nondefensive answers. All these complexities do not, however, change the fact that if you are just starting to be a therapist, and you are asked about your experience, you will probably feel on the spot. If asked, for example, how many clients you have seen, don't "try to be Freud" by saying something like "credentials must be important to you." If you do give such a response, don't be surprised if the client says, "Yes, credentials are important to me when I see someone without them." Clients are seldom stupid, and they react (understandably) quite strongly to anything they perceive as defensive and to therapists trying to be something they are not. When asked about your experience, don't try to defend yourself by listing your coursework or your informal experience. Generally, the less explanation, the better. Thus, if asked how many clients you have seen, consider a reply like this, "I'm a graduate student in training. I haven't seen a lot of people in formal counseling sessions. How do you feel about that? If it bothers you, let's talk about it." (The response is more effective if you can look directly at the client and speak in a calm and confident tone—something that may at first be difficult to do.) Such a reply: (a) models for the client the kind of straightforward honesty you hope will characterize the relationship; and (b) shows that you are mature and confident enough to readily acknowledge that your are not Fritz Perls. Nine times out of ten, clients will appreciate your refreshing candor and will take it as a sign that they don't need to worry too much about your experience. On the other hand, it is perhaps not necessary to say, "You are my third client—I am a rank beginner." While still showing a refreshing (even sprightly) candor, this response gives the client nothing to hold on to. We encourage you to be straightforward but not blunt. Only a very small percentage of clients ever ask about experience. Furthermore, if you tell them up front that you are a student when you are asking permission to tape, you will almost never get a question about your experience—you will already have simply and directly addressed the issue.

28. *How should I talk about sex?* It is important not to dance around the issue of sex. If a male client says he has "difficulties in performing," you will need to help him clarify what he means—difficulties maintaining an erection, premature ejaculation, or whatever. The client will then realize that it is just fine for him to label whatever he needs to label. Or, to give another example, suppose a client says, "And then he had his way with me." We ask, "What actually happened?" She replies, "I said 'no' but he went ahead anyway." We say, "He had intercourse with you—it sounds like rape." And then she realizes that we are not afraid of emotionally dangerous situations and difficult words. We are strong enough to be her therapist. Of course, in the example just cited we would remember for future processing the difficulty the client had in approaching the subject. Our point here is that the client will be less afraid of talking when we demonstrate that we are fearless (though sensitive) in approaching subjects that society frequently avoids. When in doubt, ask, and call things by their real names rather than using euphemisms.

29. *What should I say to a client who says, "Do you like me?"* Some of the comments we made earlier concerning the client who says, "This is just your job," are applicable here. That is, clients who have a great fear of rejection may ask this question in order to be reassured, or in order to play out a fantasy in which they become your special client. On the other hand, they may be asking this question in response to some behavior on your part (more generally rejecting, but at times suggesting positive countertransference). Clients, perhaps better than nonclients, can pick up on subtle rejections by other individuals, in this case the therapist. If you really do not like a client, he or she will figure that out sooner or later. Furthermore, most therapists find that they do not make particularly good progress with clients they dislike. The point here is that if you really don't like a client, you should consider a referral. An alternative is to seek supervision on the case so you can work though some of the countertransference issues. But, of course, there may be times when you are on the verge of seeking supervision because you find yourself not liking a client, and the client "beats you to the punch" by asking "Do you like me?" There are essentially three schools of thought on such a situation. Many therapists (influenced by psychodynamic theory) believe that the client must deal with these issues and that your thoughts or feelings about the client have no place in a response. If you agree with this philosophy, you might say, "What is it that you need from me that you are not getting?" An alternative might be, "That's hard isn't it, your wanting me to approve of you, yet my seeming not to from where you stand." At the other end of the continuum is the acknowledgment that you *don't* like certain things about the client: "You're right; there are some parts of you that I find hard to work with. I don't like the way you box me out, the way you block me out and then complain that I don't give enough." A more middle-of-the-road approach attempts to validate, at least in part, the client's perceptions without focusing extensively on the therapist: "That's a good question. I think it's fair to say that I've not always been able to see your pain—and maybe my frustration seems like 'not liking you.' Maybe I haven't seen your pain because you can't let me see it just yet or because I'm a little blind at times, or both. In any event, I think it's been hard for us to always connect in a way that makes you feel understood and valued. How are you feeling about all this?" The authors prefer something similar to the latter, although there are good therapists using each of the approaches. If you are asked the question, and you do like the client and have no reason to believe that you have not been accepting of the client, we are prone to say, "Yes I do. Have you been wondering about that?" We realize that many therapists would leave off the "Yes I do." We have no quarrel with them; we are simply telling you what we usually do. As you might expect, this question is sometimes asked when clients are sexually attracted to their therapists.

30. *What should I say if a client compliments me?* Compliments might be viewed as a mild form of the client's giving you a present. One of the first things you will want to consider is the context of the compliment. For example, did it follow a tense time in therapy? Was it embedded in a discussion of how a parent never gave to the client? Did it follow a discussion of the client's inability to express negative feelings? Your response to a compliment, therefore, must be based in part on how it registers in terms of the dynamics of the situation. In a more general sense, if the client says, for example, "I like your dress," we are prone to say simply, "Thank you." If the client says something directly about therapy such as "I really appreciate the way you've supported me while I struggled with my child's operation," we might say, "I have felt very much a part of your struggle. I'm glad to have been a positive part of that." We might add, after a pause and depending on the circumstances, "Has it been hard for you to let me be close at such a difficult time?" We recommend a middle road with regard to reacting to compliments.

To paraphrase Freud, "Sometimes a compliment is just a compliment." On the other hand, it can be much more. For example, a client might say "You have a beautiful dress," and be thinking "When I was a child, I never had nice things." Or clients might say, "You understand me so much better than I'd ever hoped when I came to therapy," and be feeling that you have been intrusive or that you know too much about them. In these last two examples, we point to the ever-present potential that a compliment, like any communication, can have multiple layers of meaning, some of which may not be readily apparent. As a trained therapist, one of your strengths is and will be a certain readiness to hear more than one message when the client speaks. We are particularly underscoring this issue in answering a question about compliments because in our culture compliments take on many meanings. When clients need to communicate something but for whatever reason find it necessary to blunt or cover their real intent, they are perhaps somewhat more prone to use communication styles that have been sanctioned by the culture. Compliments are one such style. Naturally, the personal meaning of the compliment is a part of the client's story and must be understood on a person-by-person basis.

31. *What should I do if a client makes sexual advances toward me?* The literature (e.g., deMayo, 1997) suggests that many clients do make sexual remarks during therapy and that a very small percentage threaten assault, or even do assault the therapist. Obviously, you are entitled to feel reasonably safe as a therapist, and it is not unethical to refer a client who threatens you or repeatedly sexualizes the relationship to the point of disruption. However, we believe that in the majority of cases, clients who attempt (whether directly or indirectly) to sexualize the relationship can be managed and that such behavior is merely another part of the client's pathology with which we deal. There are some general rules to follow. First, if the client is making some strong hints along this line, help him or her bring the issue into the open. Therapeutic progress is likely to be very slow or nonexistent if the client is operating on the fantasy that the two of you will one day "be together," that you as the therapist will slowly but surely (or even with dramatic quickness) fall in love with the client. Why do we say that progress will be slow? The answer is quite simple. When clients are completely immersed in a fantasy that the two of you may enter into a sexual relationship, they are very reluctant to damage their chances by revealing the "bad parts" of themselves. In fact, it will be precisely those parts that the client will seek to cover up.

We understand that a great many clients have fantasies about their therapists and that therapy may progress nicely while these fantasies continue. We are saying that when clients are consciously preoccupied with these fantasies to the point that they are making broad hints, you may expect therapeutic progress to be very slow indeed. Particularly in such cases you must be quite sensitive to the possibility of the client's reporting dramatic improvement as a way of winning your love and acceptance. A second guideline is that once the desires have been expressed, clear behavioral limits must be set (it is of course unethical to have a sexual relationship with a client). "No, I will not see you outside therapy under any circumstances." "No, even if you terminate therapy, I could never go out with you," and so forth. Third, once you have been explicit about limits, stand by them. We know one therapist who says something like this: "I will not go out with you, and you can count on that like the Rock of Gibraltar." Such a statement, as we imply above, brings enormous relief to clients since they know they can now let down their guard. They have nothing left to lose, so to speak. Clients sometimes push the issue by asking, "Do you find me attractive?" One response might be: "There are many things I respect and like about you, but under no circumstances will I see you for any reason other than for psychotherapy. I will not have a sexual relationship with you. What are your reactions to what I just said?" Fourth, be sure you do not belittle or demean the client's advances toward you. Although some clients may be what society would call "obnoxious" about this issue, another group have been very afraid to admit their feelings, even to themselves. You may be the first person they have ever "fallen in love with." They may be ashamed of their attraction to you and unsure of what to do about their feelings. For this group of people, the fact that they are sexually attracted to you is a part of the positive transference. It is a positive sign because it means that they can invest with others in a positive way. It may be their first beginning steps, and it may catch you completely off guard if you had little anticipation of it. If, for example, you communicate your surprise, this could be very detrimental. So be clear but patient. There are behavioral limits, but the client's fantasies are neither bad nor something for which he or she should be ashamed.

Sexual feelings should be discussed like other feelings. Because therapists are sometimes frightened of their own sexual impulses, they may come across to the client as punishing and rejecting. Try to be aware of your own anxiety in this area (see below), and be open and nondefensive enough to take a close look at your own behavior to rule out the possibility that you are in some way inviting the comments. Finally, be sure to thoroughly process the client's sexual attraction toward you. For some clients, there may be a very hostile component to the sexual attraction. It may be an attempt to rob you of your power or to punish members of your gender for an injustice experienced as a child. It may be a continuation of a theme in the client's life that emphasizes an attempt to obtain what is not truly desired, or an attempt to set goals that cannot be achieved. Furthermore, some clients may actually be trying to injure themselves by compromising those individuals (in this case the therapist) who might assist them. It is most certainly, ultimately, a substitution for what the client wants and needs. But all this will never be discovered if you simply set the limits and assume that everything else will fall into place.

32. *Is it ever, under any circumstances, for any reason, permissible to have a sexual relationship with a client?* No.

33. *What should I do if I am sexually attracted to a client?* Research shows that the great majority of therapists have in fact been attracted to one or more of their clients. In a study by Pope, Keith-Spiegel, and Tabachnick (1993), 508 of 585 respondents reported that they had been attracted to at least one client. Among the men, only 5% reported that they had never been attracted to a client; for the women the percentage was 24%. Slightly over 91% of the men and slightly over 97% of the women reported that they had never acted on their attraction. Certainly the percentage (although small in some absolute sense) of therapists who have violated ethical standards is disheartening; however, the point we wish to make here is that there are a very large number of therapists who are attracted to one or more clients, and who do not act on that attraction. The study showed that of the "non–acting-out" therapists, the majority felt guilty about their *feelings*. Therefore, if you find yourself sexually attracted to a client, you can be counted among the overwhelming majority of therapists, and your feelings of discomfort are quite typical.

Although a full discussion of this issue is far beyond what space permits here, we will mention five simple guidelines we believe you should follow if you find yourself attracted to a client: (a) don't try to deny (to yourself) the attraction; (b) consult with one or more trusted colleagues preferably including your supervisor; (c) as you think about the issue, distinguish clearly between your feelings and your behavior—focus on the fact that you are committed to ethical behavior, which means that you will never act on your attraction; (d) remember to consider the possibility that the client is unconsciously "setting you up," as a reflection of his or her pathology—refocusing on the client's pathology may help you regain your balance; and (e) try to decide if there is something missing in your life and seek therapy or other solutions if you conclude that you are impaired for whatever reason.

In a study of 13 supervisees who reported being sexually attracted to clients, Ladany et al. (1997) found that slightly over 50% of supervisees disclosed to their supervisors their sexual attraction. Of those who disclosed, all reported that the supervisor helped them normalize the attraction, although in some cases there were also negative reactions to the supervisor's intervention.

We recommend that you not tell the client about your attraction except in highly unusual circumstances. Goodyear and Shumate (1997) found that when therapists viewed a video segment of a therapist responding to an erotic transference either by disclosing or not disclosing his or her own attraction, the viewers rated the disclosure as less therapeutic than a nondisclosing response. Pope, Sonne, and Holroyd (1993) suggest a number of issues to consider very carefully before such disclosure, including (but not limited to) keeping the needs of the client as the focus, using consultation, being theoretically consistent, thinking about the client's reaction, and being sure that the communication not be seductive in any way. The book by Pope and colleagues (1993) is an excellent resource for reading in this area.

General Therapeutic Issues

34. *When should I make a report concerning child abuse?* This is a very complex question with a very large literature (e.g., Kalichman, 1993; see also, APA, 1997). The easy answer is, "Whenever you suspect child abuse." But this is an overly simple answer and begs such questions as, "How *much* should I suspect it before reporting?" Although state laws are subject to change, it would likely be accurate to say that in all states psychotherapists have some responsibility to report suspected child abuse. Apart from the general question of when to report, psychotherapists often face two issues. First is the issue of confidentiality: The ethical responsibility to protect confidentiality comes into conflict with one's ethical responsibility to protect the vulnerable (here, children) and the legal responsibility mandated by the state. In a survey by Pope and Vetter (1992), which looked at ethical dilemmas encountered by members of the American Psychological Association, when the issue was confidentiality, the category of "child abuse reporting" was second in frequency only to dilemmas surrounding actual or perceived threat to third parties. Thus, it is clear that psychologists often do face a conflict between keeping confidentiality and protecting children.

The second area involves the internal conflict faced by the psychotherapist who may repeatedly see the relevant state agency take little or no action when a report is made. Under such circumstances, therapists often become very reluctant to report, fearing that nothing will be done to protect the child (or worse, that the child will suffer more as a result of the report), while simultaneously, the therapeutic bond is seriously damaged.

Clearly, all these issues must play a part in the decision as to when to report. This being said, we will offer three generalizations. First, always discuss this issue with your supervisor and be sure to check the policy of the agency for whom you are working. You have a responsibility to carry out the policies of the agency except in the most extreme circumstances. Second, our general philosophy is that when in doubt as to whether you have enough evidence to report, you should report. One way of thinking about this dilemma is to ask yourself, "What happens, and what do I feel, if I report and then the child's situation is worsened?" versus "What happens, and what do I feel, if I *fail* to report and the child's situation is worsened?" Our belief is that therapists work in a cultural milieu, and when the culture decides that certain protections are needed for children, we must have a very strong, very compelling argument to go against this cultural mandate. It can be all too easy to come to the conclusion, "I am so well trained, and I have so many facts, that I can go against the law." We do believe, however, that in the final analysis, the greater good is the protection of the vulnerable child, and there may be occasions when this commitment leads us to do something that is in violation of the letter of the law, for example, when there is clear prior evidence that reporting may place the child at greater risk. We repeat, however, that such a decision must be taken only with the greatest of care, and certainly only following consultation. Third, we point out that when it becomes necessary to violate confidentiality, one must try to use the situation in the most therapeutic way possible. Furthermore, this problem of reporting child abuse underscores once more the importance of discussing with your client, at the onset of therapy, the limitations of confidentiality. We also point out that the comments we have made about child abuse are applicable concerning elder abuse—an action that is reportable (like child abuse) in some states.

35. *What should I do when a client misses an appointment?* These situations include both canceled appointments and "no-shows." Some comments apply to both types of situations. First, it is important to remember that cultural factors may influence whether, or how often, clients miss a session. For example, individuals who are members of the "working class" are much more likely than middle class people to have their car break down, be dependent on a bus that may be late, be told by their supervisor that they can't leave yet, and so forth. Thus, when making decisions about what to do and how to react to missed sessions, you will need to consider cultural factors.

Gans and Counselman (1996) describe a number of the issues relevant to clients' missing sessions, and they argue primarily that the missed session is an important event in therapy:

> While the reasons for a missed session may be completely reality-based, the thoughts, feelings, and fantasies about the missed session should be attended to with great interest. A therapeutic stance characterized by neutrality and curiosity facilitates such exploration. (p. 45)

As Gans and Counselman suggest, therapists display a wide range of differences on this issue. One of the big questions always is, "Should the client be charged for a missed session?" As a practicum student you will not be in a position to make that decision, but you should check to see if there is an agency policy. That way, if a client wants to discuss the issue, you will be prepared.

Another question that comes up is whether clients should be called if they miss a session. Again, you should first check the agency policy. Our own recommendation is that the intake form contain a question that asks clients whether they agree to be called at home (or the office). If you do not have this agreement, we think it best that you not call except under very unusual circumstances. There are simply too many possibilities for confidentiality to be (inadvertently) violated (for example, roommates who answer the telephone, caller ID, answering machines to which others may have access, etc.). Even if permission has been granted by the client, the question is still difficult to answer because it generally depends on the client. For example, clients who don't show up for their first appointment are frequently not called, nor are clients who have repeatedly "no-showed" in the past.

On the other hand, you might call an individual who has never missed a session in 20 visits (and who has given permission). Some therapists believe that any individual who no-shows should always be called as a therapeutic technique. From this perspective, clients are treated "as if" they very much wanted to be in therapy, but were prevented from doing so. The technique is continued until the client stops no-showing or until the client becomes angry because she or he is constantly being contacted, at which point the issue of commitment to therapy is processed. It is also true that many therapists *never* call clients who have no-showed. In fact, some agencies specifically prohibit it.

In our opinion, it is not advisable to get in the habit of calling individuals who do not show up. Psychotherapy is most often a voluntary endeavor for which individuals must be encouraged to take responsibility. If a client repeatedly no-shows, this issue *must* be processed in therapy. If a client just stops coming to therapy, you should consider sending him or her a letter that outlines options of either returning to therapy with you or being referred. This type of letter will help protect you against a potential malpractice suit. It also offers the client an opportunity to return in order to work out his or her reason for leaving. We know that some clients do stop coming with little or no warning; we believe that such a termination procedure generally glosses over important issues. If the client is willing to come for even *one* final session, we would see this as a very positive step.

If you do selectively choose (with permission) to call clients who no show, one very practical issue is what to say to individuals (roommates or relatives) who may answer the telephone if you call. If your client is not available, one alternative is to leave the message that you called, requesting that your client return your call. If this alternative is chosen, we recommend that you not leave a telephone number (simply say that the person you are calling has your number) since curious relatives may call back to find out where your call originated. If you leave the agency number, the relative then can ascertain that you are with a mental health facility. In fact, with electronic devices now available, the person on the other end of the telephone line can identify the number from which the call is placed; but if the client has given permission for you to call, you perhaps need not worry about that sort of situation. The potential problems that can develop when you try to call clients who have failed to show up for an appointment are just another reason why calling them is not typically done.

Finally, we would note that when you send a letter to a client, be sure to use an envelope that includes a return address that does *not* name the mental health facility. Many agencies provide two different types of stationery, one of which will have envelopes using only a post office box number. This ensures confidentiality in that if another person sees your client's mail, that person will not be able to ascertain from the envelope that your client is in counseling.

36. *Should I accept presents from clients?* From our perspective, this question cannot be answered with a simple yes or no. Some therapists take the position that a present should never be accepted from a client because the present is thought to represent an attempt to erase the dependency felt by the client. In this view, if therapists accept presents, they thereby collude with clients in pretending that dependency is not an issue. There may also be a fantasy on the part of the client that the therapist can be "bought off." In this sense, the client may be asking for forgiveness for a particular shortcoming or may in general be carrying out a theme of seeking the approval of authority figures. Furthermore, the idea of buying off the therapist contains a hostile component related to the dependency issue. That is, individuals who have been "bought" have had their power reduced and are no longer a threat. Particularly if there is monetary payment for the therapy (as in private practice or mental health centers), the proffering of a gift may contain elements of self-punitiveness (I must pay you over and over for your services since what I offer is of such little importance). A final caution is that a client may bring a gift because of sexual attraction to his or her therapist.

Despite these considerations, it is our position that it is permissible to accept a present if all of the following conditions are met: (a) The client does not evidence a pattern of responding to authority figures by giving them presents to win their approval; (b) The gift is not unreasonable by broad cultural standards (e.g., the offering of a small handmade gift is very different from the offer of a new car); (c) Some relationship has developed between the therapist and the client (e.g., it would be unwise to accept a present from a client after he or she had come to see you only once or twice); (d) The offer of a gift does not appear to be related to any recent development in therapy. It is also important to take into consideration the culture and ethnicity of the client. There are some subcultures in which it would be an insult to the client to refuse a small present that has been proffered. Whether you choose to accept presents are not, it is most important to remember that when a client offers the therapist a present it is almost always significant. At times you may want to say something similar to, "You know you don't have to do this. I care about you anyway."

We would not normally process the offering of a small present at the termination of therapy. In our view this would be a normal part of the way in which clients can say to themselves and to us, "I appreciate your help; I'm ready to stop taking from you, and can now give you something in return." Although some clients may attempt to subvert the therapeutic process with a gift, our own experience has been that these instances are rare. In general, we find that clients who bring gifts do so as an appropriate reflection of their positive attachment to the therapist. Taking into consideration the issues just discussed, we see nothing wrong with this.

37. *Is it ever appropriate to give a client a present?* To be straightforward in answering this question, let us admit that the authors themselves disagree about the answer. One of us says, "Probably not—I've never done it," and the other says, "Not often—but I have done it on one occasion." The most important question is why you would want to do this. You may be saying, "I have not done a good job of doing therapy; perhaps this present will make up for it." Certainly, if you are a beginning therapist you will want to think long and hard before giving a client a present. In addition to considering countertransference issues, you must think about how the client will understand your present. For example, you would certainly never give a present to a very immature person or to an individual with a personality disorder since she or he might be confused by what you had done. Van Denburg and Van Denburg (1992) describe a case in which a psychoanalytic therapist gave the client a congratulatory card for finishing his dissertation. In this particular case, the client is reported to have believed that the card reflected social obligation. Clearly, the nature of the therapeutic relationship (in addition to the client's personality) is a critical variable in thinking about this issue.

38. *Is it permissible to touch clients?* Most attorneys will tell you that you should not do this because you could be charged with assault and battery, sexual harassment, or any number of other breaches of duty. Orthodox psychoanalysts strongly recommend against it for theoretical reasons. Many therapists do touch clients from time to time, but we encourage you to be cautious about doing so. If you tend to touch others naturally, you are very likely to touch clients from time to time. We believe that is permissible. In fact, under certain circumstances touching may be therapeutic. Horton, Clance, Sterk-Elifson, and Emshoff (1995) found that a significant majority of clients found touch to be very helpful. It is important to remember that touching means different things to different people, and therefore, until you know a little about your client, touching is a bit risky. Certainly you should avoid obvious mistakes like hugging a client of your own gender when that client appears to be homophobic. It should go without saying that touching should involve no sexual intent on the part of the therapist. Furthermore, if either client or therapist becomes sexually aroused by touching, clearly touching should be discontinued, regardless of any "original" intentions (Kertay & Reviere, 1993). Alyn (1988) has pointed out that people who hold more power are more likely to touch persons of lesser power, thereby raising questions about the advisability of male therapists touching female clients. That is to say, touch may perpetuate the traditional experience of females feeling less powerful. If there is a consensus in the literature, it is that therapists must be clear about their motivation when they touch and that the client's needs and vulnerabilities must be carefully considered. In our own view, handshakes or something like a passing touch on the shoulder are generally quite appropriate. There is a full range of opinion on this issue among experienced therapists. As we have suggested, we are not opposed to touching when appropriate good judgment is used. Special precaution must be taken when the client has a history of being battered, raped, or assaulted, or being the victim of childhood sexual abuse (Lawry, 1998; Olio & Cornell, 1993; Vesper, 1995), especially if you and the perpetrator are of the same gender. It should be noted that in the Horton, Clance, Sterk-Elifson, and Emshoff study, the victims of sexual abuse seemed to value touch moreso than did the clients who had not been sexually abused.

39. *Is it okay to use expletives?* In general, we caution against the therapist's frequent use of expletives. We are not suggesting that you should never use a word like "damn," but we advise that the frequent use of strong expletives may be counterproductive to therapy. Most clients do not expect therapists to use such words and may be confused by the occurrence. Some clients will be offended, and the majority of others will wonder why you rely on such words to make your points or may believe you are trying to prove something by your language. At a

minimum, we strongly recommend against your use of such language prior to the client's using similar language.

40. *What should I say if the client asks, "Do you think I'm gay (or a lesbian or bisexual)?"* First, we note that there have been differences of opinion about how words like gay, lesbian, and homosexual are to be defined and used (Morgan & Nerison, 1993). These are important issues, but they are beyond the scope of this book. We strongly encourage you to read literature in the area of psychotherapy with gay men, lesbians, and persons who are bisexual (e.g., Anderson & Adley, 1997).

In response to the client's question, consider something like the following: "I never try to answer that question for my clients. As I see it, it is very important that something so central to who you are be something *you* decide about. Let's talk some more about the types of feelings you have been having for men and women." Obviously, clients are expressing anxiety about their sexual orientations if they ask you this question. On the other hand, simply because clients ask about whether you think they are gay, does not mean that they *are* gay. This is especially true of adolescents and young adults who have limited heterosexual experience. Also, some clients may have one or two sexual experiences with a person of the same gender and then conclude that they are gay, lesbian, or bisexual. It is very important that you as a therapist not jump to any quick conclusions about the person's sexual orientation. We emphasize that clients' sexual experiences with persons of the same gender, by themselves, do not tell us (or the client) what the person's sexual orientation is. Nor does experience of attraction to someone of the other gender necessarily mean that the client is heterosexual. Many people who now identify as lesbians or gay have been in heterosexual relationships or marriages in the past.

If the client is concerned about her or his sexual orientation, it is important to focus on at least seven issues: (a) the client's previous sexual/romantic experiences and how he or she felt about them at the time; (b) the client's sexual fantasies (that is, do they involve males or females?); (c) the client's emotional attractions; (d) the client's perceived goals concerning various types of sexual liaisons; (e) the client's feeling about seeking various types of relationships; (f) the client's perception of, and fears about, how others would react to his or her sexual orientation; and (g) the degree to which the person is accepting of his or her own sexual behavior and impulses. By itself, a person's sexual orientation is neither healthy nor pathological. The Diagnostic and Statistical Manual (4th ed.) published by the American Psychiatric Association (1994) does not treat sexual orientation as a part of psychopathology. If you believe that people who engage in, or have a preference for, sexual activity with individuals of their own gender are suffering from pathology, we encourage you to discuss the issue with your supervisor. Clients who are conflicted about their sexual orientation are typically (though by no means universally) very perceptive about picking up therapist attitudes toward them. If you start with the assumption that some sexual orientations are bad, you will make it very difficult for conflicted clients to explore their issues, and you may in fact be sending quite harmful messages.

It is often the case that a therapist is the very first person in whom the client has placed enough trust to talk about the issue of sexual orientation. In such a circumstance, it is obviously of great importance that you react with sensitivity and acceptance. In part because of certain cultural taboos against same-gender sexual activity, clients who are conflicted about this issue often feel isolated, fearful, and lonely. They often internalize the homophobia that is present in the culture of the United States. This internalization may result in feelings of self-rejection and even self-loathing. Even for those clients who are gay, lesbian, or bisexual, and not conflicted, problems such as a lack of social and family support may make other concerns more difficult to overcome.

Issues of mental health in the gay-male community have been greatly intensified and made more complicated by the HIV/AIDS crisis. Certainly the therapist must be sensitive to the possibility that clients who are uncertain of, or conflicted about, their sexual orientation may equate being a gay male with having or getting AIDS. These individuals need help in understanding the difference between sexual orientation and risky sexual behavior. Even if the distortion just described is not present, there may be a more general fear of being a part of a "medically vulnerable" group, or being unable to find a partner who is not HIV positive. These sorts of fears are, of course, a "fiction," but it is the kind of fear some clients have. Obviously, education and dealing with the internalized homophobia are parts of the treatment in this sort of situation.

41. *What should I say if a client says to me, "I am a lesbian (or bisexual or gay)"?* If you are not yet comfortable with someone, especially a client, saying this to you, it is time to get comfortable, or at least it is time to learn how to handle this sort of disclosure in a professional and appropriate way. In a national survey of gay men and lesbians who had seen a therapist, 63% of those responding reported that they screened their therapist for gay-affirmative attitudes and over one-third of this 63% reported doing so directly with the prospective therapist (Liddle, 1997). Clients who tell you their sexual orientation (if they are not heterosexual) fall into two general categories. In the first category are individuals who see their sexual orientation as a fundamental part of their identity. These people are nondefensive; they usually want you to know "up front" who they are and are essentially saying, "This is important to me and you should know about it if you are going to help me. If you have a problem with this, I need to know now so I can find another therapist." Individuals in the second category use this statement more defensively. They may anticipate rejection (based on prior experiences) and they may use this stated information as a way of testing your acceptance of them. In either case, your goal as a therapist is to be comfortable with this individual variable, just as you should be comfortable seeing both men and women, people of different ethnicity, people who grew up in different parts of the country, and so on. If a client says, as she sits down, "The first thing you should know about me is that I am a lesbian," you might respond, while looking very directly at her, "OK. Would you like to tell me more or do you just want to be sure that I'm comfortable with that?" You might also consider a response like this: "OK. The way I see it, sexual orientation is a therapeutic issue if it's something that concerns you; otherwise, it's not something

I tend to focus on. Do you have any questions you'd like to ask *me*?" This sort of response communicates your intention to be open and straightforward about the issue. It is important to communicate, whether directly or indirectly, your acceptance and affirmation of the person's sexual orientation, without being "fake" or patronizing and without "protesting too much." If you are anxious about the issue of sexual orientation, we encourage you to read related material, discuss with peers and/or supervisors, reflect, or discuss with your own therapist.

Earlier we made the point that sexual orientation, by itself, is not psychopathological. A correlate of this point is that, whatever a person's sexual orientation, you should never assume that this is the reason a person came to psychotherapy or that it is the "real" problem. Furthermore, you should examine your own biases (whatever your sexual orientation) to ensure that you can quite easily picture people living in happy, committed relationships (or alone), and being very satisfied with their lives, regardless of their sexual orientation. McHenry and Johnson (1993) have discussed some of the problems that arise in treatment when homophobia or heterosexism are present in either the client or the therapist and have explored a number of treatment issues such as secretiveness (see also Baron, 1996).

Although we know that HIV is not a "gay disease," and that it is an important issue for all sexually active clients, we must also be aware of the fact that many members of the gay-male community have been affected by the HIV/AIDS crisis. In many cases, clients may have had numerous close friends die, and many more may be in the midst of coping with the disease. This is not to say that the HIV/AIDS crisis figures prominently in the lives or mental health problems of all gay men; however, clinicians must be very aware of the social and personal strains that may have been created by the disease. We also encourage you to be sensitive to the uses of language and the more subtle ways in which therapists can make erroneous assumptions (American Psychological Association, Committee on Lesbian and Gay Concerns, 1991). For example, if sexual orientation has not been discussed in therapy, and a male client says, "I have difficulty in my dating relationships," the therapist might reply, "When did you first notice that you were anxious around women?" A female client might say, "My lover and I will be moving in together soon," and the therapist might reply, "How long have you known him?" Obviously, such heterosexist assumptions are to be avoided. You should realize that clients who are gay, lesbian, or bisexual sometimes use nonspecific pronouns as a way of testing potential therapists. If your responses reflect heterosexist assumptions, you fail the test and you will not be their therapist. How can we expect clients to trust us if our comments render them invisible or even nonexistent?

Finally, it is also important to remember that in any given academic class, a variety of sexual orientations are likely represented. If nothing else, the idea of sensitivity alone suggests that you should remember this as you describe your clients to your instructors and peers. The main point, however, is not sensitivity per se, but rather the need for you to avoid assumptions that may be, quite simply, wrong.

42. *What should I say if a client wants to write me a letter about something?* Although psychotherapy is primarily a verbal endeavor, there are no arbitrary rules about the mechanisms you can or should use to assist clients. If a client is having difficulty expressing feelings, it may help to write the feelings down whether in the form of a letter to you, a diary, or whatever. On a few occasions, we have known clients who wanted to write a letter and *mail* it to the therapist. This we strongly discourage—chiefly because it represents a breach of the boundary conditions. Allowing a client to mail you a letter may encourage fantasies of involvement that go beyond the client–therapist relationship. So if clients would like to express their feelings in a letter, that's fine; they should bring the letter to their therapy session and read it to you, or as a minimum, allow you the opportunity to read it in their presence.

43. *How do I know when a client should be hospitalized?* As a beginning therapist, the first rule to follow, of course, is to check with your supervisor if you believe that the client is a candidate for hospitalization. A variety of skills (as well as potential value conflicts) come into play in making judgments about hospitalization; therefore, discussions with your supervisor about the general issue should occur *before* you are faced with it. Generally speaking, you should offer hospitalization when you believe there is a definite possibility that clients might harm themselves or others. Also, offer hospitalization when clients fear they are losing control, if they are out of touch with reality, if they have not slept in two or more days, if they feel manic, or when it appears that they cannot be responsible for themselves. When offered hospitalization, many clients reject it but feel relieved that this form of support is available. As a part of your administrative briefing at your agency, you should ask about hospitalization procedures. Frequently, this will include the client's being examined (interviewed) by a psychiatrist or chief psychologist.

44. *What should I do if I think a client should be hospitalized but the client refuses?* In answering this question, we will assume you have tried your best to persuade the client to consider this option—listened to his or her concerns, reframed the issue, and the like—but the client still says no. One possibility is to set up an appointment each day for the next few days. Another is to contract with the client to call you each day at a certain time. Other options include discussing how to use the crisis line, providing your phone number, and discussing how to use the emergency room. Finally, it may be possible and appropriate in some circumstances to help the person make some arrangements with family or friends. However, if you are moving toward the end of the session and believe that the client would be a strong threat to either his or her own welfare or someone else's once the person leaves the building, we would recommend that you call a supervisor or (another senior person) into the session. This question can rightly be seen as a specific one addressing the larger question of "under what circumstances should I call a supervisor into the session?" In any event, if you are near the end of the session, and the client is still refusing hospitalization, you might say something like this: "We have been talking for almost an hour now and although I would like to see you go to the hospital, it seems as if that's not a very good option from where *you* sit. I don't mind telling you that I'm very concerned about your life because you say you want to die, you live alone, you have a loaded gun, and you refuse to give it up. Perhaps there are some alternatives to the hospital that I've overlooked. If you have no serious objection, I'd like to invite another therapist in at this point for the time we have left. I want you to know how important it is to me that we work something out; I think you and I are in agreement that this is a serious time for you." An alternative to bringing someone into the session may be to tell clients that you would like them to see the psychiatrist who is in the building. If the client leaves without any resolution of the problem, and you believe that there is imminent danger, obviously you should notify your supervisor immediately and document your actions in the client's chart.

The possibility of clients' refusing hospitalization or doing other things that you think might endanger themselves or others underscores the importance of your being familiar with the agency's policies on what to do in life-threatening emergencies. You cannot be prepared for all contingencies, but being very clear on what the general policies are for an emergency should go a long way toward helping you feel as confident as possible. Finally, throughout a crisis of this type, it is very important not to become involved in a power struggle with the client.

45. *What should I do about clients who keep talking at the end of the session?* These clients fall into three groups: (a) those who do a lot of talking as a matter of routine and merely continue this pattern at the end of the session; (b) those who make a habit of bringing up important issues at the end of sessions; and (c) those who, for any number of reasons, are testing the limits and are asking to be stopped. Clients in the first category quickly learn that when the session is over, it's over. With a small amount of help, they learn to stop themselves (assuming there are no barriers to learning). Clients in the second category are seen not infrequently. They may or may not be aware of their defensive maneuver. When confronted with their pattern they most frequently respond well and are able to discuss their fear and ambivalence. Clients in the third category tend to be more problematic. As an unconscious ruse, they may become very upset, protesting that they cannot program their feelings, and that they don't like fitting into a box. The more they protest, the more you can be sure that they are asking to be stopped—that is, the more they are saying "I can't stop myself."

Time limits are very important. First of all, you cannot afford to run past the stopping time when you have another client. If you do, the other client feels cheated, and rightly so. In the second place, running overtime gives the client a mixed message. Clients want to believe that there is some stability in the world—that they can count on psychotherapy to be consistent when other things aren't. So if you give clients 90 minutes when you promised 60, what are they to think? Are you really strong enough to be their therapist if you can't handle their "end of session" tirades or ramblings? The above comments suggest why you need to hold the line on time. (Incidentally, the rule on sticking to the schedule applies even if you have an "extra" hour following your client session). But what exactly should you do? First of all, you can help yourself a great deal by using a clock clearly visible to both you and the client. In fact, two clocks—one that you can easily see and one that the client can easily see—may be helpful. You need to be able to see the clock without interrupting the flow of therapy, and it should also be easy for the client to keep track of time. Second, be clear with clients from the beginning about what time their sessions start and what time they will end. Third, do not open up whole new areas when there is only five minutes left. If the client introduces important new material at the last minute, you can say something like this, "Well, that sounds like a very important area. I'm thinking we should begin there next session since we are almost out of time." If the client still continues to talk and shows no sign of stopping, say, "I hate to cut you off, but we really have to stop today." This sentence can be said while you shift and move forward slightly in your chair, or, if necessary, stand up. You will find that if you give clients clear, unambiguous messages, they will respond to the clarity. If you give mixed messages, you can expect them to test the limits in order to find out what the rules are.

All therapists must learn (and generally do learn with some practice) to help pace their sessions with clients. If you feel that you have cut a client off abruptly, and the client reacts non-verbally, you might make a note and ask about the reaction at the next session. Or, for example, you might say, "Last time I sort of cut you off because we ran out of time, and you seemed a little upset. What were your feelings?" This question may lead into a discussion of the therapy agreement as well as a discussion of the client's difficulty in setting and living by limits.

Be sure that you do not become apologetic for stopping the therapy session on time. Such behavior merely encourages the client to test the limits again. We are not saying that there will never be an emergency requiring you to go overtime. Furthermore, being clear on limits is neither a license nor an excuse for insensitivity. With a little practice, however, you should be going past the agreed stopping time very infrequently. The time you spend with clients is a valuable service you provide. You do not need to give an extra 15 minutes to ensure that you have made a contribution. Going overtime is not merely not good for your clients; it also is a subtle put-down of your own skills and contributions.

46. *What should I say to a client who says, "Am I crazy?"* Clients ask this question for many reasons, but most often for one of two reasons. One obvious possibility is that clients may want reassurance that they are not crazy. Since they *feel* so crazy, they believe it would be helpful to be told that they are not. Or perhaps the client is attuned to self presentation issues and wonders how she or he is coming across. Perhaps others have said, "You are crazy," and the client wants to be told otherwise. A second possibility is that clients may be seeking a very different kind of reassurance—the reassurance that you recognize how serious the problem is. Perhaps they have kept a very tight lid on their pathology, perhaps they successfully hide from others their "crazy" feelings and crazy behavior, and they wonder if you will be insightful enough to see—and brave enough to confront—the crazy part of them. As in so many cases where the client asks a hard-hitting question, our philosophy is to respond briefly with your own thoughts and then gently move the focus back to the client. This means that you have to say more than "What do *you* think?" For example, to the question you might answer, "Well, I don't use the word crazy because it's not very helpful to me. I do think your problems should be taken seriously. I know it's very disturbing to hear these voices. You know that something is wrong, and you think you may want to do something about it. And I guess that's where I come in—helping you work on that part of you that you call crazy."

47. *What should I do if a client won't say anything?* This issue arises chiefly in four situations. In one, you may be seeing a client who is rather unsophisticated about what psychotherapy is and expects direction from you. A combination of client education together with, where appropriate, your assuming at the first a little more responsibility for the direction of the session will likely have the desired effect. A second situation arises with clients who are socially anxious and who for this reason don't talk very much in the session. With such clients it is necessary to work a little harder at putting them at ease. One can generally proceed by (a) initially making some efforts not to raise their anxiety level higher than it already is; and (b) when appropriate, helping them talk about their anxiety in therapy. A third type of situation involves clients who are fairly concrete and who may typically give very short responses, with no elaboration, and then wait for guidance from you. You may need to be a little more active and provide slightly more structure for these clients.

The fourth situation occurs when you have said something that made a big impact on the client and the client stops talking in the session. This sort of situation may arise at any point in therapy. The first thing to remember is that it takes the client much longer to incorporate what you have said than it took you to say it. So, allow some time. The second point is that this type of situation involves what can be called a "working silence" (O. Bown, personal communication, 1985). Remember that while clients are silent, they are usually still thinking, reorganizing their thoughts about themselves or the world, or perhaps even "pulling themselves together." Thus, silence is not something that needs to be destroyed. Third, remember that the silence may suggest that something important has happened or is happening. Viewed this way, silence should be less likely to raise your anxiety level. Fourth, silence does not mean you have done something wrong. So you need not get busy undoing it. Fifth, clients are rarely as uncomfortable with these working silences as you are. If they become uncomfortable, they often will do something about it.

Perhaps you are still saying, "Ok, so now I have a great attitude about silence; I'll try not to get too anxious, I realize they need time to integrate things, and so on. But how long should I let them sit there before I say something? And when I do decide to say something, what should it be?" Therapists vary in their answers to these questions, particularly the first one. Part of the answer must lie in the client's nonverbal cues. If clients appear to be deeply absorbed in what they are thinking about, or if, for example, they are continuing to cry, you may choose not to interrupt them at all. On the other hand, if the client starts to look around and sighs as if to punctuate a thought, it may be time to say something. At the risk of oversimplifying a complex issue, we will say that you should be comfortable with a client's being silent for at least ten minutes. This will feel like a very long silence, but occasionally you will see clients who need this much or more time. If you sense that the client might be ready to proceed but doesn't quite know how, you might say something like, "I know you are having some thoughts and feelings. Can you tell me any of them?" or you might say simply, "I can see these things are very difficult for you to talk about," or "I sense that what I said hit you hard."

We briefly address two other issues involved with silence. First, it may at times be used as a retreat from the therapist. If the silence is more a time of retreat than a time for reorganization (of course these may be the same to some extent), this issue may need to be processed. Thus the client may be saying, "Talking with you is so painful I will be quiet." A second point that bears noting is that clients at times refuse to talk if they are angry with the therapist. In this case, silence may take on a punishing function, as expressed in the attitude, "If words are your game, I'm not playing. Now what can you do since I am not talking?" Alternatively, anger followed by silence may suggest that clients fear their anger; or more specifically, fear that it will destroy the therapist or elicit rejection by the therapist. In such a circumstance, the long-term goal is to have the client experience and express the anger in therapy, with a therapist who can withstand this anger without becoming fearful and withdrawing or punishing. These comments are meant to suggest some of the complexities involved in therapeutic silences. The main point is that silence is not something to be eliminated, but rather something to be understood in light of the client's dynamics. If you think that you are failing to say things you need to be saying (and thus in your mind contributing to silences), ask your supervisor if he or she agrees. Perhaps you are anxious but doing a good job. On the other hand, if your anxiety is impeding your performance (e.g., preventing you from responding), you need to find out what you are fearful about. On the whole, clients do talk without too much prompting. On the other hand, there are times when they want something from you and wait, whether patiently or impatiently, for you to respond.

48. *What if the client doesn't want to be there?* Since there are entire books written about the reluctant client and since we devote a chapter in this book to resistance, we will make only brief comments here concerning the issue. Rule number one is that you should avoid power struggles. If they begin by saying that you are a part of the power structure which keeps them down, you are ill-advised to disagree. If they indicate that they have more "street smarts" than you, the first session is no place to talk about how you are on to their game. Rather than being dewy-eyed about all the ways you think you might be able to help such clients with their lives, you need to keep three goals in mind: (a) maintaining the relationship so that you might be able to earn the right to help; (b) maintaining the relationship so that you will have some opportunity to see whether you can offer anything of interest to the person; and (c) maintaining the relationship since angry people typically haven't had too many good relationships. The redundancy is obviously intentional. If you are working with people who have been incarcerated for a long period of time, we encourage you to remember that these individuals have a great deal of experience with environments that are punishing, demeaning, and almost never designed for the benefit of the person. Even if these people had entered prison as well-adjusted, caring people, the environment would likely have had deleterious effects on them. Do not expect to be welcomed unambivalently and do not be surprised when you are manipulated—it may be the case of a human being who has learned to survive under brutal conditions.

49. *How do I handle clients who always blame someone else?* Clients who continually blame other people for their problems represent a challenge for therapists for two reasons. First, it is very difficult for clients to solve problems over which they feel they have no control. Most approaches to (or theories of) therapy include some attention to helping clients assume realistic control over portions of their lives. Second, therapists are sometimes prone to become angry with clients who will not "take responsibility for their behavior." Becoming angry with such clients almost never works, because in their mind there is no connection between what they are doing and your anger. Rather, they tend to think of *you* as out to get them and as lacking in understanding. Actually, there are two broad personality types represented here. One is the individual with a narcissistic personality disorder who has a rather ingrained characterological belief that others are really to blame for all his or her problems. Significant improvement with these people is very slow—almost always requiring long-term psychotherapy. The second group of people are the individuals who are much more aware of the fact that they blame others and who are often very aware that they are being defensive when they do this. Self-esteem issues, often rooted in being criticized or judged by significant others, are typically central for these persons.

50. *What should I do about clients who seem repeatedly to tell stories?* Although "telling stories" has long been recognized as a potential form of client resistance, in a much broader sense, the essence of therapy is often seen as storytelling (Rennie, 1994). Because therapy is often conceptualized in this way, this makes the question more subtle and more difficult to answer. Rennie suggested that storytelling represents both defensive and therapeutic processes. This implies that often the therapist may not be able to tell the extent to which a client is primarily avoiding material by storytelling versus wrapping the disturbance in a container we call a story. Obviously, the first question to answer is whether the therapist is sensitively listening for the signs, perhaps even just hints, of what the story means at a deeper level. It takes a while to become adept at hearing the significant portion of stories, but that is a skill beyond this discussion; therefore, for our purposes, let us assume that the client repeatedly tells seemingly pointless stories, perhaps without any discernable pattern.

In our experience, such "storytellers" fall roughly into two categories. In one category are those clients who begin to tell a story when they become anxious during therapy, whether due to a primary internal disturbance, or to a more immediate threat involving the therapist. In these cases, a combination of making process comments and moderating the client's anxiety to the extent possible tends to produce the desired result. For example, one might say something like this: "Sunil, I notice that when we start to discuss your father, you often begin to tell a story that seems, at least on the surface, to be more or less unrelated. Can you help me understand what you think is going on here?" When making interventions like this, remember that more immediacy tends to be more threatening. Also, we tend to urge students to avoid less subtle comments such as "What does this have to do with your father?" These sorts of comments almost always make clients defensive and reduce the likelihood of their delving more deeply into their feelings.

In the second category are those individuals who have developed a general characterological style (which in this case includes therapy, but often goes well beyond it as well) in which stories are told routinely and pervasively. Obviously, individuals in this category may also be prone to more storytelling when threatened, but the dynamic is much more general. In our experience, some diagnostic groups—for example, clients who have long abused alcohol—are more prone to this defense than are many other clients. If the client repeatedly tells stories that seem "nonproductive," and particularly if process comments don't seem to help, we recommend a more active approach to "cutting through" the storytelling. In these cases, do not be shy about interrupting the client. If you *don't* interrupt, the hour may end without your getting in much more than a polite "un-huh." To make things run reasonably smoothly, you might consider some sort of bridging technique that ties the seemingly pointless story to the last important area in which you were working. Or, for example, you can simply say something like, "Excuse me, but let me stop you for just a minute. I'd like for us to go back to where we were a moment ago. That seemed important. You know, I don't think I have a very good picture of what your *feelings* were when your wife said goodbye. I'm guessing that was really overwhelming. Can you tell me if I'm on target?" The main point is that although you shouldn't be blunt or insensitive, you also don't have to make long explanations of why you are interrupting.

Supervisory Issues

51. *What should I expect from supervision?* You might begin by "jumping ahead" and reading a book on supervision to learn how supervisors think about supervisees and supervision (e.g., Bernard & Goodyear, 1998; Stoltenberg, McNeill, & Delworth, 1997; Watkins, 1997). Just as there are great differences among clients who seek services, as well as among supervisees who are in training, you will find significant differences among supervisors. Nonetheless, you should expect certain things from supervisors: a reasonable amount of support, at least some specific suggestions about how you can improve your therapy skills, sensitivity to your struggles as a beginning therapist, respect for your developing therapeutic style, a willingness to help you confront your shortcomings, and a responsiveness to your expressed needs.

From yourself you should expect: some time preparing for supervision (listening to audiotapes or viewing videotapes, etc.), the courage to bring in cases with which you are having difficulty, a willingness to process with your supervisor difficulties you are having with him or her, responsiveness to suggestions about how to proceed with a case, and the ability to hear both positive and negative feedback about your therapeutic style and interventions. Perhaps the single most important sign that you are having difficulty with supervision is if you find yourself *repeatedly* failing to bring to your supervisor major concerns about your clients or you as a therapist. If you see this sign and fail to take action, you are perhaps depriving yourself of a chance for the experience of good supervision. If you have already had some good psychotherapy supervision, you know what we mean when we say that good supervision is a growth-producing and life-enriching experience. If you have tried repeatedly to work out conflicts with a supervisor and cannot seem to do so, we recommend that you request another supervisor. If the problem is *you*, you will find this out fairly soon. On the other hand, no supervisor is perfect. Identify the good things you can get from a particular supervisor and do everything in your power to benefit from what he or she offers.

One question that often comes up about supervision is whether supervisors should focus on your "dynamics" as opposed to your specific skills in therapy. Most supervisors agree that supervision is not psychotherapy, and that neither supervisee nor supervisor should try to turn supervision into something it is not. Our experience has been that a sizable percentage of supervisors (including ourselves) believe and practice the idea that supervision must at times focus on beliefs and feelings of the supervisee as they hinder the delivery of psychotherapeutic services to the client. Supervisors at university counseling centers are perhaps more likely to have this orientation than are supervisors at mental health centers. Supervisors of a psychoanalytic bent are, of course, quite committed to the idea of focusing on countertransference issues. (Countertransference is discussed in Chapter 12 of this book.) When you are just getting started as a therapist, you should expect your supervisor to spend a sizable percentage of supervision time helping you focus on what you can *do* to help your clients as opposed to focusing on your dynamics. Friedlander and Ward (1984) speculated that beginning therapists may best profit from "a cognitive-behavioral, highly task-oriented supervisor," whereas more advanced students might be better served by a supervisor taking a more psychoanalytic and interpersonal perspective. Lochner and Melchert (1997) raised questions about the scope of earlier stage models of supervision; they found that the supervisee's cognitive style and theoretical orientation influenced supervisees' preferences for supervision. In short, based on research literature, it is very difficult to draw firm conclusions about the kind of supervisor that would be best for you. Using common sense alone, it is clear that you must be able to have some sort of alliance with the supervisor to make full use of the process. An important part of this alliance is your feeling toward the supervisor and your expectations for what would be helpful.

52. *What should I do if I don't like my supervisor?* Most supervisors do supervision not because they are forced to, but because they want to, they enjoy it, and they get personal satisfaction out of doing it. They are generally very motivated to do a good job. They want you to benefit from and enjoy supervision. Therefore, in general you will find them to be responsive to your request for more understanding, less advice, more advice, or whatever you think you need to make supervision more effective. Supervisors tend to admire supervisees who can put their cards on the table and articulate their needs. They do not admire supervisees who are discontented with supervision but won't say so. Occasionally, you may get a defensive, inept supervisor. As we said earlier, in such cases make an honest attempt to work it out and, if you fail, request another supervisor.

53. *What should I do if a client brings up a problem I do not know how to treat?* This is a question that does not have a simple answer, although it is important to realize that the issue of practicing within one's competency is an ethical one (e.g., APA, 1992). Some of the factors to be considered when dealing with the question of competency include: (a) what you feel comfortable handling; (b) your supervisor's judgment about the case; (c) training you have had that might be relevant; (d) the seriousness of the problem in terms of potential behavioral outcomes; (e) the client's reaction or potential reaction to knowing that you have no experience in the area; (f) availability of potential services from another professional; (g) availability of a referral source that specializes in the problem; (h) client's level of distress; (i) degree to which intensive supervision is available; and (j) the extent to which the problem is recognized as needing a specific kind of treatment. Many times clients who are seeing therapists in training are accepting some sort of trade-off. For example, at a crowded VA hospital, the choice may be between a student therapist and a long wait. At times, clients may be aware of such a trade-off, at other times they may not. If there is a clear indication that a more experienced therapist could ideally handle the case but none is available, our belief is that this factor should, in many cases, be discussed with the client. However, not all agencies agree with this procedure. Some prefer to handle such questions internally and then once the decision is made that a therapist in training *can* see the person, the issue is not brought up for discussion with the client.

A distinction should be drawn between problems that you have never had presented to you and problems that you don't have any idea about how to approach. Just because a problem is new to you is, of course, no cause for undue concern since in part that is why you are in training. However, even if the presented issue is completely baffling to you initially, this is no cause for alarm. Because psychotherapists use such broad and far-ranging constructs (for example, anger turned inward, lack of trust, etc.), you should be able to conceptualize at least portions of any given problem, particularly after meeting with the person two or three times. For example, if a client says, "I always seem to wake up in the middle of the night and worry," you may initially have no idea what is going on but probably will start to form some hypotheses after a few sessions.

Perhaps this sounds like the green light to see any client. Not so. Let us draw a continuum with two extremes using a few of the dimensions listed above. On the one end is a presenting problem you don't know anything about—let's say the person is a veteran who appears to have post-traumatic stress disorder (PTSD). You feel very uncomfortable as the client discusses the situation. The client suggests the possibility of suicide if the issue is not resolved, a doctoral-level staff person with expertise in PTSD is available to see the person, you cannot recall having done any reading in the area, and it's never come up in class. Your supervisor doesn't know anything about PTSD and the client indicates that he is tired of being shifted from student therapist to student therapist since, as he puts it, "They never have any experience." On the other end, a client presents with what seems to be PTSD but you have a supervisor with much experience in this area. No other person is available right now to see the client, but the client reports only moderately disturbing symptoms with no homicidal or suicidal ideation. The client suggests that he saw a student once before, had a good experience, and is interested in your seeing him. Although you don't know much about PTSD, you have done volunteer work with veterans. In the first case, we would recommend referral. In the second, we would recommend that the student see the client. Probably the two most critical factors determining whether you should see someone who has a problem you think you know little about is the expertise of the supervisor available and the apparent seriousness (for example, homicide, suicide, or potential psychotic break) of the symptoms.

54. *How do experienced therapists prevent burnout?* The idea that one must take care of oneself in order to be of assistance to others is almost axiomatic within the profession. Coming from a slightly different perspective, Kant (1785/1959) expresses the idea well:

> To secure one's own happiness is at least indirectly a duty, for discontent with one's condition under pressure from many cares and amid unsatisfied wants could easily become a great temptation to transgress duties. (p. 15)

There are many potential sources of stress for the psychotherapist, including personal problems, organizational problems, and difficult clients (Coster & Schwebel, 1997; Kramen-Kahn & Hansen, 1998; Mahoney, 1997; Sherman & Thelen, 1998). Our supervisees often ask the question, "How can I avoid 'taking home' the problems of my clients?" At the risk of oversimplifying, we will suggest a few ideas about how to help prevent, and lessen the potential deleterious effects of, this potential problem (see also, Mahoney, 1991; Norcross & Guy, 1997). First, try to spend some time reflecting on your limits as a therapist. "Taking home" problems in part may suggest that you think you have more power than you do. It may be helpful for you to refocus on clients' autonomy, their right not to change, and the limitations of psychotherapy in general. Worrying about clients may be one way of telling yourself that you have the power to make something better happen if only you make the right intervention. Second (and conversely), consider that your clients are getting good treatment from you. You do not need to suffer or put yourself down by worrying. Third, consult frequently. Covering the bases during the day often does reduce worrying at night. Fourth, ask yourself whether you are taking your problems home because your clients are more interesting than your life. If so, do something about your life, not your clients. Fifth, ask yourself whether you are seeing too many clients or too many difficult clients. Sixth, take some solace in the fact that you worry about your clients. All good therapists worry about clients. If you didn't care about the pain others are in, you would not be a therapist.

Despite the general awareness among therapists that practicing psychotherapy can be stressful, one study (Murtagh & Wollersheim, 1997) found that therapists were not more depressed as a result of seeing depressed clients, but rather were able to use planful problem solving and self-controlling as a way of dealing with their feelings. Friedman (1997) makes several suggestions for preventing burnout, including, don't put more energy into therapy than your clients do. For additional discussion about getting "hooked" by clients' problems, see Chapter 12, Transference and Countertransference.

Summary

In this chapter we have given some general ideas, as well as some specific suggestions, for how we think about a number of the issues with which beginning therapists struggle. As we said at the outset, we encourage you to think about how our ideas differ from yours. We also encourage you to discuss our comments with your supervisor. Psychotherapy is a complex process practiced by a diverse group of people. The process is influenced by many contextual variables including ethnicity and gender of client and therapist. Although we have tried to stay within what we consider to be the mainstream of ideas about psychotherapy, we recognize that our definition of the mainstream, as well as our specific suggestions, are open to debate.

DISCUSSION QUESTIONS

- Which of the questions in this chapter do you think depend most and least heavily on theoretical orientation?

- Are the disagreements that professionals have about the answers to these questions a reflection of a temporary lack of knowledge by psychotherapists, the inherent and permanent uncertainty that comes with complex issues, or something else?

- Which of the questions (and comments) seem in your view to be most likely to be influenced by the values of the psychotherapist?

- What are some of the important issues about ethnicity and cultural values that you believe are raised by these questions and comments?

BIBLIOGRAPHY

Alyn, J. H. (1988). The politics of touch in therapy: A response to Willison and Masson. *Journal of Counseling and Development, 66,* 432–433.

American Psychiatric Association (1994). *Diagnostic and statistical manual of mental disorders* (4th ed.). Washington, DC: Author.

American Psychological Association. (1992). Ethical principles of psychologists and code of conduct. *American Psychologist, 47,* 1597–1611.

American Psychological Association, Committee on Lesbian and Gay Concerns. (1991). *Bias in psychotherapy with lesbians and gay men.* Washington, DC: Author.

American Psychological Association, Public Interest Directorate. (1997). *Professional, ethical and legal issues concerning interpersonal violence, maltreatment and related trauma.* Washington DC: Author.

Anderson, C. W., & Adley, A. R. (Eds.). (1997). *Gay and lesbian issues: Abstracts of the psychological and behavioral literature 1985–1996.* Washington, DC: American Psychological Association.

Baron, J. (1996). Some issues in psychotherapy with gay and lesbian clients. *Psychotherapy, 33,* 611–616.

Bennett, B. E., Bricklin, P. M., & VandeCreek, L. (1994). Response to Lazarus's "How certain boundaries and ethics diminish therapeutic effectiveness." *Ethics & Behavior, 4,* 263–266.

Bernard, J., & Goodyear, R. K. (1998). *Fundamentals of clinical supervision* (2nd ed.). Boston: Allyn & Bacon.

Borys, D. S. (1994). Maintaining therapeutic boundaries: The motive is therapeutic effectiveness, not defensive practice. *Ethics & Behavior, 4,* 267–273.

Cornett, C. (1998). *The soul of psychotherapy: Recapturing the spiritual dimension in the therapeutic encounter.* New York: Free Press.

Coster, J. S., & Schwebel, M. (1997). Well-functioning in professional psychologists. *Professional Psychology: Research and Practice, 28,* 5–13.

Dauser, P. J., Hedstrom, S. M., & Croteau. J. M. (1995). Disclosure of comprehensive pretherapy information on clients at a university counseling center. *Professional Psychology: Research and Practice, 26,* 190–195.

deMayo, R. A. (1997). Patient sexual behavior and sexual harassment: A national survey of female psychologists. *Professional Psychology: Research and Practice, 28,* 58–62.

Eells, T. D. (Ed.). (1997). *Handbook of psychotherapy case formulation.* New York: Guilford.

Friedlander, M. L., & Ward., L. G. (1984). Development and validation of the supervisory styles inventory. *Journal of Counseling Psychology, 31,* 541–557.

Friedman, S. (1997). *Time-effective psychotherapy: Maximizing outcomes in an era of minimized resources.* Boston: Allyn & Bacon.

Gans, J. S., & Counselman, E. F. (1996). The missed session: A neglected aspect of psychodynamic psychotherapy. *Psychotherapy, 33,* 43–50.

Glickauf-Hughes, C., & Chance, S. E. (1995). Answering clients' questions. *Psychotherapy, 32,* 375–380.

Goodyear, R. K., & Shumate, J. L. (1997). Perceived effects of therapist self-disclosure of attraction to clients. *Professional Psychology: Research and Practice, 27,* 613–616.

Haas, L. J., & Malouf, J. L. (1995). *Keeping up the good work: A practitioner's guide to mental health ethics* (2nd ed.). Sarasota, FL: Professional Resources Exchange.

Hawkins, I. L., & Bullock, S. L. (1995). Informed consent and religious values: A neglected area of diversity. *Psychotherapy, 32,* 293–300.

Horton, J. A., Clance, P. R., Sterk-Elifson, C., & Emshoff, J. (1995). Touch in psychotherapy: A survey of patients' experiences. *Psychotherapy, 32,* 443–457.

Jobes, D. A., & Berman, A. L. (1993). Suicide and malpractice liability: Assessing and revising policies, procedures, and practice in outpatient settings. *Professional Psychology: Research and Practice, 24,* 91–99.

Kalichman, S. C. (1993). *Mandated reporting of suspected child abuse: Ethics, law, and policy.* Washington, DC: American Psychological Association.

Kant, I. (1785/1959). *Foundations of the metaphysics of morals and what is enlightenment?* Translated by L. W. Beck. New York: (The Library of Liberal Arts) Bobbs-Merrill.

Kertay, L., & Reviere, S. L. (1993). The use of touch in psychotherapy: Theoretical and ethical considerations. *Psychotherapy: Theory, Research, Practice, Training, 30,* 32–40.

Knox, S., Hess, S. A., Petersen, D. A., & Hill, C. E. (1997). A qualitative analysis of client perceptions of the effects of helpful therapist self-disclosure in long-term therapy. *Journal of Counseling Psychology, 44,* 274–283.

Kramen-Kahn, B., & Hansen, N. D. (1998). Rafting the rapids: Occupational hazards, rewards, and coping strategies of psychotherapists. *Professional Psychology: Research and Practice, 29,* 130–134.

Ladany, N., O'Brien, K. M., Hill, C. E., Melincoff, D. S., Knox, S., & Petersen, D. A. (1997). Sexual attraction toward clients, use of supervision, and prior training: A qualitative study of predoctoral psychology interns. *Journal of Counseling Psychology, 44,* 413–424.

Lawry, S. S. (1998). Touch and clients who have been sexually abused. In E. W. L. Smith, P. R. Clance, and S. Imes (Eds.), *Touch in psychotherapy: Theory, research, and practice* (pp. 201–210). New York: Guilford.

Lazarus, A. A. (1971). *Behavior therapy and beyond.* New York: McGraw-Hill.

Lazarus, A. A. (1994). How certain boundaries and ethics diminish therapeutic effectiveness. *Ethics & Behavior, 4,* 253–261.

Liddle, B. J. (1997). Gay and lesbian clients' selection of therapists and utilization of therapy. *Psychotherapy, 34,* 11–18.

Lochner, B. T., & Melchert, T. P. (1997). Relationship of cognitive style and theoretical orientation to psychology interns' preferences for supervision. *Journal of Counseling Psychology, 44,* 256–260.

Mahoney, M. J. (1991). *Human change processes.* New York: Basic Books.

Mahoney, M. J. (1997). Psychotherapists' personal problems and selfcare patterns. *Professional Psychology: Research and Practice, 29,* 14–16.

McHenry, S. S., & Johnson, J. W. (1993). Homophobia in the therapist and gay or lesbian client: Conscious and unconscious collusions in self-hate. *Psychotherapy, 30,* 141–151.

Morgan, K. S., & Nerison, R. M. (1993). Homosexuality and psychopolitics: An historical overview. *Psychotherapy, 30,* 133–140.

Murtagh, M. P., & Wollersheim, J. P. (1997). Effects of clinical practice on psychologists: Treating depressed clients, perceived stress, and ways of coping. *Professional Psychology: Research and Practice, 28,* 361–363.

Norcross, J. C., & Guy, J. D. (1997). *Leaving it at the office: Understanding and alleviating the distress of conducting psychotherapy.* New York: Guilford.

Olio, K. A., & Cornell, W. F. (1993). Therapeutic relationship as the foundation for treatment with adult survivors of sexual abuse. *Psychotherapy, 30,* 512–523.

Pilkington, N. W., & Cantor, J. M. (1996). Perceptions of heterosexual bias in professional psychology programs: A survey of graduate students. *Professional Psychology: Research and Practice, 27,* 604–612.

Pope, K. S., Keith-Spiegel, P., Tabachnick, B. G. (1993). Sexual attraction to clients: The human therapist and the (sometimes) inhuman training system. In K. S. Pope, J. L. Sonne, and J. Holroyd, *Sexual feelings in psychotherapy: Explorations for therapists and therapists-in-training* (pp. 205–236). Washington, DC: American Psychological Association.

Pope, K. S., Sonne, J. L., & Holroyd, J. (1993). *Sexual feelings in psychotherapy: Explorations for therapists and therapists-in-training.* Washington, DC: American Psychological Association.

Pope, K. S., & Tabachnick, B. G. (1993). Therapists' anger, hate, fear, and sexual feelings. National survey of therapist responses, client characteristics, critical events, formal complaints, and training. *Professional Psychology: Research and Practice, 24,* 142–152.

Pope, K. S., & Vetter, V. A. (1992). Ethical dilemmas encountered by members of the American Psychological Association: A national survey. *American Psychologist, 47,* 397–411.

Rennie, D. L. (1994). Storytelling in psychotherapy: The client's subjective experience. *Psychotherapy: Theory, Research, Practice, Training, 31,* 234–243.

Richards, P. S., & Bergin, A. E. (1997). *A spiritual strategy for counseling and psychotherapy.* Washington, DC: American Psychological Association.

Sarason, S. B. (1985). *Caring and compassion in clinical practice.* San Francisco: Jossey-Bass.

Shafranske, E. P. (Ed.). (1996). *Religion and the clinical practice of psychology.* Washington, DC: American Psychological Association.

Sherman, M. D., & Thelen, M. H. (1998). Distress and professional impairment among psychologists in clinical practice. *Professional Psychology: Research and Practice, 29,* 79–85.

Smith, E. W. L., Clance, P. R., & Imes, S. (Eds.). (1998). *Touch in psychotherapy: Theory, research, and practice.* New York: Guilford.

Sommers-Flanagan, J., & Sommers-Flanagan, R. (1995). Intake interviewing with suicidal patients: A systematic approach. *Professional Psychology: Research and Practice, 26,* 41–47.

Stoltenberg, C. D., McNeill, B. W., & Delworth, U. (1997). *IDM supervision: The Integrated Developmental Model of Supervision.* San Francisco: Jossey-Bass.

Stricker, G., & Fisher, M. (Eds.). (1990). *Self-disclosure in the therapeutic relationship.* New York: Plenum.

Strong, S. R. (1968). Counseling: An interpersonal influence process. *Journal of Counseling Psychology, 15,* 215–224.

Sullivan, T., Martin, W., Jr., & Handelsman, M. (1993). Practical benefits of an informed consent procedure: An empirical investigation. *Professional Psychology: Research and Practice, 24,* 160–163.

Van Denburg, T. F., & Van Denburg, E. J. (1992). Premature termination in the midst of psychotherapy: Three psychoanalytic perspectives. *Psychotherapy, 29,* 183–190.

Vesper, J. H. (1995). Conflicting relationships. *American Journal of Forensic Psychology, 13,* 5–20.

Wachtel, P. L. (1993). *Therapeutic communication: Principles and effective practice.* New York: Guilford.

Watkins, C. E., Jr. (Ed.). (1997). *Handbook of psychotherapy supervision.* New York: Wiley.

Weed, L. (1968). Medical records that guide and teach. *New England Journal of Medicine, 278,* 593–600, 652–657.

Williams, M. (1997). Boundary violations: Do some contended standards of care fail to encompass commonplace procedures of humanistic, behavioral, and eclectic psychotherapies? *Psychotherapy, 34,* 238–249.

Wolberg, L. R. (1988). *The technique of psychotherapy* (4th ed., Parts 1 & 2). New York: Grune & Stratton.

Worthington, E. L., Jr. (1986). Religious counseling: A review of empirical research. *Journal of Counseling and Development, 64,* 421–431.

Worthington, E. L., Jr. (1988). Understanding the values of religious clients; A model and its application to counseling. *Journal of Counseling Psychology, 35,* 166–174.

APPENDIX

Index of Questions

Boundary/Management Issues

Personal Inquiries and Emotional Issues

3 Client Fears

At the start, I didn't listen to what you said most of the time but I watched like a hawk for your expression and the sound of your voice. After the interview, I would add all this up to see if it seemed to show love.

—a client, quoted in Hayward & Taylor, 1964

"I simply DO NOT understand, sir," Data said, "Did I miss some subtle message in your contact with the Furies?"
…Picard nodded. His fear was still there, but the control he had placed over it grew with each passing moment. "Perhaps, Data, but what you missed was not subtle. It affected the crew's emotions deeply."
"What was it, sir?"
"If we knew that, Mr. Data, we would be able to fight it."

—from *Star Trek: The Next Generation,* "Invasion: The Soldiers of Fear"

Less than 13% of individuals suffering from a psychiatric illness seek services during a one-year period (Regier, Narrow, Rae, Manderscheid, Locke, & Goodwin, 1993). Additionally, there are many individuals who need and could profit from psychotherapy but are not psychiatrically "ill" and do not seek services. Obviously, one of the reasons some individuals do not seek psychotherapy is that they fear either the process or the outcome (or both) of being in treatment. In this chapter we will review some of the concerns clients have about psychotherapy. We believe that psychotherapists who are aware of the full range of concerns clients may have about therapy will be more adept at recognizing these concerns as they are indirectly expressed by the client. Additionally, to be aware of these concerns provides a stimulus for us to think about not merely what is at stake for clients but also how we can be responsive to their concerns. One very obvious reason that we spend some time writing about client fears concerning therapy is that clients who are or become fearful about therapy may terminate prematurely.

We have at least two goals in writing this particular chapter. Our first goal is simply to alert you to a number of fears clients may have as they enter therapy.

Some of these fears are often conscious, others frequently are unconscious. Some have rather clear implications for your initial behavior as a therapist with any client; others we describe chiefly so that you can think about what issues are involved and how you might handle a situation in which the client is clearly expressing the fear. Some of the fears may be overtly expressed by the client; others may only be inferred. A few of the fears may be expressed early on, others tend to emerge much more slowly.

A second and more indirect reason for writing about client fears is that psychotherapists need a good appreciation for the many internal obstacles clients often must overcome just to arrive at a first session. A keen appreciation for these difficulties gives one an empathic frame with which to "greet" individuals and also strengthens our sense of respect for this person we call our client.

Another point we should perhaps underscore is that there may be an important relationship between concerns or fears clients have about therapy and the difficulty that brought them there. More broadly, we are saying that there is a link between the kinds of fears a person has about the process of therapy and his or her personality traits. For example, clients who are socially anxious may be concerned about pressure to talk (Kushner & Sher, 1991). Or, if a client says, "Can I be sure that what I say will be held in confidence?" we might hypothesize that the client may have difficulty placing trust in others. We say "may have difficulty" because the question is also a reasonable one by cultural standards. One might think of a continuum of client concerns about therapy. Variables of interest include the type of concern, presence or absence of situational variables likely to activate the concern, the relative sophistication of the client with regard to therapy, the emotional intensity of the client with regard to the fear, and evidence of the client's having similar concerns in other situations. At one end we might see a client who has little knowledge about therapy, who has a pending legal case, who asks about confidentiality but doesn't seem obsessed by it, and who seems easily reassured by your answer. At the other end is a client who has been in therapy several times, who has no obvious objective reason (such as legal difficulties) to be strongly interested in confidentiality, and who repeatedly asks about confidentiality despite your reassurances. In the former case you have learned little about the person as a result of the issue of confidentiality being raised. In the latter case you have probably learned quite a bit and have certainly identified an area that deserves further exploration by the client and therapist.

A number of client fears probably diminish rapidly if therapy progresses as we hope it will. Furthermore, we are not suggesting that all clients experience each of the fears we list. We are saying that these are typical and representative of the concerns clients may have about the process. For sake of discussion, we divide client fears into three broad categories: (a) how will I (the client) be treated? (b) how will I be viewed? and (c) will I like the effects of therapy? These are not conceptually distinct and mutually exclusive categories, but serve as a way to organize the material. A number of these concerns are represented in an instrument developed by Pipes, Schwarz, and Crouch (1985). Kushner and Sher (1991) have also discussed a number of fears related to therapy.

How Will I Be Treated?

Clients have both hopes and fears about how they will be treated in psychotherapy. We believe that it is a rare client indeed who has no expectations or concerns about what the therapist will be like or what the therapist will do and say. These expectations may be built on stereotypes (psychologists can read your mind, etc.) or previous interactions with the mental health system (Kushner & Sher, 1991). Furthermore, many clients will know someone who has been in treatment, and the prospective client may have developed ideas about psychotherapy from those sources.

Most clients have some sense that the relationship into which they are contemplating entering is somewhat of a one-sided affair. They understand, if only implicitly, that the therapist will not be very vulnerable, that they (the clients) will, and that the therapist will be in control of many aspects of the relationship. They also realize that they are coming to seek the help of the therapist (implying that the therapist offers something that cannot be, or has not been, found from other sources), while the therapist has not sought them out and apparently needs little from them. All of these facts (actually, *feelings*) are very much a part of clients' phenomenological world as they approach therapy. As if these things were not enough to strike fear and apprehension in the heart of the most self-confident client among us, the client is aware of two other things. First, this therapist is an unknown quantity—the client has little or no hard data about this person. Can one be certain that this unknown person will prove to be benevolent? Second, and perhaps more importantly, most clients have had a number of relationships in which the other person has proved to be, at least in the eyes of the client, untrustworthy, punishing, controlling, unforgiving, or a major disappointment in some other important way. Like Antonio in *The Merchant of Venice,* clients have been led to believe that there is often a Shylock who will demand "a pound of flesh" for services rendered. Of course, this business of expecting (fearing) that one will be treated by the therapist as one has been treated by others is a part of what will need to be examined in therapy. The point here is that clients can be reasonably expected not to place their faith immediately in the therapist.

We will now discuss some of the specific concerns clients have about how they will be treated.

1. *Will I be treated more like a case than a person?* In part, this concern is about not being respected in a particular kind of way. Taking telephone calls during the therapy hour, being inflexible in response to reasonable requests, and not bothering to remember important events about which the client has told you are examples of treating clients as if their worth as individuals is not significant. As another example, there are some agencies in which clients in the waiting room may hear therapists discussing cases down a hall or in an adjacent conference room. Even when names cannot be discerned, imagine your own reaction if you are a client and you hear a therapist (maybe even your own) say, "Well, I'm just tired of listening to this client." Here the issue is not so much confidentiality as it is a question of basic sensitivity (or lack thereof) that communicates a sense of respect for all clients.

2. *Will the therapist be honest with me?* In part because clients believe that other individuals have not been honest with them, clients are at times concerned that the therapist will not be entirely forthcoming. This fear may also represent a projection of sorts in which clients have concerns about their own capacity to be straightforward in dealing with others. There is also a popular image of psychotherapists as never willing to give their own perspective, as always turning questions back on the client. But there is also another issue as we see it that has nothing to do with clients' experiences or the image of the therapist. We believe that the concern about the therapist being honest reflects a relatively sincere and healthy desire to be able to know how one is perceived by others. If not taken to the extreme, this desire reflects the recognition that knowing how you are affecting others gives you information that may help you make desired changes in interpersonal behavior. Yalom (1995) cited interpersonal learning (input) as the most helpful (as reported by clients) of 12 curative factors in group psychotherapy. Examples of this category include, "Learning how I come across to others" and "Other members honestly telling me what they think of me."

3. *Will my problem be taken seriously?* Although clients generally come to therapy with an acute awareness of the troubles they see as afflicting them, they are not so sure that these afflictions are important to anyone else. Perhaps they have come despite great indifference on the part of, or over the expressed objection by, friends, family, or intimate partners. Even if people close to them are supportive, clients may secretly harbor the fear that their problem will seem insignificant to the busy therapist. One trap that some therapists fall into is assuming that clients who present their problem as if the problem were not serious are not highly motivated about psychotherapy. In Chapter 6, Intake Interviewing, we note that clients at times present with a problem they feel is more socially acceptable than the one that is really bothering them. It is certainly important to keep this in mind. If the therapist can be trusted with a little problem, perhaps a larger one will be forthcoming. However, the point we underscore here is that in listening to the style in which the problem is presented, we must not be too eager to accept "presentation style" as reflective of the true inner experience of the client. Clients, having learned from the culture that expression of deep anguish is rarely rewarded, are apt to titrate the strong emotions they feel. They do this not just because they do not know the therapist, but because they instinctively "dress up" their shortcomings and camouflage the "nasty" parts of themselves. Often, other people they have encountered have been willing to accept, and in fact have preferred to see, this false self. Indeed, clients themselves are often "satisfied" at one level to accept this false self. Here then is the fear: that the therapist will not take the client seriously, will be willing to accept the "dressed up" problem rather than caring enough to allow and encourage the client to be serious about the difficulties with which he or she struggles.

Individuals who have been sexually abused as children, who have been abused in intimate relationships (including therapeutic relationships), or who have suffered discrimination or cultural oppression are all wondering at some level whether they will be taken seriously by the therapist. Particularly with clients who do not share your own cultural background or ethnicity, you must be careful to communicate to them that their problems, however they may be described, are serious to you. Similarly, the therapist must be alert to clients appearing to be nonchalant about serious problems. For example, Latina/Latino or African American clients may greatly downplay incidents of racism because they have been rewarded in the broad culture for not complaining about such incidents and because they do not know how the therapist, particularly if he or she is from a different culture, might respond to descriptions of racism. Thus, when we are culturally different from our clients we must take special precaution to treat seriously what is being told us, and to be vigilant about the serious things that may be minimized or even withheld by the client. Even if the client and therapist are of the same ethnicity, clients may not trust that their own experience of racism is similar to that of the therapist. Similarly, some women clients will be especially fearful that male therapists will not take seriously their experiences of sexism, but women clients may also assume that female therapists are powerful individuals who do not have to endure the same kind of sexism to which they (clients) are subjected. One of the most serious mistakes you can make as a therapist is to confirm your client's fear that you may not take his or her problems seriously. The danger of this happening is perhaps heightened when there are large cultural differences between therapist and client. Such circumstances call for particular care by the therapist.

4. *Will the therapist share my values?* Despite our sometimes protestations to the contrary, psychotherapy is, in part, about values (Beutler, Machado, & Neufeldt, 1994; Frank & Frank, 1991; Garfield & Bergin, 1994; London, 1986; Sugarman & Martin, 1995). Jensen and Bergin (1988) concluded that there is consensus among mental health professionals about a number of values related to mental health. Braaten, Otto, and Handelsman (1993) found that regardless of whether individuals were given an informed consent form to read, one of the most important things they wanted to know about psychotherapy was the personal characteristics of the therapist. An example in this category was, "What kind of morals do they have?"

Values are evident in our (at times hidden) goals for clients and in the methodologies we use to achieve those goals. Instinctively, many clients realize this fact and are concerned about whether there will be values differences and, if so, how these differences will affect both the interaction and outcome of therapy. That is, when clients are concerned about such differences, they are expressing a concern both about whether they will like, respect, and feel comfortable working with the therapist and also about whether the therapist will exercise an influence on them that they would view as unhelpful or destructive in some important way. These are not concerns to be taken lightly. If we view psychotherapy as a life-changing process (Bugental, 1987), the person with whom one enters into this process deserves serious scrutiny. We know from a long line of research that people tend to be attracted to those they perceive as similar (Byrne, 1971). Since we obviously want our clients to be attracted to us in a basic kind of way, this desire that we share basic values does not seem misplaced. This does not mean that all of our values should constantly be up for extended discussion; however, if clients initially want some information about something that is important to them, it is seldom a mistake to provide them with some information. If a client wants to know at the outset whether we are "pro-life" or "pro-choice," we should certainly not feel bound to answer the question as framed, but neither should we try to perform a verbal ballet that leaves the client wondering whether we are capable of making commitments to a reasoned position. Individuals who practice feminist psychotherapy have frequently expressed the idea that therapists should encourage clients to ask questions about the values of the therapist. As we noted in the chapter, Questions that Beginning Therapists Ask, questions clients pose to us often have multiple purposes and we ignore this fact at the peril of good therapy. However, we must also try to strike a balance so that clients are given respect and credit for asking about the things that are important to them.

We should also point out that although clients may have some concern about whether their therapist shares their values, Epperson and Lewis (1987) found that clients strongly endorsed the statement "Counselors should make every effort to keep their own values from influencing their clients." However, this finding in no way suggests that clients think counselors should have no values; rather, the implication is that counselors should not *misuse* their influence.

5. *Will the therapist understand my problem?* This concern is often related to the one about values, and it also raises the issue of empathy (Bohart & Greenberg, 1997). Clients may wonder whether the therapist will understand what it is like to be Jewish, Latino/Latina, African American, male, female, gay, lesbian, and so on. For example, at times a client may say, "Are you a Catholic?" or "Have you seen many people in therapy who are gay?" At other times the fear may be more indirectly expressed as in, "This culture does not know what to do about women," or "White people don't understand people of color." In most such cases, clients are expressing feelings about their situation and trying to ascertain whether you have some sort of feel for what it's like to be in their shoes. Consider the following situation.

MALE CLIENT: Nobody cares about white males anymore.

FEMALE THERAPIST: Well, I agree that things can be rough. After all, reverse discrimination has become a reality.

MALE CLIENT: Well, I'm sick of it.

FEMALE THERAPIST: If I were a white male, I would be too.

Here the therapist has at least overtly suggested that she has an appreciation for the client's feelings. On the other hand (and even leaving aside the issue of whether "reverse discrimination" is a viable construct), she has perhaps been a little overly enthusiastic about trying to identify with the client. Furthermore, while we acknowledge that a discussion of cultural values and the culture's prejudice toward many subgroups can be of great effectiveness when timed well, we emphasize that these discussions should not, in our opinion, remain on an abstract level, but must be tied directly to the affective experiences of the client.

There are some differences of opinion among therapists about the degree to which the therapist should emphasize the issue of culture in discussing psychopathology. For example, feminist psychotherapists are explicit in emphasizing the role of society in contributing to client conflicts and difficulties. Worell and Remer (1992) noted:

> Since traditional sex-role socialization and the institutionalized separation and discrimination of people based on gender are judged to oppress and limit the potential of all individuals, the external environment is considered the main source of clients' problems. (pp. 91–92)

From this perspective, some emphasis is placed on helping clients analyze how society may have contributed to their problems through processes such as racism or sexism. Many therapists probably do agree that some relief from guilt and anxiety may be effected by assisting the client to identify ways in which the culture and persons in the culture help make the client more vulnerable to those feelings. Our culture has often attempted to force ethnic and racial minorities into the proverbial melting pot, and away from their ethnic identities. When people are forced away from their ethnic identities, their self-esteem is clearly at risk, and this is not due to any characterological defect.

In the broad area of multicultural research, the concern about whether the therapist will understand the client's problem has been addressed by studying client preferences (or lack thereof) for matching between their own ethnicity and that of their therapist. Currently, this research is beset by the problem of the number and complexity of interacting variables, and its conclusions are somewhat conflicting (Beutler, Machado, & Neufeldt, 1994; Helms & Carter, 1991; Lopez, Lopez, & Fong, 1991; Speight & Vera, 1997; Sue, Zane, & Young, 1994). Although there are circumstances under which a match between therapist and client on ethnicity may be important (for example, if the client expresses a strong desire for a "match"; see also Sue, 1998), sweeping generalizations are not possible at this time. Nonetheless, sensitivity to client preferences is clearly important.

6. *Will the therapist be competent to help?* Naturally, this is not a fear that is generally expressed directly. Nonetheless, we assume that many clients do have this concern. One theory about the process of psychotherapy includes as a central tenet the degree to which the client perceives the therapist to be an expert (Heppner & Claiborn, 1989; Strong, 1968). Kokotovic and Tracey (1987) found that perception of therapist expertness was related to probability of clients returning after an initial session, although only insofar as the variance overlapped with that of client satisfaction. McNeill, May, and Lee (1987) found that premature terminators viewed their therapists as less expert than did successful terminators.

Earlier we discussed the issue of clients inquiring about one's credentials. To reiterate, we do not force clients to discuss the "deep meaning" of asking about credentials. These are, in our view, legitimate and realistic concerns. In part, such questions express a concern about competency. However, as Paul Meehl once said, "The proof is in the pudding." We advocate answering questions like these straightforwardly and then demonstrating to the client by our skill and caring that we are indeed competent to help.

7. *Will I be pressured to do or say things?* Some clients bring to therapy a strange and varied assortment of conceptions and misconceptions about the therapeutic process. Both accurate and inaccurate ideas may come from friends, books, or television programs. Many clients are sophisticated enough to know that few therapists "force" their clients to do things clearly against their wills. On the other hand, this concern embodies and captures the spirit of a concern most clients do have—that of the extent to which they, rather than the therapist, will have control over the process. As therapists, we are sometimes prone to point our finger accusingly and say, "She has a great need for control," or "He is trying to take control of the sessions." We should not find it altogether surprising when people seem to want control over their lives! At its base, the desire to be in charge of one's life is viewed as a healthy one. We say this knowing that it is certainly possible for this desire to be corrupted in the sense that it may become defensive obsession. Here we are merely emphasizing that clients who are mildly concerned about whether they or the therapist will be making the final decisions about what is best for them are implicitly expressing some basic drive toward good mental health.

It should be obvious that many clients come to therapy in part because they do not feel that they are in control of what seems, in their eyes, to be happening to them. Or more pointedly, they may have had many past experiences in which they were dependent upon someone and felt they had to comply over and over or risk losing love and/or support. These people have a very keenly developed fear that new relationships will prove confining, suffocating, or demeaning. They may expect therapists to be controlling from the beginning, but more often these sorts of people have a more subtle fear—the fear that they will be forced to strike a Faustian bargain to get the help they need. This fear takes the form of, "I will let you be in charge of me in order to get from you (the therapist) what I need." That is just one powerful example of why therapists must not place clients in the position of fulfilling *therapists'* needs. Inevitably, many clients will feel that they have no choice but to comply—no matter how much is demanded of them. Not merely does this convey to clients the message of the terrible price that must be paid for getting one's needs met, it also conveys to clients the sense that love and support, rather than springing quite naturally from a relationship, must be earned by certain kinds of behavior. The issue is not just that a heavy price is paid but that the person fears that there are always *conditions* with which he or she must contend.

8. *Will I become dependent upon therapy (or the therapist) and then be abandoned?* This fear is not typically expressed early in therapy, and it is obviously not typically and overtly stated by the client the way we have phrased it. Nonetheless, it is assumed to be operative in the minds of many clients, including those who are "counterdependent," and those who are seen as "dependent" in a traditional sense (e.g., Bornstein, 1993; Bornstein & Bowen, 1995; Overholser & Fine, 1994). For a number of reasons, we expect that many clients will fear and resist being dependent upon the therapist. Broadly speaking, these concerns fall into two categories that may be reciprocally causal, but which we separate for emphasis. The first revolves around the issue of how clients view themselves and how they feel about the various "selves" they might be or wish to avoid (Markus & Nurius, 1986). Thus the idea of being dependent may conjure up associations of weakness or worthlessness. Examples would be clients who have been told by their parents all their lives such things as, "Don't ever put yourself in the position of owing someone something," or "Don't ever love someone too much," or "Love them but make sure you leave them before they leave you," or "Only the strong remain free." These messages are not typically stated overtly by parents but rather are inferred by children as they watch and listen to parents. In cases like these, clients have come to associate certain actions suggestive of dependency with a bad image of themselves. Thus they make every effort to avoid placing themselves in situations that would suggest their dependency on others. Having reached a point at which psychotherapy seems like the only alternative to a bleak or painful life, they force themselves to "submit" to the dependency they fear by seeking therapy. This does not mean that they are comfortable about entering into the relationship, and it certainly does not mean that they easily allow their dependency to develop. For each time they are reminded of their dependency they experience a kind of self-loathing: They fear that they are about to become what they have always viewed as bad.

It is often quite difficult for therapists to understand this sort of attitude toward the self. After all, we are caring, competent people in whom others are to place their trust. But that is not the point. From the client's perspective it may matter very little how caring or how competent we are—for to be dependent on anyone for any reason may activate self-hate. To appreciate what this is like for clients, you might imagine that you feel sick for a period of time and then see a physician. Medication is prescribed that you are told will help make you well. But there is a catch. The medication has the disturbing side effect of making you feel very guilty every time someone does you the least little favor. And so you work very, very hard to set up situations in which you won't feel so bad about yourself. You probably also do a lot of thinking about whether you could just take half the dosage, or take the medicine less often, or in some other way reduce the side effects. Perhaps you try to pretend that the guilt you feel really isn't guilt. In short, you struggle valiantly. But there is really no getting around the fact that you have become someone you do not particularly like—someone for whom you have little respect even though you don't feel you had much choice about the medication. This is exactly what clients do as they struggle not to be (or to appear to themselves) dependent while simultaneously disliking the person they have become. These clients may not fear the actual interpersonal consequences of dependency as much as they despise seeing themselves act in a manner for which they have always had little respect. With these clients, some attention will need to be given to their view of dependency and their view of themselves in therapy, for each time they acknowledge dependency, they may go through a period of renewed self-loathing.

Clients who view being dependent as a weakness often fear abandonment. There are a couple of reasons why this may be so. In the first place, a great many people seem to have learned the lesson that if they have been foolish, there will be a price to pay. (This is perhaps especially true of males.) Secondly, some of this fear may be a kind of projection. That is, clients are unforgiving of their perceived weakness, and perhaps imagine that under reversed conditions, they would abandon the person.

Another reason people fear being dependent is that they fear the interpersonal consequences. For example, they may fear that they would be powerless to prevent psychological abuse or they may fear that they would be powerless to prevent the loss of the person on whom they are dependent. This sort of fear of dependency is closely related to Freud's ideas of danger situations (one of which was "loss of the object," and another "loss of the love of the object," Greenberg & Mitchell, 1983). One certainly does not have to be a Freudian to believe that when individuals are dependent on another person it may remind them (whether consciously or unconsciously) of earlier experiences in which they were dependent and ended up losing, in one form or another, the relationship.

The client's fear of becoming (being) dependent upon the therapist and then being abandoned, we assume, in part reflects feelings about people in general. That is, there may be an expectation that anyone on whom the person comes to depend will in fact ultimately disappoint him or her in a major way. Such ideas (and feelings) are expressed by sentences such as, "I knew that sooner or later she would let me down," or "Nobody's perfect and that goes double for the people I've trusted," or even, "I don't intend to let him get close enough to hurt me." For people who fear becoming dependent and then being abandoned by the therapist because this has happened with others, the relationship with the therapist assumes heightened importance. This is true for two reasons. First, as clients recapitulate their problem in the therapeutic relationship, they are presenting the therapist with a powerful opportunity to create an experience that disconfirms their fear about the consequences of trusting others. Since we view some trust in others as being a requisite for good mental health, the opportunity for the client to experience that trust in others does not lead to abandonment seems of great importance. For example, Phelps, Friedlander, and Enns (1997) studied 11 cases in which clients had retrieved memories of abuse in past or ongoing psychotherapy. In all 11 cases, they found a theme involving the client's expression of trust in the therapist. If the client can place no faith in the therapist, then there is no possibility of a disconfirming experience. As we have noted, this is an assumption of the book— that the therapeutic relationship is part and parcel of the client's struggle for better mental health.

The second reason the relationship with the therapist is especially important if a person fears being abandoned is that in such instances the client, in order not to be vulnerable, tends to discount the ideas of the therapist and in general to limit the impact and influence of the therapist. Thus, a poor relationship in such instances means that a key therapeutic ingredient, therapist influence, has unfortunately been at least partially neutralized.

There are several more practical implications of these facts for the practice of psychotherapy. For example, it is quite common even for clients who have done well in therapy to have the fear near termination that they have become somewhat dependent on therapy. Furthermore, it is important to keep in mind that some clients are very prone to experience fear of abandonment if the therapist is about to go on vacation. When clients show the therapist a part of themselves that they do not like, they may feel especially vulnerable to abandonment. This is true because telling someone about the "bad them" both realistically and especially in fantasy makes them dependent upon that person in the sense that the therapist now knows how to exploit their weakness. Thus, they fear that the therapist will "damage" them and then leave. There is also a kind of potential symbolism here of the bad person (therapist) who might steal the client's secret. More specifically, once the client has confessed to the therapist, the client has lost control of what was once so well guarded. In a milder form of this fear, clients fear that they will be rejected (rather than completely abandoned) when they reveal the "bad" parts of themselves. We will discuss this issue a little later in this chapter.

It is not likely that a client will initially and overtly express concerns about being abandoned. A possible exception to this rule is when a client sees a series of therapists who are students on rotation. If you are to be a part of such a scenario, the two general rules to follow would be: (a) offer the client an opportunity to talk about the issue and (b) avoid encouraging dependency. How should you go about offering the client an opportunity to discuss the issue? Consider the following example involving a female therapist and male client:

THERAPIST: I'm Sue Smith. Dr. Jones, the psychiatrist, said you wanted to see a therapist.

CLIENT: Are you another one of those students who is in training out here? How long will you be here?
(Note: The client's use of the term "another one of" is important. At best, this sentence suggests a kind of benign curiosity about the therapist. More likely, the client has a well-developed set of expectations about what is possible with a student. The question "How long will you be here?" immediately alerts the therapist to the client's sensitivity about being left.)

THERAPIST: Yes, I'm a psychology intern. I'll be here for three months. I know Bill Johnson also interned here. I think you saw him for about three months didn't you?
(Note: Obviously, the previous therapist did not introduce the client to his new therapist. At times this may not be possible but it is generally best. Even though the client has implicitly raised the issue of being left, the therapist chooses not to process the fear immediately since she has just met the person. This is probably a wise decision.)

CLIENT: Yeah, he was around here for awhile. He helped me quite a bit. Are you going to need those audiotapes like he did?
(Note: The first sentence suggests some hostility and again implicitly raises the issue of being abandoned. If we take at face value the client's comment about being helped, we see that clients can have positive feelings about their past therapy but simultaneously still be angry about being left. Notice that by asking about audiotaping, the client, for the second time, places the new therapist in the same category as his previous one. One might assume this sentence

to carry with it elements of hostility. For example, there is the suggestion that the therapist will "need" something from the client and there is also an implicit pointed reference to the therapist's being a student. Some clients use this as leverage to reduce the therapist's power. Although these more negative purposes are certainly possible, it is also possible that the client is trying to offer the therapist what he can to be helpful. We are perhaps rightly suspicious of such a question, but we want to point out that the instinct to be helpful is not a cancer to be cut out. True, it may be overemphasized by some clients, but we need to be "on the lookout," so to speak, for behaviors that might in part represent positive, desirable aspects of the person's personality.)

THERAPIST: I'm glad you brought up the issue of taping. I will need to tape if that's okay with you. In fact, I have a form here I'd appreciate your signing if you don't mind.
(Note: Again the therapist chooses not to address the issue of the client's being abandoned. Since she is still in the first minutes of the first session, she is waiting for a more direct statement about the issue or a little more time to pass, whichever comes first.)

CLIENT: Well, I'll sign. (*Pause*) Could you tell me again how long you will be here?
(Note: The client is sending out such strong, frequent signals about the issue that the therapist should probably go ahead and try to process the issue, even though it is fairly early in the first session. One reason the therapist would be reluctant to go ahead here is that it will be very difficult for the client to express anger about the person who helped him [assuming for a moment that this is his perception] to a relative stranger. Thus the therapist will likely adopt a limited goal of making the issue as nonthreatening as possible while realizing that she will undoubtedly have to return to the issue later because any processing done now will almost certainly be incomplete.)

THERAPIST: I'll be here for three months. (*Pause*) I know that's a very short time.
(Note: The therapist does a nice job of placing the issue on the table without being overly threatening.)

CLIENT: Well, nothing lasts forever.
(Note: The client seems a little defensive, a little protective of himself and his previous therapist.)

THERAPIST: (*Nods—Pause*) Well, I was just thinking, you saw Bill for only three months and now I'm here for only three months. That can be tough. I'm guessing that's not quite enough time for you to get to know someone the way you'd really like to.
(Note: Since the client sent out such strong signals, the therapist decides to push just a little. The issue is framed in positive terms rather than a more negative one [suggesting the possibility of anger could be an example of a more negative frame]. The "positive" emphasis is appropriate here.)

In this example the therapist would likely continue both in the first session and in future sessions to afford the client the opportunity to express and explore his feelings of being abandoned. In fact, the therapist's continued alertness to this issue is one way of addressing the suggestion above that clients who will be seen for a very limited number of times should not be encouraged to be dependent on you. It is also important, however, that such limited therapy not be turned into one extended processing of the previous therapy. So, while some time should be spent in "wrapping up" the previous therapy (assuming there has been some sort of problem), some common goals for the new therapy, however limited it is to be, must also be established.

9. *Will I be engulfed by the therapist?* The obverse of the concern about losing the therapist is the fear of being engulfed by the therapist. Thus these two fears represent different aspects of one issue—how the problem of closeness (Schwartz, 1993) is to be addressed.

It is very important that the therapist not push for more intimacy than the client is capable of handling. So, for example, if the client says, "I'm not sure I can trust you," or "I'm not sure I want to tell you about it," the following sorts of comments would be inappropriate:

> "If you can't trust me, who can you trust?"
> "You can't get better until you talk about it."
> "You do realize that these sessions are confidential, don't you?"
> "Maybe if you trusted me you could trust others."
> "Why can't you trust me?"
> "Why don't you want to talk about it?"
> "Nothing ventured, nothing gained."

Each of the above responses has the effect of suggesting to clients that they ought to be open and trusting with the therapist. This is a demand by the therapist for intimacy that is inappropriate and which may heighten the client's fear that the therapist will overwhelm and engulf the client. When clients express anxiety about boundaries between themselves and the therapist, the therapist is advised to ensure respect for those boundaries in responding to the concern. In the previous example, the therapist might consider one of the following:

> "It seems reasonable not to trust others when you barely know them" (assumes initial stages of therapy).
>
> "It's tough struggling with that fear about what I might do if you show me your real self" (assumes client has been seen for a number of sessions).
>
> "It sounds like a part of you wants to go ahead and talk about it, but there's also another part—one that says, 'be careful.' I'd like for you to know that this is a place where *you* decide what's best for you."

Clients who had dominating parents (caregivers) may be especially likely to fear being engulfed by the therapist. These clients may also exhibit behaviors of the classic help-rejecting complainer. That is, clients who have never developed an easygoing acceptance of their autonomy may seek out advice and direction, but then reject that direction or subtly sabotage the ideas that were solicited. In the first place, these clients can be very frustrating. The therapist needs to be alert to the possibility of being lured into a role that repeats the client's earlier pattern of seeking help and then rejecting it. On the other hand the client who fears being engulfed may exhibit this fear by chronically remaining uncommitted to therapy. These clients stick their toe in the water, so to speak, but have a great fear of actually going for a swim. They are often quite attracted to therapy, especially initially, but then get stuck because they fear they might lose what little power and control they have carved out for themselves. Their self-image is quite fragile; there is a constant fear that someone bigger will swallow them up. For these people, being close is equated with loss of self. Typically, the therapist should move slowly, encouraging the development of some sort of self identity, and respecting client's needs to establish intimacy at their own pace.

10. *Will the sessions be confidential?* Some comments concerning this issue may be found in Chapter 2, Questions That Beginning Therapists Ask, and Chapter 5, Ethical and Legal Issues. We make a few additional comments here because confidentiality is indeed a client concern. There is a very practical reason for the profession's insistence about confidentiality. Weinberg (1984) expresses this reason well:

> Confidentiality must become a specialty of ours. Our patients often trust us with information they would want no one else to have. Moreover, they trust us to explore the recesses of their souls, and along with them to uncover other facts whose discovery is mortifying in its very prospect. They need confidence in our ability not to disclose information to anyone.
>
> Not surprisingly, most patients are slow to arrive at this state of trust. They wait a long time before being willing to reveal themselves fully. They watch us narrowly, and if we seem aghast at anything they disclose, they may worry that we will have a need to discuss it with others, and they may retreat. There's a burden on us to be absolutely above reproach. (p. 64)

Weinberg makes a second interesting point related to confidentiality in psychotherapy. It is his belief that the client should also be asked to honor the principle of confidentiality since in his view this helps the client avoid diluting the impact of the session by talking to others and seeking their support. Although we do not practice asking the client to honor confidentiality, we believe that it is an interesting idea with sound reasoning behind it.

We emphasize that it is very important to avoid any actions that might give the impression that confidentiality is being compromised. This requirement goes beyond the strict rule of not revealing a person's identity. Thus, for example, suppose that you are at a party and are asked, "Have you ever seen a client who was bulimic?" You answer, "Yes, last semester at the VA Hospital." The person says, "Did the client always act like the perfect child when growing up?" You say, "Yes, that did seem to be the case." You then go on to add, "It also seemed as if the client wanted me to be perfect. There was a great deal of hostility. The client often criticized me at length." Although you revealed no names and very little identifying information, you have communicated to the person(s) with whom you are speaking that you discuss clients at parties. Would we be surprised to learn that the listener, upon becoming a client, was concerned about confidentiality?

One of the authors once supervised a student who was seeing a client who was in prison for rape. The student told his wife one or two facts about the person, including why the client was in prison. The following week, the client, who knew that the therapist was married, asked, "Did you tell your wife why I am in prison?" The therapist had not anticipated that the client would ask such a question and was naturally very uncomfortable. The point is that it is very difficult to know how the subject of confidentiality will come up and what kind of impact your not being absolutely circumspect will have. There is, therefore, a very simple rule to follow: "Don't talk about your clients except to your supervisor."

11. *Will I be punished or exploited by the therapist?* In a study of undergraduates' perceptions of therapists and psychotherapy, Bram (1997) found that:

> ...despite generally positive impressions...[there was a] disconcertingly pervasive view of therapists as prone to act on countertransference sexual-romantic and aggressive impulses. Participants tended to overestimate the prevalence rates of sexual-romantic boundary violations committed by male and female practitioners.... Common beliefs were that an insulted therapist would retaliate against or abandon the client and that a therapist experiencing strong sexual-romantic countertransference would act out with or abandon the client. (p. 174)

Given these findings, we must conclude that some clients will enter therapy with a slightly jaundiced view of therapists, with misgivings about the kinds of intentions harbored by professionals. In the case of clients who are somewhat prone to mistrust others in general, we might anticipate a fear of being exploited by therapists using their attributed powers of understanding and insight into human behavior.

How Will I Be Viewed as a Client in Psychotherapy?

Since psychotherapy always involves the client and at least one other person, we can say that therapy is a social process. One perspective on a social phenomenon is that there are self-presentation motives operating in such processes. Baumeister (1982) has suggested that two such motives are to please the audience (i.e., to obtain rewards) and to construct one's public self congruent with the ideal self. The idea that there is a motive to please others or appear desirable has been around for quite some time in psychology. The groundwork for empirical studies was laid by Crowne and Marlow (1960) and by Edwards (1957). The idea that there is a motive to have congruence between public self and ideal self is an extension of the ideas of Carl Rogers (e.g., Rogers, 1951; Rogers & Dymond, 1954). Baumeister (1982) described the desire to obtain consistency between the public self and the ideal self as "a means of, substitute for, or prop to self-fulfillment." He also noted that there may be an accompanying "motivation to convince them [others] that one is like one's ideal self." Citing Jones (1964), Baumeister suggested that if we can convince others that we are a certain way, we may be more prone to believe it ourselves. With regard to therapy, then, the client is assumed to come with some sort of predisposition to appear reasonable, rational, and appropriate. More generally, we might say that clients come with a kind of agenda about the way they would like to be seen. Some of this agenda may reflect cultural predispositions in interpersonal environments. Perhaps most importantly, we are interested in the degree to which the client seems overly concerned about creating, maintaining, and controlling this image, whatever the image may be. Why are we so interested in this attempt by clients to control the image they create for us? There are two primary reasons and they are related: (a) we want clients to realize, ultimately, that the relationship does not depend on their being a good person, and (b) we hope they will progressively spend less and less energy maintaining an image and more and more energy identifying their own preferences, expectations, and the like.

First, as clients struggle (as they often do) to obtain our approval, we want them to understand that our approval is not contingent on their good behavior. Certainly we have the hope that the client will behave (or at least learn to behave) in a more or less civilized fashion. But in fact, most clients who seek therapy already meet that criterion—many clients more than meet it. The great majority of clients have in some basic way come to expect that if they behave in some specified way, then they will be accepted. Rogers (e.g., 1951) called these expectations "conditions of worth." Psychotherapy attempts to turn this reasoning around. If clients are fully accepted, we assume that then client's behaviors will be something that both they and others can enjoy, in part because behavior is not demanded but rather is expressive. There really are several different and powerfully positive processes at work here. The first is clients' discovery that not all the world places conditions on them. This realization is freeing in itself since clients can now dare to hope that they might be able to have good relationships. Thus, we hope that clients will come to expect helpful responses from others and that they will begin to seek out and create better interpersonal environments for themselves. Also, as they begin to see themselves as actually deserving of good treatment (not contingent on good behavior) they are less demoralized, more self-accepting, and less likely to subject themselves to rigid and punitive treatment. This is the process whereby therapists' accepting, tolerant attitude is internalized by the client. In one form or another, and by whatever name it may be called, this process seems to be present in virtually all schools of psychotherapy. Furthermore, clients are greatly relieved to learn that neither good nor bad behavior can put the relationship at risk. It is who they are, not what they do, that forms the basis for the ongoing relationship. Finally, by showing that our approval is not for sale, we underscore within the *process* of therapy that, despite the client's natural inclination to seek our approval, this is not the goal to be sought. Rather the goal is an identity for the client that is ultimately not dependent upon the therapist for validation. This does not mean that we should not be supportive. We are simply saying that as clients strive to create for us an image that they believe will bring rewards, we must help them work toward less and less dependence on this sort of approval. Simultaneously, we help them generalize this experience to their relationships with others.

The second primary reason we are interested in clients' efforts to control the image we have of them is that such efforts can take up enormous amounts of energy. We adopt an uncritical acceptance of the client in part because we want the client to be placed in an interpersonal environment where little energy is needed to maintain the acceptance of the therapist. If the client spends great effort to maintain an image with the therapist, we assume that similar efforts are made with others. Clients who work very hard at maintaining an image have very little time left over to explore, focus on, and carry out their own preferences. This leaves them frustrated because they are unable to express who they are, and anxious because their sense of accomplishment and identity is based on an image subject to the interpretive whims of others. In fact, many clients enter therapy in part because they no longer are able to maintain a balance (which they often have spent so much energy doing and which they themselves may label as a "balancing act") between what they experience as their own needs and the needs of others. In part, such "failures" in the balancing act create a crisis of self-image in which the person is left uncertain both about who they wish to be and who they think they are. When individuals are uncertain about the way they would like to be, they paradoxically engage in especially strong attempts to draw clear and coherent pictures for others of their self—hence the efforts to create and control the image the therapist has of them.

We know that clients may also have other motives that in part conflict with their need to be seen as possessing positive traits. For example, a part of their motivation for coming may be to confess or to shock. In any event, clients may be invested in creating a certain image of themselves for the therapist (Kelly, Kahn, & Coulter 1996) and perhaps to some extent for others who may be aware of the fact that the client is seeking therapy. We will now discuss some of those issues.

1. *Will the therapist think that I am a bad person?* One of the more common (though not unimportant) fears clients have is that the therapist will see them as a bad person. Exactly what is meant by "bad" varies enormously from client to client. Some will think they have treated their spouse, parents, or children badly, others will think that they are morally bankrupt because they have squandered their potential or failed to speak out about injustice, and still others may be unable to specify (or may not even be conscious of) exactly why they feel that they are a bad person. But in each case clients may fear the same type of judgment from the therapist that they have pronounced upon themselves. Hill, Thompson, Cogar, and Denman (1993), as well as Kelly (1998) found that in fact clients do appear to keep secrets from their therapists for a variety of reasons, including shame and embarrassment. Kelly found that a general tendency to self-conceal was associated with greater symptomatology; however, surprisingly, actually keeping secrets from the therapist was associated with fewer symptoms. The research investigating who is more likely to avoid therapy, high self-concealers or low self-concealers, is mixed (Cepeda-Benito & Short, 1998; Kelly & Achter, 1995).

If the therapist is uncritical and accepting, the fear is not realistic and thus becomes grist for the therapeutic mill. That is, the client's fear about rejection is something to be explored. As suggested earlier, when clients repeatedly experience *not* being thought of as a bad person they come to be more forgiving of themselves. Although the various schools of therapy differ in their emphasis on the importance of the relationship between client and therapist, most either implicitly or explicitly suggest that the therapist must adopt a forgiving and tolerant attitude toward the failures of the client. There are at least three different processes whereby clients may not experience being accepted. Since the relationship between client and therapist is so important, it is critical that the therapist be alert to each of these possibilities.

First, as we have suggested, the client may *expect* to be judged and therefore see evidence of such judgment when in fact there is little or none. This is an example of what Freud called transference. For example, if parents have been harshly critical, therapists will be expected to be that way also. More generally we might say that people probably look for cues suggesting that what has happened in the past will happen again. One reason they do this is to order their world; a part of this ordering is a constructed continuity of experience about the self. Thus, even when evidence is scant, if it is of central importance to the self, and if it is consistent with previous experience, it is likely to be information on which the client focuses. Furthermore, the client is likely to place trust in this information, even if it is at variance with other available data. This is a part of the process whereby clients actively (whether intentionally or unintentionally) maintain an ongoing fear that others think them to be bad persons. A related part of the process is that since people internalize (or emulate) individuals who have been important to them, they come to adopt the same attitude about themselves that others have had toward them. So it is not just that clients think they will be seen as bad since they have been treated that way in the past, but additionally that they have come to believe that they *are* bad persons. What people already believe about themselves requires little confirmation. The expectation that one will be thought of as a bad person, coupled with the belief that one *is* a bad person, is something that the client may bring to therapy and which may be independent of any actual thoughts or feelings which the therapist has about the client. In our view, the therapist must be alert to this possible issue and, where needed, address it repeatedly, not merely in terms of the therapeutic relationship, but also in terms of the client's interpersonal relationships outside of therapy. Consider the following example:

CLIENT: My wife said it bothered her a lot when I came home late without calling.

THERAPIST: How did you feel about what she said?

CLIENT: Well, I know I shouldn't do it. I know she must think that I'm a clod.

THERAPIST: She said you were a clod?

CLIENT: No, but I could tell by the tone in her voice. She sounded just like my mother always did when she criticized me for staying late at the playground.

THERAPIST: Well, perhaps your wife was angry. On the other hand, perhaps she was mainly concerned about you or even wondering how you felt about her. It sounds like your first assumption was that she was being critical of you—it's almost like you expected that kind of response, that you're afraid that people are likely to think of you as a bad person.
(Note: The therapist does not specifically comment on the client's statement about his mother but rather makes note of it as a potentially important issue.)

CLIENT: I know I'm basically a nice guy.
(Note: The client overtly rejects what the therapist has said. At this point beginning therapists often stop, fearing they will offend the client if they continue to press.)

THERAPIST: You know this on one level, yet at another level you continue to expect other people to pronounce judgments on your behavior—maybe the way your mother did when you were a child.
(Note: The therapist does four good things with his or her comment: (a) acknowledges the client's reality ["you know this on one level"]; (b) doesn't let an important issue drop, but does that in a way that is not threatening ["yet at another level…"]; (c) links the client's behavior to an emotionally charged part of the client's life [what he learned from his mother]; and (d) broadens the issue slightly from one of being a bad person to the more inclusive one assuming that others, rather than the client, are to be the judges of the client's behavior. Note also that the therapist is now tying the current problem to an issue [the client's mother] that was first introduced by the client.)

Clients like the one in this example are likely to expect rejection from many people including the therapist. This expectation tends to make their behavior more rigid, more defensive, less adaptable, and less inherently enjoyable to themselves. Furthermore, as we have said, the clients' expectation that they will be seen as bad persons heightens their awareness of, and sensitivity to, information consistent with their view, however limited the data are. Thus one way in which clients may feel they are being judged as bad persons is if they have come to expect bad treatment from others. This expectation is seen as a combination of direct learning experience, in which they are criticized by others, and a subsequent internalized view of themselves as bad persons. Furthermore, we emphasize that parents and significant others may be critical covertly rather than overtly, and in such cases negative self-images can be especially difficult to overcome.

A second way in which clients may experience themselves as being bad persons is if the therapist is *repeatedly* intolerant, moralistic, or judgmental. Any of several factors may produce such a situation. These factors include: (a) a long-standing personality deficit in the therapist; (b) a situation in the therapist's life that has temporarily affected his or her capacity to respond therapeutically; or (c) a client and therapeutic relationship that has raised issues that are not quite settled for the therapist, and about which the therapist is somewhat defensive. These issues will be discussed more in Chapter 12, Transference and Countertransference.

A third way in which clients may end up feeling that they are bad persons comes about when they from time to time provoke or elicit unsympathetic responses from the therapist. This may sound strange after we have emphasized how the therapist needs to have a "helpful" personality and after we have suggested that therapists' deficits may produce therapeutic failure. However, people vary widely in their capacity to elicit helpful and relationship-enhancing responses. We will discuss this issue more in Chapter 12, Transference and Countertransference, but here we merely underscore the importance of recognizing instances in which you have been somewhat critical of the client and the importance of ascertaining the degree to which the client provoked your criticism.

We have just listed some ways in which clients may end up feeling bad about themselves. There are three primary reasons why clients' fears about being seen as a bad person must be addressed.

First, clients may not be willing to discuss the things that are bothering them if they fear that disclosure would exacerbate their preexisting bad feelings about themselves. Second, the reduction of doubt about one's self-worth is frequently a therapeutic goal in and of itself. Third, fear about being seen as a bad person may set up a self-perpetuating cycle in which expectations are verified through various "cognitive errors," and then followed by defensive behavior that is self-constricting and which also elicits defensive and unhelpful responses from others.

2. *Will my friends think there is something abnormal or bad about me if I come for psychotherapy?* This fear (if it exists for a client) typically comes from some sort of interaction between cultural or environmental factors and the personality of the client. For example, certain ethnic groups may be suspicious of "professional helpers" or have a view that emphasizes taking care of your problems by yourself or within your family or community. Some religious groups believe that psychotherapy is an "instrument of the devil" and threaten to expel any member seeking help. Males may be particularly sensitive to how they imagine their friends will see them. They may believe (at times with some evidence) that their peers will think that a man who cannot solve his own problems is not a full man. Another example would be the woman who is married to a man who might physically abuse her if he knew she was coming for therapy. The therapist must be especially sensitive to these cultural and environmental factors both because they are powerful maintainers of fear and also because they can have real and potentially damaging consequences for the client. Although you can offer support for the client coming to therapy, and even possibly additional help in the case of overt threats, it is very important to avoid pressuring the client toward continuing to seek help. It is only the client who can finally decide what is best and it is the client, rather than the therapist, who will reap the potential consequences of ostracism, verbal or physical abuse, ridicule, or whatever if the client's interpersonal environment is not supportive of being in therapy.

Fortunately, these examples are not the "average" case. More typically, the client's general concern about being evaluated by others is manifested. In many cases the assumption that others would be critical is untested. In fact, there may be some advantage to the client's gathering together enough courage to mention it to the person whose opinion is feared. For example, one Chinese student mentioned that his wife did not know he was coming for therapy. The student's therapist was of the opinion that cultural factors were an issue. Although the therapist did not actually encourage him to tell his wife, the student did so and was very relieved to learn that she was supportive.

Often clients want to deal with their fear and will introduce the topic by saying "I haven't told my mother I'm coming for therapy," or, in the case of college students, they may want to know whether their parents will be informed about their visits. When clients volunteer the information that they have not told a given person about their therapy, there is almost always some sort of relationship issue involved. In the example about the mother, there is a strong possibility that dependency issues rather than evaluation issues are more central.

One way a version of this fear may be expressed is when the client says something to the effect of, "Coming for psychotherapy means I have failed—I just don't want other people to know about my failure." The primary issue, here again, is not really the fear of being evaluated by others but rather the way in which the person looks at what he or she has decided to do (i.e., seek psychotherapy).

3. *Will the therapist think that I am more disturbed than I really am?* There is something rather fundamental about the desire to be seen as we believe we really are. True, there is a fear on the part of some that they are frauds—impostors (Langford & Clance, 1993) who need to avoid being discovered. But many clients are seeking, as much as anything, to have the experience of being understood. In part they seek psychotherapy because others have failed to understand them—have failed to see the complexities and appreciate the nuances. Clients are searching for a person who is willing to go into "the heart of darkness" with them—a person who is also willing to visit their secret shrines, and stay long enough to meet their gods and devils. A part of the client wants to believe that if we can understand the exquisite balance, the peace treaty if you will, the client has worked out between these forces, perhaps we will appreciate the client. For example, there is evidence that people see themselves as having a rich, deep, and multifaceted personality (Sande, Goethals, & Radloff, 1988). This belief at times produces in clients a feeling of, for example, "If they only knew my mother, they would understand why I do what I do." But this desire to be known sets in motion a number of fears, including the fear that the therapist will "go too far" and see more pathology than the client believes is there. As is the case with many other fears, this one is influenced by both cultural factors and personality structure. Cultural factors of relevance include the popular image of the psychotherapist who "psychoanalyzes" the client and "makes a mountain out of a molehill." Certainly in our culture there is a premium placed on what might be called one's understanding of reality and a capacity to adapt to it. Clients do not want an expert sitting in judgment of them who fails to notice adaptive strengths. After all, one possible outcome of being misjudged is being placed, nonvoluntarily, in a psychiatric unit.

Obviously, some clients are concerned about this issue not so much because they fear being seen as disturbed as because they fear both that they are disturbed and that they might have this confirmed. Other clients are sensitive to evaluation, and their sensitivity may interact with an identity that is tied to a belief in one's hold on reality. In any event, the point we wish to stress is that clients are very sensitive to the issue of how disturbed they are judged to be.

4. *Will the therapist find out some things about me that I don't want known?* A fear related to the one we just discussed is the idea that clients often have "secrets" that they, at one level, do not want revealed. We say "at one level" because we believe that most clients have a rather basic desire to tell the therapist about the things that are disturbing to them. This desire, however, may be counterbalanced by the fear of being known, of being vulnerable to another person. At times clients are quite aware of withholding their "secrets"; at other times they resist talking about these secrets but are not aware of their resistance. (Additional comments may be found in Chapter 11, Resistance.)

There are several reasons that clients may fear having some things revealed. These range from potential legal difficulties to issues about power and control that have little to do with specific content. Our general belief is that when clients try to prevent us from knowing certain things about them they have symbolically placed themselves in opposition to us. This may or may not represent a pathological process, and it is not necessarily easy to know the difference. Consider the following exchange from a fifth session involving a client who came for therapy because she was intensely jealous.

THERAPIST: So as I understand it you don't, in your view, have any evidence that your husband has been unfaithful but there's a kind of nagging fear that just won't go away.

CLIENT: That's right.

THERAPIST: Well, we've talked about this for five sessions now. I'm wondering if we might talk a little about how you viewed your parents' marriage. Does that sound reasonable?

CLIENT: I really don't want to talk a lot about the past. It's not that I mind, it's just that I've never thought one could solve problems by going back in time.

At this point of the interchange, it is difficult to know whether the therapist's suggestion has set off anxiety about her parents' marriage or whether the client's statement is a philosophy of life and behavior change consistent, for example, with that of someone like Albert Ellis (e.g., 1985). One clue suggesting that the person is expressing a philosophy of life rather than a specific conflict is that she frames the issue broadly rather than saying she doesn't want to talk about her parents' marriage. Certainly we must understand that clients can appear quite reasonable in their defensiveness. However, we must also understand that we are foolish therapists indeed if we assume that every time the client "rejects" our suggestions or ideas, a pathological conflict has been identified.

What we do have to do when the client seems to disagree with our suggestion about how to proceed is to weigh as impartially as possible the evidence suggesting we might be off base against the evidence suggesting that the client is conflicted about the material. For example, if a client comes to therapy reporting difficulty in establishing new relationships, but says, "the past is past" when describing his feelings about his wife who died six months earlier, there is certainly a strong possibility that the client doesn't want to discuss something he probably needs to discuss. The psychotherapy profession has gone to great effort, both in the legal area, and in the professional attitudes fostered in training programs, to create an environment that allows clients to reveal information about themselves. By doing this, we seek to calm naturally arising and reality-based client concerns.

5. *Will I appear foolish or weak?* Most clients come to therapy in part because they believe they have not been able to solve one or more problems confronting them. Whether the problem is highly specific, as in the case of an inability to board an aircraft, or rather diffuse, as in feelings of despair about the meaning of life, clients often see themselves as weak, inept, or worthless. Having this view of themselves, they suspect that others may also. We have all experienced the sharp pain of believing that someone thinks us foolish. We have also all had the experience of scrambling to portray ourselves as not foolish. We have worked to say just the right thing that lets others know that we are insightful, that we were being ironic if we at first seemed foolish, that we are not to be trifled with. There is not so much fear here of actually being damaged, but the fear that we will seem as if we could be damaged. Men in particular are often fearful of appearing weak, vulnerable, or inadequate.

As we have suggested elsewhere in this book, clients' desires to win our approval by being "good clients" serve to fuel the fear of appearing foolish. The client who believes that you can be bought off with good behavior has a very strong motivation not to appear foolish. But, of course, it is this image of the "non-foolish" self that clients are ill-served in protecting because the image itself is a protective device preventing clients from disclosing and testing hypotheses about their worthlessness. With the successful image securely in place, clients are never able to deal with the deeper feelings of uncertainty about the acceptability of their "true self." As therapists, we must be careful to send messages that emphasize our interest in the deeper—at first unnoticed—aspects of the person. Such a message is ultimately reassuring to clients because they can then begin the process of giving up the image so carefully cultivated in previous relationships.

Will I Like the Effects of Being in Therapy?

In addition to concerns about how they will be treated and how they will be viewed in psychotherapy, clients may also have fears about the effects or outcome of psychotherapy. We now briefly discuss four such fears.

1. *Will I learn some things about me I don't want to know?* Earlier we discussed the fear that some clients have of having the therapist discover things about them they feel uncomfortable sharing with someone else. It is often the case that the deeper fear is of discovering something about oneself. More specifically, there is often a fear that a dreaded suspicion will be confirmed. Perhaps the client worries that he or she is an impostor, or uncaring, or mean, or has some other fatal flaw. In our view, the fact that clients have these types of fears makes psychotherapy both exciting and difficult. Initially, these fears may not be at all evident even though at some level the client had to fight against them to come to therapy. In short-term, highly focused therapy, these sorts of concerns may or may not be dealt with, depending on how closely they are linked to the presenting complaint and depending on how deeply such fears are buried. In longer-term therapy, this fear that one's suspicions will be confirmed becomes extremely important, for an individual will struggle valiantly to prevent knowing fully what is feared. The parallels to phobic behaviors are obvious. Individuals who are phobic consistently avoid contact with the feared object or situation. The fear some clients have of discovering (or confirming) something about themselves is a fear of massive loss of self-esteem—something that the client works hard to avoid. Typically, the fatal flaw that the person fears has no more than a small base in reality. However, this base has often been extended and solidified by repeated destructive interactions with significant others. It is perhaps a strange paradox that people both look for evidence that they have some bad characteristics but also fear the "final proof" of this fact. Because of the nature of psychotherapy, clients may indeed see entering into it as having the potential to result in such a proof.

Clients may also fear learning about, and becoming more aware of, past trauma, especially childhood sexual abuse. This fear is related to a number of others, including a fear of losing control of one's emotions and a fear of general deterioration in one's functioning. In particular, the evolving literature in childhood sexual abuse (e.g., Gold & Brown, 1997; Pope & Brown, 1996) emphasizes the reality of this fear. That is, current writing in this area points out that recovery of traumatic memories involves a clinical process fraught with many dangers and that not all clients are well-served by encouraging full recovery of these memories. Thus, clients who are beginning to have delayed memories of abuse are rightly fearful of any process that might lead to memory retrieval. It should go without saying that therapists must also have a great respect for the dangers involved in this process.

2. *Will I lose control of my emotions?* Some clients are concerned about whether they will lose control of their emotions either in the session or afterward. One particular concern that clients sometimes have is the fear that if they start crying, they may not be able to stop (Counselman, 1997). It would be fair to say that for many people the fear of losing control is rooted in reality since clients often do lose control of their emotions. Some of the concern about losing control is related to image concerns that we discussed previously. That is, clients may not want the therapist to see them while they are angry, or crying, or whatever. Many people have a view of themselves as stoic, as able to withstand and control emotional reactions. The idea that they might, for example, "break down and cry" is very frightening to them. They would not want this to happen while they are with someone, and they would not want it to happen while they are alone. In either case they experience themselves as weak, vulnerable, and lacking in dignity. This may be especially true of males.

Some people have so long overcontrolled their emotions that they fear they will either disintegrate or destroy others if they lose control. It is very important that the therapist help the client address this fear. The point is that the client is more likely to move toward better mental health if he or she (a) feels safe enough with the therapist to risk this vulnerable part of the self, and (b) actively struggles with this issue so that there is better access to the spontaneous parts of the self. It is a serious mistake, in our view, for the therapist to adopt the limited goal of having clients feel comfortable experiencing their emotions in the therapy hour and leaving to chance whether they are able to generalize this comfortableness. On the other hand, this is not to suggest that clients are encouraged to "let go" outside of therapy every time they feel like it. We are merely underscoring the idea that the client's fear of losing control emotionally is a concern about the self that includes but transcends what happens in the therapy hour.

3. *Will I find there is no hope?* Clients often see psychotherapy as a kind of "last resort." Short of suicide, they may view it as the most drastic action possible to resolve the problem. Obviously, if therapy were not to be of help, there would appear to be little hope of gaining relief. This is part of the reason clients may become so depressed in therapy if they do not feel they are making progress. It is not the lack of progress per se that brings discouragement, but rather the belief that even though they have done "the most likely to be helpful thing," they see little improvement. In such a case, the ways they have tried to solve the problem in the past have not worked, and now the one last thing in which they placed their hope seems to have come up short. How can we as therapists fail to understand how discouraging this may be? (You will find additional comments on the subject of "hope" in Chapter 6, Intake Interviewing.)

4. *Will therapy disrupt my relationships?* As psychotherapists, we know that the outcome of psychotherapy can involve the termination of, or radical change in, various relationships in which the client is involved prior to entering therapy. Some clients also realize this and may be apprehensive about it. For example, a client may say in the first or second interview, "You're probably going to tell me I should leave my husband since he beats up on me." Another client may say, "I'm not sure I want my wife to come with me to talk about this; we've had several friends who went to marital counseling and ended up getting a divorce." Generally speaking, clients' concerns about the way things are now outweigh their concerns about what might happen if they come for therapy—otherwise they wouldn't have come. Nonetheless, some clients need a kind of reassurance that you aren't out to tell them who they should sleep with, how they should treat their parents, and the like. This sort of concern can generally be successfully dealt with by consistently refusing to give advice or be critical. In this way you signal that the client, rather than you, is in charge of any and all changes that will, or might, be made in relationships with others.

A slightly different situation is presented by the sophisticated client who worries that therapy will set in motion a set of changes in the self with accompanying interpersonal forces impossible to control and which he or she fears will lead to a deterioration of some relationship. In our view, this is entirely possible, and if the client hints at this fear we tend to state rather forthrightly that relationships do change, sometimes for the better and sometimes for the worse as a result of psychotherapy. It is important to remember that in these cases, most clients are not raising some sort of unconflicted theoretical issue of how therapy changes people and their relationships. Most of the time there are issues about dependency ("I'm worried because I could never live without Bill") or self-esteem ("I don't want to hurt Julie and would think badly of myself if I ended up divorcing her") or both. There may also be unacknowledged secret wishes for a major change that the person defensively covers up by talking about fear of change.

To repeat, when clients express a concern about how therapy may affect some of their relationships, we recommend that you make it clear throughout therapy that they are in charge of their relationships, and we suggest that you acknowledge the possibility of major change if the client raises the concern. Most important, however, is the issue of being sensitive to the implied fears clients have about doing something that will affect their relationships. Consider the following example from a first session.

CLIENT: I've just been thinking so much about whether to come for therapy or not. My wife says we should be able to work these problems out by ourselves, and in some way I guess she's right. She's not willing to come to therapy.
(Note: The client is echoing some of the fears being expressed behaviorally by the spouse. By using the phrase "in some ways I guess she's right," the client "sits on the fence" so to speak and has created a complex mixture that partially hides his deep anxieties about therapy.)

THERAPIST: Well, I gather that you also have some concerns about coming.
(Note: The therapist keeps the focus on the client and does this in a way that encourages the client to take responsibility for his own concerns. This response, while it may raise the client's anxiety level, may also partially relieve him from the burden of creating a complex way to talk about his concerns. Of course, there is also the issue of the spouse's refusal [actually, *reported* refusal] of therapy. This must also be dealt with, but that, in our view, should take a backseat to the fears the client has about being there himself.)

Clients' expressed fears about how psychotherapy might affect their relationships is a mixture of reality, myth, and projection. Almost always the expressed fear represents something quite basic such as wishes, dependency, self-esteem, or control.

Implications for Short-Term Therapy

Client fears have direct implications for short-term therapy. First, a working alliance (e.g., Horvath & Symonds, 1991) between client and therapist must be established quickly for several reasons. One of these reasons is that a certain element of trust is required for clients to be able to transcend their most central fears about psychotherapy. Absent this trust, clients are likely to spend what few sessions are available trying to decide whether to put their heart and soul into this enterprise. While this decision process is being carried out in the mind of the client, one can expect less than adequate motivation and commitment. Thus, in short-term therapy it is critical that the therapist be able to create a feeling of therapeutic safety, including the fostering of confidence in the client that the therapist is competent to help.

As this implies, short-term therapy calls for a rapid assessment of any fears that might seriously hinder the progress of therapy. In particular, the therapist must ascertain whether previous involvement with the mental health system has set up expectations or created fears that might radically hinder progress. For example, clients who have had a sexual relationship with a previous therapist (e.g., Pope, 1994) would typically be ruled out as candidates for short-term therapy because of the inherent distrust they likely have of the therapist. Thus, in short-term therapy it is critical that significant client fears be identified and addressed quickly for success to be likely. This does not mean that all fears will be eliminated, and it certainly does not imply that one has to keep talking about the fears prior to addressing the presenting complaint. It does imply that in contrast to long-term therapy, where one has the "luxury" of returning again and again to the client's fear(s) about psychotherapy, in short-term therapy the heavy emphasis on identifying and holding a focus precludes spending large amounts of time on the client's fears about the process. In short-term therapy the therapist must set up conditions that help clients quickly set their fears aside in favor of commitment to a process they expect to result in symptom relief. Individuals who are characterologically fearful of others (e.g., avoidant personality disorder, paranoid, etc.) are likely to present serious challenges for the person doing short-term psychotherapy, although a diagnosis by itself is not sufficient to make short-term therapy inadvisable.

Summary

Clients may come to therapy with a wide assortment of fears. For discussion purposes we have divided these into three groups: (a) how will I (the client) be treated? (b) how will I be viewed? and (c) will I like the outcome? In part, clients' fears are seen as part of the natural process whereby all individuals, including clients, ensure for themselves a safe and orderly world. Thus, fears are not something that should necessarily be eradicated as soon as possible, but rather are to be used by both client and therapist as one of the ways to understand the client's personality organization. The process of dealing with the client's concerns about therapy is one of the many ways in which the client confronts his or her interpersonal vulnerabilities.

DISCUSSION QUESTIONS

- If you were seriously considering entering psychotherapy, what would be your greatest concerns or fears? What specific things might a therapist do to help you reduce your anxiety?

- Among all of the fears discussed in this chapter, which one(s) would you most dread having to respond to if asked directly by the client?

- Which significant client fears do you believe can be greatly reduced by directly addressing the issue early in therapy? Which do you believe can be greatly reduced only through the *process* of therapy?

BIBLIOGRAPHY

Baumeister, R. F. (1982). A self-presentational view of social phenomena. *Psychological Bulletin, 91,* 3–26.

Bergin, A. E. (1985). Proposed values for guiding and evaluating counseling and psychotherapy. *Counseling and Values, 29,* 99–116.

Beutler, L. E., Machado, P. P. P., & Neufeldt, S. A. (1994). Therapist variables. In A. E. Bergin & S. L. Garfield (Eds.), *Handbook of psychotherapy and behavior change* (4th ed., pp. 229–269). New York: Wiley.

Bohart, A. C., & Greenberg, L. S. (Eds.). (1997). *Empathy reconsidered: New directions in psychotherapy.* Washington, DC: American Psychological Association.

Bornstein, R. F. (1993). *The dependent personality.* New York: Guilford.

Bornstein, R. F., & Bowen, R. F. (1995). Dependency in psychotherapy: Toward an integrated treatment approach. *Psychotherapy, 32,* 520–534.

Braaten, E. B., Otto, S., & Handelsman, M. M. (1993). What do people want to know about psychotherapy? *Psychotherapy, 30,* 565–570.

Bram, A. D. (1997). Perceptions of psychotherapy and psychotherapists: Implications from a study of undergraduates. *Professional Psychology: Research and Practice, 28,* 170–178.

Bugental, J. F. (1987). *The art of the psychotherapist.* New York: W. W. Norton & Company.

Byrne, D. (1971). *The attraction paradigm.* New York: Academic Press.

Cepeda-Benito, A., & Short, P. (1998). Self-concealment, avoidance of psychological services, and perceived likelihood of seeking professional help. *Journal of Counseling Psychology, 45,* 58–64.

Counselman, E. F. (1997). Self-disclosure, tears, and the dying client. *Psychotherapy, 34,* 233–237.

Crowne, D. P., & Marlowe, D. (1960). A new scale of social desirability independent of psychopathology. *Journal of Consulting Psychology, 24,* 349–354.

Edwards, A. L. (1957). *The social desirability variable in personality assessment and research.* New York: Dryden.

Ellis, A. (1985). Expanding the ABC's of rational emotive therapy. In M. J. Mahoney & A. Freeman (Eds.), *Cognition and Psychotherapy* (pp. 313–323). New York: Plenum.

Epperson, D. L., & Lewis, K. N. (1987). Issues of informed entry into counseling: Perceptions and preferences resulting from different types and amounts of pre-therapy information. *Journal of Counseling Psychology, 34,* 266–275.

Frank, J. D., & Frank, J. B. (1991). *Persuasion and healing* (3rd ed.). Baltimore: The Johns Hopkins University Press.

Garfield, S. L., & Bergin, A. E. (1994). Introduction and historical overview. In A. E. Bergin & S. L. Garfield (Eds.), *Handbook of psychotherapy and behavior change* (4th ed., pp. 3–18). New York: Wiley.

Gold, S. N., & Brown, L. S. (1997). Therapeutic responses to delayed recall: Beyond recovered memory. *Psychotherapy, 34,* 182–191.

Greenberg, J. R., & Mitchell, S. A. (1983). *Object relations in psychoanalytic theory.* Cambridge, MA: Harvard University Press.

Hayward, M. L., & Taylor, J. E. (1964). A schizophrenic patient describes the action of intensive psychotherapy. In B. Kaplan (Ed.), *The inner world of mental illness* (pp. 323–344). New York: Harper and Row.

Helms, J. E., & Carter, R. T. (1991). Relationships of White and Black racial identity attitudes and demographic similarity to counselor preferences. *Journal of Counseling Psychology, 38,* 446–457.

Heppner, P. P., & Claiborn, C. D. (1989). Social influence research in counseling: A review and critique. *Journal of Counseling Psychology, 36,* 365–387.

Hill, C. E., Thompson, B. J., Cogar, M. C., & Denman, D. W. (1993). Beneath the surface of long-term therapy: Therapist and client report of their own and each other's covert processes. *Journal of Counseling Psychology, 40,* 278–287.

Horvath, A. O., & Symonds, B. D. (1991). Relations between working alliance and outcome in psychotherapy: A meta-analysis. *Journal of Counseling Psychology, 38*, 139–149.

Jensen, J. P., & Bergin, A. E. (1988). Mental health values of professional therapists: A national interdisciplinary survey. *Professional Psychology: Research and Practice, 19*, 290–297.

Jones, E. E. (1964). *Ingratiation.* New York: Appleton-Century-Crofts.

Kelly, A. E. (1998). Client's secret keeping in outpatient therapy. *Journal of Counseling Psychology 45*, 50–57.

Kelly, A. E., & Achter, J. A. (1995). Self-concealment and attitudes toward counseling in university students. *Journal of Counseling Psychology, 42*, 40–46.

Kelly, A. E., Kahn, J. H., & Coulter, R. G. (1996). Client self-presentations at intake. *Journal of Counseling Psychology, 43*, 300–309.

Kokotovic, A. M., & Tracey, T. J. (1987). Premature termination at a university counseling center. *Journal of Counseling Psychology, 34*, 80–82.

Kushner, M. G., & Sher, K. J. (1991). The relation of treatment fearfulness and psychological service utilization: An overview. *Professional Psychology: Research and Practice, 22*, 196–203.

Langford, J., & Clance, P. R. (1993). The impostor phenomenon: Recent research findings regarding dynamics, personality and family patterns and their implications for treatment. *Psychotherapy, 30*, 495–501.

London, P. (1986). *The modes and moral of psychotherapy* (2nd ed.). New York: W. W. Norton.

Lopez, S. R., Lopez, A. A., & Fong, K. T. (1991). Mexican Americans' initial preferences for counselors: The role of ethnic factors. *Journal of Counseling Psychology, 38*, 487–496.

Markus, H., & Nurius, P. (1986). Possible selves. *American Psychologist, 41*, 954–969.

McNeill, B. W., May, R. J., & Lee, V. E. (1987). Perceptions of counselor source characteristics by premature and successful terminators. *Journal of Counseling Psychology, 34*, 86–89.

Overholser, J. C., & Fine, M. A. (1994). Cognitive-behavioral treatment of excessive interpersonal dependency: A four-stage psychotherapy model. *Journal of Cognitive Psychotherapy, 8*, 55–70.

Phelps, A., Friedlander, M. L., & Enns, C. Z. (1997). Psychotherapy process variables associated with the retrieval of memories of childhood sexual abuse: A qualitative study. *Journal of Counseling Psychology, 44*, 321–332.

Pipes, R. B., Schwarz, R., and Crouch, P. (1985). Measuring client fears. *Journal of Consulting and Clinical Psychology, 53*, 933–934.

Pope, K. S. (1994). *Sexual involvement with therapists: Patient assessment, subsequent therapy, forensics.* Washington, DC: American Psychological Association.

Pope, K. S., & Brown, L. S. (1996). *Recovered memories of abuse: Therapy, assessment, forensics.* Washington, DC: American Psychological Association.

Regier, D. A., Narrow, W. E., Rae, D. S., Manderscheid, R. W., Locke, B. Z., & Goodwin, F. K. (1993). The de facto U.S. mental and addictive disorders service system. *Archives of General Psychiatry, 50*, 85–94.

Rogers, C. R. (1951). *Client-centered therapy.* Boston: Houghton Mifflin.

Rogers, C. R., & Dymond, R. (Eds.). (1954). *Psychotherapy and personality change.* Chicago: University of Chicago Press.

Sande, G. N., Goethals, G. R., and Radloff, C. E. (1988). Perceiving one's own traits and others: The multifaceted self. *Journal of Personality and Social Psychology, 54*, 13–20.

Schwartz, R. S. (1993). Managing closeness in psychotherapy. *Psychotherapy, 30*, 601–607.

Speight, S. L., & Vera, E. M. (1997). Similarity and difference in multicultural counseling: Considering the attraction and repulsion hypotheses. *The Counseling Psychologist, 25*, 280–298.

Strong, S. R. (1968). Counseling: An interpersonal influence process. *Journal of Counseling Psychology, 15*, 215–224.

Sue, S. (1998). In search of cultural competence in psychotherapy and counseling. *American Psychologist, 53*, 440–448.

Sue, S., Zane, N., & Young, K. (1994). Research on psychotherapy with culturally diverse clients. In A. E. Bergin & S. L. Garfield (Eds.), *Handbook of psychotherapy and behavior change* (4th ed., pp. 783–817). New York: Wiley.

Sugarman, J., & Martin, J. (1995). The moral dimension: A conceptualization and empirical demonstration of the moral nature of psychotherapeutic conversations. *The Counseling Psychologist, 23*, 324–347.

Weinberg, G. (1984). *The heart of psychotherapy: A journey into the mind and office of the therapist at work.* New York: St. Martins.

Worell, J., & Remer, P. (1992). *Feminist perspectives in therapy.* New York: Wiley.

Yalom, I. D. (1995). *Theory and practice of group psychotherapy* (4th ed.). New York: Basic Books.

4

Therapist Fears and Concerns

Although psychotherapists must be capable of a certain degree of detachment and objectivity, they, like those who choose the arts and humanities, must seek to experience and include the emotional and irrational. Openness toward one's own emotions and openness toward the emotions of others go hand-in-hand.
—Anthony Storr

...for ultimately, and precisely in the deepest and most important matters, we are unspeakably alone; and many things must happen, many things must go right, a whole constellation of events must be fulfilled, for one human being to successfully advise or help another.
—Rainer Maria Rilke (quoted by Najavits & Strupp, 1994, p. 114)

In this chapter we will discuss some of the concerns that beginning therapists have about doing psychotherapy. Some concerns are based in reality, others in misinformation or lack of information, and still others are part of our fantasy life—perhaps symbols of some of our struggles to be loved, to feel good about ourselves. Whatever the source of our concerns, it helps if they are taken seriously by ourselves and our supervisor. On the other hand, one of your tasks as a beginning psychotherapist is not to take *yourself* too seriously. If you must blame yourself (and you undoubtedly will) for making mistakes, try to view your mistakes (and imagined ones) as specific behaviors that you can improve rather than as global personality defects.

As we all know, fear can be constricting. It can limit our creativity and it is uncomfortable even when it does not seem to limit us. It is important to realize, however, that your fears about being a therapist are also a source of strength for you. Your fears can help alert you to areas to discuss with your supervisor; they are a constant reminder of your ethical and legal responsibilities, they underscore the fact that the person who is your client is a human being to be treated with respect and dignity, and who is entitled to the very best you have to offer. Your fears also offer a guide to those parts of you that are candidates for growth and development; they should remind you of the key truth that we all are, and will forever be, limited in multiple ways as a therapist. Even if you find yourself making the very mistake you feared you would, you will be amazed at how often you learn something very important about both yourself and the client in such instances. To fear something can easily be the first step toward harnessing and mastering it. In fact, much of mastering begins with a healthy respect for, or fear of, that which we do not understand. If you do not have some fears as a therapist, you are probably ill-suited to being one. It was Freud who pointed out that any process with great healing capacity would naturally also have the power to hurt. If you have no fears about doing therapy, you are either operating out of a dangerous illusion, or you are completely convinced that what you do is of no importance. Neither of these positions produces good therapists.

The Fear of a Client's Being Smarter Than You Are

Unless you plan to see only individuals with a low IQ, some clients will have a higher IQ than you. In addition, some clients will be more widely read, better educated, and more discerning in an intuitive way than you are. When you see such a client, it is very important to keep focused on the client and to be aware of what it is that you offer. Do not be drawn into "mind games" and do not spend your time thinking about how you wish that you were as quick as he or she is. If the client were not vulnerable, were not hurting in an important way, she or he would not be there. This is your leverage, and you should focus on this fact rather than dwelling on your own shortcomings.

Clients who attempt to use their actual or perceived "intellectual advantage" over the therapist are in part attempting to injure the very person who is trying to help. Often these individuals are acting out the same twisted, competitive, distance-producing relationships that have thus far characterized their lives. They want to be closer, but they also fear that anyone who gets close to them will dominate them (see discussion of fear of being engulfed by the therapist in Chapter 3, Client Fears). If you find that your client is repeatedly saying things like, "I've already thought of that," your first step is to seek supervision to see if in fact you are holding back and not doing your best therapy. In some instances, that will be the case, and perhaps that will be the case because you are already intimidated and your anxiety is destroying your effectiveness. In other instances, there will be nothing wrong with your interventions; rather, the client's comments will be more reflective of his or her own dynamics about what it means to be in a relationship. You do not have to have an IQ higher than your client to do good therapy. You do need to be good at what you do and that is why it is so important to stay focused on what you have to offer (in addition to the traditional focus on the client's needs).

The Fear of Clients' Getting Too Close

The issue of "closeness" in psychotherapy is an important one, although it is often ill-defined (Schwartz, 1993). Therapists may be referring to any of several different concerns when expressing a fear about clients' getting too close. One such concern is that of fearing how they will be able to handle someone being very dependent on them. In theory, most therapists understand that psychotherapy typically involves an element of dependency, especially in the beginning and middle phases. To know this in theory and to work easily with it in practice are, however, two different things. Like others in our culture, psychotherapists often believe, even if secretly so, that dependency is a "dirty" word. Fearing it in ourselves, we subtly discourage it in our clients. That is, just as we fear that our being dependent on someone will take away our power and strip us of our autonomy, so do we fear that another's being dependent on us will ensnare us in an ever-constricting prison. If we view the client's dependency as a phenomenon we must do something about, we may feel forced to intervene in certain ways or to avoid intervening in certain ways. In turn, when we feel *forced* to respond, we lose access to one of our therapeutic strengths—that part of ourselves which is spontaneous and free.

The answer to this dilemma, however, is not to avoid the dependency of our client. A part of the answer lies in a sense of self (*your* self) which does not rely on the actions or feelings of the client for its strength. Such a self can afford to allow another to be dependent. A part of what we mean by this is the lack of a need to defend oneself against the possibility of expressed dependency. For example, one supervisee offered her home phone number to a client in crisis, but spent five minutes going on and on about how this was an exception, she expected the client not to abuse the privilege, it would be a violation of the therapy contract if the client called too often, and so forth. This example illustrates a case in which the therapist feared that the client might be (or become) dependent. The central point, however, is not that the therapist was aware of potential dependency, but that the therapist prematurely (and defensively) assumed that there might be a problem. Such premature assertions about dependency are manifestations of an inner uncertainty about a conflicted area. In part, the solution is to trust oneself to handle dependency issues as they arise rather than taking defensive precautions meant to stop the dependency.

Trying to anticipate and prevent the dependency of the client is bad for at least four reasons: (a) It sends the client the wrong message about dependency (i.e., dependency is bad—it should be covered up, "I am weak if I need help"); (b) It frequently makes the client defensive (in the example in which the therapist gives the client the telephone number but does it inappropriately because of the fear that the client might become excessively dependent, the therapist should not be surprised if the client says, "Don't worry, I won't be calling you"); (c) It fails to help the client deal with dependency; and (d) In the end it frequently doesn't prevent even overtly expressed dependency. No matter how many "warnings" you issue, clients may end up calling you on numerous occasions. We also note here, however, that individuals with a personality disorder (Axis II diagnosis from the DSM-IV), clarifying therapy parameters early is generally warranted.

In addition to the issue of the client's dependency, there may be other fears related to the question of whether a client will "get too close" to us. A central construct here is the idea of boundary (e.g., Johnson & Farber, 1996; Smith &

Fitzpatrick, 1995). By "boundary" we do not mean a "wall" (with all the pejorative connotations accompanying such a term). Rather we refer to the characteristics of the relationship along the dimensions of (a) role behavior and (b) identification with the client. Although these two dimensions may be closely related, we separate them here for ease of discussion. (The word "boundary" also involves a number of other administrative and therapeutic issues that will not be discussed here.)

When we speak of boundary issues concerning role behaviors, we are referring to questions such as "What happens if I suddenly realize that I am acting more like the client's friend than his or her therapist?" First, a word of reassurance. The most critical issue is not whether you do or don't "slip out of role." Beyond such basics as acceptance, involvement, and ethical behavior, it is impossible to say with any degree of completeness what the therapist's role should be for all clients. In fact, one view of therapy is that the roles we play must be somewhat different with the varying needs our clients bring us. Therefore, it is not surprising that we will, from time to time, find ourselves taking a role that allows the client to get close to us in a way that we did not anticipate. If you spend a lot of time worrying about being in or out of role, you are quite likely to end up feeling rather constricted. Furthermore, occasionally "slipping out of role" may be precisely to express what Kegan (1982) called "our vulnerability to being recruited to the welfare of another." As Kegan suggests, it is vital that clients be able to recruit their therapists.

In Chapter 8, Listening, Chapter 12, Transference and Countertransference, and Chapter 7, The Therapeutic Stance, we discuss the issue of overidentifying with clients. Here we mention it only as a concern that beginning therapists express when they fear that they might take on the same emotion expressed by the client—say, depression. This sort of fear is frequently articulated by therapists when they say something like "I really know how this client feels—I feel that way when she describes the situation she's confronting." Again, we emphasize both the legitimacy of this fear (overidentification certainly can lead to poor therapy) as well as the advantage that comes with respecting (fearing) your own potential limits. Additionally, we point out that your fear in this area suggests that you very likely do have both the capacity and motivation to resonate with your clients. If you have a healthy respect for not doing that in the extreme, you have scarcely damned yourself by saying that you fear being well-tuned to emotional difficulties. Supervisors generally see emotional involvement with (support of) clients as something that is easier to moderate than increase.

Finally, with regard to dependency issues, we want to emphasize that concerns about clients' getting too close to you in very short-term therapy may be realistic. That is, you are right to worry about clients' becoming too dependent on you if therapy is to last only a few sessions. In such a therapy context, there is not enough time to work through strong dependency. Hence, you should not encourage dependency in very short-term psychotherapy. Although the definition of short-term therapy differs widely, in our own view any therapy lasting (or scheduled to last) less than three months should be considered short-term.

The Fear of "Making a Fool of Oneself"

Certainly it is possible to appear foolish as a therapist—particularly if one takes oneself rather seriously, adopts an unforgiving attitude toward one's mistakes, is determined to defend the importance of one's every utterance, and fails to give clients credit for being the perceptive and forgiving human beings they often are.

One way in which almost all beginning therapists fear they will look foolish is by saying the obvious. In one joke about this issue, a little boy is throwing a tantrum in the therapist's office. After 15 minutes of this, the therapist says: "You sound angry." To which the therapy-wise child replies, "Thank you, Dr. Freud."

If by saying you fear that you will say the obvious you mean you fear that a client will say "That's obvious," or "Well, of course," or "I understand that," or even, "Yes, I'd considered that," your belief that this may happen is well-founded. You will most certainly hear this sort of response from some clients. What the client says and what is actually going on in the interaction are two different things, however. Unfortunately, when clients say something like "I'd already considered that," our fear of appearing foolish makes us want to accept the client's statement as the end of the discussion. It would seem reasonable that few therapists would welcome the opportunity to continue a discussion in which the client has already anticipated one's interventions. Certainly you will see clients who actually have already given careful consideration to some parts of what you are saying. In fact, on occasions it will become clear to you (and perhaps to the client) that the client has thought more deeply about the issue than you have. One's first impulse in such circumstances can range from wanting to change the subject, to defensively pointing out that the client is being defensive by discounting your comments. If while feeling foolish you can resist, for just a minute or two, the temptation to go on the offensive, you may discover that some remarkably powerful therapeutic gains can often be had when the therapist is "caught short" so to speak. In the first place, this is your opportunity to learn more about clients and how they construct the world—more than you obviously knew when you made the remark. Second, if you are nondefensive and simply acknowledge it if you were "off base," you give clients a wonderful opportunity to teach you about their world. This acknowledgment, that in a very important way clients know more about their world than you do, places appropriate responsibility on clients for being an active part of the treatment. Your willingness to acknowledge your limitations models for clients a trust in self toward which they are working. Your lack of defensiveness shows clients that you do not need to be protected, and hence that they can count on you. By avoiding the temptation to gloss over your imperfection, you paradoxically show that you cannot be exploited, for it is the vulnerability that must be hidden that allows exploitation.

Of course, some clients *do* defend themselves by denigrating the comments of the therapist. If the client repeatedly points to the triteness of your comments, you should "get a second opinion" from your supervisor. The key is to consider the full range of possibilities. If the client is feeling powerless and is seeking to "even the match" by criticizing many of your interventions, certainly you need to address that fact. If the client "goes on the offensive" when the content of the discussion provokes anxiety, certainly that needs attending to. But it may also be that you are holding something back. Perhaps you are "playing safe" because you are afraid of the client; or perhaps you have the (mistaken) view that the client is too vulnerable and fragile to hear anything other than the obvious; or perhaps you are feeling angry or judgmental toward the client and are thus saying things that you know won't reflect your true (unacceptable) feelings.

Two other points should be made about the issue of appearing foolish by saying obvious things. In fact, much of therapy does involve the obvious. First, there is the "obviousness" of discussing the same issue over and over. As we point out in Chapter 9, on therapeutic mistakes, it is important that you do in fact go over and over things in therapy. This repetitiveness is in part how therapy works. Second, it may help to remember that just because you think you said something that was overly simplistic does not mean that the client will think the same thing. Although we know of no research to back this idea, we suspect that a great deal of therapeutic gain is achieved when therapists say very simple, obvious things, but say them at precisely the right time.

Another aspect of saying the obvious is that therapists sometimes fear that they may repeat stories, metaphors, or favorite one-liners. This is a realistic fear if you are prone to forget whether you have or have not used a story with a particular client. It is not bad to have favorite stories; most therapists over time do accumulate particular ways of expressing powerful "truths." Moreover, there may be times when repeating an image or metaphor would be very helpful. The key is to remember that you have used it before so that you don't introduce it as if it is a completely new idea. If you are concerned about this issue, consider making a few informal comments in your progress notes. These notes could include how you emphasized key points.

Therapists at times may be concerned about contradicting themselves. For example, you may be challenged by a client who points out that a couple of weeks ago you said that her anger was something she could use constructively—that it was a signal to her that she has a right to go for what she wants. In today's session, you suggested that her anger was perhaps a cover for deeper feelings of pain and worthlessness—that anger was not the real issue. At times, in such instances, the client may have misunderstood what you were saying. At other times, it may be very easy for you to resolve the apparent contradiction or it may be therapeutic for the client to struggle with the issue for a little while. But in some instances it may dawn on you that you do not really understand the phenomenon under discussion. You may feel foolish because you are confused and are not sure how both parts of what you said are true. There are two related issues here. The first is how to deal with a specific and immediate awkward situation. The second is the question of what therapists should do when they "confuse themselves," so to speak. With regard to the first issue, one idea would be to say something that would draw the client out in a way that helps you understand what the client is thinking. Let's continue the example regarding anger, with a male therapist and a female client.

CLIENT: So which is it? Is my anger a kind of positive sign that says I'm feeling better about myself?; I deserve better treatment and I intend to get it; or is it just a kind of cop-out—a cover-up that says I don't want you to see my sense of worthlessness? I know things are not just black and white but those ideas don't seem to be the same. In my view that is a real contradiction. (Note: Notice that the client is no longer focusing on her feelings but rather is attuned to the "contradiction." Certainly the therapist would need to consider how the client's personality structure might result in such a focus. For purposes of this example, however, we will put aside that issue. A second issue, which is very important to consider, is the extent to which the therapist's comments might follow gender stereotypes rather than taking full account of the individual. For example, if this therapist is threatened by strong women who feel good enough about themselves to feel angry on occasion, he may retreat immediately to the explanation that anger is a cover for a sense of worthlessness. However, for sake of argument, let us assume that gender stereotyping is not a part of the issue here. At this point in the interchange we simply emphasize that the client seems confused. Let's assume that the therapist also becomes confused and doesn't see an easy way to resolve the contradiction.)

THERAPIST: Well, sometimes I guess I do contradict myself. Does that bother you? (Note: While such candor may be helpful at times, here it is defensively motivated. The client is obviously "bothered" by the contradiction or would not have noted the contradiction in the first place. Although it is good that the therapist is somewhat attuned to process issues in cases where clients have legitimate reason for being confused, it may not be helpful to comment on the process. Certainly there are some clients for whom it would be helpful to struggle with perceived contradictions, and in such instances this last therapist comment might be helpful. However, as we said above, this example is not about the client's personality structure even though we know we can never completely rule out that consideration.)

CLIENT: Yes it does; I don't know how to make sense of my anger. I need some help here.

THERAPIST: Maybe you don't need my help. (Note: The therapist is continuing the mistake of implicitly blaming the client. The concerns of the client are not being addressed.)

CLIENT: Well I think I do or I wouldn't be in therapy. I'm just trying to figure out what my anger is about. (Note: The client feels forced to respond to the provocative comment by the therapist, but also "hangs in there" trying again to get closure on the confusing issue of anger. The client needs something from the therapist about anger. The therapist feels unsure and foolish about not being able to resolve the potential contradiction and so is avoiding addressing the issue of anger. The result is that the client is provoked and distracted from a legitimate question. The client is likely not feeling respected.)

THERAPIST: I know you are trying hard to figure out what your *anger* really means. Certainly there are times when, as you talk about it, *my* sense of what's going on shifts. I guess that's part of what we're trying to do together—take a look at some of the different ways you express your anger as well as looking at a number of perspectives in terms of what it all means. I think our goal is to arrive at a shared understanding and then maybe go on from there. (*Pause*) Of the different ways we've talked about your anger, what seems to fit best as you are thinking right now?

(Note: This is not a bad intervention. It is perhaps a little noncommittal considering that the client was asking what we assumed to be a reasonable question. The therapist has acknowledged *his* shifts in understanding without making a big issue of it. We believe that in this case such a balanced response is reasonable.)

CLIENT: There you go again putting it back on me. Why do you always do that?

(Note: Obviously the client is still angry—still feels ignored. One now begins to wonder more strongly about how the client's dynamics fit into her being upset about the contradictions.)

THERAPIST: We've been talking about anger. Now it sounds like you *are* angry. (*Pause*) Perhaps it seems that I've let you down by not answering your question.

(Note: Since the client continued to be angry, the therapist decided to make a process comment. We believe that such a comment *was* needed since the issue had shifted somewhat from search for understanding to a more immediate powerful emotion. The therapist then turns to one of the possibilities about the meaning of the client's anger to the client. The therapist has no way of knowing for sure what the central meaning of the experience is for the client. However, the therapist chooses an intervention that is perhaps related to the earlier theme of feeling worthless. There are undoubtedly other therapeutic interventions that might prove to be helpful in this circumstance. However, the point we are making here is that our goal is one of helping clients discover and articulate the personal meanings behind their actions and experiences. In this example, the therapist first became somewhat defensive because he could not resolve in his own mind how *he* actually conceptualized the problem. Toward the end of the example, however, he has made an attempt to help the client to refocus on *her* experience. We believe this later approach is appropriate.)

We said that there was a second issue—that of how we as therapists view situations in which we have essentially befuddled ourselves. In the example, we said that, at least initially, we would not "put it back on the client." We realize that some good therapists take the position that it is the client's job to struggle with what the therapist says—that if the therapist is confusing, clients should work through their feelings about this fact. We do not think that this process usually produces the best therapeutic outcome. Nor do we believe that the therapist should in such instances immediately say, "Well, I'm confused myself—I don't think I've thought enough about the construct of anger and how it applies to you." We are advocating a middle ground—a position in which it is acceptable to acknowledge some limitations including confusion, but that avoids making central to the therapy hour your own shortcomings.

In addition to fearing that they will appear foolish by saying the obvious, therapists also often fear that they will stumble when the client asks them a "tough" question. We discussed some examples of these types of questions (such as, "Do you like me?" or "Do you think I'm crazy?") in Chapter 2, Questions That Beginning Therapists Ask. To fear that you may be "put on the spot" by a client is realistic in the sense that therapy, when it is the alive and lively interchange it should be, is marked by spontaneity, unpredictability, and a certain kind of reciprocity. So, if you fear being put on the spot, you might also consider the opposite. That is, how will you enjoy doing therapy if you are successful in constructing a style that prevents clients from "punching through" on occasion? Might it not be the case that this form of vulnerability brings with it both a useful added sensitivity to the interpersonal aspect of psychotherapy as well as an opportunity to experience and confront one's limitations?

The Fear of Not Being Competent to Help

This is certainly one of the most frequent fears of beginning therapists. We discussed one aspect of this fear in Chapter 2 under the question about seeing clients who have problems you do not know how to treat. Here, perhaps we can start best by plainly saying the truth: You will undoubtedly see some clients you are not competent to help. We say this for three reasons. First, there is a certain percentage of clients for whom therapy is very unlikely to be of much benefit regardless of the therapist's skills. You will undoubtedly have some of these clients assigned to you from time to time, regardless of the type of screening being used. Second, each of us has weak areas as a psychotherapist. Even the best therapists are not going to be helpful to all "helpable" clients. Third, as a beginning therapist, you may be especially likely to fall (and place yourself) into traps and difficulties that will reduce your effectiveness.

This fear regarding competence is often a persistent, general uneasiness. It may be reflected in anxiety about seeing an intake client about whom you have no information; it may be reflected in questioning whether you should be a therapist; or it may be reflected in your reluctance to discuss what you are doing with your supervisor. This fear may be very difficult for you to deal with because one often believes that others are more self-confident and do not have such fears. Thus, the deep-seated fear that you have little to offer is often not exposed to the very kind of peer discussion that would likely make it much easier to manage. The premium that graduate school places on the appearance of competency seems to foster norms that work against open discussion of serious misgivings about one's abilities. Moreover, this problem may intensify with increasing experience, since one's expectations for oneself tend to go up.

As we see it, there are at least two ways of making your unease about your competency more manageable. The first is to try to lower your expectations about the degree to which you should be able to effect "cures." This idea of lowering your expectations carries with it a call to be more tolerant of your mistakes and of poor and questionable therapeutic outcomes. There is an invitation here to suspend judgment of yourself and the outcome of what you do a little longer. You are invited to wonder a little more about the extent to which you can be so sure that what you do is or is not effective. Certainly your intervention may not have the luster of a master therapist. But we believe that beginning therapists, by holding themselves to very high standards, often overlook many of the crucial roles they play with clients—of being a caring, respectful, interested person who struggles to understand what the client is trying to express. Using data from the Vanderbilt II study, Najavits and Strupp (1994) concluded: "…basic capacities of human relating—warmth, affirmation, and a minimum of attack and blame—may be at the center of effective psychotherapeutic intervention" (p. 121). Being warm, affirming, and nonblaming is something you can do with your very first client, and every client thereafter. Such a therapeutic stance need not await the conferring of the graduate degree. Second, see if you can identify one or two of your peers with whom you might be able to talk about your feelings of incompetence. This sounds like a very simple-minded suggestion—and it is. Nonetheless, it is very easy to overlook the possibility of grappling with this issue with friends. "Bull sessions" may be frequent, but they are often abstract. Even if they are not abstract, they may not include discussion of serious reservations about one's competency. We are not suggesting that "telling all" solves this concern about competency. We are saying that the sense of isolation that often accompanies these concerns may be reduced if you can identify even one peer you think would be willing and able to tell you about his or her struggles as you also relate yours.

The Fear of Making the Client Worse

There is nothing wrong with starting your career as a psychotherapist by being afraid that you might do damage. As we (and Freud) noted earlier, interventions that are powerful enough to be helpful are also potentially damaging. In our experience, most therapists are not actually afraid that they will *cause* a client to have a psychotic break. (In Chapter 6, Intake Interviewing, we discuss the concern therapists have about causing people to commit suicide.) Rather, what beginning therapists fear is that a client's mental state might "deteriorate" and that this process might not be recognized by the therapist. It is very important that you be concerned if clients show evidence of an impending psychotic break. Such evidence might include, though is not limited to, appearance of delusional-like thought, inability to sleep, feelings of being out of control, highly atypical behavior, and increasingly rigid and ineffective methods of coping with anxiety. It is very important that you keep your supervisor fully informed about your clients, and especially those who seem that they might have a break with reality. Keeping in touch with your supervisor is one of the key ways to avoid a big surprise with regard to a client. Nonetheless, you should expect that sooner or later a client will have a break with reality (or will perhaps attempt or complete suicide) even though you did not anticipate it. When this happens, it is obviously quite important to process the event with your supervisor. This will be a good opportunity to learn something about the limits of psychotherapists to predict behavior as well as an opportunity to see what cues you may have missed, why you missed them, and how (or whether) you can avoid missing them in the future.

The Fear of Not Liking the Client

Kottler (1993) has written:

> That clinicians have strong preferences concerning whom they prefer to work with is well known. Most everyone prefers clients who are bright, eager, verbal, perceptive, affluent, and attractive. These clients not only grow quickly, but they can be patient, polite, and grateful, and they pay their bills promptly. (p. 115)

It should be no secret that psychotherapists do not have strong positive feelings for all their clients and that they may become quite angry with some of them (e.g., Mehlman & Glickauf-Hughes, 1994). That therapists prefer some clients to others is not a problem unless therapists (a) deny it and insist they will enjoy all their clients, or (b) attempt to treat someone on an ongoing basis for whom they have a strong and active dislike. Sometimes it can be helpful to remember that disliking a client should be the beginning of a process in which you commit yourself to learning more about the client as well as more about yourself. If you try to deny that you are not all that fond of some clients, you make therapy much less likely to be effective. This is true for two reasons. First, if you pretend there is no problem, you are not motivated to solve it. Second, you are probably more likely to send mixed messages to the client if you feel one way but deny to yourself those feelings.

There are several different "surface" reasons why we may not like a client. These include value differences and disliking what clients are doing in therapy. We say surface reasons not to imply superficiality, but rather to suggest that disliking a client often has dimensions beyond that of "value differences" or anger because a client has acted badly toward someone. As psychotherapists we are interested in the multiple reasons that help produce our dislike and we rightly look primarily toward ourselves to understand the phenomenon. To understand your dislike of a client, there are several questions you may find helpful to ask yourself. These include: (a) Does this person remind me of someone in my past I did not like? (b) Are the characteristics I dislike in the person a part of my personality or a part I defend against; that is, am I overidentifying with the client and trying to keep my own self-esteem by being angry about the traits I dislike in myself? (c) Have I stereotyped the person in some way so that I am responding to only one part of the client? (d) Am I keeping this person at a distance because I fear he or she will be too dependent on me? (e) Is this a person I admire or like in some way but defend against my attraction by focusing on the behaviors I dislike? and (f) Has the client intentionally provoked me to be angry?

The assumption is made that an understanding of the basis of your dislike will lead to some diminution in your feelings. Additional changes in the way you feel may be effected as you struggle with possible alternative perspectives. For example, if you realize that you are keeping a client at a distance because you have stereotyped him or her, you might actively look for behaviors running counter to the stereotype. (You would also want to ask yourself why you were engaging in stereotyping in the first place. For example, perhaps you are unconsciously prone to make assumptions about individuals based on their ethnic, racial, gender, age, handicap, social class, or lifestyle characteristics. Most psychotherapists pride themselves on being tolerant. It is typically very difficult for us to recognize in ourselves—and to admit—that we make judgments about people based on their membership in certain groups.)

In addition to trying to understand specifically why you dislike a particular client, a general suggestion is to refocus your efforts toward identifying the pain an individual is experiencing. It is very difficult to dislike a person when you are acutely aware of his or her suffering. Unfortunately, although understandably, over the course of a lifetime, many clients have become very adept at hiding this suffering. What they show the therapist is the same toughness, the same obnoxiousness with which they have felt compelled to face the world. And so, over and over, and especially when the therapist finds himself or herself disliking a client, the client's suffering must be held in focus in the mind of the therapist.

We would be remiss if we did not also point out that seeking supervision is a rather standard procedure in cases where you are discovering that you do not like a client. Often a supervisor (or peer) can help you identify key causal elements in your feelings about a client. Good supervisors do not condemn supervisees who seek help for problems like this one. If your supervisor seems unresponsive or judgmental, this might be a good time to discuss with him or her your expectations about supervision.

All these ideas assume that the therapist is at least minimally motivated to "get beyond" the dislike of a client. We believe this is a reasonable assumption since we are convinced that the vast majority of therapists are highly motivated to deliver the best services possible. It is certainly true that a few psychotherapists are primarily motivated by a need for power or even an unconscious desire to punish. However, this book was not designed to be of much assistance in cases such as these.

When you find yourself strongly disliking clients, perhaps the clients are telling you something about themselves through their behavior. This observation is not meant to let us off the hook for what we might learn about ourselves, nor is it a subtle way of blaming the client. We are just saying that perhaps a part of the picture is that your dislike of the client reflects a kind of response the client gets from others as a result of engaging in certain types of defensive maneuvers. Such information about, and understanding of, the client may prove extremely valuable in the therapeutic process.

Finally, we will mention briefly an idea related to, but quite distinct from, disliking a client. The concern that one will be bored by clients (Geller, 1994) is often considered by individuals who think they might want to do psychotherapy full-time as a job. Furthermore, it is perhaps a rare experienced psychotherapist who has not felt bored with more than one client in her or his career. So the concern about becoming bored with clients is a realistic one in the sense that you will probably experience it. We discuss this issue more in Chapter 12, Transference and Countertransference; however, we note here Geller's idea that boredom may signal a type of rupture in the relationship between the client and therapist. Therefore, if this concern arises for you in a particular case, considering what may be going on in the therapeutic relationship is a good place to start your detective work.

Concern about the Client's Not Liking the Therapist

Generally, we as psychotherapists want our clients to like us. Some of this desire is reality-based in that clients who do not like their therapists are more prone to be dissatisfied with therapy and to terminate therapy earlier. Furthermore, since there is a strong correlation between how clients feel about us and how they feel about their therapy, we often take clients' feelings toward us as some evidence about the effectiveness of therapy. This also is a reasonable assumption as long as we do not get too caught up in *equating* therapy effectiveness with the clients' feelings about us. If you see a client long enough, there are almost certain to be some negative feelings as you fail to live up to the impossibly wonderful qualities with which the client comes to imbue you (the issue of transference is discussed in Chapter 12). Although many therapists do indeed dread having a client who is in the midst of negative transference, the concern we are addressing here is broader. We are speaking of the anxiety about whether any given client will, in a general sense, be favorably predisposed toward us. Although it is very unrealistic for us to expect that all clients will like us, we nonetheless hope secretly that a special kind of chemistry will be present in all our relationships with clients. Just as we should not expect that every client who walks through our door will be someone we are psychologically drawn toward, nor should we expect that all clients will find us to be a person they unambivalently enjoy. The client may initially and continually have a few reservations about you without making therapy either impossible or even difficult. On the other hand, as we have said, clients probably do need to believe that you have their basic interests at heart.

Aside from our realistic concern that clients who do not like us will profit less from therapy than they might otherwise, this concern reflects the basic issue of our wanting to be seen as a good person. The underlying false assumption is that to be loved by the client will adequately provide us with a strong and positive sense of self. In the worst case, we allow the client's love and admiration to become a substitute both for our own sense of self, as well as for effective therapy.

There is no point in denying that we want in some way to be liked by clients. Individuals who really do not care about how others see them are not typically drawn to the profession. The question is not whether we need what have been called narcissistic supplies from clients, but rather how we manage the need and how we try to be aware of it. As we stated earlier, it is very important to distinguish between how the client views you (feels about you), what kind of therapy you are doing with the person, and how you feel about yourself. Some of the issues involved will be unconscious ones, and that is in part why supervisors are so helpful.

A related issue is how we feel when a client does not come back or terminates prematurely. This issue will be discussed in Chapter 13, Termination.

Concern about Losing Control of the Session

As a beginning therapist, you likely have a number of fears about not being able to "control" what goes on in the session. As you probably know, there are many different philosophies among even experienced therapists about the advisability of trying to control what goes on in therapy. Furthermore, people mean various things when they talk about the therapist's responsibilities with regard to controlling the session. In our view, the chief responsibility of therapists in this area is to reasonably anticipate the consequences of various therapeutic approaches and to assist the client accordingly and in cooperation *with* the client. For example, if a client comes for the first time and seems to be having difficulty staying in touch with reality, one would certainly be advised not to ask the client to engage in some sort of fantasy. In this example, the therapist controls the content and process of therapy by not introducing a particular therapeutic technique.

On the other hand, one of the great lessons to be learned by all psychotherapists is that they cannot "control" any client. Certainly, we can often have input. But you will discover rather rapidly that clients often have a way of controlling their own lives that limits the role you will have. If you can give up your illusions of grandeur, you will be in a much better place to exercise the influence you *can* have.

All these issues aside, beginning therapists often fear that in certain kinds of ways they may lose control of what is going on. These fears of losing control are generally about prototype "emergency" situations such as a client announcing that he or she is leaving the session early, a client actually storming out of the session early, the client "going strong" at the end of the session, the client expressing attraction toward the therapist, the client threatening the therapist, or the client crying uncontrollably. Of course, there are other situations you may worry about, but the foregoing are several about which we often hear supervisees express concern or fear. There are three aspects of these various situations we would like to address. The first is the observation that each profession, as a result of the procedures it uses and the material it covers, lends itself to particular kinds of "difficulties." For example, as psychotherapists we rarely worry about whether the client is about to hemorrhage; on the other hand, surgeons must constantly worry about this issue. We make this point because it underscores what we hope will be some reassurance—namely, that there are actually a fairly limited number of high-probability difficulties that therapists tend to encounter. What this means is that there is an informal body of knowledge transmitted from therapist generation to therapist generation about what to do or not to do in these situations. For example, as we noted earlier, you do not need to spend a lot of time debating about whether you can date your clients. The answer is "No, you can't." (Of course, you should not criticize your clients for wanting to date you.)

Second, there is unfortunately no real substitute for actually encountering and having to deal with some of these difficult situations. Certainly, reading books such as this one and discussing issues in class and with your supervisor can help. But no matter how much information you have, it is not apt to eliminate all of your concerns about "losing control."

Third, it may seem paradoxical, but many of the situations involving therapist loss of control in the session are appropriately addressed in part by what we call common sense, that is, behavior suggested by common cultural knowledge. For example, if a client threatens to leave the therapist's office prior to the end of the session, few of us would be inclined to say "You can't leave." There are several reasons why we would not say such a thing, including (a) We know it would likely make the person very angry and perhaps more likely to leave and (b) Except under circumstances involving a legal situation, we would have no way of enforcing our injunction. Thus, one's lack of experience as a therapist does not mean that one lacks knowledge about the best course of action in a difficult situation.

With regard to the specific potential situations involving potential loss of control, in Chapter 2, Questions That Beginning Therapists Ask, we made suggestions regarding several of them. One on which we have not commented is uncontrollable crying. Unless the person has recently been or shows signs of being out of touch with reality, prolonged crying by the client is not something about which you should worry. You will find that crying does end. Certainly, one wrong thing to do is to rush in to stop the person from crying because you are anxious. Do not be alarmed, even if the person continues to cry for 10 minutes or longer. Remember, *crying will stop.* Of course, if you are very near the end of the session and the person is still crying uncontrollably, you will need to help the client compose himself or herself at least a little. We are not talking about "cheering clients up" or denying their feelings—obviously those sorts of interventions would be a mistake. On the other hand, we do not generally feel comfortable with a client leaving the session crying uncontrollably. Typically, under these circumstances, you would verbally recognize the importance of the issue with which you and the client were dealing, perhaps reassure the person that the two of you will be working on it together, and if you think it necessary, remind the client that she or he can call you for an additional appointment if one is needed.

If there is some evidence of psychosis, and the person's emotional state seems to be escalating, you may need to provide more cognitive structure (e.g., by saying, "Let's talk for a minute about your plans for after you leave here this afternoon"). In some cases, you may need to make specific suggestions. In part, such interventions may be needed to give the person a tie to reality. With some clients it may be important to implicitly remind them that a supportive person is in the room with them. It may sound a little strange for us to say that clients are reminded that "a supportive person is in the room with them"; however, individuals with tenuous ties to reality may withdraw far inside themselves when emotionally upset. With such clients, it is important that they be assisted in maintaining some connection to reality.

In summary, with regard to the therapist's concern about losing control of the session, we emphasize the following points: (a) It is a myth to believe that one can control another person; (b) Many difficult situations call as much for "common sense" as for intricate specialized knowledge; (c) Emergency situations calling for such specialized knowledge are not large in number and tend to be discussed in classes; (d) Concerns about losing control are perhaps best dealt with by having the good fortune, early on, of being forced to rely on your own skills—by clients who don't bother to inform you in advance of the lively situation they end up creating for you. We should also add that if you are concerned about a particular "emergency" situation, we encourage you to ask your supervisor to demonstrate, in a role play, how the situation might be handled.

Concern about Losing Control of Emotions

In addition to fearing what the client might do in a session, psychotherapists also fear what *they* may do. They may fear that they may become angry or cry, or in general that their emotions will be "stirred up" (e.g., Counselman, 1997). Our experience has been that therapists rarely "lose it" completely. Therapists don't tend to yell at their clients, sob uncontrollably, or jump up and pace back and forth as a result of emotional arousal. On the other hand, it is often the case that therapists find themselves irritated with a client, moved by a client's situation, or in some other way emotionally affected by what is going on in the therapy hour. Of course, one of the maxims accepted by many therapists is that there is often diagnostic information about the client contained in a therapist's emotional reaction. This issue will be discussed more in the chapter on transference and countertransference.

The concern about losing control of one's emotions carries with it an important dialectic. On the one hand, there is the knowledge that we will not be helpful if all we do is repeat with the client earlier unsatisfactory relationships. Furthermore, communication and therapy principles suggest that clients may have difficulty showing their problems if we continually evidence strong emotional reactions to them. On the other hand, therapists are human beings; they have emotional reactions. Furthermore, it may be helpful for clients to experience a relationship in which they know their impact is felt and can be processed.

In our view, this dialectic is resolved in part by therapists titrating their expressed emotional responses and also by their interposing cognitive processes between the experience and expression of affect. At first, these two processes may seem a bit cold, calculating, and academic. However, they are not meant to destroy spontaneity, and in fact they express what therapists actually do. We know of no therapist (or even *person* for that matter) who gives free expression to all affect or who does not routinely and frequently think about what he or she is feeling before expressing the feeling. When therapists say, as they sometimes do, "I just let the tears come to my eyes in the session because I was so moved," in part they may be suggesting that their cognitive activity did not produce a reason *not* to let tears "come to their eyes."

Another way of talking about this issue is to note that there must be some sort of balance between emotional involvement and distance. On the one hand, therapists who are completely wrapped up emotionally in their clients' problems are not likely to be of great assistance (although there must certainly be counterexamples, given the elusiveness of what heals in psychotherapy). On the other hand, as we have suggested before, therapists who have an iron grip on their emotional lives, who are not at any risk for losing control of their emotions, may find it very difficult to understand the pain others suffer. In functioning as a therapist, there are much more serious problems than being moved by the suffering of others. See Chapter 7, The Therapeutic Stance, for related material.

Concern about Making a Difference

Over and over again we have supervisees raising, in one form or another, the concern of whether they really are doing their clients any good or not. The fear, of course, is that they are of no actual help. We think it can be helpful for therapists to identify more specifically the kind of concern they are having. The fear that one is having little impact may represent any (or some combination) of several factors including the fears that (a) Psychotherapy itself is of little value; (b) Some particular clients cannot be helped; or (c) The therapist is simply ineffective at doing psychotherapy. Concerns about one's effectiveness can be exacerbated by infrequent supportive comments from one's supervisor. To the extent that this is a factor characterizing several supervisors, the therapist may be receiving some valuable feedback about where talents do and do not lie. On the other hand, and especially at the beginning of training, therapists should work toward not taking critical feedback from the supervisor *too* seriously, both because the sample of people looking at their work is too small to ensure reliability and also because frequent mistakes as a beginning therapist do not suggest poor skills later on.

Concern about the Supervisor's Evaluation

As we note in other chapters, self-presentation is a powerful motive; this holds for clients, therapists, and supervisors alike. It is altogether natural that therapists have a strong desire to please their supervisors. This desire, though it may in part be "external," is certainly not all bad in that it may reflect one's basic commitment to doing good psychotherapy. On the other hand, one of the more frequent mistakes we see made by beginning therapists is to wait for too long to discuss with their supervisors feelings of inadequacy, fear of evaluation, and so forth. Supervisors certainly may be overly critical or unsupportive at times, but they are also often quite open and responsive to expressed therapist concerns. Discussing one's fear of evaluation may not eradicate the fear, but it will often increase the supervisor's sensitivity to therapist vulnerabilities. It doesn't hurt to remember that just as the therapist wants to do a good job, so does the supervisor. Our philosophy is, "Give your supervisor the *chance* to be helpful and responsive." If you don't get the help you need, at least you will know that you made the effort.

We might also add here that, despite supervisee fears to the contrary, there are very few situations in which a supervisor actually holds, "life or death" power over the supervisee. In most training programs, if one supervisor sees only your weaknesses, that is not an insurmountable problem because you will be given other opportunities with different supervisors. Certainly, a poor evaluation is hard on anyone, but it may help to remember that training programs are not typically dictatorships in which one person holds ongoing life or death power over you. With regard to supervision, you are very rarely at the continuing whim of any one person. That being said, it should also be noted that supervisors can be unreasonable or biased (e.g., Pilkington & Cantor, 1996); under such circumstances, fear of evaluation is based in reality.

Finally, we emphasize that in *good* supervision you are going to hear in one form or another that you made mistakes. Certainly there is little reason for a supervisor to be nasty or hypercritical. But you should be very wary of supervisors who seem to be supportive of everything you do. In part, supervision is an opportunity for you to test your ideas and judgment against someone else. Whether you agree or disagree with that person's critique, it can be helpful to have it. Thus, as you worry about your supervisor being critical of you, consider that you would lose by *not* receiving criticism. Furthermore, as you worry about your supervisor's judgment of you, you might want to consider the ways you have rebounded from criticism before; perhaps you can survive better than you first feared.

Concern about the Client's Disrupting the Therapist's Life

From time to time therapists are attacked during the therapy session and/or between therapy sessions. There may be sexual assault or sexual harassment (deMayo, 1997). Romans, Hays, and White (1996) found that 64% of counseling center staff members reported that they had experienced some type of harassing behavior from a current or former client. What is perhaps more frequent than actual physical attacks are behaviors that become disruptive to the therapist's personal and professional life. These may include hang-up phone calls (either at home or at the office), following/stalking the therapist, hate mail, frivolous civil charges, and the like. It is no surprise that an intelligent, creative, and highly disordered individual can make your life extremely difficult. Do not kid yourself into believing that because you know how to set limits, impose consequences, be persuasive, and so forth that you will always be able to control the behavior of such individuals. Schwartz (1995) has described vividly the extent to which a client can disrupt one's life and the emotional consequences of becoming entangled with these highly disordered individuals:

> A woman came to my office describing her relationship with a former therapist as a fatal attraction.... The client told me about hundreds of frantic telephone calls to the therapist; police summoned to remove her from the therapist's office; nightly forays past the therapist's office; and watching other clients for hours on end.... I did not recognize these incidents as the client's warnings to me. I ignorantly thought I could provide a different therapeutic experience. Now I am in the role of the therapist–victim. My reactions vary between outrage and panic, because, once a victim, life is changed. My hands tremble, my ears listen acutely, and my head quickly turns to look over my shoulder. Being the target of hate puts me on the edge of fear and smashes the safety of my world. I was stalked and attacked like the other therapist, and after the same duration of therapy. My message machine was tied up with blank space, radio playing, and hundreds of hang-ups daily. I was interrupted with telephone emergencies under fictitious names when she assumed I was talking to clients. She engineered a stream of tow trucks, taxis, carpet services, landscapers, super shuttles at all hours, and volumes of people calling me from their beepers.... Now I sit in court testifying in my harassment case filed against her. She slanders and attempts to discredit me. I worry that the lies are believed and feel shame if judged an incompetent therapist.... I later became too afraid, even for my life. I dreamt about poking out the eyes of a monster who was trying to kill me. (pp. 78, 83)

Although incidents similar to the one just described occur very rarely, when they do they remind all therapists that we are never fully in control of what our clients do and that even very experienced therapists can be drawn into, and may find it difficult to extricate themselves from, highly destructive relationships with their clients. Because of the low level of frequency of these extremely difficult cases, therapists are often not particularly concerned about them until they find themselves in the middle of such a case. Then, the therapist is *very* concerned. In general, we believe that being concerned about the possibility of such a case is somewhat like being concerned about legal issues in psychotherapy. It should not be something that weighs constantly on you, but it must be in the back of your mind and be readily accessible should circumstances warrant it. In the case described above, there were warning signs (e.g., the client describing the large number of phone calls to her previous therapist and her description of conflict with that therapist). It is certainly the case that if all we had to do was look for warning signs and then refuse to see the client or terminate with the client, then our job would be much easier. Unfortunately, high-risk clients also need therapists, and if all we do is "bail out" when the going gets tough, then we have merely transferred the problem to someone else. That being said, if you have a low tolerance for high-risk situations, you should seriously consider referring presenting clients who report extensive behavioral conflict with previous therapists, especially if paranoid and aggressive features are prominent. Particularly while in training, you would typically be assigned only a few cases where there are such clear danger signals, and if you are uncomfortable with a case assignment, you should discuss this with your supervisor.

The typical diagnosis for individuals who represent a danger in terms of pathological involvement with the therapist's personal or professional life is borderline personality disorder (see related comments on p. 161). These individuals will often have previously received other diagnoses as well, but it is almost axiomatic that they will have had a long history of difficult interpersonal relationships, therapeutic and otherwise. It is perhaps "common clinical wisdom" that therapists who have several individuals in their caseloads with the diagnosis of borderline personality disorder are at risk for burnout. As noted above, we strongly encourage you to avoid, if possible, seeing several such individuals in your caseload. The first rule in preventing "client disruptions" in your personal life is to control the number of likely candidates at any one time. Aside from the laws of probability (which clearly apply), carrying several high-risk individuals decreases the amount of supervision time you have for each one of the cases. In turn, this diminution of supervision time increases the probability that key warning signs will be missed and that boundary management may not be implemented quickly enough to mitigate the potential problems.

If you are seeing an individual who has a diagnosis of borderline personality disorder, we strongly encourage you to maintain good therapeutic boundaries (Pam, 1994), to avoid, if at all possible, multiple roles of any sort, and to receive weekly supervision. Regardless of diagnosis, you should also exercise caution when seeing a client who reports previous conflict with therapists, or who appears consistently to engage in revenge for apparent slights.

Summary

Our fears as therapists are frequently healthy for a number of reasons. They serve to motivate us to understand the basis of our concerns, which in turn provides us with a base on which to build additional skills. They also alert us to the fact that we suffer from shortcomings—a not inconsequential insight as we work toward helping others deal better with *their* suffering. Finally, our fears about not doing a good job as therapists are friendly evidence that we care deeply about the degree to which we are or are not helpful to our clients. This caring is a primary and indispensable part of being effective as a therapist.

DISCUSSION QUESTIONS

- Can you identify your greatest fear as a psychotherapist?

- What sorts of fears do you suppose most typically plague highly competent, experienced therapists?

- Is it ever appropriate (and if so, when) for a psychotherapist to express a fear to a client?

BIBLIOGRAPHY

Counselman, E. F. (1997). Self-disclosure, tears, and the dying client. *Psychotherapy, 34,* 233–237.

deMayo, R. A. (1997). Patient sexual behavior and sexual harassment: A national survey of female psychologists. *Professional Psychology: Research and Practice, 28,* 58–62.

Geller, J. D. (1994). The psychotherapist's experience of interest and boredom. *Psychotherapy, 31,* 3–16.

Johnson, S. H., & Farber, B. A. (1996). The maintenance of boundaries in psychotherapeutic practice. *Psychotherapy, 33,* 391–402.

Kegan, R. (1982). *The evolving self: Problem and process in human development.* Cambridge, MA: Harvard University Press.

Kottler, J. A. (1993). *On being a therapist* (Rev. ed.). San Francisco: Jossey-Bass.

Mehlman, E., & Glickauf-Hughes, C. (1994). The underside of psychotherapy: Confronting hateful feelings toward clients. *Psychotherapy, 31,* 434–439.

Najavits, L. M., & Strupp, H. H. (1994). Differences in the effectiveness of psychodynamic therapists: A process-outcome study. *Psychotherapy, 31,* 114–123.

Pam, A. (1994). Limit setting: Theory, techniques, and risks. *American Journal of Psychotherapy, 48,* 432–440.

Pilkington, N. W., & Cantor, J. M. (1996). Perceptions of Heterosexual Bias in Professional Psychology Programs: A Survey of Graduate Students. *Professional Psychology: Research and Practice, 27,* 604–612.

Romans, J. S. C., Hays, J. R., & White, T. K. (1996). Stalking and related behaviors experienced by counseling center staff members from current or former clients. *Professional Psychology: Research and Practice, 27,* 595–599.

Schwartz, R. S. (1993). Managing closeness in psychotherapy. *Psychotherapy, 30,* 601–607.

Schwartz, S. E. (1995). The violent client and therapeutic failure. *Voices, Summer,* 78–83.

Smith, D., & Fitzpatrick, M. (1995). Patient-therapist boundary issues: An integrative review of theory and research. *Professional Psychology: Research and Practice, 26,* 499–506.

CHAPTER

5 Ethical and Legal Issues

There is no supreme court for ethics. Sometimes the only thing you can do is look at yourself in the mirror the next morning.

—character from *Law and Order*

Lodovico [to Iago]: *O spartan dog,*
More fell than anguish, hunger, or the sea.
Look on the tragic loading of this bed;
This is thy work…To you, lord governor,
Remains the censure of this hellish villain;
The time, the place, the torture,—O, enforce it.

—from *Othello*

Ethics

Assume that you are seeing a client, Mr. Redwolf, who comes to therapy complaining of anxiety about whether he will be able to get a promotion in his job. Thus far, you have seen Mr. Redwolf for five sessions. He reports that he has had serious conflict with his boss, Ms. Mathews, whom he accuses of being too demanding. Mr. Redwolf, who is an American Indian, appears to have no delusions or hallucinations and reports a good relationship with his wife and several close friends. He tells you that he has had a bad therapy experience with three previous therapists. Mr. Redwolf complains that his previous therapists did not care about him as a person. In your sixth session with him, he tells you that his religious beliefs are very important to him and he invites you to attend his religious services, which he describes as being quite a bit different from many Jewish, Catholic, and Protestant services in the United States. He notes that all of his previous therapists refused to attend these services, but that if you really want to understand who he is, you should attend.

Should you, or should you not, attend the religious services with your client? Why?

You and your spouse are professionals. You are a psychologist in private practice and your spouse is a professor at a local university. The two of you have maintained the last names you had prior to marriage.

You have a long-term client who is a doctoral student working on a degree in liberal arts. While this client has many problems, his academic work is not one of those. Psychologically, he has particular difficulty with issues of trust and abandonment as well as having a tendency toward perfectionism. He has briefly mentioned that he will be working with his father during the summer, but there is no further mention of the details of this arrangement.

During that summer your house is being redecorated. Your spouse spoke with a contractor who will arrange for this to be done. For the first two weeks of the project, your family stays in a house on a lake. Beginning the third week, you move back to your house. As your family prefers privacy, having workers at your house seems to be somewhat of an intrusion. Your spouse is on break from school and is assuming responsibility for talking with the contractor and for being at home when the workers are there, while you are working at the office.

Difficulties in having the job satisfactorily completed arise, which your spouse is unable to reconcile with the contractor. Due to the amount of money that you have spent—much more than you can afford to lose—you and your spouse decide to settle this matter in court. Your attorney initiates a lawsuit against the contractor due to the inferior quality of the work provided.

A few months after this, your client mentions to you that he and his father have continued to work together and that they are being sued due to communication difficulties between them and a couple who hired them to redecorate. Your client mentions the name of the contracting firm that his father owns; this name sounds familiar. Later that evening, you realize that you and your family are suing your client and his family (Bowers, 1995).

Is it ethical to sue a client's father? Would you pursue the lawsuit? If you wanted to drop the lawsuit, would you be willing to withhold information from, or mislead, your spouse in order to protect the confidentiality of your client?

Does either of the scenarios just described involve questions of ethics? If so, what standards in the APA *Ethics Code* might be applicable in each scenario? In each case, what might it mean to protect the welfare of your client? If applicable, how might you balance the interests/rights of your client against your own interests/rights?

The two therapy situations just described call for you to make some sort of determination as to (a) whether there is an ethical issue and (b) what course of action you should follow. If you discuss these scenarios with fellow students, you will probably find that there is quite a bit of difference in how the scenarios are viewed. Not only will there be differences in the preferred course of action, but you are likely to find differences in whether there is even an ethical issue involved. Some students may see serious ethical issues in each of the scenarios; other students may see one or both of the scenarios as being mainly questions of clinical judgment, rather than an ethical issue per se. The issue of what ethics is about in psychology, and how to determine an ethical course of action, is both stimulating and challenging. It is one that provokes deep (sometimes irreconcilable) arguments between fellow professionals, and it is one to which we turn our attention in this chapter.

Most people are not inclined to say things like, "The dog was wrong to have bitten that child," or "It was right of that cat to share her food with the kitten." We reserve our "moral" judgments for our fellow human beings. Whether for genetic, cultural, or individual psychological reasons, it seems scarcely possible that a human being can *not* make judgments along a moral dimension. Indeed, we view individuals who seem to be lacking in the capacity to draw moral distinctions to be flawed in the most fundamental of ways. Herein lies one of the paradoxes of the discipline of psychology. As therapists, on average, we are rightly concerned that we not be seen or experienced as "judgmental," or "moralistic." At the same time, when our colleagues behave in an unethical fashion, we should be ready to take whatever steps are necessary to protect the welfare of the client. Thus, while we tend to select for our training programs individuals who are not quick to judge others, at the same time we expect such individuals (whether they be in training or not) to have little trouble judging their own behavior and the behavior of their colleagues. While it is not necessarily impossible to resolve this dilemma, it gives us pause to consider how we can be both consistently nonjudgmental and forgiving of clients' foibles, while at the same time a faithful guardian of high standards for ourselves and other professionals. In part we are suggesting that one of the very things that may have attracted you to the field of psychotherapy—its inclination to reject moralizing in favor of trying to understand—may put you at a disadvantage when, for example, you are confronted with what to do about a colleague who is failing to protect the welfare of a client.

On the other side of the coin, the inclination to make judgments about human behavior along the dimension of "right" or "wrong" is perhaps one of the oldest of human characteristics. The idea that there is a moral dimension to human existence has been around for a very long time. Certainly since the beginning of written history, cultures have set aside roles for certain individuals to help the "ordinary" citizen do the best job possible in this regard. Almost always the role is filled in part by religious institutions and their representatives. The process used by cultures to decide what is "right" and what is "wrong" is one of extreme importance, whatever the outcome. We take this business of right and wrong quite seriously; in our brief evolutionary history, we have often made those who disagree with us pay with their reputation, if not their lives. From the Clarence Thomas/Anita Hill hearings to the witch trials of Salem, from the Paula Jones/Bill Clinton drama to the case of Salman Rushdie, from the case of Timothy McVeigh to the downfall of several televangelists, one sees clearly the inclination of Homo sapiens to engage in moral judgment. Thus, one might say that there are forces pushing psychology students away from making moral judgments about the behavior of others, but also forces that propel them toward making such judgments. The key, of course, is understanding that you are obligated to make some judgments, but not to fall victim to the self-righteousness that genetics, life experience, or a course in ethics sometimes produces.

Even though religious institutions have traditionally been the keeper of the flame with regard to morality, in the United States certain professions are granted the right to set, and have assumed responsibility for, ethical standards for their own members, under the assumption that the profession is willing to protect the public. Psychology is such a profession, and we will consider in this chapter a number of ethical issues using as a primary framework the most current ethics code of the American Psychological Association (APA, 1992). (Other relevant codes include those of the American Counseling Association [ACA, 1995] and the American Association of Marital and Family Therapy [AAMFT, 1991].)

Iago—Negative Role Model and Stimulus for Self-Awareness

As we read Shakespeare's *Othello*, we perhaps assume that we need little reflection to know our feelings for Iago. He is false; his treachery is unbounded; and he seems to know nothing of kindness, decency, or commitment to others. We do not like this man. Looking at Iago, we understand the kind of person we do not want to be, and presumably, we conjure up an image of a character whom we have rejected by our moral decisions across our lifespan. By extension, we can know some of our standards and values by experiencing our reactions to Iago. Our emotional reactions help us to define the kinds of principles in which we believe, to which we are committed, and on which we wish to act. Iago helps us understand that which we reject and that which we embrace.

Even though it may initially be helpful, this use of Iago as a rejected model is somewhat limited. Unfortunately, we often find ourselves in situations where the issue is not so much the choice between right and wrong as it is how best to implement a moral course of action. A survey by Pope and Vetter (1992) shows that indeed psychologists struggle with extremely difficult questions that often defy easy answers. We are often faced with questions such as, "What is the best way to be committed to another's welfare?" "What rights do *psychologists* have when faced with a highly disordered, life-disrupting client?" or "When does our commitment to the individual pose an excessive threat to the good of the many?" Assuming *no* evil, assuming no lack of moral commitment, we may nonetheless struggle to understand how best to carry out our moral beliefs. In the most difficult circumstances, we are faced with dilemmas in which our multiple commitments conflict to produce choices that by their very nature call for us to violate a principle we value. Thus, while our reactions to Iago help us understand that we wish to keep our promises, that we wish to honor our commitments, that we wish not to deceive others, these reactions cannot fully inform the wide range of behaviors needed in ethically ambiguous situations.

There is a *second* way in which Iago can help us, and it is less limited than the first. If we can avoid defensiveness, Iago can perhaps help us recognize in ourselves the kinds of impulses that we are so quick to condemn in others. If we can see in ourselves at least the echo of the impulses that drive Iago, perhaps this self-understanding and resulting humility can in turn help us avoid the complacency and self-satisfaction that may precede ethical violations. It is no accident that self-awareness has been valued from Socrates ("Know thyself") to Section 1.13 (Personal Problems and Conflicts) of the *Ethics Code*. To understand one's vulnerabilities, one's biases, and one's standpoint is often a key ingredient in helping us prevent and avoid ethical problems, as well as helping limit the damage when violations do occur for whatever reason.

In addition, this recognition of our frailties helps us understand that people who violate ethical standards are human beings like us, and that ethical principles, while often helpful, do not represent easy solutions to difficult problems. If we are to help colleagues who seek consultation from us on ethical problems, if we are to be the kind of professionals from whom others would *want* to seek consultation on ethical matters, we must not start from a position of self-righteousness or invincibility. Rather, we must begin with a keen awareness that circumstances can overwhelm almost anyone and that it is entirely possible for competent, ethical professionals to make errors in judgment.

Ethical Codes: Practical Origins and Relationship with Character

It is important to emphasize that in the ideal, ethical codes are built on principles of behavior we value for itself, and not on behavior that is mandated. That is, in the ideal, these codes are adopted voluntarily by members of a profession. It is perhaps also important to emphasize, however, that in the final analysis ethical codes are in fact tied to good practice in a very practical way. For example, when we say that clients should be able to discuss their problems without fear of our telling others what they have revealed (the principle of confidentiality), we adopt this stance not just because "nice people don't tattle," but also because we fear we will not be able to help people unless they can trust us not to talk about them with others. Similarly, we say that a therapist should not engage in multiple relationships, in part because experience has shown that such relationships often hinder therapy and run an inordinate risk of psychological damage to the client. In short, good ethics are good practice. In fact, there is some evidence to suggest that therapists' standards for good practice may be even more stringent than published ethical principles (Pope, Tabachnick, & Keith-Spiegel, 1988).

No matter how careful we are, we all find ourselves facing ethical dilemmas from time to time. Good solutions to these dilemmas are found in part by application of critical reasoning. Just as important, however, is that the person trying to apply ethical principles has a felt identity for the limitations of human beings. This idea is expressed well by George Eliot, as quoted by Carol Gilligan (1982):

> We have no master-key that will fit all cases [of moral decision]…[G]eneral rules [will not lead people] to justice by a ready-made patent method, without the trouble of exerting patience, discrimination, impartiality, without any care to assure whether they have the insight that comes from a hardly-earned estimate of temptation or from a life vivid and intense enough to have created a wide, fellow feeling with all that is human. (p. 148)

The necessity of having this "wide, fellow feeling with all that is human" is easily seen when we consider many of the cases in which human beings have sought to stand in moral judgment of their fellow human beings. Perhaps the first ethical principle should be, "Remember that we are all human." The idea that ethical behavior is dependent to some extent on a sense of relationship or at least a sense of empathy or sympathy has been explored by a number of writers including Gilligan (1982) and Wilson (1993). We turn now to a brief discussion of the important relationship between ethical behavior, character (or virtue), and ethical principles.

Principle Ethics and Virtue Ethics

Since 1953, when the first version of the APA *Ethics Code* was published, the term "standard" or "principle" has been used in the title of each of the revisions. Although distinctions have been drawn between rules, standards, and principles, in practical application, we can think of a standard or principle (e.g., respect the autonomy of others; do no harm, etc.) as being a rule that has been incorporated (either as a requirement or as an aspirational goal) into a formal code (such as the APA *Ethics Code).* Put in a slightly different way, when we speak of "principle ethics," we are referring in part to a belief that there is a set of "rules" by which psychologists should abide and that ethical behavior follows if we apply and abide by these "rules."

Thus questions arise: "What are the principles by which psychologists should practice?" "How can we know what they are?" "How many of them are there?" "How can we know when to apply them and how to apply them?" "How can we justify having some rules but not others?" "In general, what procedures should we use to produce such rules?" "What level of abstraction should we use when listing these rules?" "How should we resolve a dilemma in which two rules seem to be in conflict?" "Should these rules apply to all psychologists and counselors, and if so, in what way do we make allowances for multicultural perspectives and minority communities such as rural areas?" "What is the relationship between these rules and the motivation to follow them?" and so forth. (Ibrahim, 1996; Kitchener, 1984, 1996, 1999; Meara, Schmidt, & Day, 1996; Vasquez, 1996).

Ethical principles may be seen as arising from a number of sources and processes. These range from religious ideals to common sense to the products of theories of ethics. In the psychology literature, the foundation for much discussion about ethical principles was laid by Kitchener (1984), who adapted the work of Beauchamp and Childress (e.g., 1994) in medical ethics. Kitchener suggested that the five principles of autonomy, nonmalfeasance, beneficence, justice, and fidelity "constitute an initial foundation for the critical evaluation of ethical reasoning in the context of counseling and psychology" (p. 54). (The reader is referred to Kitchener, 1984, for a description of each of these principles.) Meara, Schmidt, and Day (1996), felt that truth-telling is an important enough principle in psychology to merit its own category, and they added "veracity" to the list. One might reasonably say that the specific rules or standards found in the *Ethical Principles of Psychologists and Code of Conduct* (APA, 1992) can be more or less drawn from these five or six principles. (The APA *Ethical Principles of Psychologists and Code of Conduct* contain general principles—competence, integrity, professional and scientific responsibility, respect for people's rights and dignity, concern for others' welfare, and social responsibility—which are aspirational and the ethical standards, which are enforceable rules.)

In part because any list of ethical principles raises a number of difficult-to-answer questions (see above), a second approach to the study of ethical behavior is found in the literature. Jordan and Meara (1990) and Meara, Schmidt, and Day (1996) have argued that principles must be augmented by the idea of virtue or character. They suggest that ethical dilemmas are perhaps best resolved by asking not so much what rule is to be applied, but rather, what kind of person we want to be in a given situation. A brief example from the "real world" may be helpful in understanding this idea of virtue ethics.

In January of 1997, a security guard for a Swiss bank noticed that among documents scheduled to be shredded were a number that seemed to throw light on the debate about Swiss bank accounts and holocaust victims. The guard, believing that the documents were relevant to the current controversy, and believing that the bank was trying to conceal evidence, stole the documents by hiding them in his clothes. Subsequently, his life and the lives of his wife and children were threatened and he was denounced as a traitor. When asked why he did it, he reported that he had seen the film *Schindler's List,* and was moved to action by the example set by the protagonist. In a television interview, the guard (who left Switzerland for the United States) indicated that his decision to take the documents and save them from destruction was made very quickly. He did not talk about how a course in ethics influenced him (indeed it is entirely likely that he had never had such a course), he did not talk about rules that he was carrying out. Instead, he recalled a hero from a story. He also noted that he was a religious person and that he felt it was his duty to act in this way. Thus, in a moment of decision, this individual acted on his understanding of what it meant to be a virtuous person. In turn, this is the kind of person whom we as psychologists aspire to be and whose model helps us better understand the argument that, at the deepest level, we seek not to be people who follow certain rules, but people who represent a certain kind of character.

Although the idea of virtue ethics as a construct has been criticized (e.g., Bersoff, 1996), and although it seems highly unlikely that psychologists would ever replace principle ethics with virtue ethics, it is also clear that rules alone will never provide all the help we need to act in an ethically appropriate fashion. For example, even if we have a very sophisticated understanding of the APA *Ethics Code,* and even if we have developed an effective judgment process for deciding which principle should be most honored when principles conflict, neither of these facts (whether alone or in combination) would ensure that we were motivated to engage in ethical behavior. Thus, the virtues such as "virtuous intent" and "personal investment in doing good" represent a very important component of ethical behavior.

There are a number of reasons why training in graduate programs of psychology focuses on principle ethics rather than virtue ethics. In the first place, no one has suggested that principle ethics be abandoned. It is important that you know and understand the kinds of behavior that are expected of psychologists or counselors. Second, programs do what they can to select out "bad character" during the admission process, so a certain level of "good character" is assumed. Third, just about everyone agrees that it is quite difficult for external agents to engineer changes in character when the "subjects" are adult human beings. Thus, even if those who manage training programs were motivated to change character and were committed to spending a significant amount of resources doing it, there would still be the question of how to accomplish the task. Despite the limitations of virtue ethics, we believe that some of the broader issues raised by this approach to ethics are worth considering. In particular, there may be value in asking ourselves from time to time whether we are engaging in behavior that defines the kind of person we want to be; or there may be value in asking ourselves whether a given behavior is consistent with what we think someone whom we greatly admire might do in that situation. We might also profit from asking ourselves whether we are engaging in self-deception, or rationalization, or wishful thinking. As noted above, we must be alert to the dangers of self-righteousness. If we find ourselves justifying questionable behavior on the grounds that somehow the situation is different for us than for just about everyone else, we need the virtue of relentlessly subjecting such attitude to hard-nosed examination. Thus, although there is no substitute for knowing the content of, and how to apply, a professional code of ethics, some of the broader "character" values to which psychologists should be committed remain absolutely essential to carrying out effectively our responsibilities. If we neglect these broader values, an in-depth knowledge of an ethics code will be no insurance against serious ethical difficulties.

Resources

A number of resources are available to assist psychotherapists and counselors who are confronted with ethical dilemmas or who wish to be better informed about ethical principles. These include the *Ethical Principles of Psychologists and Code of Conduct* (APA, 1992), *Standards for Educational and Psychological Testing* (AERA, 1985), Guidelines on Therapy with Women (APA Task Force on Sex Bias and Sex Role Stereotyping in Psychotherapeutic Practice, 1978), Guidelines for Computer-Based Tests and Interpretations (APA, 1986), and General Guidelines for Providers of Psychological Services (APA, 1987). One book that is keyed directly to the APA *Ethics Code* is *Ethics for Psychologists: A Commentary on the APA Ethics Code* (Canter, Bennett, Jones, & Nagy, 1994). The American Counseling Association (ACA) and its various divisions also have published several related documents including the *ACA Code of Ethics and Standards of Practice* (ACA, 1995), *A Practitioner's Guide to Ethical Decision-Making* (Forester-Miller & Davis, 1995), a casebook (Herlihy & Corey, 1996) and two publications on dual/multiple relationships (Herlihy & Corey, 1992; 1997). One may also wish to consult the *Principles of Medical Ethics with Annotations Especially Applicable to psychiatry* (American Psychiatric Association, 1995). Additionally, there have been many books and articles published about ethics in psychology in the last few years. For example, a number of articles related to ethical and legal issues in psychology have been published in the APA journals *American Psychologist* and *Professional Psychology: Research and Practice.* The *Journal of Counseling and Development*, published by the American Counseling Association, also contains articles relevant to ethical and legal issues. Additionally, one journal, *Ethics & Behavior,* is devoted entirely to articles focusing on ethics. There are also a number of texts that you may find helpful, including ones by Kitchener (1999), Welfel (1998), Corey, Corey, and Callanan (1998), Keith-Spiegel and Koocher (1998), and Bersoff (1995). Because there are so many resources available, this chapter will highlight only a few of the ethical issues related to psychotherapy. We will comment briefly on five areas in ethics (Competence, Diversity, Confidentiality, Client Welfare, and Professional Relationships), each of which involves several of the standards in the APA *Ethics Code.* (Although there are some differences between the APA code and the ACA code, there are many overlapping areas.) We chose these five areas in part based on the types of questions raised by our students. All of the standards, and the aspirational principles, are of course important and psychologists have an ethical obligation to abide by the complete set of standards (similarly, members of ACA must abide by that code). We are choosing some, rather than other, aspects on which to comment as a matter of emphasis, not importance. The Principles and Standards cited after each of the five areas (below) refers to the 1992 *Ethical Principles of Psychologists and Code of Conduct* of the American Psychological Association.

Competence.   (Principle A; Standards 1.04, 1.05, 1.06, 1.08. 2.02, 2.04, and Others)

Practice Within Your Competence.   The very first principle listed (among the General Principles) in the APA *Ethics Code* is that of "Competence." Furthermore, Standard 1.04a states explicitly:

> Psychologists provide services, teach, and conduct research only within the boundaries of their competence, based on their education, training, supervised experience, or appropriate professional experience.

The idea of being a professional is rooted in two assumptions about competency: (a) the idea that one has certain competencies that exceed those of the general population and (b) the idea that one practices *within* (that is, does not exceed) one's competency. Thus, psychologists and counselors must be competent, but they must also ensure that they do not practice outside the boundary of that competence. This is relatively easy to say, but not always easy to do. The problem lies in deciding what is meant by "competence" in a given area and exactly where the boundary lies around that area. For example, how much training does one need to implement a behavioral program of desensitization for a client who fears being on airplanes? Or, how much experience does one need in order to use the empty-chair technique in independent practice? A related question revolves around presenting problems for which there is very little research or conflicting research.

Standard 1.04c notes that when the discipline has not yet agreed on treatment standards, "psychologists must take reasonable steps to ensure the competence for their work." Again, one is left with vague ideas such as "reasonable steps." Because each dilemma may vary dramatically from case to case, it is very difficult to generalize. As a minimum, we might say that being competent implies professionally sanctioned knowledge and that you have enough knowledge of the literature to defend to other professionals your planned course of action. As Canter, Bennett, Jones, and Nagy (1994) point out:

> It would be improper for psychologists, in their professional capacity, to say or do something merely because it "felt right," it "seemed logical," or they were curious about the impact of an untried approach in a specific case (e.g., telling a spouse abuser to take his or her aggression out on the family pet in hopes that the cathartic experience would reduce the risk of additional abuse). (pp. 36–37)

When struggling with questions such as "What is competence?" or "What kind of justification do I need to proceed?" perhaps what is more important than a set of guidelines is a commitment on the part of psychologists and counselors (including those in training) to question themselves routinely when there *might* be a possibility of operating outside the boundaries of what they are qualified to do. In turn, these issues should be discussed with a supervisor or consultant. For example, on occasion a supervisor may assign you a case that you believe is outside your area of competence. If this should happen, you have an ethical responsibility to discuss the issue with your supervisor. Treatment procedures that you have read about but have not actually been trained to apply certainly demand close supervision. For example, beginning therapists might assume that with a little reading they can institute a behavioral intervention such as desensitization. We reject, and we assume other therapists do also, the idea that certain interventions are very simple ones with little training needed to implement them. As a minimum, one needs to be able to conduct a very careful assessment of whether such an intervention is called for.

At times it may also be important to inform clients of the limits of your competency. For example, suppose that a client brings you pictures drawn by his five-year-old daughter because the client is disturbed by the pictures. Suppose further that the pictures depict very frightening scenes of children being tortured and molested. If you have no training in child assessment, you must limit your comments about the pictures; it is your ethical responsibility to inform the client that you are not trained to interpret such material and that you will be happy to refer the client to someone who is.

Responsibility to Seek and Use Supervision. An integral part of your responsibility to practice with competence as a student is doing everything you can to ensure that you are receiving good supervision. This means, among other things, that you are willing to bring to your supervision sessions any information that might bear on treatment, even (or perhaps we should say especially) if such information includes serious mistakes on your part. Most beginning therapists do not need too much encouragement to seek supervision because they experience it as helpful. In some cases, however, a supervisor may be perceived as not helpful. In such cases, it is a very human reaction to withdraw and cease bringing up the more troubling aspects of one's interactions with clients (e.g., Ladany, Hill, Corbett, & Nutt, 1996; Yourman & Farber, 1996). In fact, in the Ladany et al. study, 44% of the supervisees failed to disclose all their perceived clinical mistakes, 36% failed to report all negative reactions to clients, and 25% failed to report each incident of attraction to their client. Fully 90% of the sample reported that they had on one or more occasions not disclosed negative feelings about their supervisor to their supervisor. Thus, unfortunately, it is clear that failure to disclose information is not all that atypical. Here we emphasize the importance of taking responsibility for your part in the supervisory relationship. The building of trust appears to be a key component in good supervision, which is perhaps another way of saying that the quality of the supervisory relationship is central to good supervision (Worthen & McNeill, 1996). If you do find your supervisor to be consistently unhelpful, we encourage you to consider processing the issue with him or her, or if that does not seem workable, ask for another supervisor. Your clients have a right to be seen by someone who is being actively supervised by a competent supervisor with whom the therapist is working effectively. As we have previously suggested, when in doubt as to whether you need supervision concerning a development in therapy, the rule is unambiguous: Seek supervision. Consistent failure to disclose to your supervisor important information about clients, or your interactions with them, becomes an ethical matter because you may be practicing outside your competency and because the client's welfare is at risk. It is also a legal matter, since you are practicing under your supervisor's license and he or she is held liable for your mistakes.

Personal Problems and Conflicts.   Another variable that may affect one's competence to practice is the existence of serious personal problems in the life of the psychologist (e.g., Kottler, 1993; Stadler, 1990). The 1992 APA Ethics Code contains three standards directly addressing your responsibility to be aware of, and deal appropriately with, your personal problems and conflicts (Standards 1.13a, 1.13b, and 1.13c). Essentially, one's responsibility is to avoid undertaking an activity when one's personal problems are likely to lead to poor treatment for the client. One also has a responsibility to be generally alert to the impact of personal problems and to take action (such as limiting one's practice or removing oneself from a situation) when one does become aware of personal problems that might lead to harm.

It is important to remember that Standard 1.13a contains the phrase, "…when they [psychologists] know *or should know* [italics added] that their personal problems are likely to lead to harm to a patient…" As Canter, Bennett, Jones, and Nagy (1994) point out:

> The psychologist who is unaware of his or her own personal problems may in fact be impaired. Denial or lack of knowledge, however, will not provide a sufficient excuse under this [1.13a] standard. (p. 44)

In particular, you have an ethical responsibility to be aware of how your personal difficulties may be impacting your performance as a therapist. Such impact might take the form of a temporary general decline in your therapeutic skills or special difficulty with a particular client. For example, if you are in the process of divorcing your spouse, it may be hard for you to ensure therapeutic objectivity with clients who are also in the process of a divorce. If you have just been denied a promotion, individuals who are particularly ambitious, or conversely, who are underachievers may pose problems for you. Or if there has been a recent death in your family you may fall victim to seeing death anxiety in many of your clients. Most therapists are at least somewhat aware of the potential for over- or under-identification with clients during personally troubled times. However, it is important to get in the habit of periodically thinking about how your personal life may be impacting your therapy. There is further discussion of this issue in Chapters 7 and 12, The Therapeutic Stance and Transference and Countertransference.

Accurately Represent Your Training. In an earlier chapter we noted that you should inform clients if you are a student in training (see Standards 4.01a and 4.01b, Structuring the Relationship). You also have an obligation to ensure that, for example, neither clients nor others "inadvertently" think you have a Ph.D. when you don't. It is important to emphasize that one's ethical responsibilities not only involve avoiding actually committing an overt unethical act by misrepresenting your credentials or training, but also require one to correct misperceptions that have arisen due to no fault on the part of oneself.

Responsibility to Competently and Respectfully Respond to Diversity. (Principle D, Standards 1.08 [Human Differences], 1.09 [Respecting Others], 1.10 [Nondiscrimination], 1.11 [Sexual Harassment], 1.12 [Other Harassment], 2.04c [Use of Assessment with Special Populations], and Others)

Although Chapter 10, Multicultural Counseling, discusses diversity and psychotherapy, we are also making comments here because we believe that sensitivity to issues affected by individuals' gender, age, race, ethnicity, national origin, religion, sexual orientation, disability, language, or socioeconomic status is an ethical responsibility (e.g., Payton, 1994). General Principle D (Respect for People's Rights and Dignity) summarizes our aspirational commitment to respect all people and avoid bias whenever possible:

> Psychologists accord appropriate respect to the fundamental rights, dignity, and worth of all people. They respect the rights of individuals to privacy, confidentiality, self-determination, and autonomy, mindful that legal and other obligations may lead to inconsistency and conflict with the exercise of these rights. Psychologists are aware of cultural, individual, and role differences, including those due to age, gender, race, ethnicity, natural origin, religion, sexual orientation, disability, language, and socioeconomic status. Psychologists try to eliminate the effect on their work of biases based on those factors, and they do not knowingly participate in or condone unfair discriminatory practices.

In addition to General Principle D, several Standards (some noted above) address directly issues related to diversity. The spirit of the General Principle and of the various Standards includes as a bedrock a respect for others and an appreciation for the role of diversity. Furthermore, we should all be committed not just to treating others fairly or not discriminating, but rather to *valuing* differences. Diversity must be something that we prize as reflected in our proactive behavior, whatever the context. Apart from the broad (but obviously critically important) notion of respect for others, we underscore two additional guidelines (expressed in various standards in the *Ethics Code*): (a) take into consideration ethnicity, gender, and lifestyle issues, as well as other individuating variables, when making assessments and treatment plans and when carrying out such plans (e.g., Standards 2.03, 2.04c, 2.05); and (b) deliver psychological services to clients from diverse populations only when one is competently trained to do so (e.g., Standard 1.08). These issues are discussed more thoroughly in Chapter 10, Multicultural Counseling. Here, we underscore one's *ethical* responsibility to ensure that one's training and experience with diverse clients are adequate to avoid the "one size fits all" approach to delivery of psychological services.

Because instructors in graduate psychology courses in ethics often ask students to grapple with ethical dilemmas, one way of sensitizing oneself to individuating variables is to ask oneself how the optimal behavior in the dilemma might change depending on the ethnicity, gender, sexual orientation, religion, and so forth of the actors in the dilemma. Even if hypothetically changing the variables in the dilemma does not affect your judgment about the best course of action, merely considering protagonists from other cultures, handicapping conditions, and the like will be a pointed reminder that ethical behavior occurs in a context and that preferred courses of action may change when the context changes. Furthermore, a change in the story may help you identify hidden assumptions you have, both about individuals from diverse populations, and also about how ethical behavior is to be identified.

It is a part of psychology's evolving understanding of behavior to recognize the importance of variables such as ethnicity, age, religion, sexual orientation, and so forth. It is a part of our evolving understanding of *ethics* to recognize that these variables are also bound up in ethical demands. Psychologists who are competent and ethical understand the importance of individual differences, especially those related to ethnicity, gender, disability, sexual orientation, and the like. These variables are now recognized as extremely influential in human behavior; failure to appreciate the role of such variables is both a clinical error and an ethical shortfall.

Questions have been raised about how documents such as the APA *Ethics Code* can be applied to minority communities (Payton, 1994; see also Pedersen, 1997). It must be recognized that ethics codes, by their very nature, are typically products of the dominant culture and are conservative in the sense that they tend to preserve the status quo. A part of our growing sensitivity to the role of culture in virtually every part of human behavior is an increasing appreciation for how thoroughly questions with ethical overtones are infused with cultural influences. From how a question about ethics gets framed, to which values are seen as significant in a dilemma, to the action preferred to best resolve an ethical dilemma, we see the influence of culture. Furthermore, in the scholarly literature, we are beginning to see a greater inclination to view certain behaviors as ethically problematic when such behaviors, in the recent past, might have been viewed as unrelated, or at least marginally related, to ethics. An excellent example of this process may be seen in a book review, written by Daniel (1994), that was published in the journal *Ethics & Behavior*. Daniel criticized the reviewed book and suggested that the author, by omitting a discussion in her book of the trauma caused by racism, had in fact committed an ethical violation. The author responded with a vigorous defense of what she had written (Herman, 1994) and called on Daniel to retract her statements that framed the omission as an ethical issue. Subsequently, several additional comments were printed in the journal; the spirit of the published comments can be captured by the title of one of them: "It's About Time!" (Sanchez & Nuttall, 1995). That this sort of debate is now appearing in the professional literature is a sign of the vigorous emergence of cultural factors into the mainstream of professional attention. Thus, it is important to underscore that respect for diversity means more than some vague appreciation for differences. Rather, it also means that our understanding of ethics, and what is to be seen as the proper purview of ethical analysis, is put at risk and must be constantly reevaluated. This is a challenge to our profession and to each of us personally.

Another example of scholarly work outlining the effects of culture on ethics is that by Gilligan (1982), whose perspective on moral development emphasized the role of gender in helping shape our beliefs about what is moral and how one goes about deciding whether an action is or is not moral. Gilligan articulated a new view of how women and men approach moral issues. Her analysis suggested that whereas men often focus on an ethic of justice, women more often focus on an ethic of care in pursuing moral or ethical behavior. More broadly, Gilligan's work can be seen as addressing the issue of how what we "bring to the table" in trying to understand our ethical responsibilities is a reflection of our socialization within a particular kind of culture.

Confidentiality and Privileged Communication.   (Principle D; Standards 4.01a [Structuring the Relationship], 5.01 [Discussing the Limits of Confidentiality], 5.02 [Maintaining Confidentiality], 5.03 [Minimizing Intrusions on Privacy], 5.04 [Maintenance of Records], 5.05 [Disclosures], 5.06 [Consultations], 5.07 [Confidential Information in Databases], 5.08 [Use of Confidential Information for Didactic or Other Purposes], 5.09 [Preserving Records and Data], and 6.26 [Professional Reviewers]).

Perhaps no part of the ethical code has been written about as much as has this principle. Confidentiality is certainly a keystone of psychotherapy. It is an ethical principle rather than a legal one. The principle essentially says that, except under certain conditions, the therapist is bound not to disclose to anyone the contents of the client's communication to the therapist. The parallel legal construct is privileged communication. Privileged communication is a right held by the client that prevents the therapist, except under certain conditions (e.g., child abuse, felonies, situations in which individuals make their mental health a legal issue, and others), from testifying in court as to the content of the psychotherapy sessions. Thus, statutes or rulings specifying when privileged communication does not hold represent a limited and particular example of when psychologists may be compelled to break confidentiality. Further, psychology licensure laws and other related administrative statutes, as well as civil case law, may address a variety of related issues, including conditions under which (a) breaking confidentiality is permitted (b) breaking confidentiality is required; and (c) privileged communication between therapist and client does not hold. Glosoff, Herlihy, Herlihy, and Spence (1997) have given a good overview of the issue of privileged communication. DeBell and Jones (1997) and Knapp and VandeCreek (1997) have described an important case, Jaffee v. Redmond, which established precedent for privileged communication in federal courts.

The repeated emphasis in the literature on the importance of confidentiality is there not only because confidentiality is so central to the process of therapy, but perhaps also because there are so many ways in which we may inadvertently compromise this principle. Mythology (Warner, 1967) records what was perhaps the first case in which confidentiality was accidentally breached. The story involved Midas, who, following his predicament with the "golden touch," became embroiled in a dispute as to whether Pan or Apollo played better music:

> All agreed with the judgment of the mountain god—all except Midas, who kept disputing it and calling it unjust. Apollo then decided that he was unworthy to have human ears. He made them move from the base. In all other ways Midas was human: only as a punishment for his bad taste, he had the ears of an ass.
>
> Naturally he was ashamed of them and covered them up in a purple turban which he wore upon his head. But the servant who used to cut his hair discovered his secret. He dared not tell others what he had discovered, but he could not bear to keep the secret to himself. So he went out and dug a hole in the ground. Kneeling down he whispered into the hole: "King Midas has asses' ears." Then he carefully put back the earth and went away, relieved that he had spoken the words, even though no one had heard them. But a crop of whispering reeds sprang up in the place, and, when they were full-grown and swayed by the winds of the autumn, they repeated the words that were buried at their roots, "Midas has asses' ears," they said to every breeze, and the breezes carried on the news. (pp. 129–130)

Although psychologists do not typically whisper confidential information into a hole in the ground, they are nonetheless at risk, from time to time, for failing to protect confidential information. For example, students may make "personal" notes about clients and then leave them on a desk where a roommate or housemate might accidentally see them. Or, one may "gossip" to a fellow staff member about a client when the fellow staff member did not need to know about the case and in fact may be acquainted with the client through some "outside" contact. Some therapists like to use stories to illustrate points and may be tempted to use a story from a recent client to make a point to another client. Unfortunately, it may take less for one of your clients to recognize another of your clients in a story than you might think.

Most therapists are very committed to confidentiality; it is a value that is strongly held by most psychologists, and graduate programs tend to strongly emphasize it. Perhaps the greatest threat to client confidentiality is not poorly trained clinicians or psychopathic psychologists, but rather the accidental or poorly considered actions of which we are all capable from time to time. For example, Pope and Vasquez (1991) gave an example of mental health charts being left temporarily in a hallway. They also give a number of other examples or situations in which confidentiality may be put at risk, including the issue of the disposition of client files that are "out of date," the question of what to do about your answering machine at home if you live with someone, and the problem of therapy rooms that are not adequately soundproofed. Thus, confidentiality is not just an abstract value to which we swear alliance, but rather, it is also something that must be safeguarded in many quite different ways. To reiterate what you have undoubtedly heard many times, it is extremely important to protect client confidentiality if at all possible. In a survey of directors of APA-accredited clinical and counseling psychology programs in the United States and Canada, Fly, van Bark, Weinman, Kitchener, and Lang (1997) found that of eight types of ethical violations, graduate students were most likely to have violated the principle of confidentiality.

Of course, there are frequently times when clients are willing to have you reveal what would otherwise be considered confidential. The client may be *asking* that you reveal information so that another professional can have access to the knowledge, so that a family member can help them, or so that an insurance company will reimburse them. The client may also be willing for you to reveal information if you request permission to (e.g., if you believe that you need to inform her or his partner, spouse, or parents about their suicidal thoughts). Of course, a signed release of information form is needed whenever information is to be provided to companies, agencies, individuals, or other professionals. As noted earlier, there are times when you do not need a release of information to reveal confidential information; however, these are the exceptions.

One issue that can be particularly difficult arises when clients are using a third party (such as an insurance company) to pay for treatment. Even in the more traditional, and typically less intrusive, model of "fee for service" insurance, the dates of service and diagnosis are recorded as a minimum. In Health Maintenance Organizations (HMOs) and other forms of managed care, the insurance company typically takes a much more active role in monitoring the case. Case summaries, treatment plans, explanations of the need for additional sessions, and the like, may be required if payment is to be received from the insurer. In general, although there are large variations, almost all companies with an HMO structure require a periodic review of cases if they are to continue paying, and they will request information from the therapist. Under such circumstances, psychologists are very concerned about confidentiality (e.g., Sank, 1997) and rightly so.

It is important for therapists to inform clients of these sorts of situations before they arise. Although we as therapists are not necessarily expected to be familiar with all companies and their policies, we are expected to inform clients of the range of requirements mandated by third-party payers. Sections 5.01a and 5.01b of the *Ethics Code* require that psychologists discuss the limitations of confidentiality, unless "not feasible" or "contraindicated," at the onset of therapy and as conditions change. If insurance may be used by a client, it is wise to obtain a signed release of information at the very beginning of therapy. Such a release need not detail all possible information that *might* need to be made available to the insurance company, but as a minimum it should outline that continued payment by the insurance company may be conditional on whether information is provided. It is also important that clients understand that once you have released information to the insurance company, you are not in control (and the client may not even be in control) of the uses to which the data are put. Even if the client signs such a statement, it may be necessary, depending on the specificity and range of requested information, and the type of initial release signed by the client, to obtain a more detailed signed release at the time that disclosure is requested.

Another area that often involves problems in terms of confidentiality is college counseling services. Sharkin (1995) has outlined three types of "strains" on confidentiality in therapy on campus, including entangled therapeutic relationships, incidental encounters, and third-party inquiries. Each of these types of strains is in fact present in locations other than college campuses, but the campus environment does raise the probability of certain types of problems. In particular, because of the administrative structure of universities, referrals to the counseling center not infrequently come from a third party on campus. As we noted earlier, it is very important that you do not break confidentiality (without a signed release of information) by telling the referring party any details, including even the fact that the person did come for counseling. As Sharkin points out, it is very important in a community such as a university that you help educate sources *before* they make a referral so that when they do make one they will not expect feedback on the situation.

Among the areas that have raised a number of questions about confidentiality have been HIV-positive and AIDS-related issues (Harding, Gray, & Neal, 1993; Lamb, Clark, Drumheller, Frizzell, & Surrey, 1989; McGuire, Nieri, Abbott, Sheridan, & Fisher, 1995; Melton, 1988; VandeCreek & Knapp, 1993) in therapy, especially in light of the famous Tarasoff case (see discussion later in the chapter). Because of the potentially devastating impact on the client's life should confidentially be breached about HIV status, it is obviously very important that therapists do everything in their power to protect the confidentiality rights of such clients. A question that has been repeatedly discussed is whether therapists' obligations under the Tarasoff rulings should or should not apply to cases in which HIV-positive individuals disclose to the therapist the identity of an individual with whom they are having unprotected sex and whom they have not informed of their HIV status. Consider the following vignette:

Five years ago, Mr. Smith tested positive for HIV. He is in psychotherapy because he cannot decide whether to tell his dying father about his condition. He reports that he has had unprotected sex with seven or eight women in the last five years and that he only told one of them about his HIV status. He reports that he is currently living with a woman, that they do not practice safe sex, and that he has not told her of his HIV status. The therapist tries repeatedly to have him tell the woman or at least start using some protection, but he adamantly refuses. His attitude seems to be, "let her take her chances like I did."

Under these circumstances, do you believe that the therapist would be justified in "warning" the woman with whom the client lives? Do you believe that you could continue treating this person and not have strong feelings about what he has done and is doing? If you *would* have strong feelings, do you believe that such feelings would interfere in your treatment to such an extent that you could not ethically (because of your inability to provide good therapy) continue treating the client? In general, how long would you be willing to see a client who was engaging in behavior similar to that of this client?

Clearly, therapists who are told the identity of a partner who does not know that she or he is being exposed to HIV have an ethical responsibility to do everything they possibly can inside therapy to remove or reduce the threat. Whether there exist HIV-related situations in which the therapist may or should breach confidentiality is an exceedingly difficult question. Clearly the values of the therapist enter into the decision, but again we emphasize that before one considers breaching confidentiality, one must do everything short of that first. It is also important to know state law concerning disclosure of confidential information related to HIV. Some states forbid disclosure, some allow disclosure, and others have no specific information or have ambiguous information.

Client Welfare. (Principle E [Concern for Others' Welfare], Standards 1.14 [Avoiding Harm], 1.15 [Misuse of Psychologists' Influence], 1.16 [Misuse of Psychologists' Work], 1.17 [Multiple Relationships], 1.18 [Barter (With Patients or Clients)], 1.19 [Exploitative Relationships], and others)

Whether directly or indirectly, the entire APA code and the entire ACA code are designed (at least in theory) to protect the welfare of clients. In particular, Standard 4 (with each of its substandards) directly addresses the kind of relationship we are to have with our clients. Additionally, a number of the General Standards (Standard 1 with substandards) apply quite directly to our therapeutic relationships. Fisher and Younggren (1997) have said, "Perhaps the most valuable aspect of the new APA ethics code is the extent to which it specifically addresses the rights of client-patients receiving psychotherapy and the responsibilities of psychologists providing such services" (p. 588).

Commitment to the Client. It is very important that you be clear on who is your client, and to whom you have primary responsibility. This is especially true for cases in which legal issues are involved (e.g., child custody, forensic evaluation, etc.). It is also important that you be clear with your client about what responsibilities you have to the agency if you are employed by one. Most therapists begin with the assumption that the person who is coming to see them is the person for whom they have responsibility. This is a good starting assumption; however, there may be complications. For example, what should you do if a client tells you that his or her mother is threatening suicide? What should you do if a person calls you on the telephone and says, "Your client is my roommate and he is scaring me to death with all his talk about guns"? What should you do if a client says, "I'm going to take everything I can from my husband in the divorce settlement"? What if a client says, "My roommate treats me like dirt, so I'm going to get his girlfriend in bed"? Principles of good therapy aside, in each of these cases you must remember who is your client. It is not your job to save the client's mother from suicide or comfort a roommate who is frightened (although one would scarcely be blase about such dangerous situations), or to ensure a fair divorce settlement, or to uphold commonly accepted notions of decency and trust. Naturally you may (and probably would like to) have some impact on these situations. But it is very important that you keep focused on the fact that the client who came to see you is where your loyalty, energy, and commitment must lie. Certainly if other people are in danger from the client you may need to take some action; however, in the midst of action, you must never forget the welfare of your client.

Marital and family therapy represent more of a conceptual problem in terms of being clear on one's obligations and being clear on who is the client. A complete discussion of the perspective various therapists take on this issue is beyond the scope of this book. However, as we suggested earlier, it is advisable to set up the therapy situation so that you are as clear as you can be on your primary responsibilities and so that clients are clearly informed of your commitments.

Similarly, prison settings represent a great challenge to psychologists in their effort to keep clear in their own minds and with others both who their clients are and what their commitments to confidentiality mean in such a setting (Monahan, 1980; Weinberger & Sreenivasan, 1994). If you are employed in a correctional facility, it is critical that you read some of the available resources (such as those just cited) and that you initially spend time clarifying as much as possible the role that the administration sees you performing. Obviously, you need to know if your own view of your role differs significantly from that of your employer. In most correctional facilities, it would not be unusual to find questions emerging about role conflict. The key is to do as much "homework" as possible, not with a goal of eliminating difficulties, since that is perhaps not a realistic goal, but with a view to minimizing the difficulties that do inevitably arise.

Multiple Relationships.   In psychology, the concept of a "multiple relationship" draws primarily on role theory. That is, psychologists (or persons training to be psychologists) are involved in a multiple relationship when they attempt to perform more than one role with a client. There is a substantial body of literature that outlines many of the issues and dangers inherent in multiple relationships (e.g., Herlihy & Corey, 1997; Kitchener & Harding, 1990; Simon, 1992; Smith & Fitzpatrick, 1995; Sonne, 1994). Multiple relationships that are sexual in nature present a special problem; there is ample evidence that they are almost always deleterious to the client (Pope, 1994). The *Code* addresses multiple relationships (with former, current, and potential clients) in a number of standards including Standards 1.17,

1.18, 1.19, 4.05, 4.06, and 4.07. The *Code* states, "Psychologists do not engage in sexual intimacies with current patients or clients," (Standard 4.05), and "Psychologists do not accept as therapy patients or clients persons with whom they have engaged in sexual intimacies," (Standard 4.06). Furthermore, the *Code* says, "Psychologists do not engage in sexual intimacies with a former therapy patient or client for at least two years after cessation or termination of professional services," (Standard 4.07a). The ACA ethics code has a similar provision.

The general principle concerning multiple relationships is that professionals attempting to carry on relationships that involve conflicting or potentially conflicting roles are subjecting the other person to a set of unreasonable risks. They are also subjecting themselves, and at times other people as well, to a similar set of risks. In general, the problem is that as we try to carry out two conflicting responsibilities, we lose objectivity. In turn, the loss of objectivity is thought to have both emotional and behavioral consequences. The idea that multiple relationships are to be carefully evaluated—if not avoided—has a long history. For example, the military typically discourages intimate relationships between officers and enlisted personnel. Similarly, in the play *Becket* (Anouilh, 1960), King Henry II tells his friend, Thomas Becket, that he wants Becket to be Archbishop. Becket responds with several "excuses," but finally realizes that the King is serious:

BECKET: My Lord, I see now that you weren't joking. Don't do this.

KING: Why not?

BECKET: It frightens me.

KING: Becket, this is an order!

BECKET: (Gravely) If I become Archbishop, I can no longer be your friend. (p. 72)

Thus Becket recognizes the danger of multiple relationships, and attempts to warn Henry of one of the consequences. Of course the King did not heed Becket, and tragedy followed.

Even though engaging in multiple roles is clearly fraught with dangers, The APA *Ethics Code* is in fact rather ambiguous about the extent to which multiple roles (outside of sexual ones) are prohibited (Sonne, 1994). Section 1.17 begins with a disclaimer that notes that "In many communities and situations, it may not be feasible or reasonable for psychologists to avoid social or other nonprofessional contacts with persons such as patients, clients, students, supervisees, or research participants." This disclaimer is in recognition that several "situations" (e.g., rural areas and communities of minorities) present special challenges in terms of overlapping roles (Payton, 1994; Podrygula, 1995; Schank & Skovholt, 1997). For example, in some rural communities, there might be only one local psychologist within 50 or even 100 miles. The likelihood is great that psychologists who work in such settings will be faced with multiple roles that are not easy to avoid. Schank and Skovholt give several examples (based on a survey) that demonstrate vividly that working in rural areas is a challenge in terms of what to do about possible and actual multiple roles. Here are two short examples from their study:

> When I moved here, I got a membership to the YMCA to go to exercise classes. After running into a couple of clients in the locker room, I decided that this was just so uncomfortable for me. So I'm not going to continue my membership in the YMCA. It was just really awkward. It's not like there are a huge number of athletic clubs here that you can have a choice of which one you go to. (p. 47)

In this example, do you believe that it is reasonable or necessary that a psychologist forgo being a member of an athletic club (assuming there is only one in town) solely to avoid running into clients there? Here is another example from that same survey:

> I think there are a lot of variables. If I can avoid a situation I will. Let's say it is a function like a hockey party. My kids are on the hockey team. The kids want to go, and they want the parents to go. So you are at this function [with clients]. You're not going to say to the kids, "Gee, I can't go to the hockey banquet." So you just go.... Sometimes you just kind of live with it. My older kids have friends who have been my patients in the past. I prefer that they not come over to our house, but you can't say to your kids, "Don't invite so and so." (p. 47)

If you were the psychologist in this example, how would you feel about having a client in your home? How should one go about making a decision that pits one's responsibilities to one's family against one's responsibility to one's clients?

Another example of possible multiple role relationships would be the small church whose members are predominantly African American, that would like their "member psychologist" (who is African American) to conduct a personal growth/therapy group with special emphasis on sharing one's experience of racism. Where does the line between routine church activities end and delivery of psychological services begin? What accommodations should be made in such circumstances, especially when minority communities are involved and the number of minority psychologists is very small? Thus, questions about multiple roles can be extremely difficult to answer, and it is easy to see why the individuals who drafted the APA *Ethics Code* found it so difficult both to be clear about "rules," but also to allow the kind of flexibility required by complex situations (Herlihy & Corey, 1992; St. Germaine, 1993). In any event, the *Code* sets three criteria, any one of which may preclude engaging in multiple roles: (a) the relationship *reasonably* [italics added] might impair the psychologist's objectivity; (b) the relationship might interfere with the effective performance of the psychologist's duties; or (c) the relationship might harm or exploit the other person. Gottlieb (1993) has developed a decision-making model designed to help psychologists avoid multiple relationships that are exploitative and Schank and Skovholt (1997) listed four safeguards designed to minimize risk when multiple relationships appear inevitable. Greenberg and Shuman (1997) have discussed the "irreconcilable conflict between therapeutic and forensic roles." Thus, it is generally preferable that one avoid multiple relationships and it is virtually axiomatic that psychologists and counselors should apply a rigorous standard before choosing to engage in one. As is so often the case in life, "an ounce of prevention is worth a pound of cure."

One area of multiple relationships now receiving some attention is that of nonsexual relationships between therapists and their former clients (e.g., Anderson, 1996; Anderson & Kitchener, 1996; Anderson & Kitchener, 1998; Lamb, Strand, Woodburn, Buchko, Lewis, & Kang, 1994; Pipes, 1997). Although the 1992 APA *Ethics Code* specifically prohibits sexual relationships with former clients for at least two years, the *Code* does not address directly what other behaviors might (or might not) be prohibited. We believe that relationships with former clients should as a minimum be prohibited if they are exploitative or likely to exploit the client. Perhaps future revisions of the *Code* will address this issue; however, in the meantime, we encourage you to think very seriously before engaging in a nontherapeutic relationship with a client who has terminated. This caution is particularly warranted when the ex-client was or is vulnerable or when therapy was especially intensive. For further discussion of this issue, see Chapter 13, Termination.

Providing Clients with Adequate Information and Informing Them of Their Rights. One of the changes made in constructing the 1992 *Ethics Code* was that for the first time the *Code* contains a standard (4.02a) that explicitly requires that psychologists obtain informed consent to therapy and related procedures. Standard 4.01a requires that psychologists discuss issues "such as the nature and anticipated course of therapy, fees, and confidentiality." Standard 4.02a outlines what is implied in "informed consent" (capacity to consent, possessing necessary relevant information, consent freely given, consent documented). Standard 1.07 (Describing the nature and Results of Psychological Services) is even broader and states that "psychologists provide assessment, evaluation, treatment, counseling, supervision, teaching, consultation, research, or other psychological services to an individual, a group, or an organization, they provide, using language that is reasonably understandable to the recipient of those services, appropriate information beforehand about the nature of such services and appropriate information later about results and conclusions." Section 2.09 (Explaining Assessment Results) contains similar language regarding assessment procedures.

In addition to the specific language now contained in the APA *Code,* the idea that clients should routinely be informed of their rights has received considerable attention in the professional literature over the years (e.g., Everstine, Everstine, Heymann, True, Frey, Johnson, & Seiden, 1980; Handelsman & Galvin, 1988; Handelsman, Kemper, Kesson-Craig, McLain, & Johnsrund, 1986; Hare-Mustin, Marecek, Kaplan, & Liss-Levinson, 1979; Talbert & Pipes, 1988). The Everstine et al. and Hare-Mustin et al. articles give good discussions of clients' rights and make specific proposals for the kind of written information a client should receive. Handelsman et al. and Talbert and Pipes concluded that clients typically do not receive extensive information about their rights. Based on a review of the literature, Talbert and Pipes identified 19 possible elements of an informed consent form including (a) the right to switch therapists; (b) a statement about referrals to other psychologists; (c) mention of community resources as an option; (d) the right to end therapy; (e) a statement concerning risks of unpleasant emotions; (f) a statement concerning risk of change in relationships; (g) the limits of confidentiality; and other risks, rights, and information. Handelsman & Galvin (1988) provided an excellent example of a document that might be given to clients to help them understand their rights. We think that this document is an especially good one because, by listing questions a client might want to ask the therapist, it encourages client–therapist interaction.

There are perhaps a number of reasons why therapists are reluctant to use extensive written descriptions of informed consent for therapy, but perhaps one concern is how to describe all the various conditions under which confidentiality might be broken, including exceptions to privileged communication. (As previously described, informed consent to therapy includes, but is not limited to, discussing confidentiality.) As noted in Chapter 2, Questions that Beginning Therapists Ask, the conditions vary by state; the exceptions to privileged communication alone can be rather long (Glosoff, Herlihy, Herlihy, & Spence, 1997). Because each of the circumstances under which one might break confidentiality can be quite complicated, it is understandable why therapists might be reluctant to try to put all of this in writing. Furthermore, therapists do not always agree on the advisability of spelling out the many possible negative consequences of psychotherapy. Nonetheless, it is now an ethical requirement that psychologists obtain informed consent for psychotherapy. The exact content and form of that consent may vary depending on the client and the therapist.

Termination When Client Is Not Benefitting from Psychotherapy. Standard 4.09 addresses this issue directly. Our obligation is to terminate the therapy relationship when it becomes, in the words of the *Ethics Code*, "reasonably clear that the patient or client no longer needs the service, is not benefitting, or is being harmed by continued service." The point is also made that the therapist should offer, when needed, to assist the client in locating alternative sources of help. Perhaps the slightly broader issue here is that the client's progress in, and satisfaction with, psychotherapy should be periodically discussed with him or her. Unfortunately, clients often want to protect the feelings (or at least what they imagine to be the feelings) of the therapist and hence may be reluctant to articulate their dissatisfactions. At times the therapist may be subtly or unconsciously encouraging the client to be satisfied when he or she is not. Such unconscious needs on the part of the therapist are especially detrimental because they keep clients locked into a process that is not helpful while simultaneously communicating to them that they ought to be satisfied with what they are receiving. Unfortunately, this process often is a recapitulation of earlier interpersonal learning environments, so many clients may be especially vulnerable to a cycle in which their needs are not met, the psychotherapist communicates that their needs are being met, the clients feel guilty, blame themselves for lack of progress, and ultimately conclude that their needs are unimportant. This process is at complete variance with our intention to have clients reach a point at which they can recognize, articulate, and act upon their fundamental needs. It is also at complete variance with our ethical responsibility to protect the welfare of our clients.

A different—but obviously related—situation involves the client who uses therapy as a sort of crutch. Clients who have essentially decided to stay in therapy indefinitely for general support, but who are no longer committed to change, should be assisted in reassessing the role of therapy in their lives. We have an obligation to terminate if therapy is not benefitting the client.

Professional Relationships.

Relationships with Supervisors. Earlier we discussed the importance of working closely with your supervisor. It is important to remember that the *Ethics Code* now specifically prohibits sexual relationships between supervisors and supervisees (Standard 1.19b). Glaser and Thorpe (1986) as well as Robinson & Reid (1985) provided evidence that sexual relationships between graduate students and professors often are later perceived by the former students as harmful. Although sexual feelings and sexual attraction between supervisees and supervisors may be normal, acting on them is inconsistent with the *Ethics Code.* The relationship between supervisor and supervisee is inherently asymmetrical in terms of power; engaging in sexual intimacies in such a relationship is a recipe for disaster. Furthermore, the research cited above suggests that individuals who engage in sexual intimacies with their professors are more likely to later engage in sexual relationships with their clients. If you believe that your relationship with your supervisor is at risk for becoming sexualized, consider consultation with a peer, a trusted faculty member, or your therapist.

Respect for Other Professionals. We have an ethical responsibility to show respect for other psychotherapists. The *Ethics Code* (Standard 4.04) cautions psychologists to proceed carefully when considering whether to offer services to a client being seen by another mental health professional. Although the client's welfare is clearly the preeminent value in such a circumstance, it also shows a lack of respect for other professionals not to consider carefully one's course of action when a potential client is already being seen by a therapist. The issue of using caution when offering services to clients who are currently being seen by other therapists is a good example of how ethical practice goes hand in hand with good clinical judgment.

Unfortunately, the various helping professionals (e.g., psychology, counseling, psychiatry, and social work) do not always seem to respect each others' competencies. Nonetheless, we must take as our ideal the broad-minded recognition of both common and diverse strengths among these professions. Stereotyping and making caustic remarks about other professions do not advance our own profession. Certainly there may be legitimate disagreements. However, and in particular where a client's interests are concretely involved, our ethical responsibility is to ensure that clients can benefit from the full range of available services.

Conduct of Colleagues. If you observe unethical behavior by a colleague, supervisor, or other professional, you have an obligation to take action that you believe will lead to a resolution or correction of the problem, while ensuring that confidentiality rights are not violated. Actions to be considered include talking with the person (Standard 8.04 [Informal Resolution of Ethical Violations]) or making a report to a state or national organization/board (Standard 8.05 [Reporting Ethical Violations]). The chief points we emphasize here are the importance of (a) trusting your intuition when something bothers you and (b) seeking consultation from peers, supervisors, and/or the APA Ethics Office if you are wondering if something is ethical. By "trusting your intuition" we mean simply that if something seems wrong, it is inappropriate to shrug it off by saying something like, "Well, that person has a Ph.D. and I don't, so she probably knows what she is doing," or "I guess there will always be differences," or "I don't have all the facts," and so forth. Even though you should not ignore your intuition that something is unethical, neither should you completely trust your intuition when your "gut feeling" is that a behavior (either a colleague's or your own) is ethical. If you are unsure, no matter which way you are "leaning," you need to seek consultation.

As we suggest in Chapter 9, Mistakes That Therapists Make, if a client complains of the behavior of a colleague, you have an obligation to try to get all the facts in the case. Certainly any serious allegations should be thoroughly discussed with clients, and they should be informed fully as to their rights and the various options available to them. This is a good example also of the importance of being committed fully to your client's welfare. (Also see related information in Chapter 2, Questions That Beginning Therapists Ask.)

If a client suggests that a helping professional has used unethical behavior, it is very important that you honor the client's requests concerning what action he or she would like to take (Schoener, Milgrom, Gonsiorek, Luepker, & Conroe, 1989). For example, your client may initially say, "I just want to write my previous therapist a letter." Under those conditions you should not pressure the client to file a lawsuit, or take some other more drastic action. Conversely, if the client says, "I intend to sue," you certainly should not stand in his or her way, but neither should you assume that a lawsuit is what the client really wants. Perhaps she or he just wants an opportunity to confront the other therapist. The key point is that after informing clients of all their options, you should work with them to help them select the option that is most likely to help them accomplish their goal. Naturally, one's theoretical orientation, as well as one's personality, influences the degree to which one would want to be actively and continuously involved in the course of action chosen by a client who has been adversely impacted by unethical behavior (e.g., Pope, 1994).

Record Keeping and Legal Issues

Record Keeping

Record keeping is an ethical issue in so far as it bears on the welfare of the client. Although keeping good records has always been a good idea, the APA *Ethics Code* now requires (Standard 1.23a [Documentation of Professional and Scientific

Work]) that psychologists document their work. Furthermore, there is a requirement (Standard 1.23b) that psychologists who believe that records might come under legal scrutiny are obligated to ensure that such records are kept in a manner consistent with adjudication standards. Forensic assessments (Standard 7.02) are particularly demanding in this regard, although beginning psychotherapy students are not typically involved in such assessments. In Chapter 2, Questions That Beginning Therapists Ask, we commented briefly on some principles of record keeping, such as whether it is permissible to keep personal notes and what you should write in progress notes. For a good summary of issues involved in record keeping, see an article by Soisson, VandeCreek, & Knapp (1987). Quoting the Specialty Guidelines for Clinical Psychologists (American Psychological Association, 1981), Soisson et al. note that in the absence of state or federal statutes, a full record is to be kept for at least 3 years and the summary disposed of no sooner than 15 years. The Specialty Guidelines for Counseling Psychologists (American Psychological Association, 1981) stipulate that a full record must be kept for 4 years, with disposition of the summary allowed no sooner than 7 years. We recommend that you follow the more conservative guideline in cases of doubt.

As each set of Specialty Guidelines and Soisson et al. point out, clients have a right to have access to the information in their files. The laws spelling out the exact nature of this right varies from state to state and from agency type to agency type (Haas & Malouf, 1995). For example, agencies receiving federal or state funding may be governed by quite different laws than are agencies (or independent practitioners) that do not receive such funding. The ethical responsibility is to allow clients to know what is in their files, although there is no ethical requirement to show the client every piece of paper in the file. Particularly if the agency receives federal funding, there may be a *legal* requirement that the client be shown his or her file upon request. There are typically exceptions if the therapist has strong reason to believe that allowing the client complete and immediate access to his or her file would jeopardize the client's well-being. Although clients have both ethical and legal rights regarding access, it should be emphasized that the therapist has an ethical responsibility to exercise good clinical judgment. For example, almost certainly it would be considered unethical to give clients files containing extensive technical notes likely to upset them, and immediately leave the room and not provide explanation. Naturally, you should be familiar with the laws of your state concerning this matter, as well as any guidelines currently being used by the agency where you are working.

Finally, with regard to this issue of record keeping, we underscore the potential clinical significance of clients asking (or demanding) to see the contents of their file. As we said above, clients certainly have legal rights in this area. Nonetheless, it is important to try to understand in a nondefensive way what clients are concerned about when they make such a request. Some clients may be legitimately concerned about legal issues, wondering about the kind of information that may be available to their insurance company, or concerned about some other important aspect related to their records. Other clients may actually be more interested in hearing from you what your impressions are of them, but they may be afraid to ask or be more comfortable with a "legal approach." In such instances, the nature of your relationship with the client is the real issue and should be processed. It is very important to remember that not every client request or demand represents a hidden challenge to, or implicit criticism of, the therapist. Clients will, from time to time, take positions with which we are in disagreement. This is as it should be and clients who raise potential differences with us must be respected for their positions, even as we carefully consider the clinical or deeper meaning of those differences.

Malpractice

Malpractice in psychotherapy has been described by a number of writers (e.g., Appelbaum & Gutheil, 1991; VandeCreek, Knapp, & Herzog, 1987). To prove malpractice, the person filing the case must show four things: (a) that the defendant owed a "duty" to the plaintiff (this is normally established by pointing to the existence of the therapeutic relationship); (b) that the defendant failed to perform the duty (established by showing that the defendant failed to provide a standard of care expected of someone with similar training and experience); (c) that the plaintiff suffered harm (this might be either physical or psychological damage); and (d) that the defendant was the direct and proximate cause of the damage. In particular, the last of these four can be very difficult to prove since psychotherapists chiefly use words as their mode of intervention.

A number of "grounds" for malpractice have been identified including: (a) unauthorized release of information; (b) negligent treatment of suicidal or aggressive patients; (c) a sexual relationship between patient and therapist; (d) failure to diagnose properly; (e) improper hospitalization; (f) failure to keep adequate records; and (g) failure to treat properly (Deardorff, Cross, & Hupprich, 1984; Soisson, et al., 1987). Appelbaum (1993) has discussed some of the legal liability issues that may arise with managed care.

Duty to Warn and Protect

The most famous of all legal cases involving psychotherapy is commonly referred to as the Tarasoff case, previously mentioned. In reality this case involved two different decisions which are called Tarasoff I and Tarasoff II (*Tarasoff v. Regents of the University of California,* 118 Cal. Rptr. 129, 529 P.2d533 [1974]; *Tarasoff v. Regents of the University of California* 17 Cal.3d 425 551 P.2d 334 [1976]). This case has been described and discussed frequently (e.g. Fulero, 1988; VandeCreek & Knapp, 1993). Since the case has been so widely publicized, we will not review the details; but to summarize, a client threatened (during a psychotherapy session) to kill his "girlfriend," and subsequently carried out the threat. Although the therapist informed the campus police of the threat, he did not warn the "intended victim." For this "failure to warn," the defendants were found negligent. From this first finding by the court, called Tarasoff I, a now rather famous quote came: "The protective privilege ends where the public peril begins." Informally the court finding produced what came to be called the "duty to warn." Since 1974, countless counselors and therapists in training have undoubtedly been told that they have a legal responsibility to break confidentiality and to warn individuals whose lives have been threatened by a client. In actuality, one's duty may be much greater than merely "warning" the intended victim. Tarasoff II suggested that psychotherapists have a duty to *protect* intended victims. This duty presumably extends one's obligations to actions such as initiating commitment proceedings.

The decision about when to break confidentiality if danger to others seems possible is a very difficult one. Consultation with peers is highly recommended. Consultation with an attorney may also be appropriate. Clearly, every threat made by all clients cannot be acted upon by breaking confidentiality. Some issues that must be taken into consideration include the specificity of the threat (that is, is the intended victim clearly identified or easily identified by logic?), options available to the therapist (e.g., if the individual is psychotic, medication, or more medication, if applicable, may be possible [Mills, 1985]); previous violent actions by the client; available means to carry out the threat (e.g., if the client threatens to use a gun, does he or she own one?); and presence or absence of evidence as to whether the client's impulse control is deteriorating. There is an evolving legal literature on the conditions requiring one to break confidentiality when threats have been made; however, the many court decisions are too numerous to describe here; students are encouraged to read one of the available summaries of this literature (e.g., VandeCreek & Knapp, 1993).

Truscott, Evans, and Mansell (1995) have outlined a model for clinical decision making when a dangerous client is being treated on an outpatient basis. Their model emphasizes assessment of risk and assessment of the strength of the therapeutic relationship. The therapist should seriously consider breaking confidentiality if the relationship is weak and cannot be strengthened and the risk is high and cannot otherwise be reduced. Monahan (1993) has outlined a number of guidelines for limiting the risk of legal liability in cases of dangerous clients. A number of other resources are available to help therapists learn more about risk assessment and risk management (e.g., Appelbaum & Gutheil, 1991; Bednar, Bednar, Lambert, & Waite, 1991; Roth, 1987; Simon, 1987).

We emphasize that you should avoid being unduly influenced by the fact that the client has a history of threatening violence but not carrying it out. If the client has never acted on a threat, certainly he or she is less likely (statistically speaking) to carry out a threat now. But do not be "lulled" into the mistake of automatically thinking, "This is another bluff." Violence is very unpredictable, and this may be the occasion when all the necessary ingredients come together.

Subpoenas and Compelled Testimony

From time to time, psychologists (and more rarely, psychologists in training) receive subpoenas or court orders. Such demands made by the legal system may arise from any of several sources including, but not limited to, criminal or civil charges against the psychologist, his or her client, or parties connected to a client;

divorces involving legal disputes, especially when children are involved; and situations in which a client or former client is being evaluated for commitment or release from commitment. Receiving a subpoena or court order can be quite anxiety provoking because of a number of factors including threat of contempt citations, substantial time required to deal with the demands, potential threat to one's malpractice insurance, potential civil lawsuits, potential conflicts with ethical standards, and potential harm to clients. In part because laws governing the procedures to be used to compel, and prevent, the production of testimony and/or documents vary from state to state, it is impossible to make general statements about one's options under such circumstances. However, as a psychologist in training, you should follow the most obvious advice: Except under compelling and extreme circumstances, you should take no action before consulting with your supervisor.

If you do find yourself involved in a legal dispute, it is important to determine whether your supervisor is in fact qualified to help you with this problem. Many excellent clinical supervisors have little experience with the legal system; therefore, it may be necessary for you to obtain some consultation with your own attorney and/or another psychologist, in addition to consulting with your immediate supervisor. If you have any reason to suspect that a case might "develop" some legal issues, you should bring this topic up for discussion in supervision. The Committee on Legal Issues of the American Psychological Association has published an article (APA, 1996) outlining some strategies to use under circumstances involving demands from the legal system. We recommend that you read this article as a first step in becoming knowledgeable about what to do under these circumstances (even though you are not likely to need to act on the information until after you are a practicing psychologist).

Summary

We have commented on several of the ethical standards of psychologists and also touched on some of the legal issues of interest to psychotherapists. A distinction can be drawn between ethical and legal behavior. An action may be ethical but illegal, or, as is more frequently the case, legal but unethical. On the other hand, ethical and legal issues often become closely intertwined, especially in psychotherapy. In one example of how this can happen, charges of malpractice raise the question, as they inevitably do, of whether the therapist has violated the standard of care—that is, whether the therapist did something that other psychotherapists would not normally do, or failed to do something other therapists normally would do. When these failures involve areas of ethical concern (such as in multiple relationships), ethical and legal issues cannot be completely separated.

Ethical principles are important both because they represent a special set of values in which we believe deeply, and also because they help lay the foundation for effective psychotherapy. We have emphasized the broadness of one's ethical responsibilities. One's duty is not merely to avoid making mistakes, but also to be proactive. In particular, keeping up with new developments in the field and being sensitive to ethnic, gender, and lifestyle issues as they may affect diagnoses and psychotherapy are examples of our responsibility to be proactive.

DISCUSSION QUESTIONS

- When considering an ethical dilemma, have you ever asked yourself what some-one you respect a great deal would do in that situation? In what way does such a process assist you differently than consulting the APA *Ethics Code?*

- How do you make the decision about whether you are competent to see a particu-lar client?

- When two standards of the APA *Ethics Code* appear to be in conflict, how do you go about resolving the conflict?

- Go back and reread the two scenarios at the beginning of the chapter. How do your personal feelings about the situations affect how you think about an ethical course of action?

- When was the last time you felt angry because you thought someone had violated an ethical ideal in which you believe? What was it that made you the angriest about the perceived violation?

- When was the last time *you* violated an ethical ideal in which you believe? What does it feel like when you conclude that you have violated one of your ethical standards?

- Would you say that you are more or less ethical than the average counseling or psychology graduate student? How do you believe that your fellow students will answer this question?

- Do you believe that the APA ethical standards should be applicable to all psychol-ogists regardless of their cultural or ethnic backgrounds and regardless of the cul-tural or ethnic backgrounds of their clients? Why or why not?

BIBLIOGRAPHY

American Association of Marital and Family Ther-apy (AAMFT). (1991). *Code of ethics* (Rev. ed.). Washington, DC: Author.

American Counseling Association (ACA). (1995). *Code of ethics and standards of practice.* Alexan-dria, VA: Author.

American Educational Research Association (AERA), American Psychological Association, & Na-tional Council on Measurement in Education.

(1985). *Standards for educational and psychologi-cal testing.* Washington, DC: American Psycho-logical Association.

American Psychiatric Association. (1995). *Principles of medical ethics with annotations especially appli-cable to psychiatry.* Washington, DC: Author.

American Psychological Association. (1981). *Specialty guidelines for the delivery of services: Clinical psychologists, counseling psychologists, industrial/*

organizational psychologists, school psychologists. Washington, DC: Author.

American Psychological Association. (1986). *Guidelines for computer-based tests and interpretations.* Washington, DC: Author.

American Psychological Association. (1987). *General guidelines for providers of psychological services.* Washington, DC: Author.

American Psychological Association. (1992). Ethical principles of psychologists and code of conduct. *American Psychologist, 47,* 1597–1611.

American Psychological Association, Committee on Legal Issues. (1996). Strategies for private practitioners coping with subpoenas or compelled testimony for client records or test data. *Professional Psychology: Research and Practice, 27,* 245–251.

American Psychological Association, Task Force on Sex Bias and Sex Role Stereotyping in Psychotherapeutic Practice. (1978). Guidelines on therapy with women. *American Psychologist, 33,* 1122–1123.

Anderson, S. K. (1996). Nonromantic/nonsexual relationships with former clients: Implications for psychologists' training. In K. Kitchener (Chair), *Training of ethical psychologists— Implications of current research.* Symposium conducted at the annual meeting of the American Psychological Association, Toronto, Canada.

Anderson, S. K., & Kitchener, K. (1996). Nonromantic, nonsexual posttherapy relationships between psychologists and former clients: An exploratory study of critical incidents. *Professional Psychology: Research and Practice, 27,* 59–66.

Anderson, S. K., & Kitchener, K. (1998). Nonsexual posttherapy relationships: A conceptual framework to assess ethical risks. *Professional Psychology: Research and Practice, 29,* 91–99.

Anouilh, J. (1960). *Becket.* New York: New American Library.

Appelbaum, P. S. (1993). Legal liability and managed care. *American Psychologist, 48,* 251–257.

Appelbaum, P. S., & Gutheil, T. G. (1991). *Clinical handbook of psychiatry and the law* (2nd ed.). Baltimore: Williams & Wilkins.

Beauchamp, T. L., & Childress, J. F. (1994). *Principles of biomedical ethics* (4th ed.). New York: Oxford University Press.

Bednar, R., Bednar, S., Lambert, M., & Waite, D. (1991). *Psychotherapy with high-risk clients: Legal and professional standards.* Pacific Grove, CA: Brooks/Cole.

Bersoff, D. N. (1995). *Ethical conflicts in psychology.* Washington, DC: American Psychological Association.

Bersoff, D. N. (1996). The virtue of principle ethics. *The Counseling Psychologist, 24,* 86–91.

Betan, E. J. (1997). Toward a hermeneutic model of ethical decision making in clinical practice. *Ethics & Behavior, 7,* 347–365.

Bowers, M. A. (1995). *The influence of consultation on ethical decision making.* Unpublished doctoral dissertation, Auburn University, Auburn.

Burke, C. A. (1995). Until death do us part: An exploration into confidentiality following the death of a client. *Professional Psychology: Research and Practice, 26,* 278–280.

Canter, M., Bennett, B. E., Jones, S. E., & Nagy, T. F. (1994). *Ethics for psychologists: A commentary on the APA ethics code.* Washington, DC: American Psychological Association.

Corey, G., Corey, M. S., & Callanan, P. (1998). *Issues and ethics in the helping professions.* Pacific Grove, CA: Brooks/Cole.

Daniel, J. H. (1994) Exclusion and emphasis reframed as a matter of ethics. *Ethics & Behavior, 4,* 229–235.

Deardorff, W. W., Cross, H. J., & Hupprich, W. R. (1984). Malpractice liability in psychotherapy: Client and practitioner perspectives. *Professional Psychology: Research and Practice, 15,* 590–600.

DeBell, C., & Jones, R. D. (1997). Privileged communication at last? An overview of *Jaffee v. Redmond. Professional Psychology: Research and Practice, 28,* 559–566.

Everstine, L., Everstine, D. S., Heymann, G. M., True, R. H., Frey, D. H., Johnson, H. G., & Seiden, R. H. (1980). Privacy and confidentiality in psychotherapy. *American Psychologist, 35,* 828–840.

Fisher, C. B., & Younggren, J. N. (1997). The value and utility of the 1992 Ethics Code. *Professional Psychology: Research and Practice, 28,* 582–592.

Fly, B. J., van Bark, W. P., Weinman, L., Kitchener, K. S., & Lang, P. R. (1997). Ethical transgressions of psychology graduate students: Critical incidents with implications for training. *Professional Psychology: Research and Practice, 28,* 492–495.

Forester-Miller, H., & Davis, T. E. (1995). *A practitioner's guide to ethical decision-making.* Alexandria, VA: American Counseling Association.

Fulero, S. M. (1988). Tarasoff: 10 years later. *Professional Psychology: Research and Practice, 19,* 184–187.

Gilligan, C. (1982). *In a different voice.* Cambridge, MA: Harvard University Press.

Glaser, R. D., & Thorpe, J. S. (1986). Unethical intimacy: A survey of sexual contact and advances between psychology educators and female graduate students. *American Psychologist, 41,* 43–51.

Glosoff, H. L., Herlihy, S. B., Herlihy, B., & Spence, E. B. (1997). Privileged communication in the psychologist-client relationship. *Professional Psychology: Research and Practice, 28,* 573–581.

Gottlieb, M. C. (1993). Avoiding exploitive dual relationships: A decision-making model. *Psychotherapy, 30,* 41–48.

Greenberg, S. A., & Shuman, D. W. (1997). Irreconcilable conflict between therapeutic and forensic roles. *Professional Psychology: Research and Practice, 28,* 50–57.

Haas, L. J., & Malouf, J. L. (1995). *Keeping up the good work: A practitioner's guide to mental health ethics* (2nd ed.). Sarasota, FL: Professional Resource Exchange.

Handelsman, M. M., & Galvin, M. D. (1988). Facilitating informed consent for outpatient psychotherapy: A suggested written format. *Professional Psychology: Research and Practice, 19,* 223–225.

Handelsman, M. M., Kemper, M. B., Kesson-Craig, P., McLain, J., & Johnsrud, C. (1986). Use, content, and readability of written informed consent forms for treatment. *Professional Psychology: Research and Practice, 17,* 514–518.

Harding, A., Gray, L., & Neal, M. (1993). Confidentiality limits with clients who have HIV: A review of ethical and legal guidelines and professional policies. *Journal of Counseling and Development, 66,* 219–223.

Hare-Mustin, R. T., Marecek, J., Kaplan, A. G., & Liss-Levenson, N. (1979). Rights of clients, responsibilities of therapists. *American Psychologist, 34,* 3–16.

Herlihy, B., & Corey, G. (1992). *Dual relationships in counseling.* Alexandria, VA: American Association for Counseling and Development.

Herlihy, B., & Corey, G. (1996). *ACA ethical standards casebook* (5th ed.). Alexandria, VA: American Counseling Association.

Herlihy, B., & Corey, G. (1997). *Boundary issues in counseling: Multiple roles and responsibilities.* Alexandria, VA: American Counseling Association.

Herman, J. L. (1994). Reply to Daniel's "Exclusion and emphasis reframed as a matter of ethics." *Ethics & Behavior, 4,* 237.

Ibrahim, F. A. (1996). A multicultural perspective on principle and virtue ethics. *The Counseling Psychologist, 24,* 78–85.

Jordan, A. E., & Meara, N. M. (1990). Ethics and the professional practice of psychologists: The role of virtues and principle. *Professional Psychology: Research and Practice, 21,* 107–114.

Keith-Spiegel, P., & Koocher, G. P. (1998). *Ethics in psychology: Professional standards and cases* (2nd ed.). New York: Random House.

Kitchener, K. S. (1984). Intuition, critical evaluation and ethical principles: The foundation for ethical decisions in counseling psychology. *The Counseling Psychologist, 12,* 43–55.

Kitchener, K. S. (1996). There is more to ethics than principles. *The Counseling Psychologist, 24,* 92–97.

Kitchener, K. S. (1999). *The foundations of ethical practice in psychology.* Hillsdale, NJ: Lawrence Erlbaum.

Kitchener, K. S., & Harding, S. S. (1990). Dual role relationships. In B. Herlihy & L. B. Golden (Eds.), *Ethical Standards Casebook.* Alexandria, VA: American Counseling Association.

Knapp, S., & VandeCreek, L. (1997). *Jaffee v. Redmond:* The Supreme Court recognizes a psychotherapist-patient privilege in federal courts. *Professional Psychology: Research and Practice, 28,* 567–572.

Kottler, J. A. (1993). *On being a therapist* (Rev. ed.). San Francisco: Jossey-Bass.

Ladany, N., Hill, C. E., Corbett, M. M., & Nutt, E. A. (1996). Nature, extent, and importance of what psychotherapy trainees do not disclose to their supervisors. *Journal of Counseling Psychology, 43,* 10–24.

Lamb, D. H., Clark, C., Drumheller, P., Fizzell, K., & Surrey, L. (1989). Applying Tarasoff to AIDS-related psychotherapy issues. *Professional Psychology: Research and Practice, 20,* 37–43.

Lamb, D. H., Strand, K. K., Woodburn, J. R., Buchko, K. J., Lewis, J. T., & Kang, J. R. (1994). Sexual and business relationships between therapists and former clients. *Psychotherapy, 31,* 270–278.

McGuire, J. M., Nieri, D., Abbot, D., Sheridan, K., & Fisher, R. (1995). Do Tarasoff principles apply in AIDS-related psychotherapy? Ethical decision making and role of the therapist homophobia and perceived client dangerousness. *Professional Psychology: Research and Practice, 26,* 608–611.

Meara, N. M., Schmidt, L. D., & Day, J. D. (1996). Principles and virtues: A foundation for ethical decisions, policies, and character. *The Counseling Psychologist, 24,* 4–77.

Melton, G. B. (1988). Ethical and legal issues in AIDS-related practice. *American Psychologist, 43,* 941–947.

Mills, M. (1985). Expanding the duties to protect third parties from violent acts. In S. Rachlin (Ed.), *Legal encroachment of psychiatric practice* (pp. 61–68). San Francisco: Jossey-Bass.

Monahan, J. (Ed.) (1980). *Who is the client: The ethics of psychological intervention in the criminal justice system.* Washington, DC: American Psychological Association.

Monahan, J. (1993). Limiting therapist exposure to Tarasoff liability: Guidelines for risk containment. *American Psychologist, 48,* 242–250.

Payton, C. R. (1994). Implications of the 1992 ethics code for diverse groups. *Professional Psychology: Research and Practice, 25,* 317–320.

Pedersen, P. B. (1997). The cultural context of the American Counseling Association Code of Ethics. *Journal of Counseling and Development, 78,* 23–28.

Pipes, R. B. (1997). Non-sexual relationships between therapists and their former clients: Obligations of Psychologists. *Ethics & Behavior, 7,* 27–41.

Podrygula, S. (1995, August). Ethical issues: The realities of rural practice. In P. L. Craig (Chair), *Ethical issues in rural practice.* Symposium conducted at the meeting of the American Psychological Association, New York, NY.

Pope, K. S. (1994). *Sexual involvement with therapists: Patient assessment and subsequent therapy, forensics.* Washington, DC: American Psychological Association.

Pope, K. S., Tabachnick, B. G., & Keith-Spiegel, P. (1988). Good and poor practices in psychotherapy: National survey of beliefs of psychologists. *Professional Psychology: Research and Practice, 19,* 547–552.

Pope, K. S., & Vasquez, M. J. T. (1991). *Ethics in psychotherapy and counseling: A practical guide for psychologists.* San Francisco: Jossey-Bass.

Pope, K. S., & Vetter, V. A. (1992). Ethical dilemmas encountered by members of the American Psychological Association: A national survey. *American Psychologist, 47,* 397–411.

Rave, E. J., & Larsen, C. C. (Eds.). (1995). *Ethical decision making in therapy: Feminist perspectives.* New York: Guilford.

Remley, T. P., Herlihy, B., & Herlihy, S. B. (1997). The U.S. Supreme Court decision in *Jaffe v. Redmond*: Implications for counselors. *Journal of Counseling and Development, 75,* 213–218.

Robinson, W. L., & Reid, P. T. (1985). Sexual intimacies in psychology revisited. *Professional Psychology: Research and Practice, 16,* 512–520.

Roth, L. (1987). *Clinical treatment of the violent person.* New York: Guilford.

Sanchez, W., & Nuttall, E. V. (1995). It's about time! *Ethics & Behavior, 5,* 355–358.

Sank, L. I. (1997). Taking on managed care: One reviewer at a time. *Professional Psychology: Research and Practice, 28,* 548–554.

Schank, J. A., & Skovholt, T. M. (1997). Dual-relationship dilemmas of rural and small-community psychologists. *Professional Psychology: Research and Practice, 28,* 44–49.

Schoener, G. R., Milgrom, J. H., Gonsiorek, J. C., Luepker, E. T., & Conroe, R. M. (1989). *Psychotherapists' sexual involvement with clients: Intervention and prevention.* Minneapolis, MN: Walk-In Counseling Ctr.

Sharkin, B. S. (1995). Strains on confidentiality in college-student psychotherapy: Entangled therapeutic relationships, incidental encounters, and third-party inquiries. *Professional Psychology: Research and Practice, 26,* 184–189.

Simon, R. (1987). *Clinical psychiatry and the law.* Washington, DC: American Psychiatric Press.

Simon, R. I. (1992). Treatment of boundary violations: Clinical, ethical and legal considerations. *Bulletin of the American Academy of Psychiatry and the Law, 20,* 269–288.

Smith, D., & Fitzpatrick, M. (1995). Patient-therapist boundary issues: An integrative review of theory and research. *Professional Psychology: Research and Practice, 26,* 499–506.

Soisson, E. L., VandeCreek, L., & Knapp, S. (1987). Thorough record keeping: A good defense in a litigious era. *Professional Psychology: Research and Practice, 18,* 498–502.

Sonne, J. L. (1994). Multiple relationships: Does the new ethics code answer the right questions? *Professional Psychology: Research and Practice, 25,* 336–343.

St. Germaine, J. (1993). Dual relationships: What's wrong with them? *American counselor, 2,* 25–30.

Stadler, H. A. (1990). Counselor impairment. In B. Herlihy & L. Golden (Eds.), *Ethical standards casebook.* Alexandria, VA: American Association for Counseling and Development.

Strasburger, L. H., Gutheil, T. G., & Brodsky, A. (1997). On wearing two hats: Role conflict in serving as both psychoterapist and expert witness. *American Journal of Psychiatry, 154,* 448–455

Talbert, F. S., & Pipes, R. B. (1988). Informed consent for psychotherapy: Content analysis of selected forms. *Professional Psychology: Research and Practice, 19,* 131–132.

Tarasoff v. Regents of the University of California, 118 Cal. Reptr. 129, 529 P. 2d 533 (1974). (Tarasoff I).

Tarasoff v. Regents of the University of California, 17 Cal. 3d 425, 551 P. 2d 334 (1976). (Tarasoff II).

Truscott, D., Evans, J., & Mansell, S. (1995). Outpatient psychotherapy with dangerous clients: A model for clinical decision-making. *Professional Psychology: Research and Practice, 26,* 484–490.

VandeCreek, L., & Knapp, S. (1993). *Tarasoff and beyond: Legal and clinical considerations in the treatment of life-endangering patients* (Rev. ed.). Sarasota, FL: Practitioner's Resource Series.

VandeCreek, L., Knapp, S., & Herzog, C. (1987). Malpractice risks in the treatment of dangerous patients. *Psychotherapy: Theory, Research and Practice, 24,* 145–153.

Vasquez, M. J. T. (1996). Will virtue ethics improve ethical conduct in multicultural settings and interactions? *The Counseling Psychologist, 24,* 98–104.

Warner, R. (1967). *The stories of the Greeks.* New York: Farrar, Straus, & Giroux.

Weinberger, L. E., & Sreenivasan, S. (1994). Ethical and professional conflicts in correctional psychology. *Professional Psychology: Research and Practice, 25,* 161–167.

Welfel, E. R. (1998). *Ethics in counseling and psychotherapy: Standards, research and emerging issues.* Pacific Grove, CA: Brooks/Cole.

Wilson, J. Q. (1993). *The moral sense.* New York: The Free Press.

Woody, R. H. (1997). Dubious and bogus credentials in mental health practice. *Ethics & Behavior, 7,* 337–345.

Worthen, V., & McNeill, B. W. (1996). A phenomenological investigation of "good" supervision events. *Journal of Counseling Psychology, 43,* 25–34.

Yourman, D. B., & Farber, B. A. (1996). Nondisclosure and distortion in psychotherapy supervision. *Psychotherapy, 33,* 567–575.

6   Intake Interviewing

To try to explain to someone that the weather inside's not good is very difficult.
—a client, quoted in Straker & Waks, 1997

We cannot be casual when people in pain come to us for aid.
—James F. T. Bugental

Philosophy of the Intake Session

The Client's Vulnerability

Perhaps the first and most important consideration in the first session is to remember that the client is usually in a state of vulnerability, hence sensitivity on the part of the therapist is an obvious necessity. It is unfortunately the case that students are sometimes placed in initial practicum settings with little or no training in how to talk to individuals in a crisis. This problem may be compounded by reliance on screening instruments that do not accurately detect psychological problems (Shedler, Mayman, & Manis, 1993).

Even if you have had considerable training, there may be a fear on your part that you will not get through the "intake form" in the time allotted or that you will fail to ask a key question if you do not race "full steam ahead." It is imperative that you remember in this first session that the person who sits across from you is often a person with hopes and dreams that have been dashed. There may also be great fears, gnawing suspicions (not infrequently of the therapy process in general, and you in particular), and towering rage that has perhaps been camouflaged beneath a tranquil exterior. Often these people have come to therapy only under great pressure (whether internal or external) and in spite of the deepest of misgivings. Perhaps they have put aside, for the moment, their abiding fear that no one can help them; or perhaps they have promised themselves that they will make one more effort to carve out for themselves the kind of life for which they long. It is into this emotional whirlwind that the therapist steps.

In many cases, clients have pondered for a very long time (maybe years) whether they will seek therapy. In the intake session, that magic moment that they have so feared yet in which they have placed so much hope has arrived. At such a time, your behavior—the way in which you respond to them—may have a tremendous impact. In such circumstances it is imperative that you remember that the intake questions exist for the purpose of helping the client, not vice versa. We are not suggesting that the questions are unimportant—far from it. Rather we point to the importance of responding with sensitivity as individuals begin the process of trying to explain what has gone wrong in their life. No therapist wants to be guilty of overidentifying with clients; however, it is imperative that what the client is saying is registering with you as important, that it make to you some difference whether this person goes on in pain or is able to change. How you will be able to do this without, for example, making your own self-esteem dependent upon the client's progress, is another question—one of enormous complexity. Nonetheless, we believe that one of the therapist's greatest tools is that she or he is able, with each new client, to resonate to the expressed pain.

We are suggesting that doing therapy involves a process in the therapist that is far more personal than setting out to repair a broken clock. If you can (and do) sit in intake after intake and feel nothing, you probably need either to (a) get in therapy yourself, or (b) get a new clientele with whom you can identify at least a little, or (c) find another vocation. One of the important things therapists must do in the first session is find a part of the client to which they can make a connection. Look for the client's pain, look for his or her vulnerability, look for the fearful person lurking beneath the mask. Those are aspects of the person that will make you want to help. Conversely, if you are consistently overwhelmed by the problems people bring to the intake session, you will of course need to take action on that problem.

Respect for the Client

A word that often comes up in discussing how we treat (or don't treat) clients is "respect" (e.g., Hymer, 1987). As you approach conducting intake interviews, a good starting point is to consider what kind of respect you would like shown to you if you were the client. It is a well-established fact that a significant percentage of clients come for an intake session and then never return. Naturally, there are many reasons for this fact. But one reason most certainly is that clients come expecting to be treated with respect, and for some reason, some are not.

A part of showing respect for clients is to ensure that from the beginning clients be given credit for the strengths they have, including their willingness to come for therapy. There should be an implied promise that they will also get credit for progress in therapy. Naturally, some clients will take every opportunity to degrade their own accomplishments. A few will accept appreciatively recognition of their achievements and strengths; the majority will have some ambivalence about recognition offered by the therapist. To the extent that ambivalence or rejection of accomplishments (as remarked upon by the therapist) are prevalent, a potent therapeutic area has been opened and is thus easily identified by the intake therapist. This is one of the positive outcomes of recognizing the client's strengths. A second is that even when ambivalence is present, a part of the client that is healthy can begin to use this feedback, and to that extent the client will feel respected. Naturally, we are not suggesting that during the intake session the therapist counterpose an appreciation for the client's strengths to the concerns, self-doubts, and personal limitations expressed by the client. To say to a client who has just expressed doubts about his or her appearance, "Well, you look nice today," is an example of an attempt gone wrong to recognize client strengths. A general rule in the intake session is "don't contradict the client."

Therapists often are well-trained to recognize pathology; perhaps less frequently are they attuned to the strengths of the client. It is important to remember that most people, including clients, appreciate acknowledgment of, and feel respected when someone takes the time to notice, strengths such as persistence, commitment, caring, and the like that they have demonstrated. Again, we emphasize that this is not (should not be) a "glossing over" process, but rather reflects the therapist's deep respect for the full person. This recognition of the client's strengths also speaks to the idea of communicating hope and involvement, which we discuss below.

Tarachow (1963) has commented on the importance of giving clients credit:

> ...He thus also gets part of the credit in case he gets well. Never rob a patient of that. If you rob a patient of that credit, you will not permit him to be cured. A patient must be able to take as much credit for the improvement as you do. If the cure becomes something you do to the patient or for the patient, you rob him of something that is quite important and he will certainly resent it. If you take the tack, I will help you, I will do this for you, the patient will come session after session, week after week, waiting for you to cure him. He will bring his body. You are supposed to give him the cure. Patients can become spectators of their own treatment. So, divide the burden, divide the responsibility, divide the credit, divide the blame.... (p. 168)

One example of not showing respect is to communicate that you know more about clients' lives than they do. When doing an intake session, you must realize that *you* are the untutored one—it is *you* who are here to learn and to listen. And if you do that well, if within an informed framework you have a respectful and patient eagerness to know clients, clients will let you know their secrets—they will teach you what you need to know of them, and they will also forgive some of your inevitable stumbling, fumbling efforts to be effective. What we say here is no paean to what is called, among other things, soft-hearted, muddle-headed listening and thinking. If caring for others in even a deep and mature fashion is all one brings to the job of being a psychotherapist, one might as well choose any of several other vocations. Kegan (1982) has described in cogent fashion distinctions between listener, psychologist, and therapist.

> In part, it is a professional helper's persistent recognition that her own meaning for a set of circumstances might not be the same as her client's that leads us to call her

a sensitive listener; her understanding of what goes into the way her client makes meaning and what is at stake for him in defending it that leads us to call her a psychologist; and her understanding of what to do with her understanding that leads us to call her a therapist. It is advisable that before people become therapists they pursue the first two callings. (p. 3)

Thus being a good therapist is much more than listening well. However, in the intake session it is seldom necessary for you to perform heart-stopping displays of clinical acumen; what you first want to have happen is for clients to go away believing that they have been listened to—that their problem has been *heard*. In his short story "Misery," Anton Chekhov (1918/1959) gives a powerful example of one's desire to be heard. A sledge driver, Iona Potapov, tries repeatedly, and unsuccessfully, to tell other people about the recent death of his son. Chekhov writes:

> The misery which has been for a brief space eased comes back again and tears his heart more cruelly than ever. With a look of anxiety and suffering Iona's eyes stray restlessly among the crowds moving to and fro on both sides of the street: can he not find among those thousands someone who will listen to him?
>
> ...His son will soon have been dead a week, and he has not really talked to anybody yet.... He wants to talk of it properly, with deliberation.... He wants to tell how his son was taken ill, how he suffered, what he said before he died, how he died.... He wants to describe the funeral, and how he went to the hospital to get his son's clothes. He still has his daughter Anisys in the country.... And he wants to talk about her too.... Yes, he has plenty to talk about now.

Chekhov ends his story with a poignant scene of a man who cannot find another human being to respond to him:

> He puts on his coat and goes into the stables where his mare is standing. He thinks about oats, about hay, about the weather.... He cannot think about his son when he is alone.... To talk about him with someone is possible, but to think of him and picture him is insufferable anguish....
>
> "Are you munching?" Iona asks his mare, seeing her shining eyes. "There, munch away, munch away.... Since we have not earned enough for oats, we will eat hay.... Yes,... I have grown too old to drive.... My son ought to be driving, not I.... He was a real cabman.... He ought to have lived...."
>
> Iona is silent for a while, and then he goes on:
>
> "That's how it is, old girl.... Kuzma Ionitch is gone.... He said good-by to me.... He went and died for no reason.... Now suppose you had a little colt.
>
> ...And you were own mother to that little colt.... And all at once that same little colt went and died.... You'd be sorry, wouldn't you?..."
>
> The little mare munches, listens, and breathes on her master's hands. Iona is carried away and tells her all about it. (pp. 14–16)

Thus does Chekhov illustrate dramatically the very basic human need to be able to tell one's story.

Communicating Hope and Involvement

If the first thing to remember about the intake session concerns the client's vulnerability and our concomitant responsibility to respond with sensitivity and respect, a second process we must nurture is the one of communicating a certain degree of hopefulness concerning the client's problems. In absolutely no way do we want to imply that the therapist should downplay the seriousness of the presented problem (such an act would represent a lack of respect as a minimum), nor do we mean to suggest that the client should be misled into thinking there is hope where there seems to us to be none. In fact, there may be times at which we would do a client a great disservice by offering certain kinds of hope if the client suffers from a "disease of hope" (Omer & Rosenbaum, 1997). For example, therapists should avoid suggesting to clients who seek (hope for) the perfect relationship that what we offer as therapists may allow them to achieve their dream. Thus therapists must be careful about the *kind* of hope they offer; nonetheless, as Frank (1973) noted, "…unless the patient hopes that the therapist can help him [sic], he will not come to therapy in the first place, or if he does, will not stay long; and his faith in the therapist may be healing in itself" (p. 137). If you are conducting short-term therapy, it is especially important that you communicate hope and involvement. The client must be engaged from the start. Clients who do not get some idea from you that you believe that what you have to offer can be helpful to them are not likely to put their heart and soul into the process. Particularly in short-term therapy, you cannot afford to have clients who have only "one toe in the water," so to speak.

You will find that clients often ask very directly about this issue of hope. For example, they may ask in a seemingly joking fashion, "Well, Doc, is there any hope for me?" or they may be more oblique by saying something like, "I'm not sure I can get better," or "I've just about given up hope," or "I can't see any reason to get my hopes up," or even "I'm tired of trying." In each of these statements the client is in all likelihood, among other things, pleading with the therapist to provide some glimmer that things might be better. This plea is a treacherous pitfall into which many an unsuspecting therapist has fallen. Although experienced therapists differ widely in how they respond to such pleas, the majority probably tread a middle ground so that they do hold out some hope yet avoid being unrealistic (Frank in 1973 noted that success in therapy seems to be related in part to the congruence between patient expectation of therapy and their actual experience in therapy). Furthermore, therapists try in the intake session to resist starting a pattern in which the therapist is expected to assume responsibility for the "cure." Tarachow (1963) has described more than one of the problems that can arise if you give the client a "good prognosis" in the first session. In the following discussion with psychiatric residents, Tarachow reveals a subtle reason for not promising a cure:

DR. TARACHOW: What are the dangers of giving a good prognosis without any reservations or even with qualifications? What are the dangers of giving a prognosis to a patient at the end of the first interview?

RESIDENT: Well, the patient has the need to counteract you, as the person or the therapist; this person may rebel against being helped because it now presents a challenge to him [sic] not to be helped, to show you up.

DR. TARACHOW: Yes that may well be true. A patient who is stubborn and perverse will want to upset your apple cart. On the other hand, a patient may have been afraid to do something. A patient presented himself for treatment; he was afraid to play the saxophone. That was his phobic symptom. In my youthful and enthusiastic fervor I told him, "Why of course, I'll help you play the saxophone." He never returned because I had simply burdened him with more anxiety. He had had enough anxiety while not even touching the saxophone, before he came to see me. My ready promise of a cure was a threat that he would have to play it; he did not return. But these are still not the issues I am after.

RESIDENT: I was going to mention the second point, but you apparently are not after that, that you might frighten the patient. He had mixed feelings about coming to treatment in the first place, as you brought up, and if you promise him a cure this may frighten him.

DR. TARACHOW: Well, all of these things are true and you should be aware of them. Premature mention of cure may be disastrous. But something else is more central and you should be aware of it. It is the following: By the end of the first interview the patient has not told you very much. He [sic] has perhaps avoided telling you his worst problem. He has avoided telling you why he thinks he is incurable. You know, patients have various levels of thinking. While talking to you they are thinking of something else at the same time. With all the completeness that I say we can attain in the first interview, there is still the other factor. The patient cannot tell you all, either consciously cannot tell you or because he has forgotten or because he is ashamed. But for the moment we shall deal with things he consciously cannot tell you. He cannot tell you the things which he regards as his most shameful problems. So, at the end of this interview at which he has not even told you what bothers him most, you tell him that you can cure him. He regards you as a fool, and correctly so, and he need not return to you. The best attitude is to indicate that you think you can help the patient to help himself. (pp. 166–167)

Thus, Tarachow's discussion highlights three reasons for not offering too much: It may raise resistance, it may frighten the client, and more subtly, the client may lose confidence in you.

We shall also note that some clients are asking not just is there hope, but also, how much will it cost in terms of anxiety, psychic pain, and the like. In these cases, for both ethical and legal reasons as well as for psychotherapeutic ones, it is best to tell the client that some degree of cost will be involved. These costs need not be described in rigorous detail (in fact they cannot be reliably predicted), but neither should they be underplayed. Strong commitment to ongoing therapy may actually be made more difficult for the client if we describe the process as easy. It is also important for a number of reasons to give the client the best estimate we have of how long therapy may take. In clinics where there is a limit imposed on how long therapy may continue, this information should also be communicated in the initial session, and of course that factor would also have to be considered along with others in deciding with the client whether this is the place for him or her.

Cultural Variables and the Interviewer

There are many ways in which intake interviewers may be biased or in which they may make errors of judgment based on stereotypic thinking (Spengler, Strohmer, Dixon, & Shivy, 1995) or just plain ignorance. Perhaps one should speak of the possibility of both diagnostic classification bias as well as interviewer bias. Although a comprehensive discussion of bias is beyond the scope of this book, we do want to introduce for further consideration and reading two areas about which the intake interviewer must be concerned. These include gender issues and cultural/racial/ethnicity issues. We are discussing these issues under the broad category of Philosophy of the Intake Session because we believe that from the moment clients walk through the door, their behavior within therapy, the diagnosis they will receive, the way they talk about their life and their troubles, and the nature of the interaction with the therapist are all impacted by clients' cultures (in the broadest sense of that word) as well as by the culture of the therapist or intake interviewer. Furthermore, the very process by which clients reach treatment (source of referral) varies by ethnicity (Akutsu, Snowden, & Organista, 1996), as do the coping mechanisms clients use in trying to solve their problems (Chang, 1996).

Gender Issues

Gilbert (1987) expresses directly the idea that gender is an important interpersonal variable:

> Gender effects are powerful and pervasive. Knowing whether a person is male or female not only is essential to comfortable interpersonal interactions but also often makes a significant difference in how we relate to that person, both within and outside of the therapeutic setting. (p. 555)

At least since the classic study by Broverman, Broverman, Clarkson, Rosenkrantz, and Vogel (1970), there have been concerns about the linkages between gender and mental health issues in assessment. Writers in this area (e.g., Brown & Ballou, 1992; Worell & Remer, 1992) have emphasized a number of problems with the psychiatric diagnostic system, including the disregarding of the environmental context, differential diagnosis based on gender, use of internal pathology constructs, and differential prevalence rates for men and women. Furthermore, sexist attitudes on the part of therapists and the use of theoretical systems that are believed to be inherently sexist are issues of concern. A review of gender differences in diagnosis is provided by Hartung and Widiger (1998).

The key point we stress here is that interviewers must be aware of the ways in which their gender stereotypes may influence their behavior with clients, diagnostic judgments about clients, and treatment recommendations. Furthermore, interviewers should be familiar with the feminist critiques of the diagnostic system itself and be aware of ways in which that system may work to the detriment of clients. For example, it would be very unhelpful to label a woman who stays with her partner as masochistic when her partner has threatened her life if she attempts to leave the battering situation. Similarly, the diagnosis of "borderline personality disorder" is often used with women when a more appropriate diagnosis might be Post Traumatic Stress Disorder. (Brown & Ballou, 1992; Worell & Remer, 1992).

Cultural/Racial/Ethnicity Factors

Padilla and Medina (1996) have addressed what it means to conduct assessment in a culturally sensitive way:

> We believe that assessment is made culturally sensitive through a continuing and open-ended series of substantive and methodological insertions and adaptations designed to mesh the process of assessment and evaluation with the cultural characteristics of the groups being studied.... Assessment is also made culturally sensitive through an incessant, basic, and active preoccupation with the culture of the group or individual being assessed. (p. 4)

There really is no substitute for a good awareness of the client's cultural group, including knowledge about norms and practices that bear on the diagnosis of mental disorder. If you are not familiar with the culture of your client, it is imperative that you receive close supervision on the case. Ethical codes (e.g., American Psychological Association, 1992) increasingly emphasize one's ethical obligation to be competent in multicultural assessment and therapy prior to assigning diagnoses, treating, and so forth. Certainly a part of this knowledge is to be familiar with the cultural aspects of the most widely used diagnostic system in the United States, that embodied in the Diagnostic and Statistical Manual of Mental Disorders, Fourth Edition (DSM-IV; American Psychiatric Association, 1994).

One reflection of the profession's increasing awareness of the importance of culture is the DSM-IV's emphasis on cultural aspects of many of the diagnostic categories. Here are three examples from the DSM-IV:

> **Delusional Disorder (297.1):** An individuals's cultural and religious background must be taken into account in evaluating the possible presence of Delusional Disorder. Some cultures have widely held and culturally sanctioned beliefs that might be considered delusional in other cultures. (pp. 298–299)
> **Depersonalization Disorder (300.6):** Voluntarily induced experiences of depersonalization or derealization form part of meditative and trance practices that are prevalent in many religions and cultures and should not be confused with Depersonalization Disorder. (p. 488)

Avoidant Personality Disorder (301.82): There may be variation in the degree to which different cultural and ethnic groups regard diffidence and avoidance as appropriate. Moreover, avoidant behavior may be the result of problems in acculturation following immigration. (p. 663)

Although all descriptions of the diagnostic categories in the DSM-IV do not have information about cultural variables, as the examples show, a number do, and this trend represents improvement. The DSM-IV also includes an Axis (Axis IV: "Psychosocial and Environmental Problems") where conditions often relevant to clients of diverse cultures can be noted, including problems of the social environment (e.g., acculturation issues and discrimination), housing problems, economic problems, and problems with access to health care services.

Finally, the DSM-IV also contains an "Outline for Cultural Formulations and Glossary of Culture-Bound Syndromes." Thus, even though its level of specificity is perhaps still lacking in the multicultural area for some diagnoses, the DSM-IV is a clear improvement over its predecessors in terms of sensitivity to cultural issues (Smart & Smart, 1997).

Assessment of individuals from diverse ethnic and cultural groups (e.g., Dana, 1993; Harris & Kuba, 1997; Suzuki, Meller, & Ponterotto, 1996) may be complicated by a number of factors, including language differences (Yansen & Shulman, 1996), racial identity (e.g., Helms, 1995; Kohatsu & Richardson, 1996), acculturation status (Carter, Sbrocco, & Carter, 1996), and the assessor's bias or ignorance concerning the culture of the client (American Psychological Association, 1993), or lack of knowledge about research in the area of psychotherapy with culturally diverse populations (e.g., Friedman, 1994; Sue, Zane, & Young, 1994). (See also, Ladany, Inman, Constantine, & Hofheinz, 1997; Ridley, Mendoza, Kantiz, Angermeier, & Zenk, 1994.) For example, Carter, Sbrocco, and Carter have suggested that the interaction of racial identity and acculturation may have important implications for epidemiology and treatment response of African Americans.

Although specific recommendations concerning the assessment of clients from diverse cultures are beyond the scope of this book, we want to emphasize that assumptions made about one cultural group do not necessarily generalize to other groups. We also strongly advise that you not read one or two articles about assessment with a particular ethnic group—for example, African Americans—and then conclude that you are ready to do assessments of African American clients. Reviews of the research literature (e.g., Sue, Zane, & Young, 1994) clearly show that drawing general conclusions based on research findings is a very risky undertaking. A part of the reason that generalizations are so risky is that there are wide differences *within* all cultural groups and that social class and other social variables often interact with ethnic and cultural variables. The fine line that must be tread by the interviewer lies between general knowledge of the cultural or ethnic group on the one side and sensitivity to individual differences on the other. To summarize, there is no substitute for a "variety of awareness": the client's culture, culturally sensitive assessment instruments, your own identity in terms of ethnicity, your biases, the limitations of the diagnostic system, and research in the area of multicultural assessment and multicultural psychotherapy.

Overview of the First Session

Aside from being sensitive to the client's vulnerability and the client's cultural environment, one of the more important things to consider in the first session is that the intake is a time during which clients have an opportunity to "present" themselves in any of many ways. Kelly, Kahn, and Coulter (1996) concluded that "…although clients may be willing to present themselves as low in well-being to their counselor, they may try to look like good people" (p. 300). Thus, the self-presentation aspects of the intake interview must never be too far from your mind.

In most mental health settings, clients who present themselves for treatment are first and routinely assigned to an individual for an intake interview. Who does the interview, how thorough it is, over what period of time it extends, the uses to which the information will be put, whether the person doing the intake will also be the client's therapist, whether the intake will include tests, and the overall purpose of the intake interview are all issues that depend in large measure on the type of agency and the policies of that agency. Expressed another way, there is tremendous variation both between agency types (for example, community mental health center versus a Veterans Administration Medical Center) and within any given type (for example, private practitioners vary widely among themselves in terms of what they do and don't cover in an intake session). Obviously, the theoretical orientation of the person doing the initial interview will also impact the form and content of the interaction. Thus, it would be erroneous and misleading to speak of *the* intake interview. Roughly speaking, this chapter will describe intake interviewing as practiced at many community mental health centers and some university counseling centers. When we come to the part of the chapter that describes the topics to be covered in an intake interview, we will be describing an outline that is a composite of outlines used at agencies of various types. There are a number of chapters and books that you might find helpful in learning to do intake interviews (e.g., Akiskal & Akiskal, 1994; Hersen & Turner, 1994; Morrison, 1995b; Othmer & Othmer, 1994a; Othmer & Othmer, 1994b; Sommers-Flanagan & Sommers-Flanagan, 1993; Turner & Hersen, 1994). A discussion of complex differential diagnoses is beyond the scope of this book.

Many clinics require that the intake therapist assign clients a diagnostic category from the DSM-IV. Because psychiatric diagnoses are used and discussed in so many settings and university courses, we recommend that students purchase a copy of this reference book. If you are unfamiliar with the DSM-IV, there are a number of relevant training guides and casebooks (e.g., Frances, First, & Pincus, 1994; Spitzer, Gibbon, Skodol, Williams, & First, 1994).

Clinics with a primary theoretical orientation to the exclusion of other orientations will typically encourage or mandate a specific type of intake. The most obvious of these would be a clinic specializing in behavior therapy. If your placement is in a specialty clinic (other examples might include alcoholism treatment facilities and family therapy clinics), you will presumably have had some previous training/coursework readying you for such a placement. This chapter will not attempt to cover specialty intakes.

During the intake there are at least a few things to be determined and accomplished that do not generally depend on clinic orientation or even policy guidelines, since all organizations/centers offering therapy do share some commonalities. For example, no matter where you work, one of the things you naturally are trying to ascertain during the first session is the nature of the presenting complaint. We will discuss this particular aspect of the intake interview when we give a comprehensive outline. At this point we will mention two things all intake sessions typically should include.

Is Psychotherapy (at This Agency)
What the Client Needs/Wants?

One important outcome of an intake session is that you as the therapist should have some idea about whether the individual is in the right place for the help she or he is seeking. A part of answering the question is, of course, predicated on finding out for what the client is asking. If a client wants her husband to stop beating her, she may need a therapist but she may also only need an attorney and/or the police. If a client is seeking biofeedback, there is the question of whether the agency provides such a service. If a client wants to be in a group because he is lonely, the clinic may or may not be the place for him. If the client abuses drugs and alcohol, the alcoholism treatment program may or may not be appropriate.

It is also important to note that clients, even in cases that seem fairly straightforward to us, do not always know how to ask for what they want or may be initially reticent to be specific. In such cases clients may go on and on about a problem, for example, how upset they are about their job, when all they really want is information about career options. As therapists, we are rightly skeptical when an individual makes what at first seems to be a simple request for help related to problems we see as complex. We should also be careful, however, to do our best to find out what the client is asking for before we plunge in deeply to assess the problem. Thus, there are at least three reasons why we should not be too quick to come to a decision about what the problem is: (a) clients may have little insight about what is really bothering them and be trying to solve the wrong problem; (b) clients may consciously or unconsciously be holding back on telling you the real problem as they see it because they are fearful; (c) clients may not even be asking for what we think they are asking for—at times we simply misjudge people because we are too eager to "get started."

Of course there are also cases in which clients attempt to intentionally deceive the therapist or in which clients are malingering (Rogers, 1997). A discussion of these issues is beyond the scope of this book; however, common sense would suggest that one might expect these problems more frequently within a nonvoluntary client population (e.g., prison inmates).

We also emphasize that clients' expectations (anticipations and preferences) about their role and the therapist's role in psychotherapy are seen as potentially important ingredients in the process and outcome of therapy (e.g., Tracey & Dundon, 1988). We should also note, however, that some data suggest that expectancies are not related to process and outcome in simple ways (Hardin, Subich, & Tichenor, 1988; Tinsley, Bowman, & Ray, 1988). Garfield (1994) concluded that research interest in expectancies has diminished. Despite mixed results in the research, we nonetheless view the intake session as an important opportunity to discuss with clients their initial expectations about psychotherapy. These discussions may be particularly important depending on client ethnicity and acculturation.

Case Disposition and Assessment of Seriousness

A second important outcome of the intake session is related to the first: At the end of the intake session you must be able to decide, at least preliminarily, what action is to be taken. There are several "subcategories" that fall under this heading. First, we should note that before you can take action on a case you will have to know both the general guidelines used by the agency following intake and also what special supports or services are offered. One model that is widely followed involves having, a day or two after the intake session, a group discussion concerning the case by the professional staff working at the center. This procedure, called "staffing the case," may involve psychologists, psychiatrists, social workers, and trainees. The outcome of the staffing is to decide on a general course of treatment and the assignment of an individual therapist when appropriate.

Another part of deciding what action is to be taken involves an assessment of seriousness of the situation. Circumstances involving suicidal or homicidal threats or ideation require that you bring the case to the attention of your supervisor as soon as possible. If, for example, you do an intake session on Monday with a client who is suicidal or homicidal, you should not wait until a Friday staffing to discuss it with your supervisor. Assessing suicidal potential will be discussed later in the chapter. However, assessment and treatment of the violent (or potentially violent) individual (e.g., Roth, 1987) is beyond the scope of this book.

In addition to the special circumstance of homicide and suicide, another important issue in assessing seriousness is the question of whether the individual is psychotic. Most clinics require or at least strongly encourage the intake therapist to make a referral to the clinic psychiatrist if this is suspected. Cases requiring the utmost care are those in which homicidal or suicidal states are mixed with a picture of psychosis. For example, clients may report hearing voices that tell them to hurt themselves or someone else. (These are called "command" hallucinations.) Later in the chapter, we will outline the mental status exam, which helps determine if a person is psychotic. At this point, however, we will make a few general comments about psychosis that may serve as a review for the reader.

Despite widespread use of the DSM-IV, staffing and supervision frequently focus on more broad categories such as "psychosis." Thus the question is often asked, "Is the client psychotic?" or "Do you see any signs of psychosis?" The exact meaning and intention of such questions vary from professional to professional and from clinic to clinic. In its broadest sense, the term is meant to include any behavior, thought content or process, or emotion observed by the therapist or reported by the client suggesting a gross distortion of reality, particularly if the break with reality appears to be uncomprehended by the client. As the DSM-IV points out, the definition of "psychosis" has varied widely. Even in the DSM-IV, different disorders emphasize different aspects of psychosis. In general, one or more of the following should be present before the word psychosis is appropriate: (a) delusions; (b) hallucinations; (c) illogical thought; (d) incoherence of speech (including more severe, as in the case of nonsensical statements, and less severe, as in the case of tangential statements, inability to follow a line of reasoning, etc.); or (e) behavior that is grossly disorganized or catatonic. Presence of any of the above five symptoms, particularly if severe in form and uncomprehended by the client, generally justifies a broad diagnosis of psychotic.

Another component to considering what action should be taken after the intake session is deciding which staff therapist might be appropriate for this particular client. As we mentioned, some agencies have the staff meet to discuss each new client, and the decision about who will be the therapist is made at the staffing. Other agencies allow the intake therapist to make an assignment based in part on type of problem, client dynamics, client preference if expressed, and on the case load currently assigned to each staff therapist.

One of the long-debated questions concerning assignment of a therapist is the extent to which expressed client preference should be taken into consideration. Some therapists view "preference" as an early testing of boundaries, a bid for control, or as an expression of fear or anger. Our perspective is that if the client expresses a preference in terms of gender or ethnicity, the intake therapist should discuss with the client the basis for the request. Such a discussion may illuminate important therapeutic considerations. In some situations, such as those of sexual abuse (regardless of client gender), we would try to grant the request with no further questions since the basis for the request is quite clear. If the request for a particular type of therapist seems reasonable and can be honored, we believe that it generally should be. In some situations, the intake therapist may suggest that the person rethink her or his preference. Consider the following example of a client initially seeking services for anxiety on the job.

CLIENT (MALE):   I would like to see a male therapist.

THERAPIST: Any particular reason for your request?

CLIENT: Yes. My mother was an alcoholic and I can't trust women very easily.

THERAPIST: It's possible you might be able to see a male therapist. I'm not sure who is available right now. It sounds like you wonder if you could make yourself vulnerable to a woman after growing up with an unpredictable mother.

CLIENT: Well, I think you might feel the same way if you had been through what I've been through.

THERAPIST: Yes, I think I very well might. (*Pause*). Let me throw out an idea. Could it be important for you to work with a woman as a therapist for that very reason? I'm guessing, and it's just a guess at this point, that a part of you would like to learn to trust women with some of the vulnerable things about yourself. So one way to work on that would be to face the challenge right from the beginning. What do you think?

In this example, if the client still expressed a preference for a male therapist, he should be accommodated if possible. Furthermore, if there are clear time limits for the therapy, it would likely be best to grant the request from the beginning, since working through the mistrust might take a long period of time, leaving unattended the client's presenting problem. As we noted earlier, in short-term therapy it is especially important that the client have, from the beginning, some degree of trust in the therapist so that the work of psychotherapy can begin quickly and so that it is not constantly threatened with disruption by a poor relationship. Thus, there are two considerations in assigning a therapist to a client who has expressed a preference: the anticipated length of therapy and the intensity of, and/or objective reasons for, the request for a particular therapist.

If the request for a particular type of therapist seems to be filled with a fair amount of emotion, or if there are other "objective" reasons that might support the request (e.g., if the client requests a therapist of her own ethnicity), then we recommend that the request be granted if possible. In Chapter 3, Client Fears, we discussed the importance of clients' feeling that their problems will be taken seriously, that their values will be shared by the therapist, and that the therapist will understand their problem. Honoring the client's request for a "match" on gender or ethnicity is one way of addressing these concerns.

Another consideration about action to be taken after an intake interview is whether the individual should be referred to individual or group psychotherapy. Assuming that each of these modalities is available, there are a few general guidelines that are generally followed by many therapists faced with this decision. As a rule, clients who are extremely hostile should not be referred to groups because such clients frequently disrupt the group process over a considerable number of sessions. Also, clients who are expressing severe stress likely to result in suicide, homicide, or reactive psychosis should be initially referred for individual psychotherapy. A third group of individuals who should initially receive individual therapy is comprised of persons who are painfully socially anxious. These individuals need to make at least a little progress toward feeling better about themselves before being in group therapy, since otherwise they are likely to retreat so far that they profit minimally from the group. Those individuals who are in the midst of a psychotic reaction should also not be put in groups, and individuals suffering from a personality disorder should be evaluated with special care prior to referral to groups.

Referral following intake will be affected by whether your agency has a waiting list and, if so, the criteria for being placed on a waiting list as opposed to being seen more or less immediately. If it appears that clients must be placed on the waiting list, it is very important that they understand what alternatives are available and what they should do in the event of a crisis while they await an available therapist.

Finally, in terms of disposition, a decision must be made about whether to refer the client for an evaluation regarding the appropriateness of medication. This evaluation, like ones involving psychoses, will usually involve referral to a consulting psychiatrist. The general rule here is, "when in doubt, refer." Clients to be evaluated for medication include individuals who are incapacitated with anxiety, individuals who are very depressed or manic, and the individuals who appear to have a thought disorder or are otherwise out of touch with reality.

Conducting the Intake Interview

Again, it must be remembered that the structure of the intake interview depends heavily on the agency type as well as the theoretical orientation of the therapist. For example, clients being seen for "Prescriptive Psychotherapy" (Beutler & Hodgson, 1993) will have a somewhat different intake procedure than will clients seen by therapists endorsing a strong feminist theory (e.g., Brown, 1994). Whatever your theoretical orientation, however, you can benefit from the literature on the limitations of clinical judgment (e.g., Garb, 1998).

Client Forms

In most agencies, the client will be asked to complete a form prior to seeing an intake therapist. These forms may range in complexity from a "name-address" card to a form several pages in length asking for a report on symptoms, family history, previous psychotherapy, and so forth. If the client fills out any form more involved than "name-address," we encourage you to look it over (assuming it is available to you, and it usually is) for any clues about the client's personality. The carefulness (or lack thereof) with which clients approach this task, items they leave out, the detail with which they describe their problem, and so forth all convey information to you about them. Clients not infrequently use such forms to underscore how they are feeling. For example, if a question asks about age of parents and the client writes, "My mother died 5½ months ago," you can see in the response the energy that is going into struggling about that event. As you look over the intake form, you should be formulating very tentative hypotheses and raising questions in your mind about the client. The point is not to place the client in a fixed category, but rather to begin the process of collecting data that will assist you in being sensitive to clients and their difficulties.

Rationale for Questions

In the intake session, depending on the agency, a large number of questions may be asked. The need for some of these will be obvious to the client. For example, most people coming to a clinic expect to be asked something such as, "What brings you here today?" or "How long have you had this problem?" On the other hand, the client may not have any idea why certain other questions are asked. For example, in a mental status exam (to be discussed later in the chapter), we may ask them to count backwards from 100 by 7s. Or we may ask them the meaning of certain proverbs. Later, after the mental status exam and during another part of the intake, we may ask such questions as, "Do you take drugs and if so, what are they?" or "Have you ever been in trouble with the law?" or "When did you have your first significant sexual experience?" In the mind of the client, these questions may range from the unnecessary to the intrusive. Particularly if they have never previously received psychological help and are not psychologically sophisticated, they will probably not understand why they should be asked these questions if their presenting problem concerns something like anxiety on the job.

Thus, before preceding deeply into the intake, you will need to describe briefly for the client the kinds of questions you will be asking. Our experience has been that this explanation need not (and indeed, should not) take long. One mistake you may be tempted to make is to overexplain the need and basis for the questions. This tendency to go into too much detail comes in part from the training one receives in graduate school, where elaboration is reinforced, and also from a defensive fear that the client may demand to know something more about the questions than we will be able to answer. Or, perhaps one more step removed, we may become obsessive about our tools when we are least confident of our ability to use these tools.

One thing you may wonder about is timing. That is, at what point in the hour should you move into asking the questions you are expected by your agency to have answered by the clients, yet which the client does not seem to be addressing as he or she talks about the presenting problem? The timing will vary from client to client. If the client is in great crisis, you may delay some of the more standard questions that don't seem to have direct bearing on the case until a second session. In some clinics the assigned therapist is expected to complete intakes that for whatever reason were not completed by the intake therapist. We have found comments similar to the following to be effective: "I need to ask you a few more questions that we ask all clients to answer. Some of these may even sound a little strange to you. But we do need to ask them." As you ask questions that your agency requires but which may seem unrelated to a presented symptom, you should look for links that might not have occurred to the client. For example, one intake question we may ask the client concerns interests and hobbies. If a socially anxious client answers, "Stamp collecting, reading, and crossword puzzles," we might say something like, "Are there other interests you have that you can't pursue because you are anxious?" It may or may not have occurred to a client that hobbies may in some sense reflect his or her presenting problem. By linking what at first seemed to be irrelevant questions to the client's problem, we make the intake process smoother, enhance the credibility of the therapeutic process, and begin that process by fostering insight.

Description of Format

It cannot be emphasized enough that clients often come to therapy in a state of anxiety about their life, of fear and distrust about the therapeutic process, and of ignorance concerning what will be expected of—and what will happen to—them. We believe that people who are given some knowledge about what to expect, and who have a grasp of the format to be followed, are more receptive to therapy for two reasons. First, knowledge in the face of uncertainty can have a direct ameliorative effect on the concomitant anxiety. Second, by describing for the client what is to be expected, we communicate our respect for his or her right to know what should and will happen. As in the case of describing the questions for the intake sessions, the description of the overall format for receiving help from the agency should be brief. Normally, the description will include the following: (a) whether the intake lasts more than one session; (b) how contact is to be made after the intake; (c) when the client will know who his or her therapist will be; (d) what procedures are to be followed regarding testing, and in general what testing will cover and how long it will take; (e) a description of any psychiatric consult that seems needed; (f) an opportunity for any questions he or she would like to ask about therapy; and (g) a short role-induction procedure describing in very general terms what is expected of them in therapy (some clients will obviously not need this part of the description, and many therapists prefer not to comment on it except under unusual circumstances).

Some of the clients who do not need to be seen or evaluated by a psychiatrist will be disappointed upon being told they will not see a psychiatrist; some clients who do need to be evaluated by a psychiatrist will be upset by this development. The issue of the working relationship between the individuals who deliver psychological services and the psychiatrist is an important one. If you are not comfortable with this issue, the client's anxieties about the power and status of various help-givers are sure to be magnified by your own anxiety. Thus, when you are getting started, you might want to practice with a fellow student answering questions such as, "Why can't I see a real doctor?" or "Is it really necessary for me to see a psychiatrist?"

In inpatient settings such as VA hospitals, a psychiatrist generally will see all patients who are admitted. If you have been assigned to do intakes in such a facility, the topics you cover as well as the description of the overall format that you will provide the client will vary depending on when the psychiatrist (as well as other treatment team members such as social workers) sees the client and what topics are covered. It is imperative that you understand how the help you are providing fits into the overall scheme of service delivery by the agency.

Mental Status Exam

Depending on the agency, the intake therapist may be asked to administer a mental status exam. In other agencies, this part of the interview may be handled by a psychiatrist. In either case you should be familiar with the components of the mental status exam and have some understanding of how the exam is administered. As we have noted previously, the thoroughness of this part of the interview varies widely by agency. In hospital settings, the examination is usually rather thorough; in private practice it is usually brief if used at all; in terms of usage, community mental health centers probably fall somewhere between these two types of agencies. Also, as noted earlier, we emphasize that cultural factors may greatly influence the responses given by the client. If you are unfamiliar with the culture of the client, you need supervision in giving or interpreting a mental status examination.

We divide the examination into five major parts. Each part, in turn, consists of one or more components. Various components may be left out of the examination in cases where the probability of obtaining useful information is very low. For example, a client seeking service from a private therapist and presenting with moderate anxiety about a job change might not be asked about hallucinations without some evidence to suggest a more serious problem. The five major parts—Behavior, Thinking, Feeling, Data-Gathering Apparatuses, and Symptomatology—are described below.

Behavior

Appearance.   As an examiner, there are two key issues on which to focus. The first is merely to describe what clients are wearing (dress, high heels, etc.) and how they look (neat, disheveled, etc.). The second is to consider whether clients' dress and appearance are consistent with their age, occupation, and socioeconomic status. A student presenting in blue jean cutoffs is not viewed the same as a business executive presenting in the same attire.

Interview Behavior.   Here we are interested in what clients actually do during the interview. For example, is he constantly tapping his foot? Does she sit rigidly erect? Does he smile through most of the interview? Does she speak softly or loudly? Are any speech impediments noted? The concept of behavior also includes the client's characteristic way of interacting with the examiner. For example, we note whether the client was generally cooperative, suspicious, coy, and so forth.

Thinking

Judgment.   When we say "judgment" we are speaking of the client's ability to make effective decisions in both the social and personal realm. This aspect of thinking may be assessed in one of three ways. First, questions from tests such as the Wechsler Adult Intelligence Scale may be used. Examples include, "What would you do if you were in a theater and saw a fire?" and "What would you do if you found a letter that someone had dropped that had a stamp on it?"

A second way to make this assessment is to ask one or two questions of your own making, such as, "If you wanted to change jobs, how would you go about it?" or "If you met a stranger who wanted to borrow $1,000, what would you do?" A third way to make this assessment is to try to draw inferences based on the person's responses to other parts of the interview. For example, in the complete intake interview we ask the question, "How have you tried to solve your problem?" In addition to having therapeutic implications, the answer to the question gives us some information about the person's judgment.

Thought Content.   Quite literally, we mean by this category the sorts of things the person seems to be thinking about. There are several specific types of phenomena in which we are interested: (a) delusions, (b) obsessions, (c) homicidal ideation, (d) suicidal ideation, (e) ideas of reference, and (f) ideas of influence. Cultural factors may influence the reported intensity of, the content of, and the "reality" of delusions, obsessions, ideas of reference, and the like. For example, an African American client may report that his supervisors are conspiring to prevent his being promoted and that they discuss him during lunch hours. This may or may not be a delusion.

If any client reports homicidal ideation, you should, at a minimum, discuss this issue with your supervisor immediately following the session. In the session itself, you should ascertain whether the person has previously acted on aggressive feelings, what weapons he or she is in possession of, whether there is an identifiable person who is being threatened, to what extent the individual seems to be rational, and the extent to which the conflict seems to be escalating. Courts have frequently ruled that you have a duty to protect third parties if you become aware that their lives are in danger (VandeCreek & Knapp, 1993). Because of the potentially conflicting ethical, legal, and clinical issues, as well as the difficulty in predicting violence, homicidal ideation is among the most difficult situations faced by therapists. If you are a beginning therapist, consultation and supervision are a must. If for none other than legal reasons, you are required to take seriously statements such as "I could have killed her," even though your initial impression may be that the statement is nothing more than a metaphor.

We will discuss the issues of the suicidal client in greater detail later in the chapter.

Thought Processes.   We are interested in at least two aspects of thought process: form and rate. By form, we mean both the degree of logic inherent in the apparent stream of thought and, more broadly, the degree to which associations of words, phrases, and concepts are organized and "tight." Loosely organized thoughts may include, for example, circumstantial or tangential thinking. At the extreme end of the continuum would be phenomena such as "word salad," in which one sentence, phrase, or word follows another but appears to the objective observer to be unconnected. The rate of thought is reflected, in part, by rate of speech but is also inferred when clients say things like, "My thoughts are coming too fast—I can't say them."

Intellectual Functioning.   There are several aspects of intellectual functioning that are typically checked in a complete mental status exam. These include: (a) abstract versus concrete thinking (often checked by asking the client the meaning of proverbs such as, "People who live in glass houses should not throw stones," or "A rolling stone gathers no moss"); (b) ability to concentrate (often checked either by memory for digit span or by serial 7s or both); (c) fund of information (checked by asking questions such as, "How far is it from New York to Paris?" or "Name three presidents of the United States after 1900)." It is important to remember that many cultural groups (especially, but not limited to, immigrants), may not be familiar with proverbs used by the examiner and may not have had an opportunity for access to the fund of knowledge assumed by the culturally insensitive intake interviewer. Thus, intellectual assessment (e.g., Suzuki, Vraniak, & Kugler, 1996) is another particular area that must be carefully considered as we assess the culturally different.

Memory.   Three types of memory (immediate, recent, and remote) are checked. Some variations in definition exist, but "immediate" normally refers to a few seconds and may be checked by digit span or by asking the person to repeat the last question you asked. Recent normally includes the last 6 months and remote is anything longer than 6 months. Individuals suffering from an organic impairment may do poorly on this aspect of the exam. Individuals who are anxious may also do poorly on the immediate recall task due to their inability to concentrate.

Orientation.   Here we wish to know whether individuals are "oriented" to person, place, and time. Thus, we ask them if they can tell us where they are, what the approximate date and time of day are, and who they are. Disturbances as to time are seen most frequently, followed by place and person. We expect individuals to be within 1 or 2 days of the actual date, and within 2 or 3 hours of the actual time. Special circumstances may change these expectations, but the great majority of clients will fall within the boundaries indicated, and those who do not should be carefully evaluated.

Insight.   In this category we are interested in whether persons realize that they have a problem and to what extent they have an appreciation for how it came about.

Feeling

Some authors make a distinction between affect (by which they mean level of intensity or degree of lability) and mood (by which they mean general feeling tone of the session). In any event, the mental status exam includes (by whatever name) observing to what degree the client's affect changes quickly (labile affect), and to what degree intensity of affect is or is not manifested.

Data-Gathering Apparatuses

Sensorium.   This category represents our desire to know whether the person's five senses are functioning adequately. Hearing impairments and blindness are examples of phenomena reported.

Perceptual Processes.   The presence or absence of hallucinations is noted. If not brought up by the client, the subject may be introduced by asking something such as the following: "People often have unusual experiences when they are under stress as you have been; has anything unusual happened to you lately?" If the patient says no, but there is reason to believe hallucinations might be present, a follow-up may be added: "For example, some people in crisis see or hear things that other people don't; has anything like that happened to you?"

Symptomatology

We are interested in any psychological symptoms or any physical symptoms that might have their basis in psychological functioning. Because of their severity and/or frequency, one especially notes depersonalization, derealization, phobias, other anxiety states, depression, eating disorders (Allison, 1995; Foreyt & Goodrick, 1994), and alcohol (Sobell, Toneatto, Sobell, & Shillingford, 1994) or drug abuse (Milby & Schumacher, 1994). One should also be alert to the possibility of the client's having been a victim or perpetrator of child abuse (American Psychological Association, Committee on Professional Practice and Standards, A Committee of the Board of Professional Affairs, 1995), childhood sexual abuse (Coutois, 1988; Gold & Brown, 1997; Herman, 1992; Koraleski & Larson, 1997), rape, or battering (e.g., Carden, 1994; Gauthier & Levendosky, 1996). Recent activities that appear to have the potential to harm self or others are noted here irrespective of whether the client has denied suicidal or homicidal ideation.

Formal Intake Interview

We have already noted that the areas covered during an intake session vary from setting to setting. What follows is an outline of a rather complete intake interview divided into five major sections. Although all items in the categories may not be completed in all agencies, most agencies do—in one form or another or under one name or another—cover the five major areas.

Presenting Complaint

One of the most important aspects of an intake session is to begin the process of discovering what brought the client to therapy. We say "begin" because a significant percentage of clients cannot or will not tell you straightaway what is truly bothering them. This does not mean that you should be intensely suspicious of the client's motives; rather it means that you maintain a readiness to discover deeper levels of what the client wants or needs. Whether you do or do not have reason to believe that the client is "holding back" his or her real reason for coming, there are several aspects of the presenting complaint that will need to be explored. First, we are interested in the *duration of the symptom* (complaint). For example, did the headaches start last week, a year ago, or in the first grade? How long has the person been depressed? When was social anxiety first noticed? Second, when possible, we would like to know the *circumstances surrounding onset.* For example, was there a stressful event? Did the symptom begin suddenly or gradually? Third, we wonder about the *degree to which the symptom(s) disrupts the person's life.* For example, a complete DSM-IV classification includes a global assessment of the individual's functioning. Fourth, we look for *obvious consequences of the symptom.* Although behaviorists, among the many theorists of psychotherapy, are perhaps the best known for studying consequences, in reality all schools of therapy are interested in the consequences (outcome, end product, result, etc.) of symptoms. For example, family therapists are often interested in what the symptom does for the family. Psychoanalysts are interested in the motivational state of individuals who have symptoms and thus by inference are interested in what state for the individual is brought about by the symptom. Gestalt therapists are concerned with the process whereby individuals create certain outcomes. The "complete" set of consequences of the symptom will, of course, not be known at the end of an intake session (if ever). Nevertheless, this is the time for both therapist and client to begin understanding, for example, how the individual's problem fits into the larger picture of his or her lifestyle, how the client accomplishes goals, what the client gets out of these goals, and so forth.

Fifth, we want to know *how the person has tried to solve his or her problem.* This information tells us something of the person's resources and coping mechanisms and also helps us identify interventions that might be unsuccessful. For example, the client who reports dissatisfaction with a job and has never brought the issue to the attention of his or her boss represents a situation requiring a different intervention than a person who has had several nasty fights with a superior. Gaining a grasp on how the person has tried to solve his or her problem also enhances the client's belief that the therapist understands the subtleties and nuances of the problem, the difficulties inherent in trying to solve it, and the credit due the client for struggling valiantly. Of course, such a belief on the part of the client is easily destroyed if the therapist suggests (particularly if covertly) the stupidity of trying to solve it that way. Rather than passing judgment, the therapist is encouraged to acknowledge the efforts made by the client. Later, you may be able to suggest an alternative perspective on the problem. In the initial session, however, you have not yet earned the right to help the client. You are therefore encouraged initially to do some struggling yourself to understand how the other person is struggling prior to offering bits of wisdom or interpretation.

Sixth, we would like to know *how the individual came to this particular mental health clinic.* For example, was it a referral; if so, from whom and under what circumstances? Was the person pressured into coming? Has something happened recently to make coming seem more necessary or desirable? For example, has the symptom become more pervasive or intense, or in some way begun to make the person's life more difficult? Perhaps the most typical pattern is for an individual to be suffering from a problem over a period of time and then to have an experience that seems to galvanize him or her into action.

Finally, in terms of presenting complaint, we need to get some idea of *what the person expects in terms of symptom relief or other help.* Naturally, we understand that an individual's expectations and goals may change over the course of therapy. Nevertheless, the initial expectations, particularly concerning symptom relief, are something we ignore at the risk of premature termination. For example, Satterfield, Buelow, Lyddon, and Johnson (1995) found that clients in particular stages of change (contemplation or maintenance; cf. Prochaska & DiClemente, 1986) may have an expectation that counselors will assume responsibility for directing the change process.

Current Functioning and Living Situation

Some of the information of interest in this category should be obvious. For example, we want to know if the person is living with anyone else. Are there children, parents, siblings, housemates? How is leisure time used? Where is the person currently employed?

The ability to locate and keep a job has long been one of the important practical measures of an individual's level of functioning. Furthermore, we note whether the individual's current employment situation appears to be commensurate with education level, tested intelligence (if known), level of aspiration, and other known strengths and weaknesses. Answers to these questions provide a piece of the diagnostic puzzle. For example, individuals who have a dependent personality disorder frequently report stress in their jobs. As we ask about current living situation, we must keep in mind the many cultural variables that may be operating in a client's life. For example, discrimination (Utsey & Ponterotto, 1996; White & Parham, 1990) can have serious and ongoing effects on the client's level of stress. Intake interviewers who are not sensitive to such issues run the risk of making a diagnosis that is quite inaccurate.

Is the person currently suffering from a significant disease? What drugs, whether legal or illegal, are being taken, how often, and in what amounts (for example, how much liquor is being consumed and in what pattern)? In particular, questions about current alcohol abuse should be asked in fairly specific terms. Drug abusers are notorious for denying and minimizing their habit. Therefore, answers to such questions as, "Are you a heavy drinker?" or "Do you have any problems with alcohol?" or even "How often do you become intoxicated?" are rarely illuminating. If you have any suspicions that alcohol abuse is likely, you should ask specifically about the number of beers consumed each day, the number of ounces of hard liquor, or the like. You will need to ask about all categories of alcohol (hard liquor, beer, wine) since a significant percentage of individuals, in an effort to deny their problems, may think of drinking problems as referring only to individuals who consume hard liquor.

When we ask about current illnesses and medications, we do so not out of idle curiosity, but rather because we now know some very important links between the physical and the emotional. For example, diabetics are often subject to fluctuations in blood sugar levels, which in turn may produce irritability and loss of concentration. Long-term use of steroids may produce a type of psychosis. Hyperthyroidism may produce anxiety and panic attacks. We do not want to treat an individual for neurosis when, in fact, the problem lies in the thyroid gland.

Finally, in this category we include questions about recent significant events—job loss, new baby, moving, divorce, death, promotions, and so forth. We ask about this issue, not merely because significant events can help produce symptoms, but also because it is often easier for clients to feel understood when they know you have some grasp of the important happenings in their lives.

Family History

Systems of psychotherapy vary widely in their emphasis, or lack thereof, on the importance of the family in the development of psychopathology. Perhaps even more diverse are perspectives on the role of the family in *ameliorating* psychological problems. In most settings, however, it is customary to get at least a few basic facts about the family of origin. We usually ask (if this information is not asked on the forms completed by the client) for the parents' ages, whether married, divorced, and/or remarried, date of death if deceased, and parental occupations. A question is also usually asked about siblings, how old they are, and their occupations. Also of primary interest is a short description by the client of the family environment during formative years, a brief description of father and mother, and any psychological problems in the family that were noted by the client.

As suggested earlier, if your theoretical orientation is, for example, family systems theory, you will ask many more questions under this category.

Personal History

There are a number of questions typically asked under this category. We need to know whether there was any trauma during birth (especially important are events that might suggest the possibility of organic problems), presence of scars (which may suggest a history of aggression—fights—or accident-proneness and hostility turned against the self), and history of operations and severe illness (which may suggest a propensity to somatize conflicts).

Personal history also includes marriages, divorces, birth of children, legal difficulties, and past drug usage (important in understanding possible organic problems, acting out, and tendencies to retreat or escape from problems). One question that you may want to consider asking routinely is whether the client is currently involved in a legal dispute or has any reason to believe that such a situation might develop. Although we may like to think that we conduct therapy largely independent of legal considerations, you may find your life much simpler when you are dragged into the middle of a lawsuit if you have taken just a few precautions (e.g., record keeping) as a result of knowing that it was a possibility. Custody disputes (always a possibility in divorce with children) are notorious for making the life of the psychologist extremely unpleasant. Custody evaluations require particular skill and training (e.g., Ackerman, 1995; Ackerman & Ackerman, 1997; American Psychological Association, 1994; Stahl, 1994).

An intake session also frequently includes asking for information about the person's development of interpersonal relationships, sexual development, and work/school history. As noted earlier, while asking about interpersonal and sexual relationships, do not make any assumptions about the client's sexual orientation. Also, do not make any assumptions about gender when someone refers to "my spouse," "my partner," or the like.

Finally, we are interested in the individual's perceptions of his or her strengths and weaknesses, how those developed, and what specific events the client sees as having contributed significantly to the kind of person he or she is today. Like other areas of the intake session, a number of the areas just described may be omitted or deemphasized, depending on time available, the personality and complaint of the particular client, and the rules of the agency.

Previous Treatment

It is very important to ask about previous psychological treatment, and there are several things you need to know. First, obviously, you want to know when such treatment took place. Second, we ask about the general circumstances surrounding the treatment; that is, what it was for, living circumstances at the time, and so forth. Third, the therapist should ascertain what specific type of treatment was received (drugs? desensitization? electroshock?) and how long it lasted. Fourth, the client should be asked about his or her perceptions as to the success or failure of the treatment. And finally, you should at least briefly inquire about the client's expectations as a result of having received the treatment. It is important that you ask clients whether they are currently being seen by, or have recently stopped seeing, a mental health professional. In a small percentage of cases, clients who are still in treatment with another professional will seek additional services simultaneously.

In fact, the therapist may spend many sessions slowly discovering the impact of previous treatment; the above questions are not meant to deny the subtleties involved in this process.

Optional Questions.   Like psychotherapy, intake interviewing is in part a creative process. Thus, while there are indeed a number of areas that should be "checked" during an intake interview, the ways in which these questions are asked are not bound by any rigid rule. You will discover, if you have not already, that most experienced therapists have developed particular questions they like to ask in an intake interview—questions they believe are especially helpful in assisting them to understand the client.

You will find it very difficult to learn about such nonstandardized questions by reading books. Seeking out opportunities to observe experienced therapists and asking supervisors to talk informally about how they conduct intakes are two ways of learning about this type of question. To give you some idea of what we mean when we talk about questions that are not part of a standard intake session, we have given four examples below. These are for illustration only—you are encouraged to develop your own creative questions.

Is there anything else about you that we have not discussed that you think I should know? Actually, some version of this question is often asked at the end of the intake. Notice, however, the particular way in which this question is asked. The phrase, "that you think I should know," not merely asks "Is there anything else?" but structures that issue in such a way that the client is made to feel an active part of the therapy. In particular, the client is faced with the dilemma of asking himself or herself what the key ingredients will be in the interchange to follow. Implicitly, the issue of trust is also raised. Furthermore, the client, not the therapist, is responsible for deciding what is important. Such a question, particularly following many questions whose importance are set by the therapist, springs the client–therapist encounter into an entirely different phase. The answer to this question is important and often very illuminating since we cannot hope to ask about all important things in the client's life. Just as important however, is the set of processes set in motion by asking the question.

Is there anything about you that most people tend to misunderstand that you would like me to understand? This question is a variation of the first one but emphasizes more heavily the special relationship between client and therapist. It also raises more straightforwardly (and therefore more threateningly) the issue of vulnerability. Like the first question, it allows the client to teach the therapist about himself or herself.

Finish this sentence: "When I can't seem to get my way I _____." Such a question directly assumes clients' conscious awareness of how they deal with frustration. It also sets in motion a process of thinking about how one achieves goals and gives clients permission to begin thinking about their own needs in relationship to the ways they do or do not act on those needs.

Many people come to therapy after having promised themselves something about how they will be in therapy. Are there any promises you have made to yourself that you would like me to know about at this time? The phrase "at this time" allows the threatened client to acknowledge (to himself or herself) the importance of the issue without being forced to discuss it prematurely. The word "promise" is one most people are at ease with and allows them to talk about threatening material in a familiar context.

We emphasize strongly that these questions are not normally good ones to ask all clients. We encourage you to think of the intake session as a time to "get a few facts," but more importantly also as a time to begin the creative process of understanding deeper aspects of the client.

Dimensions of Interest to Therapists

As we have said more than once, the kinds of "intake" questions one asks, and even the number of questions asked, certainly depend in part on one's theoretical persuasion. Nonetheless, we recognize that legal and ethical constraints meld with what we will call "common clinical procedures" to produce a set of intake procedures common to many settings. Similarly, we can say that there are some dimensions that psychologists, as a group, tend to be interested in when thinking about clients. These dimensions are often implied in academic coursework, but they are often brought into clear relief only when one reaches practicum. Listed below are a few questions that address dimensions of interest to psychologists. Again, the implicit model is somewhat eclectic, but you will find that if you are prepared to address these issues, the questions asked in staffings about the client you saw for intake should not catch you completely off-guard. Put another way, the questions listed below are examples of those often asked by psychologists when an intake session is described in a staff meeting.

1. *How does the client's relationship with one type of person differ from his or her relationship with other types of people?* For example, does the person interact differently with men than women? Does the client have special difficulty with authority figures?

2. *How does the client present himself or herself?* For example, does she appear confident? Does she emphasize her intelligence? Does he present himself as a victim? Does he suggest that he usually handles things by himself?

3. *How does the client handle anxiety?* There are very few if any systems of psychotherapy that do not acknowledge the centrality of the role of anxiety in pathology. Therefore, how the person goes about attempting to control significant anxiety is always important. Of interest are both the intrapsychic processes used by the client (denial, projection, etc.) and the interpersonal ones (retreating, attacking, seeking support, etc.).

4. *Does the client differentiate reality from fantasy?* As discussed earlier, when you are seeing a client, a part of the assessment you are making is an attempt to understand the degree to which the person is "in touch with reality." A slightly different but related question often asked by colleagues when you present a case is something like, *"What is the level of insight for this person?"* Some theorists, for example Ellis (1995) and Beck (Beck & Weishaar, 1995), make the client's ability to think logically about reality, the self, and the future a hallmark of good mental health.

5. *For what is the client asking?* We commented earlier about this component of the intake interview. We repeat it here to remind you that professionals often ask this question in staffing.

6. *What are the themes in the client's comments?* Of course, this question is one that should be asked about all client sessions, not just intake sessions. It is especially important to ponder this question in the case of the individual who presents with several concerns. That is, is there an underlying theme that connects the several complaints? For example, do the client's temper outbursts seem to happen when she or he feels humiliated, or does the client seem to return throughout the session to the issue of feeling inadequate?

7. *What feelings does the client evoke in the therapist?* This sort of question is frequently asked for two reasons. First, it may alert the individual who will see the person in therapy as to potential difficulties in terms of countertransference. Second, and more broadly, an awareness of what types of feelings are being kicked off in the intake interview gives us some clue as to how the clients interact with others and the feelings they help produce in those others.

8. *What has changed to bring the client in now?* We have discussed this issue earlier and mention it again to emphasize that it is a question frequently asked at staffings.

The foregoing questions are listed as examples only and are meant to give you a brief idea of some of the kinds of dimensions in which psychologists as a group tend to be interested.

Assessment and Testing

As we noted earlier, the intake interview is a part of the overall attempt to formulate some understanding of clients and their problems. In the Introduction to this book, we noted some of the issues that face psychologists in terms of assessment. Certainly the intake session is one place where the "rubber hits the road" as far as assessment is concerned. As we pointed out in the Introduction, and earlier in this chapter, assessment is a very different matter depending on one's theoretical orientation. Nonetheless, in keeping with our "common clinical wisdom" approach, we are assuming that the majority of psychologists have a common ground in assessment that includes gathering some data in an intake interview, and that the diagnostic categories of the DSM-IV are considered at least roughly informative by many therapists. In addition to using the intake interview in the pursuit of assessment and a diagnostic category, psychologists also use a variety of other techniques, including objective and projective tests (personality, intellectual, etc.), nonstandardized instruments, observation, client self-report, data gathered from other people, analysis of objects constructed by the person (e.g., diaries), and the like. The tests that are routinely assigned for clients to take vary widely, although Watkins, Campbell, Nieberding, and Hallmark (1995) concluded that there have been few substantive changes over the past 30 years in terms of the assessment instruments typically used by clinical psychologists.

Some agencies have a battery of tests that they administer to all clients, and then a wide range of other assessment instruments that may be administered depending upon the judgment of the intake therapist or a consulting psychiatrist or psychologist. A discussion of what instruments you should use under what conditions is beyond the scope of this book. However, as discussed below, it is critical that you know something about the instruments that will be assigned. Even if you will not be utilizing the results, another professional presumably will. As an intake therapist you need to be able to describe (in general and layperson's terms) for the client the reasons why the selected testing procedure is being followed. Before doing any type of assessment, including assigning objective tests, you should take appropriate coursework preparing you for this endeavor. The few comments we make here about testing are designed to highlight critical areas; in no sense should reading this brief section be seen as a substitute for appropriate training in assessment.

We emphasize again the role of cultural variables in assessment and testing. Ritzler (1996) has noted a number of conditions that can reduce the validity of personality assessment in a multicultural environment:

1. The subject of the assessment is not acculturated to the culture of the psychologist administering the test or the psychologist interpreting the results.
2. The assessment methods are administered in a language other than the native language of the subject.
3. The assessment methods are not sensitive to the cultural background of the unacculturated subject.
4. The psychologist interpreting the assessment results does not understand the cultural background of the subject.
5. The referral question is not appropriate for the native culture of the unacculturated subject.
6. In reporting results, the psychologist does not explain the cultural effects in a way that can be understood by referring professionals with cultural backgrounds different from that of the subject. (pp. 115–116)

Testing Pitfalls

As an intake therapist who may describe testing procedures to clients, you must keep in mind that testing is a sensitive area for some. For almost all clients it may become a problem area if not handled well. For example, it is not uncommon for clients to respond to a request that they be tested with the feeling that they are being treated more like a case than a person. Or they may be offended by what they perceive to be the intrusiveness or irrelevancy of some or many assessment questions (e.g., on the Minnesota Multiphasic Personality Inventory [MMPI]). If prone to paranoia, clients may fear that the testing will "trick" them into revealing things they prefer to leave unsaid. At an unconscious level, some clients may welcome the opportunity to "expose" themselves, yet be frightened by this very opportunity (Schafer, 1954).

On the other hand, if clients are dependent or naive, they may welcome the opportunity to jump headlong into "finding out" things about themselves via testing instruments. Often clients will say something like, "I'd like to take that test that tells you what kind of people you work best with," or "Can I take some personality tests to find out about myself?" or "I want to take the test that would tell what I should major in." In such cases we try to steer a middle course in which the tests are acknowledged as potential contributions to self-knowledge while they are also described as adjuncts to therapy. An obvious general rule is that any client requesting a test must be evaluated closely in terms of whether the test requested is the assessment instrument of choice. Of far greater importance than whether a test is or is not given is the client's motivation for *requesting* it and the client's personality functioning as revealed by the ensuing discussion.

Test Selection and Description

Although this part of the chapter is about testing more than therapy, we include it as a brief reminder since, as we noted, the intake therapist at times recommends tests to be administered.

In terms of selecting tests, there are a few principles that should be followed. First, any written test must be in a language that the client can read and comprehend. This obviously can be a problem for recent immigrants, as well as a number of other individuals whose first language is not English.

Second, never select a test based on some vague desire to "understand" the client. Testing is a form of referral (in the consultation sense). The basic rule in referral is that there must be a referral question—a reason for the testing and assessment. Thus, all tests are assigned on the basis that a question to which we do not know the answer needs to be answered.

Third, no test is assigned that has not been taken by the person assigning it. If the agency for which you work routinely assigns a personality test with which you are unfamiliar, you must make a point to take the test yourself. Obviously, you must also read the manual. Reading reviews in the Mental Measurement Yearbooks is also highly desirable. If you are not involved in interpreting or directly using the results, you may be tempted to shortcut some of the foregoing principles. If your ethical responsibility to know what you are assigning is not sufficient inducement to carry out the recommendations listed, let us suggest that, as a practical matter, other treatment team members, as well as the clients themselves, will expect you to have done so; you may save yourself a great future embarrassment by taking time to do at least the minimum.

Once the test has been selected, there is the question of how to describe it to clients. In most settings, there should be a brief discussion of each of the following with the client: (a) a general description of the instrument; (b) why it was selected for the client; (c) how the results of the test will be used and who has access to the results; (d) how long it will take to complete the instrument; and (e) any necessary description of the administrative procedure to be followed (when the test is to be taken, whether it will be oral or written, etc.). Again, a middle course is to be steered in which one adequately covers the points without trying to provide too much technical information. Special care must be taken with clients whose testing is likely to become a part of a legal proceeding. In those cases (e.g., criminal issues, child custody, competency issue, etc.), test selection is critical and the use of informed consent is also very important.

Occasionally, clients may question you about a test, even going so far as to ask, "Is this test valid?" Under such circumstances, the vast majority of clients are not asking a technical question about validity coefficients, but rather are saying something like, "Will it really help me to take the test?" For example, one student described the MMPI to a client by saying that it had been normed on persons who were mentally ill but was now used more widely. This description is a poor one for a number of reasons; we cite it here as an example of overresponding, which in turn makes the client more, not less, anxious.

Finally, we would like to emphasize that to many clients there is a certain amount of magic in tests; however; your specialty is psychology, not magic. Therefore, avoid describing tests in mysterious terms. Schafer (1954) vividly describes what he calls the "oracular aspect" of the tester's role:

> Still another contribution to the tester's oracular conception of his role may be made by the patient; patients commonly ascribe magically insightful and influential powers to doctors, therapists, and their agents. The tester, when he chose clinical psychology as his life work, may have been seeking just such an oracular role. Testing—or therapy—may be to him a royal road to omniscience—short, broad, smooth, and well-marked. One sees this conception in blatant form in many young graduate students of clinical psychology for whom there is no response they cannot interpret, no contradiction they cannot resolve, no obscurity they cannot penetrate, no integration they cannot achieve. (p. 23)

We encourage you to resist the temptation to assign tests, particularly multiple tests, if you cannot clearly outline how each will be used to benefit the client in therapy. Reasons such as, "So I can get a handle on what is going on" are not an adequate basis for assigning tests.

The Suicidal Client

The comments we make here are applicable to therapy sessions other than the intake session. We include them here because any good intake includes a sensitivity to the possibility of suicide.

Client Cues and Suicide

There are a number of risk factors we use in the evaluation of potential for suicide. There has been a great deal of research on suicide and demographic variables. We will not discuss these at length because contextual and interacting variables are always present in individual cases, making generalizations dangerous. We will mention that for most age groups, men more often than women complete suicide. Caucasian men who are past middle age and not married may be particularly vulnerable.

As discussed at the beginning of the chapter, one goal of the intake session is to make an assessment of how serious the problem is that the client and therapist are confronting. Certainly, if there is a strong possibility for suicide, a serious problem is at hand. How do we approach the issue?

The first thing you need to know about suicide is that if you have any reason to believe that it is an open option for the person, you should do a complete assessment of the potential. An even safer route is simply to ask the client directly about the issue during the intake (earlier in the chapter we listed homicidal and suicidal ideation as a component of thought content). Therapists doing intakes vary as to whether they ask directly about the issue in the absence of cues. Hahn and Marks (1996) recommended that there be routine assessment of suicide risk factors at intake; they found that only 3% of clients presenting at a university counseling center objected to the routine assessment of past suicide attempts. At a minimum, we can certainly say that if cues are evident in the interview, ask! Whether cues are or are not present, asking about suicide is never wrong. Among the numerous myths about suicide perhaps the worst is, "if you ask about suicide, and the person had not considered it, you are putting the idea into his or her head and he or she may go and do it." Without getting into a debate about whether this is or is not theoretically possible, let us say most emphatically that we have never known a good, experienced therapist who was timid about asking clients about suicide. On the other hand, beginning therapists almost always are fearful of asking a direct question unless the client brings it up. It is very important that you work on your anxiety about the issue, for example, by discussing it with your supervisor. As we are suggesting, this myth about suicide is widespread among beginning therapists. Therefore, there is nothing unusual about your fear. You can take solace in the fact that there is, as far as we know, consensus among experienced therapists that asking about suicide does not *cause* suicide. Alternatively, it is entirely possible that by not asking a client about suicidal thoughts, you will lose an opportunity to help prevent suicide.

If you do not routinely ask your clients about suicide, there are some cues that should prompt the question. First, we believe that any person who reports moderate or severe depression should be asked about suicide. Second, a person who has recently engaged in an activity potentially dangerous to his or her life should be considered a suicidal threat (for example, driving a car at a high rate of speed on narrow roads). Third, if the client makes philosophical or abstract statements about life and/or death, this should be considered a cue (for example, "Most people are cowards, they can't face the idea of dying," or "Why should I get upset? Life is so transient anyway"). Fourth, you should be sensitive to any behavioral cues that suggest suicide. For example, get more information if the client "lets slip" something like "I'm making a will." Finally, the client may make vague or not so vague reference to suicide (for example, "I'm not sure I can go on," or "Is it really worth living like this?" or "People would be better off if I were not around," or even "I guess the only way I could get even with them is to kill myself"). If any of the above cues are present, it is the foolish therapist indeed who does not ask about suicide.

Let us suppose that one or more of the cues are available and you ask rather directly, "Have you considered killing yourself?" Let us further assume that the client answers something like this: "Well, once or twice I have thought about it; it scares me now to think about the possibility." This sort of situation, and the many variations of it, call for a further assessment of suicidal potential.

Assessment of Risk.   In this discussion we will mention a number of questions, the answers for which help provide a clearer picture of the degree of risk. We cannot emphasize strongly enough the fact that even when risk for suicide does not seem to be high, the presence of any risk is to be taken seriously.

1. *What is the history of previous suicidal attempts?* The more attempts that have been made and the greater the lethality, the greater the risk when suicide has been threatened.

2. *What is the frequency of the suicidal ideation?* Generally, a person who thinks about suicide once a month is at less risk, all other factors being equal, than a person who thinks of it each day.

3. *What is the nature of the suicidal ideation?* Highly specific thoughts about suicide are considered more dangerous than vague ones. We refer here not to the nature of the plan (discussed below) but rather to specific thoughts ("If I were dead, I wouldn't have to suffer any more; what would be the easiest way to die?") compared to general ones ("Life is the pits.")

4. *What is the typical duration of the ideation?* For most people, thinking about suicide is difficult; when the thought comes into our minds, we tend to block it out or stop it in some way. The person who is no longer able, or who no longer has the inclination, to stop thinking about it is at greater risk than the person still able to block out thoughts after a few minutes. So if every time a person thinks about suicide (whatever the frequency) he or she dwells on it for 3 or 4 hours, that is generally more serious than the person who only thinks about it for 5 minutes.

5. *How strong is the person's ego?* By this we mean such things as how capable do individuals seem to be in terms of resisting dangerous impulsivity, does their rational self-interest appear to be intact, to what degree do they exhibit confidence in their judgments, and to what extent do they appear to be confused?

6. *Is there a social network that the person perceives as caring?* The assumption is made that individuals who commit suicide are not well connected to friends or relatives. Of course the number of casual friends has little to do with suicide.

7. *What is the individual's assessment of his or her likelihood of committing suicide?* For example, we often say something like this: "We have been talking for a while today about your fears that you might try to kill yourself; is this something you think you might actually do or is it more that you are trying to say how bad you feel?" You will find that people give very different answers to this question, ranging from, "Yes, I might do it," to "No, I was just thinking about it; I don't think I would really do it."

8. *Is there a plan?* This question is a must when making an assessment of risk. Any case in which there is a plan is generally considered by therapists to be much more dangerous than a situation involving no plan. On the other hand, just because there is no plan does not eliminate risk, especially for individuals prone to impulsiveness.

9. *Is the plan specific?* For example, "I'd get my father's gun; he keeps it loaded and I know where it is" would represent higher risk than, "I guess could get a gun—I don't know where."

10. *Are the means readily available?* For example, individuals who have collected enough pills to kill themselves are at greater risk than someone who proposes to start saving prescriptions.

11. *How lethal is the plan?* We emphasize that any plan to end one's life is in one sense lethal. Nonetheless, the situation is *very* serious with a threat such as firearms because the outcome of their use for suicidal purposed is so often fatal.

12. *How likely is rescue?* Assuming the same means (let us say, "taking pills when I get home from work" as an example), individuals who live alone and whom no one visits are a greater risk than individuals who frequently have people stopping by to visit.

13. *What has been the person's coping style in similar situations?* Individuals who have had a serviceable coping style in the past but who can no longer use that style are generally considered at greater risk than individuals who still have that option open but aren't exercising it for some reason.

14. *What is the person's perception of suicide on others?* Individuals who say something to the effect of, "Nobody would care; nobody would miss me; the people who know me (or my family) would clearly be better off if I were gone," are considered a greater risk than individuals who say, "Well, I think it would hurt my father and I wouldn't want to do that." When we say that individuals in the former category are a greater risk, we are of course not referring to instances in which people say they don't want to hurt someone but unconsciously do want to hurt them.

15. *What diagnostic category comes closest to describing the person?* We ask this because there are some diagnoses which make suicide more likely. These include agitated depression, psychotic depression, manic-depressant depression, involutional melancholia, and command hallucinations of a self-injurious nature, particularly when combined with delusions. Chronic alcoholism raises the probability for any individual.

16. *Is the person psychotic?* Psychosis, in and of itself, does not automatically imply great suicidal risk. However, psychoses in general make prediction more difficult.

17. *Are there behavioral suggestions of suicide?* We listed this earlier under "cues." Behavioral cues should also be considered risk factors. These include making a will, giving away prized possessions, checking on insurance policies, and organizing business affairs.

18. *To what degree are helplessness, hopelessness, and exhaustion present?* The feeling of helplessness suggests that individuals perceive that they have no control over what is happening to them. Hopelessness suggests that the situation, as far as clients can judge for themselves, will not get any better. The presence of exhaustion suggests that clients have already struggled to the point that they believe they have few or no resources left.

19. *Can the client identify any reasons why she or he wants to live?* Individuals who still have something positive to "hang on to" are generally a little lower in risk than individuals who can think of no reason to go on living.

Each of the above items is relevant to the degree of risk in a given situation. In more general terms, and as a way of summarizing this section, be sure to check the suicidal history, the nature of any plan, the general ego strength, level of involvement with others, and whether there are behavioral indicators present.

When working with suicidal clients, record keeping is especially important (e.g., Jobes & Berman, 1993). Sommers-Flanagan and Sommers-Flanagan (1995) noted that when an assessment of suicidal potential has been made, therapists should document that they have:

> (a) conducted a thorough suicide assessment, (b) obtained relevant historical information, (c) obtained previous treatment records, (d) directly evaluated suicidal thoughts and impulses of the patient, (e) consulted with one or more professionals, (f) discussed limits of confidentiality with the patient, (g) implemented appropriate suicide interventions, (h) provided appropriate resources to the patient (e.g., telephone numbers), and (i) contacted authorities (e.g., police, hospital personnel) and family members if a suicidal patient is at high risk. (p. 42)

Working with Suicidal Clients.   One area in particular that is beyond the scope of this book, but which we believe merits serious attention, is the role of the mental health professional in rational suicide or hastened death (Farberman, 1997; Werth, 1996). These cases may arise in many circumstances, but the AIDS crisis has primarily focused our attention on this area. Issues include complex differential diagnosis and serious philosophical dilemmas. If you have not already done so, we encourage you to do some reading in this area and to give some thought as to your own philosophy about hastened death.

As with the issue of making an assessment of suicidal risk, space permits only a brief discussion of principles for working with suicidal clients. We list a few principles as a way to help you begin thinking about what to do when you are confronted with a suicidal person.

1. *Make an assessment of the risk* (see comments above).

2. *A contract is used by some therapists.* In other words, you essentially ask clients to agree not to kill themselves while they are in treatment with you. If they won't agree to this, you might try for a contract until the next therapy session. Thus, some therapists essentially say, "I'm going to make an investment in you. I'll stick with you when the going is tough. Would you be willing to promise to stick with me?" You will find some clients willing to do this, some not.

3. *Avoid power struggles.* The client already feels like she or he has lost control. Threatening suicide is thus an attempt to get control back (death being the ultimate control, in one sense). The last thing the client needs is another power struggle. If you have a good relationship with the client, this may enable you to engage in more limit-setting with the client; however, research shows that limit-setting has serious limitations when the urge toward self-damage is great (Straker & Waks, 1997).

4. *Offer involvement.* This is the greatest power you have. Don't promise more than you feel or can give.

5. *Take all threats seriously and communicate the fact that you intend to do so to the client.* Unfortunately, you may on occasion hear a person (maybe even a therapist) say, "The client hinted at suicide but I didn't say anything because I didn't want to reinforce that kind of behavior," or "The client threatened suicide but it was obviously just an attempt to manipulate me." We do not believe that such formulations are particularly helpful. Rather, they are often dangerous. It is very important to distinguish between recognizing some of the dynamics of suicidal threats (yes, such threats can be used to bring about desired ends, including "getting attention") on the one hand, and how you will react on the other. Just because we may view a behavior (in this case a suicidal threat) as instrumental in attaining a variety of goals does not mean that we should not respond to it. In any event, we generally do try to help clients discuss all aspects of their feelings.

6. *Make suicide seem real and don't glorify it.* We generally call suicide "killing yourself" so as to make it seem real.

7. *Find out what the client hopes to accomplish by committing suicide.* This will tell you something of the problem and may point toward a solution.

8. *Offer hospitalization if actualization of threat seems likely. Make sure such action is the client's choice, if at all possible.* An individual who is very frightened by his or her ideation may find relief in just knowing that this option is available.

9. *Share responsibility—consult with supervisor and peers.* This can help relieve the pressure even if you don't get any new ideas, which you usually do.

10. *Watch for countertransference; be aware of your own feelings and attitudes about death and suicide.* To the extent we are uncomfortable about death, it will be hard for us to listen well to someone considering death.

11. *Help the client be aware of and focus on the ambivalence.* If the client is discussing suicide with you, he or she has not yet decided to die. As a therapist you must "take advantage" of the ambivalence.

12. *Attempt with the client's assistance to remove means to carry out any expressed plan (e.g., guns, pills, etc.)* This is a simple principal, but one that helps save lives, especially with impulsive people. Obviously, not all clients will permit this action.

The foregoing principles are meant to raise a number of the issues important in working with suicidal individuals. As we said earlier, we encourage you to read more on the important topic of suicide (e.g., Bongar, 1991; Maris, Berman, Maltsberger, & Yufit, 1992).

Summary

The intake session is a critical contact between a client who (presumably) is asking for help and a person who proposes to be of assistance. Although agencies may vary in the degree to which they require information about clients, psychologists generally agree that the first contact must include the following: (a) finding out in at least a general way why the person is seeking help; (b) helping the client ascertain whether psychotherapy is the best form of assistance for the problem; (c) assessing the seriousness of the situation; (d) ensuring as best one can that the client experiences being respected (is taken seriously, is listened to, etc.). Within this framework, much latitude exists in terms of specific questions asked by the therapist, amount of detail sought, and degree to which potentially relevant areas are explored at the initiative of the therapist. Clients in crises should not be pelted with questions from an agency outline. Therapists best proceed with (a) some faith in their capacity, over the long haul, to make sense of confusing problems; (b) tolerance for clients who cannot or will not "lay the facts on the table"; and (c) a commitment to respond with respect and caring for the individual seeking help.

DISCUSSION QUESTIONS

- What are some practical ways to communicate hope and involvement without giving "false hope" or appearing to be insincere?

- Many therapists do not like to ask a great number of closed-ended questions. Which of the many questions described in this chapter do you see as not necessary for an intake interview? Can you think of situations in which you would be sorry if you did *not* ask some of the questions to which you object?

- In your opinion, is it important to know a DSM-IV classification in order to deliver good psychotherapy? If not, what assessment system do you think should be used (if any)?

BIBLIOGRAPHY

Ackerman, M. J. (1995). *A clinicians guide to child custody evaluations.* New York: Wiley.

Ackerman, M. J., & Ackerman, M. C. (1997). Custody evaluation practices: A survey of experienced professionals (revisited). *Professional Psychology: Research and Practice, 28,* 137–145.

Akiskal, H. S., & Akiskal, K. (1994). Mental status examination. In M. Hersen & S. M. Turner (Eds.), *Diagnostic interviewing* (2nd ed., pp. 25–54). New York: Plenum.

Akutsu, P. D., Snowden, L. R., & Organista, K. C. (1996). Referral patterns in ethnic-specific and mainstream programs for ethnic minorities and whites. *Journal of Counseling Psychology, 43,* 56–64.

Allison, D. (Ed.). (1995). *Handbook of assessment methods for eating behaviors and weight-related problems.* Thousand Oaks, CA: Sage.

American Psychiatric Association. (1994). *Diagnostic and statistical manual of mental disorders* (4th ed.). Washington DC: American Psychiatric Press.

American Psychological Association. (1992). Ethical principles of psychologists and code of conduct. *American Psychologist, 47,* 1597–1611.

American Psychological Association. (1993). Guidelines to providers of psychological services to ethnic, linguistic, and culturally diverse populations. *American Psychologist, 48,* 45–48.

American Psychological Association. (1994). Guidelines for child custody evaluations in divorce proceedings. *American Psychologist, 49,* 677–680.

American Psychological Association, Committee on Professional Practice and Standards, A Committee of the Board of Professional Affairs. (1995). Twenty-four questions (and answers) about professional practice in the area of child abuse. *Professional Psychology: Research and Practice, 26,* 377–385.

Beck, A. T., & Weishaar, M. (1995). Cognitive therapy. In R. J. Corsini & D. Wedding (Eds.), *Current psychotherapies* (5th ed., pp. 229–261). Itasca, IL: Peacock.

Beutler, L. E., & Hodgson, A. B. (1993). Prescriptive psychotherapy. In G. Stricker & J. R. Gold (Eds.), *Comprehensive handbook of psychotherapy integration* (pp. 151–163). New York: Plenum.

Bongar, B. (1991) *The suicidal patient: Clinical and legal standards of care.* Washington, DC: American Psychological Association.

Breiere, J. (1997). *Psychological assessment of adult posttraumatic states.* Washington, DC: American Psychological Association.

Broverman, I. K., Broverman, D., Clarkson, F. E., Rosenkrantz, P. S., & Vogel, S. R. (1970). Sex-role stereotypes and clinical judgments of mental health. *Journal of Consulting and Clinical Psychology, 34,* 1–7.

Brown, L. (1994). *Subversive dialogues: Theory in feminist therapy.* New York: Basic Books.

Brown, L. S., & Ballou, M. (Eds.). (1992). *Personality and psychopathology: Feminist reappraisals.* New York: Guilford.

Carden, A. D. (1994). Wife abuse and the wife abuser: Review and recommendations. *The Counseling Psychologist, 22,* 539–582.

Carter, M. M., Sbrocco, T., & Carter, C. (1996). African Americans and anxiety disorders research: Development of a testable theoretical framework. *Psychotherapy, 33,* 449–463.

Chang, E. C. (1996). Cultural differences in optimism, pessimism, and coping: Predictors of subsequent adjustment in Asian American and Caucasian American college students. *Journal of Counseling Psychology, 43,* 113–123.

Chekhov, A. (1959). Misery. In D. H. Green (Ed.) and G. Garnett (Trans.), *Great stories by Chekhov* (pp. 11–24). New York: Dell. (Reprinted from *The schoolmistress and other stories,* 1918, New York: Macmillan.)

Coutois, C. (1988). *Healing the incest wound.* New York: W. W. Norton.

Dana, R. H. (1993). *Multicultural assessment perspectives for professional psychology.* Boston: Allyn & Bacon.

Ellis, A. (1995). Rational emotive behavior therapy. In R. J. Corsini & D. Wedding (Eds.), *Current psychotherapies* (5th ed., pp. 162–196). Itasca, IL: Peacock.

Farberman, R. K. (1997). Terminal illness and hastened death requests: The important role of the mental health professional. *Professional Psychology: Research and Practice, 28,* 544–547.

Foreyt, J. P., & Goodrick, G. K. (1994). Eating disorders. In M. Hersen & S. M. Turner (Eds.), *Diagnostic interviewing* (2nd ed., pp. 241–256). New York: Plenum.

Frances, A., First, M. B., & Pincus, H. A. (1994). *DSM-IV guidebook.* Washington, DC: American Psychiatric Press.

Frank, J. D. (1973). *Persuasion and healing* (Rev. ed.). Baltimore: Johns Hopkins University Press.

Friedman, S. (Ed.). (1994). *Anxiety disorders in African Americans.* New York: Springer.

Garb, H. N. (1998). *Studying the clinician: Judgment research and psychological assessment.* Washington, DC: American Psychological Association.

Garfield, A. L. (1994). Research on client variables in psychotherapy. In A. E. Bergin & A. L. Garfield (Eds.), *Handbook of Psychotherapy and behavior change* (4th ed., pp. 190–228). New York: Wiley.

Gauthier, L. M., & Levendosky, A. A. (1996). Assessment and treatment of couples with abusive male partners: Guidelines for therapists. *Psychotherapy, 33,* 403–417.

Gilbert, L. A. (1987). Female and male emotional dependency and its implications for the therapist-client relationship. *Professional Psychology: Research and Practice, 18,* 555–561.

Gold, S. N., & Brown, L. S. (1997). Therapeutic responses to delayed recall: Beyond recovered memory. *Psychotherapy, 34,* 182–191.

Hahn, W. K., & Marks, L. I. (1996). Client receptiveness to the routine assessment of past suicide attempts. *Professional Psychology: Research and Practice, 27,* 592–594.

Hardin, S. I., Subich, L. M., & Tichenor, V. (1988). Expectancies for counseling in relation to premature termination. *Journal of Counseling Psychology, 35,* 37–40.

Harris, D. J., & Kuba, S. A. (1997). Ethnocultural identity and eating disorders in women of color. *Professional Psychology: Research and Practice, 28,* 341–347.

Hartung, C. M., & Widiger, T. A. (1998). Gender differences in the diagnosis of mental disorders: Conclusions and controversies. *Psychological Bulletin, 123,* 260–278.

Helms, J. E. (1995). An update of Helms's White and People of Color racial identity models. In J. G. Ponterotto, J. M. Casas, L. A. Suzuki, & C. M. Alexander (Eds.), *Handbook of multicultural counseling* (pp. 181–198). Thousand Oaks, CA: Sage.

Herman, J. L. (1992). *Trauma and recovery.* New York: Basic Books.

Hersen, M., & Turner, S. M. (Eds.). (1994). *Diagnostic interviewing* (2nd ed.). New York: Plenum.

Hersen, M., & Van Hasselt, V. B. (Eds.). (1998). *Basic interviewing: A practical guide for counselors and clinicians.* New York: Lawrence Erlbaum.

Hymer, S. (1987). Respect in psychotherapy. *Journal of Contemporary Psychotherapy, 17,* 6–21.

Jobes, D. A., & Berman, A. L. (1993). Suicide and malpractice liability: Assessing and revising policies, procedures, and practice in outpatient settings. *Professional Psychology: Research and Practice, 24,* 91–99.

Kegan, R. (1982). *The evolving self: Problem and process in human development.* Cambridge, MA: Harvard University Press.

Kelly, A. E., Kahn, J. G., & Coulter, R. G. (1996). Client self-presentations at intake. *Journal of Counseling Psychology, 43,* 300–309.

Kohatsu, E. L., & Richardson, T. Q. (1996). Racial and ethnic identity assessment. In L. A. Suzuki, P. J. Meller, & J. G. Ponterotto (Eds.), *Handbook of multicultural assessment: Clinical, psychological, and educational applications* (pp. 611–650). San Francisco: Jossey-Bass.

Koraleski, S. F., & Larson, L. M. (1997). A partial test of the transtheoretical model in therapy with adult survivors of childhood sexual abuse. *Journal of Counseling Psychology, 44,* 302–306.

Ladany, N., Inman, A. G., Constantine, M. G., & Hofheinz, E. W. (1997). Supervisee multicultural case conceptualization ability and self-reported multicultural competence as functions of supervisee racial identity and supervisor focus. *Journal of Counseling Psychology, 44,* 284–293.

Maris, R., Berman, A. L., Maltsberger, J. T., & Yufit, R. I. (Eds.). (1992). *Assessment and prediction of suicide.* New York: Guilford.

Maxmen, J. S., & Ward, N. G. (1995). *Essential psychopathology and its treatment* (2nd ed.). New York: Norton.

Milby, J. B., & Schumacher, J. E. (1994). Drug abuse. In M. Hersen & S. M. Turner (Eds.), *Diagnostic interviewing* (2nd ed., pp. 189–210). New York: Plenum.

Morrison, J. (1995a). *DSM-IV made easy: The clinician's guide to diagnosis.* New York: Guilford.

Morrison, J. (1995b). *The first interview* (Rev. ed.). New York: Guilford.

Morrison, J. (1997). *When psychological problems mask medical disorders: A guide for psychotherapists.* New York: Guilford.

Omer, H., & Rosenbaum, R. (1997). Diseases of hope and the work of despair. *Psychotherapy, 34,* 225–232.

Othmer, E., & Othmer, S. (1994a). *The clinical interview using DSM-IV* (Volume 1, Fundamentals). Washington, DC: American Psychiatric Press.

Othmer, E., & Othmer, S. (1994b). *The clinical interview using DSM-IV* (Volume 2, The Difficult

Patient). Washington, DC: American Psychiatric Press.

Padilla, A. M., & Medina, A. (1996). Cross-cultural sensitivity in assessment: Using tests in culturally appropriate ways. In L. A. Suzuki, P. J. Meller, & J. G. Ponterotto (Eds.), *Handbook of multicultural assessment: Clinical, psychological, and educational applications* (pp. 3–28). San Francisco: Jossey-Bass.

Prochaska, J. O., & DiClemente, C. C. (1986). The transtheoretical approach. In J. C. Norcross (Ed.), *Handbook of eclectic psychotherapy* (pp. 163–200). New York: Brunner/Mazel.

Ridley, C. R., Mendoza, D. W., Kantiz, B. E., Angermeier, L., & Zenk, R. (1994). Cultural sensitivity in multicultural counseling: A perceptual schema model. *Journal of Counseling Psychology, 41*, 125–136.

Ritzler, B. A. (1996). Projective methods for multicultural personality assessment: Rorschach, TEMAS, and the Early Memories Procedure. In L. A. Suzuki, P. J. Meller, & J. G. Ponterotto (Eds.), *Handbook of multicultural assessment: Clinical, psychological, and educational applications* (pp. 115–135). San Francisco: Jossey-Bass.

Rogers, R. (Ed.). (1997). *Clinical assessment of malingering and deception* (2nd ed.). New York: Guilford.

Roth, L. H. (Ed.). (1987). *Clinical treatment of the violent person.* New York: Guilford.

Satterfield, W. A., Buelow, S. A., Lyddon, W. J., & Johnson, J. T. (1995). Client stages of change and expectations about counseling. *Journal of Counseling Psychology, 42*, 476–478.

Schafer, R. (1954). *Psychoanalytic interpretation in Rorschach testing.* New York: Grune & Stratton.

Shedler, J., Mayman, M., & Manis, M. (1993). The illusion of mental health. *American Psychologist, 49*, 974–976.

Smart, D. W., & Smart, J. F. (1997). DSM-IV and culturally sensitive diagnosis: Some observations for counselors. *Journal of Counseling and Development, 75*, 392–398.

Sobell, L. C., Toneatto, T., Sobell, M. B., & Shillingford, J. A. (1994). Alcohol Problems. In M. Hersen & S. M. Turner (Eds.), *Diagnostic interviewing* (2nd ed., pp. 155–188). New York: Plenum.

Sommers-Flanagan, J., & Sommers-Flanagan, R. (1993). *Foundations of therapeutic interviewing.* Boston: Allyn & Bacon.

Sommers-Flanagan, J., & Sommers-Flanagan, R. (1995). Intake interviewing with suicidal patients: A systematic approach. *Professional Psychology: Research and Practice, 26*, 41–47.

Spengler, P. M., Strohmer, D. C., Dixon, D. N., & Shivy, V. A. (1995). A scientist–practitioner model of psychological assessment: Implications for training, practice and research. *The Counseling Psychologist, 23*, 506–534.

Spitzer, R. L., Gibbon, M., Skodol, A. E., Williams, J. B. W., & First, M. B. (1994). *DSM-IV Casebook: A learning companion to the diagnostic and statistical manual of mental disorders, fourth edition.* Washington, DC: American Psychiatric Press.

Stahl, P. M. (1994). *Conducting child custody evaluations: A comprehensive guide.* Thousand Oaks, CA: Sage.

Straker, G., & Waks, B. (1997). Limit setting in regard to self-damaging acts: The patient's perspective. *Psychotherapy, 34*, 192–200.

Sue, S., Zane, N., & Young, K. (1994). Research on psychotherapy with culturally diverse populations. In A. E. Bergin & A. L. Garfield (Eds.), *Handbook of psychotherapy and behavior change* (4th ed., pp. 783–817). New York: Wiley.

Suzuki, L. A., Meller, P. J., & Ponterotto, J. G. (Eds.). (1996). *Handbook of multicultural assessment: Clinical, psychological, and educational applications* (pp. 3–28). San Francisco: Jossey-Bass.

Suzuki, L. A., Vraniak, D. A., & Kugler, J. F. (1996). Intellectual assessment across cultures. In L. A. Suzuki, P. J. Meller, & J. G. Ponterotto (Eds.), *Handbook of multicultural assessment: Clinical, psychological, and educational applications* (pp. 141–177). San Francisco: Jossey-Bass.

Tarachow, S. (1963). *An introduction to psychotherapy.* New York: International Universities Press.

Tinsley, H. E. A., Bowman, S. L., & Ray, S. B. (1988). Manipulation of expectancies about counseling and psychotherapy: Review and analysis of expectancy manipulation strategies and results. *Journal of Counseling Psychology, 35*, 99–108.

Tracey, T. J., & Dundon, M. (1988). Role anticipations and preferences over the course of counseling. *Journal of Counseling Psychology, 35*, 3–13.

Turner, S. M., & Hersen, M. (1994). The interviewing process. In M. Hersen & S. M. Turner (Eds.), *Diagnostic interviewing* (2nd ed., pp. 3–24). New York: Plenum.

Utsey, S. O., & Ponterotto, J. G. (1996). Development and validation of the Index of Race-Related Stress (IRRS). *Journal of Counseling Psychology, 43*, 490–501.

Vacc, N. A., & Juhnke, G. A. (1997). The use of structured clinical interviews for assessment in counseling. *Journal of Counseling and Development, 75*, 470–480.

VandeCreek, L., & Knapp, S. (1993). *Tarasoff and beyond: Legal and clinical considerations in the treatment of life-endangering patients* (2nd ed.). Sarasota, FL: Professional Resource Exchange.

Watkins, C. E., Jr., Campbell, V. L., Nieberding, R., & Hallmark, R. (1995). Contemporary practice of psychological assessment by clinical psychologists. *Professional Psychology: Research and Practice, 26,* 54–60.

Werth, J., Jr. (1996). *Rational suicide? Implications for mental health professionals.* Bristol, PA: Taylor & Francis.

White, J. L., & Parham, T. A. (1990). *The psychology of Blacks: An African-American perspective* (2nd ed.). Englewood Cliffs, NJ: Prentice Hall.

Worell, J., & Remer, P. (1992). *Feminist perspectives in therapy.* New York: Wiley.

Yansen, E. A., & Shulman, E. L. (1996). Language assessment: multicultural considerations. In L. A. Suzuki, P. J. Meller, & J. G. Ponterotto (Eds.), *Handbook of multicultural assessment: Clinical, psychological, and educational applications* (pp. 353–394). San Francisco: Jossey-Bass.

APPENDIX A

Outline of an Intake Interview

General Considerations

- Vulnerability of the client
- Assessment of whether therapy is appropriate
- Assessment of seriousness
- Therapist awareness of cultural factors

Mental Status Exam

- Behavior (appearance; interview behavior)
- Thinking (judgment; thought content; thought processes; intellectual functioning; memory; orientation; insight)
- Feeling
- Data gathering apparatuses (sensorium; perceptual processes)
- Symptomatology (e.g., depersonalization, derealization, anxiety disorders, depression, eating disorders, drug abuse, domestic violence, etc.)

Formal Intake

- Presenting complaint
- Current functioning and living situation
- Family history
- Personal history
- Previous treatment

Dimensions Often of Interest to Therapists

- Relationships the client has with various types of people
- Client self-presentation
- How the client handles anxiety
- Capacity of the client to differentiate reality from fantasy
- What the client is asking for
- Themes in the client's comments
- Therapist feelings evoked by the client
- Recent changes that have brought the client in at this time

APPENDIX B

Assessing Suicidal Potential

- History of previous suicidal attempts
- Frequency of suicidal ideation
- Nature of suicidal ideation
- Duration of suicidal ideation
- Strength of the person's ego
- Social network which the person perceives as caring
- Individual's assessment of his or her likelihood of committing suicide
- Existence of a plan
- Specificity of the plan
- Readily available means to carry out the plan
- Lethality of the plan
- Likelihood of rescue
- Person's coping style in similar situations
- Person's perception of suicide on others
- Diagnostic category closest to describing the person
- Presence of psychosis
- Behavioral suggestions of suicide (e.g., self-injurious behavior)
- Presence of helplessness, hopelessness, and exhaustion
- Client's identification of reasons he or she wants to live

7

The Therapeutic Stance

People are not convinced by the truth so much as inhabited and colonized by it; they will not come back to you and say that you were right so much as they will, after...periods of incubation, repeat your ideas to you as though they had thought them up themselves.

—Robert Grudin

The patient needs an experience, not an explanation.

—Frieda Fromm-Reichman

As indicated in Chapter 3 on Client Fears, many of the clients you see will approach their first session with ambivalence and some anxiety. This may be especially true if they have never been in counseling before, but have stereotypes about what it may entail. You may have a client, as one of our students did, who arrived at the first session with her puppy, whom she said she might later need if the therapist made her cry. Or perhaps you will find, as another of our students did, that the client had brought a tape recorder in her purse so that she could later listen back to the session and decide how she felt about it! Other clients who have been in therapy before will have expectations based on their previous experience(s) that will inevitably affect their ways of dealing with you.

The atmosphere and the norms that indicate to your clients what therapy with *you* will be like are conveyed from the very beginning of your first session with them (Teyber, 1997; Trevino, 1996). Whether you feel prepared for the first session or not, your clients will be responding to the conscious and unconscious cues you reveal, and their behavior will adjust accordingly. If you are timid and self-conscious, they will likely understand that they must take charge of the session if anything is to happen. If you are calculated and impersonal, they will sense your lack of empathy and may well feel that this is a dangerous place for them to disclose. If you are uncomfortable with your therapeutic power and compensate by adopting an unprofessional chatty or flirtatious manner, they will tend to respond by treating you like a cohort. What we are suggesting is that it is primarily up to you, the therapist, to set the climate for the client (Bugental, 1987; McClure, 1996) Further, we believe this communication will in fact take place in subtle ways, regardless of your awareness or wishes. It is thus very important to give considerable thought to what your function as a therapist is and to what your expectations for yourself and your clients must necessarily be if client growth is to be facilitated.

The Therapeutic Relationship

During the last decade, there has been a resurgence of theory and research regarding the therapeutic relationship (Sexton & Whiston, 1994), much of it engendered by the conceptualizations of Gelso and Carter (1985). These writers suggested that the therapeutic relationship is composed of three parts: the working alliance, the transference configuration, and the "real relationship." The working alliance is a joining of the client's reasonable self with the therapist's "therapizing" self for the purpose of the work. Such issues as the goals and the tasks of therapy make up this component. The transference configuration consists of the client's repetition of past conflicts that are displaced onto the therapist, and the therapist's reactions to the client. The "real relationship" centers on those features of the relationship that are primarily undistorted by transferential material (Gelso & Carter, 1994). Hill (1994) suggests that the "real relationship" is conceptually unclear, and she recommends that it be considered genuineness and openness on the part of both the client and the therapist—very similar to Rogers's (1961) definition of congruence. (For further discussion of this topic, see the chapter entitled Transference and Countertransference.)

For a review of many of the major research studies on the therapeutic relationship undertaken, we refer you to the January 1994 issue of *The Counseling Psychologist* focusing on this topic. Many, but not all, of these studies looked at the working alliance, but the review also covers a separate body of research that works from within a process research model (that is, examining how the client and therapist interact with each other in a complementary fashion and under which circumstances that is important for predicting a positive therapeutic outcome). To summarize the results rather globally, what we know at this point is that the therapeutic alliance is a powerful predictive factor for psychotherapy outcome (Coady & Marziali, 1994), and that complementary interactions apparently are less important in some stages of therapy than others in predicting a positive therapeutic outcome (Sexton & Whiston, 1994). For a more conceptual understanding of the therapeutic relationship, you may want to look at the constellation of articles in the July 1994 issue of the *Journal of Counseling Psychology.*

Other writers have used similar terms to define this essential part of the counseling relationship that makes it "work." Teyber (1997), for example, refers to the "collaborative relationship," indicating that within such a relationship clients come to believe that the therapist is someone who sees their predicament and distress, is moved by their pain, has their best interests at heart, and has a commitment to help them. Eaton, Abeles, and Gutfreund (1988) and others have written in similar terms about the therapeutic alliance. When we talk about the "therapeutic stance" in this and other chapters, we are referring to the part of the relationship over which the therapist has control, the attitudes, expectations, goals, and tasks that can be offered in therapy, regardless of the client's desire or ability to match them.

When students run into difficulties with their clients, they often see their choices as bipolar: Either they can submit to their clients' expectations and styles, or they can dominate and impose their own agendas. Such a conceptualization misses the crucial understanding that therapy, like other relationships, is an interactive process. One can and must offer one's self—judiciously and professionally, but still unmistakably—to the relationship. The key word here is *offer*, as opposed to *impose*. The therapist's own maturity and interpersonal skills are, of course, requisite; otherwise, the client will be invited to participate in yet another immature, dysfunctional relationship—hardly an appealing prospect!

If you can view one of your primary therapeutic responsibilities as the consistent offering to your clients of what might well be the first caring, nonexploitative relationship in their lives, you will have taken a major step toward clarifying your therapeutic role. This approach to therapeutic responsibility will demand that you fully internalize your professional training, not hide behind it in some plastic two-dimensional role, so that what you know is blended with who you are.

Bowlby (1988) describes the therapeutic role in terms of his attachment theory. He suggests that the therapist's major task is to assume the role of an attachment figure, who provides a secure, trustworthy base from which clients can explore and reassess their working models of attachment figures and of themselves. Other writers (e.g., Dolan, Arnkoff, & Glass, 1993; Farber, Lippert, & Nevas, 1995; and Sable, 1997) have elaborated on Bowlby's ideas and suggest that much of what a good therapist does is what a good parent should do—respond sensitively and empathically, set limits without becoming critical or punitive, provide direction and guidance of the clients' tasks, and offer support and hope when the client falters. Theorists and researchers across orientations agree that the therapeutic relationship accounts for a great deal of client progress (up to 45% of the variance, according to Horvath & Greenberg, 1989).

Oliver Bown, as quoted by Rogers (1951), makes the point even more strongly that therapists must find a way to offer themselves fully to the therapeutic relationship. He suggests that the therapist must be willing to need the client, not in specific, pointed ways, but in the experiencing of a deep, profound desire for human connection with him or her. To hold back, according to Bown (Rogers, 1951), to hide behind a professional facade, teaches the client at an unconscious level, "'Do not be free in this relationship. Do not let yourself go. Do not express your deepest feelings or needs, for in this relationship that is dangerous" (p. 162). Bown goes on to suggest that when he is free to act on his motivation for relational connectedness he is left with the sense of giving everything he can to the therapeutic relationship—which in turn leaves him with no sense of withholding or guilt. And that certainty within himself frees him to say no to specific client demands or requests, without a feeling of rejecting or letting down the client.

This understanding of boundaries or limit-setting, that it grows out of the reality of who the therapist is and what she or he can offer, is a subtle but extraordinarily important concept for therapists to grasp. For many of us, setting limits is associated with punitiveness, which we see, accurately, as antithetical to a therapeutic experience. To understand that having limits in the therapeutic relationship is instead not only allowable but indeed something we offer, to fully internalize that learning, can be very freeing.

Irvin Yalom (1980), who argues eloquently for the therapeutic relationship to be a model that can teach clients what positive relationships can be like, also writes about the myth of the "ultimate rescuer." Many clients, he believes, will come with the unconscious hope not of learning to be more completely self-responsible but of having you rescue them from their pain and isolation and humanness. They will seek in you the ultimate rescuer that their parents and spouses and friends have failed at being. One of the ways you will help them take responsibility for themselves is for you to fail in this role, and the most important way for you to achieve this therapeutic failure is to acknowledge your limits regarding who you can be and what you can do. As Yalom says,

> ...one priceless thing the patient learns in therapy is the limits of relationships. One learns what one can get from others but, perhaps even more important, one learns what one cannot get from others.... The ultimate rescuer is seen in the full light of day as only another person after all. It is an isolating moment but...an illuminating one. (pp. 406–407)

The concept of boundaries is one which is especially discussed in psychodynamic circles, but all theories of psychotherapy, and certainly the Ethics Code of the American Psychological Association, 1992, suggest that there are some activities that are inappropriate within the therapeutic relationship. It is up to the therapist to maintain the boundaries seen to be in the best interests of the client. "Crossing" boundaries is a term meaning that, after careful reflection, the therapist decides that the usual "rules" might not apply. For example, changing an appointment so that a client can attend an important ceremony, extending a session past the usual time, accepting late payment—these behaviors may be facilitative for some therapeutic relationships and not for others. "Violating" boundaries, which occurs when the therapist acts out of his or her own needs without sufficient regard for the effect on the client, is experienced by clients as confusing—sometimes initially affirming but setting up expectations for continuity in what may become burdensome or unfair ways. In this manner, boundary violation recapitulates what some clients experienced with their parents when they were expected to manage a "role reversal" and take care of them.

As an example of an apparently innocuous boundary violation, consider the situation in which a therapist in private practice was told by her client, a building contractor, that her toilet needed a new part. After several weeks of reminders, the client offered to repair the toilet himself if the therapist would get the part. Although she refused, several sessions later she asked his advice about another construction difficulty she was having. What is wrong with this picture? In the first place, the client was paying money for time that was being used to meet the therapist's needs instead of his own. In the second place, if his advice turned out to be unhelpful, her feelings in regard to the situation would have a tendency to contaminate their therapeutic relationship. And third, in this case, his need to be special was so high that once she let him move into the "helper" role, he began to seek other opportunities to prove his worth to her.

A very serious example of boundary violation occurred when a therapist mentioned parenthetically to his female client that he would enjoy kissing her. Although he immediately got back on task, in that and in subsequent sessions, the client later admitted that she no longer felt safe. For her (not necessarily for all clients), the idea was an attractive one and she did not want him to change his perception of her as a potentially attractive sexual partner. Accordingly, discussing any concerns she might have wanted to explore regarding her sexuality or insecurities about men now became off limits.

The idea of boundaries, then, is to protect the client from being exploited, set up for false hopes, or led to feel that he or she must acquiesce in order to maintain a good working relationship. The rationale underlying this concept is that as real and authentic as the therapeutic relationship might be, clients are by definition in the more vulnerable position. They are looking for emotional/psychological help and are frequently paying for that; the therapist is not. Accordingly, the therapist must take special care to safeguard the relationship as a place, almost certainly the *only* place in the client's life, where therapeutic work can take place and the client can make changes.

The ideal therapeutic relationship, then, in our view, is one in which the therapist is committed to being fully present, to offering the best of who she or he is, and also to unashamedly offering realistic limits or boundaries. While it is similar to other healthy forms of love and caring in several key aspects, it is different in one very important way: The therapeutic relationship is not reciprocal. This lack of reciprocity will be experienced by the client as both blessing and curse. On the one hand, having your undivided attention frequently feels wonderful. (As a client said, "Therapy means never having to ask how your week was!") It is your commitment to providing an environment in which the client's potential can be actualized that makes therapy work. On the other hand, clients will at times rail against the lack of reciprocity and perhaps feel enormous vulnerability because you don't need them as much as they need you. They may worry, and rightly so, that in ten years you will have forgotten much of what they spoke of, while they may remember whole sessions with considerable clarity. The lopsidedness of that arrangement can be quite disturbing to them. Arguing with them that the benefits of therapeutic nonreciprocity outweigh the costs is probably less helpful than your understanding their vulnerability. They are right. Nourishing as the therapeutic relationship may be for them, one of its realities is that typically you will be more important in their life than they are in yours. The sadness they (and you) may feel because of that inequity is partly what will motivate them to leave, to outgrow their attachment to you in favor of potentially more reciprocal relationships. If you have done your job right, they will leave because, in this important aspect, they want more than you can offer.

Having clear goals, maintaining boundaries, and offering a consistently respectful and supportive relationship does not mean that you will behave exactly the same with each client. Some clients will respond to your humor; some will not. Some will be oppositional enough that you will find yourself most effective by making nondirective "asides"; others will respond best to direct, almost blunt, interventions. Some will be threatened by too much intimacy; others will respond naturally and easily to it. (Beutler & Consoli, 1993; Dolan, Arnkoff, & Glass, 1993). Good therapists "orchestrate" themselves differently so that their style can create unique relationships with each client. For a further discussion of this kind of orchestration, we refer you to the special section on The Relationship of Choice: Matching the Therapist's Interpersonal Stance to Individual Clients in the Fall 1993 issue of *Psychotherapy: Theory, Research, Practice, Training.*

An assignment we sometimes find helpful for our graduate students is for them to write down their tentative definitions of psychotherapy. Take a sheet of paper, if you will, and try it. What is therapy, really? What makes it different from friendship or mentoring? Why does it work? What are the essential healing ingredients? After you have a working definition at the top of the page, draw a line vertically down the middle. On the left side of the page, referring back to your definition, list the specific tasks the therapist must assume for this kind of therapy to work. You might want to consider such things as building the relationship, having an adequate knowledge base, adherence to ethical considerations, self-awareness, and the like. Now on the right side of the page, write down your formulation of tasks that clients must carry out to benefit from therapy. Some of these tasks will parallel the therapist's, and others may occur to you that have no apparent therapist parallel. These tentative lists should be important in helping you clarify your expectations for yourself and your clients and thus aid in creating the kind of climate you believe is important in therapy.

Therapist Tasks

Many of what we consider specific therapist responsibilities are spelled out at greater length in other chapters. At this point we will provide only a quick and somewhat arbitrary review. We will not cover at all, in this summary, your specific legal and ethical responsibilities, although we assume you give them careful consideration.

Clear Therapeutic Priorities

Your primary task can be stated very simply: You are responsible for helping the client. That is your function. If you keep that firmly in mind at all times, it will simplify many ongoing therapeutic decisions you will need to make. Your function is not to be entertained, or to make the client like you, or to enjoy hearing yourself say wise things. When you wonder how or if to express anger, or whether to comfort or confront, or whether or not to self-disclose or tell a joke or use hypnosis, the question always to ask yourself is, "Will it help this client at this time?" You may not know the answer in every instance, but at least you will be asking yourself the right question. As we have underscored many times, the client's needs come first in the therapeutic hour, and your preferences must be secondary.

Emotional Availability

As discussed in several parts of this book, we believe that one of your primary responsibilities as therapist is to be emotionally available to your clients. They need to be able to sense your understanding and support in order to feel safe enough to risk being vulnerable with you. Put another way, to trust you, they must experience you as trustworthy. As Bachelor (1988) suggests, clients may "receive" your empathy in several modes, but the importance of your experiencing and then communicating to them your understanding of their inner world is clear. If your biases interfere with your ability to empathize with certain client situations or feelings, it is up to you, perhaps with the help of your supervisor, to work through those biases. (Related material can be found in the chapter Transference and Countertransference.)

Objective Assessment

Another task of yours is to offer, in addition to your emotional availability, objectivity. You need to be able to assess your client's behavior and mood and thought processes well enough to diagnose, plan effective treatment, and evaluate progress. Further, you must not identify so closely with them that you lose the ability to understand their contributions to their dilemmas and concerns. There is a difference between empathy and gullibility. If you totally buy into your clients' versions of life, accepting their renditions of blame and hopelessness and impotency as the absolute truth, then you have little to offer them beyond a fused relationship. To use the familiar term, you need to learn to listen with a "third ear" if your goal is to encourage their growth rather than just to support their conceptualizations.

Therapeutic Knowledge and Skills

Another of your responsibilities as a professional is to gain a thorough grounding in theory and skills that are helpful in therapeutic sessions and to keep that base up-to-date. Actually, this flows directly from your primary goal of being helpful to another. Ongoing professional development feels like an obligation only to those who have become more invested in making money or meeting credentialing requirements or making superficial attempts to stay out of ethical hot water than in offering a quality helping relationship. To the professional whose top priority is being of help to her or his clients, staying up-to-date through reading, workshops, consultations, and conferences is second nature. Appropriate guilt for therapists comes from realizing that they have wasted a client's time and money by not staying abreast of current advances in theory and treatment. There is no way to know everything about therapy, of course, but the conscientious, thoughtful accumulation of knowledge is as expected of therapists as it is of other professionals. The damage to clients caused by negligence can be just as harmful, whether the cause was fraud or being "too busy to read."

Professional development should not be limited merely to learning approaches that reinforce one's own biases. If, for example, there is considerable evidence that eating disorders respond to a particular type of intervention, but the therapist prefers a different approach, it would be unprofessional for the therapist to deal with his or her cognitive dissonance by ignoring the new literature. Somehow, we must come to terms with newly emerging information, even when we don't like it, and must attempt to assimilate it into our own theoretical base. This is especially important when working with multicultural clients.

Self-Understanding

The kind of self-knowledge just alluded to—awareness of one's biases—is another important responsibility that therapists assume in order to provide clients with professional help. Hopefully, students will not only have a personal commitment to self-awareness and continued growth, but will also have supervisors who can help them pinpoint areas they may need to address. We are strong advocates of students' entering therapy to work on relevant issues. Whether or not you elect that route, however, it will be important for you to identify and explore issues and biases that interfere with your providing effective therapy. Such prejudices as sexism, racism, heterosexism and ageism should be obvious, of course, but it is also important to continue to evaluate other assumptions one makes about certain behaviors and groups of people as new relevant information comes to light.

Students evidence the most general need to explore their propensity to assume a rescuer role (which, of course, complements the client's hope for an ultimate rescuer). It is very helpful for student therapists to identify when and how they tend to assume responsibility for rescuing certain kinds of clients and to recognize that their urgency to make sweeping changes for clients may well represent a lack of respect for the clients' actual and potential strengths. Some students have found it worthwhile to look closely at their role in their own family of origin. They sometimes discover that their inclination to assume responsibility for others is rooted in the identity they formed as a result of early family patterns or in unresolved childhood grief (Bowlby, 1988).

Client Tasks

In the early stages of learning to provide effective therapy, it may be just as important to reach a beginning understanding of your client's responsibilities as of your own. Most beginning therapists, if they err in one direction or the other, expect too little—or perhaps the wrong things—of their clients, often for many sessions, before they start to grow impatient and then suddenly feel annoyed because their clients aren't "trying" hard enough. Giving thought ahead of time to what your clients will need to bring to the process in order to benefit from therapy should help you in conveying such expectations from the beginning. You cannot force your clients to meet your expectations, of course, but you can indicate matter-of-factly and consistently that therapy will have more impact if they carry their part of the load.

Different theoretical perspectives imply different tasks that the client is to assume. If you are operating from a specific theoretical orientation and/or are working on a very brief time frame, it is especially important to clarify for the clients what tasks they should assume (Callaghan, Naugle, & Follette, 1996). With experience, you will gain new ways that fit your style to encourage clients to approach therapy responsibly. Ultimately, of course, you may need to terminate clients who are not committed enough to therapy to fulfill their responsibilities.

The guidelines we offer here regarding client tasks are clearly not "cook-book" rules. We hope that you will give careful thought to how they apply to each of your clients and consult with your supervisor about such issues as timing, confrontation strategies, and relevant cultural issues.

Openness to Help

As mentioned earlier, we assume that the clients you will be seeing in therapy are "voluntary." By this we do not mean that they must be totally free from ambivalence, that they will show no resistance, or that they will necessarily be compliant. We do suggest, however, that they must be at least somewhat open to being helped. If their investment in defending against your input is very high—for whatever their reasons—you need to be aware of that process, and at some point you will probably need to address that issue with the client. Sometimes informal humor, or empathy, or strategic interventions will serve to defuse some of their defensiveness, but it must be acknowledged that ultimately such clients have veto power. You cannot "do therapy" without minimal client cooperation.

It may help you understand the therapist's basic helplessness when faced with unyielding client defensiveness if you identify with the client for just a moment. Imagine that someone with whom you were locked into a power struggle forced you somehow to see a professional whom you distrusted and/or feared. If you were completely convinced that making yourself vulnerable to this person would result in a major loss of power or sense of failure for you, there would probably be little the stranger could do to "seduce" you into trusting him or her. There are some things a therapist could perhaps say or do that might make trust easier for you, but you could not be controlled. Trust cannot be forced, only encouraged.

A typical situation that students encounter occurs when a client they have been seeing individually seems to be at a point where he or she can benefit from relationship counseling. Often this is with a family member, but not always. Before you automatically pursue this avenue, remember that not much is likely to happen therapeutically if the newcomer feels coerced or defensive. It is not enough for your *client* to be open to help; if the relationship is to be addressed, then all persons in it will need to share a certain amount of that openness. While some experienced therapists have a facility for persuading reluctant clients to invest in therapy, the task can be daunting. Best to try to work ahead of time to ensure willing participation than to walk blindly into the situation and assume you can somehow work magic! Talking with your supervisor about ways for the client and/or you to approach the "newcomer" may forestall angry or disappointed clients.

Exploration of Affective Issues

Another factor that influences the success of therapy is the client's willingness to explore affective issues. Even if your approach is largely cognitive–behavioral, you will need for your clients to introduce those problem areas to which they experience negative emotional reactions. While this seems too obvious to deserve mention, it is surprising how many clients are reluctant to do it. One of the common reasons for this hesitancy may be that they may want you to like them, to be proud of the progress they have made, and they may fear that they have used up their quota of your acceptance. You may need to remind them (and perhaps yourself as well) that hiding problem areas rarely results in their disappearance, fervently as one may wish it. Further, the more deeply the personality restructuring hoped for in therapy, the more crucial it is for clients not just to introduce affectively ladened material but to explore it as openly as possible. Not much happens therapeutically if the client and/or the therapist retreats from emotional explorations into mere intellectual discussion of important issues. Clients benefit most from therapy when they are willing to give up the control involved in "rehearsing" material and can instead let themselves respond spontaneously in the therapeutic moment, although this may be more difficult for clients from certain cultures.

(It may be of interest to you that openness to help and affective self-exploration were targeted by Czogalik and Russell, 1994, as two of the four key client processes obtained in their P-technique factor analysis of client participation in therapy.)

Willingness to Make Behavioral Changes

A final responsibility of clients we would like to mention is being willing to make different choices in behavior when they leave the therapist's office. Again, this seems obvious. Nonetheless, many people continue to come to therapy less because they want to change than because they want others to change. Or perhaps they want the therapist to make the changes feel risk-free, and so they wait for an injection of courage. Or sometimes they come because they like the intimacy of therapy and wish to continue it indefinitely. When it begins to occur to a therapist that some of her or his "best" clients—those who are open and trusting and transparent and willing to explore virtually any topic—do not seem to be making much progress, it often helps to ask them what all of this exploration has led them to do differently outside of their therapy sessions. Significant changes for clients will not occur until they experience life in new ways, and an indigenous part of that process is almost always their first attempting to making risk-taking changes. Increased psychological freedom tends to accompany change, not necessarily precede it (Fried, 1980; May, 1981).

Guidelines for Early Sessions

We assume you are somewhat familiar from previous courses with the usual three-stage model (e.g., Egan, 1994) of the counseling process. Our comments at this point are intended to build on the relationship-building skills you have already practiced in a prepracticum environment.

1. *Take time before the session to relax and remind yourself of your role.* Just as athletes and performers often take a few minutes before they go "on" to regain their focus, many therapists find it helpful to take a few minutes before (and between) seeing clients to prepare themselves to leave their own issues behind so that they can be maximally available for the demands of the therapeutic hour. As we discuss in the next chapter, Listening, doing therapy is often a nonlinear process, so the more relaxed and aware you can be, the better you will be at picking up cues and listening around the edges to your clients. Some therapists do relaxation exercises, some do ego-strengthening imagery, some listen to music. Find the approach that works for you. You will not be very helpful if half of your attention during a session is on the exam you have to prepare for or the argument you just had with a friend or the trip you leave on right after this session.

2. *When in doubt, listen.* As discussed throughout this book, there is so much to understand about any given client, it is critical that the therapist listen intently to what is being said. Your focused, concentrated listening should be available to the client from the very beginning, as you both try to identify and sort through his or her main concerns. Since clients often feel defensive when cross-examined, we suggest saving your questions for the crucial issues, rather than wasting them on minor details.

3. *Interact unapologetically.* Your best qualities, whatever they are—humor, warmth, playfulness, sensitivity, artistry, analytical skills, and so forth—need to be available for you to use therapeutically. Tentativeness and tiptoeing around clients not only provide them with a poor model of how to relate but cost you credibility. Obviously, we are not suggesting that you are licensed to behave totally impulsively. What we are underscoring here is that you should work to include in your professional style the best part of your typical interpersonal behaviors. This is seen to be especially important in brief therapy, where your genuineness facilitates the creation of a relationship more quickly than might be required elsewhere (Gelso & Carter, 1994).

4. *Offer appropriate hope.* Many of your clients will come to their first session feeling anxious and demoralized. As Tracy and Dundon (1988) indicated, clients' expectations will vary widely. Some of them will have reasonable expectations for the help therapy can provide, some will have an investment in proving to you that nothing will help, and some may want to be rescued from their responsibilities for making changes. All of them deserve your support and willingness to offer appropriate hope. "Appropriate" is the emphasized word, here, since offering unrealistic hope can be almost as damaging as offering none at all (Omer & Rosenbaum, 1997).

One source of hope that you can almost always offer, whether you state it this directly or not, is your belief in clients' potential to change. People do change; we are in the process of changing all the time as we respond to external stimuli and deal with our own changing motivations. Certainly, deep, lasting personality changes are more difficult to achieve and take more time than simple behavior adjustment, but both are possible and, in fact, often interact.

Another source of hope you can offer new clients results from your listening analytically. The accurate and empathic labeling of client concerns is potentially relieving to many clients. When a large part of one's life seems out of control and overwhelming, it can feel very helpful to recognize that the concerns have some parameters. The challenge for the therapist is to summarize the issues with enough empathy that the client does not feel discounted. For example, a therapist, after listening for 30 minutes to a new client, may well say something like, "Let me play back to you what it sounds like, and tell me if I'm on target. One area of your life that's driving you crazy is your relationship with your mother-in-law. You seem to get along fine with the rest of your family and your husband's, but you feel like throwing in the towel with her. And a second area you've indicated you may want to focus on is the stress you're experiencing at work with your boss, who, even though you've tried pretty hard for months, seems to be very critical. Are those the two areas you see as most important for us to work on?" That approach serves to begin the process of negotiating target issues with the client but does not convey the same condescending distance as a summary like, "So, you need to improve your relationship skills with your husband's mother and work on your authority problems with your boss. Right?" Helping clients see some sort of order to the chaos of their lives is a way to renew their hope that progress is possible, but that order needs to be suggested respectfully and empathically.

A third avenue for instilling hope is to offer therapeutic direction, especially if that direction includes references to your client's perceived strengths. Often this involves offering a new perspective. For example, to follow up on the mythical client we just alluded to, the therapist might say, "One thing that strikes me about you, Mrs. Smith, is your willingness to be very honest with yourself and me about your feelings regarding your mother-in-law. I think that if we can get to the root of some of those reactions—and perhaps also take a look at your feelings about your husband's role in this—you may discover that there are some new ways to deal with her that don't leave you so frustrated." Even if, in your initial assessment, there is no immediate relief possible as, for example, in dealing with a client's anticipatory grief regarding a dying wife, you may be able to ease his confusion by saying something such as, "I know what you're going through now is very painful for you. At this point in your life, there just don't seem to be a lot of options. Coming to therapy, though, may help in a couple of ways. You'll have some support so you won't have to make sense of it all alone, and as things shift a bit in your wife's condition, we may be able to discover some alternative ways for you to be there for her and still take care of yourself."

5. *Negotiate when possible.* The give-and-take in the therapeutic relationship is a reflection of mutual respect and should be present from the first session. Negotiating, in this context, means your finding a middle ground between dogmatism and tentativeness. To be clear in your perceptions and your statements of them is certainly desirable, but it is equally important to be flexible. The client, ultimately, must be the expert on himself or herself. Hence, you will probably find it helpful to blend most of your empathic, clarifying, or challenging interventions with the attitude, if not the actual words, of, "This is what it sounds like to me. Does that fit with your understanding? Do you agree? Does what I've said make sense for you? If not, how would you change it?"

The alliance you are trying to forge between the two of you can be created only when you and the client both work, and you work *together.* You will likely convey this respectful willingness to "negotiate" with the client by saying things like, "You've mentioned three main issues. Which would you like to begin with?" "Which would be a better time for you for our regular session, Tuesday at 2:00, or Wednesday at 4:00?" "I'm not sure what you mean by 'feeling down.' Does that mean you feel mainly bored, or depressed, or angry, or what?"

6. *Mix empathy and challenge.* In our experience, it is not uncommon for student therapists to begin by being warm and empathic and then, when they have decided that the listening/exploring stage should be over, to become quite task-oriented and dry. Their attitude seems to convey an OK-the-fun-is-over-now-down-to-business message, and the sudden switch can leave clients feeling bewildered and vaguely betrayed. We think it works better to blend empathy and challenge, hopefully from the beginning of the first session. The empathy should emerge automatically from the therapist's understanding of the client's subjective world, and there is no reason for that understanding, or the verbalized communication of it, to decrease over time. Challenging the client to do more—to change an unproductive behavior, to be more honest about her or his conflicted feelings, to take more interpersonal risks, and the like—is not in contrast to empathic understanding, but is an adjunct to it.

The inexperienced therapist, for example, who has been suppressing her or his impatience with a depressed client's reluctance to make behavioral changes, is likely after about three sessions of forced "empathy" to have a dialogue something like:

THERAPIST: So, how was last week?

CLIENT: (*Sighing heavily*) Oh, about the same.

THERAPIST: (*Exasperated*) You know, for you to feel better, you are going to have to push yourself harder! Lying around just guarantees that the depression will never lift. You don't want that, do you?

Such an exchange is likely to be in marked contrast to the fourth session with a therapist who, from the beginning, has communicated both an empathic awareness of the client's depressed affective state and the conviction that depression will probably lift somewhat when the client takes a more active stance in life. Examples of interventions more likely to convey this mixture of challenge and empathy are: "I can tell you're feeling pretty gloomy about things. I wonder, even with your feeling depressed, if there are some little things you might do differently to help yourself?" or "Sometimes when we feel depressed, it's almost like walking under water—everything requires so much effort it hardly seems worth attempting. Is that what you're feeling?...(wait for answer, perhaps allow elaboration). Still, one thing that psychologists have found over and over is that when depressed folks can get a little momentum going, their mood often improves. Let's talk about some things you could do that might help you but wouldn't require an inordinate amount of energy...."

7. *Set appropriate limits.* As we discussed earlier, the clearer you can be about your tasks as therapist and what you see as the client's tasks, the easier it will be to set specific, appropriate limits that reinforce those responsibilities. If, for example, you are to work with a client who has a history of irresponsible behavior and the client appears for the first appointment 15 minutes late, it is almost surely inappropriate to "take up the slack" for that client by continuing an extra 15 minutes at the end of the allotted hour. Other limits you may need to clarify and enforce might have to do with prompt payment, early cancellations of appointments, completion of homework assignments, and such treatment contingencies as attendance at AA meetings. As you state and enforce appropriate limits, we want to reemphasize that it is important to be able to do that nonpunitively and matter-of-factly. If, in fact, you find yourself angry with your client for "making" you enforce limits (such as ending sessions on time), it is time for you to take a look, with your supervisor, at your own countertransference issues.

8. *Align yourself with client strengths.* Your clients, like the rest of us, have the potential to demonstrate courage and resilience and strength, as well as the capacity for self-destructive passivity and manipulativeness. If, in the first session, you can identify and align yourself with the healthy part of the client's personality and refuse to collude with his or her pathology, you will have begun to establish the kind of "therapeutic alliance" we have previously referred to. In effect, you will be inviting them to join you in certain forms of relating (e.g., mutual respect, caring, honesty, commitment to focusing on important issues, etc.) and refusing to collude with them in nonproductive forms of relating (e.g., game playing, flirting, tangential storytelling, trying to please or impress you, etc.). In our experience, the expectation conveyed by therapists that good therapeutic work will come from their clients derives from the therapist's genuine respect for clients. Such expectations tend to permeate their interactions from very early in the first session.

9. *Indicate a willingness to learn.* Particularly if you have a suspicious or hostile client, it is important to demonstrate appropriate humility. Paradoxically, therapists often gain credibility by acknowledging outright and unapologetically that the client will need to teach them specifics about the client's life. Such client contributions certainly include, but are not limited to, information about that client's background, feelings, and motivations; education regarding the client's culture and life context; and ongoing feedback to the therapist about his or her therapeutic impact. The distinction that we are suggesting here is that you are the expert on therapy but that clients need to be the experts on themselves (Koile, 1988). This guideline is especially important in cross-cultural and cross-gender therapy, where our own experiences—different from the client's—have led us to unconscious assumptions and values. We will talk more about this in the chapters on Multicultural Counseling and Resistance.

10. *Self disclose very selectively.* Unless you have strong empirical support for making an exception, the usual guideline is to disclose little "outside information" about yourself, especially in the first sessions. As we see it, such interventions are likely to cost you, under almost any given scenario. If you acknowledge a present or past similarity to the client (e.g. "Yes, I went through graduate school as a single parent also") and the client *is* impressed, then you may become the kind of a role model that she or he believes has all the answers. If the client was *not* impressed, if for example all single parents by definition are failures, then you have lost credibility. And if the client has no particular reaction at all, but simply responds with a polite nod, you have wasted his or her time and money. Most students self-disclose, not because the client needs it, but because they are struck by a similarity and want to indulge in this kind of social discourse. As a fallback position, you may want to use a technique that a therapist we know adopts when she truly believes her experience has something to offer the client. She says, "I know someone who…" and then relates the relevant information.

We do not want to convey that therapist self-disclosure is taboo and must be avoided at all costs, rather that it is often used impulsively and inappropriately. Later in your training, if you are drawn to narrative approaches to therapy (e.g., Eron & Lund, 1996), you may find that some forms of self-disclosure fit in this paradigm. Also, as you gain experience and knowledge of clients from different cultural and subcultural groups, you may find that in certain instances limited self-disclosure can facilitate client self-disclosure.

Summary

The therapeutic relationship is one that is created anew with each combination of therapist and client. It is incumbent upon therapists to clarify for themselves what the substance and the parameters of the relationship need to be to promote client growth, and then to actively work to promote such a climate. What the client experiences with you may have more lasting impact than any specific interventions you might make (Bergin & Garfield, 1994; Walborn, 1996). Defining for yourself what your therapeutic stance needs to be—and what clients also need to offer to the process—can help you create these norms from the beginning of therapy.

DISCUSSION QUESTIONS

- Choosing the three or four theories of psychotherapy with which you are most familiar, describe your understanding of the "ideal" therapeutic stances inherent in each theory.

- In recent films and books depicting therapists, how professionally are their stances depicted? Why do you suppose that films often portray mental health professionals as violating boundaries?

- Henry Thoreau once said, "If I knew…that a man [sic] was coming to my house with the conscious design of doing me good, I should run for my life." What implications, if any, does this attitude have for an appropriate therapeutic stance?

BIBLIOGRAPHY

Bachelor, A. (1988). How clients perceive therapist empathy: A content analysis of "received" empathy. *Psychotherapy, 25,* 227–240.

Bergin, A., & Garfield, S. (Eds.). (1994). *Handbook of psychotherapy and behavior change* (4th ed.). New York: Wiley.

Beutler, L. E., & Consoli, A. J. (1993). Matching the therapist's interpersonal stance to clients' characteristics: Contributions from systematic eclectic psychotherapy. *Psychotherapy, 30,* 417–422.

Bowlby, J. (1988). *A secure base: Clinical applications of attachment theory.* London: Routledge.

Bugental, J. (1987). *The art of the psychotherapist.* New York: W. W. Norton.

Callaghan, G. M., Naugle, A. E., & Follette, W. C. (1996). Useful constructions of the client-therapist relationship. *Psychotherapy, 33,* 381–390.

Coady, N. F., & Marziali, E. (1994). The association between global and specific measures of the therapeutic relationship. *Psychotherapy, 31,* 17–27.

Czogalik, D., and Russell, R. R. (1994). Key processes of client participation in psychotherapy: Chronography and narration. *Psychotherapy, 31,* 170–182.

Dolan, R. T., Arnkoff, D. B., & Glass, C. R. (1993). Client attachment style and the psychotherapist's interpersonal stance. *Psychotherapy, 30,* 408–412.

Eaton, T. T., Abeles, N., & Gutfreund, M. J. (1988). Therapeutic alliance and outcome: Impact of treatment length and pretreatment symptomology. *Psychotherapy, 25,* 536–542.

Egan, G. (1994). *The skilled helper* (5th ed.). Pacific Grove, CA: Brooks/Cole.

Eron, J. B., & Lund, T. W. (1996). *Narrative solutions in brief therapy.* New York: Guilford.

Farber, B. A., Lippert, R. A., & Nevas, D. B. (1995). The therapist as attachment figure. *Psychotherapy, 32,* 204–212.

Fried, E. (1980). *The courage to change.* New York: Brunner/Mazel.

Gelso, C. J., & Carter, J. A. (1985). The relationship in counseling and psychotherapy. *The Counseling Psychologist, 13,* 155–244.

Gelso, C. J., & Carter, J. A. (1994). Components of the psychotherapy relationship: Their interaction and unfolding during treatment. *Journal of Counseling Psychology, 41,* 296–306.

Greenson, R. R. (1967). *The theory and practice of psychoanalysis.* New York: International Universities Press.

Hill, C. (1994). What is the therapeutic relationship? *The Counseling Psychologist, 22,* 90–97.

Horvath, A. O., & Greenberg, L. S. (1989). Development and validation of the Working Alliance Inventory. *Journal of Counseling Psychology, 36,* 223–233.

Koile, E. (1988). Workshop on Marital and Divorce Therapy, Austin, TX.

Leitner, L. M. (1995). Optimal therapeutic distance: A therapist's experience of personal construct psychotherapy. In R. A. Neimeyer & M. J. Mahoney (Eds.), *Constructivism in psychotherapy* (pp. 357–370). Washington, DC: American Psychological Association.

May, R. (1981). *Freedom and destiny.* New York: W. W. Norton.

McClure, F. (1996). Case study of Sheila: A 15-year-old African/American female. In F. McClure and E. Teyber (Eds.), *Child and adolescent therapy: A multicultural-relational approach.* Ft. Worth: Harcourt Brace.

Omer, H., & Rosenbaum, R. (1997). Diseases of hope and the work of despair. *Psychotherapy, 34,* 225–232.

Rogers, C. R. (1961). *On becoming a person.* Boston: Houghton-Mifflin.

Sable, P. (1997). Disorders of adult attachment. *Psychotherapy, 34,* 286–296.

Sexton, T. L., & Whiston, S. C. (1994). The status of the counseling relationship: An empirical review, theoretical implications, and research directions. *The Counseling Psychologist, 22,* 6–78.

Teyber, E. (1997). *Interpersonal process in psychotherapy: A relational approach.* Pacific Grove, CA: Brooks/Cole.

Tracy, T., & Dundon, M. (1988). Role anticipations and preferences over the course of counseling. *Journal of Counseling and Development, 35,* 3–13.

Trevino, J. G. (1996). Worldview and change in cross-cultural counseling. *The Counseling Psychologist, 24,* 198–215.

Walborn, F. (1996). *Process variables: Four common elements of counseling and psychotherapy.* Pacific Grove, CA: Brooks/Cole.

Yalom, I. (1980). *Existential psychotherapy.* New York: Basic Books.

8 Listening

> *The greatest compliment that was ever paid me was when one asked me what I thought, and attended my answer.*
>
> —Henry Thoreau

> *A dream destroyed…*
> *Who will I tell?*
> *There's no one listening…*
>
> —Jeffrey Dodds

There is a vast difference between social listening and therapeutic listening. (Ottens, Shank, & Long, 1995). Social listening is largely a matter of not interrupting, of nodding from time to time, and smiling when appropriate. Mainly it involves encouraging someone to continue talking, but at the same level. The purpose of such listening is to maintain contact with the other person that allows for mutual safety and for information, often superficial, to be exchanged. In the process of this exchange, most people are probably asking internal questions such as, "Am I bored? Do I want to change the subject? Have I just told too much about myself and does the sharing seem out of balance? How much longer before I can excuse myself? Oh, my—that's just like something I know about; I can't wait to tell my story!" Usually slowly and gradually we come to know another person and to let them know us, perhaps with the hope that we may strike up a friendship and spend more time together.

Therapeutic listening, while it usually requires attention to some of the same social expectations of not making comments that would unnecessarily contradict or humiliate the other person, is a much more difficult skill to master (Duan & Hill, 1996; Ridley, Mendoza, Kanitz, Angermeier, & Zenk; 1994). Many therapists from different orientations have stressed the need for therapeutic listening, but writers from the person-centered, object relations, and multicultural counseling areas are especially good resources. Additionally, writers discussing brief psychodynamic approaches also provide discussion and models that you may find useful (e.g., Patton & Meara, 1992; Sable, 1997). The classic works of Rogers (1951; 1961) and of Kohut (e.g., 1984) are still timely and enlightening.

Empathy

Titchener (1909) was the first to coin the term "empathy," which he understood as a perceptive awareness of another's feelings. Mead, in 1934, added to the current understanding of the term a cognitive component, the ability to understand. Rogers (1951,1961) and his followers (e.g., Boy & Pine, 1982; Carkhuff and Anthony, 1979; Duncan, Solovey, & Rusk, 1992; Egan, 1994) considered empathy to be one of the three ingredients that led to client progress. Rogers discussed the term at length, explaining that it was the ability to walk in the client's shoes, to understand her or his world so well that you could resonate to the meanings and feelings *as if* (his italics) they were your own. He believed that being heard by someone at this level, with an absence of judgment and in an authentic atmosphere, was necessary and sufficient to lead to the client's increased self-awareness and self-acceptance, which in turn would lead to psychological health and growth.

Kohut (1984), in very similar fashion, suggested that the best definition of empathy was the capacity to think and feel oneself into the inner life of another person. He referred to the attunement of the continuous flow of moment-to-moment experiences of clients as "prolonged" or "empathic" immersion in their psychological field. Kohut's understanding of the *function* of such attuned listening was a bit different from Rogers's. His thought was that being heard at this level was not sufficient for client psychological growth, although it did serve secondarily to establish a meaningful supportive bond between the therapist and client. Rather, his emphasis was more traditionally psychoanalytic: The primary function of empathy was to allow for the gradual understanding of the client's inner experiences and the emergence of specific developmental needs (self-object transferences), which could then lead to specific therapist interpretations and other interventions (Rowe & Isaac, 1989).

As Duan and Hill (1996) explain, the term "empathy" has been used to refer to three possibly overlapping constructs: a personality trait, a situation-specific cognitive-affective state, or a multiphased experiential process. They suggest that future research should focus on the assessment of both intellectual empathy (taking the perspective of another) and of empathic emotions (experiencing vicarious emotions), which they speculate may be separate processes that have been confused in apparently contradictory research findings.

Our understanding of empathy is consistent with Duan and Hill's speculation. We believe that empathic listening involves both aspects—the intellectual understanding of clients' situations, and the ability to resonate vicariously to their affective tone (both in what they felt in situations they may be describing, as well as in how they feel in the immediate moment of sitting in the room with their therapist.) We believe that both kinds of understanding are almost always helpful, if not sufficient, for clients to be helped very fully.

To be able to listen therapeutically is a difficult skill that is never fully mastered. One must remain in close emotional contact with the client, but also more clearly separate. Losing oneself or being personally flooded with client affect greatly reduces one's therapeutic potential. Similarly, distancing oneself is equally destructive. Distancing often feels safer for therapists and helps ensure their objectivity, but it can leave the client, especially the client exploring painful or shameful material, feeling alone and incredibly vulnerable. As discussed in the previous chapter, few therapists, even the most behaviorally trained, deny the importance of the therapeutic alliance that is forged by emotional bonding. Allowing oneself to resonate to the client's feelings, without merging or overidentifying with the client, however, requires much practice.

Let us imagine a hypothetical client, Helen, who comes to an agency for counseling. She is trying to deal with the death of her ten-year-old son, Jeff. Imagine that only two therapists are available to see her—one, too prone to be distant with clients, and the other too prone to overidentify (fuse) with clients. The dialogue with the first therapist might go something like this:

CLIENT: (*In tears*) I just don't know how to keep going. I miss him so much, and I feel so guilty!

THERAPIST: Helplessness is a common enough reaction, and your guilt is probably irrational. Both will diminish in time.

CLIENT: (*Sobbing*) But how do I make it through today? And tomorrow? My other children need me, but I can't seem to do more than go through the motions of taking care of them!

THERAPIST: Sounds like the grief has been a springboard into questioning your adequacy as a mother.

CLIENT: Oh, I don't know. I just know I hurt so much! Can't you help me?

THERAPIST: The grieving process takes time, you know. First one goes through denial, then anger, then…

The therapeutic stance of this therapist is one of self-insulation. Rather than trying to stay in emotional contact with Helen as she expresses her reactions to her son's death, the therapist emotionally backs across the room and responds with intellectual interpretations and explanations. Helen is likely to leave feeling angry and exposed, even if she felt intellectually understood. Probably she will not return.

The dialogue with the second therapist might go something like this:

CLIENT: (*In tears*) I just don't know how to keep going. I miss him so much, and I feel so guilty!

THERAPIST: My God, it must be terrible for you! I don't know how you're doing as well as you are. To lose a child…!

CLIENT: (*No longer crying*) It's the guilt that's the worst part. I keep feeling that I should have been able to help him more.

THERAPIST: (*Beginning to tear up*) Oh, I know. The worst feeling in the world must be to watch a child die and not be able to help. I can't imagine anything worse! It's my worst nightmare—losing my child!

CLIENT: Can you help me?

THERAPIST: (*Reaching for tissue*) Oh, yes, I really want to help. This really hurts, though, doesn't it? How awful you must be feeling! (*begins to weep again*)

This therapist has so completely identified with what Helen is *assumed* to be going through that no therapy can take place. By abdicating objectivity and separateness, the therapist is left with little to offer but emotionalism. At best, Helen is likely to feel overwhelmed by such "empathy." Perhaps she will realize that her assigned role requires a switch from client to comforter. More likely, she will feel angry and uncomfortable with the therapist's presumptuousness and self-indulgence and will not return for a second session with this therapist either.

What does Helen need, then, rather than distance or emotional engulfment? She needs a therapist who has the ability to tolerate and resonate to her pain without needing either to dilute or to identify with it out of her or his own needs. To be such a therapist requires a great deal of emotional strength. It is a bit like swimming very close to a deep, powerful whirlpool; the challenge is to be close enough to the emotional energy to understand what the client must be experiencing without getting swept under oneself. We are of no help as therapists if we are either drowning with the client or miles away on dry land.

Several things help keep therapists on track when dealing with heavy client affect. There is no substitute, as we have suggested several times in other chapters, for obtaining one's own therapy to deal with present or unfinished business. Affect that we have disconnected from its roots within us can be conceptualized as floating, ready to be magnetized by perceived similar affect in clients. We may feel caught off guard and overwhelmed when listening empathically to our clients if we find our own feelings "hooked"; we then are in the dilemma of having to listen to ourselves as well as to the client.

The other primary ingredient in our listening that keeps us able to listen without overidentifying with clients is our curiosity. Roth (1987), Bouchard and Guerette (1991), and Rowe and Isaac (1989), for example, all comment on the importance of not assuming that we know too much about what clients are feeling or experiencing. Once we have made up our minds, it is tempting to quit listening for new information. As Anderson and Goolishian (1988) indicated, the more quickly a therapist understands the client, the less opportunity there is for dialogue, and the more opportunity there is for misunderstanding. With Helen, for example, we don't know until we understand her better what roots within her led to the nuances of her pain. We do know, from a great deal of research and likely from our own knowledge, that losing a child is usually very painful, and we can perhaps imagine what losing our own child might be like. But until we listen more, we can't understand Helen. Was she neglected as a child, did she make promises to herself that she would always protect her own children, and does she now feel as if she abdicated her role as mother?

Had she distanced herself before her son died, and is now feeling regret about that? Might she have relied excessively on her son emotionally, having no other confidants, and now be feeling deprived? These different underpinnings will likely lead to different nuances of pain within her, and we can be of little help until we can let our comprehension emerge as we understand her better. Clearly, identifying with her and assuming she feels as we might in that situation is unproductive.

Therapists' curiosity is partially informed, among other ways, by research they have become familiar with, by biographies they have read, by people they have known well, by clients they have seen before, by what we they learned theoretically. One's own experience is merely one more possible source of understanding. And so as we listen to Helen, we are trying to be emotionally available and capable of resonating to what she feels, but we are also allowing our intellect to inform us of possible models for understanding parental grief, possible interventions we may make, and possible signals to look for that may lead to different hypotheses about what she needs. The outcome of this two-part inner experience within us is a simultaneous processing of information by our cognitive and empathic capabilities. It is this interchange between two parallel internal processes that in part distinguishes the professional therapist from the "good listener." One student referred to this as "listening with my right brain *and* my left brain, and letting them exchange information." Another described the balance as "having my mind and heart engaged simultaneously."

As this two-part exchange takes place, Ottens, Shank, and Long (1995) propose that what optimally helps this process is abductive logic. They point out that the linear problem-solving approach that many novice therapists engage in is less helpful than one in which a dynamic, nonlinear process is employed: selecting clinically relevant clues (acts toward the therapist, client expectations of others, acts toward others, and how client treats himself or herself); generating working hunches based on those clues; synthesizing client information in a nonlinear, dynamic approach; and constructing meaning out of disparate, incomplete, or semiconcealed client sources. While this process sounds complicated, Ottens et al. suggest that movie-watchers engage in it as they try to make sense quickly of a character's dynamics, and in fact they suggest that watching videotaped movies and stopping to gather and make sense of the ongoing clues is a good training practice for students to employ.

We would like to stress that this kind of therapeutic listening is a professional stance that can be learned, although much practice is necessary before the balanced awareness becomes relatively automatic. Our experience in working with many student therapists has led us to conclude that far too large a percentage of them underestimate the amount of practice this complex skill requires before it becomes a ready part of their repertoire. Most quality professionals—from concert pianists to tennis pros—practice hours a day for several years before they expect excellence of themselves. Whether you consider therapy an art or an accumulation of skills, it is important to work regularly and patiently at improving your abilities. Difficult as it may be to learn, this therapeutic listening process will be of immense benefit both to you and to those with whom you work.

For you, it is a process that allows (indeed, requires) you to use all of yourself. Your feelings, your associations, your humor, your theoretical and research understandings, your insight—all of these will become increasingly available as you sit with a client, listening and trying to understand him or her as deeply as possible. If you find yourself leaning too far in the intellectual and distant direction, your emotional resonance to the client should pull you back upright, and if you begin to fuse and overidentify, your cognitive components should serve to rebalance you. There will surely be times when you will feel yourself off balance, but your recovery will become quicker as you practice.

For the clients on the receiving end of such therapeutic listening, there is often a dawning sense of relief. Finally they are in an environment that offers the emotional closeness they need to feel safe (or at least safer) and the clarity and objectivity that help them free themselves from painful patterns of thinking, feeling, and behaving. This combination of safety and clarity offers clients hope. In time, many clients consciously or unconsciously incorporate their therapists' listening stance into their own relationship with themselves and begin to offer themselves what has been so helpful in therapy (Harrist, Quintana, Strupp, & Henry, 1994). They begin to experience, within themselves, the combination of patient compassion and encouragement to try new approaches that they have found in therapy. In a sense, the therapist thus provides a model for the client of how to listen to himself or herself.

Signals of Poor Listening

Once you have something of an idea of what therapeutic listening feels like within yourself when you offer it, it is often helpful to pinpoint those states in which listening clearly is not occurring. (We will not address the obvious here—the times your mind wanders to tonight's dinner menu, etc.) During the therapeutic hour then, when you find yourself drifting into one of these other stances, hopefully your alarm bells will go off so that you can bring yourself back on center. Alarm is an appropriate brief reaction, for in a sense, you will have begun to approach unethical behavior. Listening to the client means that you are putting her or his needs first, which of course is your primary ethical obligation; not listening almost always is an indication that your own needs have superseded the client's. Therapy is slipping toward exploitation, however subtly.

Performance Anxiety

Most beginning therapists have urgent needs to be helpful, especially if the client is paying for therapeutic services. There is a point, though, when the desire to help the client becomes a desire to do it "right," and instead of listening to the client, students begin listening to themselves, as they feverishly attempt to retrieve from their data banks what they are supposed to say in the current situation so that their supervisor, fellow students, own therapist, or whoever will be proud of them. The client's needs may be overlooked as the student becomes preoccupied with looking good (Teyber, 1997). It is crucial to remember that clients have come to you, and you have agreed to see them, because they need something a professional can offer. That is the contract. That is what you promise implicitly each time you close the door and ask the client to sit down. Any time you put your own needs ahead of the client's—including your perfectionist needs to look good—you have violated that contract, even if your intentions were good. Since it is difficult to pay attention simultaneously to your own performance anxieties and to what the client is telling you, we encourage you to spend session time listening to the client, and to try to deal with your own anxieties with your supervisor.

Therapist Overidentification

As mentioned earlier, when therapists lose their objectivity and overidentify with their clients, they lose their ability to help. The client may as well have gone to a support group—which would probably be free, as well as likely have listeners with more direct experience with his or her problem! Whenever you feel convinced that you thoroughly understand a client, we suggest that you actively generate new hypotheses that might explain his or her dynamics and check them out. This client is neither entirely like you nor like anyone else. Maintaining this awareness of individual differences is especially important when you are doing cross-cultural counseling (Trevino, 1996). When clients feel misunderstood or "overunderstood," when they sense that you have boxed them into some preconceived model, they are likely to feel frustration and a desire to withdraw. If the experience continues for more than several minutes, the therapeutic relationship may be jeopardized. Henry and Strupp (1994) were referring to similar destructive processes when they remarked, "A little bit of bad process goes a long way."

Disapproval of Client Affect

It is easy to be a supportive therapist when you like your clients, sympathize with their values, and are proud of the changes they are making. It is trickier to establish an alliance when you disapprove of their behavior (e.g., child abuse, excessive dependency, dangerous irresponsibility, etc.). Many therapists manage by distinguishing between the client's needs or feelings (which can often be supported or at least validated) and client behavior (which might require therapeutic confrontation). But what do you do when you don't like their feelings? What most beginning therapists do—inappropriately—is quit listening.

Let's go back to the example of Helen. Suppose she left the first agency, where she had access to only those two inadequate therapists, and has somehow located you. You get off to a good start. You avoid the errors of the other two and successfully establish a good therapeutic relationship. During the fifth session, Helen begins to talk of her earlier desire as a teenager to have a baby "to play with" and reports that this child, Jeff, was born when she was 18 years old. During her sixth and seventh sessions, she discusses her deteriorating marriage, and you begin to suspect that she had turned to Jeff to meet her emotional needs for intimacy. Perhaps you have some trouble accepting that. By the tenth session, her neglect of the other two children has become a clear pattern, one that began before Jeff's terminal illness. You find yourself feeling increasingly judgmental of her narcissism and immaturity. The more you listen, the clearer it becomes that the family system was dysfunctional from the beginning and that Helen and Jeff's relationship had been particularly enmeshed. Now, as you try to help her explore her grief, you discover yourself thinking that she has no right to feel what she does, that she shouldn't have been so symbiotically attached to him in the first place. Each time she mentions her sense of loss, you notice your inclination to minimize her feelings so that they will be more in line with what you think of as typical parental grief. In short, you disapprove of what seems to you to be grief over an exploitative and dysfunctional relationship.

To be able to help Helen, you will need to find some way to follow the advice of one of the authors' supervisors: "No, no! You have to start where they're *at!*" You could pretend, if you wanted, that by ignoring certain client feelings they would go away, but doing that would waste the client's time and money, damage the therapeutic relationship, and increase your own frustration. Better to remind yourself that your client needs very much to be heard and that your job is to help her express and understand the various textures of what she feels, and make whatever new choices she can that will help herself and her family. If, in fact, Helen's family relationships are dysfunctional, they will much more likely improve through her acknowledging and exploring what is, rather than by denying feelings and motivations because of your disapproval.

Another important listening skill is paying attention to the patterns that evolve regarding the client feelings you have trouble accepting. Granted that many motivations lead to dysfunctional client behavior, why do only certain of these feelings and motivations hook you? What you may discover is a form of countertransference seldom discussed—that is, when the client elicits reactions from you, not which you previously felt toward someone else, but perhaps which you felt toward yourself in a similar situation. For example, a therapist who judged herself harshly for feeling ambivalent in an earlier relationship may well find that she has little patience with a client struggling with ongoing ambivalent feelings about his wife. A therapist who spent many years struggling to overcome his dependency on an autocratic father may find himself dealing with very judgmental reactions toward the passive, dependent wife of an alcoholic. Taboos that we have imposed on ourselves we are likely to impose on others, regardless of their intrinsic wisdom or applicability.

Therapist Overcontrol

Another signal of obstructed listening is therapist attempts to change the client's behavior. Often this takes the form of advice giving, lecturing, rescuing, and other variations of controlling. It is not that offering a client information or advice is always inappropriate; sometimes, in fact, clients truly could benefit from some psychoeducational interventions. Generally, most experienced therapists are very careful about the kind of advice they offer, but doing so is not always untherapeutic. What we are suggesting that you monitor is your motivation for wanting to do these things. Again, the issue is whose needs are you meeting, yours or the client's? If you feel disappointed, hurt, or annoyed when your wisdom is ignored, that is a very strong indication that your motivation was self-serving.

Therapists attempt to change or control clients as a result of crossing boundaries and trying to take responsibility for improving the client's life. Berger (1987) talks about "dispassionate compassion" as the proper stance to take in therapy. When we start feeling passionate regarding our clients, when we feel a strong need to help them or change their minds or teach them a lesson, then we have once again lost the separateness that is the hallmark of therapeutic intimacy. It is not enough to care for our clients. We must learn to care well, and that means, among other things, letting them be responsible for making their own choices. As Rosenthal (1971) explained:

> This is part of the paradox of therapy. I am dependent upon the patient for my very existence as a therapist, and therefore for that measure of my self-esteem which derives from my being a therapist; yet to be effective and uncorrupted by the demands of the patient, my self-esteem must be independent of him. If I don't care, I can't help…; if I care too much, that is, if I want too much for myself, I can't help…. It's like learning not to slam down on your brakes on icy pavement. (p. 6)

Sometimes that can be very hard. When clients you like continue to behave in ways that sabotage their deepest goals or do things that are clearly self-destructive, it is not easy to remain dispassionate. If, for example, the abused wife you have been seeing suddenly decides to move back in with her husband, you are likely to be frustrated and very concerned, and it will be difficult not to overreact.

There are two points we would like to make that may be helpful to remember when you are tempted to overcontrol. First, if lectures or simple advice were going to work in these situations, they probably would have worked before now. Very likely, either the client's friends or family have been delivering lectures or advice for years, or the client himself or herself has been trying to control the behavior with self-threats and judgments. That approach rarely works, so there is no need to try it again. Second, and more to the point, a major paradox may occur. Deep changes sometimes occur when the client feels accepted as is, when there is an absence of therapeutic pressure to be or feel differently. Strangely, when you can offer acceptance and permission not to change, many clients—especially those who already place too many expectations and burdens on themselves—feel freer to change more. And even in those situations when no immediate change is forthcoming, at least the client will not feel it necessary to lie to you about nonexistent changes in order to maintain your goodwill.

Certainly, there will be many times when you will point out to clients that their behavior seems to be in discord with their goals or perhaps with others' welfare. There may be times when you will choose to do that forcefully. But before you do it, check your emotional urgency by asking yourself: If I offer this intervention and it is ignored or resisted by the client, can I accept that and maintain therapeutic contact? When your answer is no, we encourage you to consider that your real work may need to be with yourself rather than with the client and to explore with your supervisor the sources of your urgency.

Levels of Listening

One difficulty that many beginning therapists have is in deciding how and what kind of direction to give to a client's revelations. The guidelines seem contradictory: On the one hand, supervisors encourage acceptance and respect so the client can feel free to explore important issues, but on the other hand, they insist that the client should not be allowed to wander indefinitely or to manipulate the therapist. Further, different theories suggest different directions and interventions. While the issue of how and when to provide direction to a session is too complex to address comprehensively here, we can say that the level at which the therapist listens greatly influences the direction of a session. We would suggest that being able to listen at the three levels discussed below is important, regardless of the theory you espouse. Interventions you should make during and after you listen will vary according to theory, but the more fully you can listen, the better the therapist you will be, regardless of your theoretical orientation.

Listening for Content

Students typically fear that if they have several clients, they will somehow get them mixed up and end up saying, "So, how's the snake phobia?" to the career client. While seasoned therapists do occasionally forget important client material, such lapses are unusual if the client was given full attention during each session. Particularly if the therapist was in tune emotionally, he or she likely constructed images or other impressions as the client's "story" unfolded, and these visualizations can be the avenue to remembering considerable material.

It is impossible, of course, to remember every single thing every client says. Nor would it be particularly wise to try. If you are using all of your energy trying to memorize each piece of data the client offers, you will surely miss the essence of the communication. Clients thankfully tend to be quite forgiving of small lapses; they do, however, feel hopeless and betrayed if the essence is discounted or forgotten. The question to ask yourself as you listen, is, "What does the client mainly need me to understand?"

Keeping this guideline in the forefront of your mind, especially in the initial sessions, will do two things for the therapeutic process: (a) It will mean that the questions you ask will not be wasted on trivia. No client appreciates being interrupted during an emotional outburst to be asked, "Wait. What time did you say that happened?" He or she will, conversely, be more tolerant of questions like,

"Help me understand why this is so infuriating for you. Was this episode the final one in a long string of similar incidents?" (b) It will focus your listening and subsequent responses in such a way as to discourage client rambling or unnecessary storytelling. In effect, you will convey the message, "I want to get to the heart of your concern so I can help you as fully and quickly as possible."

On those rare occasions when you do forget important information, our suggestion is that you be honest. A simple statement like, "I'm sorry. Tell me again about…" is generally easily accepted by most clients.

There is one thing you can be sure of if you are listening for content as well as you should be: Some of your favorite stereotypes and biases will be shattered. You will find mothers who are homicidal, ministers with sexual obsessions, school board members having affairs with high school students, skid row alcoholics who write beautiful poetry, and liberal professors who have unexamined biases. The child you thought was skipping school because he was dealing drugs is instead staying home to take care of his sick sister. The son who has talked about hating his abusive uncle for eight sessions discloses nonchalantly that he carries his uncle's picture with him in his wallet. You will discover that we humans are capable of dazzling courage and selflessness, as well as dangerous sociopathy and closed-mindedness. In short, you will discover that your clients are as complex as you.

Listening for Feelings

If you have been progressing through a typical counseling training sequence, you have probably practiced "reflecting feelings." Perhaps you have learned how to paraphrase and pinpoint affect in a variety of ways, from the brittle "you-are-feeling-(blank)-because-" formula to more elegant narrative techniques. How you let your clients know that you understand what they are experiencing emotionally is much less important than that you do it. Our impression, in accord with Omer's (1997), is that many of the "yes, but" responses that therapists complain of from their clients are less "resistance" than they are a manifestation of the client's feeling misunderstood. Unless you have a clear reason to believe otherwise, we suggest you take each "yes, but" as a signal from the client that you are inappropriately moving into your own agenda and need to slow down instead and listen again to what the client is trying to tell you.

To resonate most effectively to clients' feelings, you will be paying attention to what they say, as well as to their nonverbal communication (Grace, Kivlighan, & Kunce, 1995). There are differences between sadness, melancholy, nostalgia, depression, and grief. As you listen to the nuances of feelings that your client expresses, both verbally and nonverbally, it is worth the time it takes to pinpoint as accurately as possible what emotions he or she seems to be experiencing. The look of surprised relief that comes across the face of the client who hears you accept, clarify, and express accurately the depth and breadth of her or his feelings—that look is worth the effort. For some beginning therapists, this will require enhancing their affective vocabularies. Other therapists will learn to capture the client's emotional state with a metaphor, an image, a line from a song.

What that look of relief represents, besides a more relaxed client, is that you have begun to earn the right to intervene. As Earl Koile (1977) pointed out, being heard is a prelude to the client's ability to hear you. And if he or she cannot hear you, then all of the therapeutic wisdom and insight you offer is wasted. Influence is not automatically accorded to you because of your training. You must earn influence anew with each client, and your ability to make the client feel heard is your primary avenue toward earning it.

As you listen for your client's feelings, you will find that they may arise in relation to situations or issues that are different from what you might expect, and that they flow into other feelings as the meaning and association shifts for the client, often in front of your eyes. (Psychodynamic writers often refer to your following their shifts as "tracking affect.") Do not expect that this will necessarily be very logical. As Grafton (1992), speaking in Kinsey Millhone's voice, said: "Emotion doesn't travel in a straight line. Like water, our feelings trickle down through cracks and crevices, seeking out the little pockets of neediness and neglect, the hairline fractures in our character usually hidden from public view" (p. 177).

If you are distrustful of your own feelings, you will have a very difficult time aiding clients in exploring theirs. Part of the personal work that usually accompanies professional growth as a therapist is the increased commitment to tolerating and exploring one's own painful or contradictory emotions. Surprisingly, some therapists tolerate their own and others' "negative" emotions well but block on "positive" ones such as joy, delight, and love. Discovering which emotions make you feel especially vulnerable and out of control is essential, since until you can gain greater acceptance of them within yourself, you cannot hope to be of much help to your clients as they explore similar ones. Never assume you will be able to "fake it"; clients can pick up on very subtle cues regarding what you are uncomfortable with, and you may inadvertently teach them that they cannot trust you to help in exactly the areas they most need assistance. There is no alternative—you must work on yourself to gain greater familiarity and competence with the whole range of human emotions.

One therapist we know learned this at the probable expense of a vulnerable client. She was completing her internship and had begun to earn a reputation as a therapist familiar and helpful with grief and loss issues. Accordingly, when she was assigned a 19-year-old woman concerned about losing her remission from leukemia, she assumed she could be helpful. She was, after all, relatively comfortable with sadness, fear, anger, hope, and longing. During the fourth session, her client began shaking. The client whispered that she was remembering her fear, not of the disease itself, but of the depersonalization she experienced in the large cancer hospital she'd been in for months of treatment. Within minutes, she was in a state of panic at the thought of having to possibly reexperience that, if in fact she lost her remission. Sensing her panic, the therapist moved immediately into empty reassurances and immediate problem solving. It would not be that bad, the client was older now with more resources, they would figure out how to be more assertive with the hospital staff, and so on. Her words seemed to have no impact on her client's fear, and the client did not return for another session. In retrospect, the therapist realized that she had taught her client that she could talk about many things with the therapist but not her terror. The therapist could not handle that; the client would have to deal with it by herself. The therapist slowly realized that she had treated her client's panic as she treated her own—by running from it. That experience, and the learning that followed, prompted her to tolerate her own panic more willingly and to explore it in more depth with her own therapist.

Before we leave the topic of listening for feelings, we want to add a point which has not been often addressed. As you search for a way to let the client know that you can resonate to their feelings, remember that different cultures, different age groups, and the different genders have some feelings that are considered almost taboo. You would probably not say to a 16-year-old gang member, for example, "Boy, you must have been terrified!" Your additive empathy might be on target, but terror is something he is unlikely to want to acknowledge, at least until the therapeutic alliance is well in place. Similarly, the conservative, middle-class engineer, who mentions in the first session that his father's death last week was difficult, may respond better initially to "Yeah, it's really tough to lose your dad," than to "Under all the attempts to maintain control, you must be feeling like a lost child." Our earlier point, that your empathy should include not only an awareness of their feelings about a given topic, but also your awareness of their immediate experience being in the room with you, is what should make this fine-tuning your word choice come more easily. As Omer (1997) indicated, we want our empathic comments to allow the client to say, "That's me!" We want to make it easy for them to acknowledge their feelings, not defend against our word choice that makes them feel too vulnerable or misjudged.

Listening for Themes

Adler (1931) talked about "guiding fictions." Michael Novak (1970) called them "myths." Bowlby (1988) refers to inner "working models," and cognitive therapists tend to refer to them as "schemas." Regardless of the terminology used, the gist of these constructs is the idea that all of us grow up, and usually live out, certain unquestioned assumptions about ourselves in relation to the rest of the world. For those of us who are lucky, these scripts are relatively functional and allow us some degree of flexibility and happiness. For those less lucky, the scripts are more likely pessimistic, cynical, and hopeless. Life has somehow taught these people, or perhaps they have taught themselves as they tried to make sense of life, that there were few options available to them and most of those wouldn't work. Many of your clients will come in with these unconscious negative or unrealistic assumptions; part of your role may be to help them identify and change the ones that sabotage their greater fulfillment of potential. While the following discussion is presupposing a clientele without an Axis II disorder, we encourage you to read material focusing on how a thematic approach helps in the understanding and treatment of clients with personality disorders (e.g., Beck, Freeman, & Associates, 1995).

As you listen then for these deeper themes, it may help to focus on three overlapping areas: themes regarding self, themes regarding others, and themes regarding life or fate.

1. *Themes regarding self.* Listening to a client, do you hear a pervasive sense of inadequacy? Does it seem as if he or she has trouble claiming the right to set limits or to disagree with authority or to make mistakes? Are the client's self-doubts so overwhelming that much energy is spent second-guessing others so as not to offend them? Or, conversely, is his or her self-assessment so grandiose that negative feedback is routinely discounted or distorted? What is the client's capacity for self-affirmation in stressful or rejecting environments? Obtaining this overall sense of the client's resiliency and self-esteem can be very helpful as you form your diagnostic impressions and treatment goals. Among other things, this gross barometer can give you a sense of how quickly to look for client progress, since, everything else being equal, the lower the client's overall self-esteem, the slower change is likely to occur.

We suggest you also look for exceptions to the pattern you have found. The client who seems overwhelmed with anger may experience relief and peace when playing the piano. The business professional who is controlling and perfectionistic may become quite sprightly when playing with a grandchild. These fluctuations sometimes appear as almost untouched compartments within the client, and exploring them can dramatically enrich your understanding of his or her dynamics. Much of what you will probably be attempting with your clients—a metagoal, of sorts—is aiding them in achieving a healthier relationship with themselves. (In the last decade, Polster, 1995, and others have been conceptualizing an individual as "a family of selves," an approach that can lead to a variety of interventions aimed at increasing understanding of, and reliance on, the various subselves. Similarly, Quintana & Meara [1990] defined intrapsychic characteristics "as interpersonal processes turned inwardly.") As a client of one of the authors said, "I am beginning to treat myself the way I try to treat others, and it feels damn good." As clients learn to treat their human frailties with more acceptance and matter-of-factness, and as they learn to treat themselves with a balance of nurturance and realistic demands, a side benefit is that their relationship with others will likely improve also.

2. *Themes regarding others.* In a later chapter, we will examine in greater depth some of the typical patterns that emerge in relationships. At this point, we want to highlight some of the most obvious themes you are likely to hear with clients. You will quickly discover that much of how they treat others is related to how they treat themselves. The client, for example, who feels one-down and apologetic is likely to defer to those seen as more powerful (although with some frequency this deference may be cloaked in counterdependency). The relative power that a client accords to himself or herself and to others is probably the first pattern you will notice. Not uncommonly, you will experience this directly as you relate to them. As you help clients deal with their relationships with significant others, you will probably be helping many of them assume more power and use it effectively.

It will behoove you to have a good understanding of power and influence and the effects of using them in different ways. You may also have some clients whose style is more powerful than their self-image, leaving them bewildered as to why they elicit some of the negative responses they do; these clients may need your help learning to orchestrate themselves to be "softer" when others feel threatened. Again, as with other patterns, it is helpful to look for exceptions to the rule as you sense the client's behavior changing in different roles. Some shy, "powerless" people, for instance dramatically rise to the occasion when they take a role that requires decisiveness and assurance (e.g., teacher, doctor, etc.).

Another similar theme to listen for is trust: Whom do your clients trust? Do they typically trust one gender more than the other? Do they tend to trust people who deserve their trust? Is their trust all or nothing, or are they able to trust tentatively and continue to evaluate the other person? How do they respond when their trust is violated? Have they attempted to cover their vulnerability with an overlay of distrust and cynicism? It should go without saying at this point that many of these patterns will be hinted at in their relationship with you, since the intimacy of therapy provokes such strong reactions. You may want to look also at the distance clients prefer to keep in relationships—which may or may not be a reflection of trust—and whether their needs and those of their associates are being met by their chosen stance. Many, but not all, clients desire more intimacy than they have in their lives and need to learn to approach others and to invite them closer. Some, however, may be quite comfortable having a relatively formal style with only a few close associates, but their formality and distance may be troublesome to others. It may be important for you to monitor yourself at this point, lest you automatically try to impose your style on someone who is managing fairly well with his or her own.

We would like to suggest attending to a set of themes that cuts across some of those previously mentioned. To get a measure of the client's overall relationship skills, ask yourself, "What is his or her capacity to say yes to others and to say no?" For healthy relationships, both sets of skills are necessary. To be able to affirm others and to accept affirmation is crucial if bonding is to occur. It is also important, however, to be able to protest, to resist undue influence, if necessary to reject—and to be able to respond to these "nos" from others. Saying and hearing the word "no" is frightening for most clients, since associations with parental rejections are so strong, but the skill is vital if clients are to learn to be both in relationship but separate. Again, we would note that your comfort in saying "yes" and "no" to the clients, in affirming and setting appropriate limits, is what he or she will take away more clearly than the specific lessons you try to impart.

Behavioral patterns may be as important to identify as emotional ones. One theoretical orientation, Functional Analytic Psychotherapy, an interpersonal approach based on radical behavioral principles, focuses entirely on identifying clinically relevant behaviors (CRBs) of clients who present with problematic interpersonal behaviors, often with an AXIS II diagnosis. The focus of therapy is on identifying the CRBs that are manifested *in session*, and providing feedback from within a supportive, caring relationship (Callaghan, Naugle, & Follette, 1996). While this may be only a part of what you choose to do as you help clients identify relationship themes, we encourage you to identify behaviors as well as feelings. Sometimes a client discusses feeling disappointed and needing to withdraw from an angry spouse, for example, but fails to convey that he or she stonewalls every opportunity when resolution of a conflict could occur. Relationship patterns, *as they are manifested*, are often a relevant therapeutic topic.

3. *Themes regarding life.* Although listening to your clients' themes in relation to themselves and in relation to others will teach you a great deal about their general approach to life, we believe you will find that the whole is indeed more than the sum of the parts. There are overarching values, dreams, and fears that seem to determine the stance a client takes toward his or her life that are often subtle and unconscious but extremely powerful forces. To get an intuitive sense of your client's stance (or combination of stances), you will need to give up your intensely focused listening and instead rely on listening "around the edges."

One way to look at your clients' approach to life is to see their possible choices as lying on a continuum. To modify some of Rollo May's (1981) thinking, we suggest that one end of this continuum be categorized as surrender, the other end as rebellion. Two less extreme points might be called cooperation and challenge.

Most people have one preferred stance, although many of us shift somewhat when circumstances change. As you consider your clients and their adopted postures, consider also your own, and try to obtain some objective assessment of the costs and benefits of each approach in different life conditions. Surrender, or resignation, is typically associated with a victim stance. These individuals in effect relinquish their own will and bow to forces perceived as greater. It may help to distinguish between "giving up," which often signals passivity and premature abdication of responsibility, and "giving in," which is seen by many as the appropriate religious or psychological response to life and death. Both are subcategories of surrender, but the latter certainly involves more conscious choice and is usually considered more clearly psychologically defensible.

Cooperation is often an optimistic, sometimes playful approach to life. People who cooperate often see themselves as "lucky," so fate is perceived as ultimately on their side. Some cooperators are surely just naive to the deeper injustices and sorrows of life, but not all fit this stereotype. Others are strong, positive, inviting people who have a knack for approaching people and situations in such a way as to elicit positive results. The third group, challengers, are recognized by their ability to focus easily on perceived inconsistencies. Often they refuse to accept usual ways of behaving and thinking and offer instead new, innovative suggestions. For these questioners, their integrity feels subtly undermined by automatically accepting traditional guidelines, and they feel more alive and engaged when adopting a somewhat combative approach to life. Such people often register dissatisfaction with established norms and can be difficult to work or live with, but they demonstrate considerable energy and adventurousness as they forge new, creative pathways.

Rebels are at the extreme end of the continuum. Certainly, social revolutionaries fall in this category, but so also may cancer patients who defy medical "wisdom" and live longer, parents who circulate petitions demanding changes in unfair school policies, a biracial couple attending a school dance in a racist community, and a whistle-blower speaking out on military harassment. Those who defy what others see as inevitable are often seen as "problems," and they frequently face the disapproval of authority figures. These clients may threaten your own sense of morality or good common sense, but their courage and vision is sometimes both inspiring and enlightening to those in the other three categories.

Part of your job as a therapist may be to listen to your clients well enough to help identify their chosen stance, aid them in assessing how such a stance both costs and benefits them, and encourage them to make their choices in relation to life more fully conscious and intentional.

The Empathic Process

Various writers have described the empathic process as comprised of stages (e.g., Trevino, 1996). The cyclical model of Barrett-Lennard (1981) is one that some students find especially helpful as they struggle to make sense of and master the complex skills involved in listening and responding. This model identifies three pieces of the interpersonal empathic process: therapist's resonating to the client, therapist's expression of the client's inner world, and client's receipt of that expression. The emotional closeness required by the first of these skills should be obvious by now. A mistake that some beginning therapists make, however, is to distance themselves as they struggle with ways to construe and express their understanding, and then to overlook how the client has received their intervention. Once you master maintaining emotional connectedness *throughout* your contact with the client, you will find that your empathic interventions come more easily and that you will quickly realize if they have not been received well. This gives you the opportunity to recover at once. This is especially important, since client defensiveness, as indicated by a study conducted by McCullough, Winston, Farber, Porter, Pollack, Laikin, Vingiano, and Trujillo (1991) correlates negatively with therapeutic outcome. That is when you stop, ask them if they would modify your words somehow, and "negotiate" with them, as we discussed in the previous chapter.

As one student said in peer supervision to another, "It's like you're dancing a slow dance with the client. Just because it's your turn to lead doesn't mean that you *let go* of her! You have to stay in touch with her to see if she's still following!" A similar metaphor that we sometimes use is that you are keeping your hand on the emotional pulse of the client all the way through the session. After an intervention on your part, it is especially important to "check their pulse," that is to watch their face and body posture and see if you get the "That's me!" reaction that Omer (1997) talked about. If not, you should be able to tell immediately and realize that you need to recover.

Summary

Therapeutic listening requires that therapists be able to offer not only an objective analysis of the client's psychological problems and personality style, but also consistent emotional availability. This balance of intellectual analysis and empathic understanding is a skill that generally can be learned by students, although it does require much practice. Part of such learning often involves becoming aware of why one is not listening and then making appropriate corrections. Therapists from different theoretical orientations tend to listen for different kinds of material, at different levels. Whether one listens at strictly content level, more deeply for feelings, or more deeply still for client themes, the depth of the listening often determines the direction in which the client will move. As a general guideline, the more fully the client feels understood, the more influence he or she accords the therapist.

DISCUSSION QUESTIONS

- What are your "hot topics" that often lead to an immediate emotional reaction? How might this affect your work with clients who introduce such a topic? What is your own emotional investment (i.e., your history with the topic) that leads to your overreaction, and how can you deinvest yourself of it when working with clients?

- Which is easier for you—emotionally resonating to a client's world, or intellectually hypothesizing a client's motivations? How can you work on the more difficult skill? Under which circumstances have you been able to manage using both skills simultaneously?

- Imagine that you are a famous therapist whom people flock to from all over the world. What situations have you heard or read about recently that involve people you might have difficulty empathizing with (e.g., serial killer, teenage mother whose child perished in a fire when mother left her alone to attend a party, child who witnessed mother's death in an accident, etc.)? If this person came to you and referral were not an option, how would you begin the psychological process of assuming an appropriate listening stance?

BIBLIOGRAPHY

Adler, A. (1931). *What life should mean to you.* Boston: Little Brown.

Anderson, A., & Goolishian, H. (1988). Human systems as linguistic systems. *Family Process, 27,* 371–393.

Barrett-Lennard, G. T. (1981). The empathy cycle: Refinement of a nuclear concept. *Journal of Counseling Psychology, 28,* 91–100.

Beck, A., Freeman, A., & Associates. (1995). *Cognitive therapy of personality disorders.* New York: Guilford.

Berger, D. (1987). *Clinical empathy.* Northvale, NJ: Aronson.

Bouchard, M. A., & Guerette, L. (1991). Psychotherapy as a hermeneutical experience. *Psychotherapy, 28,* 385–394.

Bowlby, J. (1988). *A secure base: clinical application of attachment theory.* London: Routledge.

Boy, A., & Pine, G. (1982). *Client-centered counseling: A renewal.* Boston: Allyn & Bacon.

Callaghan, G. M., Naugle, A. E., & Follette, W. C. (1996). Useful constructions of the client-therapist relationship. *Psychotherapy, 33,* 381–390.

Carkhuff, R., & Anthony, W. (1979). *The skills of helping.* Amherst, MA: Human Resource Development Press.

Cummings, E. M., & Cicchetti, D. (1990). Toward a transactional model of relations between attachment and depression. In M. T. Greenberg, D. Cicchetti, and E. M. Cummings (Eds.), *Attachment in the preschool years: Theory, research, and intervention.* Chicago: University of Chicago Press.

Duan, C., & Hill, C. E. (1996). The current state of empathy research. *Journal of Counseling Psychology, 43,* 261–274.

Duncan, B. L., Solovey, A. D., & Rusk, G. S. (1992). *Changing the rules: A client-directed approach to therapy.* New York: Guilford.

Egan, G. (1994). *The skilled helper* (5th ed.). Pacific Grove, CA: Brooks/Cole.

Grace, M., Kivlighan, D. M., & Kunce, J. (1995). The effect of non-verbal skill training on counselor trainee nonverbal sensitivity and responsiveness and on session impact and working alliance ratings. *Journal of Counseling and Development, 73,* 547–552.

Grafton, S. (1992). *"I" is for innocent.* New York: Henry Holt.

Harrist, R. S., Quintana, S. M., Strupp, H. H., & Henry, W. P. (1994). Internalization of interpersonal process in time-limited psychodynamic psychotherapy. *Psychotherapy, 31,* 49–57.

Henry, W. E., & Strupp, H. H. (1994). The therapeutic alliance as interpersonal process. In A. O. Horvath and L. S. Greenberg (Eds.), *The working alliance: Theory, research, and practice* (pp. 51–84). New York: John Wiley.

Kohut, H. (1984). *How does analysis cure?* Chicago: University of Chicago Press.

Koile, E. (1977). *Listening as a way of becoming.* Waco, TX: Regency Books.

MacDonald, G. (1996). Inferences in therapy: Processes and hazards. *Professional Psychology, 27,* 600–603.

May, R. (1981). *Freedom and destiny.* New York: W. W. Norton.

McCullough, L., Winston, A., Farber, B. A., Porter, F., Pollack, J., Laiken, M., Vingiano, W., & Trujillo, M. (1991). The relationship of patient–therapist interaction to outcome in brief psychotherapy. *Psychotherapy, 28,* 525–533.

Mead, G. H. (1934). *Mind, self, and society.* Chicago: University of Chicago Press.

Novak, M. (1970). *The experience of nothingness.* New York: Harper & Row.

Omer, H. (1997). Narrative empathy. *Psychotherapy, 34,* 19–27.

Ottens, A. J., Shank, G. D., & Long, R. J. (1995). The role of abductive logic in understanding and using advanced empathy. *Counselor Education and Supervision, 34,* 199–211.

Patton, M. J., & Meara, N. M. (1992). *Psychoanalytic counseling.* New York: Wiley.

Polster, E. (1995). *A population of selves: A therapeutic exploration of personal diversity.* San Francisco: Jossey-Bass.

Ridley, C. R., Mendoza, D. W., Kanitz, B. E., Angermeier, L., & Zenk, R. (1994). Cultural sensitivity in multicultural counseling: A perceptual schema model. *Journal of Counseling Psychology, 41,* 125–136.

Rogers, C. R. (1951). *Client-centered therapy: Its current practice, implications, and theory.* Boston: Houghton-Mifflin.

Rogers, C. R. (1961). *On becoming a person.* Boston: Houghton-Mifflin.

Rosenthal, V. (1971). Transcending the role of the psychotherapist. *Voices, 7,* 2–7.

Roth, S. R. (1987). *The art of wooing nature.* Northvale, NJ: Aronson.

Rowe, C. E., & Isaac, D. S. (1989). *The "technique" of psychoanalytic counseling.* Northvale, NJ: Aronson.

Sable, P. (1977). Disorders of adult attachment. *Psychotherapy, 34,* 286–296.

Teyber, E. (1997). *Interpersonal process in psychotherapy: A relational approach.* Pacific Grove, CA: Brooks/Cole.

Titchener, E. (1909). *Experimental psychology of thought processes.* New York: Macmillan.

Trevino, J. G. (1996). Worldview and change in cross-cultural counseling. *The Counseling Psychologist, 24,* 198–215.

CHAPTER

9 Mistakes That Therapists Make

What's terrible is to pretend that the second-rate is first-rate. To pretend that you don't need love when you do; or you like your work when you know quite well you're capable of better.
—Doris Lessing, quoted in *The Quotable Woman*

When we can begin to take our failures nonseriously, it means we are ceasing to be afraid of them. It is of immense importance to learn to laugh at ourselves.
—Katherine Mansfield, quoted in *The Quotable Woman*

Imagine that you are an intern working in a large university counseling center. A 19-year-old African American woman, who is a sophomore, seeks services with an initial presenting complaint of loneliness, lack of friends, and depression. She believes that a part of her problem is that there are relatively few African American students on the campus, but she also believes that there is much covert racism on campus and that such racism is affecting her ability to find friends who are not African American. She describes one or two specific examples of what appears to be racism, but she describes several other situations as involving racism, but which in your view could be either racism or any of several other problems. As you talk with her, you notice that when you ask about the racism, she seems very responsive to your questions, she elaborates, and seems very involved in the process. On the other hand, as you ask about her family, previous psychological difficulties, and other topics, she seems quickly to bring the discussion back to the racism issue. She is conversant with many African American writers such as Louis Gates Jr. and Cornell West—people whom she quotes liberally.

Given the above information, does it seem to you that you might profitably spend a couple of sessions or more of psychotherapy discussing racism with this client? Would you view it as a therapeutic mistake to spend a substantial portion of these sessions focusing primarily on the racism inherent in the culture of the United States (as opposed to focusing the issue on her own experience of racism)? Does your view of whether the therapist should spend substantial therapy time discussing racism depend on the ethnicity of the therapist? What else, if anything, would you want to know to answer these question with some degree of confidence? How (if at all) would your answer to these questions be affected if you knew that the woman's insurance would cover only five sessions?

The case just described raises a number of questions about what it means to make a mistake as a psychotherapist. What criteria should we use? How are we to make sense of a situation in which one supervisor recommends a course of action and another supervisor sees that course as a clear mistake? Kottler (1993) gives a good example of why confusion often obtains as we think about whether various interventions do or do not represent mistakes. Kottler solicited feedback from various supervisors, after giving them a verbatim quote from a client and a student therapist:

CLIENT: Nobody can believe that the state department requires seventy-one credits beyond a bachelor's degree to get a license to teach elementary school.

COUNSELOR: Now, you weren't sure you even wanted to teach because you want to teach students who were willing and interested in learning.

> Supervisor 1: Good direction but awkwardly worded.
>
> Supervisor 2: Why did you say that?
>
> Supervisor 3: This confrontation seems premature.
>
> Supervisor 4: I am unsure of what you are trying to do here.
>
> Supervisor 5: Good restatement.
>
> Supervisor 6: This statement appears unwarranted.
>
> Supervisor 7: Excellent response! You are moving the client closer to the real issue. (pp. 73–74)

These sorts of differences are the stuff of which supervisee nightmares are made and the kind of evidence often cited by skeptics who wonder about the value of supervision, if not the value of psychotherapy. So, perhaps a good place to start the discussion of mistakes that therapists make is to recognize that many interventions seen as "mistakes" by one supervisor will also be seen as a good intervention by another.

Although it may sound a little strange, we hope that while you are in training you will make quite a few mistakes as a therapist, because making mistakes is a great way to learn (assuming you have good supervision). In clinical training, you are expected to make mistakes; you have a license to fail. After you have your Ph.D., you will place more pressure on yourself. So your years of training should be "the good old years." Perhaps more so than at any other time in your life, you will be rewarded for being able to recognize your shortcomings. So, we wish for you a tolerant attitude toward your shortcomings as a therapist, a good time talking about them with your supervisor, and the healthy expectation on your part that you will commit, and are entitled to, a reasonable number of them.

Mistakes and Theoretical Orientation

Let us divide the behavior of therapists roughly into three categories. In the first category, we have unanimous (or near unanimous) agreement on what should be done. For example, it is generally agreed that it is a mistake to have a sexual relationship with a client or to discuss one of your cases publicly at a cocktail party. In the second category, we have therapeutic interventions and behaviors about which the majority of therapists probably agree but which do elicit differing opinions among therapists. For example, touching clients, disclosing something about yourself, and expressing some of your feelings are things that the majority of therapists likely believe can be helpful at one time or the other but about which you will most certainly find some disagreement. In the third category are behaviors about which we assume we do *not* have a clear consensus among therapists. As implied above, there are actually a large number of behaviors in this category. The fact that experienced therapists may disagree on the best or ideal intervention at a given time does not, however, keep them from agreeing on many basics. So even though there are many interventions that fall into category three, there are still many that fall into category one or two. It is behaviors that we believe fall into these two categories that we will focus on in this chapter. Even though in the book we make an effort to discuss mainly "mistakes" on which there is general agreement, we recognize (as suggested above) that when an intervention is labeled a mistake, that judgment, and especially any elaboration of the judgment, will be strongly influenced by the theoretical orientation of the therapist. For example, a mistake in person-centered therapy might not be a mistake from a cognitive–behavioral perspective. Although we try to discuss issues that transcend theoretical orientations, we realize that the extent to which you (and your supervisor) agree or disagree with our comments will be influenced by your theoretical orientation. It should also be noted that when we try to define mistakes we are forced to make assumptions about what is good mental health—assumptions that may have a very elusive character (Bugental, 1988).

We turn now to a discussion of various mistakes.

Common Mistakes

Trying to Solve the Problem before You Understand the Problem

We discussed this issue briefly in Chapter 6, Intake Interviewing, noting that it takes some time to find out what the problem is—what its salient features are. Although we are not behavior therapists, we think it fair to point out that this is a system of psychotherapy that emphasizes careful analysis of the problem before trying to solve it. You may or may not believe in a "behavioral" approach to therapy, but thinking carefully about what the problem is and how best to approach the solution is an area in which most of us could use some improvement.

The previous comments are not meant to suggest that therapy cannot begin until the client has answered hundreds of questions (the issue of questions is addressed below). Part of what we are saying is that problems are frequently very complex, with interlocking pieces. For example, consider the case of a woman who comes to a university counseling center and says, "I am depressed; I think it's because I'm flunking in one of my courses." In such a case you may begin to ask many questions about school. Perhaps the client acknowledges that school is very important—that she has never made less than a C before and that if she does now she thinks the world will end. You don't think she's trying to punish her parents. You don't think she's delaying "going into the real world." The figures she gives you suggest that many students do fail this particular course. She seems to be taking appropriate steps about her low grade. She has hired a tutor, she has talked to the instructor, she is studying for tests with friends, she has been to the study skills center. She reports that she is not particularly anxious during the tests. You don't see any additional behavioral steps that can be taken to help her improve her grade. Perhaps this area is just not her "cup of tea." You think, "If her grade went up, she would not be depressed." But you don't see how that's going to happen and you don't think you have much to offer there. She reports that she has never been depressed before except once briefly when she made an F on a test. It seems that the depression is situation-specific and reactive. If she does make a D in the course she can't seem to think of anything that will happen that will be all that bad—she will just feel bad. You are ready as a therapist to deal with her high standards for herself. She is depressed, you think, because a failing grade in a course means *she* is a failure. She overidentifies with her achievements. Maybe her parents gave her subtle messages about how she needs to achieve for them. So, you see the depression and you think you understand the cause. You are ready to solve the problem with psychotherapy. You spend five sessions focusing on the issue of high standards. The client admits that she is impatient with herself. She starts to understand, you think, that she does not have to be perfect. Therapy is progressing. She is still depressed, but you say to yourself, "These things take time." But wait. In the sixth week of therapy, *any* one of the following occurs:

Scenario #1: The client's mother calls and says, "I know Karen is seeing you. I'm very concerned because she seems to be getting more depressed, and last night on the phone she sort of hinted at suicide. I guess she told you about the fact that her fiance died one year ago this week."

Scenario #2: Your client's roommate calls. "I know I probably shouldn't be calling you, but I was afraid that Karen hadn't told you that she's bulimic. I thought you should know."

Scenario #3: At the end of the sixth session Karen says, "Well, I guess making a bad grade in calculus isn't so bad after all." She pauses. You say, "So you're not a failure even if your grade isn't all that hot." "Right," she says. "After all, even my older sister, who had a four-point in everything else made a B in calculus."

Scenario #4: At staffing that week a case is being presented. A female client has come seeking services. She is a lesbian who broke up with a lover two months ago. She wanted to tell the two sets of parents about the relationship. Her lover, who turns out to be Karen, wasn't ready to "come out."

No therapist can always zero in on the key issue in the first session or two. (In fact, many cases turn out not to have a single *key* issue.) However, each of the scenarios above is likely a preventable surprise in that if the fictitious therapist had not been so intent on solving the problem of high standards, he or she perhaps would have learned something of the more pressing concern earlier. A good rule of thumb is to repeatedly ask yourself, "Is there something I might be missing here?" or "What cues do I seem to be minimizing?"

Similarly, therapists sometimes fail to solicit concrete, relevant information. For example, a client told her therapist that she had been referred for counseling by Child Protective Services as a prerequisite to her regaining custody of her son. She explained that she had "given" her son to her brother, but that it "hadn't worked out." Her agenda was to learn some parenting skills. During supervision, the therapist realized that, in her attempt to make her client more comfortable, she had not asked for more concrete information. As the story later unfolded, the brother had filed charges against the boy after the *second* time his home was burned down by the young man! Clearly, a quick course of parenting skills would be insufficient in helping this mother cope with her child. This is another example of how important it is that therapists understand the problem before they try to solve it.

Focusing on Someone Other Than the Client

A mistake that is very easy to make when you are just starting out as a therapist is to allow yourself to be drawn into an extended (even repeated) discussion about someone in the client's life other than the client. Consider the following in which a client talks about his family, including his alcoholic mother:

CLIENT: I'm about to tell my brother that this time I am not going to be the one to rescue Mother.

THERAPIST: What do you think your brother will say?

CLIENT: Well, I don't know but I think it's his turn. I've done it so much. I'm just sick of it. It seems like somebody's got to do it; we can't leave her in that house by herself—she has almost died three times. But this time it's up to my brother.

THERAPIST: Will your brother do something about the situation?

CLIENT: Well, my brother is the kind of guy who…

In this example, the therapist makes the almost immediate mistake of focusing on the brother rather than the client. Perhaps the client's brother is indeed important in the client's dynamics. Certainly we know that the family is. But that is not the issue. We emphasize here that the focus of individual therapy should be on the client and not on others. If the brother is a part of the picture, we should deal with that part by seeing how the client's distress is related to the brother. The place to start is with the client, not the brother. So even if the brother is important in the client's distress, the focus must start, and work through, the client. (Naturally, these comments are about individual therapy and do not apply if you are doing family therapy.)

Consider a second example in which a client talks about her parents who, "Treat me like a little girl":

CLIENT: I love them a lot but I just can't be their little girl forever. They are just so hard to talk to about this.

THERAPIST: Parents can be difficult. Yet I also am guessing that something inside *you* makes this issue tough for you to handle.

CLIENT: Well, when someone says "You're my little girl and you always will be," what can you say?

THERAPIST: Perhaps it's tough to get clear in your mind about the kind of relationship you want.

CLIENT: What does it matter if I am clear? I just can't hurt their feelings by saying "I'm not your little girl." They're going to treat me like that no matter what I do.

THERAPIST: Parents are human too. Do you think that maybe your parents are afraid of losing you completely?

CLIENT: I think you are probably right. They have always centered their life around us kids. I'm the last one and they must be feeling sort of lonely.

THERAPIST: Well, for example, have your parents started any new activities since you moved to college—something to "fill the void"?

CLIENT: I don't think so. Maybe they could start having more friends over. I could mention that to my mom.

This example illustrates something that happens many times. In the first two interventions the therapist keeps the focus on the client. However, the client repeatedly talks about her parents. In the third intervention the therapist should have stayed with the client, perhaps addressing the client's sense of helplessness, her sense of responsibility, perhaps even her love for her parents. Instead, the therapist slips into talking about the parents. At first glance the intervention may seem fine. It is likely an accurate statement, and it communicates compassion for the parents. Notice that the client even "reinforces" the therapist for what the therapist has said. Having been reinforced, the therapist continues to focus on the parents, now expanding the focus to include an analysis of the *parents'* problem. The client's problem is now nonexistent.

We are not saying that it is wrong to discuss with clients how someone else may be feeling or the motivation for someone else's action. We are saying that such an "educational procedure" should take back seat to a focus on what is troubling the client.

Not Asking about Previous and Current Treatment

As noted in Chapter 6, Intake Interviewing, prospective clients should be asked if they are currently being seen in treatment. If so, only in very unusual circumstances should you make a commitment to see such a client in an ongoing relationship prior to contacting the other therapist. An exception to the rule would be if the other therapist seems to be engaging in unethical behavior and the client asks that you not contact him or her. Even in such a situation, there are obvious reasons why you need to contact the other therapist, with the client's permission of course.

One reason it is a mistake to begin treatment without consulting with the other therapist is that the client's version of what happened in therapy may be at variance with the facts of the case. In many instances, this may merely reflect the issue of client and therapist having different perspectives on therapy. In other cases, such discrepancies may highlight serious client pathology. For example, in a private practice setting, a prospective client told a therapist that the issue of termination was thoroughly discussed with a previous therapist. After seeing the client for several sessions, the therapist learned that in reality there had been no termination, and that the client had in fact abruptly stopped coming in the middle of therapy, which was a recurrent pattern for him. Needless to say, the therapist who was now seeing the client was thus in a difficult position.

As noted in Chapter 5, Ethical and Legal Issues, we have an ethical obligation to proceed with caution when offering services to a client who is already in therapy. Failure to ascertain such information is clearly inconsistent with a careful and thoughtful approach in these circumstances. Thus, it is very important to "check the facts," whenever possible, if clients say that they have been in therapy, and especially so if they indicate that they are currently seeing a therapist. In extreme situations, failure to ask about previous treatments might later form the basis for a malpractice suit. Certainly clients have a right to choose their therapists, and of course informed consent must be obtained when you seek information from previous or current therapists.

Too Much of One Thing

In a prepracticum or in a first counseling methods course students often are told, or may get the impression, that there are a number of rules of the form "don't do this" that guide therapeutic practice (this chapter might be viewed as one set of such rules). So for example, you may be told, "Don't give advice," "Don't give too much reassurance," and "Don't ask too many questions." When it comes to such stereotypic interventions as advice, reassurance, asking questions, and the like, the problem generally is not that you should not do it but rather (a) that the timing is bad or (b) that you may rely on it too much. We will delay for the moment the question of timing and discuss the issue of the "too much" mistake.

Here is an exercise you can try. After you have seen a few clients and audio- or videotaped the sessions, choose a few ten-minute segments at random. Before reviewing the segments, make a list of the stereotypic responses you believe are *generally* not good interventions. Add to this list any mistakes you fear you make too often. Then review a few segments of tapes from three or four clients and make a tally mark each time you hear yourself giving advice or whatever. After listening to eight or nine segments, you should be able to get a fairly good idea of the types of interventions on which you are overrelying. You should also begin to get a sense (this is more difficult) of the types of situations in which you are likely to rely on a particular form of intervention. For example, do you start to ask a lot of questions if the client becomes angry? Do you tend to give advice when the client seems indecisive?

Each of us as therapists makes mistakes. For some of us, one of the mistakes we make is to rely over and over on the same sort of response. One of your jobs in becoming a therapist is to identify the types of responses of which you make "too much" use, especially if one of these types falls into a category that we as therapists consider "suspect" anyway (for example, giving advice).

Therapists' Behaviors Inappropriate to Their Role

There is a "class" of behaviors, one might say, into which many beginning therapists fall from time to time. That is the group of social behaviors (within the session) that are clearly inappropriate to the role. Examples of this class include chatting, nervous laughter, and telling jokes with no therapeutic point. We emphasize that in order to make judgments about what behaviors are appropriate for the role, one must also make some assumptions about the client's culture. That is to say, although some behaviors clearly conflict with the role of being a therapist (e.g., having sex with a client), with regard to other behaviors, it becomes more difficult to specify whether the behavior is or is not inappropriate without being familiar with the client's culture. With this caveat, we will describe a few of the "role violations" that we have observed in supervision.

"Chatting" is one of the social interactions that we all practice with our friends from time to time. However, it is generally not a form of interaction we should practice with our clients. What do we mean when we use the word "chatting?" Examples include giving detailed (and literal) answers when clients ask you a question about yourself or your interests and talking about things such as the weather for the first few minutes of the session. If the client begins the session with, "Isn't today a lovely day," there is nothing wrong with saying, "Yes, it certainly is." In general, you should not go on to comment on the possibility of whether this winter will be tougher than the last one, the unpredictability of the weather, and so forth. In some cultures, however, chatting for just a few minutes at the beginning of therapy may be necessary to "break the ice" and help clients understand that you will be able to identify with them. For example, using "small talk" with Mexican American clients may enhance the therapeutic relationship and facilitate communication between client and therapist (Gonzalez, 1995; Ruiz & Langrod, 1992).

Another issue that comes up from time to time is the question of how humor should be or can be used in psychotherapy. On occasion, clients may tell you a joke. In our view, it is a therapeutic mistake to merely laugh at the joke and not be in any way curious or concerned about what the joke means. We are not suggesting that you should never laugh at a client's joke. However, we recognize that much humor is based on anxiety, subtle (or not so subtle) ridicule of various ethnic groups, and taboos. In such cases, laughing at the joke makes you a part of the ridicule, the rebellion, or whatever theme underlies the joke. Laughing communicates that you hold the values expressed by the joke. Since most clients realize they are not in therapy to "have a good time," they do not tell jokes; hence, when this norm is violated, the issue should be carefully noted by the therapist. In most cases the content of the joke should be carefully considered by the therapist, although the therapist may choose not to make any comments to the client. For example, one should ask oneself, "How is the theme in the joke related to the issues that the client brought to therapy or is now dealing with in therapy?"

There are at least two other issues that should be considered when clients tell a joke. The first is how the telling of the joke fits into the pattern of the session. Was it used to reduce anxiety about a subject? Did it follow your being confrontational about an issue? The second is what the telling of the joke suggests in terms of your relationship to the client. For example, might the client be attempting to make you a friend rather than a therapist?

Perhaps you are asking, "Well, what if they *do* tell a joke? Am I supposed to just look at them?" Certainly there are many funny jokes that do not communicate a value to which we object. These jokes we tend to feel free to laugh at unless we believe that the joke is expressly designed to undermine therapeutic progress. Laughing at the joke does not mean you give up your right as a therapist to process it. At times you will laugh spontaneously at a joke, only to realize almost instantly that the joke subtly communicates a value to which you object or that makes a powerful statement about the difficulties of the client. In such cases we recommend that you say something such as the following: "I find myself laughing at the joke you told, yet I'm realizing now how much *you* feel like that 'drunk' in the story." If the joke, for example, is racist, sexist, or in some other way does violence to our value system, we do not laugh. We do try very hard to understand what the client is trying to communicate. As we see our job, it is to understand (and help clients understand) why they ridicule others. Our job is not to tell clients that their values are wrong but rather to help them understand (if this is an issue in therapy) how their values and their distress are linked.

Another example of a behavior inconsistent with the role of the therapist is laughing in order to reduce your anxiety. By definition, nervous laughter means that you are laughing because you are anxious and not because you are truly amused. Beginning therapists, however, often do find themselves laughing in response to something a client said, and then realize in supervision that they laughed because they were uncomfortable with the statement. Reviewing a few of your audio- or videotapes should be enough to help you ascertain whether you are prone to this sort of mistake. There are several reasons why nervous laughter is to be avoided. The first is that you are sending a mixed message to clients. You are verbally saying, "I thought that was funny," while in reality you did not think it was funny. If there is one thing clients don't need more of it is mixed messages. Of course, there are many other ways to send mixed messages, and these should also be avoided (for example, emotionally withdrawing from the client—for whatever reason—while in the same session saying something such as "Your lack of trust keeps you from making contact with people"). Mixed messages, including laughing when you are not amused, make it very difficult for clients to learn to trust the environment (other people), because they can never be quite sure what the environment really *is*.

A second reason to avoid nervous laughter is that whatever is making you nervous is something about which you need to learn. If you "laugh off" these situations, it is unlikely that you will ever discover what is making you anxious. If you do not become aware of what is making you anxious, you are operating with a blind spot with all your clients.

A third reason to avoid this type of laughter is that you could and should be making a more effective intervention than laughing. Laughing when you are nervous may help you be less nervous, but it does not help clients explore their feelings or grapple with their problems. Fourth, laughing is often a form of reinforcement. Clients from time to time tell stories to avoid an issue. If you laugh (rather than help them go deeper into their feelings), they are likely to tell more stories.

Finally, you should entertain the hypothesis that these situations may be produced by a kind of collusion between you and the client. Perhaps your laughing is in a sense encouraged by the client. Perhaps the client wants you to laugh rather than trying to help him or her go deeper into the problem. Some clients have become very adept at making others laugh in order to keep interactions on a superficial level. So even if you find yourself truly amused by some clients (as you most certainly will), appreciate and enjoy their humor but keep open the possibility that the effectiveness of therapy may be reduced by this "strength" of the client.

Since we have raised the issue of nervous laughter and telling jokes, we want to emphasize that the use of humor in psychotherapy can be a very effective tool (Richman, 1996; Strean, 1994). If you view therapy as a procedure devoid of levity, you will probably not last long as a therapist. In the first place, it will be hard for you to find enough rewards to keep you doing therapy. In the second place, unless you are *very* good at what you are doing, your clients will be less than likely to return for very many sessions of this grim procedure.

Simply expressed, our philosophy is to have some fun at being a therapist. We also want to encourage our clients to use strengths, such as the ability to see humor in a situation, in order to deal with adversity. On the other hand, as therapists we must be alert to when we allow ourselves or our clients to use laughter as a way of avoiding that with which we must deal. Certainly we also want to make sure that our humor is not perceived by clients as demeaning or condescending.

Setting the Client Up for Failure

All therapists presumably want the best for their clients. We want clients to be less anxious, to be creative, to have friends, to enjoy life, to be sensitive, caring people.

In our exuberance to have this happen, we sometimes push clients, whether subtly or overtly, into behaviors for which they are not ready. Of course, part of our job is to encourage and support new behaviors for the client, and there are judgment calls to be made as to when he or she is ready to confront mother, invite a potential date to dinner, or look for a new job. Certainly it is possible to conspire with clients to help them avoid taking a slightly risky step for which they *are* ready. However, we emphasize here the necessity of not pushing clients into situations for which they are not prepared. We are sometimes prone to believe that we have easy answers to difficult problems. Most clients cannot and will not make dramatic changes quickly. If you push them toward something for which they are not ready, and you are *lucky*, they will resist you, think you foolish and lacking in understanding, and probably feel guilty because they are not living up to your expectations. If you are *unlucky*, these clients will perhaps either fail and regress, or quit therapy altogether before being "forced" to do something they "know" they cannot do. It is very important to communicate that therapy is a shared endeavor. If clients seek help in making behavioral changes, it is imperative that they receive the message from you that they will not be pushed into doing something for which they are not prepared. (Additional comments concerning this issue are found in Chapter 3, Client Fears, Chapter 6, Intake Interviewing, and Chapter 8, Listening.)

Perhaps you are asking, "What if the client has a great fear of failure and wants to be able to handle failure in a more satisfactory way?" For example, a college student may say, "I want to be able to ask people out for a date and not let it bother me when they say, 'No.'" Your work with the client might then involve having her ask someone for a date when the probability for success was not particularly high. The critical issue here is ensuring that the client is ready to try this and that she is not just responding to subtle, or not so subtle, pressure from you. More generally, however, we would encourage you to take the time to ascertain in what way the reported symptom might be part of a larger issue—in this case, for example, perhaps ambivalence over establishing intimate relationships.

Trying to Be a Friend

Most beginning therapists know they should not be "just a friend" to a client. They know, for example, that you should not be having a beer with a client every Friday afternoon. There are a number of actions (innumerable, in fact) that, if taken, suggest that you are perhaps more a friend than a therapist. For example, you should not loan or give money to clients (such requests are most likely to be made in a hospital setting). Don't make a habit of "chatting" with them during the therapy session, don't try to rescue them from difficult situations, refrain from giving advice, and don't comment on the client's personal appearance unless this is an issue in therapy. There are some people with whom you will be very tempted to establish a friendship. For example, there will be those clients who have no friends. You may be tempted to just "let them talk since they have no one to listen to them." Although there are undoubtedly some cases in which the client's "just talking" is therapeutic, more often we view such an arrangement as the therapist selling himself or herself short. You are not spending five or six years of your life training to be just "someone who listens," and most of your clients are asking for something more. Social listening may be a component of what you do, but do not allow it, except in very select cases, to define your function as a therapist.

You should not delude yourself by using more complex conceptualizations to justify allowing the client to treat you like a friend and vice versa. For example, at times we have had students explain their "friendship chatting" behavior with a client by saying that the client needed to learn how to self-disclose in a nonthreatening environment. While this may very well be true, do not let it become an excuse for failing to carry out your appropriate role as a psychotherapist.

Occasionally you may have clients who have such similar interests and/or intriguing ways of viewing situations that you may find yourself wishing you knew them outside of therapy so you could just enjoy spending time with them. Of course you cannot do that, but the idea of the two of you sharing ideas about mutual interests may be especially tempting if you have a legitimate dual relationship—if for example, you attend the same church or temple or are both graduate students in the same college. In these instances, your professionalism will be challenged in an ongoing way, as you remind yourself to keep the process focused on therapeutic issues, rather than being seduced into discussing interesting but irrelevant topics.

Not Tolerating Silence

We discussed silence to some extent in Chapter 2, Questions That Beginning Therapists Ask. We want to emphasize again that silence is not necessarily bad. It is not a signal that you need to say something. One of the most common mistakes that beginning therapists make is not being able to tolerate silence. If you are comfortable with therapeutic silence, the client is more likely to be also, and thereby less likely to fill the airways with stories and tangential comments. One of our supervisees, in reflecting on his propensity to say *something* during silence, labeled what he was doing as "production therapy." In production therapy there is a limited amount of time, and products (words) must be produced at a high rate. It is often amazing when we consider the size of the "insight leap" we expect from our clients after only a few seconds of silence. So, give your clients, and yourself, time to reflect on what has been said. We encourage you not to slip into "production therapy."

Asking Too Many Questions

We previously broached this topic when discussing intake interviewing and in the case in which we provided several possible scenarios that might follow if a therapist fails to consider possible causes for a problem. Furthermore, we noted in the discussion of "Too Much" mistakes, that questions are one example of a response on which we might rely excessively. Because we believe that this response is used far too often (particularly after the initial interview), we emphasize here that you should refrain from subjecting the client to an ongoing barrage of questions. Beginning therapists know they shouldn't offer much advice, shouldn't give too much reassurance, shouldn't argue with clients, shouldn't "chat," and so forth. Having been left with a response repertoire seemingly limited in scope, they easily fall back on the old standby: a question. Yes, you have an ongoing need for information. You will find, however, that clients are much more interested in answering your questions if you provide a little variety. After all, this is an interchange between humans even if there are special ground rules. Consider the following example:

CLIENT: My ex-husband came in my house when he dropped the kids off this time.

THERAPIST: How did you feel about that?

CLIENT: I didn't like it. He won't let me in his house so why should I let him in mine?

THERAPIST: Why did you let him in?

CLIENT: I really didn't know what to say. Well, maybe I did want to talk to him.

THERAPIST: Why *did* you want to talk to him?

CLIENT: We have a lot of problems with the kids—we *do* need to talk.

In this scenario, the therapist's repeated questions, although they are not necessarily bad ones, pushed the client toward feeling "on the spot." The result is a defensive maneuver in which the client answers the questions on a superficial level. Now consider the following version:

CLIENT: My ex-husband came in my house when he dropped the kids off this time.

THERAPIST: How did you feel about that? I get the impression that's not how it's been before.

CLIENT: You're right. It's a change. It made me angry. He won't let me in his house so why should I let him in mine?

THERAPIST: That's a good question.

CLIENT: Well, maybe I did want to talk to him.

THERAPIST: I think part of what you are saying is that it's hard right now for you to be clear in your mind about how *you* want the relationship to be.

CLIENT: Well, it just seems like this house business is so much like our marriage was. It was always a question of him taking over and me giving in.

In this version, the therapist, while still eliciting information, goes about it in a way that helps the client feel less defensive. Here the therapist takes more responsibility for actively trying to understand rather than merely rolling out a list of questions, however well-crafted these questions may be. One informal guideline we sometimes offer students is to avoid more than two or three questions in a row, lest they be perceived as cross-examining their clients.

Not Going into Deeper Levels

This mistake might also be called the "Taking Things at Face Value" mistake or the "Failing to Follow Up" mistake.

THERAPIST: Have you ever thought about seriously injuring yourself?

CLIENT: Sometimes I think I'd be better off dead. (*Laughs*) I was just kidding—I'd never do anything like that.

THERAPIST: Well, have you ever considered hurting anyone else?

Here the therapist makes a very serious mistake. The therapist seems to accept at face value, and without further exploration, a statement that denies suicidal thoughts just expressed by the client. Instead of going on to the issue of homicidal intent, the therapist should have said something like this: "Well, perhaps you *were* kidding. (*Pause*) Or maybe you were not. Maybe you were being honest about the way you really *do* feel sometimes. How often have you felt like that?"

As another example of not following up on an important issue, consider the following interchange:

THERAPIST: We talked last week about your mother and how critical of you she often is. How are you feeling about that?

MALE CLIENT: I just decided to ignore it. It doesn't bother me any more.

THERAPIST: So things are OK now?

MALE CLIENT: Yeah.

THERAPIST: Well, do you have some concerns other than your mother?

We are not saying that you should always disbelieve clients. On the other hand, there are many instances when clients do not go into detail and will not do so unless you ask them directly or assist them in exploring their deeper feelings, beliefs, hopes, and the like. In the prior example, after the client says "It doesn't bother me any more," the therapist should have sensed that the client had become anxious about his relationship with his mother and was ready to deny problems as a way of escaping the anxiety. The therapist, by his or her comments, makes it a little too easy for the client to continue the denial. A better response, for example, might have been: "I think what's coming through most clearly to me is that you would sure *like* to be able to 'ignore it.'" Perhaps you are wondering about what you should do if the client continues to deny the problem. Let's continue the example.

THERAPIST: I think what's coming through most clearly to me is that you would sure like to be able to "ignore it."

(Note: At this point the therapist uses the language of the client—"ignore it"— rather than the more threatening "ignore your mother.")

CLIENT: That's what I've done this week and it worked.

THERAPIST: It's tough, I gather, thinking about how *you* feel when she criticizes you. Somehow it's tempting to block it all out.

(Note: Since the client continues to deny the problem, the therapist again chooses a phrase, "block it all out," that is somewhat general in tone.)

CLIENT: Well, as they say, "If it works, do it."

THERAPIST: Would I be wrong in assuming that it's hard work to ignore your mother?

(Note: Here the therapist picks up on the word *work* and uses it as a bridge to bring the issue of "mother" into the picture. The intervention is perhaps a little risky in that the client has been somewhat defensive about exploring his feelings. Most people would agree, however, that it is hard to ignore your mother. By at first using the client's language, and then by connecting the client's behavior to a broader cultural norm, the therapist has focused on a key element of the problem, while simultaneously placing client and therapist together on the same side of the issue.)

CLIENT: Well, maybe a little bit. I just don't intend to let it destroy my life.

THERAPIST: I sense that in some ways your mother's criticism has felt destructive to you—that you really *would* like to ignore her because it hurts so much when she doesn't seem to approve of you.

In this example, notice how the therapist refused to buy into the client's superficial explanation of "ignoring it works for me." Also, notice that the therapist doesn't say "Why don't you stop denying that your mother is important to you?" Part of what the therapist is trying to do is talk about the issue in a way that allows the client to show a more vulnerable part of himself. In pursuing this goal, the therapist first addresses the hopes of the client ("want to ignore it"), then how the client feels when he thinks about being criticized, then addresses again the desire to "block it out," and finally makes the discussion more concrete by talking about the difficulty in ignoring mother. At this point the therapist "reaches" the client, who opens the door by speaking about what he doesn't want ("to let it destroy my life") rather than continuing the platitude of "I'll ignore it." Notice that the therapist was not dissuaded by the repeated assertions ("I ignore it") of the client. Rather, the therapist continued a pattern of interventions that differed somewhat in their slants but all of which continued the focus of client and mother. So in part, your ability to help the client go into deeper levels will depend on your willingness to trust your intuition about problem areas and also on your skill in selecting and using a variety of ways to approach a problem. Resist the temptation to accept from clients explanations that you do not believe. As we imply, you are not issued a license to bang people over the head with reality; rather we are encouraging you to repeatedly pursue (with adroitness) any issue you feel is central to the client's problem. Additional material concerning this issue can be found in Chapter 11, Resistance.

Poor Phrasing of Interventions

At first glance, the idea that the way we say things is important seems rather simple. After all, psychotherapy almost always involves verbal communication. The principle itself is simple. Every therapist would agree that how and when you say things has an impact on the kind of response you are going to receive. So, there are various types of interventions that should be avoided because we know that their impact is to cause clients to withdraw, to distort, or to feel that we are not helpful. If any of these actions or feelings on the part of the client persist over time, therapy is likely to be ineffective at best and more likely than not will be terminated. First, the client should not be criticized or blamed. To criticize is not our role, and if we are critical, clients will tend to see us as a member of the large group of people who have already been nasty to them. Most therapists don't directly criticize their clients. However, clients feel criticized when, for example, we are impatient with them, or when we imply that they are not really interested in solving their problems, or when we imply that their behavior was lacking in some important way.

Suppose a client tells a story about the previous evening. He came home drunk and his wife locked him out of the house. He is now very angry about it, he says. Perhaps you think: "I don't blame her." You are tempted to set him straight, to tell him that she was justified. Instead, depending on how long you have been seeing the client, you might say, "I can see you are very angry. I wonder if it seems easier for you to try to change her than to stop drinking," or "I can see you are very angry. I'm guessing that the helplessness you felt as you tried to get in the house was a little like the helplessness you feel when you think about trying to stop drinking."

There are some phrases you should typically avoid since within our culture they tend to set off defensiveness (not to mention the fact that they are vague). Examples include "You are feeling sorry for yourself," "Complaining won't change things," and "You are a defensive person." You will find that you will make the mistake of poor phrasing only rarely if you are aware of what clients are feeling and thinking and act on the basis of having some appreciation for the predicaments in which they perceive themselves to be. This procedure does not mean that you support or condone all the activities of the client but rather that your *focus* is on clients' difficulties, not on correcting their values.

Not Finding Out How the Client Has Tried to Solve the Problem

As we discussed earlier, a thorough intake interview should include some idea about how the person has tried to solve the presenting problem. You might be surprised, however, to learn that many therapists plunge into trying to help the client solve the problem without ascertaining what solutions have been found wanting, so to speak.

One thing that you can find out by pursuing this issue is some idea about how clients may be setting themselves up for failure. It will also give you some idea about what dimensions of the problem seem most central to the client, which aspects seem (to the client) resolvable and which do not, and how sophisticated and informed the client is or is not about therapy. By asking clients how they have tried to solve the problem, you begin the process of helping them see themselves as able, within some (perhaps limited) area, to take action or make changes, which will help ameliorate the problem. Even if clients cannot at all see themselves in this light at the beginning of therapy, it may give them some "working hope" to hear such a question. Even in the difficult cases for which the question touches off feelings of helplessness and exhaustion, the process of therapy may be started by a discussion of these feelings.

As therapists we are prone to make this mistake because we may see ourselves as possessing special skills to solve problems. In this technocratic view of ourselves, we fail to remember that the client is both a participant in the process and the central source of our data about the problem.

Allowing Too Limited a Time to Deal with Termination

In our view, it is a mistake to terminate therapy without giving the client ample opportunity to discuss and think about what the termination means. Weiner (1975) expresses well the classic view of the importance of not terminating too hastily:

> Although the conduct of the psychotherapy is governed largely by relative rather than absolute principles, an absolute prescription can be written with respect to termination: never terminate psychotherapy with the session in which termination first comes up for discussion, regardless of how appropriate it is agreed to be. (p. 280)

The philosophy expressed by Weiner may seem a bit dated in an era of short-term therapy and managed care. Certainly his advice must be tempered by the setting in which you are working as well as your theoretical orientation. Here, we chiefly emphasize that if you have seen someone several times, try to avoid terminating abruptly. As an absolute minimum, try to contract for *at least* one or two more sessions if the client brings up termination abruptly.

Of course, you can't force clients to return and you should not place pressure on them to do so. Nonetheless, abrupt terminations are to be avoided if possible, particularly in therapy that lasts for more than a few sessions. As noted above, what one labels as a mistake depends quite heavily on one's theoretical orientation. Thus, for example, individuals endorsing a solution-focused brief therapy model such as that outlined by Walter and Peller (1992) may be inclined to agree with the idea that "every session is the first, every session is the last," (p. 140). If this is your philosophy, then you will be less inclined to be concerned when the client decides rather abruptly to terminate services. At the same time, it is important to emphasize that one's beliefs about whether one should be concerned with abrupt termination must be consistent with one's theoretical orientation, including beliefs about clients, the nature of psychotherapy, and the process of change. Our own view of psychotherapy, while acknowledging the possibility of quick and dramatic change, tends to see change as more typically involving a slower process and the therapy relationship as typically being central to significant change. From this perspective, the abrupt breaking of a therapy relationship is significant. The sudden rupturing of a relationship that is part and parcel of the improvement process must leave one wondering what powerful forces have elicited this rupture.

There are at least four reasons why therapists fail to allow enough time to deal with termination. One is that the therapist may be underestimating the client's dependency on therapy, in part because the therapist does not feel dependent on the client. A related point is that dependency has long been recognized as troubling for many individuals, and the problem can be especially difficult in psychotherapy (e.g., Bornstein & Bowen, 1995). A lack of client dependency may also be problematic, but our point here is that when a therapist "misreads" the dependency of the client, thinking that the client is not dependent when in fact she or he is can be a serious problem. A second reason is that the therapist may not want the therapy to end and may be expressing the desire unconsciously by not bringing up the subject. Third, the therapist may be a bit ignorant about generally expected client reactions. Fourth, the therapist may fear that the client will have a strong reaction to the subject of termination and be apprehensive about what the client might do when the subject is broached.

Not Setting Limits

In Chapter 2, Questions That Beginning Therapists Ask, we addressed some of the potential events that may call for you to set appropriate limits. These include things such as missing appointments, wanting to start early or late, and repeatedly calling you at home. In our efforts to be understanding and tolerant, we may occasionally lose sight of the fact that it does clients a great disservice to allow them to use (ultimately) dysfunctional strategies in pursuit of their goals in therapy. For example, let us say that a woman comes seeking help for her failing marriage. We recommend marital therapy. The husband comes and treatment seems to be progressing. After 8 to 10 sessions the woman indicates that she wants to see the therapist for individual sessions also, in order for her to work on how to deal with her aging parents. The therapist assumes that there may be some connection between the request and how therapy is progressing, but the connection is unclear and the idea of simultaneous marital and individual therapy is not at variance with the theoretical orientation of the therapist. The therapist and the woman agree that the individual sessions will not focus on her relationship with her husband. In the second individual session the woman says, "It is so much easier to talk to you when my husband is not in the room. I just feel safer. Today I'd like to talk about why I don't seem to trust my husband." As in previous examples, there are many aspects to the client's statement on which we might focus. The central point we make here is that in such an instance, you cannot allow yourself to be drawn into breaking your previous agreement. This is an example of a situation in which it is imperative that limits be set.

If you are not strong enough to set and hold to limits, your clients cannot possibly trust you with their problems that make them feel so out of control. Limit-setting needs to be offered matter-of-factly, not out of a desire to punish. For example, one therapist realized this in her work with a client who had a serious personality disorder. The therapist had at first tolerated phone calls at home because the client seemed in crisis. After the fourth call in one week, the therapist was angry for being "taken advantage of" and ready to set overdue limits. Her supervisor helped her realize that she had, in effect, reinforced the client's behavior, so it was no surprise it had continued. The supervisor helped the student therapist approach limit-setting more matter-of-factly and helped her construe the process as supporting the client.

Holding Too Much Back from the Client

As we have said previously, individuals who have chosen to be therapists generally have a very strong urge to protect and help others. This urge helps make you a good therapist because a caring attitude serves as both a motivator for you to help and a personality feature to which your clients will be drawn. Unfortunately, this positive, caring attitude may at times lead us to make the therapeutic mistake of holding too much back from the client. If you are wondering whether saying a certain thing to a client would be helpful or not, you might ask yourself whether *you* would be strong enough to have a therapist say that to you without your becoming defensive. If the answer is "yes," perhaps the client is stronger than you are giving him or her credit for. On the many occasions when we have asked our supervisees, "What would you like to say to the client?" we have found more often than not that the therapist's instincts were right on target and that the client would, we believed, benefit from the intervention contemplated by the therapist. This is obviously not an excuse to blast the client with every raw insight you have. It is, instead, encouragement to see your clients as resilient, coping human beings who may not need as much protection as you might at first believe.

There is a second reason why therapists at times make the mistake of holding things back from the client. They may not trust themselves to handle the difficult situation that they fear will follow talking about an "unpleasant" or emotionally charged topic. For example, perhaps the therapist senses that therapy has become a "chore" for the client, and that the client is "putting in time" more than actively participating in therapy. Naturally, there is the intellectual puzzle of trying to understand why this is happening. But there is also a very personal, emotional issue for the therapist when thinking about broaching a topic that may lead to a statement such as "I no longer find your comments to be all that helpful," or "We just don't seem to be clicking any more." Thus, holding back your thoughts may at times reflect your fears about yourself and how you are viewed by the client.

Discussing a Problem Only Once

One fear most therapists have is that they will "say the obvious"—or perhaps more to the point, we as therapists fear that the *client* will say or imply that we are making a comment that is obvious (see Chapter 4 on therapists' fears). As a defense against this fear, we may make the mistake of discussing something once with the client and then assuming that the issue has been "dealt with." A number of years ago one of the authors heard a counselor describing a marital case in which one spouse had had an affair. The counselor, who had apparently been poorly trained, indicated that he had said something like the following to the couple. "We will discuss this affair thoroughly, but then we will put it behind us. We will not bring it up again. We will lay the issue to rest." This view of therapy is a naive one. The assumption that an issue can be talked about one time and then "laid to rest" is simply not valid. Nonetheless, it is easy to fall into the trap of believing, for example, that if you discuss the client's angry feelings toward his or her mother once, it would be redundant to talk about the issue again.

Suppose a client is prone to being very self-critical. You point out that as a child he learned to criticize himself before his father could. The client agrees. He says, "So now that I'm an adult maybe I have no one to fear, but I still act as if I do." You say, "That's right. Now you need not be afraid. The only tyrant left is yourself." He says, "Well, I'm through being a tyrant. I'm going to give myself a long vacation. It feels good to figure this out—to know I don't have to be afraid so I don't have to worry…" Is this the end of the matter? Does the client live happily ever after? Probably not. Certainly he has taken a first crucial step toward reducing a personal characteristic (self-criticism) that he finds very bothersome. It would be a great mistake, however, to assume that just because he has had this insight, the issue of his self-criticism will not need to be discussed again.

As behavioral scientists, we do not completely understand why it is so, but there seem to be aspects of well-learned behavior that make it very difficult to change quickly, especially if the behavior involves strong emotions. It is important to remember that psychotherapy is a predominantly verbal interaction that often has very real limits in terms of how quickly and the extent to which it can produce behavioral (including attitude and emotional) change (Vaughan, 1997). One of the "techniques" therapists use to enhance the power of psychotherapy is to use a certain kind of repetitiveness. Going over the issue again and again with the client is typically necessary for several reasons.

For example, those of us who are not behaviorists still recognize the powerful force the environment plays in eliciting and maintaining behavior. After we discuss an issue with clients, they go back out into the interpersonal world with which they had reached an accommodation based on neurotic behavior patterns. This interpersonal world is typically not as supportive and understanding of the changes being tried by clients as was the therapist. Often this interpersonal world fights back and clients struggle to remain a part of their world yet make the changes they talked about in therapy. In such instances, the therapist and the healthy part of the client have one hour (or so) a week to influence the client, whereas the environment has 167 hours a week of influence. The client is certainly a part of these other hours (and so is the therapist to the extent that the client identifies with the therapist), but it doesn't take a genius to figure out that a ratio of 167 to 1 is a bit unbalanced. One of our primary tools to offset this imbalance is that as therapists we help the client *focus, repeatedly,* on an issue. This does not mean, of course, that you repeat verbatim what you have said before. Part of your success as a therapist depends on your ability to stay creative in your interventions— being able to help the client focus on problems in several different ways.

Some environments are in fact very supportive of the changes the client is making. Yet, since the client has constructed an elaborate inner world to make sense of previous experience and get ready for new experiences, new perspectives tend to be short-lived at first. Thus, while in the powerfully supportive and limited time space of a therapeutic hour, the old perspective may be temporarily swept away, it is not one insight that must be added, or one idea that must be changed. It is an interlocking grid of assumptions, adaptations, and emotional reactions that make clients prisoners in their own houses. So, even when the environment is very supportive, what we might call a "one discussion cure" is very rare—not unheard of—just rare. We point again to the efforts of theorists and researchers such as Beutler, Consoli, and Williams (e.g., 1995) who emphasize that problem complexity is a key variable in making an assessment of the client and deciding what kind of therapy should be implemented. Complicated problems usually take time to solve. We must go over and over an issue with a client because it is only through this repetition that the underlying grid is slowly changed. In truth, we would not want it any other way. For if a large and lasting change in personality structure could be the result of a one-time discussion, our clients (and we) would be the unwitting dupes of countless interpersonal con artists. We know of course that some people are more easily duped than others. We also know that each of us has a constructed identity and belief world that, by its interlocking nature, is more suited to gradual evolution than to easy and quick transformation.

Moralizing or Passing Judgment on the Client's Problem

Psychotherapists, like all other human beings, do and should have moral standards. There is general agreement in the profession, however, that the role of the therapist is not to pass judgment. We perhaps adopt this role of being non-judgmental in part because it seems to fit our personal values. Perhaps to an even greater degree, we adopt this role because passing moral judgment is thought, in the majority of cases, to decrease the probability of change. The stance we assume is one of trying to understand clients, rather than to judge them. William Styron (1976), in his novel *Sophie's Choice*, describes an emotionally wrenching scene in which Sophie is brought to Auschwitz with her two children. In the "selection" line, the Nazi physician tells Sophie that she can keep one of her children, but that she must *choose* which one is to live and which one is to die. One is tempted to label the physician as evil and stop at that point. The narrator, however, does what psychotherapists must do as they sit across from the client—he attempts to understand the forces that have set in motion this aberration, this terrible deed:

> I have always assumed that when he encountered Sophie, Dr. Jemand von Niemand was undergoing the crisis of his life: cracking apart like bamboo…The renewed horror scraped like steel files at the doctor's soul, threatened to shred his reason. He began to drink, to acquire sloppy eating habits, and to miss God. *Wo, wo ist der lebende Gott?* Where is the God of my fathers?
>
> But of course the answer finally dawned on him, and one day I suspect the revelation made him radiant with hope. It had to do with the matter of sin, or rather, it had to do with the absence of sin, and his own realization that the absence of sin and the absence of God were inseparably intertwined. No sin! He had suffered boredom and anxiety, and even revulsion, but no sense of sin from the bestial crimes he had been party to, nor had he felt that in sending thousands of the wretched innocent to oblivion he had transgressed against divine law. All had been unutterable monotony. All of his depravity had been enacted in a vacuum of sinless and businesslike godlessness, while his soul thirsted for beatitude.
>
> Was it not supremely simple, then, to restore his belief in God, and at the same time to affirm his human capacity for evil, by committing the most intolerable sin that he was able to conceive? Goodness could come later. But first a choice. After all, he had the power to take both. This is the only way I have been able to explain what Dr. Jemand von Niemand did to Sophie when she appeared with her two little children on April Fools' Day, while the wild tango beat of "La Cumparsita" drummed and rattled insistently off-key in the gathering dusk. (pp. 592–593)

We are not suggesting that the narrator has an accurate understanding of the physician's behavior and motivations. Rather, our emphasis is on the fact that the narrator *attempts to understand* the physician at a level that goes beyond merely making a moral judgment. Of course, to understand some of the forces propelling the physician in no way excuses him for his terrible deed. In our view, however, clients can seldom be helped by therapists who pass moral judgments to the exclusion of helping the client struggle toward an understanding of his or her needs, and this includes clients who have violated acceptable moral standards. This is a part of the special relationship we offer clients—we are committed to helping that part of the client that sought expression of a healthy need, but which did so in an ill-chosen or regrettable form.

It is important to remember that cultural factors often influence how we view the "acceptability" of a problem. Furthermore, many potential mistakes with ethnic minority clients may be avoided by the therapist's being familiar with research and theorizing concerning racial or ethnic issues (Sue, Zane, & Young, 1994; Suzuki, Meller, & Ponterotto, 1996).

Not Being Open to Feedback from the Client

If there is one grand consensus in the theory and research literature of psychotherapy, it is that the relationship between the therapist and the client is important.

Therefore, actions that tend to rupture that relationship are clearly a mistake. The context of the therapeutic relationship includes the typical assumption that clients, perhaps particularly because of their roles, are frequently deferential to the therapist (Rennie, 1994). In his study, Rennie (1994) found that fear of criticizing the therapist was one component of this deference. Thus, when clients are dissatisfied with therapy, they must overcome both a general predisposition to be deferential, and a more specific concern about being critical of the therapist. Rhodes, Hill, Thompson, and Elliot (1994) studied retrospective accounts by clients concerning misunderstandings between therapist and client. (See also, Safran, Muran, & Samstag, 1994.) Rhodes et al. tentatively concluded that if clients perceived a problem with the therapist or the therapy process, whether they (clients) felt free enough to assert their dissatisfaction was critical in terms of continuing in therapy. The researchers also suggested that talking about misunderstandings between therapist and client is a very valuable part of therapy. Thus, if you do not create a climate in which clients feel that they can disagree with you, and if you do not respond therapeutically when clients have concerns about things you have done or said, you have blundered badly. Interpersonal inflexibility may be a characteristic of some clients (Mallinckrodt, 1996); it should be the characteristic of no therapists.

Summary

All therapists, whether experienced or inexperienced, make mistakes. We agree with Earl Koile (personal communication, 1974) that the issue is not whether one makes a mistake, but rather, how one recovers from it. Vaughan (1997) expressed directly a related idea: "The good thing about making mistakes as a psychotherapist is that patients almost always give you a second chance if you look for it" (pp. 126–127). The mistakes we make as therapists provide the foundation for an increasing sensitivity to the way people make sense of their world, the ways in which they may be caught by what they experience, and the high drama with which their struggles are played out. In turn, this increased sensitivity, coupled with developing technical skills, enables us to respond better to those who seek our assistance. When we make big mistakes as a therapist, we are reminded of our limits. Whatever other things are to be learned from a mistake, surely this reminder is a valuable one.

DISCUSSION QUESTIONS

- If you have been in psychotherapy, can you point to any mistakes you believe were made by your therapist? If so, do you believe that your therapist would agree with your assessment about what was a mistake? Why or why not?

- Other than having a sexual relationship with the client, in your own opinion, what are two or three of the worst mistakes a therapist can make? What empirical findings can you cite that support your concern about these particular mistakes?

- What role does the client's culture play in determining whether an intervention is a mistake or not? Can you give a specific example of an intervention that would frequently be effective with persons from a particular culture, but frequently be a mistake with clients from a different culture?

- If a client accuses you of being a racist, should you deny it, agree with it, or force the client to deal with his or her own feelings rather than discussing your thoughts on the matter? If you believe that your answer depends on the situation, describe situations in which each of these approaches would be a mistake.

BIBLIOGRAPHY

Beutler, L. E., Consoli, A. J., & Williams, R. E. (1995). Integrative and eclectic therapies in practice. In B. Bongar & L. E. Beutler (Eds.), *Comprehensive textbook of psychotherapy* (pp. 274–292). New York: Oxford.

Bornstein, R. F., & Bowen, R. F. (1995). Dependency in psychotherapy: Toward an integrated treatment approach. *Psychotherapy, 32,* 520–534.

Bugental, J. F. T. (1988). What is "failure" in psychotherapy? *Psychotherapy, 25,* 532–535.

Gonzalez, F. (1995). Working with Mexican-American clients. *Psychotherapy, 32,* 696–706.

Kottler, J. A. (1993). *On being a therapist* (Rev. ed.). San Francisco: Jossey-Bass.

Mallinckrodt, B. (1996). Capturing the subjective and other challenges in measuring transference: Comment on Multon, Patton, and Kivlighan (1996). *Journal of Counseling Psychology, 43,* 253–256.

Rennie, D. L. (1994). Clients' deference in psychotherapy. *Journal of Counseling Psychology, 41,* 427–437.

Rhodes, R. H., Hill, C. E., Thompson, B. J., & Elliott, R. (1994). Client retrospective recall of resolved and unresolved misunderstanding events. *Journal of Counseling Psychology, 41,* 473–483.

Richman, J. (1996). Points of correspondence between humor and psychotherapy. *Psychotherapy, 33,* 560–566.

Ruiz, P., & Langrod, J. (1992). Substance abuse among Hispanic-Americans: Current issues and future perspectives. In J. Lawinson, P. Ruiz, R. Millgram, & J. Langrod (Eds.), *Substance abuse: A comprehensive textbook* (pp. 868–874). Baltimore: Williams & Wilkins.

Safran, J. D., Muran, J. C., & Samstag, L. W. (1994). Resolving therapeutic alliance ruptures: A task-analytic investigation. In A. Horvath & L. Greenberg (Eds.), *The working alliance: Theory, research, and practice* (pp. 225–255). New York: Wiley.

Strean, H. (Ed.). (1994). *The use of humor in psychotherapy.* Northvale, NJ: Jason Aronson.

Styron, W. (1976). *Sophie's choice.* New York: Bantam.

Sue, S., Zane, N., Young, K. (1994). Research on psychotherapy with culturally diverse populations. In A. E. Bergin & A. L. Garfield (Eds.), *Handbook of psychotherapy and behavior change* (4th ed., pp. 783–817). New York: Wiley.

Suzuki, L. A., Meller, P. J., & Ponterotto, J. G. (Eds.). (1996). *Handbook of multicultural assessment: Clinical, psychological, and educational applications.* San Francisco: Jossey-Bass.

Vaughan, S. C. *The talking cure: The science behind psychotherapy.* New York: G. P. Putnam's Sons.

Walter, J. L., & Peller, J. E. (1992). *Becoming solution-focused in brief therapy.* New York: Brunner/Mazel.

Weiner, I. B. (1975). *Principles of psychotherapy.* New York: Wiley.

10 Multicultural Counseling

Culture, in all of its early uses, was a noun of process: the tending of something...

—Raymond Williams

The problem of the twentieth century is the problem of the color line.

—W. E. B. DuBois

The last two decades have seen the stabilization of a new paradigm in counseling (Hollis & Wantz, 1995; Ponterotto, 1996). Referred to in various terms—cross-cultural counseling, multicultural counseling, diversity counseling, transcultural counseling, among others—this new approach has had far-reaching impact. The shift was jump-started by the Civil Rights and Women's movements of the 1960s and 1970s, when many ethnic minorities and women (as well as supporters of the Gay Pride movement, the Gray Panther group, and others) awoke to the realization that their marginalized status could be disputed (Das, 1995; Helms, 1994). No longer were such individuals as willing to accept the dominant culture's definition of their differences as a reflection of their inferiority or inadequacy. Increasingly, they relied on their own perceptions of their experiences, values, and goals, and their demands increased that mainstream psychology and counseling (education and theology were similar targets) adjust its thinking. The concept of "worldview" became common even to the lay public, with the implication that one worldview was not by definition more valuable or valid than another. The debates that ensued between the "old" and the "new" were sometimes scholarly and polite, sometimes less so. (After one heated debate, one of the participants who had been chided by a friend for not playing by the rules and being polite, responded humorously with a line from *Butch Cassidy and the Sundance Kid: "Rules? Rules* in a knife fight?"!)

One has only to review the psychology and counseling journals, or to see the new divisions in APA that have arisen in the last 20 years, however, to see evidence of the shift; there is a dramatic increase in articles and books and discussions about marginalized groups and subgroups. Especially within the last decade, it can be seen that research designs have become increasingly sensitive to the need for information about diverse groups (Ponterotto, 1996), and even the concept of multicultural counseling itself is in the process of refinement, as indicated by recent articles by Patterson (1996), Ho, (1995), Fowers and Richardson (1996), Weinrach and Thomas (1996), and others. The paradigm shift, then, is still in process, but gaining in momentum and sophistication (Sue, 1996).

The purpose of this chapter is to provide a brief overview of this new approach in counseling, especially as it relates to the student therapist. We assume that you have had already, or soon will have, a course in multicultural counseling, so we will not provide a comprehensive review of the very important literature on various cultural groups and subgroups or the needed mental health services of each group. Our intent instead is to help you integrate multicultural counseling into the knowledge of counseling you have already gained through this book and other training. We especially hope that you will be excited about the challenges this approach offers to increase your self-awareness and your counseling skills so that you can serve a wide diversity of clients. We do not assume that you will take unquestioningly everything that we or other writers say about multiculturalism, but we do hope that you will consider afresh the ideas, even if you have heard them before and/or feel a little uncomfortable with their implications.

Key Concepts

As a number of writers have suggested (e.g., Axelson, 1993; Hays, 1995; Ho, 1995; Pedersen, 1991), in a sense, all counseling is multicultural. While the following concepts are especially relevant in situations when your client is from a different cultural group than yourself, we think you will find them helpful in understanding all clients and your reactions to them.

Worldview

Traditionally in anthropology and in early cross-cultural counseling approaches, worldview was viewed solely as encompassing the broad, general understandings of the world, understandings grounded in culture; a separate aspect of the person was individual characteristics that made up the personality (Schwartz, 1992). More recently, anthropology has suggested that worldviews are organized into *systems of thought* within a given individual that range hierarchically from abstract to more specific, and that culture is intricately related to the person in a dynamic and unified manner (e.g., Schwartz, 1992; Wolcott, 1991). Any given person is thought to have abstract perceptions that are central, such as those regarding relationships (e.g., Beutler & Bergan, 1991; Carter & Helms, 1987), as well as specific views regarding, for example, understandings about marriage, how conflict should be handled, and the like. All of these perceptions are interrelated and, according to D'Andrade (1991), they tend to be consistent. Internal inconsistencies are considered bothersome, and the worldview system will attempt to minimize them. For example, if relationships in general are thought to be hierarchical, then a view of a specific relationship such as in marriage or counseling will tend to be conceptualized in a hierarchical configuration. This newer understanding of worldview is used as the basis for a model of counseling proposed by Trevino (1996), which we will explore in more depth later in the chapter.

Royce and Mos (1980) developed a different approach to the dimensions encompassed by worldview than Kluckhohn's (1956) much-used set of human nature, interpersonal relationships, nature, time, and activity. This newer approach proposes that there are three broad categories of worldview: rationalism (reliance on logical reason to make sense of the world), metaphorism (reliance on symbolic meaning), and empiricism (reliance on the senses). Research indicates that these dimensions are related to preferences for different counseling approaches (e.g., Neimeyer, Prichard, Lyddon, & Sherrard, 1993), but the model has yet to be tested across cultures.

Internalized Culture

A related concept is one used by Ho (1995)—internalized culture. He points out that one may grow up in a group or subgroup and not necessarily internalize all, or even most, of its assumptions. Most of you would not be in graduate school if your socialization as members of gender groups had been total: The men would presumably be less interested in fostering deep helping relationships and the women would not have aspired to professional degrees. Often other factors—temperament, family influences, one's choice of heroes, religious beliefs, to name a few—have profound enough effects that not all of an aspect of one's culture "takes" (Ibrahim, 1991). There are also instances (e.g., family traveling with military), when one's situation simply didn't expose one very much to one's identified cultural group so the values and assumptions were not internalized for those reasons. As Ho (1995) explained:

> ...the conception of culture most relevant to counseling pertains not to the culture external to the individual but to the culture internalized by the individual through enculturation. Internalized culture may be defined as the cultural influences operating within the individual that shape (not determine) personality formation and various aspects of psychological functioning.... An appreciation of the distinction between cultural differences and individual differences within a culture is crucial to multicultural counseling. (p. 5)

What Ho is alluding to here is that knowledge of large cultural groups can teach us between-group differences, but that effective counseling requires an appreciation for within-group (individual) differences also (Ibrahim, 1991; Sue & Sue, 1990). Learning about the probable effects of different cultural groups' "press" provides counselors with hunches about what *may* be important to the client. It helps us to listen for what clients may not be saying, for what is so obvious to them that they think it warrants no discussion. We must still test our hypotheses to know if and how the normative effects are pertinent to this particular client.

An example may clarify this. A client seen by one of the authors was a physician in the United States, but born and reared in Mexico. One would have expected that, had she internalized the culture's usual gender role for women, she would have been much more interested in getting married and raising a family than in pursuing a career in another country (e.g., Espin, 1985). So, did her parents encourage her to aspire to a medical career? As she told her story, that did not appear to be the case; her mother's injunctions were for her to obey and cater to her father and other males, and her father was largely absent. She did not have members in her extended family that served as professional women role models or as encouragers. The two factors that seemed to make a difference for her were the upper-middle-class status of the family (which meant that she took piano and swimming lessons, mingled with adults at parties, etc. and which perhaps diluted some of the usual socialization) and her own intelligence and temperament. She described herself as being "a tomboy," always rebellious and wanting to play with the boys, whom she thought had more fun than girls. She apparently was a gifted student and loved attention, so making good grades was easy and gratifying for her, and accordingly education seemed a natural goal to pursue. Individual differences seemed to explain more about her than cultural influences in the early stage of understanding her dynamics.

One of the issues she wanted to address in therapy was her tolerance of her husband's rage. He stopped short of physical abuse, but his reaction to his own vulnerability was angry tirades that lasted for hours. As therapy progressed, it eventually became apparent that her feistiness and strength extended to almost all areas of her life except when conflict arose with her husband. At those times, as she said, she didn't have a clue how to respond. Nothing in her cultural background or later learning had provided her with any models other than passivity with male anger. This emerging understanding was helpful to both her and her therapist, as the process of developing a new stance took longer than she thought it should and caused her to feel shame. Understanding the cultural pull toward passivity in the face of male anger helped her to be more patient with herself. Much as she had tried to extricate herself from what she perceived as the negative effects of her culture, there were still undercurrents tugging her back and which needed acknowledgment. (It should be noted that there were many things about her early culture that she delighted in and discussed proudly, and that this willingness to embrace what she saw as the positive aspects of her culture-of-origin increased as therapy continued.)

Multifaceted Identity

Consistent with this understanding of internalized culture is the notion that there are multiple cultural factors that affect one's identity. Gender and ethnic origins probably account for a considerable portion of this identity (Brown, 1990; Davenport & Yurich, 1991; Hays, 1996), but other cultural effects, important life events, birth order, and similar factors usually also contribute to a greater or lesser extent.

Hays (1996) proposes a model for assessing cultural factors that have been indicated through psychological research studies as warranting attention. Her ADRESSING model, designed to aid counselors in understanding a client's self-identification, involves the following factors:

Age
Disability
Religion
Ethnicity/race
Social status
Sexual orientation
Indigenous heritage
National origin
Gender

Hays (1996) goes on to offer specific suggestions of how to understand which of these components may be important to a client's identity. She recommends asking the client to describe himself or herself, by asking a question such as, "Would you describe yourself for me—both how you see yourself and how others see you?" In listening to the response, the counselor can note mentally which of the aspects of the model are self-identified by the client as important. Regarding the implicit challenges of this model to the counselor, Hays (1996) notes, "The potential biases and areas of inexperience that require the counselor's most careful consideration are those that correspond to the client's salient identities" (p. 336). She reminds us that, with the exception of social status, specializations in counseling and psychology have been developed concerning each of the groups targeted in her model, and each of these specializations has published both empirical and conceptual literature that can inform us in our work.

Culturocentrism

Another term for culturocentristic is "culturally encapsulated" (Lee, 1995, p. 80). Both terms refer to the idea that an individual's concept of the world, often as a result of minimum exposure to other cultures, is narrowly based on the worldview of his or her own culture, with little or no understanding that other frameworks exist that have value and validity for the individuals within them. Instead, often out of naiveté, one assumes that one's internalized culture is the "right one." Even understanding that one has been raised in a given culture, which has by definition no more claim to virtue than any other culture, is sometimes a difficult notion to remember consistently. Our own culture, which has nurtured and "tended" us, is difficult to question or even to fully identify.

As Cole (1996) indicated, culture is often hard to analyze, because we take it for granted: "Like fish in water, we fail to 'see' culture because it is the medium within which we exist. Encounters with other cultures make it easier to grasp our own as an object of thought" (p. 8).

Another similar analogy is to say that culture is "in our bloodstream." Until we have reason to view it otherwise, it is something we assume as naturally as we think of the day being made up 24 hours, some of which are light and some of which are dark. We plan our activities accordingly, and unless we are suddenly in a position in which our work is done on different shifts, we tend to eat breakfast in the morning, and two later meals within about 12 hours after breakfast. To think of breakfast as something one might eat at 10 P.M., before one begins an 11 P.M. shift, may seem quite strange at first. We are, all of us, culturocentric at first.

Within our culturocentrism, normal cognitive processes predispose all of us toward the formation of stereotypes and biases as we attempt to generalize and categorize vast amounts of information about others (Hamilton & Trolier, 1986; Stephan, 1989). Many of these stereotypes are shorthand ways to understand people who seem to be different from us. If we are members of a dominant group, viewing as outsiders those who do not "belong," such stereotyping can lead to oppression of the minority group. As Hays (1996) noted:

> When…biases are held by a dominant group and thus reinforced by political, social, and economic power, the results are the "-isms." That is, Racial Bias + Power = Racism, Gender Bias + Power = Sexism, Age Bias + Power = Ageism…. This conceptualization helps counselors to see the connections between racism, sexism, and other forms of oppression. (p. 335)

As multicultural writers (e.g., Lee, 1995; Pedersen, Draguns, Lonner, & Trimble, 1996; Sue, Ivey, & Pedersen, 1996) have emphasized over and over, to be able to help clients from a different culture(s), one must first have an awareness of one's own previous culturocentrism. We have talked with students about some of the incidents that led to their beginning awarenesses that others had quite different inner or external lives. These are some of the examples they gave:

- I remember when my best friend was confirmed in the Catholic Church. She got to take a new name for herself. I thought that was so cool! Her family also prayed before meals, which we never did.
- When this new family moved next door, I used to go over there a lot to play with the kids. No one drank over there, and the parents didn't yell all the time. Up until then, I'd assumed all families were like mine.
- My mom drove me through some ghettos so I could see how other people lived, and I couldn't quite comprehend it. I asked why people would live like that and she told me they had almost no choice. I felt really bad for them.
- I remember we took a trip to the city and the taxi driver yelled at me for opening the door into traffic. I didn't know you couldn't open any door you wanted to.
- My uncle was killed in Viet Nam, and that December his family skipped Christmas because it felt too bad to be without him. What would that be like, to feel so bad you wanted to skip the holidays? I couldn't imagine.

These early instances serve to open our eyes to the fact that others have different outer and inner worlds than our own. We are faced with this same relativity of experience when we are engaged in couple counseling: it becomes clear that the same event can mean two dramatically different things to the two people involved, depending on their vantage points. Learning about other cultures is an extension of a similar awareness, in that one realizes that some of the things that two or more groups take for granted can be very different. What we become aware of are both similarities and major differences in worldviews (Axelson, 1993; Sue & Sue, 1990).

In addition to inquiring about beginning social awareness, we have also asked our students to describe experiences in which they "crashed" from their own culturocentric world into profound empathy or understanding for some one else's. We have found that some of these instances occurred in counseling, but often the experiences predated their graduate training and indeed may have been a determining factor in their decisions to choose counseling as a profession. Some of these examples include:

- When I was in the fourth grade, the teacher had all of us say what we got for Christmas. I was rehearsing my list in my head, trying to make it as long as my friends', when the girl in front of me, "Dora Sanchez," said she got a basketball. That was all she said and she said it with such dignity. I suddenly imagined what she felt as she listened to all us "white girls" reciting so many gifts. It made me feel so ashamed.
- I did two years in the Peace Corps in Ethiopia. The culture shock I felt was unbelievable, both when I saw the poverty over there, and then when I came back to all our waste and materialism in America.
- I have watched my brother struggle with being gay. He confessed it to a priest, he's stayed celibate for three decades, he's been in therapy several times—and still he feels terrible about being *wrong*. He's internalized all this homophobia and feels bad about himself *every day.*
- I was seeing a client who was a second-generation Cambodian American. She came to the counseling center because she had been beaten and kicked out of the family by her father who wanted her to stay home and help with the family restaurant instead of go into pre-med. I was feeling so bad for her being torn between her family and her ambitions, and really kind of mad at her father, and then it suddenly hit me how bad her dad must have felt that after getting his family out by one of those boats and trying so hard to save his family and his culture, and now here his daughter was apparently defying all that. I don't know who I felt worse for, the father or the daughter.
- When I read Alice Walker's book about how girls' genitals are mutilated in some African tribes, their clitoris just cut out with a stone and their vaginas sewn up—without anesthesia of course—I kept thinking about it. *Women can't let this go on!*
- My best friend has breast cancer. I have watched her go through agony because of having to have a breast removed (all the pain and the fear that she

was less feminine and also that her husband wouldn't find her attractive anymore), as well as going through chemo. She's in remission now, but she lives in fear of cancer coming back. It's such an out-of-control feeling. I hadn't realized how lucky I was to have good health.

- When I was a school counselor, I once called the parents of a little Asian American girl to ask for a conference because the child seemed depressed. I later found out that she was punished because I called; in her culture, any attention from a school authority figure must mean that she had done something wrong and was in trouble. I felt so guilty for adding to her problems. I just didn't have a clue about her culture.
- The O. J. Simpson trial did it for me. The opinion polls were devastating. They were so clear you couldn't ignore them. There is an enormous gulf between black and white America. It is much bigger than I ever realized. Very depressing.

These are examples of jarring experiences that can serve to awaken awareness of one's culturocentrism and/or biases. Often this happens when members of some privileged group (by reason of ethnicity, gender, age, sexual orientation, religion, living without disability, etc.) suddenly awaken to others' realities. One of the processes that underlies effective counseling is the awareness of one's own culturocentrism and the willingness to reexamine long-held assumptions and biases.

Multiculturalism

We feel strongly that racism is a pervasive problem in the United States and that racial issues require continued theoretical and research focus, especially among psychologists. There is always something lost when one broadens a focus to other groups before the first is fully addressed, and racial issues are far from being fully addressed. Nonetheless, we think it is imperative for therapists to realize that other forms of oppression exist and cause pain, and that being a member of more than one oppressed group can lead to double or triple (or higher) jeopardy. As counselors, you will need to have an understanding of the interactive effects of the environment on your clients (Ridley, Mendoza, Kanitz, Angermeier, & Zenk, 1994). Accordingly, we are echoing the recent views of Weinrach and Thomas (1996), Gutierrez (1996), Welfel (1998), and Hays (1996), who use the term multiculturalism in a way that goes beyond ethnic or racial origin. Our definition is based less on this traditional anthropological construct than on an awareness of groups that experience deliberate or inadvertent marginalization by the mainstream culture(s). Accordingly, minority or marginalized status can arise from many sources, including racial or ethnic heritage, skin color, gender, age, language, socioeconomic status, religion, sexual orientation, and physical appearance or limitation. As we use the term, *multicultural counseling* can be defined as counseling clients who belong to any one or more of these groups (visibly identifiable or invisible) that is different from the counselor's. For a somewhat different perspective on multiculturalism, see Helms (1994).

Evolution of the Multicultural Focus

Understanding how this paradigm shift has unfolded in psychology and counseling is fascinating in itself. We are presenting a brief overview for you, however, not simply because of academic interest in the heritage of the movement, but because we think that the process the field has gone through—the varied emphases and modifications of those emphases, and emerging models and the controversy that surrounds them—can also provide students with insight into conceptual dilemmas that counselors sometimes face as they attempt to be open to new ideas.

Beginning Roots

As indicated in the beginning of the chapter, the 1960s Civil Rights and Women's movements provided much of the impetus behind what Pedersen (1991) has called the "Fourth Force" in counseling (i.e., multicultural counseling; psychoanalysis, behaviorism, and humanistic approaches representing the first three). As you have no doubt heard or remember, that decade was a time of rebellion against long-held traditional standards, much questioning of authority, and enough anger and energy to transform storms of isolated complaints into organized sociopolitical currents that eventually pervaded much of the strata of traditional thought. While what sparked some of the conflict may have been young adults' questioning that they should follow the government's expectation of fighting in the Viet Nam war, in psychology, the focus of the anger was the belief by many that the ethnocentric views of white males had thus far dominated the field of psychology. Often, members of "nonmainstream" groups felt that their values and experiences had been devalued. The multicultural perspective brought new conceptual and research emphases to the field of psychology. Their perspective was not quickly accepted by all scholars in mainstream psychology and counseling. The following example illustrates some of the difficulties involved in breaking free from long-held and ingrained assumptions:

Imagine if you can that some outside party with authority and power had the ability to unilaterally evaluate your family. Suppose this person had lost a spouse to cancer and his or her values centered around a family's willingness to devote half of its net income to the American Cancer Society. If your family were defined and evaluated using that criterion, our guess is that it would not get sterling marks. Because that would be a new experience for you, perhaps you would have the clarity to protest vigorously about the imposition of such a value, commendable as it might be in some ways. You might point out as worthy of praise the support that your family members give each other, or the fun had collectively on weekends, or the way conflict is resolved respectfully. Perhaps you would point to other family charitable projects, such as spending a weekend helping to build a house for Habitat for Humanity, as meritorious. At any rate, we expect you would object strenuously to being defined and valued by outside criteria that bore little direct relevancy to many of your own values and experience.

If, however, this imposition of values was not new, but instead part of the mainstream culture you and your ancestors had grown up in, it would not be as easy or obvious to you that you should protest. Presumably, you might have felt all along that your values and approaches were worthy, but if you had grown up with the "give half to the Cancer Society" view being dominant, what would it have taken for your family to feel entitled to *demand* a new criterion? Unfairness may be easy to recognize when we have been accustomed to respect, but much harder to note when one has lived with its absence in the culture historically and one's role models have accommodated the dominant group's assumptions, perhaps without question.

Questioning the assumptions and values of the dominant groups was truly a revolution. It should not be assumed, however, that all protesters were equally enlightened about oppression of similar groups. Their own culturocentrism sometimes became painfully obvious. A true example:

During the 1960s, much of the energy to protest societal norms took place on college campuses. At one well-known university, the student protesters—men and women of a variety of racial and ethnic groups—all concerned about equity and justice and the dispensing with demeaning stereotypes, gathered to stage a campus protest. They eventually succeeded in occupying the floor of a university building. That night, flushed with the success of their efforts, they gathered to plan the next day's activities and to formulate strategy. At some point in the planning, several of the men mentioned that they were hungry, and turning to the women in the group, indicated that their contribution would be to prepare supper. It was not until the women vigorously pointed out the irony of the situation (and many women in the 1960s, even protesters, might not have thought to question their presumed role as preparers of the meal) that the men realized they had violated their own values of equity and shared input by falling prey to lingering sexist biases.

We are describing this early protest stage because an understanding of its origins is important to the appreciation of the shift in perspectives. These roots set the stage for the writing and research of the next wave of the multicultural movement. Although the direction came from several groups' insistence, we will summarize here only the evolution of literature in the racial/ethnic and the women's movements, since these groups generated their own counseling theories, sets of practices, expectations for training, and research design guidelines. It should be noted that although for the purposes of this chapter we are combining the two areas under the broad umbrella of multiculturalism, the two groups were in fact usually independent and often wary of each others' influence. For clarification, we also want to emphasize that the focus on racial/ethnic minorities was, until recently, *the* targeted concern of "multicultural" counseling; the inclusive definition we are using in this chapter is part of the recent evolution in the field and was not used historically.

First Decade

We will somewhat arbitrarily define the first stage of organized work in the multicultural and feminist psychology communities as taking place in the 1970s. As described by Sue (1996), one of the first and most dedicated advocates of what was then called cross-cultural counseling, early proponents of this movement made several important points in their protests:

1. Traditional counseling and psychotherapy failed to adequately consider the importance of race, culture, and ethnicity in the counseling process.
2. There was little understanding about the history, experiences, lifestyles, and worldviews of culturally different populations.
3. The standards used to judge normality–abnormality or the characteristics of "good counseling" were often based on European American norms.
4. The role of counseling professionals was too narrowly defined and seldom included systems intervention knowledge or skills to deal with the sociopolitical forces affecting clients' lives.
5. Education and training of psychologists and counselors needed to change in order to produce culturally aware and competent mental health professionals.

In a similar review of the historical roots of feminist therapy, Enns (1993) commented on the influence of the Consciousness Raising (CR) groups of the 1960s and 1970s on feminist psychologists. As she noted, CR groups' insistence on political activism's being part of the protest affected many of the goals of psychologists (both men and women) who were part of the Women's Movement. In her catalog of the targets of this group of psychologists, Enns mentions:

1. Sexism in the culture and its negative effects on women
2. Traditional therapy with its hierarchical therapist–client relationships, which served to reinforce women clients' lack of power
3. Psychological theories and therapeutic goals that encouraged adherence to masculine or biased criteria of psychological health
4. Diagnostic criteria that pathologized women's functioning and ignored men's parallel issues. Although she did not mention this as a separate focus, perhaps seeing it as part of her first item, we will note that it was at this point also that feminists began protesting the usage of the "generic masculine," that is, using "men" or male nouns and pronouns to refer to the entire population (e.g., "all *men* are created equal"). This attention to language and how it shapes—as well as defines—reality eventually resulted in changes in the APA Style Manual, many government documents, and other public statements by various organizations.

The objectives referred to in Sue's and Enns's lists obviously have much in common, although this is somewhat more obvious now than it was then.

Much of the literature of this era was designed to document the pervasive and destructive effects of racism and sexism and how they were manifested in counseling situations. Casas (1984) described the multicultural counseling research of this era as falling into three broad categories: (a) Racial ethnic minority client variables, including sociocultural characteristics; counselor preference; presenting problems; and utilization of services, among others—much of which has since been criticized as being done from an ethnocentric European American perspective (e.g., Ponterotto, 1988; Sue & Sue, 1990); (b) Therapist variables, including racial ethnic bias of therapist and underrepresentation of minorities in the psychology profession; and (c) Techniques, service and settings, and outcome variables. Many of these writings/studies were theoretical and still need empirical support (Gutierrez, 1996). In feminist counseling, the foci were somewhat similar: (a) Chodorow (1978), among others, questioned personality theorists' "white male" culturocentristic assumptions about women's development and psychopathology; (b) sex/gender bias, precipitated by the study by Broverman, Broverman, Clarkson, Rosenkrantz, and Vogel, 1970, was the focus of hundreds more articles; and (c) nonsexist, sex-fair, and feminist counseling, discussed in both theory and research articles, was a third focus. Overlapping some of these areas was the interest in androgyny and in the theory and outcome of assertiveness training for women (Enns, 1993).

Second Decade

The 1980s saw a continuation and refinement of many of the ideas of the 1970s, with research not always providing the expected results. In both the areas intended to document racism and sexism in the counseling, studies yielded less than definitive results (Casas, 1984; Enns, 1993). The two groups demonstrated an increased emphasis on training, with standards of competency suggested by both multiculturalists and feminists. (We will discuss these standards in the next section of this chapter.) Similarly, both groups addressed the ethical issues arising from diagnosing diverse clients using criteria developed in the main by European American males and presumably reflecting their culturocentric biases; accordingly, the *DSM-IV* was intentionally designed to be more culturally sensitive. In response to the accusation that much of the two sets of literature tended to be atheoretical and even possibly to contribute to further stereotyping by ignoring within-group differences, both groups developed important models and theories upon which more sophisticated research could be conducted.

During this decade also, arguably because of the primary influence of these two groups, traditional research designs themselves came to be questioned as often inherently biased and ethnocentric. *The Counseling Psychologist* explored the question of whether white researchers should even conduct cross-cultural research, and a number of guidelines were proposed to help preclude researcher bias. Similarly, feminist researchers raised questions about traditional designs, and increasingly qualitative methodology was employed so that findings regarding diverse groups could be based on the groups' own experience and ways of explicating that experience, rather than on a researcher's predetermining the areas that would be considered important. Both groups increasingly conducted research looking at specific subgroups (e.g., adolescent women) and at individuals who might be members of more than one minority group (e.g., Latina lesbians).

Increasingly during the 1980s, feminist psychologists became more diversified in their descriptions of what feminist psychology and therapy meant. (This diversification was less evident among the multiculturalists.) By the end of the

1980s, four major groups of feminist therapists had been identified (Enns, 1993): (a) Liberal feminists, whose goals were to help individuals overcome socialization that limited their potential; differences between sexes were minimized; (b) Cultural feminists, who saw women's approaches to life as historically devalued and whose goal was the feminization of culture; (c) Radical feminists, who viewed oppression of women as the most fundamental form of oppression in society, embedded in patriarchy; their goals included dramatic transformation of institutions so that sexism could be eradicated; and (d) Socialist feminists, who focused on multiple oppressions associated with all minority groups' status and who believed that society should be changed at its very roots through attention to multiple forms of oppression. Other branches of feminist theories included existential feminism, lesbian feminism, postmodern feminism, and Womanist (based on the experiences of African American women) approaches, as well as others (Jaggar, 1983).

Acculturation Theory and Research.   In keeping with the newly acknowledged need to investigate groups on the basis of smaller units than ethnicity, one of the major areas of focus for multiculturalists during this time was the effects of acculturation. The broad, general area of acculturative stress, especially of Latino immigrants, was the subject of dozens of studies (e.g., Ponce & Atkinson, 1989) during the 1980s. Asian Americans also began to be considered as a focus of research, as well as generational acculturation differences and stresses (e.g., Das, 1995).

Racial and Ethnic Identity Development.   These models include descriptions of stages of reference group identity, not personal identity (Wehrly, 1995). Atkinson, Morten, and Sue's (e.g., 1989) model of minority identity development (MID) was the focus of much publicity during the 1980s and was presented as a schema in 1993. Cross's (e.g. 1987) model of Black Identity Development became a focal point for considerable research during the 1980s. Similarly, Helms (1984) presented a black and white model of racial identity development, Kim (1980) proposed his Asian American racial identity development model, Ruiz (1990) presented a model of Chicano/Latino identity development, Hardiman (1982) described her white racial identity model, and Ponterotto (1988) outlined a model for racial consciousness development among white counseling students. All of these models indicated the process that individuals hypothetically take in claiming their own racial identities in relation to other racial groups. All indicate that not everyone goes through all stages, and in fact recycling is not unusual.

Women's Development.   One of the areas among feminist psychologists that attracted a great deal of attention during this time were the theories—especially the Self-In-Relation Theory originating from the Stone Center at Wellesley—of women's development. In brief, the notion here is that in most families the mothers are the primary caretakers of the children, and that boys' development is different from girls' because boys need to separate their identities from their mothers in order to meet the cultural definitions of masculinity, while girls can stay *in rela-*

tion to their mother as they develop their identities as women (e.g., Miller, 1984). The implication of this, in accord with Gilligan's (1982) work, is that women's values, including their moral values, are often embedded in relationships rather than in autonomy and separateness.

Third Decade

Researchers and writers in the 1990s have continued and elaborated on many of the previous themes, as well as proposed new models and theories. Some of the early goals of multiculturalists and feminists have seen at least partial attainment. One of the areas that shows the most demonstrable improvement is in graduate training, where, according to Ponterotto (1996), 89% of the APA-accredited Counseling and Clinical Psychology programs required at least one multicultural counseling course. This does not guarantee, of course, that other courses have been modified to include relevant implications for diverse groups, but it is a significant step. Secondly, with the combined influences of the women's and multicultural groups, diagnosis is increasingly culturally sensitive although by no means completely informed (e.g., Smart & Smart, 1997). A third development was that research and conceptual writing is much more likely than before to consider within-group differences and to examine the difficulties inherent in being a member of more than one minority group (e.g., Wade, 1995).

Psychological Literature.   There continues to be research and conceptual writing that distinguishes between men's and women's experiences. For example, studies regarding gender differences have been published in the dimensions of aggression (Campbell, 1993), career development (six articles in the April 1997 *Journal of Counseling Psychology*), and power strategies (Sangrestano, 1992). Women as the object of sexual harassment and other forms of sexual violence and abuse continues to be a primary focus for many feminist psychologists (e.g, Crossman, 1994). The concept of androgyny has lost much of its support (Enns, 1993), but the difficulties in complying with cultural expectations of gender roles have been well-documented; this is the special focus of much of the current research on men (e.g., Good & Wood, 1995; Hetzel, 1997). Indeed, the 1990s have evidenced a new focus on men's issues, as indicated by the new division of APA and by increased attention to the difficulties of men, especially from marginalized groups, living up to the demands of "masculinity."

The models of racial identity development have served to generate dozens of research studies, including such targets as gifted African American adolescents and biracial children (Kerwin & Ponterotto, 1995). Ponterotto (1996) considers the conceptual breakthrough in the refinement of theories of racial and ethnic identity and of acculturation as one of the most noteworthy aspects of 1990s multiculturalism, and cites articles showing application of these theories to groups as diverse as American Indians, Asian Americans and biracial individuals, as well as African Americans, Hispanic Americans, and white Americans. Helms's model has especially received attention. While her ideas are not without controversy (e.g., Behrens,

1997; Rowe, Bennett, & Atkinson, 1994), they have provided a model that can be tested and modified through continued research findings.

Counseling and Psychotherapy Literature.   Specifically in the area of counseling and therapy, many more articles and books have been written that provide specific focus on targeted cultures and subcultures, in contrast to "generic" therapy approaches. Some of these suggested treatment approaches in individual and group therapy to specific groups, such as Asians (e.g., Bracero, 1996), bilingual Spanish-speaking clients (e.g., Santiago-Rivera, 1995), Native Americans (e.g., Herring, 1992), African Americans (e.g., Ottavi, Pope-Davis, & Dings, 1994), and sexually abused women (e.g., Rose, 1991), to name only a small percentage.

Another branch of the literature on counseling diverse clients has focused specifically on cross-cultural counseling. For example, Todisco and Salomone (1991) discussed white therapist/black client dyads, Shay (1993) wrote about male therapists working with couples, and Hays and Gelso (1993) focused on heterosexual male therapists counseling gay men and lesbian clients.

Finally, there has been considerable discussion in the literature about appropriate multicultural counseling in general. Racial and ethnic, heterosexist, and gender bias are still the focus of considerable discussion, and guidelines and models for cultural sensitivity and multicultural counseling have been proposed and discussed. We will review some of the important points in these writings later in the chapter.

Diagnostic and Assessment Literature.   There are two broad sources of concern for multicultural counselors in the area of assessment and diagnostics. The first area is with the measures and criteria themselves being biased when applied to diverse groups. Members of marginalized groups have often been overdiagnosed with certain disorders or misdiagnosed altogether (Sinacore-Guinn, 1995). Mwaba and Pedersen (1990), for example, found that culturally appropriate behaviors that do not match Western standards may be viewed as pathological. Difficulties assessing specific cultural groups have been noted, such as Rogler, Cortes, and Malgady's (1991) discussion of the specific difficulty in assessing Hispanics, and Brown and Ballou's (1992) book regarding the assessment of women. Similarly, feminists have protested the continued pathologizing of women's behavior and the concomitant underdiagnosing of complementary or parallel men's patterns (e.g., Caplan, 1991.)

In addition to focus on the *DSM*, continued attention has been given to culturocentric bias in many other assessment instruments, which are often not normed on diverse or culturally different groups. Helms (1992), for example, wrote about ongoing difficulties in making standardized testing culturally equivalent. In schools, legal challenges have been raised to many forms of educational and psychological testing, using evidence that such measures tend to discriminate against African American and Latino children (Walsh & Betz, 1995; Welfel, 1998). An especially helpful resource for responsible assessment of diverse groups is *The Handbook of Multicultural Assessment,* edited by Suzuki, Meller, and Ponterotto (1996).

The second large area of concern was counselor–therapist bias. Malgady, Rogler, and Constantine (1987), for example, discussed counselors' vulnerability to inferential bias in working with racial or ethnic minorities. Similarly, gender may also be the cause of differential diagnoses, as indicated by numerous studies (e.g., Robertson & Fitzgerald, 1990). In addition to the plea for better training of students and professionals in diagnosing and assessing diverse groups, several specific suggestions have been made to aid therapists in their diagnostic interviews. Brown (1986, 1990) recommended an analysis of gender role as part of the intake procedure.

Standards and Principles for Working with Diverse Groups

The counseling and psychology professional associations have adopted through the years several versions of standards for multicultural counseling, many of these originating in special interest groups and then supported by the professional organizations. For example, Fitzgerald and Nutt, in 1986, published practice guidelines for delivery of services to women that were later approved by Division 17 (Counseling Psychology) of the American Psychological Association. In 1993, *The American Psychologist* published guidelines for Providers of Psychological Services to Ethnic, Linguistic, and Culturally Diverse Populations; these were suggested by APA's Board of Ethnic Minority Affairs, and were originally written by the board's task force on the delivery of services. Similarly, Sue, Arredondo, and McDavis (1992) published in *The Journal of Counseling and Development* the guidelines for counseling competencies for work with ethnic minority individuals that the Professional Standards Committee of the American Association for Counseling and Development (now called the American Counseling Association) endorsed. These standards were revised and published in 1996 in the *Journal of Multicultural Counseling and Development* (Arredondo, Toporek, Brown, Jones, Locke, Sanchez, & Stadler, 1996).

In keeping with our belief that multicultural counseling is an approach that includes delivery of services to *all* cultural groups and subgroups, and based on the documents just discussed, we summarize below ideas that guide multicultural counseling. Counselors and therapists of individuals from diverse cultural groups:

1. Are aware of the influence of their own cultural heritage and their biases and values that reflect that heritage; these biases and values (both positive and negative) are consistently reviewed, and harmful attitudes are challenged by one's self in an ongoing manner. They monitor these attitudes through consultation, supervision, or therapy.
2. Have a respect and appreciation for culturally different heritages, beliefs, attitudes, and behaviors that are different than their own.

3. Are knowledgeable about cultural groups and subgroups, particularly with regard to biological, psychological, and social issues that have negative impact on such groups of individuals.

4. Are aware that the assumptions and precepts of theories relevant to their practice may be culturocentric and therefore less valid and useful, even harmful, when applied to individuals from some cultural groups.

5. Are aware of the power that their professional position may accord them, especially with some cultural groups and subgroups, and are committed to using that power to enhance individuals' psychological well-being.

6. Recognize the limits of their expertise and refer to more culturally knowledgeable professionals when necessary. When this is not feasible, they seek culturally knowledgeable consultation and education.

7. Are knowledgeable of the biases in assessment instruments and diagnostic criteria that are used, and do not use invalid or questionable approaches.

8. Interpret test data and other professional material in terms that are understandable and relevant to the needs of those addressed.

9. Interact in the language requested by the client or make appropriate referrals. When neither option is feasible, a culturally knowledgeable translator or paraprofessional from the client's culture is used.

10. Provide culturally appropriate structure for clients as necessary, negotiating and/or clarifying expectations and roles of both the counselor and the client.

11. Respect the roles of family members and community structures and hierarchies of diverse clients.

12. Recognize and are aware of all forms of oppression and their effects on the psychological functioning of individuals from diverse groups.

13. Work to eliminate sexism, racism, and other forms of biases and practices, both in institutions and in individuals.

14. Actively pursue activities, both intellectual and experiential, that expand knowledge of cultural groups and subgroups.

15. Build and maintain expertise in counseling interventions that may be helpful with specific cultural and subcultural groups of individuals.

The assessment of these competencies, as well as more specific ones, has been the object of various objective measures, most notably the Multicultural Counseling Inventory constructed by Sodowsky, Taffe, Gutlin, and Wise (1994). Although somewhat limited in usefulness because of its self-report measure, you may find it helpful to review it as an aid to self-awareness. For a review of the literature on this and other instruments, consult Pope-Davis and Dings (1995).

Counseling Models and Considerations

The previous guidelines provide students with some of the structure that defines a broad multicultural approach, but the professions have only recently begun to grapple with the "What do you *do*?" question that students legitimately ask when wondering how to spend 50 minutes with a "multicultural" client. Guidelines are often very general or prohibitive (i.e., what not to do), rather than offering much direction or help. In this section we will provide an overview of several approaches, as well as describe our own evolving understanding of appropriate multicultural counseling.

Emic versus Etic

A usual distinction among multicultural writers is between "emic" or "etic" approaches; emic approaches look for differences and follow a *culture-specific* approach, and etic approaches look for similarities between individuals and follow a *universal* counseling (primarily person-centered) approach (e.g., Das, 1995). Our impression is that this debate about the "correct" approach is often based on writers' "worst case scenario" fears. Worried that therapists will settle for the easy answers of one model or theory of counseling and never reach beyond it, they settle into positions advocating either the emic or the etic guidelines. In our experience, supported by a number of research studies showing that experienced therapists tend to be integrative rather than relying strictly on any one theory or approach, good therapists borrow from a number of theoretical roots (hopefully with some integrity) and try to orchestrate themselves to meet the needs of an individual client. Certainly that is the approach we have been advocating in our Introduction and Listening chapters. Good therapists do have well-honed facilitative skills, but they also have a number of therapeutic schemas that help them particularize their approach to a given client. We agree with Patterson (1996), who, in reference to the emic/etic (specific/universal) debate, said, "…the universal is the process, and the specific deals with the content in the therapy" (p. 230).

Ridley et al.'s Model of Culturally Sensitive Counseling

Ridley et al. (1994) made several noteworthy contributions to multicultural counseling in their article on cultural sensitivity. First, echoing many other multiculturalists writers' points, they provide five presuppositions that underpin their model: 1. Cultural sensitivity depends on an idiographic understanding of the personal meaning clients derive from a number of overlapping cultural groups of which they are members (i.e., understanding clients' multifaceted identities). 2. Cultural sensitivity requires that counselors accept their naiveté with respect to their *a priori* understanding of incoming stimuli from culturally different clients (i.e., recognize their culturocentrism and reach beyond it). 3. Cultural sensitivity is a prerequisite for culturally responsive counseling interventions. 4. Cultural differences between counselors and clients may interfere with counselors' effectiveness in perceiving, collecting, interpreting, and organizing client information. 5. Cultural sensitivity is grounded in the information-processing theory of perceptual schemata.

Ridley et al. (1994) provided an operationalization of this information-processing theory of perceptual schemata. For purposes of summarizing this fairly technical material, we will paraphrase the components of their model.

Counselor Cultural Self-Processing.   Counselors acknowledge their cultural biases and personal agendas in order to avoid ignoring, distorting, or underemphasizing incoming cultural information to the detriment of the client. Accordingly, counselors must be self-analytic and actively work to eliminate prejudicial or stereotypic perceptions of culturally different clients.

Purposive Application of Schemata.   Secondly, counselors work purposefully to perceive and collect data that are relevant to therapeutic action. That is, as they listen empathically, they are placing relevant information into working schemas, from which they can understand the client and make appropriate interventions. Collecting cultural information randomly and then not applying it to therapeutic intervention is not helpful and may be damaging to the client. Rather, the information must be organized and channeled into beneficial treatment planning and intervention.

Maintaining Plasticity.   While schemas are necessary to understanding and planning, when they become too rigid they result in stereotyping and/or misperception. If instead of looking for quick answers, counselors can stay open to new material and have evolving mental structures of the meaning of client information, they can reconfigure their schemas as new information arises. Put another way, counselors need to be able to develop "hunches," and tolerate ambiguity as they confirm, modify, or dispense with those hunches as new client information becomes available.

Active-Selective Attention.   Rather than the usual process of "tuning out" cultural information (much as one ignores seeing one's watchband when looking for the time), counselors in multicultural settings need to learn to pay specific attention to cultural data coming from the client. As Ridley et al. (1994) said, "The degree to which they are able to use active-selective attention is expected to correlate with the degree to which counselors are able to apply cultural sensitivity schemata to accurately understand culturally different clients" (p. 132). In other words, counselors need to listen with the "third ear" to client feelings and meanings that may be quite subtle but crucial to their identity.

Counselor Motivation.   Cultural sensitivity depends on the counselor's willingness to acquire (outside of therapy) relevant cultural knowledge and (inside of therapy) client information so that idiographically based cultural schemas can be developed and refined. In other words, one has to work at this. There is no substitute for learning about cultural groups or subgroups, nor is it possible to substitute that "outside" information for learning about this particular client.

We find this approach to counseling both "emic" and "etic." It is a process which we believe is indigenous to all good counseling, but is *especially* relevant when working in a multicultural setting. Predetermined, rigid approaches for understanding and treating clients can be disrespectful and damaging, even if they were learned as the "proper" multicultural approach and implemented with good intentions.

You may know a good deal about the grief process, for example, and also a bit about a Latina's ethnic and gender socialization. By now, you likely have some schema for working multiculturally. Those schemas are somewhat in place before an intake session with a self-referred woman from Guatemala who indicated on her biographical information form that she has two deceased daughters. As the client tells her story, you keep those schemas available for use, but also available for modification, so that you can get the essence of the client's inner world and counseling needs as quickly as possible. Suppose in this case, you are trying empathically to follow Hays's (1996) ADRESSING model and are gathering information about the client's self-perceived identity. You listen for the suggested aspects of age, disability, race/ethnicity, and so forth and find that at this point the client's identification with her country and her heritage are minimal—in fact, something from which she is actively trying to disassociate herself. As her story unfolds, she tells of her young daughters' visit to her parents' house for a weekend two years ago. Her brother, who had been politically active (as she had) and the subsequent recipient of political threats and intimidation, had been visiting her parents also that weekend. As she tells the story, she is walking from the bus to the house with her two nieces in hand when she sees a crowd outside, and police inside hosing down the floor, "as if," she says, "they were washing away blood." There are no signs of her parents, her daughters, or her brother, nor has she ever heard from any of them again. She turns and runs, holding onto the nieces, and with footsteps running after her, is able to find a cab with an open door and escapes with the driver's help. She was able to escape to Chicago with her nieces, but continues to feel great loss and guilt about the lost family members, especially her daughters. Her presenting problem is grief. Obviously, the cultural context cannot be divorced from the problem. Her identities as a Guatemalan, as a woman, and as a Roman Catholic, are very important to understanding who she is and what some psychological resources may be. But it is as a mother that she grieves, and as both a mother and a political activist that she feels guilt for endangering and, in her mind, abandoning her children. Family and Political Activism are not listed as identity components to Hays's model, but they are clearly the chief parts of this client's identity that are most salient here. Her early and recent experiences in Guatemala and her gender expectations for child-raising are certainly significant and relevant parts of her identity, and color in pervasive ways the tapestry of who she is, but at this point in time, they are not the primary aspects. It would be inappropriate to ignore them and treat her as a middle-class European American bereaved woman, and it would also be inappropriate to focus entirely on prespecified multicultural identity components and thereby ignore the source of this woman's pain.

Trevino's Worldview and Change Model

Earlier in the chapter in our discussion of worldview, we mentioned Trevino's (1996) two-stage approach. She addresses how change might be effected in counseling within the context of the client's worldview. Following the more recent conceptualization in anthropology that an individual's worldview varies in levels of abstraction, and that specific worldviews fall within the domain of a general worldview (Kearney, 1984), she proposes a change model. Within this model, the counselor should be able to understand and operate within the client's general worldview. At this level, the client needs to experience validation and support rather than discrepancy between his or her own worldview and the counselor's. Within this general worldview, however, are specific views, and she suggests, citing previous research on the counseling change process, that discrepancies in this area between the counselor and the client are what facilitates change. The outcome, then, is that the general worldview is left intact, but the specific view is changed.

We illustrate this change process by use of our own example. A friend of one of the authors has a doctoral degree in Theological Studies and is a pleasant, calm, friendly person by temperament and choice. Very little ruffles him, and when he is upset, his coping style is to *always* remain respectful and if necessary be quietly assertive. He had the opportunity to study for a year in Greece, and his father-in-law visited him at the end of his year-long stay. One afternoon the two of them were in city traffic and the driver of the car in front of them unexpectedly slammed on his brakes. Unable to stop in time, Dave's car tapped the back bumper of the front car but caused no damage. As his father-in-law tells the story, he was astounded at that point to see both mild-mannered Dave and the Greek driver hurtle out of their respective cars and proceed to shout obscenities and gesture wildly at each other. After five minutes of this, they each returned to their cars and drove off. Dave picked up the conversation he had been having with his father-in-law as if nothing out of the ordinary had taken place. When asked about it later, Dave said he had previously discussed the driving habits in that city with a Greek associate and was advised as to how to drive in a culturally congruent fashion, as well as how to handle the inevitable conflicts that would arise. In effect, Dave's general worldview about the importance of peace and harmonious, respectful relations stayed intact, but his specific view on how to deal with aggressive drivers in this city in Greece changed.

In the initial stage of Trevino's model, the counselor strives to understand the client's general view of the world and view of the specific problem domain. The counselor strives for congruence with both views, thereby enhancing the therapeutic relationship. In the second, intervention, stage of counseling, congruence with the client's general worldview is maintained, but the counselor encourages exploration of alternative, discrepant, perspectives within the specific problem domain.

While Trevino does not specify this, she implies that during the intervention stage, the empathic appreciation of the client and his or her worldview is communicated clearly, so that the relationship is not jeopardized by the client's feeling unappreciated or forced into changes that seem to assault the client's values and identity.

Synthesis and Modification of the Models

Considering Hays's model (presented earlier in the chapter), Ridley's model, and Trevino's model concurrently, there seem to be several complementary pieces:

1. Understanding the client's general worldview is crucial. Among other requirements, this means having enough psychological knowledge to begin the process of informed listening without superimposing one's own agenda or worldview. Remember that, as the quotation at the beginning of this chapter stated, culture is the world that has "tended" them, that has provided structure and meaning to a world that would have been impossible to navigate otherwise.

2. As the counselor listens and responds empathically, two things happen: The client feels affirmed, understood, and supported, and the counselor begins to construct an understanding of how the specific problem domain is causing difficulty. Ridley's explanation of the counselor's internal process of constructing schemas while remaining open to new information, in concert with Hays's suggestions regarding which cultural pieces of the client's identity are likely important enough to inquire about, provides both a process (etic) and a culture-specific (emic) understanding of this initial phase of counseling.

3. During the intervention stage, the client's general worldview should not be challenged but is consistently supported by the counselor; change results when the counselor, maintaining the therapeutic alliance (a relevant term from another body of literature), provides alternative, discrepant constructions within the specific problem domain.

This synthesized approach, we believe, has great merit. It offers a complex but understandable approach that answers the "But what do you *do*?" question.

Our own understanding of counseling and therapy in general, including multicultural counseling specifically, is that additional guidelines may be helpful:

1. As you listen to the client's description of their presenting concern, try to understand the client's multifaceted identity. Ask yourself also whether the issue seems *predominantly* to be intrapsychic or interpersonal. In the case of the Guatemalan bereaved mother, the issue is primarily intrapsychic, although there are certainly interpersonal components. In the case of an 18-year-old African American female who is feeling alienated in a predominantly white university, her focus is probably primarily interpersonal. By the end of the first session, you should have a feeling for the cultural components of this specific client's identity and an understanding of those components' dynamic relationships with the presenting problem.

2. If the client's difficulties are primarily *intrapsychic*, we suggest you follow your usual models for addressing intrapsychic conflict, paying particular attention to the need for offering support and respect to all aspects of the self that are in conflict. Polster (1995) and others' descriptions of subselves may be a helpful way to construe the conflicted area and to work toward reconciliation of the parts.

3. If the clients' difficulties are primarily *interpersonal,* try to ascertain whether the approach most congruent with their general worldview and identity is to work toward changing themselves or trying to interact and effect change with the other party/parties. While you may choose to offer therapeutic considerations of the positive and negative effects of proceeding one way or the other, bear in mind that those effects are inextricably linked with the client's identity.

4. Whether the clients' decision is to work on changing themselves and/or the environment causing the problems, consider employing a solution-focused approach first (i.e., asking them what they have done before in similar situations that helped). This conveys respect and precludes your superimposing your own agenda on them.

5. If they have no previous solutions to implement, and no models for such solutions in their repertoire, a psychoeducational approach may be appropriate. For example, the client who wants to cope with the situation by "not worrying so much," may be helped by learning relaxation skills, cognitive restructuring, and the like. The client who instead wants to adopt a more interactive approach may be helped by role-playing conflict resolution strategies, defining priorities, and so forth.

6. Regardless of whether the therapeutic focus is intrapsychic or interpersonal (and within that second context, whether change is hoped for internally or externally), provide for consistent therapeutic reassessment. Is the client happy with the direction the two of you are proceeding? If the focus has been primarily intrapsychic, should that be reassessed? If it has been on changing the system, is that eliciting intrapsychic conflict that now needs to be addressed? In other words, when you encounter the resistance we discussed in an earlier chapter, ask yourself and the client if the direction of the therapeutic focus needs to be reconsidered.

Improving Your Multicultural Skills

As should be apparent by now, we and other writers concerned about multiculturalism believe that simply being a well-meaning counselor is not enough. As Ridley et al. (1994) noted, "Many well-meaning counselors have good intentions, but, we ask, do they have the *right* intentions?" (p. 132). We hope that, like us, you will find the process of informing and modifying your culturocentric views to be exciting and enlightening enough to compensate for the occasional deep discomfort.

There is no substitute for actually doing cross-cultural counseling. If at all possible, do at least one practicum in a cross-cultural site. Try to obtain supervision from a knowledgeable professional who is a member of the cultural group or subgroup with whom you are working. If your program does not have such sites on the approved practicum placements, encourage that they be sought out, and if all else fails, seek one out yourself and see if you can get it approved.

In the meantime, you can begin the process of becoming more culturally sensitive by investing yourself in three different areas. We emphasize that these do not substitute for the actual face-to-face encounter in the therapeutic dyad, but they are necessary and entirely in your control.

First, we suggest that you undertake a respectful but diligent self-analysis of your cultural heritage. Some students enjoy writing this out in autobiographical form, others prefer talking it out with other students. The goal here is to be honest, nondefensive, and empathic with yourself. The one area in all the multicultural literature on which there is complete consensus is in this belief that self-awareness and self-confrontation are imperative.

Secondly, we suggest you "stretch" yourself through reading, watching movies, listening to music, and the like in which the focus is a cultural group or subgroup different from your own. Read biographies and autobiographies and historical fiction about individuals in contexts different from your own. Watch movies and television series that deal with people unlike you. Listen to music that originates from a different culture or subculture than yours. As you undertake these activities, try to identify with the person unlike you so that you can increase your empathy for her or his situation and coping patterns. Do this especially in areas in which you think you have some unresolved stereotypes and biases, and do it with the notion in mind of correcting your old views. Keep doing this for years. Reading one book about each ethnic group will hardly provide you with the kind of breadth of understanding you need. We believe you will find that this process of self-education and embracing diversity is both fun and provocative.

Finally, we suggest that you actively involve yourself in activities in which you feel culturally different. Gutierrez (1996) looked at nonacademic, informal activities that are related to multicultural competency. The areas of travel, associating in work or recreation with individuals from different cultural groups and subgroups, and actually experiencing being a minority for a period of time are the factors especially related to multicultural competency as measured by the MCI. If you are going to travel to a different country, spend some time away from the usual tourist sites and strike up conversations with the "real" people you encounter. Have discussions with members of another cultural or subcultural group and share your preoccupations and worries, to check for similarities and differences. Attend a church where you will be in the minority. You will be struck by how different some people are from you in some ways, and also by the similarity in basic human concerns about relationships and the like. Use your emerging professional skills on behalf of others. For example, consider volunteer work in nursing homes where you can take the opportunity to confront any lingering stereotypes you have of individuals who are older and/or living with a disability. Work in an AIDS hospice and see the similarities between your existential concerns and the residents'. This emphasis on *doing* something rather than simply increasing your sensitivity is reflected in the standards of the two professional organizations, both of which imply an ethical obligation to serve as change agents. Jane Addams, the human rights advocate, said it well: "The good we secure for ourselves is precarious and uncertain…until it is secured for all of us and incorporated into our common life" (*Teaching Tolerance*, 1998).

Summary

Multicultural counseling, as we have defined it, involves the counselor's sensitivity to all aspects of the client's identity, with special focus on those areas of culture and subculture that we have reason to believe may be particularly important to the client and which are intertwined with the presenting problem. An understanding of oppression and its effects, of ones' own culturocentric biases, and of the usual difficulties that various cultural groups and subgroups encounter can provide the counselor with a respectful, empathic stance from which to understand any particular client's concerns. Important in all counseling, but especially in cross-cultural counseling, is the counselor's willingness to tolerate ambiguity while constructing therapeutic hypotheses and the counselor's sensitivity to the impact of various interventions on the therapeutic alliance and on the client's worldview.

DISCUSSION QUESTIONS

- Which worldviews, cultures, and subcultures do you have the most trouble understanding empathically? What can you do to remedy this?

- If you were an international student in a non-Western country and sought counseling, what would you most need the counselor to understand and respect about you? What would you most fear happening in this cross-cultural counseling dyad in which you are the client?

- How will you honor the ethical mandate to counter oppression and the ethical mandate to honor the client's worldview if that worldview intrinsically promotes oppression (for example, of women in many cultures)?

- What universal values, if any, do you think transcend culture and should be used to promote change in any context (e.g., basic human rights, etc.)?

BIBLIOGRAPHY

Arredondo, P., Toporek, R., Brown, S. P., Jones, J., Locke, D., Sanchez, J., & Stadler, H. (1996). Operationalization of the multicultural counseling competencies. *Journal of Multicultural Counseling and Development, 24,* 42–78.

Atkinson, D. R., Morten, G., & Sue, D. W. (1989). *Counseling American minorities: A cross-cultural perspective* (3rd ed.). Dubuque, IA: W. C. Brown.

Atkinson, D. R., Morten, G., & Sue, D. W. (1993). *Counseling American minorities: A cross-cultural perspective* (4th ed.). Dubuque, IA: W. C. Brown.

Axelson, J. A. (1993). *Counseling and development in a multicultural society* (2nd ed.). Pacific Grove, CA: Brooks/Cole.

Behrens, J. T. (1997). Does the White Racial Identity Attitude Scale measure racial identity? *Journal of Counseling Psychology, 44,* 3–12.

Beutler, L. E., & Bergan, J. (1991). Value change in counseling and psychotherapy: A search for scientific credibility. *Journal of Counseling Psychology, 38,* 16–24.

Bracero, W. (1996). Ancestral voices: Narrative and multicultural perspectives with an Asian schizophrenic. *Psychotherapy, 33,* 93–103.

Broverman, I. K., Broverman, D. M., Clarkson, F., Rosenkrantz, P., & Vogel, S. (1970). Sex-role stereotyping and clinical judgments in mental health. *Journal of Clinical and Consulting Psychology, 45,* 250–256.

Brown, L. S. (1986). Gender role analysis: A neglected component of psychological assessment. *Psychotherapy, 23,* 243–248.

Brown, L. S. (1990). Taking account of gender in the clinical assessment interview. *Professional Psychology, 21,* 12–17.

Brown, L. S., & Ballou, M. (Eds.) (1992). *Personality and pathology: Feminist reappraisals.* New York: Guilford.

Campbell, A. (1993). *Men, women, and aggression.* New York: Basic Books.

Caplan, P. J. (1991). Delusional dominating personality disorder (DDPD). *Feminism and Psychology, 1,* 171–174.

Carter, R. T., & Helms, J. (1987). The relationship between Black value-orientations and racial identity attitudes. *Measurement and Evaluation in Counseling and Development, 19,* 185–195.

Casas, J. M. (1984). Policy, training, and research in counseling psychology: The racial/ethnic minority perspective. In S. D. Brown & R. W. Lent (Eds.), *Handbook of counseling psychology* (pp. 785–831). New York: Wiley.

Chodorow, N. (1978). *The reproduction of mothering.* Berkeley: University of California Press.

Cole, M. (1996). *Cultural psychology: A once and future discipline.* Cambridge, MA: Belknap Press of Harvard.

Cross, W. E. (1987). A two-factor theory of Black identity: Implications for the study of identity development in minority children. In J. S. Phinney & M. J. Rotheram (Eds.), *Children's ethnic socialization: Pluralism and development in minority children* (pp. 117–133). Newbury Park, CA: Sage.

Cross, W. E., Jr. (1995). The psychology of nigrescence: Revising the Cross model. In J. G. Ponterotto, J. M. Casas, L. A. Suzuki, & C. M. Alexander (Eds.), *Handbook of multicultural counseling* (pp. 73–92). Thousand Oaks, CA: Sage.

Crossman, L. (1994). *Date rape and sexual aggression by college males: Incidence and the involvement of impulsivity, anger, hostility, psychopathology, peer influence, and pornography use.* Unpublished doctoral dissertation, Texas A&M University, College Station, TX.

D'Andrade, R. G. (1991). The identification of schemas in naturalistic data. In M. J. Horowitz (Ed.), *Person schemas and maladaptive interpersonal patterns* (pp. 279–301). Chicago: University of Chicago Press.

Das, A. (1995). Rethinking multicultural counseling: Implication for counselor education. *Journal of Counseling and Development, 74,* 45–52.

Davenport, D. S., & Yurich, J. (1991). Multicultural gender issues. *Journal of Counseling and Development, 70,* 64–71.

Espin, O. (1985). Psychotherapy with hispanic women. In P. Pedersen (Ed.), *Handbook of cross-cultural counseling and therapy.* Westport, CT: Greenwood.

Enns, C. Z. (1993). Twenty years of feminist counseling and therapy: From naming biases to implementing multifaceted practice. *The Counseling Psychologist, 21,* 3–87.

Fitzgerald, L. F., & Nutt, R. (1986). Division 17 principles concerning the counseling/psychotherapy of women: Rationale and implementation. *The Counseling Psychologist, 14,* 180–216.

Fowers, B. J., & Richardson, F. C. (1996). Why is multiculturalism good? *American Psychologist, 51,* 609–622.

Gilligan, C. (1982). *In a different voice.* Cambridge, MA: Harvard University Press.

Good, G. E., and Wood, P. K. (1995). Male gender role conflict, depression, and help seeking: Do college men face double jeopardy? *Journal of Counseling and Development, 74,* 70–75.

Gutierrez, B. (1996). *Reported experiences which influence psychologists' degree of multicultural competency.* Unpublished doctoral dissertation, Texas A & M University, College Station, TX.

Hamilton, D. L., & Trolier, T. K. (1986). In J. F. Dovidio and S. L. Gaertner (Eds.), *Prejudice, discrimination, and racism* (pp. 127–163). New York: Academic Press.

Hardiman, R. (1982). *White identity development: A process oriented model for describing the racial consciousness of White Americans.* Unpublished doctoral dissertation, University of Massachusetts, Amherst.

Hays, P. (1996). Addressing the complexities of culture and gender in counseling. *Journal of Counseling and Development, 74,* 332–338.

Hays, J. A., & Gelso, C. J. (1993). Male counselors' discomfort with gay and HIV-infected clients. *Journal of Counseling Psychology, 40,* 86–93.

Helms, J. (1984). Toward a theoretical explanation of the effects of race on counseling: A Black and White model. *The Counseling Psychologist, 12,* 153–165.

Helms, J. (1992). Why is there no study of cultural equivalence in standardized cognitive ability testing? *American Psychologist, 47,* 1083–1101.

Helms, J. (1994). How multiculturalism obscures racial factors in the therapy process: Comment on Ridley et al., Sodowsky et al., Ottavi et al., and Thompson et al. *Journal of Counseling and Development, 41,* 162–165.

Herring, R. D. (1992). Seeking a new paradigm: Counseling Native Americans. *Journal of Multicultural Counseling and Development, 20,* 35–43.

Hetzel, R. (1997). *Gender role conflict and perceived social support as predictors of psychological distress in men.* Unpublished doctoral dissertation, Texas A & M University, College Station, TX.

Ho, D. Y. F. (1995). Internalized culture, culturocentrism, and transcendence. *The Counseling Psychologist, 23,* 4–24.

Hollis, J. W., & Wantz, R. A. (1994). *Counselor preparation: 1993–95: Vol. II: Status, trends, implications* (8th ed.). Muncie, IN: Accelerated Development.

Ibrahim, F. A. (1991). Contribution of cultural worldview to generic counseling and development. *Journal of Counseling and Development, 70,* 13–19.

Jaggar, A. M. (1983). Political philosophies of women's liberation. In L. Richardson & V. Taylor (Eds.), *Feminist frontiers* (pp. 322–329). Reading, MA: Addison-Wesley.

Kearney, M. (1984). *World view.* Novato, CA: Chandler & Sharp.

Kerwin, C., & Ponterotto, J. (1995). Biracial identity development: Theory and research. In J. G. Ponterotto, J. M. Casas, L. A. Suzuki, & C. M. Alexander (Eds.), *Handbook of multicultural counseling* (pp. 181–198). Thousand Oaks, CA: Sage.

Kim, J. (1980). *Processes of Asian-American identity development.* Unpublished doctoral dissertation, University of Massachusetts, Amherst.

Kiselica, M. S. (1998). Preparing Anglos for the challenges and joys of multiculturalism. *The Counseling Psychologist, 26,* 5–21.

Kluckhohn, C. (1956). Toward a comparison of value-emphases in different cultures. In L. D. White (Ed.), *The state of social sciences* (pp. 116–132). Chicago: University of Chicago Press.

Lawler, A. (1990). The healthy self: Variations on a theme. *Journal of Counseling and Development, 68,* 652–654.

Lee, C. C. (1995). Reflections of a multicultural road warrior. *The Counseling Psychologist, 23,* 79–81.

Malgady, R. G., Rogler, L. H., and Constantine, G. (1987). Ethnocultural and linguistic bias in mental health evaluation of Hispanics. *American Psychologist, 42,* 228–234.

Miller, J. B. (1984). The development of women's sense of self. *Work in Progress* (No. 12). Wellesley, MA: Stone Center Working Papers Series.

Mwaba, K. A., & Pedersen, P. (1990). Relative importance of intercultural, interpersonal, and psychopathological attributions in judging critical incidents by multicultural counselors. *Journal of Multicultural Counseling and Development, 18,* 107–117.

Neimeyer, G. J., Prichard, S., Lyddon, W. J., & Sherrard, P. A. D. (1993). The role of epistemic style in counseling preference and orientation. *Journal of Counseling and Development, 71,* 515–523.

Ottavi, T. M., Pope-Davis, D. B., & Dings, J. G. (1994). Relationship between white racial identity attitudes and self-reported multicultural counseling competencies. *Journal of Counseling and Development, 41,* 149–154.

Patterson, C. H. (1996). Multicultural counseling: From diversity to universality. *Journal of Counseling and Development, 74,* 227–235.

Pedersen, P. (1991). Multiculturalism as a generic approach to counseling. *Journal of Counseling and Development, 70,* 6–12.

Pedersen, P. (1996). The importance of both similarities and differences in multicultural counseling: Reaction to C. H. Patterson. *Journal of Counseling and Development, 74,* 236–237.

Pedersen, P. B. (1997). The cultural context of the American Counseling Association Code of Ethics. *Journal of Counseling and Development, 76,* 23–28.

Pedersen, P. B., Draguns, J. G., Lonner, W. J., and Trimble, J. E. (Eds.). (1996). *Counseling across cultures* (4th ed.). Thousand Oaks, CA: Sage.

Polster, E. (1995). *A population of selves: A therapeutic exploration of personal diversity.* San Francisco: Jossey-Bass.

Ponce, F. Q., & Atkinson, D. R. (1989). Mexican American acculturation, counselor ethnicity, counseling style, and perceived counselor credibility. *Journal of Counseling Psychology, 36,* 203–208.

Ponterotto, J. G. (1988). Racial consciousness development among white counselor trainees: A stage model. *Journal of Multicultural Counseling and Development, 16,* 146–156.

Ponterotto, J. G. (1996). Multicultural counseling in the twenty-first century. *The Counseling Psychologist, 24,* 259–268.

Ponterotto, J. G., Casas, J. M., Suzuki, L. A., & Alexander, C. M. (Eds.). (1995). *Handbook of multicultural counseling.* Thousand Oaks, CA: Sage.

Pope-Davis, D. B., & Dings, J. G. (1995). The assessment of multicultural counseling competencies. In J. G. Ponterotto, J. M. Casas, L. A. Suzuki, & C. M. Alexander (Eds.), *Handbook of multicultural counseling* (pp. 287–311). Thousand Oaks, CA: Sage.

Ridley, C. R., Mendoza, D. W., Kanitz, B. E., Angermeier, L., & Zenk, R. (1994). Cultural sensitivity in multicultural counseling: A perceptual schema model. *Journal of Counseling Psychology, 41,* 125–136.

Robertson, J., & Fitzgerald, L. F. (1990). The (mis)treatment of men: Effects of client gender role and life style on diagnosis and attribution of pathology. *Journal of Counseling Psychology, 37,* 3–9.

Rogler, L. H., Cortes, D. E., & Malgady, R. G. (1991). Acculturation and mental health status among hispanics. *American Psychologist, 46,* 585–597.

Rose, D. S. (1991). A model for psychodynamic psychotherapy with the rape victim. *Psychotherapy, 28,* 85–95.

Rowe, W., Bennett, S. K., & Atkinson, D. R. (1994). White racial identity models: A critique and alternative proposal. *The Counseling Psychologist, 22,* 129–146.

Royce, J. R., & Mos, L. P. (1980). *Psycho-Epistemological Profile manual.* Edmonton, Canada: University of Alberta Printing Office.

Ruiz, A. S. (1990). Ethnic identity: Crisis and resolution. *Journal of Multicultural Counseling and Development, 18,* 29–40.

Sangrestano, L. M. (1992). The use of power and influence in a gendered world. *Psychology of Women's Quarterly, 16,* 439–447.

Santiago-Rivera, A. L. (1995). Developing a culturally sensitive treatment modality for bilingual Spanish-speaking clients: Incorporating language and culture in counseling. *Journal of Counseling and Development, 74,* 12–17.

Schwartz, T. (1992). Anthropology and psychology: An unrequited relationship. In T. Schwartz & C. A. Lutz (Eds.), *New directions in psychological anthropology* (pp. 324–349). Cambridge, England: Cambridge University Press.

Shay, J. J. (1993). Should men treat couples? Transference, countertransference, and sociopolitical considerations. *Psychotherapy, 30,* 93–102.

Sinacore-Guinn, A. (1995). The diagnostic window: Culture- and Gender-sensitive diagnosis and training. *Counselor Education and Supervision, 35,* 32–42.

Smart, D. W., & Smart, J. F. (1997). DSM-IV and culturally sensitive diagnosis: Some observations for counselors. *Journal of Counseling and Development, 75,* 392–398.

Sodowsky, G. R., Taffe, R. C., Gutlin, T. B., & Wise, S. L. (1994). Development of the Multicultural Counseling Inventory: A self-report measure of multicultural competency. *Journal of Counseling Psychology, 41,* 137–148.

Stephan, W. G. (1989). A cognitive approach to stereotyping. In D. Bartal, C. T. Graumann, A. W. Kruglanski, & W. Stroebe (Eds.), *Stereotyping and prejudice* (pp. 37-57). New York: Springer-Verlag.

Sue, D. W. (1996). Multicultural counseling: Models, methods, and action. *The Counseling Psychologist, 24,* 279–284.

Sue, D. W., Arredondo, P., & McDavis, R. J. (1992). Multicultural counseling competencies and standards: A call to the profession. *Journal of Multicultural Counseling and Development, 20,* 64–88.

Sue, D. W., Ivey, A. E., & Pedersen, P. B. (1996). *A theory of multicultural counseling and therapy.* Pacific Grove, CA: Brooks/Cole.

Sue, D. W., & Sue, D. (1990). *Counseling the culturally different: Theory and practice.* New York: Wiley.

Sue, S., Zane, N., & Young, K. (1994). Research on psychotherapy with culturally diverse populations. In A. E. Bergin & S. L. Garfield (Eds.), *Handbook of psychotherapy and behavior change* (4th ed., pp. 783–817). New York: Wiley.

Suzuki, L. A., Meller, P. J., & Ponterotto, J. G. (1996). *Handbook of multicultural assessment.* San Francisco: Jossey-Bass.

Suzuki, L. A., & Valencia, R. R. (1997). Race-ethnicity and measured intelligence: Educational implications. *American Psychologist, 52,* 1103–1114.

Todisco, M., & Salomone, P. R. (1991). Facilitating effective cross-cultural relationships: The White counselor and the Black client. *Journal of Multicultural Counseling and Development, 19,* 146–157.

Trevino, J. G. (1996). Worldview and change in cross-cultural counseling. *The Counseling Psychologist, 24,* 198–215.

Wade, J. C. (1995). African American men's gender role conflict: The significance of gender identity. Paper presented at the annual meeting of the American Psychological Association, New York, NY, August, 1995.

Walsh, W. B., & Betz, N. E. (1995). *Tests and assessment* (3rd ed.). Englewood Cliffs, NJ: Prentice Hall.

Wehrly, B. (1995). *Pathways to multicultural counseling competence.* Pacific Grove, CA: Brooks/Cole.

Weinrach, S. G., & Thomas, K. R. (1996). The counseling profession's commitment to diversity-sensitive counseling: A critical reassessment. *Journal of Counseling and Development, 74,* 472–477.

Welfel, E. R. (1998). *Ethics in counseling and psychotherapy: Standards, research, and emerging issues.* Pacific Grove, CA: Brooks/Cole.

Wolcott, H. F. (1991). Propriospect and the acquisition of culture. *Anthropology and Education Quarterly, 22,* 251–278.

Worell, J., & Johnson, N. G. (Eds.). (1997). *Shaping the future of feminist psychology.* Washington DC: The American Psychological Association.

CHAPTER

11 Resistance

If change were too easy and mental structures too fluid, the result would be greater instability, not quicker psychotherapy.

—Harry Guntrip

I cannot hurry, for I have so much more at stake than you.

—Louise White

Several years ago, one of us supervised a student who received feedback from two clients within one week. This student had just read about resistance and thought it might be helpful to share with his clients whenever he thought that was what they were doing. Watching tapes of the sessions, the supervisor came across: "Well, hell yes I'm 'resistant'!" the first client told her therapist. "All these new ways of doing things may seem easy for you to say, but let me tell you—they ain't so easy to implement! Gimme a little while to make sense of them! And the reason I'm late is, the city bus picked me up late. I got the first damn one I could after I got off of work. Get off my back, why don'tcha?" This is a fascinating transaction from the supervisor's perspective. The client's style was certainly a bit abrasive. Perhaps this same defensive posture causes her trouble in other aspects of her life and might merit attention in therapy at some point. But the content of what she said, the fact that she was protesting an easy labeling of her failure to capitulate with the therapist's agenda, seemed quite legitimate.

The second client, a psychology student who had been in therapy before, said something similar to our student: "You know, it's true I came in here and we had a contract to work together on something. But it's like someone with a bunch of broken bones going to a doctor to get them fixed. It's a lot easier for the surgeon to say 'Let's do this in 15 minutes 'cause I got another patient' than it is for the patient to go through that. Slow down and give me a little time!" The student was actually lucky to get this feedback from these two clients. Others had simply quit coming, with no explanation, and the student was left wondering what it was about "them" that precluded a therapeutic alliance.

Regardless of what they call it, writers from most schools of thought note that clients don't always follow the therapist's agenda. For the student, whose confidence in her or his own skills is still evolving, it may be tempting to personalize this. And, as in the above cases, sometimes the therapist *is* the problem. But in general, if our empathic abilities are in tune, we should be able to sense when we have moved too fast or too far away from the clients' experience and go back to "pick them up." An analogy that may capture some of this is of two people ice skating; one is quite proficient and has done it for years and knows this stretch of ice very well, and the other is a rank beginner. If the goal is to get to the other side of the lake together, the first skater will need to take the second skater's anxiety and lack of expertise into perspective and slow down when the skating partner seems to be lagging behind. For those of you who have been in therapy, it may be easier to understand the client's inability to maintain a steady rapid pace. Indeed, some research (e.g., Hill, Corbit, Kanitz, Rios, Lightsey, & Gomez, 1992; Tracey, 1986) suggests that resistance is not only inevitable, but may be instrumental in the counseling process. Thinking of resistance as part of the package, as an expected part of the client's difficulty in making changes, gives the therapist more compassion, as well as providing the possibility of devising some creative interventions to help.

Contemporary Understandings of Resistance

Resistance is a term used so loosely and often so naively that it is difficult to know what others mean when they say it. Beginning therapists may use it ubiquitously to describe virtually anything the client does that makes them feel inadequate. Although behaviorists generally don't use the term, Davison (1973) mentions it as a substitute term for "counter-control," and it could describe, for example, a client who refused to do her assignment from the last session and is now crying rather than recommitting herself to the new behavior. Conversely, many therapists would view automatic deference to the therapist's agenda as resistance (e.g., Rennie, 1994) and assume that the client was unwilling to explore difficult material. It depends, then, on what his or her definition of and goal for therapy is, to know what a given therapist means by saying a client is "resisting." The literature seems to provide three, possibly overlapping, understandings of resistance.

Psychodynamic

Psychodynamic writers and others who partially rely on such approaches view resistance as the client's avoidance of pain (e.g., Bauer & Kobos, 1987; Strupp & Binder, 1984; Teyber, 1997). Patton & Meara (1992) specifically discuss this "pain" as aggressive feelings or loss; Teyber's (1997) suggestion is that shame is a probable contributor. This kind of resistance is most obvious when the therapy involves uncovering work—exploration of suppressed feelings (which, arguably, would not have needed suppression if they were that easy to accept!). The client who says she needs help in resolving the grief over a deceased family member, but who seems to change the subject whenever painful feelings arise, is a "classic" example. This definition of resistance also helps us understand, however, the client with a low sense of efficacy who is trying to take on a new large project. If the therapist is using a cognitive/behavioral approach to help her get started and maintain momentum, but each new step feels to her that this is another opportunity for humiliating failure, her "resistance" to following through on homework assignments might be construed not so much as lack of motivation or as counter-control, and more as the reluctance to undertake a task that seems certain to end in failure, shame, and even lowered self-esteem (in other words, as matching the psychodynamic definition of resistance).

Behavioral

Another approach to resistance is to define it in behavioral, rather than intrapsychic, terms. Bischoff and Tracey (1995), for example, define resistance for the purposes of their research study as "any behavior that indicates overt or covert opposition to the therapist, the counseling process, or the therapist's agenda." This approach to resistance certainly makes research easier to do; one can look at content analyses or transcriptions of tapes and simply note when and under which circumstances clients do not follow the therapist's guidance. Although this sounds suspiciously like the subjective definition of the threatened therapist—that he or she had to be "right," and that the client's resistance indicated a failure on the client's part to cooperate—those connotations are not necessarily appropriate in many cases of researchers' findings. Using the Client Resistant Scale that he developed, Mahalik (1994), for example, found in analyzing the first and third film sets of "Three Approaches to Psychotherapy" that certain types of therapist behaviors—interpretation (what others might call advanced empathy), open questions, and minimal encouragement—were the most effective response modes, that closed questions was the least effective response mode, and that providing information was connected to greater opposition of expressing painful feelings, to the therapist, and to insight. This process approach to resistance can be helpful to students when they review their tapes of sessions. Discovering what approaches "work" with a given client and which ones do not can help the therapist orchestrate his or her style accordingly.

Social Constructionism

A final broad approach to resistance is one that urges therapist caution and humility before defining client behavior in such a way. This approach, in opposition to what was seen as an inherent arrogance in psychoanalytic interpretations, stresses that therapist direction might have been wrong. As Omer (1997) says, "The arguments against the concept of resistance have changed with the years. In the last decade, however, they have converged upon one unifying theme: since therapists have no privileged access to the truth, their formulations cannot claim to be more acceptable than those of clients." This approach has been espoused through the years by a variety of therapists representing various theoretical orientations, especially from those with a phenomenological basis. It has gained great momentum since the blossoming of constructivist and social constructionist approaches to therapy (e.g., Neimeyer & Mahoney, 1995; Rosen & Kuehlwein, 1996), which in general posits that the client's attempt to find meaning will be a joint construction of that meaning arising from an ongoing dialogue between client and therapist. The therapist is not assumed to have the "answer," but rather will, in working with the client's narrative, help construct meaning (McAdams, 1993).

Writing from within this approach, Omer, (1997) suggests several reasons why clients will "resist" therapists' formulations: (a) the formulations are experienced as offensive, (b) they are in contrast to the client's feelings, (c) they entail values or goals unlike the client's, (d) they seem abstract or foreign, (e) they conflict with other, accepted, understandings, or (f) they are delivered in the wrong tones or in improper words. He refers to such formulations as, by definition, coming from an "external narrative," and directs therapists confronted by impasses with clients to acknowledge the externality of the previous approach and propose a more empathic one instead.

While we cannot wholly agree with all aspects of social constructionism, we do believe that much of what the approach offers tends to confirm our own understandings of the optimal therapeutic process. We especially concur with Omer's six possible reasons for clients' "balking," and suggest that student therapists look to such possibilities first, before they assume more intrapsychic explanations.

Resistance

For the purpose of this book, we will define resistance as "an intrapsychic or interpersonal process marked by ambivalence about claiming and exploring little-known feelings and motivations within one's self." The ambivalence is rooted in the conflict between urges toward growth and completeness on the one hand, and fear of pain or punishment on the other.

Consider a client one of the authors had, whom we will call Raquel. Raquel had been an abused child, beaten regularly by her father and relatively ignored by her mother. She came for therapy because she wanted to be more assertive with her husband rather than continue to acquiesce through fear of his displeasure. As she worked to improve her assertion skills, she simultaneously began to explore her fears of standing up for herself. She acknowledged that she almost never felt angry with her husband, even when intellectually she knew her needs were being discounted. What happened to the anger? She didn't know. As nearly as she could tell, she had never assumed that her feelings and needs should be considered. She did, however, admit to behavior that seemed to be superficially passive-aggressive, and traced it back to childhood. Even with her father, whom she greatly feared, she had exhibited such behavior. Believing that perhaps under such behavior might lurk some justifiable, self-affirming anger, the therapist encouraged

Raquel to continue her exploration of her memory of those times. Surely, in addition to all the fear toward her dad, must there not have been some anger? Raquel experienced enormous anxiety at such a notion—anger toward her father was simply unthinkable!—and missed the next session. Only over a period of months was she able to slowly accept her early rage as justifiable and healthy. Why the resistance to such an appropriate feeling?

Consider what Raquel must have been like at four or five years of age: lonely, unsupported by her mother, and frightened of her father. Even when she tried very hard to second-guess her father and be "good," she received almost daily beatings. Simply thinking about expressing anger to him must have seemed terribly dangerous, especially since at that age admitting feelings seems tantamount to acting on them. Small wonder, then, that Raquel "resisted" experiencing anger as a child. By the time she entered therapy as an adult, she had been out of her parents' house for years and her father had in fact died. Neither time nor death had been of much help, however, in erasing the old pattern of repressing anger—a pattern that had helped her survive as a child, but which now was dysfunctional.

Raquel's resistance exemplifies the way we see resistance operating generally. A pattern of coping with anxiety-provoking feelings, often originating in early childhood and an adaptive pattern at the time, continues into the present in a client's life and is demonstrated both in and out of the therapy session (Bauer & Kobos, 1987). Trying to strip away the resistance without dealing with the resulting fear can leave the client feeling overwhelmingly vulnerable and out of control. Good therapists do not assault resistance in an adversarial way; they "woo" the client, to use Roth's (1987) word, into trusting them enough to gradually expose the underlying feelings and motivations. That is a fearful process, for Raquel, as it is for all of us, to venture into the hidden places within oneself. We fear opening Pandora's box, lest all sorts of painful and evil aspects fly out.

In Raquel's case, the fear was related to early associations of the expression of anger to the expectations of severe punishment. Similarly, someone shamed as a child for showing sadness or pain may be understandably reluctant to explore such feelings later in life. Other clients' fears may be less related to specific early episodes than to damage that they would incur on their self-image by admitting to what they would consider to be illegitimate feelings. In either case, the issue often is that the client does not feel entitled to certain feelings (Wile, 1984). Much of the therapeutic "working through" of resistance is thus dependent on the therapist's ability to help the client feel entitled to feelings and needs which the client had previously assumed must be denied.

Encouraging entitlement is not as simple as it sounds. Clients are likely to sense the power of unexplored material, and perhaps even overestimate such power (Langs, 1981), and look to you, the therapist, for reassurance that their feelings will not overwhelm and destroy them. Whether that reassurance is asked for overtly or not, your faith in the process will need to be somehow conveyed. Unless you have personally explored similar material within yourself, it will be difficult for you to be helpful with your client. We offer you the caution we have given our students: Never ask a client to do what you would not be willing to do yourself.

We want to underscore a point that should be obvious by now. Clients do not demonstrate resistance out of irresponsibility, or obstinacy, or dishonesty. They resist because they are ambivalent about change and self-exploration; they want greater freedom, but fear the pain that might be necessary. As Singer (1970) indicated, "Resistance reflects both the patient's disbelief in an alternative way of life, reflects…desperate holding on to familiar self-esteem-furthering operations and at the same time…intense fear that any other approach to living would be self-esteem shattering" (p. 235).

We encourage beginning therapists, rather than to personalize their clients' resistance or be annoyed by it, to realize that without resistance, they would probably be out of a job. If every client were perfectly ready to change and able to do it, if it were really that easy, there would be little need for psychotherapists. When we view client resistance as a signal of fear, that thus deserves our support and empathy, rather than as some annoying obstacle we must batter down, it becomes easier for us to do our job of continuing to maintain the therapeutic alliance while encouraging client self-exploration.

Bugental's (1978) definition of the therapeutic alliance is worth noting. He refers to it as "a bond between what is best and most dedicated in the therapist and what is most health-seeking and courageous in the client" (p. 72). Your ability to offer the best of yourself rather than withdrawing or becoming adversarial when you sense resistance is what inspires the client to persevere even when he or she is fearful. If you become impatient, you add to clients' sense of unentitlement, since now you have communicated to them that they do not have the right to their own fear!

True resistance, as we define it, is a process marked by client inner conflict. As Taft (1933/1973) explains eloquently, it is a reflection of the inherent ambivalence of the human being toward growth and individuation. To quote more fully (Taft, 1933/1973)

> However speculative it may sound and however differently it may express itself in any particular case, the fact remains that always, at bottom, every serious blocking in a human life is the expression of an unsolved or rather unaccepted conflict between the will to become more and more individualized, to develop one's own quantum of life, and the reluctance to pursue wholeheartedly a course which is beyond control of the individual will and which inevitably leads to the annihilation of this dearly bought individuality. (pp. 284–285)

Distrust

There is a related process that is often mistaken for resistance. For lack of a better term, we will call this process distrust. Distrust, in contrast to resistance, has an interpersonal root. It arises, not primarily out of ambivalence within the client, but rather out of the interaction the client has with the therapist. Its origins are not so much fear of growth, as fear or anger or mistrust of the therapist. In both cases, the client balks at further therapeutic self-exploration, but the reasons behind the two processes vary. (Note that this discussion bears marked similarity to Omer's 1997 list of "external narrative" mistakes that therapists may make.)

The primary reason, we believe, that clients become mistrustful (either temporarily or permanently) of continuing with therapy is that from their perspective the therapeutic alliance has either been broken or was never satisfactorily forged in the first place. Clients who feel attacked or accused or unsupported are likely to "put on the brakes," less perhaps because they are unwilling to proceed, than because they are unwilling to proceed *with this person*. Their trust in the therapist is at least temporarily shaken, and they feel unsafe and discounted. As Wile (1984) points out, in ordinary human discourse, when people feel criticized, they often respond with anger and/or defensiveness. It should come as no great surprise that they respond similarly in therapy also. In effect, their balking is a protest. It is a way to say to the therapist, "Do not do to me what I do to myself. Do not attack and criticize me; I can do that at home, for free, by myself. I need your support and understanding."

Obviously, it makes little difference at this point whether the therapist intended to criticize or slight the client. It is the client's perception that matters, and until the client feels reassured and supported again, not much therapy will be taking place. We agree with the supervisor who told his supervisee when he heard a tape of a client becoming reluctant and balking, "This is an important process. Nothing else is more important. This is where you stop and park your truck!"

We underscore again that the relationship you offer is often what is healing to the client. To clients who have felt discounted and wounded, and who often discount and wound themselves, having a therapist listen to their protests—however inarticulately they may have been voiced—is indeed a corrective emotional experience. As one terminating client told her therapist after years of therapy, "What you did that I remember most, what helped more than anything else, was when you listened to me that time I got so mad at you. You didn't get defensive or angry, although you didn't cave in either. You listened to me and even changed some of your behavior. I was amazed!" We agree with Stone (1981) that the possibility of therapist error needs to be consistently acknowledged, and that (as in the prior situation) a willingness to listen to client feedback and change behavior can increase the therapist's credibility.

Lewis and Evans (1986) suggest three reasons other than broken alliances for clients to balk at the interpersonal process inherent in therapy. First, they suggest that the client may be experiencing fear or anxiety, some of which may be what we earlier referred to as fear of individuation, but which they believe often has the clear interpersonal focus of fear of control by the therapist. Since we dealt rather extensively with this and other client fears in a previous chapter, we will not further expand on this factor.

The second reason Lewis and Evans suggest for client reluctance to proceed in therapy is that they may not believe that the interactions the therapist is suggesting will be helpful. We think this may especially be operating with beginning therapists, who often do not take the time or do not know how to explain briefly to clients why they are recommending a course of action. If clients want to know why they should explore painful feelings, can you give a brief explanation in layperson's terms? If you wanted a client with an eating disorder to monitor food intake and she objected because of shame and embarrassment, could you explain convincingly why the benefits should outweigh the cost? When you suggest a role play, an empty chair, or other interventions, do you understand the rationale and believe in it enough to explain it to clients, if that seems necessary? We are not suggesting that you always expect client opposition and offer lengthy explanations to fend off their possible questions. We do believe, however, that when you sense reluctance on the part of the client, you should be willing to explore the source of their reservations and if necessary be able to explain briefly why you think it would be helpful for them to do what you have suggested. (Again, to gain an appreciation of their perspective, it may help to imagine yourself going to a physician because you have what you believe is a sinus infection. You want an antibiotic. If the physician were to suggest an unexpected and possibly painful treatment instead, wouldn't you want an explanation? And if you asked for one, and the physician couldn't or wouldn't give it, wouldn't you be offended?)

Finally, Lewis and Evans suggest that clients may appear uncooperative because they simply do not understand what the therapist expects of them. Unless they have been in therapy before, they may have only vague and misinformed ideas about how to proceed. Even if they have been in therapy, their first therapist's orientation and expectations may have been quite different. When our students complain that their clients are being too superficial, telling too many stories, changing the subject, and so forth, we often ask if they have explained what they want the clients to do differently. Delineating roles and responsibilities is not always done directly, and clients can often pick up on fairly subtle clues, but some beginning therapists are sufficiently unclear themselves about the roles that they offer few clues at all. So if clients seem to be doing the "wrong" things, our first suggestion is that therapists clarify for themselves and their clients what behavior would be more helpful. Our second suggestion is that they not expect that one persuasive five-minute explanation will be sufficient to change a lifelong pattern of relating, and that instead, it should be assumed that clients' new behaviors, both in and out of therapy, will need to be encouraged and reinforced over time.

Other writers, such as Dowd and Wallbrown (1993) and Brehm and Brehm (1981) refer to interpersonal "reactance." By this they mean, "The natural tendency to react against or resist pressures or influence from others" (Kleinke, 1994, p. 105). (It should be noted that Bischoff and Tracey, 1997, as well as others have found empirical support for this phenomenon in therapy.) While this kind of reactivity can be carried to the point of characterological oppositionalism, we also need to remind ourselves that this unwillingness to be unduly influenced by others is the basis for our maintaining a strong sense of self or identity. It would not be helpful if clients simply bought into everything we suggested and became our clones. Reactance is likely to be activated if clients had (or their view of things was that they had) domineering or controlling parents who felt threatened by independent thinking. In such cases, the client was likely to grow up feeling the need to fight for his or her identity, and to view any "parental" influence (including what may be coming from you) as highly suspicious. Even when the client agrees that it makes sense, it may feel quite uncomfortable for them to cooperate. One therapist, when faced by such consistent oppositionalism, said with some humor, "Does it feel like it used to when your parents told you what to do?" (The client agreed.) "You know, my favorite definition of maturity is 'doing what you want to, even if your parents approve!'"

Before we leave this topic of client mistrust, we would like to suggest one more reason for the client's balking at the therapist's input. It might be that the therapist is simply wrong. Foreshadowing the social constructionism emphasis, Singer (1970) noted with some irony:

> It must also be remembered that practitioners of psychotherapy are not necessarily oracles of wisdom, and therefore the patient's outright rejection of some interpretation or confrontational comment…is frequently a sign of remarkable well-being. Indeed it would indicate gross pathology were a patient to accept as gospel truth the therapist's misconceptions or inconsequential and irrelevant interpretations. (Or he [sic] would have to be very hostile to the therapist, because in accepting his silly pronouncements and pontifications, the patient would allow the therapist to live unchallenged in a fool's paradise.) (pp. 225–226)

Transference Resistance

The third related process we wish to discuss that involves the client's balking is called by Freud (1926/1981) "transference resistance." If resistance, as we defined it, is an intrapsychic phenomena, and distrust an interpersonal one, transference resistance is somewhere between the two. Or more succinctly, the resistance is in fact intrapsychic, but as the client manifests it, it appears interpersonal. Allen Wheelis (1973, p. 42) described transference resistance when he said, "The trigger for anxiety is the giving of an account for which I may be judged." It is as if the client is so certain that what he or she is experiencing is unacceptable that the therapist is presumed to be unaccepting and critical, all evidence to the contrary. Thus a simple empathic comment on the therapist's part, such as, "That must have been really tough for you," can elicit an angry, "What? Do you think I'm such a baby I can't take it?" The process is transference in the sense that the client is transferring onto the therapist feelings that probably rightfully belong to an earlier relationship. In terms of present dynamics, however, the mechanism is a form of projection. The client's own self-judgments and worst fears about himself or herself are projected onto the therapist, with no awareness that the therapist may in actuality be feeling quite understanding and compassionate.

Clients exhibiting transference resistance often present themselves quite combatively; they require consistent support from their therapists as they sort out what they fear the therapist is feeling (or might feel) from what she or he actually is experiencing. If the therapist can remain emotionally available to the client and deal over and over with the immediacy of their relationship, gradually most clients will come to claim more readily their own fears, which can then be dealt with therapeutically. Prime requirements are the therapist's patience and ability to convey nondefensively "not guilty" when accused of being judgmental, assuming you were *not* being judgmental. The classical psychoanalytic way to deal with transference resistance was to remain emotionally neutral and to offer an interpretation of the process (Menninger, 1958). Therapy with a more supportive, interpersonal focus lends itself to a somewhat different approach. We believe that brief, supportive clarifications will work best: "Sounds like you felt judged just now. Actually, I was feeling pretty good about what you were saying." Or as one therapist said after a series of accusations, "You know, I don't have to feel about you the way you feel about yourself." Another therapist sometimes used humor: "Well, I agree that someone in this room might feel critical of you, but it isn't me. Who's left?" Whatever the style used, the goal is to help clients acknowledge and then deal with their projected self-judgments, after which the resisted material can be more easily explored.

Resistant or Distrustful Behaviors

As we briefly describe behaviors that therapists have come to recognize as potentially signaling resistance, distrust, or transference resistance, we will not attempt to differentiate between the three processes. The behaviors could signify any of the three processes—or perhaps none. We list some of these, not so that in cookbook fashion you can identify them and then apply the appropriate remedy, but rather so that you can approach your clients with heightened awareness of processes that might profit from further exploration. Otani (1989) classifies resistant behaviors as response quantity resistance, response quality resistance, response style resistance, and logistic management resistance. For purposes of this discussion, however, we will categorize these client process behaviors in terms of how they affect most therapists; behaviors are categorized as disarming, innocuous, and provocative. We would like to repeat at this point that clients do not use such behaviors as maneuvers to win at some imagined therapeutic chess game; rarely are they trying to outfox you.

Disarming Behaviors

Some of your clients will probably be charming, socially skilled, and very likable. They will be quite practiced at being engaging, and you may find yourself wishing that you had met them in another context so that you could be friends. The problem such clients may have is that it is such second nature for them to read others' cues and be accommodating that they have trouble exploring difficult feelings and motivations that might be less socially acceptable. They will need your encouragement and permission to give up their usual interactive style and be more transparent. You will need to resist the temptation to collude with them to stay "likable" and avoid such problematic issues.

Some behaviors that beginning therapists seem to find disarming that might perhaps signal resistance, distrust, or transference resistance are:

- humorous, charismatic storytelling
- mild flirting
- asking about therapist's feelings, personal life, and the like especially when done with genuine tact and concern
- praising therapist's skills, wisdom, and so forth
- psychologically sophisticated "safe" self-disclosure (e.g., I know I'm resisting, but…")

Whether your clients present with such styles or resort to them under pressure, it will be important for you to be empathically curious enough to invite them to explore the deeper issues that may lie underneath. One therapist we know said to a client that fit in this category, "You're a great storyteller and I enjoy hearing them, but I worry that we're not paying attention to what we really need to. What do you think?" and, lightly, to another, "I don't know if you know it, but you could come in here next time and never say anything funny and I would still like you!"

Innocuous Behaviors

There is another set of client behaviors that again may be either stylistic or situational. These behaviors are more clearly seen as defensive (i.e., self-protective) and less engaging than those in the previous list and so are more clearly identified by beginning therapists as potentially warranting attention. Our impression is that students sometimes feel helpless when confronted by them. It can be frustrating to sense that there is something in the client under the surface, ask the client, and be met by denial. What then? The frustration that therapists feel is as often directed at themselves as at the client, since they feel inadequate and directionless. Some of these "innocuous" behaviors are:

- changing the subject away from affect-ladened issues
- an unemotional recounting of powerful experiences
- becoming helpless and passive
- becoming "confused"
- retreating into silence
- obsessing about trivial details when describing an event or situation

We suggest that when you see such client behaviors, one of your hypotheses should be that they don't know how to "do" therapy and are falling back on typical behaviors, for what seems good reasons from their perspective. If you have evidence to justify this hypothesis, it may well help if you can explain to clients what they need to do differently for your kind of therapy to work, and why.

For example, one of the authors had a dependent, insecure client who seemed to find it necessary to recount long stories in infinite detail. She had to start at the beginning, recount every incident with meticulous thoroughness, and then move chronologically through the event piece by piece to the end. After suggesting that maybe they could "fast forward to the end," and "jump to the chase," to absolutely no avail, the therapist realized that the client was probably manifesting the same behavior with her that she had done with herself. Presumably the client had gone over and over the details, rehearsing them thoroughly, probably to reassure herself that she was blameless and entitled to feel bad. If that were the case, then skipping a detail, in her mind, could mean that the therapist might not get the whole picture and might judge her negatively. So the following set of interventions was made: "I can tell by your face that you get frustrated when I interrupt and ask you to slow down and tell me what you were feeling, and then sometimes I want you to skip portions and tell me how it all ended and what it meant to you. Must be confusing! 'What *does* the woman want?!'" (Client agreed.) "Tell me what's the worst that might happen if you leave out an important detail. Are you worried that I might not "get it"? (Client tentatively agreed and launched into another long story!) "I'm sorry to interrupt, but I'm looking at the time and realize we only have 15 more minutes. Let me tell you what I want. If you could just give me the essence of what happened, in just a paragraph or two instead of a page, I could figure out better what it all meant to you. That's what I really want to know, what it was like for *you*. The details are interesting, but we don't have time to do both, and you are more important than the details. I promise I'll believe that it was very important, even if you skip some of the specifics. Can we try that focusing-on-the-essence idea for the rest of the session? Before you leave, you can tell me how it was for you."

Provocative Behaviors

Finally we want to describe behaviors that are alarming and provocative enough that "counterresistance" is likely, even for very experienced therapists (Strean, 1993). In our experience, these kinds of behaviors are most often evidenced by clients with personality disorders or more severe pathology. Since your typical reaction outside of therapy would very likely be to become punitive or to withdraw, neither of which is generally therapeutic, it is especially important that you be prepared to deal professionally with such behavior:

- punitive, withholding silence
- accusations of therapist's unhelpfulness, biases, learning, uncaring, and the like
- demands for a closer, personal relationship (e.g., the film *What About Bob?*)
- pattern of missed sessions, tardiness, emergency midnight calls, and the like
- sexual overtures toward the therapist

Mehlman and Glickaf-Hughes (1994), in their article about therapists' hateful feelings toward clients, quote Groves's (1978) list of client types that engender hate: dependent clingers, entitled demanders, manipulative help-seekers, and self-destructive deniers. While we think "hate" is a stronger affect than most experienced therapists feel, we agree that these categories can be added to our list.

One approach to dealing with such behaviors is to say matter-of-factly and nonpunitively, "Before we can proceed, we need to get something out of the way. I know therapy is a strange place—different expectations and goals and all that. Maybe I should go back over why I'm here and what I'm doing, and see if you still want to come. It may be that this just doesn't fit with what you're looking for...." On inpatient wards, when the patient makes a clearly sexual suggestion or overture, many staff members have learned to say calmly but firmly, "No, that's inappropriate behavior. We don't do that here." That is the stance we think is most helpful when dealing with very provocative behaviors.

One therapist, in conducting an intake session, was asked by the client, "Can I talk about sex in here?" The therapist, assuming it was a matter of some concern for him, said, "Sure, if it's important to you," to which the client said, "Do you like oral sex?" After a pause to gather her wits about her, the therapist said, calmly, "Oh, I see, you thought we could share experiences. No, I don't ever do that with clients. I was thinking you had some sort of concern you wanted to talk about regarding yourself. Sorry I misunderstood," and proceeded with the intake (noting in supervision that she had clearly gotten some unexpected diagnostic information!).

Working through Resistance/Distrust

Writers as theoretically diverse as Ellis (1985), Milman and Goldman (1987), and Teybur (1997) suggest that the therapist's ability to properly handle client resistance is a crucial therapeutic skill. There is some experimental evidence that level of client resistance should be used in considering type of psychotherapy (e.g., Beutler, Engle, Mohr, Daldrup, Bergan, Meredith, & Merry, 1991). Beutler and his colleagues (e.g., Beutler & Consoli, 1993; Beutler, Consoli, & Williams, 1995) have identified client resistance as one of the critical dimensions of assessment (with treatment implications) in their approach to therapy—systematic eclectic psychotherapy.

We will now briefly outline several approaches to understanding resistance as framed by various theoretical orientations.

Psychodynamic Approach

The crucial ingredient in this approach, the goal of which is client uncovering of affect and eventual insight, is to refuse to adopt an adversarial stance and instead to "join" with the client, thereby providing client support, lessening his or her fear, and encouraging the exploration of avoided material. Bugental (1978) outlined this as a three-part process: First, the therapist, in a warm, nonchallenging way, draws the client's attention to the behavioral manifestation of the resistance as nonthreateningly as possible. For example, you might say, "For the last five minutes you've hardly looked at me," or "Lately I notice you've been late for our appointments." The second step may be combined with the first step or, with more fragile clients, not made until after the first has been noted many times; it puts the behavior in a context. For example, you might say, "As we've been talking about your sexual abuse by your dad, for the last few minutes, you've talked very rapidly and looked away." The final and most important step is to invite the client to explore the process. This might be merged with the first two, but may be quite separate. With genuine curiosity, you may say something like, "I notice that for the last couple of sessions you've been more distracted, and I remember your being upset with me the session before when I suggested you look at your feelings about your brother's success. Are you feeling differently about coming here now that I've brought him up?"

The therapist, in order to invite such exploration, clearly needs to be willing to hear anything the client says, whether the material is intrapsychic or has arisen out of the client's feelings about the therapeutic relationship. If the issue is interpersonal, we believe it is very important for the therapist to be open to client feedback rather than to automatically chalk off the client's reactions as transference. If in fact the therapist erred in some way, he or she needs to be able to acknowledge the mishap nondefensively. This not only reestablishes the therapeutic alliance by legitimizing the client's feelings and showing respect and influence, but it also provides a good model for the client that making mistakes is a normal part of human life and does not have to diminish one's self-esteem.

"Joining" with resistance does not mean that the therapist is not setting limits. Especially with clients with poor impulse control, your task will be to continue to set limits nonpunitively and still remain emotionally supportive enough to encourage client self-exploration.

Narrative Approach

This and the following three approaches are especially useful in brief therapy, where relatively quick change is hoped for. There are a number of avenues that this narrative approach can take, and the last ten years has seen a plethora of books and articles available on this topic (e.g., Eron & Lund, 1996). We summarize them here, but before using them, be familiar with them and do not use them without supervision. To summarize briefly, images, stories, and narrative self-disclosure can be used to help the clients get a different perspective on themselves or their situation. For example, one client, Chantal, a college sophomore putting herself through college, had been raised by poorly educated working-class grandparents. They and others in the family were actively critical and disparaging of her interest in studying art and music in college. After several weeks of counseling to help her work on study skills, Chantal was still held back from wholeheartedly investing in school because of her preoccupation with her family's massive disapproval. In one session the therapist said something like,

> Think about a pasture someplace that has some dandelions growing in it. I don't know about you, but I like dandelions—good, hearty flowers that can grow almost anywhere and provide a lot of color. Often they are the first ones up in the spring. Of course, the plants have stickers on them, and you wouldn't want to step down on one barefoot, but otherwise they are perfectly nice plants. Now imagine that, in this family of dandelions, all of a sudden a rose bush was born. A rose bush, of all things! Not only was it different, it needed more stuff—pruning, fertilizing, and all that. You can imagine the dandelion family's reaction when the rose requested those things: 'Hey, don't be so high-falutin'! You don't need all that junk; use some regular manure, it'll do fine. Works for us!' I guess some rose bushes would tell themselves they should listen to the family, but it sure would deprive the world of some prize-winning roses, huh?

Similarly, using clients' own images and metaphors, and empathically adding to them, can sometimes be very helpful.

Paradoxical Interventions

These interventions are used when a more straightforward approach does not seem indicated. They involve sidestepping the resistance, rather than using or working through it. The two usual categories of such interventions are compliance-based and defiance-based (Kleinke, 1994). As she describes the contexts for each, compliance-based interventions involve "prescribing the symptom," and are used with clients who are not highly reactive to help them gain a sense of control by flowing with and experiencing their symptoms. For example, you might use this with a client presenting with a concern about overeating. Telling the client to gain one pound before she returns in a week is an example of symptom prescription.

For highly reactive, defiant clients, conversely, the technique suggested is "restraining." (Laypersons are familiar with the more obvious forms of this technique as "reverse psychology.") Along these lines, the therapist might suggest delaying change, (e.g., "We don't want you to rush into this, take your time."), forbidding change, (e.g., "Don't try to make any changes until we can thoroughly explore what all this means. It might take months before we can really understand it."), and predicting a relapse if things are going well. Again, it should be remembered that these approaches are to be used with truly reactive, oppositional clients.

Agreeing with Part of the Client's Stance

This is an approach that we find helpful with resistant clients, although we have not seen it described by anyone else. The idea is to listen closely to the content of the client's position (e.g., "hypnosis is bad and the work of the devil, my church told me so,") and to legitimize part of it; then add exceptions. For example, in this instance you might say to a client's husband, who accompanied his wife to a session, who was angry because you were using hypnosis to help the client quit smoking, "Boy, I know what you mean! Some of those guys that do all that hypnosis on stage and make people look stupid, who'd want to do that stuff? You can't help wondering what makes them do that—a need for power, or what?! Pretty weird! Like you, I wonder if people like that might ever try to use hypnosis to get people to really veer off from their values! Of course, what Sandy and I are doing is a lot different, since we always agree ahead of time what she wants to work on, but I can really understand your concern!" In fact, there often is a partial basis to many concerns that are raised to our approaches, and being able to legitimize those concerns and show how what you're doing is different can sometimes provide reassurance and also enhance your professional credibility.

Informed Consent

This is another approach that is helpful when all else fails. This approach is useful with clients who insist that they have no choice (often because of ideological/religious belief systems) but to behave in a certain way. The therapist does not attempt to attack or change the client's belief system, but *adds information to it*, leaving the client to deal with his or her cognitive dissonance. For example, you might say to a father who refuses to let his daughter back into the house because she married a person of another race, "Well, you might need to honor that instinct to punish her that way. I couldn't tell you not to do that. But you may want to know, as you continue to struggle with your reactions to the situation, that as psychologists what we know when parents do that is that the kid tends to withdraw and that many of the values that the parent has tried so hard to teach her over the years get thrown out along with the relationship. I would hate to see you lose the positive influence you have had. Think about it, and see if that's o.k. with you." In more extreme situations, you might employ the same tactic, "Well, it looks like you've made up your mind what you want to do, even though it's illegal. I know you won't do it recklessly, but will make a clear decision. Let's see, we're looking at losing your job; 10 years, minimum, in the can (which is no picnic, as you know); alienating your family, and not seeing your grandkids grow up." After such an intervention, change the subject! Plant the seed and then move on. With stubborn clients like this, even if they are inclined to change their minds, they can't if they think you'll believe you "won." It is hard enough for them to reconsider their position without feeling like they have lost face also.

Summary

In dealing with resistance, reluctance, or transference resistance, it is easy for the therapist to be tempted into an adversarial role. From our perspective, doing so jeopardizes the therapeutic alliance and thereby sabotages some of the most valuable aspects that therapy has to offer. As one comes to view clients balking as a normal, expected component of the therapeutic process, it will be increasingly easy to stay respectful and emotionally available to them while simultaneously and empathically implementing an intervention that will help get the therapy back on track so that the clients' goals can be attained.

DISCUSSION QUESTIONS

- How will you distinguish between resistance and distrust in a cross-cultural counseling situation? What ideas do you have for making a cross-cultural client more comfortable with you?

- How do you feel about using paradoxical techniques? Do you see the implementation of them as counter to your values or theoretical orientation?

- Imagine a range of "provocative" resistant behaviors. Rehearse in your mind how dealing with clients manifesting each of these would feel to you, and how you might respond from within an appropriate therapeutic role. Role-play in class, and see if you all can brainstorm a number of appropriate responses that you can add to your repertoire.

BIBLIOGRAPHY

Bauer, G. P., & Kobos, J. C. (1987). *Brief therapy: Short term psychodynamic intervention.* Northvale, NJ: Aronson.

Beutler, L. E., & Consoli, A. J. (1993). Matching the therapist's interpersonal stance to clients' characteristics: Contributions from systematic eclectic psychotherapy. *Psychotherapy, 30,* 417–422.

Beutler, L. E., Consoli, A. J., & Williams, R. E. (1995). Integrative and eclectic therapies in practice. In B. Bongar & L. E. Beutler (Eds.), *Comprehensive textbook of psychotherapy* (pp. 274–292). New York: Oxford University Press.

Beutler, L. E., Engle, D., Mohr, D., Daldrup, R. J., Bergan, J., Meredith, K., & Merry, W. (1991). Predictors of differential and self-directed psychotherapeutic procedures. *Journal of Consulting and Clinical Psychology, 59,* 333–340.

Bischoff, M. S., & Tracey, T. J. G. (1995). Client resistance as predicted by therapist behavior: A study of sequential dependence. *Journal of Counseling Psychology, 42,* 487–495.

Brehm, S. S., & Brehm, J. W. (1981). *Psychological reactance: A theory of freedom and control.* New York: Academic Press.

Bugental, J. (1978). *Psychotherapy and process.* Reading, MA: Addison-Wesley.

Cullair, S. (1996). *Treatment of resistance. A guide for practitioners.* Boston: Allyn and Bacon.

Davison, G. (1973). Counter-control in behavior modification. In L. Haverlyncy and E. Mash (Eds.), *Behavioral change.* Champaign, IL: Research Press.

Dowd, E. T., Hughes, S., Brockbank, L., Halpain, D., Seibel, C., & Seibel, P. (1988). Compliance-based and defiance-based intervention strategies in the treatment of free and unfree behavior. *Journal of Counseling Psychology, 35,* 370–376.

Dowd, E. T., & Wallbrown, F. (1993). Motivational components of client reactance. *Journal of Counseling and Development, 71,* 533–538.

Ellis, A. (1985). *Overcoming resistance: Rational-emotive therapy with difficult clients.* New York: Springer.

Eron, J. B., & Lund, T. W. (1996). *Narrative solutions in brief therapy.* New York: Guilford.

Freud, S. (1926/1981). Inhibitions, symptoms, and anxiety. *Standard edition,* Vol. 20. London: Hogarth Press.

Groves, J. E. (1978). Taking care of the hateful patient. *New England Journal of Medicine, 298,* 883–887.

Hill, C. E., Corbit, M. M., Kanitz, B., Rios, P., Lightsey, R., & Gomez, M. (1992). Client behavior in counseling and therapy sessions: Development of a pan-theoretical measure: *Journal of Counseling Psychology, 39,* 539–549.

Kleinke, C. L. (1994). *Common principles of psychotherapy.* Pacific Grove, CA: Brooks/Cole.

Langs, R. (1981). *Resistance and interventions.* New York: Aronson.

Lewis, W., & Evans, J. (1986). Resistance: A reconceptualization. *Psychotherapy, 23,* 426–433.

Mahalik, J. R. (1994). Development of the Client Resistance Scale. *Journal of Counseling Psychology, 41,* 58–68.

McAdams, D. P. (1993). *Stories we live by.* New York: Morrow.

Mehlman, E., & Glickauf-Hughes, C. (1994). The underside of therapy: Confronting hateful feelings toward clients. *Psychotherapy, 31,* 434–439.

Menninger, K. (1958). *Theory of psychoanalytic technique.* New York: Basic Books.

Milman, D. S., & Goldman, G. L. (Eds.). (1987). *Techniques of working with resistance.* Northvale, NJ: Aronson.

Neimeyer, R. A., & Mahoney, M. J. (Eds.). (1995). *Constructivism in psychotherapy.* Washington DC: American Psychological Association.

Omer, H. (1997). Narrative empathy. *Psychotherapy, 34,* 19–27.

Otani, A. (1989). Client resistance in counseling: Its theoretical, rational, and taxonomic classification. *Journal of Counseling and Development, 67,* 458–461.

Patton, M. J., & Meara, N. M. (1992). *Psychoanalytic counseling.* New York: Wiley.

Rennie, D. L. (1994). Clients' deference in psychotherapy. *Journal of Counseling Psychology, 41,* 427–437.

Rosen, H., & Kuehlwein, K. T. (Eds.). (1996). *Constructing realities.* San Francisco: Jossey-Bass.

Roth, S. R. (1987). *The art of wooing nature.* Northvale, NJ: Aronson.

Singer, E. (1970). *Key concepts in psychotherapy* (2nd ed.). New York: Basic Books.

Stone, L. (1981). Notes on the nonenterpretive elements in the psychoanalytic situation and process. *Journal of the American Psychiatric Association, 29,* 89–118.

Strean, H. (1990). *Resolving resistances in therapy.* New York: Brunner/Mazel.

Strean, H. (1993). *Resolving counterresistances in therapy.* New York: Brunner/Mazel.

Strupp, H., & Binder, J. (1984). *Psychotherapy in a new key.* New York: Basic Books.

Taft, J. (1933/1973). *The dynamics of therapy in a controlled environment.* Gloucester, MA: Peter Smith.

Teyber, E. (1997). *Interpersonal process in psychotherapy: A relational approach.* Pacific Grove, CA: Brooks/Cole.

Tracey, T. J. G. (1986). The stages of influence in counseling and psychotherapy. In F. J. Dorn (Ed.), *The social influence process in counseling and psychotherapy* (pp. 105–114). Springfield, IL: Thomas.

Wheelis, A. (1973). *How people change.* New York: Harper Colophon Books.

Wile, D. (1984). Kohut, Kernberg, and accusatory interpretations. *Psychotherapy, 21,* 353–364.

Williamson, J. D. (1990). *Psychological reactance and individual needs for control.* Unpublished master's thesis, University of Kansas, Lawrence.

12 Transference and Countertransference

> *"We thought Oz was a great Head," said Dorothy.*
> *"No, you are wrong," said the little man, meekly. "I have been making believe."*
> *"Making believe!" cried Dorothy. "Are you not a great wizard?"*
> *"Hush, my dear," he said. "Don't speak so loud, or you will be overheard—and I should be ruined. I'm supposed to be a Great Wizard."*
> *"And aren't you?" she asked.*
> *"Not a bit of it, my dear; I'm just a common man."*
>
> —from *The Wizard of Oz*

> *The idea of mother means, first of all, unqualified, unwavering love, no matter how obnoxious and unadorable the years have rendered us. And, second, it signifies that once there existed another living soul who knew about and had been in intimate contact with our purest and most unblemished childhood self, the self we still believe we are, the self with whom we still commune in our interior conversation, the self that, despite all the evidence to the contrary, still insists, still knows, that we are good.*
>
> —Tova Reich

A 22-year-old college senior sought psychotherapeutic services from a university counseling center. She was involved in a committed relationship, and she reported that this relationship was a very positive one. She was the oldest of four children. Her mother had died when she was six years old and her father when she was 10. She and her siblings were raised by a loving uncle and aunt. In many respects, the client acted as a "mother" to her younger siblings and, despite the fact that her aunt and uncle were very supportive, she had an extremely difficult time adjusting to her parents' deaths. The client identified herself as a lesbian and seemed to have no concerns about her sexual orientation. She sought treatment when her minister's wife seemed, in her estimation, to pull away from her emotionally. She reported a similar pattern of feeling abandoned when a college teacher for whom she had great respect seemed very friendly initially and then, in the client's view, pulled away emotionally.

The therapist assigned to this client was a middle-aged female psychologist with a psychodynamic orientation. She had substantial experience with college students and clients who were lesbians. Her own mother, to whom she was very close, had been seriously ill for a number of months when she began seeing the client. Beginning with the intake session, the psychologist was aware of several interlocking dynamics. First, the client's sexual orientation placed her at risk for being rejected by homophobic individuals who discovered, or were told, her sexual orientation. Thus, the therapist was aware that the previous interpersonal rejection (or perceived rejection) might be rooted in an unfortunate reality. Second, the therapist was very aware that the client had repeatedly suffered from interpersonal loss and rejection, and the client might well feel abandoned when therapy ended because of graduation or when the client was unable to elicit from the therapist responses she felt she needed. Third, the therapist was cognizant of the impact her relationship with her own mother might have on how she felt about and interacted with the client.

The client initially formed a powerfully positive attachment to the therapist and idolized her. This was followed by some feelings of disappointment and rejection when the therapist declined to attend the client's sister's wedding. The client was able to resolve her feelings of anger and disappointment about the wedding as well as her feelings of abandonment by the minister's wife. She concluded that the college teacher had probably been frightened by her sexual orientation, but that the minister's wife pulled away in part because she and her husband were scheduled to leave within the year. Furthermore, the client came to understand that, at times, her own fear of rejection caused her to withdraw from others, thereby unconsciously provoking others to withdraw. Overall, psychotherapy was successful, but the client did repeatedly struggle to accept the support of the therapist without fearing rejection. Because therapy would have to end at graduation, the therapist was particularly sensitive about the client's not developing too much dependency on her, while at the same time using the therapeutic relationship to help address the client's fear of rejection. Following three or four of the therapy sessions, the therapist realized that her emotional reactions to the client were being created in part by her own fear that her mother would die. In order to ensure that she did not unconsciously withdraw from the client, the therapist monitored both her feelings about her own mother as well as the client's need to control interpersonal distance in therapy.

This example illustrates the tangled web that contains the client and the therapist, as well as the previous and current relationships each brings to therapy. Both the therapist and the client are vulnerable to a certain amount of distortion in the therapeutic relationship. Although some close relationship disturbances (including ones in the therapeutic relationship) may be produced by external reality (e.g., a homophobic culture), others are the product of our own struggles toward appropriate interdependence, closeness, self-acceptance, and feelings of safety. For the client, these distortions in the therapeutic relationship are called "transference"; for therapists, they are called "countertransference."

The concepts of transference and countertransference are perhaps not quite as widely used as they were a number of years ago; however, a number of researchers, (e.g., Gelso, Kivlighan, Wine, Jones, & Friedman, 1997; Patton, Kivlighan, & Multon, 1997) have made vigorous efforts to define, measure, and investigate these variables. Although many therapists do in fact find great utility in these constructs, many others, for a variety of reasons, are perhaps seldom prone to utilize them. Among the factors contributing to skepticism about these constructs are the rise in popularity of cognitive-behavioral and technical eclecticism orientations to psychotherapy; feminist critiques of the power of the therapist and how best to approach that issue (including emphasis on egalitarian relationships between clients and their therapists); multicultural critiques that raise questions about how to define "distortions" from a mythical norm; short-term therapy, whose frequent emphasis on coping mechanisms, focused symptom relief, and expedient use of time preclude an emphasis on transference; and humanistic orientations to therapy that emphasize that all parts of the therapeutic relationship are "real."

Despite the limitations just outlined, and even though we are in agreement with many of the critiques, we believe that there are still several elements in the constructs of transference and countertransference that good therapists of many persuasions can find useful (Patton & Meara, 1992). Our aim is to discuss these ideas in a way that is compatible with many theoretical orientations. Although our comments about these issues are directed mainly at individual therapy, it is important to emphasize that work with groups and couples (e.g., Solomon & Siegel, 1997) also entails similar ideas.

Transference

Components of the Client–Therapist Relationship

Traditionally, in order to discuss transference, writers have referred to three components of the therapeutic relationship: the real relationship, the working alliance, and the transference relationship (Gelso & Carter, 1994; see also Sexton & Whiston, 1994). The term "real relationship" refers to the part of the therapeutic relationship that is based solely in the reality of the client and therapist meeting and talking, with interactions in this "real relationship," and perceptions by the client and therapist, being relatively free from distortion. Gelso and Carter see the real relationship as having two central features, genuineness and realistic perceptions. Although problems with using genuineness as part of the criteria for the real relationship have been noted, as have concerns about the idea of a distortion of reality (Greenberg, 1994), there seems to us to be heuristic advantage in using the idea that there is a part of the relationship between therapist and client that can be relatively free from distortion. For example, suppose that the therapist is 30 minutes late and offers no apology or explanation. If the client becomes angry and expresses the idea that the therapist is insensitive, this action would be a part of the real relationship, since in North American culture it is considered rude to keep a person waiting for 30 minutes with no explanation. (This example also high-lights how cultural factors may help define what is or is not considered transfer-ence versus the real relationship—see discussion below.) Or, if a client, based on several sessions with the therapist, comes to see that the therapist has a good sense of humor, this perception may be nondistorted and be a part of the real rela-tionship. Some therapists are offended by the term "real relationship," fearing that its use demeans a part of the therapeutic relationship by suggesting that some of what the client feels is not real. We have little interest in engaging in this debate, but we do believe that some client perceptions are much more accurate than others and that understanding when these variations occur can be very helpful in therapy. If a client, whose father constantly berated him, believes that you are angry at him when you are not, that is a very different case than believing you are angry when, in fact, you do feel that way.

The "working alliance" (e.g., Bachelor, 1995; Horvath & Greenberg, 1994) refers to the special rules that surround the therapeutic encounter. For example, the ideas that clients will talk about their problem, that the therapist is entitled to ask questions, and that the therapist will not, except under very unusual circum-stances, divulge the content of the conversation, all refer to the working alliance. The bond that develops between therapist and client is also seen as a part of this alliance. On the one hand, Gelso and Carter (1994) see the working alliance as being composed, at various stages of therapy, of differing amounts of "real relationship" and "transference relationship." On the other hand, Multon, Patton, and Kivlighan (1996) have suggested that the "real" relationship is more or less synonymous with the working alliance. Thus, there are differences among researchers as to the rela-tionship among the three components of the real relationship, the working alliance, and the transference relationship. In any event, the working alliance (at times also referred to as the therapeutic alliance or the helping alliance) represents the shared effort between psychotherapist and client under the conditions of psychotherapy. It has been viewed as a transtheoretical construct that is critical to the therapeutic process (e.g., Horvath & Luborsky, 1993). The working alliance has been of partic-ular theoretical and empirical interest in recent years (e.g., Bachelor, 1995; Horvath & Symonds, 1991; Kivlighan & Shaughnessy, 1995; Mallinckrodt, 1993).

Finally, the term transference is reserved for all the remainder of the behav-iors and attitudes of the client toward the therapist. Another way of saying this is that transference is represented by actions and feelings by the client that are based neither in the reality of two people having a conversation, nor in the reality of the psychotherapy treatment arrangement (or contract), but rather, are based prima-rily on the false assumption that the therapist is very much like someone in the cli-ent's past. It is important to emphasize that this "person in the client's past" may be an actual person or a "person" constructed in the imagination of the client who represents parts of one or more people, who themselves may be either real or imagined. For example, clients may have been mistreated by their parents and other adults, but longed for a protector and savior to come to the rescue. In turn, the therapist may be treated as if she or he were in fact that savior. This, too, would be considered transference.

Definitions

Although there are ongoing challenges in rigorously defining transference (Carter, 1996; Richardson, 1997), there are several characteristics on which many therapists tend to agree. As noted above, the central tenet in transference is that feelings and attitudes toward a person early in life are transferred (or displaced) onto the therapist. A key assumption is that the therapist has done nothing (or very little) to evoke these feelings. If the client says "Why are you angry with me?" after the therapist repeatedly frowns, we have learned little about the client. If, however, the client asks this question and there have been no frowns (or similar behaviors, verbal or nonverbal) by the therapist, an important therapeutic issue has perhaps come into focus. Freud first viewed transference as an obstacle to treatment but later came to believe that transference was the key to a successful outcome in psychotherapy (Storr, 1980).

It was a part of Freud's genius to discover that under certain conditions clients may behave toward their therapists as if their therapists were their primary caregivers from childhood. It is now generally accepted that this sort of transference is greatly influenced by the therapist's behavior and that its "recognition" by the therapist is highly (though perhaps not completely) dependent upon the therapist's theoretical orientation. In short, therapists who are not predisposed to psychoanalysis may not see a great deal of transference.

Another way that the word transference is sometimes used is to describe any overly emotional reaction to something the therapist does or says. In this view transference *may* be the result of displaced attitudes, but may also more generally represent "exaggerated" reactions to internal conflicts or a stressful environment without reference to any specific person. In classic psychoanalytic theory this second definition is subsumed by the first. The definitions of transference as displaced attitudes and transference as exaggerated reactions are actually compatible from a theoretical perspective. We are drawing a distinction here only because you may hear people use the term in either way.

Multon, Patton, and Kivlighan (1996) suggest a number of criteria that can be used to detect transference: (a) intensity (i.e., the strength of the reaction is not congruent with the precipitating event); (b) inappropriateness (i.e., the irrational character of the response); (c) tenacity (i.e., the tendency for the client's feeling to persist despite the therapist's actual behavior), (d) capriciousness (i.e., the erratic events that evoke the feelings), and (e) ambivalence (i.e., the shifting of positive and negative feelings toward the therapist).

An example of transference can be found in *Moby Dick* (Melville, 1930). Even though there is a partially rational reason for him to be angry with the white whale, Ahab reacts to the whale with emotions that go far beyond what reason alone might suggest:

> …ever since that almost fatal encounter, Ahab had cherished a wild vindictiveness against the whale, all the more fell for that in his frantic morbidness he at last came to identify with him, not only all his bodily woes, but all his intellectual and spiritual exasperation. The White Whale swam before him as the monomaniac incarnation

of all those malicious agencies which some deep men feel eating in them.... Deliriously transferring its idea to the abhorred White Whale, he pitted himself, all mutilated, against it. All that most maddens and torments; all that stirs up the lees of things; all truth with malice in it; all that cracks the sinews and cakes the brain; all the subtle demonisms of life and thought; all evil, to crazy Ahab, were visibly personified, and made practically assailable in Moby Dick. He piled upon the whale's white hump the sum of all the general rage and hate felt by his whole race from Adam down; and then, as if his chest had been a mortar, he burst his hot heart's shell upon it. (p. 267)

Like the white whale, the therapist may become the focus of the pent-up frustrations, the difficulty of changing, and the dashed hopes of the client. It is a part of the therapist's job to be the object of this anger and disappointment without retaliation, and in fact, to do so in a continuing environment of care and respect for the struggles of the client.

Types of Transference

Generally we speak of two types of transference: positive and negative. One may also speak of specific transference (when a client treats the therapist as if the therapist were a specific person in the client's past) as contrasted with general transference (when the client treats the therapist the way most people in the culture treat authority figures). The literature on transference contains other constructs as well, such as transference neurosis, mirroring transference, and twinship transference. Although a discussion of all these issues is beyond the scope of this book, here we highlight what is meant by positive and negative transference.

It is generally assumed that the majority of clients who remain in therapy for a period of time have rather quickly grown to like or at least respect their therapists. The initial *liking* is sometimes called positive transference. It is transference in the sense that the client does not really know much about the therapist but is presumed to be responding to the noncritical, accepting demeanor of an authority figure on whom the client is counting for help. Most clients who do not develop some minimal liking for the therapist are assumed to drop out of treatment. Positive transference is even better illustrated by the period (if it occurs) when the therapist, in the eyes of the client, "can do no wrong, has no faults, and always understands exactly what the client is thinking and feeling."

Negative transference (or whatever you would prefer to call it), if present early in therapy and left unaddressed, may at best greatly impede treatment and at worst contribute to client dropout. For example, Gelso, Kivlighan, Wine, Jones, and Friedman (1997) found that negative transference that was not resolved was associated with less successful psychotherapy outcome.

There are primarily two types of negative transference. The first may happen quite early in therapy (perhaps even in the first session). These situations involve clients who are mistrustful and/or hostile toward the therapist because the therapeutic relationship reminds them of an earlier important relationship that was difficult for them, and about which they have ambivalent or negative feelings. (These situations often contribute to the client's "resistance," discussed in Chapter 11.) The second type of situation, when it occurs, happens later in therapy. These situations arise when clients realize that the therapist cannot and will not fulfill all their needs and is not perfect. The second type of negative transference is not likely to emerge in short-term therapy.

A general rule (and it is *very* general because of the complexity of this issue and wide differences among therapists) is that positive transference is not something you should comment on at the beginning of therapy. Furthermore, negative transference should be controlled, particularly at the beginning of therapy. This is typically done by the therapist's avoiding confrontations, being supportive, and avoiding falling into roles representing people with whom the client has had difficulty getting along in the past. For example, if the client says, "My father always gave me too much advice," the therapist is advised to studiously avoid giving advice initially. Later the therapist may wish to help the client work through the dependency issues involved in resenting the father's advice. This process might indeed entail some degree of negative transference. As we said, however, this would (should) not happen near the beginning of therapy. The risks of the client's dropping out are far too great.

One important point to remember is that negative and positive transference often accompany each other. In particular, negative feelings may follow strongly positive ones. For example, when clients can initially find no fault in the therapist, they have thus set up a situation in which they are easily disillusioned when the therapist does not perform in a consistently perfect fashion. Certainly some clients will evidence primarily positive or primarily negative transference. Perhaps just as often, and especially in settings where one sees numerous clients with serious disorders, one will see a pattern of overvaluation and idealization of the therapist, alternating with a pattern of irritated discontent as the client discovers that the therapist does not measure up to the ideal person the client imagined the therapist to be. Corey and Corey (1998) give several examples of transference situations, including, "Clients who make you into something you are not" (e.g., a parent, a former spouse, etc.), "Clients who see you as a superperson," "Clients who make unrealistic demands on you," "Clients who are not able to accept boundaries," "Clients who displace anger onto you," and "Clients who easily fall in love with you" (pp. 91–93).

Development of Transference

There are several reasons why transference develops. An understanding of these factors contributes to a wider perspective on the psychotherapeutic process and to an enhanced ability to deal with transference issues.

Neutrality or Anonymity of the Therapist.   We mentioned at the beginning of the chapter that a key assumption when we say we observe transference is that the therapist has done little or nothing to evoke the attitudes that have been "transferred." This assumption was originally tied to the idea of the psychotherapist as "mirror" or "blank screen." That is, if the therapist revealed nothing of himself or herself, the client was assumed to be "transferring" from someone else any emotion that was felt about the therapist. Although many therapists do not consider themselves to be a "blank screen," it is still true that therapists do not routinely discuss their personal life, they do not disclose all their felt reactions to the client and his or her behavior, they do not talk about their reading habits, their preference for friends, or their preferred vacation spots, and they do not frequently express political or religious preferences. Thus the client will never know a therapist in the same way that he or she knows close friends—there will always be an element of mystery about who this person is. This mystery is addressed through fantasy—through a process whereby clients fill in the gaps of their knowledge with imagination based on their experiences with other people. Sometimes these fantasies are very close to reality—clients may combine a natural perceptiveness with the bits and pieces of reality they pick up from the therapist to form a quite accurate picture of the therapist's reactions to a given event. At other times, clients may be far "off-base" as they guess, imagine, fantasize, or distort the reactions or feeling states of the therapist. It is these distortions that constitute transference, and, as suggested above, they are produced in part by the fact that therapists leave much of their lives (interior and exterior) a mystery to their clients.

Therapist's Role as Authority.   Because therapists are people to whom others go to receive help in solving problems, their role, by definition, may be seen as involving the exercise of authority. Furthermore, the long dependency of childhood, during which one must count on parents and others to provide help and advice, seems to endow many individuals in a more or less permanent fashion with an inclination to look to others for answers. This sort of inclination, which is sometimes called dependency, may be acted out toward the therapist because of the therapist's role as an authority figure. More generally we might say that there is a *propensity* for clients to act toward the therapist in ways that are typical of how people in general behave toward authority figures within the culture. It is obvious that the client's dynamics will interact with this general propensity. However, when clients behave in a somewhat different manner toward the therapist, they may be expressing a kind of cultural norm rather than childhood conflicts. Thus, acting toward the therapist in a stereotyped (as an authority) fashion can also be thought of as transference.

Expression of Clients' Conflicts.   In defining transference, we said that one way to think of transference is to view it as a displacement of feelings from others (perhaps including generalized expectations about the world) onto the therapist. This "inappropriate" (or perhaps a better word would be "inaccurate") generalization occurs in part because clients' emotional distresses make them less interpersonally flexible (Mallinckrodt, 1996) and more apt to engage in self-defeating behavior such as attacking the therapist with little or no provocation. For example, a female therapist may say to a male client, "You seem to have a hard time making a commitment to a job." The client replies, "You're just like my mother—always on my case." This is an example of transference, but it also reflects *why* transference occurs. Here the client has responded to the therapist not on the basis of "reality" (assuming the comment about commitment was not made in a critical tone and is not part of a larger pattern of criticism), but rather on the basis of strong feelings about his mother and how he felt he was treated by her. The assumption is that feelings are not transferred if they are not "in conflict," so to speak, with other feelings. Traditionally the word "conflict" refers to the psychoanalytic idea of different drives or structures competing with each other. Perhaps another way of describing this phenomenon (in a more generically clinical way) is that strong feelings that have not been integrated into the person's self-concept seem to "erupt" in situations that are similar in some ways to, but quite distinct from, the original situations in which the feelings were experienced.

As in so many other cases, therapists of different theoretical persuasions use different language to describe the same phenomenon. For example, a person-centered therapist might use the term "conditions of worth" to describe the original experience of the client, with the concomitant unacceptability to the client of angry feelings toward the mother. In turn, the experience of having had "conditions of worth" is carried forward by the client into the therapeutic relationship.

Again using the example given, therapists using a more cognitive approach might talk about the client's inaccurate generalization from mother to therapist and also about the client's (faulty) assumption that he is constantly being judged harshly by others. Such therapists also talk about helping the client modify his assumption that it is necessary for others to like him—an assumption that perhaps originated with his desire to please his mother. Thus whatever theoretical perspective one takes, there is an assumption that transference, whatever one may call it, occurs in part because clients have had earlier experiences that predispose them to this sort of process. At times these earlier experiences may be described as involving conflicted feelings, unacceptable feelings, lack of integration of feelings, or early learning predisposing one to faulty assumptions or faulty generalizations.

Discussion of Earlier Emotional Experiences.   Clients who are seen by therapists who do not emphasize earlier experiences when doing psychotherapy probably do not show transference to the degree that clients do when the therapist does emphasize these earlier experiences. Certainly this is not to say that a focus on the present eliminates transference. However, we think that Rogers (1951) was basically correct in suggesting that a primary focus on the present in psychotherapy tends to retard further development of basic transference attitudes. We are not suggesting that the therapist *should* focus on the present. We are merely underscoring the fact that one reason transference occurs is that therapists often *do* focus on earlier experiences.

Permissive and Encouraging Attitude of the Therapist.   The accepting stance taken by the therapist encourages the expression of vulnerability and previously unacceptable ideas and feelings. Because the therapist is an integral part of the process whereby the client confronts such feelings, he or she may become an easy target for the client's strong feelings, whether they be feelings of relief or anger, or whatever.

Client Dependency on the Therapist.   Earlier we discussed the fact that the therapist's role as an authority figure sometimes contributed to the client's reenacting
the dependency of childhood. There is another sense in which transference may be
directly fostered by dependency. For example, in long-term therapy, and especially in cases of severe childhood trauma, the therapist may become a critical part
of the client's social support system and the client's tie to reality. In the process of
"remaking" themselves, clients may come to be profoundly dependent on their
therapist by the very nature of the support needed for transformation and healing.
Dependency and transference issues may become particularly important with clients who are incest survivors and who also have poor adult attachments (e.g.,
Alexander & Anderson, 1994). In such an intense interpersonal environment, and
especially when the therapist becomes so very important to the client, the client
tends to become alert to the smallest of slights—the nuances of both real and imagined rejection. Often these clients may come to believe that the therapist is the one
person in the world who understands, and it is this person to whom they form
extraordinarily powerful feelings that may swing dramatically if judgment or
rejection is perceived. In this type of environment, intense feelings toward the therapist will naturally form. In some sense, these feelings are a part of the real relationship and the working alliance, because the therapist is providing such a key
part of the client's grip on the world and self. Nonetheless, the feelings of such
intense dependency (including attachment, anger, etc.) must be attenuated for psychotherapy to have been successful. In this sense, the feelings represent a distortion
of what should be and what will be; they are thus seen as partially transferential.

Importance of Using Transference

There are a number of reasons why, in our view, the therapist should not merely
be aware of, but should also "use," transference. As we said earlier, one's ideas
about transference certainly depend upon one's theoretical orientation. Nonetheless many therapists agree that clients (like people in general) bring certain
assumptions about and predispositions toward the other person to any interpersonal encounter. We will briefly mention three reasons why we think it is important to focus, at least to some degree, on these predispositions of the client.

Power of Immediacy.   Most therapists agree that many clients, left to their own
devices, often talk abstractly about their problems. Such abstract and emotionally
removed discussions frequently do little to alleviate the client's suffering. Rogers,
for example, talks about movement of the discussion from the "there and then" to
the "here and now." Gestalt therapists emphasize the power of being "in the
now," and cognitive therapists may ask questions like, "What is your thinking
about suicide right this minute?" Each of these therapies, in its own way, is
addressing the issue of *immediacy*. Because transference, by definition, is partially
about current attitudes and feelings, a focus on this issue brings the client and
therapist together "in the now." There is hardly anything more immediate than
talking to another person about your current relationship with her or him.

Power of Analyzing Repeating Themes.   We have said that in our view one of the most important things a therapist can do in longer-term therapy is to help the client understand the themes that seem to be repeated in his or her life. Because transference *is* a repeated attitude or feeling, it gives the therapist a uniquely potent opportunity to help the client look closely at a repetition. We say "uniquely potent" because transference combines the immediacy just discussed with a repetition.

Power of Interpersonal Encounter.   In this book we have emphasized in numerous ways the importance of the relationship between the client and the therapist. To the client's vision of a disturbing universe, the therapist brings hope and perspective. The therapist also offers what may be the only nonexploitative relationship the client has ever known. One might say that this relationship offers the client the opportunity to straighten out the twists and kinks of previous ones. So it is precisely when these "twists and kinks" make themselves manifest that a kind of maximum leverage has been created for change. We have said that transference combines the power of immediacy with the power of analyzing repeating themes. To those two important processes we now add a third—the power of an interpersonal encounter. In our view, it is certainly possible to help many clients without focusing on transference issues. However, a focus on transference combines at least three forces, each of which is seen by many therapists as often contributing to behavior change within the context of psychotherapy.

Cultural Considerations

Earlier in our example of the therapist's being 30 minutes late, we noted how cultural factors must be considered in deciding what is or is not transference. Mallinck-rodt (1996) gives an excellent example that raises similar conceptual challenges:

> Consider a Euro-American male therapist and an African American male client who comes from a peer group that has experienced many negative interactions with authorities and representatives of "the system." If this client's individual experiences with a harsh and punitive father lead the client to behave with moderate deference and expressed gratitude toward the therapist's initial offers of help, Euro-American observers may conclude that there is no transference or distortion, whereas this client's peers might be shocked to see one of their friends depart from the group's typical stance of antipathy toward a system that has failed them, a system the therapist represents. Who, then, is the best arbiter of whether what one observes is appropriately cooperative or an "Uncle Tom" capitulation? Transference or undistorted reality? It is clear that considerations of culture, together with the influence of neighborhoods, schools, the workplace, and other social networks, must be included in a determination of what is "reasonable" and "undistorted" for a given client. (p. 255)

Thus, in particular as applied to transference, the complexity of cultural factors raises broad questions about how individuals from one culture can define the "reality" of individuals from another culture and, by extension, what role culture plays in defining deviation (Mallenckrodt, 1996).

When thinking about the practical implications of the relationship between cultural diversity and transference, it is important to remember that the pattern of child caregiving is not the same in all cultures. Thus, for example, one should not assume that parents are the chief object from which transference feelings arise. For any given client it may be a grandmother, an uncle, or even an individual not related by blood. Such cultural considerations underscore the difficulty, articulated by social constructivists (e.g., Neimeyer & Mahoney, 1995), of finding a common ground for defining "reality" and its "distortions."

Transtheoretical Perspectives

Orthodox psychoanalysis aside, the concept of transference may be seen in a rather broad context. That is, technical transference (displacement of specific feelings) is only part of a much larger issue involving prior learning experiences (e.g., Andersen, Glassman, & Chen, 1995), including attachment (Mallinckrodt, Gantt, & Coble, 1995a, 1995b; Robbins, 1995). In broader views of transference, clients' behaviors may demonstrate parallels to behavior toward earlier figures, but this process of behavior transfer characterizes all people to one degree or another. Each person brings to an interpersonal encounter a set of prior learning experiences that in turn shape expectations, behaviors and attitudes toward the person encountered. These expectations and attitudes are in operation before the other person says or does anything. The learning experiences that help shape client expectations involve childhood experiences with parents, siblings, and peers; emotional involvement in sexual relationships; the experience of working with, supervising, and being supervised by others; books and articles that have been read (for example, about human nature or psychotherapy) and information obtained from friends and acquaintances about a variety of issues including psychotherapy. Thus, when clients come for therapy, they have already formed some impressions about what a psychotherapist does or does not do. These impressions in turn affect the behavior emitted by the client toward the therapist. Furthermore, research suggesting that a lack of flexibility in interpersonal perception may be a central cause of client problems, by extension, suggests that transference might profitably be viewed as a special example of a more generalized problem of inflexibility (Mallinckrodt, 1996).

We assume that most therapists agree that previous experiences shape how clients will respond to their therapists. Therapists, however, depending on their theoretical orientation, vary widely in terms of how much *emphasis* is placed on this idea that one's previous experience shapes one's feelings and attitudes toward the therapist. In particular, therapists are at odds about how strong the relationship is between therapeutic effectiveness and the degree to which transference is discussed and processed. Therapists who are more cognitive-behavioral in their orientation, while acknowledging the role of prior experience on attitudes toward the therapist, do not emphasize this construct. Psychodynamic therapists, as well as interpersonal therapists, are typically more interested in the construct and see it playing a more pivotal role in treatment. However, we emphasize that whatever your theoretical orientation, you should be alert to how the client may jeopardize her or his progress by acting as if you are like hurtful and unhelpful people in the past. Progress may also be hindered if clients continually view you as able to solve all their problems.

Carl Rogers (1951) takes a position on transference that overlaps but also contrasts somewhat with the traditional psychoanalytic position. Rogers distinguishes between what he calls the transference attitude and the transference relationship. Rogers says:

> If transference attitudes are defined as emotionalized attitudes which existed in some other relationships, and which are inappropriately directed to the therapist, then transference attitudes are evident in a considerable proportion of cases handled by client-centered therapists. (p. 218)

Although Rogers goes on to say that in contrast to psychoanalysts, client-centered therapists do not foster the development of a transference *relationship*, it is clear from the quote that he does give credence to the idea that many clients have feelings about their therapists that are based less on the reality of the current situation than on feelings about prior relationships. Thus theorists as diverse as Freud and Rogers agree that feelings are often "transferred" to the therapist. Furthermore, there seems to be agreement on several aspects of transference (again, however labeled), including the need for clients to come to a clearer or more "realistic" understanding of how they may be distorting the efforts of their therapists based on their own distortions. This agreement is a good example of what we call common clinical wisdom.

As noted above, the degree to which the therapist attends to the construct of transference is heavily dependent on theoretical orientation. However, there does seem to be some common ground. Most orientations, whether implicitly or explicitly, give some emphasis to rationality—that is, to the client's capacity to distinguish between what is "real" or "reality based" from what is not. Even the person-centered perspective (which is much more focused on the phenomenology of experience rather than on "reality") talks about ongoing treatment as involving progressively less and less distortion of experience and as involving a movement toward a more accurate understanding of one's experience. Thus, although various theories may place different emphases on the importance of transference, and may suggest different ways of using it, we are underscoring that most therapies have as one of their goals the capacity of the client to differentiate between the figures in one's past life and the figures (including the therapist) in one's current life. There is also the related capacity to respond to current figures, including the therapist, based on objective experiences in the present. Gelso and Carter (1994) give the following example:

> The client (a 26-year-old woman) and therapist had worked together for 2 years in analytically oriented therapy when the client began talking about difficulties at

work with a reportedly critical supervisor. As the therapist began asking questions to try to understand the client's experience and the degree of reality or transference in the situation, the client reacted to her with hurt and anger, feeling misunderstood and criticized. At the same time, the client was able to say, "I feel upset but I need to remember that you always try to help me understand. So I need to trust that this is what you are doing now." The work was then able to proceed. (p. 301)

Some therapists believe that the process whereby one comes to be able to make this distinction, both emotionally and intellectually, is the essence of therapy. Other therapists would see this distinction as part of a larger issue of the need to think rationally. In any event, the therapist obviously gains little by commenting on culturally typical behavior. Thus, in the prior example of the hypothetical therapist who was 30 minutes late, there would be little point in saying to the client, "Do you always get upset when people make you wait?" If the client were to repeatedly bring up the issue for several sessions even though the therapist had apologized, the therapist would certainly be remiss if he or she did not help the client look at this process, since the issue involves strong feelings and/or distortion, whether one does or does not view this as a "transference issue."

Even though we believe that attention to "transference reactions" (whether labeled as such or not) often may be helpful, this focus also has limits. While being alert for the many ways in which clients may repeat with us previous unsatisfactory relationships, we must also be keenly aware of the here-and-now, actual relationship that exists between us and the client. Yalom (1980), has expressed well the idea that it is a mistake to be overly infatuated with transference:

> To summarize, a singular focus on transference impedes therapy because it precludes an authentic therapist-patient relationship. First, it negates the reality of the relationship by considering the relationship solely as a key to understanding other more important relationships. Secondly, it provides therapists with a rationale for personal concealment—a concealment that interferes with the ability to relate in a genuine fashion with patients. Does this mean that therapists who faithfully maintain a detached, objectifying, "interpretation-only" posture toward patients are ineffective or even destructive? I believe that, fortunately, such therapists and such courses of therapy are exceedingly rare. Here lies the importance of the "throw-ins" in therapy: therapists despite themselves and often unbeknownst to themselves reach out in a human manner in off-the-record moments. (pp. 413–414)

Summary Comments on Transference

A number of processes involved in, and related to, transference have been discussed. Here we wish to emphasize three aspects of the discussion. First, transference, while it is sometimes described in rather mysterious terms, is perhaps best seen as an example of the larger process by which individuals come to have expectations and feelings about current interpersonal relationships based on previous interpersonal experiences. Second, there are a number of characteristics of typical therapeutic relationships that tend to make transference more likely to occur there than in other relationships. Third, we have emphasized that powerful forces are often involved in transference. If these processes can be activated and used in a thoughtful manner, the possibility of behavior change is enhanced.

Countertransference

Definitions

Countertransference as Reaction to Transference.   There are a number of ways in which countertransference has been defined. The original definition was, of course, Freud's and emphasized that countertransference was a reaction to the transference of the client rather than a reaction based on the reality of the therapeutic situation. For example, if a male client became angry with the therapist because the therapist reminded him of his father, and then the therapist became very upset because the client was angry, this would be an example of countertransference. Thus the use of the word "countertransference," using the original definition, was limited to those cases in which the client had engaged in "transference."

Countertransference as General Unconscious Attitudes or Behavior.   Another way in which countertransference is sometimes viewed is that it is any unconscious attitude or behavior on the part of the psychotherapist that is prompted by the needs of the therapist rather than by the needs of the client. For heuristic purposes it may be helpful to think of this process as involving either (a) a temporary need or (b) a long-standing need.

We will discuss first the case of a therapist need that is temporary in nature. For example, a therapist might be having serious conflict in an intimate relationship, be sexually attracted to a client, and say to the client, "You seem to be attracted to me." This would be an example of projection in that the impulse (or feeling) experienced by the therapist was unacceptable and then "projected" onto the client. Projection in this particular case might be considered countertransference because the behavior of the therapist was based on the needs of the therapist rather than on the needs of the client. Another example would occur when the therapist displaces a feeling from someone else to the client. For example, if a therapist is angry with his wife and later that day angrily confronts the client about an issue, this also might be called countertransference. Or if a gay male therapist cannot decide whether to come out to his parents, he might overemphasize to a gay male client the importance of gay pride in good mental health. Another example would be that of a therapist who has recently been given a speeding ticket by a police officer and fails to be empathic with the police officer he is currently seeing as a client. Finally, clients who are in great distress (e.g., divorce) may provoke crisis-driven countertransference reactions from their therapists (e.g., Wallerstein, 1997). In such circumstances, the therapist may not be responding to transference per se and may not be acting out some basic personality flaw. Rather, the intense reaction (partially driven by culture) may be almost inevitable given the emotional situation. Nonetheless, therapists must learn to work through their own emotional reactions.

In each of the examples just cited, we are emphasizing that the therapist may try unconsciously to solve a current problem by using the client. One of our jobs as therapists is to try to recognize (perhaps with the help of a supervisor) when we are doing this.

Therapists may also have long-standing character styles that reduce their effectiveness with particular types of clients or even all clients. For example, a therapist may have difficulty working with angry clients because she was punished severely as a child for being angry. Another therapist may have difficulty confronting *any* client because his parents were always very indirect with him and merely dropped hints when they were upset about something. A European American male who grew up in a privileged family may have great trouble understanding the feelings of powerlessness in clients who are not so privileged. An African American therapist may have difficulty empathizing with European American males because throughout her educational experiences those individuals never seemed to be supportive of her academic efforts. Or a European American female therapist who left the world of business because she could not seem to break through the glass ceiling may repeatedly and impatiently emphasize to women of color that they are responsible for breaking through that ceiling.

In the book, *Listening as a Way of Becoming,* Koile (1977) gives an example of a good way to become aware of the areas in which we may be vulnerable to countertransference. You are asked to imagine that a person (one could say client) is coming to visit you. You realize that you don't want to see this person—that you don't want to listen to what the individual has to say. What is this person like that you don't want to see? What is it that this person will discuss and how will he or she discuss it that makes it difficult for you to listen? In a slight variant of that exercise, try to think of someone whom you would look forward to seeing.

More broadly we might ask what types of strong feelings, preferences, assumptions, and expectations do you bring to the therapeutic encounter that are likely to impede your effectiveness with clients? As we have suggested, these impediments may grow out of either a temporary situation in which we find ourselves or may be part of a long-standing personality style.

Therapists' Mistakes Signaling Countertransference

The most blatant example of countertransference is having a sexual relationship with the client. This issue is discussed in the chapters, Questions That Beginning Therapists Ask, and Ethical and Legal Issues; thus we will make only a few comments here about that type of countertransference. Such a relationship is considered countertransference because it places the needs of the therapist above the needs of the client. In a more classical sense, the attraction is seen as being based on such a very limited sample of the client's behavior (namely, the time spent in therapy), that at least some of the feelings must be a result of a distortion or an elaboration of an infantile wish on the part of the therapist. We understand that therapists, like everyone else, may quickly and easily recognize attractive personality features. To allow such a perception to blossom, without taking corrective action, into a feeling of "being in love" or to act on feelings of attraction, is so clearly in violation of professional standards, and so preventable (at least the behavioral part), that we call such instances countertransference. Therapists certainly differ in terms of when they begin to label attraction as countertransference. However, we believe that the majority of responsible professionals recognize that strong and recurrent feelings of attraction to clients, while understandable and perhaps at times almost inevitable, are feelings that cannot be acted upon. Furthermore, if such feelings are strong and continue undiminished, one must at least *consider* the possibility that they are reflective of a problem in the therapist's life. In any event, such feelings represent a threat to the therapeutic process if ignored or treated cavalierly by the therapist (Pope, Sonne, Holroyd, 1993).

One way we think of countertransference is that there are certain response styles that therapists frequently fall into as a reaction to clients about whom they have strong feelings. Certainly any "error" on the part of the therapist potentially represents countertransference. However, we want to highlight four response styles that we think are especially tempting for therapists because these styles, in situations other than therapy, may be appropriate. We are making no assumption here about whether transference is or is not involved. We merely wish to mention four responses that therapists may fall back on when they have strong feelings about a client.

The All-Knowing Therapist.   One way we may deal with strong feelings about a client is to fall back on the dangerous assumption that we are an expert on this particular client. This assumption may in turn compound the problem by distancing us from the emotional experience of the client or leading us to give advice when it clearly is not needed.

Being Bored.   Another way of controlling one's strong feelings about a client is to become bored during the therapy hour. It is certainly the case that clients may at times have their own unconscious reasons for wanting the therapist to be bored. Furthermore, some clients obviously are more interesting than others. Putting aside these issues for the moment, we are emphasizing that when therapists have strong feelings about their clients, one way to reduce the intensity of those feelings is to suddenly find that the client is not very interesting. Therefore, if you find yourself becoming bored with a client, one question you have to ask yourself is whether you have some strong feelings of which you have been unaware or only dimly aware.

Being Especially Nice.   Particularly if one has strong negative feelings about a client, a role that is very easy to fall back on is that of being very nice to the client. Psychoanalysts would label such a response as reaction formation. We are underscoring how therapists use "being nice" defensively because it is such a subtle process that often goes undetected for long periods of time. One reason therapists often do not realize what they are doing is that "being nice" is a culturally valued behavior. If you have a client with whom you are interacting in this way, you should consider the possibility that you have strong negative feelings about the client but are dealing with these feelings by being nice. A related possibility is that by treating the client so gingerly, you are failing to acknowledge the client's coping skills.

Rescuing Clients.   Just as some clients appear to be searching for someone who will solve their problems for them, so too are there some therapists who have difficulty refraining from becoming this rescuer. One example of when this process is likely to be activated is when therapists are not feeling good about themselves. When we are feeling ineffective in our personal or professional lives, it may become more and more important to us that we be able to help our clients. Clients who are "clearly in need of help" thus become the medium whereby therapists can elevate their self-esteem and renew their trust in themselves. In monitoring themselves for this type of countertransference, a danger signal therapists should look for is an opinion on their part that says, "The client has no one but me to turn to." In the first place, this conclusion is frequently (though certainly not always) inaccurate. In the second place, even when the client has no other social support, the job of the therapist is not to rescue the client but to help the client develop the internal and external resources needed to solve the problem.

Detecting Countertransference

An ongoing series of similar therapeutic errors, especially if they have been discussed with a supervisor and a number of alternatives have been provided, may suggest countertransference. Another way of saying this is that simple lack of information about how to proceed with a client may certainly impede progress, but lack of information alone is not considered countertransference. When a mistake is repeated numerous times, particularly with multiple clients, however, countertransference is likely taking place. In such an instance we look for something a little more subtle than lack of information, something that is more basic to who the therapist is. We suggest that if you find yourself having the same difficulty over and over, even though you are receiving what seems to you to be good supervision, it will be helpful to consider how your feelings, assumptions, and expectations about the client may be getting in the way.

In addition to analyzing your therapeutic "errors," there are a number of other ways in which you can increase the likelihood of your recognizing a countertransference reaction before too much time has passed. One idea is to compare your feelings across different types of clients. If you are like most therapists, you will find that there are some types about whom you have stronger feelings, both negative and positive. If you can identify some of these types of clients, you can be ready to monitor yourself a little more closely when you begin seeing them. By "types of clients" we mean not merely personality style (e.g., aggressive, dependent, etc.) but also problem type (e.g., alcoholism, depression, etc.).

If you are seeing a client and are wondering whether some of your actions are motivated more by your own needs than by the needs of the client, you might ask yourself how another therapist whom you respect might handle the case. (It obviously would be important to select for comparison someone who had the same general theoretical orientation as you.)

Another thing you might do to recognize countertransference is to look for the presence of extreme emotions. We have said that therapists often devise ways, typically unconscious ones, to reduce strong feelings they have about their clients. On the other hand, these "reduction processes" don't always work immediately, and you may be able to catch yourself before your feelings "go underground," so to speak.

Lack of client progress is of course always a potential signal that one is acting more out of one's own needs than out of those of the client. Of course there may be many other reasons for a lack of client progress, including a straightforward lack of skill on the part of the therapist, low client motivation, client characterological deficits, an environment that makes client change more problematic, or a poor match between client and therapist.

Another way to check for countertransference reactions is to think about ways in which the client is very much like you, or people close to you, and to think about how the client is very *unlike* you or someone close to you. The general assumption is that therapists are probably more prone to countertransference reactions if they identify very closely with the client or if they find it very difficult to identify with the client. Corey and Corey (1998) give several examples of behaviors or feelings that may signal countertransference, including, "I hope he cancels" (p. 96; e.g., you find yourself tense before the client arrives or relieved if she or he cancels).

Using Countertransference as an Adjunct to Diagnosis

Although the first view of countertransference was that it, like transference, represented an impediment to treatment, the view now taken by many therapists is that the therapist's emotional reactions to the client are a source for understanding the difficulties of the client. In this view, countertransference is not exactly something therapists want to have happen, but they see it as rather inevitable and then strive to understand how it can help them be better therapists. Strong emotional reactions to the client are often a product both of one's own "issues" as well as of the client who is seen as helping to elicit such reactions (Homqvist & Armelius, 1996). Clients who suffer from serious personality disorders are particularly well-known to elicit a wide variety of countertransference from therapists (Schultz & Glickauf-Hughes, 1995). For example, Brody and Farber (1996) asked therapists to read clinical vignettes and imagine that they were working with the clients who were described. When reading about a client diagnosed as "borderline," therapists anticipated feeling relatively more anger, irritation, and frustration when compared with their anticipation when the client was depressed or schizophrenic. One way of thinking about this finding is that when you find yourself experiencing high levels of anger with a client, you should consider the possibility of using your reaction as a part of the diagnostic picture. As another example, therapists who find their self-esteem being lowered in therapy with a client who frequently devalues the therapist may use their "countertransference" to better understand, and help the client better understand, the kind of pathology from which the client suffers. Similarly, the therapist who feels helpless in the treatment process may come to understand that reaction in part as being diagnostic of clients who need to make sure that they are always in control.

If we become dissatisfied with a client's progress, we are interested in whether our standards may be too high or whether we are overidentifying with the client and demanding progress for *ourselves*. On the other hand, we should also wonder how it is that the client is able to set up a situation that involves our worrying so much about him or her. As another example, suppose that we realize that we have started giving the client repeated advice. While we should certainly wonder what about us had caused a lapse into this role, we should also be interested in the traits of the client that made it easier for us to do this.

The client's role in helping to elicit countertransference (often involving emotional reactions) from us is important for at least three reasons. First, the client, whether consciously or unconsciously, may be reducing treatment effectiveness through these behaviors. Second, the kinds of reactions the client is getting from us very likely parallel the reactions he or she is receiving from many other people. If we seem to routinely become angry at the client, there is a good chance that a number of other people do also. In such a case (as an example), it becomes much more clear to us (and we hope, subsequently to the client) how the client fails to achieve his or her interpersonal goals. In turn, this understanding sets the stage for the client to "recapture" some of the power that has been missing in his or her life. Finally, there may be instances in which our failure to hide our emotional reactions to clients, which in some very technical sense might be considered countertransference, may actually prove to be therapeutic in that clients may experience their power to evoke reactions from us. We are not suggesting this as a technique, but merely pointing out that the process may at times have positive consequences.

Importance of Recognizing Countertransference

It must be strongly emphasized that countertransference, unrecognized, poses serious challenges to the integrity and well-being of the therapeutic process. Deciding when a therapist's behavior represents countertransference and when it represents creative therapy, or simple lack of skill, is heavily dependent on both cultural factors and the theoretical orientation of the therapist. Nonetheless, if you are punishing your client because something about her reminds you of your father, or if you are bored with a client because something about him reminds you of your own passivity, or if you constantly give advice to the client who seems similar to your daughter, you can scarcely be delivering high-quality psychotherapy.

Even if you believe that the construct of countertransference is too imprecise to be of much help to you, you will likely still agree that there may be situational events in the life of a therapist, or certain personality characteristics of therapists, that predispose them to therapeutic errors. Gelso and Carter (1994) give a good example of a therapist "catching himself" in a therapeutic error, which was caused (at least in his understanding) by a temporary problem in his personal life:

> The client (a 35-year-old woman) and therapist had worked together for 2 years, twice a week, in analytically oriented therapy. By all measures, they had a very sound working alliance. However, the client became increasingly frustrated because each time she brought up her difficulties with her children, the therapist seemed to respond nonempathically and at times even critically. In this case, the client perceived the therapist's nonempathy and judgment realistically and responded with realistic hurt and frustration. She expressed these observations and feelings to the therapist during one session, and the therapist became aware that, in fact, his conflicts with his parenting of his own children were interfering with the empathic process with his client. Having grasped his countertransference reaction, the therapist was able to regain his empathic stance during exploration of the client's parenting. (p. 299)

In the example just cited, the therapist, in his own view, made a mistake (failed to be appropriately empathic), whether you do or do not label it as "countertransference." Our emphasis here is not on the terminology, but rather, in the simplest of terms to observe, that good therapists must be able to recognize, in a reasonable amount of time, when their personal problems are affecting their work with clients.

There are at least two reasons why it is very important to be able to recognize how one's personal problems and/or personality characteristics impede therapy. First, at the simplest level, this sort of situation means that your clients are not being helped. You are making therapeutic errors, which means that clients are not receiving the kind of treatment to which they are entitled and which is, in fact, reasonably to be expected. Obviously, we would like to be able to rectify this type of situation; we want to correct any mistakes that are within our power to correct.

Second, countertransference is especially important because it describes a circumstance under which there is a tendency for the therapist to confuse his or her own distortions with the imagined distortions of the client. At best, as in the example given by Gelso and Carter (1994), the therapist fails to be appropriately supportive of the client (leading, unfortunately, to the client's dissatisfaction, with the concomitant possibility of premature termination). The worst part of countertransference is that the therapist is at risk for communicating to clients that they do not understand the world, or that they only imagine the nonsupportiveness of the therapist. The therapist who is in the midst of countertransference is likely to suggest, in any of a hundred different ways, that the client does not understand what is really going on. Unfortunately, the great tragedy is that the *therapist* does not understand what is really going on; yet the client is left to face the message that this highly credible, well-trained professional, on whom he or she has perhaps become dependent, lacks confidence in the experience of the client and in fact sees the client as being dead-wrong about her or his problem. This amounts to nothing less than a betrayal of the therapist's professional responsibility. If clients suggest to you that you seem angry with them, or impatient, or bored, it is critical that you listen carefully to what is being said and consider that the client might be right, and to wonder, if that is so, what might be going on with you. You can certainly encourage clients to talk more about such expressed feelings, but it is also important that you examine your own feelings, to understand both what they are and what may be creating or contributing to them.

Summary Comments on Countertransference

We use the word countertransference to describe situations in which the psychotherapist acts toward the client on the basis of the therapist's needs rather than on the basis of the client's needs. This process may occur as the therapist attempts to solve a more or less temporary problem in his or her life, or it may occur as the therapist acts out long-standing problems that have become character traits. In order to deal with their strong feelings about clients, therapists may lapse into roles that are dysfunctional in terms of therapy, but which do have the property of temporarily reducing the therapist's anxiety. There are a number of ways in which the therapist may recognize countertransference, including being aware of repeated therapeutic mistakes, comparing feelings across different types of clients, comparing one's responses to the responses of other therapists, being aware of extreme emotions, noting a lack of client progress, and being aware of similarities/dissimilarities between oneself and the client.

Implications of Transference and Countertransference for Short-Term Therapy

In short-term therapy, we usually do not expect to see the development of transference in the same way that one might expect to see it in longer-term therapy. In the first place, the client has less time to develop a set of elaborated fantasies about the therapist. Second, there is much less time for the client to become dependent on the therapist. In general, a certain amount of dependency is seen as being almost a necessary condition for transference to develop. Third, in many cases involving clients who are insured by managed care, only a few sessions of psychotherapy are authorized for payment. Under these conditions, the therapy will perhaps often have a cognitive-behavioral flavor, with a strong emphasis on coping behavior, and is likely not to be highly interpersonal or psychodynamic. Cognitive-behavioral orientations do not tend to emphasize the constructs of transference and countertransference. Fourth, we might venture that therapists who practice short-term therapy do so with the prior inclination that, in such cases, they will not encourage dependency, and they will not encourage deep exploration of transferential material. Thus, whatever the client's inclination, and whatever the limitations of the therapy are as a function of the structure of short-term therapy, therapists themselves are likely to exert some control over the development of transference. This control is exerted through a number of mechanisms, including being more directive, being more active, being less inclined to interpret comments in a way that might lead to discussions about transference, and repeatedly emphasizing the strengths of clients to solve their own problems.

Does all this mean that the constructs of transference and countertransference have little or no place in short-term therapy? Our answer to this question is that when clients significantly distort their interactions with the therapist, for whatever reason, this is a very important part of the therapeutic process. We do not believe that transference is typically a key ingredient in short-term therapy, but we do believe that interpersonal distortions are quite important, and especially so when they involve the very person who is trying to help the individual. For reasons discussed throughout the book, we believe that the therapeutic relationship is a powerful vehicle for change and that clients can be greatly helped, even in a short-term environment, when the client and therapist together help the client take advantage of this power. Distortions that in any way diminish this power must be attended to.

Countertransference may also be of importance in short-term therapy. Again, for reasons discussed above, when the therapist's personal feelings are transferred to the client, rather than worked out in supervision or personal life, therapy is vulnerable to diminished effectiveness. No matter what our theoretical orientation, and no matter what the length of therapy, it does little good for us to confuse our own lives with the lives of our clients. It is a part of common clinical wisdom that therapists must be aware of their own "personal issues" and must be able to separate themselves from their clients.

DISCUSSION QUESTIONS

- What are some of the practical limits of considering a feeling or behavior on the part of the therapist countertransference as opposed to being a part of the real relationship? For example, when might you be justified in being angry at a client without its being considered countertransference?

- When clients are sexually attracted to their therapists, is this attraction ever a part of the real relationship, or is it always more appropriately seen as transference?

- When therapists are sexually attracted to their clients, is this attraction ever a part of the real relationship, or is it always more appropriately seen as countertransference?

- If you believe that the constructs of transference and countertransference are not very helpful, how do you conceptualize some or all of the processes that have been labeled using that terminology?

- In addition to issues discussed in this chapter, what are some other implications of cultural diversity for the concepts of transference and countertransference? What is the relationship between transference and the stereotypes some clients have of therapists who are from a different ethnic group?

■ If you and the client are not of the same ethnicity, how might you know whether the client's distortion of some aspect of your personality is based on ethnicity rather than on something else? Does it matter what the source is of a distortion?

BIBLIOGRAPHY

Alexander, P. C., & Anderson, C. L. (1994). An attachment approach to psychotherapy with the incest survivor. *Psychotherapy, 31,* 665–675.

Andersen, S. M., Glassman, N. S., & Chen, S. (1995). Transference in social perception: The role of chronic accessibility in significant-other representations. *Journal of Personality and Social Psychology, 69,* 41–57.

Bachelor, A. (1995). Clients' perception of the therapeutic alliance: A qualitative analysis. *Journal of Counseling Psychology, 42,* 323–337.

Brody, E. M., & Farber, B. A. (1996). The effects of therapist experience and patient diagnosis on countertransference. *Psychotherapy, 33,* 372–380.

Carter, J. A. (1996). Measuring transference: Can we identify what we have not defined? *Journal of Counseling Psychology, 43,* 257–258.

Corey, M. S., & Corey, G. (1998). *Becoming a helper* (3rd ed.). Pacific Grove, CA: Brooks/Cole.

Dyckman, J. (1997). The impatient therapist: Managed care and countertransference. *American Journal of Psychotherapy, 51,* 329–342.

Gabbard, G. O. (1998). *Transference and countertransference in the treatment of narcissistic patients.* Washington, DC: American Psychiatric Press.

Gelso, C. J., & Carter, J. A. (1994). Components of the psychotherapy relationship: Their interaction and unfolding during treatment. *Journal of Counseling psychology, 41,* 296–306.

Gelso, C., Kivlighan, D. M., Jr., Wine, B., Jones, A., & Friedman, S. C. (1997). Transference, insight, and the course of time-limited therapy. *Journal of Counseling Psychology, 44,* 209–217.

Greenberg, L. S. (1994). What is "real" in the relationship? Comment on Gelso and Carter (1994). *Journal of Counseling Psychology, 41,* 307–309.

Homqvist, R., & Armelius, B. (1996). Sources of therapists' countertransference feelings. *Psychotherapy Research, 6,* 70–78.

Horvath, A. O., & Greenberg, L. S. (Eds.). (1994). *The working alliance: Theory, research, and practice.* New York: Wiley.

Horvath, A. O., & Luborsky, L. (1993). The role of the therapeutic alliance in psychotherapy. *Journal of Consulting and Clinical Psychology, 61,* 561–573.

Horvath, A. O., & Symonds, B. D. (1991). Relation between working alliance and outcome in psychotherapy: A meta-analysis. *Journal of Counseling Psychology, 38,* 139–149.

Kivlighan, D. M., Jr., & Shaughnessy, P. (1995). Analysis of the development of the working alliance using hierarchical linear modeling. *Journal of Counseling Psychology, 42,* 338–349.

Koile, E. (1977). *Listening as a way of becoming.* Waco, TX: Regency Books.

Luborsky, L., & Crits-Christoph, P. (1998). *Understanding transference: The core-conflictual relationship theme* (2nd ed.). Washington, DC: American Psychological Association.

Mallinckrodt, B. (1993). Session impact, working alliance, and treatment outcome in brief counseling. *Journal of Counseling Psychology, 40,* 25–32.

Mallinckrodt, B. (1996). Capturing the subjective and other challenges in measuring transference: Comment on Multon, Patton, and Kivlighan (1996). *Journal of Counseling Psychology, 43,* 253–256.

Mallinckrodt, B., Gantt, D. L., & Coble, H. M. (1995a). Attachment patterns in the psychotherapy relationship: Development of the client attachment to therapist scale. *Journal of Counseling Psychology, 42,* 307–317.

Mallinckrodt, B., Gantt, D. L., & Coble, H. M. (1995b). Toward differentiating client attachment from working alliance and transference: Reply to Robbins (1995). *Journal of Counseling Psychology, 42,* 320–322.

McHenry, S. (1994). When the therapist needs therapy: Characterological countertransference issues and failures in the treatment of the borderline personality disorder. *Psychotherapy, 31,* 557–570.

Melville, H. (1930). *Moby Dick.* New York: Random House.

Multon, K. D., Patton, M. J., & Kivlighan, D. M., Jr. (1996). Development of the Missouri Identifying Transference Scale. *Journal of Counseling Psychology, 43,* 243–252.

Neimeyer, R. A., & Mahoney, M. J. (Eds.). (1995). *Constructivism in psychotherapy.* Washington, DC: American Psychological Association.

Patton, M J., Kivlighan, D. M., Jr., Mutlon, K. D. (1997). The Missouri Psychoanalytic Counseling Research Project: Relation of changes in counseling process to client outcomes. *Journal of Counseling Psychology, 44*, 189–208.

Patton, M. J., & Meara, N. M. (1992). *Psychoanalytic counseling.* Chichester, England: Wiley.

Pope, K. S., Sonne, J. L., & Holroyd, J. (1993). *Sexual feelings in psychotherapy: Explorations for therapists and therapists-in-training.* Washington, DC: American Psychological Association.

Richardson, M. R. (1997). Toward a clinically relevant model of counseling research: Comment on Patton, Kivlighan, and Multon (1997) and Gelso, Kivlighan, Wine, Jones, and Friedman (1997). *Journal of Counseling Psychology, 44*, 218–221.

Robbins, S. B. (1995). Attachment perspectives on the counseling relationship: Comment on Mallinckrodt, Gantt, and Coble (1995). *Journal of Counseling Psychology, 42*, 318–319.

Rogers, C. (1951). *Client-centered therapy: Its current practice, implications, and theory.* Boston: Houghton Mifflin.

Schultz, R. E., & Glickauf-Hughes, C. (1995). Countertransference in the treatment of pathological narcissism. *Psychotherapy, 32*, 601–607.

Sexton, T. L., & Whiston, S. C. (1994). The status of the counseling relationship: An empirical review, theoretical implications and research directions. *The Counseling Psychologist, 22*, 6–78.

Solomon, M. F., & Siegel, J. P. (1997). *Countertransference in couples therapy.* New York: W. W. Norton.

Storr, A. (1980). *The art of psychotherapy.* New York: Methuen.

Twemlow, S. W. (1997). Exploitation of patients: Themes in the psychopathology of their therapists. *American Journal of Psychotherapy, 51*, 357–375.

Wallerstein, J. S. (1997). Transference and countertransference in clinical interventions with divorcing families. In M. F. Solomon & J. P. Siegel (Eds.), *Countertransference in couples therapy* (pp. 113–124). New York: Norton.

Yalom, I. D. (1980). *Existential psychotherapy.* New York: Basic Books.

CHAPTER

13 Termination

In the final analysis, termination, separation, and death are the bedrock of human existence, for which psychotherapy, whether it is time limited or unlimited, can offer no cure.

—H. Strupp and J. Binder

From now on, wherever you go, or wherever I go, all the ground between us will be holy ground.

—farewell message to a healer, quoted by Henri Nouwen

The term "termination" refers to the last stage of therapy, presumably following some sort of beginning point and then a middle "working" stage. Rice, Alonso, and Rutan (1985) and others have suggested that this final stage is the one in which students have had the least training; we agree with that. However, until the last decade, there were a number of books and articles that students could seek out as resources, even if their professors and supervisors chose not to focus on this stage. Even writers from a wide variety of theoretical orientations had quite a lot to say about termination. Recently, however, there has been a notable absence of new work coming out, either conceptually or empirically.

We suggest that there may be two reasons. Those in academic or medical settings may feel that they have little to contribute to an already large body of literature on the termination of therapy. What is new to be added, they may feel? In marked contrast, those therapists in private practice or in agencies now dealing with managed care may have given up considering termination issues out of necessity. How can one plan for termination, using any of the classically oriented models, when neither the therapist nor the client has the final say in when termination will take place? In the current marketplace, a psychologist may be seeing someone with PTSD, for example, and be authorized by the insurance case manager to work with her or him for five sessions, then told to call back and report progress. At that point, under many policies, the *case manager* will decide if and for how much longer the therapist can work with the client. Not uncommonly, the therapist will be authorized for five more sessions, and then told to call back for further negotiation. Some companies are fairly lenient or at least predictable, some are not. Therapists may be put in the position of having to call clients to cancel the next session because no more are authorized. (How to deal with this when ethically we are warned against abandonment has been the subject of considerable controversy.) Treatment planning becomes problematic at best, and allowing enough time for termination is an aspiration that case managers have little sympathy with, to say the least.

In this chapter, we will provide some of the traditional ways to think about termination. Some of you will be doing your training in agencies untouched by managed care, and/or may be working in the future with clients who can see you for more than a few sessions. Or you may be working with EAP referrals, who are authorized for a given number of sessions (often as few as three, but at least the number is known ahead of time.) Even if that is not the case, the issues that clients and therapists were traditionally expected to have to deal with are often still there in the managed care scene, they are just difficult to use as a basis for making many therapeutic choices. We will also provide you with some generic guidelines that we hope will be helpful regardless of the setting, client, or theoretical orientation of yourself or your supervisor.

Psychodynamic Conceptualization of Termination

The stages or steps of therapy are never quite as clear-cut as beginning, middle, and end. Sometimes the therapeutic alliance is never really forged in the beginning stage, and even with the most responsible clients, motivation will ebb and flow in the course of treatment, thereby making the middle stage hard to track. Still, most therapists seem to feel that they know intuitively when therapy is going well and in retrospect can often identify the turning points that marked a client's progress. Even experienced therapists often have difficulty with the awkwardness of the final stage, however, and so therapy may simply stop.

Traditionally, termination has been considered difficult because it deals with loss (Strupp & Binder, 1984). The assumption in this classical understanding of termination is that the therapeutic relationship will have been intense and will have lasted long enough that both therapist and client are heavily invested in the process. Presumably, heavily affective, probably developmental, issues will have been explored at some length, and all aspects of the therapeutic relationship—the working alliance, the transferential configuration, and "real" relationship (refer to the chapters Transference and Countertransference and The Therapeutic Stance)—will have been activated. For clients, their therapist will have become their "elected surrogate parent" (Simonton, 1988), and giving up this parent is seen as a necessary piece of their separation–individuation work, just as separating from their real parent figures is. With this understanding, then, it becomes clear that this last stage of therapy can "make or break" the treatment, and difficult as it is for both parties, the issues must be explored thoroughly.

Maholick and Turner (1979) for example, spoke to the importance of this stage in their discussion of the loss and powerlessness issues that often bring clients into therapy in the first place. They suggested that these issues are likely to be reactivated by termination with their therapists, and a poorly handled termination is likely to recapitulate the negative experiences they have had in previous losses.

In somewhat more existential terms, Martin and Shurtman (1985) discuss the importance of coming to terms with loss:

> Therapy, like life itself, ends. If as therapists we minimize the termination process or do not permit ourselves to be as emotionally available as we can be during the final sessions, what are we implying to the client about how to conduct one's waking activities during an experience that has a certain end? Might we not then be teaching the need to defend oneself against loss and death instead of the need to live life to its fullest? (p. 95)

The psychodynamic model, then, assumes that the ending of the relationship will be painful for both the therapist and the client. Further, it is assumed that therapists will be unable to stay emotionally available to the client unless they have acknowledged and largely worked through their own anxiety. To expand a bit upon Martin & Shurtman's (1985) conceptualization of the process, therapist anxiety about termination often originates from five possible sources:

1. The therapist's own dynamics and inability to deal with loss in his or her own life. If therapists have major unresolved losses, or if they are very cautious and afraid to invest in relationships because of possible rejection or other ending, that fearfulness will make them protective of themselves and of their clients in facing the pain that comes from loss.

2. Concern over the loss of one's professional role. Sometimes one may get so attached to clients that it is easy to forget that one's role was foreshadowed from the beginning as time-limited. The therapist wonders how her or his clients can manage without the therapist's support and guidance, much as a parent worries when a child goes out into the world without the parental safety net. Similarly, if one's work with this client has gone well and been a source of self-esteem for the therapist, the client's leaving can feel like a partial loss of the therapeutic role. Especially if the rest of the therapist's life is not going well, giving up this source of fulfillment and gratification can be difficult.

3. The therapist's reaction to the client's termination anxiety. If clients have strong reactions to leaving, and some of them will, therapists may experience countertransferential feelings of guilt, self-doubt, anxiety, or similar feelings. This may be especially true if it is a therapist-initiated termination, if the therapist has felt ambivalent about the client, and/or if the client accuses the therapist of not caring, of being arbitrary, or the like.

4. Uneasiness about the implied importance of termination. Sometimes, therapists are so mindful of wanting to do a "successful termination" that they get performance anxiety, rooted in the fear that they will somehow damage their clients if they handle termination poorly. Instead of relying on their own training and experience, they may find themselves deferring to an outside expert on how to do it "right."

5. The literal loss of a meaningful relationship. As we have discussed earlier, there is, or should be, a "real" component to the therapeutic relationship. As transference issues are worked through, presumably this component becomes stronger. Especially with clients whom therapists have felt fond of from the beginning, letting go is personally painful. As one counselor said after a particularly sad termination, "They should post a warning in graduate school that termination can be hazardous to your health."

Any one or a combination of these sources of anxiety can lead to this last stage being so painful that therapists may make sure to end therapy abruptly rather than risk going through the third stage at all.

In the psychodynamic formulation of termination, clients are *expected* to have a quite difficult time letting us go. Quintana (1993) summarizes these expected client reactions to termination as "a plethora of neurotic affective, cognitive, interpersonal, and defensive reactions related to grief reactions." Bauer and Kobos (1987) list a variety of client reactions that the therapist must be prepared to deal with: new problems or regression, desire to stay in therapy to obtain a more complete self-understanding, bargaining, anger, devaluing treatment, desire to terminate early, and therapist idealization. Yalom (1980) discusses his dilemmas in dealing with a client who was so upset when he initiated discussions of termination that she threatened suicide if he insisted on going through with it. (He did, and she did not suicide.) In short, therapists are warned that they should be prepared for quite emotional client reactions.

Other Conceptualizations of Termination

While most therapists we know who have been in practice for several years agree that sometimes termination can be painful, much of the research does not seem to bear that out. Quintana and Holahan's (1992) survey of therapists reported generally positive client reactions to termination. Similarly, in Fortune's (1987) and Marx and Gelso's (1987) studies of clients' reactions to termination, the large majority reported positive reactions.

There seem to be three obvious explanations for this: (a) Therapists and clients are colluding to avoid the pain. (b) Termination might actually be less traumatic than the psychodynamic model suggests, and/or (c) The concept of termination has changed from a final, irrevocable but necessary break to a more developmental understanding that clients may well "terminate" and return in a few months or years. There is some research support for this last hypothesis. Kramer (1986) found that about 76% of therapists invited clients to return. Along these same lines, Budman and Gurman (1988) found in their study that 50% to 66% of terminated clients do indeed return to therapy within a year. Quintana (1993), apparently referring to the managed care marketplace we alluded to earlier, explains this by noting that the nature of current practice lends itself to repeated episodes of psychotherapy without necessitating a formal end. Or, as one of our colleagues commented, "With only a few sessions a year paid for by many companies, clients have come to use us like they use family physicians. When something is wrong they come for help, and then leave until they need us again."

Quintana (1993) proposes that even when the psychodynamic termination-as-loss model is invoked, another understanding that might be more useful than the assumption of trauma is what he refers to as the termination-as-development model. Using psychodynamic understandings of the internalization, he suggests that loss might be less painful for clients who have used such developmental processes as introjection, identification, and ego identity internalization in their work with their therapists. He quotes Edelson (1963):

> The problem of termination is not how to get therapy stopped, or when to stop it, but how to terminate so that what has been happening keeps going inside the patient.... It is a problem of facilitating achievement by the patient of the ability to hang on to the therapist (or the experience of the relationship with the therapist) in his [or her] physical absence in the form of a realistic intrapsychic representation. (p. 23)

Or, said more succinctly by a client, "I don't think I'll miss you too much—I have the eternal Donna inside."

This construal of termination sees the shift in the client's life caused by termination as similar to other transitions the client has had and will make in the future. Part of the process of development involves interacting and learning from others, and then moving on into new stages of life. This is true, it is argued, with one's parents, with mentors, and with friends, and therapy is no exception. Part of being somewhat autonomous requires that we "outgrow" previous constructions of relationships and construct new ones that better fit our emerging identities.

Guidelines for Termination

Our understanding, while rooted in some of the foregoing conceptualization, assumes that each termination process is unique. It grows out of the process between the two individuals involved and the issues that have been the therapeutic focus. The ending of a therapeutic relationship between a client with an eating disorder and her behavioral therapist will probably be quite different from the process between the same client and her analyst if she had instead chosen to enter long-term psychoanalysis. The guidelines we offer here are intended to be generic. We will suggest separate emphases for termination when the decision for that termination comes from each of four different loci—when the therapist makes the decision (often because of agency guidelines), when the client makes the decision, when the decision is mutually agreed upon, and when the decision is made by an unpredictable third party such as a managed care company. Before we discuss each situation separately, however, we would like to offer some general guidelines.

First, you should keep in mind that the purpose of therapy is to help the client change. Termination, accordingly, should have as its top priority the consolidation, maintenance, and generalization of client gains. Asking clients to take stock for themselves and list their original goals and how far they have come in attaining them is a focus that is often helpful periodically in therapy, but especially in termination. You should also be able to offer your own perspective of their progress to terminating clients. Additionally, many therapists talk about, or perhaps even role-play, probable scenarios that are likely to arise in the client's life in an attempt to facilitate transfer of learning to the future. When you terminate, you will want clients to have obtained their money's worth, to leave stronger or with more skills than when they entered. Further, you want them to experience these accomplishments as *theirs*, not to defer to you in gratitude.

Next, we agree with Kramer (1986) that termination needs to be discussed overtly—not just at the end of therapy, but from the early sessions on. Endings of relationships are so frequently nonverbal and/or impulsively acted out that, as Kramer says, there is much to be gained by bringing the termination process into the open where it can be discussed freely. With time-limited therapy (as in a counseling center with a ten-session limit) it is especially important to keep the termination date in perspective as one of the limits built into the therapeutic relationship that serves to channel and focus the client's energy and attention. Lamb (1985) provides a model for the content of each of the last seven sessions so that termination issues are highlighted and virtually inescapable. Even if no specific termination date is set, however, the fact that therapy will not continue indefinitely should be in the client's awareness all along. No client, if it can possibly be avoided, should have to repeat earlier traumatic abandonment experiences by being subjected to an abrupt termination.

Another general guideline we offer for your consideration is that you maintain your therapeutic stance with the client right through the final moments of the last session, rather than dilute the experience by becoming "friends," even if the client is insistent. We are aware that there is some controversy over this issue, but we feel strongly that it is almost always in the client's best interest to follow the conservative "once a therapist, always a therapist" approach. It should be obvious that we are not proposing a rigid formality to your style that would preclude any warmth or self-disclosure. Rather, maintaining a therapeutic stance means that you honor your primary commitment to the client's growth and needs and do not allow yourself to slide into a social, chatty relationship simply because that makes you feel better. Boyer and Hoffman (1993) found support for the hypothesis that counselors who have had more severe grief reactions following a personal loss experienced more dysphoria during termination. This seems to confirm the psychodynamic assumption that it behooves the therapist to work through his or her own losses in order to be emotionally available to terminating clients.

Finally, a guideline regarding possible future contact with your client. Some clients may ask if the two of you can be "friends." Our impression is that the client who suggests this probably does not mean that he or she wants an equal, reciprocal relationship but instead secretly hopes that the therapeutic alliance (which called for your offering the best of yourself in the service of their needs) can simply be continued indefinitely, for free. This is, after all, probably the only way he or she has experienced you, and it is not unreasonable to want to continue having access to such a warm, wise person! In our experience, it is quite likely that clients will feel disappointed and betrayed if you interact with them in a new social way that suggests that you are no longer primarily focused on their growth, may sometimes be distracted and irritable and bored, and in fact may cancel or even forget social engagements with them. In short, we feel that therapy and friendship have somewhat different foundations and that it is ill advised and potentially damaging to the client to try to shift the structure from one set of goals and norms to another. (We are also aware that in small communities it can be quite difficult to keep relationship distinctions from getting blurred, but we feel that therapists in such situations should at least avoid the trap of naively assuming that all clients can be believed when they insist they can handle equality.)

You will need to think about your position on later contact and find a way to share that in a nurturing way with your client. A position taken by one therapist we know is, "I'm touched by your request for more contact with me. You have been important to me, too, and saying good-bye is hard. I will miss seeing you so regularly. But I don't know how to care differently about you. The *way* that I listen and feel when I am with you, the ways that I think about you and the areas where I feel responsibility for helping you—these are part of how I am with you that it's too late for me to change! 'Watering that down' to a friendship level is something I can't manage." What she is saying is that her therapeutic stance is something that is indigenous to their relationship and that there is no way to remove it and still have a relationship.

Having stated this rather conservative stance, we also acknowledge that our reservations are not universally shared. Salisbury & Kinnier (1996), in their study of counselor behavior and attitudes, found that almost two thirds of the counselors they surveyed felt that under some circumstances such posttermination friendships might be acceptable. Certainly, professional ethical codes do not specifically prohibit such relationships. Nonetheless, as Herlihy and Corey (1992) warned, in dual relationships there is indeed a risk for harm, and that potential harm must be the counselor's primary concern. (For an excellent discussion of the ethical issues involved in a variety of posttherapy relations—including, but not limited to, friendship—see Anderson and Kitchener, 1998.)

Client-Initiated Decision

Premature termination is a term with decidedly negative connotations. The use of it presupposes the therapist's objective assessment that the client is acting out his or her resistance to the exploration of important clinical material. Sometimes, of course, this is so unmistakable that even the client would not deny it. The substance abuser who resumes the use of drugs and misses his next session, the abused spouse who calls to cancel because she is moving back in with her husband, the anorexic client who no-shows after losing three more pounds—these clients, if pressed, would probably acknowledge that they had made choices that would be considered dysfunctional but that they preferred the immediate gratification of their present behavior to therapeutic exploration.

Other clients, however, may terminate simply because they have different goals from their therapists. Wolberg (1988) found that most clients regard symptom relief as the best measure of positive gain, which, to say the least, is in contrast to the analyst's criterion of the resolution of transference or the self psychologist's expectations that the self will be stronger. Symptom relief, from many clients' perspectives, must seem considerably easier to attain! Other clients may terminate because they do not believe they are being helped, because of financial considerations, or for a variety of other reasons. In short, we urge you not to automatically make hasty, negative judgments regarding clients' motives for considering termination.

If clients simply cancel or fail to keep appointments and do not reschedule, you will be on safer grounds both ethically and legally (dissatisfied clients occasionally sue on malpractice grounds) if you communicate by letter to indicate your willingness to continue meeting with them and/or to refer them to another professional. Some therapists additionally offer a free session to help the client explore his or her reasons for terminating. The goal here is to offer continued professional help without in any way attempting to coerce the client into remaining in therapy.

Assuming you have the opportunity to discuss with clients their reasons for terminating, it will be important to avoid taking an adversarial stance. If, in fact, you want your clients to become more autonomous, you must be able to support their independence, even if that means they leave therapy against your advice. You may still, of course, offer your clinical opinion, but we suggest you do so as nondogmatically as possible. You may, for example, want to say something like, "My concern is that you have more work to do in the area of...I will respect your opinion, since you must make the decision, of course, but I'd like for you to consider what I've said. Can you tell me your reaction?" If clients insist on terminating after all, we believe you will have the most therapeutic impact if you back off at that point, review with them the progress you have seen them make, and then suggest that at some later date, if old or new issues arise, they may want to contact you or another professional. If you are quite worried about their well-being, one possibility is to say something along the lines of, "I really do hope things will go OK for you. I'd feel a lot better, though, if I knew that if your depression/anxiety/ anger worsens, you'd contact me or another professional. Will you do that?"

Therapist-Initiated Decision

There are two kinds of situations in which you as therapist may find it necessary to discontinue therapy with a client. We will consider these separately, since both your own motivations and the client's are likely to be quite different in the two scenarios. In the first, more common situation, your decision has nothing to do with a particular client. The decision to terminate is demanded by your own situation. You are an intern, and it is time to rotate to another unit, or you work in an agency that has an eight-session limit and you of course must adhere to that limit, or you accept a new position somewhere else. Or perhaps you decide to retire or change careers. Whatever the precipitating cause, your clients' dynamics have not and cannot influence your decision. Depending on your clients' reactions to being helpless, they will find this either more or less easy to tolerate and understand than if your decision in fact had anything to do with them (as it does in the next scenario). You can assume that none of your clients will be very grateful for the disruption, but their relative helplessness will be a relief to some of them. For these individuals, knowing that at least they were not at fault will help them accept the situation. They will not need to wonder, as perhaps they have when experiencing other losses, what they could have done differently. Other clients, however, especially if they have been abused or neglected historically, may find their helplessness to influence your decision almost intolerable. It may provoke intense feelings of abandonment, rage, or despair.

Given these considerations, it should be obvious that your clients need to be given as much notice as possible about your plans. Preferably, you can tell them at the beginning of therapy, so they can pace themselves accordingly. We would also encourage you to allude often to the time frame during the course of therapy (as in, "Well, we're about halfway through our ten sessions. Are we on the right track as far as accomplishing your goals?" or "What did you want to focus on in our last four sessions?"). We suggest that you ask specifically what your clients' reactions are to finishing up therapy with you, that you listen nondefensively to any strong feelings they have, that you acknowledge the legitimacy of their situations, and that you demonstrate that you are somewhat affected by their reactions, even if you cannot change the final outcome. Expressing some regret and any positive feelings you have for them can serve to lessen their sense of powerlessness. Obviously, you will also offer a referral and facilitate it as much as possible if the client wishes. Helping clients see what choices are still available to them can also reduce their feelings of helplessness.

In the second scenario, you are not forced to end therapy with a client because of outside forces; instead, you choose to initiate termination because in your professional judgment staying in therapy with you will not enhance the client's growth. If clients were not grateful for the disruption in their lives in the previous situation, you can be sure that in this instance they will be even less so. Some will react stoically, some will withdraw or terminate precipitously at the first hint of rejection, and others may act out to the point of threatening suicide, as Yalom's did. Before you make such a decision, it is crucial that you consult with your supervisor or, lacking a supervisor, with other professionals.

Your choice to initiate termination will probably be based on your view that the client is holding onto symptoms out of dependency on you and a desire to avoid termination. We have also seen situations such as a husband's wanting to continue therapy indefinitely because as long as he keeps coming, his ambivalent wife remains hopeful that their relationship will improve and puts few demands on him. Sometimes the reason for clients' position is obvious to you; at other times, the cues are so subtle that it is only gradually that you come to understand that the client may never choose to terminate if left to his or her own devices.

Whatever the specifics of the case, the judgment is made in consultation with your supervisor that therapy is not providing help to the client. At this point, you will, following ethical guidelines, have to decide whether to encourage your client to let you make a referral or to suggest that she or he terminate therapy altogether. Clearly, decisions such as this are some of the most difficult ones therapists are called upon to make. In most cases, you will be able to suggest termination as a possibility, discuss it with your clients, help them work through their reactions, and they will accept the suggestion over time. Occasionally, this may take place quite quickly, especially if the client was feeling "ready" but needed your permission to leave. At other times, several weeks may be required. Our point is that you will usually be able to avoid the power struggle that ensues when clients feel "kicked out" if you emphasize your clients' strengths and progress made and suggest that the time has arrived for them to try their wings. If that is too fearful for them to imagine, you may suggest that at least they try a "vacation" of several months away from therapy. Keeping your approach positive and supportive, as opposed to critical and impatient, is very important. No one, including clients, likes to leave important relationships feeling rejected.

The instance of court-referred clients merits separate discussion. You may be working with clients, often spouses or parents convicted of abuse, who are seeing you as a condition of parole or probation. Some of these clients are truly invested in using therapy as an opportunity to make change. But we have seen students move into overdrive trying to accommodate and motivate clients whose agenda is to jump through the required hoops as painlessly as possible, rather than to make substantive change. We strongly encourage you to make it clear to them that you will be glad to help them change, but that you have specific expectations. Clarify the limits under which you will work, and then *stick to them.* If you instead collude with them to "work the system" and pretend that change is taking place when it is not, or if you find yourself working much harder than they are to schedule appointments, for example, you have not only not helped them, you have reinforced any ideas they have that manipulation works better than true change. Should you start feeling "set up," that is the time to matter-of-factly remind them of the limits and clarify that you have no choice if the limits are not honored but to notify the court of noncompliance. (We expect that you will have already obtained a release of information to communicate with relevant parties.) Mandated therapy works when the client himself or herself somehow takes responsibility for investing in the process; your job is not to accommodate clients' lack of investment, but to help them make changes.

Mutual Decision

Ideally, and more frequently than you might imagine, you and your client will agree with each other that therapy has run its course. That does not mean that there will be no pain in its ending but rather that acceptance and a mutual acknowledgment of the meaningfulness of what has happened will be a predominant theme.

Various writers have suggested "cues" that signal the emergence of this third phase of therapy. Kramer (1986) concurs with the traditional view that transference issues tend to be replaced by a more egalitarian exchange between the therapist and client. Roth (1987) reports that themes regarding loss and separation, especially in patients' dreams, precede and coincide with termination. You may see similar cues, as well as others, such as an expressed desire on the part of the client to decrease the frequency of sessions, a lack of things to talk about, or clearly self-congratulatory client expressions of progress. Whether the therapy has been within a specific or open-ended time frame, such cues are signals that, if you have not already, it is time to begin the overt discussion of termination.

As in the previous discussions of more unilaterally initiated termination, much of your job will be to affirm the gains the client has made and facilitate the consolidation and generalization of changes. You will also need to be available to encourage and help the client explore the full range of his or her feelings—from gratitude and acceptance to anger and grief. Some clients will not have a lot to explore. For them, the ending of therapy may represent a graduation, a chance for more free time and more money to spend, or just a simple acknowledgment that they have accomplished what they came for and are ready to move on. Our impression is that difficulty in termination is often a function of the intensity of the previous work, the psychopathology of the client (hopefully, not the therapist!), and/or the level of transference. As you help these clients recognize their feelings, their assumptions, and perhaps their coping styles, you may find that quite stressful. At this final stage, perhaps more than at any earlier time, your faith in clients' strength and resiliency will be tested.

What you need to strive for is to be as helpful and emotionally available to the terminating client as you would be if the person were discussing losing someone else important in their lives. In that situation, we imagine that you would ask them to explore their feelings, perhaps challenge self-defeating assumptions they were making, acknowledge the reality of the loss, offer support and confidence in their strength, and perhaps consider targeted grief-oriented interventions (letting them write a letter to you and perhaps read it aloud, providing an imagery experience where they tell their therapist how they feel and what they want to keep and use that therapy has offered, etc.) The important thing to remember is that the focus is on them, and that while they may need responses from you regarding your own feelings and impressions, this is not the place for you to deal with *your* loss issues.

Unpredictable Decision by Outside Party

Managed care is under increasing consumer and legislative attack, and many mental health professionals are hopeful that within a few years the situation will improve. But for the foreseeable future, an outsider whose commitment may be to company profit rather than to client welfare will be making decisions about the kind of work you can do with managed care clients. Working under these increasingly common situations is quite difficult. As indicated earlier, not having any idea how long you can work with a client makes treatment planning problematic and a termination "stage" almost obsolete. It is very important to be honest with clients about the situation you are both in, so that they can monitor their dependence on you and the process.

Many therapists find that therapy of this sort tends to be problem solving. Diagnosis is crucial, since this is usually the basis for case managers' allocation of authorized sessions. The first session, then, is less of an intake per se, and instead utilizes a diagnostic–problem definition approach. Obviously, it is important to identify as quickly as possible the major issue, and then our impression is that most therapists, regardless of their preferred theory, do cognitive or solution-focused work as an "opener." This needs to be done without sacrificing the therapeutic alliance. In fact, very brief therapy usually requires even more attention to the alliance so that you can keep to a minimum client defensiveness or misunderstandings. If those therapeutic approaches prove unsuccessful, you will need to renegotiate with the case manager, perhaps with new diagnostic information.

With no specific termination stage to rely on, it becomes even more important to ensure that clients are consolidating and generalizing their learning. Therapists often use homework assignments between sessions to maximize client investment during this therapeutic interlude in their lives, an approach that lessens the destructive effect of abrupt endings. The therapeutic stance tends to be more overtly supportive than usual, since it is often crucial for clients' sense of efficacy to increase quickly. If the managed care company provides coverage of no more sessions, you should consider offering a final one at reduced or no charge, especially if you sense that you have become very important in the client's life.

Final Session

Given the awkwardness and mixed feelings both you and your clients will likely be experiencing, it may be tempting to reach for an easy, systematic approach to bring therapy to a close. We urge you to remember that one of your primary responsibilities is to stay emotionally available to your clients, and hiding behind a set of procedures will hardly facilitate that. At the same time, it is generally not helpful to your clients to encourage them to explore new, difficult material in the last session.

Generally speaking, the last time you meet with a client will be a time for the two of you to say good-bye. As Lamb (1985) indicates, this can be accomplished in a variety of ways, including further expressions by therapist or client on the meaningfulness of therapy and leave-taking, or review of progress made by the client and an exploration of her or his future plans. Sometimes clients, especially after long-term therapy, wish to give a gift to the therapist. While the acceptance of gifts, even during the last session, is somewhat controversial, it is our position that the ritual of gift giving is an important one for some clients and may help them accept the finality of the situation. We see the therapist's willingness to accept small gifts as a symbolic acknowledgment of the client's feelings, and in most cases we think it is more helpful to accept graciously a small gift than to encourage the client to explore the motivations behind the giving. (Expensive, valuable gifts are infrequently given and in our opinion should not be accepted.)

Another thing that therapists occasionally do, especially if they have routinely done this throughout the course of therapy, is to solicit their clients' feedback. If a therapist has never done this with a given client, it would be inappropriate to shift the power balance of the final session by doing so now. But if some mutual give-and-take and focus on the therapeutic relationship has been part of your style all along, then briefly asking the client what he or she found helpful or difficult in therapy may provide you with valuable feedback. If you ask, be prepared to live with some ambiguity, since what you get will be the client's very subjective assessment. Asking for in-depth clarification, even if you are bewildered by his or her answer, would be an unfair burden to a client in a final session and would probably increase the client's defensiveness.

Finally, we remind you again that in addition to acknowledging the range of your clients' feelings about you—including their gratitude for your help—you nonetheless should give them much of the credit for their progress. It may be tempting to let them idealize you and your therapeutic power, but they need to leave therapy in touch as much as possible with their own strengths and resources. Your acknowledging the value of their struggles and gains will help them further internalize your belief in their abilities.

Summary

In some ways, the approach to termination has shifted in the last decade, as the traditional model of a clear ending to longer-term therapy has often given way to a model wherein clients seek therapy as needed, often to deal with situational issues. What termination means varies with each case. It is based on the kinds of expectations, therapeutic issues, and therapist–client relationship that had previously evolved. Your goals as therapist will be to maximize the possibility of continued growth and change when clients are no longer seeing you, and to explore, if appropriate, what their losing you might mean for them. They will need your continued emotional availability until the end, as well as your support and acknowledgment of their progress.

DISCUSSION QUESTIONS

- If clients knew you well enough to see how you have dealt with loss in your personal life, would that be a good model for them? Do you have unresolved loss issues that might impact your ability to work with terminating clients, and if so, how can you address them?

■ What kinds of clients do you think you will have the most trouble giving up? What is it about them that would make it difficult for you? If you can imagine being in their shoes, having had you as a therapist and now finding it time to say good-bye to you, what therapist attitudes or behaviors make that easier or more difficult to do?

■ Do you think there is merit to the traditional approach to viewing termination as a necessary separation–individuation loss? What cultural or gender biases might underpin that understanding?

BIBLIOGRAPHY

Anderson, S. K., & Kitchener, K. (1998). Nonsexual posttherapy relationships: A conceptual framework to assess ethical risks. *Professional Psychology: Research and Practice, 29,* 91–99.

Bauer, G. P., & Kobos, J. C. (1987). *Brief therapy: Short term psychodynamic intervention.* Northvale, NJ: Aronson.

Boyer, S. P., & Hoffman, M. A. (1993). Counselor affective reactions to termination: Impact of counselor loss history and perceived sensitivity to loss. *Journal of Counseling Psychology, 40,* 271–277.

Budman, S. H., & Gurman, A. S. (1998). *Theory and practice of brief therapy.* New York: Guilford Press.

Edelson, M. (1963). *The termination of intensive psychotherapy.* Springfield, IL: Thomas.

Epstein, R. S. (1994). *Keeping boundaries: Maintaining safety and integrity in the psychotherapeutic process.* Washington, DC: American Psychiatric Press.

Epston, D., & White, M. (1995). Termination as a rite of passage: Questioning strategies for a therapy of inclusion. In R. A. Neimeyer and M. J. Mahoney (Eds.), *Constructivism in psychotherapy.* (pp. 339–354). Washington, DC: American Psychological Association.

Fortune, A. E. (1987). Grief only? Client and social worker reactions to termination. *Clinical Social Work Journal, 15,* 159–171.

Herlihy, B., & Corey, G. (1992). *Dual relationships in counseling.* Alexandria, VA: American Association for Counseling and Development.

Kitchener, K. S. (1992). Posttherapy relationships: Ever or never? In B. Herlihy and G. Corey (Eds.), *Dual relationships in counseling* (pp. 146–154). Alexandria, VA: American Association of Counseling and Development.

Kohlenberg, R. J., & Tsai, M. (1991). *Functional analytic psychotherapy: Creating intense and curative therapeutic relationships.* New York: Plenum.

Kramer, S. (1986). The termination process in open-ended psychotherapy: Guidelines for clinical practitioners. *Psychotherapy, 23,* 526–531.

Lamb, D. (1985). A time-frame model of termination in psychotherapy. *Psychotherapy, 22,* 604–609.

Maholick, L. T., & Turner, D. W. (1979). Termination: That difficult farewell. *American Journal of Psychotherapy, 33,* 583–591.

Martin, E., & Shurtman, R. (1985). Termination anxiety as it affects the therapist. *Psychotherapy, 22,* 92–96.

Marx, J. A., & Gelso, C. J. (1987). Termination of individual counseling in a university center. *Journal of Counseling Psychology, 34,* 3–9.

Penn, L. S. (1990). When the therapist must leave: Forced termination of psychodynamic therapy. *Professional Psychology, 21,* 379–384.

Pistole, C. (1991). Termination: Analytic reflections on client contact after counselor relocation. *Journal of Counseling and Development, 69,* 337–340.

Pope, K. S., & Vasquez, M. J. T. (1991). *Ethics in psychotherapy and counseling: A practical guide for psychologists.* San Francisco: Jossey-Bass.

Quintana, S. M., (1993). Toward an expanded and updated conceptualization of termination: Implications for short-term, individual psychotherapy. *Professional Psychology, 24,* 426–432.

Quintana, S. M., & Holahan, W. (1992). Termination in short-term counseling: Comparison of successful and unsuccessful cases. *Journal of Counseling Psychology, 39,* 299–305.

Rice, C., Alonso, A., & Rutan, J. (1985). The fights of spring: Separation/individuation, and grief in counseling centers. *Psychotherapy, 22,* 97–100.

Roth, S. R. (1987). *Psychotherapy: The art of wooing nature.* Northvale, NJ: Aronson.

Salisbury, W. A., & Kinnier, R. T. (1996). Post-termination friendship between counselors and clients. *Journal of Counseling and Development,* *74,* 495–500.

Simonton, S. (1988). Workshop on psychotherapy with the cancer patient. Little Rock, AR.

Strean, H. (1993). *Resolving counterresistances in therapy.* New York: Brunner/Mazel.

Strupp, H., & Binder, J. (1984). *Psychotherapy in a new key.* New York: Basic Books.

Teyber, E. (1997). *Interpersonal process in psychotherapy: A relational approach.* Pacific Grove, CA: Brooks/Cole.

Vaughan, S. C. (1997). *The talking cure: The science behind psychotherapy.* New York: G. P. Putnam's Sons.

Wolberg, L. R. (1988). *The technique of psychotherapy.* New York: Grune & Stratton.

Yalom, I. (1980). *Existential psychotherapy.* New York: Basic Books.

PART TWO

Overview

We conclude this book with three chapters. We have set the first two apart because books on psychotherapy typically do not use these topics as chapter headings (an exception would be Yalom, 1980), and yet, in our view, these are two ideas that are used repeatedly by a wide variety of psychotherapists. Whatever the therapists' theoretical orientations, we believe that they *think about* their clients' relationships with others, and their clients' capabilities to be responsible. Almost any typical definition of mental health includes, either implicitly or explicitly, these two constructs. Yalom suggested that psychotherapists "throw in something" in therapy that they don't (or perhaps can't) describe, which is nonetheless an essential ingredient in their work. To this we add that therapists, if you listen to them at all, slip into using certain constructs over and over, even if those constructs do not occupy a central role in their stated theory. Responsibility and relationships are two such constructs that we believe are part of what is "thrown in" that makes therapy effective.

We are also adding some comments about therapy. Although in this edition we have modified each chapter to include a brief approach into our conceptualizations, this final chapter offers a more systematic overview of the basic elements of brief therapy as it is typically practiced.

CHAPTER

14 Responsibility

I think one must finally take one's life in one's arms.

—Arthur Miller

No one can walk my path for me.

—Greg Pipes, age 10

"I'm getting sick of this," Judith Viorst (1986) quotes a seven-year-old boy as saying. "Everything I do you blame on me" (p. 153). Most of us have no trouble at all resonating to this child's annoyance. Learning to take responsibility for one's choices is usually a slow and fitful process, often cluttered with a concomitant willingness to accept responsibility for happenings (both good and bad) beyond one's control. It is not easy to sort out how and for what one must claim authorship. Nonetheless, this issue is an undercurrent in most therapeutic work, for clients can make changes only in areas where they can claim responsibility (Bauer & Kobos, 1987; Branden, 1994). In this chapter we will address some of the transtheoretical ways of thinking that therapists sometimes bring to client issues of responsibility. We will give a composite definition for your consideration, and, since that definition draws heavily from three separate theoretical orientations, we will summarize those three approaches first. We will also offer some "common clinical wisdom" distinctions relevant to responsibility, as well as other therapeutic considerations you may find helpful in working with clients.

Terminology Issues

Despite its widespread use in common clinical practice, responsibility is a construct whose usage is somewhat problematic for several reasons. Our first reservation has to do with the moral overtones that often swirl around the word, bringing associations of parental expectations and punishments, as well as societal demands for acceptable behavior. Sometimes we may have been criticized for being "irresponsible," and the accusations made little sense to us since we had nicely constructed rationalizations for the behavior in question.

345

Secondly, there is little research that specifically targets responsibility as the variable of interest. Despite this particular limitation, there are hundreds of articles and books available on related issues—self efficacy (e.g., Bandura, 1997), self-esteem (e.g., Branden, 1994), self-control (e.g., Rosenbaum, 1993), and self-regulation (e.g., Zimmerman, 1989), to name a few. We think such sources offer very helpful insights and empirical results that can serve as the basis of potential therapeutic interventions and with which we strongly encourage you to acquaint yourself. These constructs are tidier and much easier to measure than responsibility; they lend themselves to increasingly sophisticated research designs.

A third reservation regarding using responsibility as a therapeutic construct is that it is easily used in *non*therapeutic ways. Rather than listening closely and understanding the intricacies of client motivations and behavior, it may be tempting with frustrating clients to simply label dysfunctional or unappealing behavior as "irresponsible" and be done with it. We have, nonetheless, stayed with our original impression that such a chapter belongs in a transtheoretical text on psychotherapy. In spite of our reservations, the construct is implied in most approaches to counseling and psychotherapy, and we believe it offers clarity that may be useful to both the therapist and the client.

Theoretical Contributions

The three therapeutic approaches that most specifically address client responsibility are existential psychotherapy, reality therapy, and gestalt therapy. We will briefly examine each of these to identify their distinctive contributions, as well as to delineate the underlying themes.

Existential Psychotherapy

With its proclamation that meaning in life could not be reached by looking to divine or ultimate sources, but was necessarily relative and individual, existentialism seemed to imply to some that there was no reason to do anything, since all values were arbitrary and relative and no action could be said to be ultimately more meaningful or worthwhile than another. Construed this way, existentialism is reduced to little more than nihilism. The existential psychotherapists, notably Rollo May (1983) and Irvin Yalom (1980), however, bring a different perspective to this otherwise rather bleak picture of the human condition. Since we cannot attribute what happens to us to divine intervention, they suggest, and since others are only human and not capable of providing meaning to us or of "rescuing" us from our situations, we must rely ultimately only on ourselves. No one else is responsible for me; I make my own choices. Even if I derive a grim satisfaction from blaming someone else (my parents, for example) for failing me in major ways, only I can be responsible for making my life better. No one else can do it for me or tell me the "right" thing to do. I must live, in Sheldon Kopp's (1975) words, "within the ambiguity of partial freedom, partial power, and partial knowledge" (p. 32) and make the best decisions I can.

This focus on decisions and choices, and the need for the individual to accept responsibility for the consequences that ensue, is one of the cornerstones of existential psychotherapy. The therapist with such an approach would try to listen carefully to where his or her clients find meaning in their lives—or, put another way, to what their deepest needs and goals are—and would then aid them in learning to make conscious decisions that are meaningful and consonant with their values. The client who makes such conscious choices is considered "responsible"; the client who, conversely, adopts a passive attitude and simply waits hopefully (or hopelessly) for life to improve is "irresponsible." Irvin Yalom's (1980) discussion sums up the existential therapist's position:

> Responsibility means authorship. To be aware of responsibility is to be aware of creating one's own self, destiny, life predicament, feelings, and if such be the case, one's own suffering. For the patient who will not accept such responsibility, no real therapy is possible. (p. 218)

Reality Therapy

William Glasser's (1965) reality therapy was in some ways similar to existential therapy. Although he has made major modifications in his theory in recent years (see Glasser, 1984), his early ideas have considerable relevance for the topic of responsibility. Glasser defined responsibility as the ability to fulfill one's needs and to do so in a way that does not deprive others of the ability to fulfill theirs. This presupposes the making of conscious choices that the existential therapists stressed. Glasser, however, felt that clients who are badly demoralized (or, in his terms, have a failure identity) cannot learn this responsible decision-making process without the active involvement of a responsible role model. Reality therapy, then, stated explicitly that the therapist must be responsible for himself or herself—as a personal life style, not as a mantle put on for an hour a week. Reality therapy also defined what the basic human needs are (the assumption is that when we need something, we are likely to value it, which translates in existential terms to discovering what has meaning for us). According to reality therapy, all of us have two basic needs: to love and be loved and to feel worthwhile. The job of the reality therapist is to help the client learn to take responsibility for getting those needs met.

Although Glasser did not spell this out at length, learning how to love others and accept love in return is no small task for many clients. If he was right that the need for interpersonal contact and affirmation is innate but that one's ability to get that need fulfilled is a learned process, then we believe it follows that much therapeutic work should often focus on intimacy skills. As Fromm (1956), Bowlby (1980), and others have pointed out, the simple forming of attachments is a fairly primitive process, but learning how to create and maintain those bonds in mature, fulfilling relationships is much more complex. Narcissism must be transcended enough to allow for empathic responsiveness; giving ourselves must become a creative, rewarding act, distinguished from depleting ourselves; we must be able to allow vulnerability in ourselves in order to be able to fully receive; and we must know how to protect and assert ourselves when necessary rather than acquiesce or dominate.

Unfortunately, many clients have no idea that these are learned skills that are usually gained with struggle and determination, and hope instead that nourishing relationships will just "happen." For clients to take responsibility for getting their needs met to love and be loved, they must be willing to examine and probably change some of their behavior and attitudes. Similarly, the reality therapist's goal of helping clients learn to assume responsibility for feeling worthwhile was also more difficult than it might appear. As Glasser (1972) pointed out, we cannot respect ourselves until we behave in ways that deserve respect. The client with a "failure identity" is one who expects failure and in fact often courts it. In reality therapy, he or she must be confronted over and over with the "reality" that certain behaviors sabotage the possibility of attaining important goals and that different behavioral choices would be more successful.

Gestalt Therapy

Gestalt therapy's approach to responsibility is to break it down to "response-ability: the ability to respond, to have thoughts, reactions, emotions in a given situation" (Perls, 1969, p. 65). Being able to respond honestly is possible, according to Perls, only when we relinquish our defenses and allow ourselves to become aware of our true feelings and motivations, however inconsistent they may appear. Before we can take responsibility for ourselves, we must first make contact with and "own" all of our discrepant parts. The ideally responsible person, from the Gestalt therapy perspective, is one who does not defend against his or her awareness of feelings and sensations and in fact welcomes them, one who can see others clearly and realistically without projecting disowned parts of the self onto them, and one who is self-supporting enough to risk the rejection of others by refusing to automatically acquiesce to their expectations. One's sense of identity comes from one's awareness of and experiences of one's self, rather than from others' feedback. What is hinted here is an extreme portrait of the rugged individualist, strong and courageous and self-supporting, capable of making independent decisions in the face of others' expectations. The other side of this concept of total self-responsibility is the concurrent Gestalt insistence that we are not responsible for others. They, like us, must learn to become aware of and trust in themselves, and we do them no favors if we try to protect them from reality and take responsibility for making their decisions. The assumption is that each of us is equally strong, at least potentially, and that each must rely primarily on herself or himself. Perls's I-do-my-thing-and-you-do-your-thing "prayer" captures this spirit and is given as a directive for productive relationships. Needing or depending on someone else is thus seen as being suspiciously close to being irresponsible.

The role of the Gestalt therapist is to aid clients in working through their defensive impasses by facilitating their awareness of their ongoing feelings and sensations. Therapeutic work is in the "here and now," with the assumption that increased awareness will lead to more responsible behavioral choices.

Responsibility, Newly Defined

To underscore some of the key components of responsibility, then, as derived from our overview of these three therapeutic systems: (a) Each of us is ultimately responsible for making his or her own decisions. No one, including a therapist, can "rescue" another from that. (b) Awareness of what one wants is crucial. Responsibility can then be taken for living one's life in a way that is most likely to achieve those goals. (c) Awareness of external reality is also crucial. We must give up our defenses of denial, avoidance, projection, and so forth, so that we may see others and our environment as realistically as possible. (d) We are as responsible for what we don't do as for what we do. Passivity and helplessness are no excuse. If we want something to be different, we must actively work for it to happen. If you find one or more of the three approaches particularly relevant to your own experiences and ways of thinking, we encourage you to read more widely from the original works. Our brief summary obviously cannot begin to do justice to the complexity of the theories. Let us turn now to a transtheoretical definition of responsibility.

Drawing from these other definitions, we will define responsibility as "the ability to be aware of one's own needs and those of relevant others, and the willingness to make proactive behavioral choices in accordance with that awareness." First, we want to underscore some of the points in this definition, after which we will examine some of the implications this definition might have for your work with clients.

One of the benefits of using this definition of responsibility is that it avoids the assumption that acceptance of complete individuation or isolation is the healthy approach to life. Multicultural and feminist psychologists have argued persuasively that many cultures and many women do not view themselves outside of the context of their relationships, nor should they be forced to. Guisinger & Blatt (1994) have continued this line of thinking in their proposal that self development and interpersonal relatedness are both reciprocal and dialectical, with greater development in each sphere made possible by concomitant development in the other. It is within this context that we discuss responsibility.

Ability to Be Aware

As indicated by the choice of words, this definition emphasizes awareness as an *ability*, a learned process, that involves a committed refusal to be controlled by one's defenses. Defenses, as Freud indicated, are presumably in place to defend the ego against assault. Defenses are great coping devices; they allow us to continue to feel intact when our own motivations or external situations appear to be quite threatening. In some extreme situations (e.g., overwhelming loss, life-threatening catastrophes, etc.), strong defenses are clearly necessary, at least until individuals have time to get their psychological feet back under them. But in most of our everyday activities, defensiveness is antithetical to self-awareness, and giving way to the desire to defensively distort reality costs us much more than we gain. There is perhaps some truth to the saying: "You shall know the truth, and the truth shall make you free—but first it shall make you very uncomfortable."

When we tell ourselves that our boss is crazy about us, even though we were just passed up for the third time for a promotion, when we insist to ourselves that we very much want to maintain a relationship although we give it less and less time, when we nurse our resentment of others and refuse to examine how the disowned parts of ourselves are remarkably similar to their most irritating qualities—when we engage in these forms of self-deception, we make it impossible for much change to occur. Learning to "catch ourselves in the act" of being defensive (there are often idiosyncratic kinesthetic signals to the sudden rigidity of defensiveness such as tightened jaw muscles and closed body posture) and then stopping ourselves to examine the possible underlying feelings is a process we can practice, although never fully master.

If I tell you your hair is red when in fact it is black, you are likely to deny the allegation fairly matter-of-factly (and maybe also with amazed amusement), but unless the color of hair carries some symbolic meaning for you, you will probably not get very defensive in your denial. If, on the other hand, I tell you the person you are falling in love with also elicits feelings of resentment and fear from you, you are likely to protest vigorously, especially if you have a variety of hopes already tied up in the relationship. That immediate protest, as opposed to the previous calm denial, is the hallmark of defensiveness. Clients who come to believe, however, that self-awareness is a stronger ally than defensiveness, may be willing to pause and ask themselves, "Could it be true? Have I ever had even an inkling that this could be?" Often what clients find is that, underneath the defensiveness, there is some basis of truth to the charge they wanted so badly to deny, but that admitting the truth—or more likely, the partial truth—is not nearly as devastating as they had feared.

Why is it then that so many clients have a phobic response to self-awareness? There are different reasons, of course. Some clients are afraid of discovering feelings that will contaminate their self-image. Often that self-image has strong family or cultural reinforcers in its roots, and admitting to certain feelings may seem tantamount to jeopardizing one's position in the family/culture/gender. Other clients may be afraid that if they admit to an unwanted motivation, it will give it more power and permanence. Still others fear—perhaps with cause—that if they become aware of new things within them they will be called upon to make new changes, to disturb the status quo. And most frighteningly, some are reluctant to explore their deeper feelings because they sense a hollowness within themselves and fear that if they explore very deeply they will find nothing at all.

Exploring and owning one's feelings, of course, are just the first steps. In time, themes of meaning begin to emerge, and finally some of the core needs that make up one's identity can be inferred. This kind of in-depth awareness of one's needs is close to what many therapists are hoping clients can attain in the process of learning to take responsibility for how they lead their lives.

Needs

The word "needs" in this definition merits some discussion. What clients *want* is often immediate gratification and an end to trouble. We see nothing wrong or evil with this. We want that, too! But sometimes, pursuing what we want forestalls our getting what we need. In the country-western song entitled, "The Whiskey Ain't Workin' Anymore" a rejected lover looks for comfort in whiskey, or when that doesn't work, in a honky-tonk angel. While many therapists would agree that as a short-term solution those might provide some limited comfort, in the long term they are is not likely to work so well. A psychologist sitting at the bar might suggest that what the fellow really *needed* for his life to improve, is help with his grief process, better relationship skills, and probably some confrontation to work through sexist attitudes. While we feel safe in asserting that such a perspective would probably not be welcomed by the gentleman in question, the psychological perspective distinguishing between wants and deeper needs has considerable validity.

Relevant Others

Let us return to the second part of our definition. Some situations that bring clients to therapy involve only the clients themselves. The student who seeks career counseling, the retired person looking for new interests, the assembly-line worker wanting advice on how to deal with sexual harassment can all probably make decisions that are in their best interests without giving too much thought to others' needs. But many decisions impact others, and the therapist will need to be sensitive to the clients' relevant others in helping them with their choices.

Being aware of relevant others' needs is a similar but more difficult challenge than being aware of one's own. Most people are fairly good at letting us know, either overtly or covertly, what they want from us. They interact with us in patterns that are designed (often unconsciously) to elicit certain reactions from us that complement their own expectations and behaviors, and we find ourselves expressing the nurturance or anger or detachment, or the like, that many others in their lives express. But, in a corollary to the previous discussion, what people indicate they want from us and what they really need are often two different things. As almost any parent can confirm, adolescents are prone to say that they want to make their own decisions with no parental interference, but what they usually need is continued guidance and limit setting (if of a different sort). Similarly, clients may insist that they want a mutual, perhaps sexual, relationship with their therapist, although considerable theory and research indicate that clients in fact need the reassurance of knowing that their therapist is nonseducible. Understanding what someone else needs, as opposed to wants, requires that we be able to keep from automatically reacting to his or her expectations and instead let ourselves respond to the whole three-dimensional human being before us—to the strengths as well as the weaknesses, to the hopes and fears and dreams, to her or his future development as well as to the present person. If in interacting with others we ask ourselves, "How can I best respond, so that their maximum potential can be tapped and facilitated?" then we are likely to be close to responding to their needs rather than to expectations or roles.

Once we know what we need and have at least a tentative guess about the needs of the other person(s) involved, then the challenge becomes one of orchestrating our behavior so that our choices are an attempt to meet both sets of needs. The more flexible we can be in terms of seeing that needs can often be met in several ways (as opposed to the assumption that there is a fixed, one-to-one ratio between what we need and how we must act), the more likely we will be able to behave in responsible ways that are fulfilling for both of us.

Imagine the following scenario: A married couple, Maria and Rafael, come to you for counseling. As they begin to tell their story, they both affirm that they love each other very much but seem to be consistently angry with each other. At some point, you ask them how they have shown their love for each other in the past week, and Rafael says, "Well, I took her dancing last Friday," and Maria says, "Last night when we were over at his mother's house, instead of watching the game on TV I spent the whole evening in the kitchen helping his mother." They look at each other for a moment, and then Maria blurts out, "But I don't need you to take me dancing! We went dancing the week before! What I need is for you to listen to me the way you used to!" And Rafael says, "Honey, thanks for helping my mother, but what I really wanted you to do for me last night was to have a beer with me and relax in front of the TV and let my mother look after the kids." What becomes increasingly clear over time is that their desire to show love and affirmation of each other is genuine, but they are locked into preconceived ideas of the specific ways that affirmation should be demonstrated. When they can begin to listen more deeply to each other and also increase their behavioral flexibility, it is likely that they will disappoint each other far less often. The challenge of trying to understand and meet each other's needs in ways that are consonant with their own becomes much less formidable if they can each stay open to a variety of optional responses. Once the concept of orchestrating themselves to meet both people's needs is internalized, the challenge of working out the specifics can be stimulating and fun. In this way then, they can find ways to be responsible to themselves within the context of the relationship.

Proactivity

We must be willing to act, to consider our options and then take decisive action, rather than to wait passively for circumstances finally to force us into reacting. If we are aware of our needs and goals in life, they can provide a magnet which gives direction and meaning to the taking of calculated risks. It may help to remind ourselves that "all important decisions must be made on the basis of insufficient data" (Kopp, 1975, p. 32). Knowing that there are no guarantees that our risk-taking behaviors will be successful, we nonetheless make the choices that seem most likely to meet our own and others' needs.

Proactivity, then, is the major mechanism for giving ourselves some control over our lives. It is by behaving proactively that we are most able to control our destinies, to invite life to meet our needs by having first made self-affirming choices. The opposite of proactivity—passivity—tends to elicit predictable negative consequences. When we are unable or unwilling to throw the weight of our actions on the possibility of fulfilling our own needs, but instead simply sit and wait for things to improve, we set ourselves up for victimization. In its extreme forms, such passivity is evidenced by fear, paranoia, learned helplessness, and massive projection of responsibility.

A couple of final words about our definition. First, options that seem obvious to the therapist often do not seem viable to the client. Sometimes this is because of fear of trying something new, but it may also be because what seems obvious to us might not fit with the context the client must live in. We need to be wary in assuming that choices are equally possible for everyone. Secondly, the concept of "choices" implies the ability to renounce some alternatives. While it is true that frequently in life clients can find ways to compromise or negotiate enough to at least partially have two seemingly incompatible things, some avenues truly are mutually exclusive. Renunciation is always painful—occasionally so difficult that staying in limbo indefinitely seems preferable to the anguish of truly choosing one course and renouncing the other—but unfortunately life sometimes does involve saying yes to one thing and no to another. Allen Wheelis (1956) said it well:

> Some people sit at the crossroads, taking neither path because they cannot take both, cherishing the illusion that if they sit there long enough the two ways will resolve themselves into one and hence both be possible. A large part of maturity and courage is the ability to make such renunciations, and a large part of wisdom is the ability to find ways which will enable one to renounce as little as possible.

Therapeutic Distinctions

In this next section, we will discuss some distinctions that many therapists find useful in working with clients. In our discussion, we will imply or suggest outright that clients might be helped by "learning" certain things. We mean "learn" here not in the sense of accepting a logical explanation and perhaps being able to repeat it later—say, as in high school one memorized the factors leading to the Civil War. Nor are we referring simply to cognitive restructuring. We use the term "learn" heuristically to imply a new, richer understanding of one's self and one's relation to the rest of the world, a different stance to reality. In this respect, learning is a cumulative process that allows for new creative approaches to old problems.

Something shifts deep inside the client that gives him or her a feeling of increased lightness and flexibility. Instead of being locked tightly into their former perceptions and assumptions, they see new possibilities. They begin to ask themselves, "Why not?" Your role in "teaching" them is less to offer explanations—although that may occasionally be a well-timed part of the process—than to provide an atmosphere in which your clients can discover new learnings. As Glasser (1965) indicated, people learn to be responsible primarily through interacting with responsible adults, so it is important that you take your role as their "model" seriously. Learning, in therapy as elsewhere, often takes place at an unconscious and nonverbal level.

Responsibility *for* versus Responsibility *to*

Although this is a somewhat overused and simplistic distinction, clients who are unfamiliar with it may find it freeing. When we feel responsible for others, we are likely to see them as an extension of ourselves. Thus, a mother who feels responsible for her six-year-old's rudeness will probably feel anger, humiliation, and embarrassment. She is blaming him for being rude, but also herself for not having taught him to be more polite. If you ask her what her fantasies are, she is likely to say that she fears that others observing her son's behavior are thinking something like, "Oh, dear. Why hasn't that child's mother taught him how to behave?" If instead of feeling responsible for him, however, she felt responsible *to* him, she would probably feel more concern than embarrassment and would ask herself what experience she could provide that would encourage her son to be more sensitive to others' feelings. The focus would switch then from blame and punishment to a more constructive problem-solving mode.

This distinction between for and to can be a powerful one for someone who hears it for the first time, and the magic of it is not just semantic. In the example, the mother is not in full control of her son's behavior, so it is theoretically unrealistic for her to feel full responsibility. At best, she can influence him to behave in certain ways. Feeling responsibility enough to him that she uses her influence wisely is a much more realistic expectation of herself. Of course, the issue gets clouded because she may indeed be held legally responsible for his behavior, and observers may actually feel judgmental not only of her son, but of her too. Nonetheless, she will probably be more effective in changing her son's behavior if she can adopt in large part this "responsible to" attitude. As a general rule, as individuals become chronologically and psychologically more adult, it is reasonable for us to feel less and less responsible *for* their behavior and happiness and more responsible *to* them so that ideally, with equals, we identify with them very little and see them as essentially responsible for their own choices. For example, the alcoholic's husband, with this ideal attitude, would feel little embarrassment or protectiveness for his wife's irresponsible behavior and would not feel obligated either to nag at her to change or to "cover" for her alcoholism with her acquaintances. He would ask himself what he could do in order to be responsible to her, and he would refuse to shield her from the consequences of her behavior.

Responsibility versus Obligation

If you ask people off the street what their "responsibility" is, they will probably recount a lengthy list of obligations. They are responsible for going to their job, for rearing their children, for taking out the trash every second day, and so on. From many of them, you will get the impression that they simply go through the dreary motions of performing these endless obligations, and the only joy in their lives is a vague sense of virtue for having done what was "right." From others, you may get the feeling that they are driven by an anxious compulsion to meet another's expectations and demands and accordingly feel intense guilt for being "irresponsible" if they are unable or unwilling to comply. It is almost as if both of these groups are still children, trying hard to please a demanding parent so that they can "earn" approval or love. This kind of empty or compulsive acquiescence to someone else's perceived demands is a long way from Perls's concept of response-ability. In contrast to a full, conscious choice that one's identity will be enhanced by responding to one's own or another's real need, automatic compliance smacks of subservience or cowardice. One is afraid *not* to comply, and hopes to forestall possible abandonment or punishment by acquiescing. In short, this act of "responsibility" is made from a position of weakness, not strength. Trying to earn love by always doing what someone else demands or expects is futile. For one thing, love cannot be earned. But even if it could be, what is one supposed to do when two significant others make conflicting demands at the same time? In therapy, such compulsive pleasers need help in becoming more fully self-affirming so that risking another's disapproval is less terrifying. One part of this process may be aiding them in coping with their guilt at saying no; helping them to distinguish between a loved one's superficial demands and deeper needs can be another important step.

Responsibility versus Selfishness

A related misunderstanding is the assumption that accepting responsibility for trying to get one's own needs met somehow makes one "selfish." For someone who has been socialized, or may have even consciously chosen, to put oneself in a nurturing, care-taking role, even considering acting in one's own best interest can feel foreign or evil. Much meaning has been derived from actively giving to others (as opposed to the previous section, which described one's giving out of obligation), and it can be very difficult to entertain the idea that one's own needs are also valid. Women may be especially immersed in this self-sacrificial attitude and often appear genuinely bewildered that their efforts are unappreciated or exploited by others (e.g., Lemkau and Landau, 1986). Why, they wonder, do others take for granted what is given and often give so little back? If you suggest that they might need to clarify what they need and actually ask for it, they tend to become acutely uncomfortable. That would make them selfish! They are caught in the bind of wanting others to validate needs about which they themselves are ambivalent.

Contrary to Norwood's (1985) belief, we feel that the issue here is not that clients give or love too much. The problem is that they are not sure that they deserve to receive. Because they cannot truly affirm their own needs, they put themselves in a position where those needs can be ignored or exploited. As you work with them in therapy to begin the process of self-affirmation, what typically emerges is their fear that the pendulum will swing too far and that if they validate their own needs they might turn into selfish monsters. Such clients need help in understanding that their operating position does not have to swing from "you, not me" to "me, not you." A third possibility—"me *and* you"—is available to them if they can expand their awareness and responsiveness to include others' needs as well as their own. They must eventually believe that their needs to receive in reciprocal relationships are valid and in fact can contribute to deeper, richer interactions with others (Davenport, 1982).

One way to begin this change in attitudinal sets is to suggest that clients have two major responsibilities in healthy relationships—responsibilities to give and responsibilities to receive. Learning how to affirm their own needs and receive from others is not a luxury; it is a requirement if they hope to have mature, fulfilling relationships. Refusing to validate and assert their needs often has at least three negative consequences: (a) Their anger at being discounted builds, frequently leaking out in destructive ways or perhaps increasing to explosive proportions that can eventually destroy the relationship. (b) Their own self-respect suffers, since at some level they realize they are partners in the conspiracy to deny their own needs. (c) Significant others in their lives are placed in the position of having to guess what the client needs or, as one husband said, "playing twenty questions in the dark." This can get wearisome very quickly, and the client's self-denial can be perceived by others as less virtuous than manipulative. At its core, self-denial is in fact often self-protective and manipulative. It is almost always a shield from rejection. Eventually, most clients usually acknowledge that they know what they need but are afraid of asking and being refused. It feels safer, at least in the short run, not to ask. Besides, they may believe, as one woman told her therapist, "If I don't ask for very much, then when I do ask for something, I deserve to get it!"

Self-Responsibility versus Control

At the other end of the continuum is the client who is psychologically sophisticated, skilled in interpersonal techniques, and sensitive to the cues of others. "Jim" comes to you because in spite of all he has learned about relationships, he is beginning to feel desperate at 35 because he would like to be married. He wants to know what he is doing wrong so he can take responsibility for himself and fix it. As you listen to Jim explain what he does and how he thinks in regard to women, you are at first impressed with his openness to feedback and his willingness to change. Here is a client to make up for the passive, resistant ones with whom you work! Gradually, however, you begin to get suspicious that somehow he is trying too hard. Although his communication skills are excellent and his openness is genuine, he seems to operate from the assumption that if he just learns enough he can be *in control* and will then find the perfect mate for whom he longs. In the meantime, his single-minded determination seems to be frightening off the women he dates. Jim is having difficulty distinguishing between taking responsibility for himself and trying to control others. His willingness to examine his own behavior and change it is admirable, but it is not enough. He must also accept his ultimate powerlessness to build a relationship unilaterally. All the interpersonal skills in the world will not compensate for his dates' lack of motivation, immaturity, or disinterest in marriage.

One of the perils in learning self-responsibility is that clients can get a lopsided view of the world and may forget that others have the right to say no to them. An important distinction for such clients, alluded to earlier in this chapter, is the difference between control and influence. We are rarely in full control, especially of other people; taking responsibility for ourselves affords no guarantees that others will respond as we want them to. If we are willing, however, to settle for *influencing* others and can give up our illusion of control, it will be easier for us to direct our efforts into responding spontaneously to the cues we pick up in the moment from ourselves and from those with whom we are interacting. When Jim can begin to see and appreciate his dates as complete, full individuals rather than as "potential wife" objects, then he will be better able to ascertain what the two of them might be capable of creating together in the way of a relationship.

A related confusion between responsibility and control is sometimes seen in clients who are extraordinarily self-disciplined. Well-trained athletes, for example, are accustomed to demanding a great deal from themselves both physically and psychologically. In return, they are rewarded for this self-discipline by seeing their performance improve and by receiving honors and acclaim from others. The line between feeling responsible to their bodies and believing that they can control their bodies may grow dim, and their self-esteem may plummet when their bodies no longer function as well because of aging or illness. It may be very difficult for them to accept that they no longer have the same power to make their bodies "obey" them, particularly when they are bombarded by well-intentioned holistic health messages that imply that poor health might have been avoided if they had taken the right combination of vitamins, minerals, and herbs, found the perfect diet, exercised in just the right way, practiced meditation faithfully, and so on. Such clients may need help discovering what they can control and what they can't. Eventually they, like the rest of us, need to understand that aging and death are not punishments for poor self control, nor are they something one can choose to defer indefinitely. People age and get sick even if they don't smoke, always watch what they eat, and get regular checkups.

Self-Responsibility versus Self-Blame

A final similar distinction that clients may benefit from learning is that accepting responsibility for their behavior is not the same as indulging in heavy self-blame. As clients become more aware of how their present behavior sabotages their attainment of present goals, they may go through a period of examining past choices and blaming themselves for having contributed to their own unhappiness.

A certain amount of regret for one's past self-destructive behavior is appropriate. Some guilt, too, for the harm that one has caused others may be a necessary component of developing increased self-awareness and self-responsibility. But an inordinate and continued pattern of blaming oneself can easily become self-indulgent and frequently makes it more difficult to assume responsibility for making present changes in one's life. If possible, learning self-responsible ways of behaving should be accompanied by learning to treat one's self with the same kind of compassion one would ideally try to offer others.

The alcoholic who looks back over the last 20 years and sees the damage she caused her family, the father playing with children in the yard who looked away for just the instant it took for his three-year-old to dart into the street and get hit by a car, the daughter crying at the father's funeral because she hadn't told him she loved him—all of these people, in order to go on with their lives, must eventually move beyond total remorse over their past behavior to a more balanced perspective of their "true" responsibility in the situation. From there they may find at least partial self-forgiveness and a commitment to living out their futures in a way that indicates they have learned from their past experiences.

Often, as Yalom (1980) points out, a part of this process involves separating one's neurotic guilt (emanating from imagined transgressions) from one's real guilt (which flows from an actual transgression against another) and then possibly attempting to make reparation for the actual damage caused. This reparation may be a concrete act or gift for the person harmed, or it may be a symbolic way of making amends. What is important is that such an act allows the person to accept and experience herself or himself as qualitatively different than the previously perceived irresponsible "guilty" self. The client is thus more fully freed from the past and can better respond to present and future potentialities.

Therapeutic Considerations

In working with clients who are not "responsible," several considerations may be helpful.

Signals of Irresponsibility

First, it is important to be able to recognize those client attitudes and behaviors that signal an unwillingness or inability to accept responsibility. Some of these are obvious, but others are subtle enough to lead even quite experienced therapists off the track.

Helplessness.   The client who seems truly desperate and afraid of taking any action at all is likely to hook our rescuer tendencies. If the situation is truly critical (e.g., the client has just been raped, received devastating news, etc.), it may be necessary for the therapist or other outsider to be fairly directive and assume a certain amount of supportive responsibility that would ordinarily be the client's. The goal, however, should be for the client to reassume responsibility as quickly as possible for making as many decisions as he or she can. Clients who go from crisis to crisis or who have adopted a helpless lifestyle may at times elicit our annoyance rather than our sympathy, but they too need us to believe in and call forth the potential potency that lies beneath their helplessness.

Confusion.   A related symptom of unwillingness to take responsibility is exhibited by the client who regularly gets "confused" when a certain issue is addressed. She or he may be otherwise quite articulate and expressive but feel suddenly blocked or bewildered when asked questions about specific relevant areas. It is important for beginning therapists to keep in mind that clients are rarely deliberately evasive in order to spite their therapists. Rather, confusion is a defense employed presumably because the material feels too dangerous to the client to be explored. Stepping back a pace to try to understand with the client what is so potentially threatening about the topic is usually more effective than a frontal assault on the resistance.

Displacement of Responsibility.   Clients often wait, sometimes in subtle, barely perceivable ways, for their therapists or some other authority figure to make their important decisions for them. The responsibilities of making crucial decisions, especially ones that involve renunciation, may seem too burdensome or fearful for them to accept. While it is appropriate with such clients to be wary of being led into taking too much responsibility, beginning therapists may err in the other direction and disengage emotionally or react punitively whenever they sense client dependency. Clients who tend to displace responsibility for themselves onto others certainly need well-timed confrontation, but they also benefit from supportive exploration of their options. The client who asks, "What should I do?" may be helped by a response such as, "That depends on what you want to accomplish. What is your goal?" The therapist's role here is to help the client clarify his or her needs and then to facilitate the development of an appropriate plan of action that is consistent with the client's values.

Compulsive Action.   Although decisive activity is often equated with the assumption of responsibility, it may at times signal the opposite. "Burying oneself in work" is a common enough phenomenon that nonprofessionals are aware of it and understand that it is usually an attempt to avoid experiencing painful feelings. The therapist working with a compulsively active client will probably need to make a clinical assessment regarding the client's ego strength and ability to face whatever it is that is being avoided. Returning to our definition of "responsibility," until clients are aware of the avoided feelings, little progress can be made in assuming greater self-responsibility. Letting these negative feelings—usually shame, fear, or anger—into their awareness, however, will likely require trust in their therapists' support, as well as confidence in their own abilities to maintain their equilibrium.

Client Change

A second consideration in working with clients lacking a strong sense of self-responsibility is that lectures and demands rarely work. As tempting as it may be to simply exhort, "Get a grip! Be more responsible!" these parental statements of exasperation/encouragement tend to be more therapeutic for the therapist than the client. The actual process of client assumption of responsibility is likely to be sporadic, slow, and ongoing. Clients usually change because they become less afraid to. For most clients, this requires a strong and supportive alliance with their therapist that will allow the examination of fears and assumptions that are currently hindering their development, the gradual replacement of these old dysfunctional ways of thinking and feeling with healthier ones, and increased confidence and ability to tolerate failures as they begin to acquire new skills to add to their repertoire. They change, not because someone tells them to, but because it now makes more sense to them experientially. They change because they have interacted with a therapist whose ways of thinking and making decisions—at both a personal and professional level—have provided a firsthand model of how to be responsible for oneself. As one client told his counselor, "You know, you leak out around the edges. It's not so much what you say, it's who you are that I listen to."

Acceptance of Ambiguity

In spite of the distinctions made earlier, responsibility is a concept fraught with ambiguity. There will be many, many situations in therapy when it will be impossible for you or the client to have a clean, clear understanding of exactly what that client's responsibility to himself or herself should be. Exactly when should parents feel less responsible for their children's attitudes and behaviors? Is one as responsible for the effects of one's behavior on another as for the underlying intent? How much does a client's physical deterioration affect the amount of responsibility that the client should feel for his or her psychological stability? For that matter, in what ways and for how long is a therapist responsible for or to a given client? These questions, and many other similar ones, raise issues that clients and therapists struggle with continually. Certainly, therapists should not fall into the trap of having to manufacture simple solutions just to make the client feel more comfortable. It is the very act of struggling with such questions that helps clients clarify their goals and values. Their eventual choices have more meaning exactly because they have struggled. The challenge for therapists should not be to understand perfectly, but instead to help the client in his or her own attempts to find tentative answers. Omniscience is not a requirement for therapists; the willingness to struggle with ambiguity is.

Summary

Encouraging clients to assume appropriate responsibility for their lives is one of the generally accepted metagoals of psychotherapy. In this chapter we reviewed the concept of responsibility from three theoretical perspectives, and discussed treatment implications of defining responsibility in a particular way. Being able to help clients delineate responsibility from other less desirable processes can often be quite liberating for clients who have misunderstood what responsibility actually entails. The therapist's own understanding, and her or his ability to serve as a responsible model, are crucial if consistent messages are to be communicated. As with other aspects of therapy, it is often who the therapist is, as much as what he or she says, that conveys the message.

DISCUSSION QUESTIONS

- What are your views on using forms of psychological disturbance as a legal defense against legal penalties? Are "mentally ill" people less responsible for the consequences of their actions?

- Brickman and his associates (1982) suggested that therapists consider whether any individual client is (a) the cause of the problem, and (b) responsible for the solution for the problem. Under which client circumstances might either one, both, or neither, be your assessment?

- Might the definition of responsibility used here need to be modified with clients from very different cultures? Can clients remain loyal to a culture that values hierarchical roles and still be proactively responsible?

BIBLIOGRAPHY

Atkinson, D. R., Worthington, R. L., Dana, D. M., & Good, G. E. (1991). Etiology beliefs, preferences for counseling orientations, and counseling effectiveness. *Journal of Counseling Psychology, 38,* 258–264.

Bandura, A. (1997). *Self-efficacy: The exercise of control.* New York: Freeman.

Bauer, G. P., & Kobos, J. C. (1987). *Brief therapy: A short term psychodynamic intervention.* Northvale, NJ: Aronson.

Bowlby, J. (1980). *Attachment and loss: Vol. 3, Loss: Sadness and depression.* London: Routledge.

Branden, N. (1994). *The six pillars of self-esteem.* New York: Bantam.

Brickman, P., Rabinowitz, V. C., Karuzan, J., Coates, D., Cohn, E., & Kidder, L. (1982). Models of helping and coping. *American Psychologist, 37,* 368–384.

Davenport, D. S. (1982). Women—and the daimonic. *The Counseling Psychologist, 10*(3), 76–78.

Fromm, E. (1956). *The art of loving.* New York: Harper & Row.

Glasser, W. (1965). *Reality therapy: A new approach to psychiatry.* New York: Harper & Row.

Glasser, W. (1972). *The identity society.* New York: Harper & Row.

Glasser, W. (1984). *Control theory: A new explanation of how we control our lives.* New York: Harper & Row.

Guisinger, S., & Blatt, S. J. (1994). Individuality and relatedness. *American Psychologist, 49,* 104–111.

Harcum, E. R. (1989). Commitment to collaboration as a prerequisite for existential commonality in psychotherapy. *Psychotherapy, 26,* 200–209.

Higgins, R. L. & Berglas, S. (Eds.). (1990). *Self-handicapping: The paradox that isn't.* New York: Plenum.

Kleinke, C. (1994). *Common principles of psychotherapy.* Pacific Grove, CA: Brooks/Cole.

Kopp, S. (1975). *No hidden meanings.* Palo Alto: Science and Behavior Books.

Lemkau, J., & Landau, C. (1986). The selfless syndrome: Assessment and treatment considerations. *Psychotherapy, 23,* 243–249.

May, R. (1983). *The discovery of being.* New York: W. W. Norton.

Murdock, N. L., & Fremont, S. K. (1989). Attributional influences in counselor decision making. *Journal of Counseling Psychology, 36,* 549–559.

Norwood, R. (1985). *Women who love too much.* New York: Pocket Books.

Overholser, J. C. (1996). Elements of the Socratic method: V. self-improvement. *Psychotherapy, 33,* 549–559.

Perls, F. (1969). *Gestalt therapy verbatim.* Lafayette, CA: Real People Press.

Rosenbaum, M. (1993). The three functions of self-control behavior: Redressing, reformative, and experiential. *Work and Stress, 7,* 33–46.

Schlenker, B. R., Weigold, M. F., & Doherty, K. (1991). Coping with accountability: Self-identification and evaluative reckonings. In C. R. Snyder and D. R. Forsythe (Eds.), *Handbook of Social and Clinical Psychology* (pp. 96–115). New York: Pergamon.

Viorst, J. (1996). *Necessary losses.* New York: Ballantine.

Viorst, J. (1998). *Imperfect control.* New York: Ballantine.

Wheelis, A. (1956). Will and psychoanalysis. *Journal of the Psychoanalytic Association, 4,* 285–303.

Worthington, R. L., & Atkinson, D. R. (1993). Counselors' responsibility and etiology attributions, theoretical orientations, and counseling strategies. *Journal of Counseling Psychology, 40,* 295–302.

Yalom, I. (1980). *Existential psychotherapy.* New York: Basic Books.

Zimmerman, B. J. (1989). A social cognitive view of self-regulated academic learning. *Journal of Educational Psychology, 81,* 329–339.

CHAPTER

15 Relationships

We are all of us calling and calling across the incalculable gulfs which separate us...

—David Grayson

To love...is to be vulnerable. Love anything and your heart will certainly be wrung and possibly broken. If you want to make certain of keeping it intact...lock it up safe in the casket or coffin of your [self]. But in that casket—safe, dark, motionless, airless—it will change. It will not be broken; it will become unbreakable, impenetrable, irredeemable.

—C. S. Lewis

Sullivan (1954) suggested that all client problems stem from relationship issues. While we think that position is debatable, we do agree that for many clients such issues tend to be their central focus. Psychologists certainly see individuals suffering from simple phobias, problems with physical pain, panic attacks, and a few other concerns that do not seem to fit that pattern (although arguably they partially originate from intrapsychic relationships), but in general depression, anxiety, and the like, have an interpersonal aspect to them. In this chapter we will try to synthesize the knowledge and approaches that psychologists can draw on to inform their therapy. If you have not already begun, we strongly urge you to begin familiarizing yourself with this body of literature. The more you know about typical interpersonal dynamics and psychodynamic, cognitive, and skills-based interventions, the better position you will be in to offer therapeutic interventions to clients from a wide range of backgrounds and agendas. Other kinds of writing—biographies, memoirs, therapists' writing about their work, fiction—especially when it is about individuals from different cultures or in situations very different from your own, provide a rich context for understanding human relationships. In the meantime, we hope that this chapter, and some of the information in Chapter 10, Multicultural Counseling, will be of help to you as you try to conceptualize client difficulties and the appropriate counseling approach(es) to pursue.

Basic Assumptions about Relationships

There are a few underlying assumptions about relationships to which therapists from a variety of orientations adhere, less out of theoretical loyalties than because they seem to be substantiated in their clinical work. As in other chapters, we offer a partial summary of these assumptions here, not as a group of constructs with an absolutely pure theoretical base and certainly not as a comprehensive analysis of all important views on the subject, but as a starting point for your own thinking. We encourage you to add to or modify the ideas we will summarize here, and to be willing to challenge your theoretical biases as your clinical experience increases.

Importance of Early Experiences

Freud, of course, was especially adamant that childhood experiences affect adult behavior in profound, pervasive ways. As you probably know, there is considerable disagreement regarding his emphasis on several crucial issues, including his views on childhood sexuality, his insistence on the importance of very early experiences (to the exclusion of later ones), and the specifics of his stage theory. Nonetheless, many clinicians do accept his basic premise that many adult behaviors are rooted in childhood interpretations of events. The assumption here is that clients do not feel and behave the way they do arbitrarily; they respond to present events at least partially because of attitudes and responses developed at a much earlier age. In effect, life "taught" them to make certain assumptions and to react in specific ways, although much of this learning probably took place at an unconscious level. For more on this developmental perspective, you may want to focus your attention on writers coming from the object relations and self psychology approaches (e.g., Hamilton, 1988), those that write about brief psychodynamic therapy (e.g., Davanloo, 1990), and theory and research based on Bowlby's attachment model (e.g., Sable, 1997a), although some of the older books on Adler's theory offer interesting complementary perspectives.

Sable (1997b) and others have found consistent empirical confirmation for Bowlby's assertions that attachment style can be measured and that everyday details of parenting have lasting effects on personality. This area of research has undergone significant growth during the last decade and continues to provide insight into the origins of adult attachment styles. Terminology and classifications of styles have undergone slight variations as the theory has evolved. Sable (1997b) provides a summary of the research that designates styles, and she identifies secure, anxious/ambivalent (preoccupied), insistent self-reliance (avoidance), and disorganized (extreme avoidance). This body of research offers parallels to some of Millon's theories regarding underpinnings of personality disorders, but empirical study of the relationship between the two approaches has only begun (e.g., Fonagy, Target, Steele, Steele, Leigh, Levinson, & Kennedy, 1997).

Clarifying with the client what these patterns of beliefs/expectations/feelings/behaviors are can be helpful in the therapeutic process in at least two ways. First, it helps counteract the sense of shame and hopelessness that many clients feel at not being able to will themselves to change more quickly. Having some of their reactions understood and validated helps them feel less "crazy." Second, once some of these assumptions are clarified, conscious, responsible choices are more easily made by the client regarding how to begin the process of formulating major new perceptions and making appropriate behavioral changes.

A case example may be illustrative. One of the authors recently had an EAP referral for a 19-year-old man who said he wanted help with his drinking problem. When asked about his drinking behavior, "Larry" said that he drank two six-packs a night, more on weekends. Larry indicated that he couldn't remember when he'd started drinking. The first time he had intentionally gotten drunk, he thought, was right before his parents split up—when he was six. He said he'd heard stories of his mother putting beer in his bottle when she ran out of milk. His mother is an alcoholic, as are his maternal grandparents. There was quite a lot of evidence, in other words, to justify psychological intervention with substance abuse as a focus.

Larry indicated that the reason he was coming in for counseling now was because his girlfriend told him she wouldn't marry him if he didn't get help. This sounded somewhat promising; apparently he had a fairly level-headed person in his life. He said she had recently moved out, which had caused a problem because then he had no one to take care of his two children, aged 2 and 4, except his mother, who was unreliable. (He did say he made it a point not to give his children beer so they would go to sleep, even though he was tempted when he was tired.) His girlfriend's moving out had made getting to work, and even keeping this appointment difficult. Living with him now were his 19-year-old wife and her boyfriend. He said that now that his girlfriend was gone, he sometimes got jealous seeing his wife with someone else. Interesting arrangement! He wanted them gone so his girlfriend could move back in, hence the urgency in receiving counseling. Certainly it seemed as if his present relationships merited some attention.

Larry said that as a child he lived with his mother, who was "o.k., except when she was drunk." He indicated that she used to take him with her when she would go to a local pool hall to "hook," and that waiting in the car on winter nights had sometimes bothered him. He had a number of stepfathers and "uncles," he wasn't sure how many. When he was 12 he went to live with his dad and stepmother, but he said, with some bewilderment, that they had *rules* he was supposed to follow, so he had to leave. He moved back with his mother, got his present wife pregnant, and eventually dropped out of school to get married and support his family. He was currently driving trucks for a food deliverer, making $6 an hour.

Larry's situation is not as unusual as it sounds. Many clients coming for counseling, especially EAP and court referrals, have similar disturbed backgrounds. Knowing his background helped the therapist see how entwined were his drinking behavior (virtually the only stable, gratifying thing in his life) and his expectations for what relationships and life might offer. Long-term therapy was clearly not an option. But as the therapist worked from a more crisis–solution-focused approach, she was able to be empathic about his difficulties in making substantive changes from his past ways of understanding what life was all about. In addition to helping him extricate himself from the disarray his life was in, she was in a position to drop seeds such as, "Think about what you wish you could have had from your parents... (pause for answer). Can you do some of that for your own kids? What would that feel like?" and "Your girlfriend sounds like she wants a real different life from what your mom did. No hooking, no drinking, promises kept. It's gotta feel strange being around this woman who is so different and wants so much more. Do you think you want some of what she wants?"

Another brief example: A client, "Sarah," also seen by one of the authors, was a 20-year-old female depressed over the breakup with her boyfriend. After the crisis, she stayed in therapy to take a look at her assumptions and behavior patterns in romantic relationships. Two months into therapy, she came in very anxious, aware that in a new relationship she was falling back into an old pattern of possessiveness/petulance/anger. She was furious with herself. As we explored the origins of that constellation of feelings, she emotionally recounted a terrible time she had when she was 7 and her parents were divorcing. She said, "I still remember what it felt like—it was like being in a hurricane and everything was blowing and scary and loud and completely out of control and I remember thinking, 'If I can scream louder than all of this, I'll be back in control.'" At that time her parents saw a psychologist, who had the parents put her on a behavioral contingency plan to control her temper tantrums. This was internalized by her as something like, "act nice and don't make trouble, and whatever you do, ignore those feelings because they will just make you act bad again." So she had learned to control her panic by repressing it and focusing on utilizing "nice" instead of "bad" behavior.

"Sarah" was able to experientially identify the panic under the acting out and relate that to what had happened that morning with her new boyfriend. It gave her and her therapist a quick understanding of her current intrapsychic experience when she felt out of control, allowed both of us to empathize with the "part of her" that was scared but causing trouble with the behavioral patterns, and provided the basis for some tentative intrapsychic and interpersonal changes she could make the next time she felt like that.

There are two points that are important to remember. First, there is general agreement among clinicians that what shapes a person's belief system is less what happened to her or him than the sense the person made of the events. Our current state of knowledge does not provide a complete understanding for us of how it is that the same event early in life can have radically different impacts on different children. On the other hand, in spite of individual differences, we know that strongly negative events have a typical impact on children. That is, for children who are subjected to more and more negative events, it becomes increasingly unlikely that they will be left unaffected by these events. For example, overt abuse or negligence leave typical wounds on almost any child. It is important to remember that your work is not to judge the accuracy or morality of the client's story nor to decide whether an event should or should not have affected the client but to help him or her understand the impact it did have and continues to have on present patterns.

Second, the deeper, more pervasive and unconscious the beliefs, the longer it will take the client to change them. This "working through" process is addressed in part through "therapeutic repetition" and in part through focus on affect. We mention it here to remind you that consistent compassionate patience is an important part of what you offer in therapy. In doing short-term therapy, one thing you can do is provide interventions that, in addition to helping with the current situation, will also lend themselves to possibly "seeping down" after the client terminates.

Implications of Persistent Patterns

A usual assumption that therapists make, and that clients very much resist making, is that persistent patterns of behavior (e.g., marrying substance abusers, losing jobs, getting manipulated by others, etc.) are at least partially the result of the client's dynamics and expectations (e.g., Bauer & Kobos, 1987; Strupp & Binder, 1984; Teyber, 1997). It is probably not just fate, bad luck, or unfairness that explains why a pattern of bad things keeps happening. We emphasize the word *pattern*. Isolated problems that have very little to do with clients' choices can arise, and some recurring events happen (miscarriages and being a member of a marginalized group, as examples) that dramatically affect clients' quality of life but seem to be almost entirely outside of their control. But as a general rule, at least most of the patterns in relationships that clients discuss are partially "courted" by the clients themselves (one explanation of which may be their attachment styles, as discussed earlier). Almost always, such structuring of unfortunate patterns takes place unconsciously, which helps explain, of course, clients' angry resistance when confronted with the possibility that they are partially responsible. They do not *feel* responsible. They feel, in fact, helpless and often ashamed that sheer force of will is insufficient for them to extricate themselves.

The client who insists she wants her grown child out of the house but cannot find a way to get her to move is usually quite conscious of her anger and resentment but much less aware of how and why she has trouble enforcing limits. Nor is she aware that this difficulty has probably been evidenced in other relationships. The first approach used by many therapists with such a client in individual therapy will be educational and behavioral—helping her clarify her position relative to her daughter, teaching her assertive skills, and the like. But if that approach doesn't work, many times the therapist and client will step back a pace to examine what expectations, fears, guilt, and hopes keep her "stuck" in this and other relationships. Perhaps she will discover that, like many women, her identity seems to be at stake when important relationships feel threatened and that setting limits is perceived as threatening rather than enhancing (Gilligan, 1982). Or perhaps she will uncover promises she made to herself as a child about the way she would treat her children. Regardless, discovering some of the less conscious roots to her present behavior may aid her in feeling freer to take decisive action. As noted above, you can expect a strong defensive reaction if you suggest outright that the client has had a part in structuring the pattern that is being bemoaned. Any confrontations or interpretations you make will need to be phrased as empathically and tactfully as possible to enhance the likelihood that they will be heard. Strupp & Binder (1984) refer to this as the "principle of least possible confrontation" p. 107. For more on this topic, see Chapter 11, Resistance.

Complementary Expectations

An easy trap for beginning therapists to fall into is taking sides. (This is especially likely to happen if they hear only one point of view, but it is not uncommon when working with couples.) Typically, they will side with whomever they see as the underdog. What the client is having to go through seems so clearly unfair and unjust that they may focus exclusively on how the environment is blocking the client's progress. They may work very hard to help the client be more assertive, more proactive, more self-affirming—only to see that again and again he or she chooses to stay in relationships that appear totally unpromising. After this happens with a few hundred clients, many therapists become jaundiced and cynical. Why bother to help, they wonder, when clients keep sabotaging their best efforts?

The alternative to either naively buying into the client's point of view or to feeling angry and disillusioned if immediate change is not forthcoming is to understand from the beginning that the client is part of a system. We refer you to the complicated and often very insightful literature on systems therapy, one proposition of which is that people gravitate toward others with similar or complementary expectations. It is uncanny how predictably a person with low self-esteem and a difficulty setting limits finds an abuser for a mate.

Various writers have described typical patterns that they have observed. Strean (1985) identifies several of the couple patterns the psychodynamic writers have noted, including dominant/submissive, detached/demanding, romantic/rational, and love-sick/cold. By the time such a couple comes for counseling, the patterns between them are often very entrenched, and each of the partners feels completely justified in his or her position. The issue, as we see it, is not that clients feeling one down in destructive relationships do not feel that they need more. With few exceptions, they feel angry, hurt, or bewildered. The problem is that they do not believe they can *get* more. Their assumption, their belief about how life works, may be that they must settle for what they can get if they want to have any relationships at all, and to insist on mutuality and reciprocity will drive everyone away. That assumption, unsurprisingly, sets them up for exploitation. Conversely, someone who expects to be treated with respect, and will tolerate nothing less, frequently has a variety of rich and fulfilling relationships

We think you will find that your therapy is more effective if you resist the temptation to think of clients in terms of "games" they are playing. We also suggest that you not be overly infatuated with the concept of "secondary gains." The amount of human pain some clients experience is staggering. Many (though not all) of these clients would not tolerate such pain if they truly believed that there were other options. It will probably be more helpful if you see your task, as one therapist said, as getting them to the point where they can "believe in the impossible." Until they can begin to believe that they can have reciprocal, rich relationships they will probably continue to structure the same patterns and norms as before, albeit with new partners. (We note again at this point a consideration that threads throughout this book—that the relationship you offer clients can be crucial in this process of helping them to experience and thus believe in the "impossible." Your relationship with them is not equal or reciprocal in the usual use of the term, but the essential quality ingredients of respect and empathy and clear limits should be undeniable.)

Ambivalence about Intimacy

A final assumption about relationships is that people seem both to fear and to long for intimacy. Judith Viorst (1986) said it well: "And while we fiercely protect the boundaries of self…we also yearn to recapture the lost paradise of that ultimate connection" (p. 25). Finding a balance between isolation and engulfment is an ongoing dilemma for all of us. While there has been recent speculation that women consider relationships "safer" and more identity-enhancing than men (Gilligan, 1982; Kaplan, Miller, Stiver, & Surrey, 1991), this seems to be a matter of degree, not sharp distinction. Our impression is that part of the human condition is the strong, sometimes overpowering, need for affirmation from others and the concurrent vulnerability one feels if that affirmation is not forthcoming. Clearly, some people let their need for affirmation show more transparently than others. In working with these clients, you will sense an almost tangible longing. But those who try to deny their need (individuals with avoidant personalities, acting-out adolescents, abusive partners, etc.) are also transparent in their obsession with relationships. Their need to avoid pain and humiliation is simply the flip side of their need for intimacy.

Most student therapists are so relationship-oriented by nature that it comes as no great surprise to them that clients need human attachments. What is harder for them to understand is that the same clients who work so hard to attain intimacy sometimes also work very hard to sabotage their own efforts. Eventually, most therapists come to appreciate the power and potential danger of loving, and it begins to make more sense to them why clients are so ambivalent about intimacy. Person (1988) said it well: "While it is true that love can be an agent for personal growth and change, it is also a loose cannon on the deck of human affairs."

What are humans afraid of, in relation to intimacy? The answer seems to be that we are usually afraid of two things—engulfment and/or abandonment. People who are afraid of engulfment are likely to be quite consciously wary of being trapped, making commitments prematurely, or giving up their freedom.

(While it makes sense that this kind of fear would have its roots in early experiences of being controlled or smothered, that explanation does not always seem to apply.) Abandonment fears, conversely, are excruciatingly painful but for the opposite reason: The terror, as one client described it, is similar to being "lost in space, forever, all by myself." Our experience is that most people have both sets of fears, to a greater or lesser extent, but that one set usually predominates in a given individual (and that, predictably, such fears will be part of what the client brings into therapy). As you might guess, two people with complementary sets of fears often manage to find each other with considerable regularity and then set up a painful and enmeshed "dance" of approach/avoidance.

Dysfunctional Styles

The risk in categorizing and describing typical dysfunctional styles is that the categories will necessarily be somewhat arbitrary and will thus lend themselves to superficial treatment. We encourage you to see each client as a complex and multidimensional human being whom you will never fully understand. We offer the following descriptions in the hope that you will find the descriptions useful as you try to understand and help your clients, rather than simply relating to them by reacting to the dysfunctional styles, as others in their lives do.

Your task is to make sure you have more to offer them than automatic reactions and to maintain your therapeutic position of "compassionate dispassion." We believe that, at base, dysfunctional relationship styles derive from an attempt to control others so that one's needs for affirmation can be met, while the risk of pain is kept to a minimum, and that such a style was usually forged early in life. Given the vulnerability clients feel when their needs for acknowledgment and affirmation are unmet, there is a certain logic to their trying to control the ones in their lives whom they perceive as potential need satisfiers. Regardless of your personal feelings about such a "control" issue, this is perhaps less a moral issue than a practical one: Control rarely works in interpersonal relationships, and when it does, there is almost always a big cost. (For a theoretical discussion of one theory that draws on control as a central construct, see Rappaport, 1996.)

The controlling styles and underlying dynamics that are simplest to identify are those that rely on overt domination, such as physical or verbal abuse. The typical abusive partner, for example, is frequently "hooked" by jealousy and defiance—behaviors that make him or her feel inadequate and out of control. Their strong needs for attachment and their fears of abandonment lead them to defend against painful feelings of vulnerability by becoming abusive, in hopes that the offending partner will be bullied back into line. They may be relatively unaware of either the increasing resentment they engender or the damage they do to the trust in the relationship each time they resort to such tactics. Like other controllers, only perhaps more dramatically, they end up "winning the battle and losing the war." They succeed in getting their way in the short run, but they irreparably damage the relationship over time. At a bare minimum, such clients need help in learning new behaviors that are more functional, in understanding the long-term effects of their behavior, and in facing the reality of their helplessness to make others love them.

Only slightly less obvious in the attempt to dominate are clients commonly known as the "bulls in the china closet." These people are less overtly abusive than they are strong-willed and self-righteous. It simply does not often occur to them to treat others' needs and ideas with much respect; they operate in life as if their integrity depends on never being influenced by someone else. Often they bear some of the marks of the "detached personality" (Bowlby, 1973). Listening to others and accommodating their needs is thus quite difficult for them, and they tend to wear out both their friendships and work relationships quickly. Such clients have little experiential understanding of the creative give-and-take that leads to mutuality and reciprocity. If they cannot dilute their compulsive need to control others enough to acknowledge and respect others' separateness, they are likely to continue to sacrifice intimacy for dominance.

Another controlling style, often manifested by clients with narcissistic personality disorders, is one based on subtle, manipulative deception. The client who consciously pretends to be sick or helpless in order to gain her family's attention, the smooth adolescent who relies on false protestations of love to seduce his dates, the employee who lies about sick relatives to gain his boss's sympathy—individuals who make lifestyles of such tactics seem to do so because they do not trust their personal power to elicit affirmation from others. Rather than simply ask for what they want, they rely on untruthfulness to justify their requests. You may never see in your office the ones who have well-developed styles, for they are getting reinforced enough by others to make changing seem too risky. It is the ones who have been "caught" in the dishonesty or are in enough pain that they cannot deny their vulnerability who may be open enough to explore what they are up to and make some changes. As the first two groups substituted dominance for affirmation, so this group seems to substitute attention. At best, they have learned something about drawing others toward them but little about maintaining attachments in nonexploitative ways.

At the other side of the continuum from these overt controllers are the dependent individuals who attempt to control by pleasing. Frightened by the possibility of being abandoned or rejected, they become quite practiced at picking up on others' cues and trying to accommodate them. Their own preferences and needs are often ignored by both themselves and the other party as they focus on being pleasant, undemanding, and, as one client said, "irresistible." The resulting pain, anger, and diminishing self-respect frequently *do* lead many of these folks into therapy, where they need to learn to affirm their own needs more and to allow exploitation less. It is unlikely that they are consciously aware that their self-denial is a form of control and that they, like other controllers, are defending against feelings of vulnerability by sacrificing true intimacy for, in this case, the hope of a permanently harmonious relationship.

The group that is least likely to be viewed as exercising much control interpersonally is made up of very passive individuals. Certainly, there are many situations when relatively powerless people are abused and dominated. Especially when these are the very young, or ill, or elderly, or the victims of violent crimes like rape or murder, their choices are so limited as to be almost negligible. It is unconscionable to hold someone accountable when he or she has no power; such "blaming the victim" is both unfair and dishonest, and it contributes to clients' guilt (Ryan, 1971). Nonetheless, therapists who automatically champion the underdog in less extreme situations may be blinding themselves to the reality that some individuals who feel trapped and passive at least theoretically could make changes or extricate themselves from destructive relationships. As Perls (1969) reminds us, underdogs or "martyrs" often have more power than is immediately apparent. Part of your job as therapist will be to help your clients feel more empowered, when possible, and to encourage them to use that power wisely. You will discover that some individuals have become so accustomed to contact with an abuser that they have difficulty imagining themselves living without him or her. Placating, sometimes alternating with more assertive or aggressive behavior, tends to characterize some of the patterns of such individuals, as they search for a way to maintain contact with a minimum of pain.

The final group of controllers we wish to mention is one that attempts to maintain contact with others by adopting a combative style. They want engagement that is relatively equal—but without the vulnerability of intimacy. And so they fight, not just occasionally, but as a relationship habit. If two people with this style are in a relationship, they find ways to stay available to one another, but as adversaries; they succeed in forging attachment, but the bond is predicated upon conflict rather than cooperative relating.

McKay, Fanning, and Paleg (1994) identified eight basic fallacies that can lead to poor relationships. These are the cognitive underpinnings that keep dysfunctional styles in place, and we list them for those of you who work with individuals and couples utilizing cognitive approaches:

1. *tunnel vision*—focusing on the negative aspects of another and ignoring the positive ones
2. *assumed intent*—believing that on the basis of a few cues, one can know what another is thinking or intending
3. *magnification*—similar to catastrophizing; making mountains out of molehills
4. *global labeling*—as in "you always," "you never," "he is just irresponsible"
5. *good/bad dichotomizing*—seeing people and situations in bipolar ways
6. *fractured logic*—consists of a premise and conclusion that are independent of each other (e.g., "She obviously must hate me because she didn't support me in that discussion")
7. *control fallacies*—feeling completely responsible or completely powerless
8. *letting-it-out fallacy*—the belief that when others are wrong, you should punish and rage at them

Relationship Skills

Specific Skills

Many of the clients you will see will be very unhappy in some of their relationships, will ask for help in improving them, but will nonetheless feel quite sure that good relationships are more contingent on luck or chemistry than on aspects they can directly influence. They will ask for new ideas, but their underlying beliefs may keep them from implementing those ideas consistently. As indicated earlier, our suggestion is that helping them explore some of their early problematic attachments can be very helpful, but it is also possible to work on relationship issues almost entirely in the present, with either an individual or a couple.

What is it that people who have good relationships *do*? What different assumptions do they make? How do they think and behave differently from those in painful relationships? Sperry and Carlson's (1991) description of healthy patterns is, unsurprisingly, very much the opposite of the previous list of cognitive distortions. Healthy relationships are characterized by a willingness to see truth as relative instead of absolute, by an assumption of positive intent of others, by a belief that conflict can be resolved. (This, as you've probably noted, is another way to say that these individuals have the ingredients necessary for "secure" attachments.) They are often in relationships with individuals with whom they share a sense of mission. We would add, from our own experience and from drawing on others' writings, that they have a secure enough sense of their own identity that they can tolerate ambiguity and conflict without becoming desperate, and that they have ways of joking and playing that provide pleasure to both, and that they have the capacity to commit themselves to relationships without feeling trapped or anxious.

Other writers have discussed the specific behaviors that typify healthy relationships. Many of these fall into the broad category of communication skills, and a number of manualized procedures have been developed to enhance such skill-building in individuals and couples. Similarly, several-session and weekend workshops are popular for couple enrichment. Young and Long (1998) provide a summary of some of these, including PREP, RE, PAIRS, and Marriage Encounter. Many of these approaches cover the same basic elements, although the presentation of information and format of activities differ considerably. Some have a religious/spiritual flavor, which many participants find helpful.

Young and Long (1998) provide their own list of healthy couple behaviors, which they suggest that therapists reinforce when they see them in individuals or couples, and teach clients if they are lacking them.

1. *responsibility*—taking responsibility for one's role and refraining from blaming the other
2. *alignment of goals*—collaboration on some mutual goals
3. *encouragement*—offering support, acceptance, and confidence

4. *open communication*—expressing feelings openly and honestly
5. *empathic listening*—portraying respect and caring for the other's feelings and beliefs
6. *willingness to analyze and discuss the relationship*—identifying strengths and concerns in the relationship by both parties
7. *demonstration of affection*—expressing verbally and nonverbally one's valuing of the other, especially when differing opinions are expressed
8. *support of positive goals of the relationship*—creating appropriate boundaries so that relationship goals will be supported
9. *commitment to the equality of the relationship*—mutual sharing of workload and new goals and interests

To conclude this section, we would like to offer you one final perspective, since it comes out of considerable research effort. John Gottman, drawing on his background as a mathematician and research psychologist, has spent over twenty years observing couples' conversations and has identified patterns that lead some couples to stay together and others to split up. Four of his research findings are particularly noteworthy and can serve as the basis for various therapeutic interventions.

First, Gottman (1994) found that there were three different conflict interactional styles found in happy marriages. One style, probably the one that you would most expect, is based on mutual validation. These couples seemed to find it easy to communicate, stay calm even during conflict, empathize easily with the other's positions, and problem-solve efficiently. They were, as Gottman said, the psychologist's dream! The second style he described as "volatile"—couples who had a good time fighting and a good time making up. They were louder, often argued about trivial things, maintained high levels of engagement throughout their interactions, and also knew how and when to de-escalate arguments before they became destructive. The third successful style were conflict-avoiders. From the outside it was as if they avoided conflict by using understatements and hints. But because they spoke the same language, they communicated effectively and could resolve conflicts to their mutual satisfaction.

Second, Gottman found that happy couples had difficult moments in their relationship also—there were misunderstandings and frayed nerves and frustrations with each other. But the ratio of good interactions to bad ones was at least 5:1. This ratio seems magic: Fall below it and the relationship is in danger.

Third, he found that four communication blunders in conflict led to divorce: *criticism* (attacking another's personality instead of behavior), *contempt* (insulting or psychologically abusing the other), *defensiveness* (denying responsibility, making excuses, whining, negative body language, cross-accusations, etc.), and *stonewalling* (withdrawing into stony silence).

Finally, Gottman identified four skills that couples in conflict can learn that lead to successful resolution of the conflict and accordingly a happier relationship. These he described as *learning to calm down, speaking nondefensively* (this includes praising and admiring, moving toward anger in the partner instead of defending against it, reading facial expressions, complaining about behavior rather than personality traits, etc.), *validating* (apologizing, complimenting, etc.), and *overlearning* (continuing to practice these skills, even when you don't feel like it!).

Global Skills

We believe you will be more likely to help such clients if the suggestions you offer for present changes are not isolated into unrelated behaviors but instead fit into a contextual understanding of qualities and skills that tend to lead to deeper, richer relationships. You will discover as you read through the rest of this section that the skills mentioned not only overlap but are somewhat arbitrarily defined. They reflect the qualities of a mature, healthy adult who is relatively free of some of the control issues just discussed.

Self-Respect.   Without a belief that what they have to offer others is valuable and that they themselves are lovable, clients will continue to structure relationships that are unfulfilling, if not destructive. To build good relationships with others requires at least a marginal respect for oneself. We prefer the words *self-respect* or *self-affirmation*, old-fashioned as they may be, to the ubiquitous term *self-esteem*. Esteeming oneself is difficult to do if one has long ago internalized negative ways of relating to oneself and especially if one is behaving in ways that are nonestimable. Respecting oneself and affirming one's strengths and potential, conversely, are closer to conscious choices one can make in an ongoing way. As clients make new choices and refuse to collude with others in allowing themselves to be treated in ways that lack respect and affirmation, their relationships and views of themselves are likely to improve substantially. In a sense, they create their own "self-esteem," not by giving themselves empty self-affirmations, but by experiencing the rewards of making different choices.

Honoring One's Needs.   People who build healthy relationships tend to be relatively unapologetic about what they need and expect from others (Branden, 1985). Rather than ruminating about whether or not they have the "right" to need something, they behave in ways that suggest that reciprocity and mutuality are the only real options they will consider. They are more likely to see their needs as a contribution to the relationship—something that allows for their receptiveness to others' caring—and not simply as an inroad for possible injury and exploitation. Knowing and affirming what one needs from another is not, of course, a license to make childish demands to be rescued from self-responsibility. One must still be willing to grow up. But grown-ups, as well as children, have legitimate needs for deep, enhancing, mutual relationships, and your clients may benefit from your help in believing and acting on this concept.

Setting Limits.   A related skill that enhances relationships is the ability to set limits. Actually, this ties in closely with both respecting oneself and honoring one's needs; we should set limits or say no when, for example, someone purposely or inadvertently treats us in unacceptable ways. Many of your dependent clients will be quite fearful of saying no. It will probably be necessary for you to recouch this kind of "limit setting" for them in such a way that it is seen as part of the responsibility they have to define for another how they want and do not want to relate, rather than making the other person guess.

Setting limits does, in fact, involve some risks. Someone may like the individual less because of a stand he or she takes. On the other hand, not setting limits often involves higher risks in the long term, since the usual consequence is increased resentment and the gradual erosion of identity. For your clients to have more successful relationships, they will need to believe that the more clearly they define themselves and the various roles from which they operate, the more likely others will be to respect them. They will discover that limits are not, after all, just reflected by their no's; they can affirm, or say yes, more freely also when they can differentiate what they value and are willing to tolerate from what they cannot.

Listening and Responding.   As was discussed in Chapter 14, Responsibility, healthy relationships require that both parties have the ability to understand and respond with some consistency to each other's needs. Listening in the relationship thus becomes part of the ongoing process, since one's own and the other's needs and feelings are often in flux. One does not accomplish much by listening once and then stopping. The commitment to listen works best when it is directed to the continual exploration and discovery of the evolving issues relevant to the relationship. As Gilbert and Rachlin (1987) point out, such listening and nurturing have traditionally been more expected of women than of men but, especially among dual-career couples, need to be reciprocal for the relationship to thrive. Many of our clients will explain that they like to be needed, just not *too much* (perhaps because that would require them to set limits). As they work through some of their own dependency and responsibility issues, they will find it easier and more fun to listen and respond to others. With your help, they may even discover that listening and responding can be creative acts, from which they emerge more fulfilled and enhanced.

Tolerating Ambiguity and Conflict.   Healthy relationships tend to be characterized by harmony, cooperation, and pleasure. Conflict, nonetheless, is inevitable, since no two people have matching identities. Fearful as many of your clients will be of it, it is not the conflict of desires or preferences or values that is so destructive; it is the way the individuals deal with those conflicts that largely determines the prognosis of a relationship. Conflict is a test of one's ability to remain separate but still in a relationship. For your clients to do that, they will have to have a strong enough sense of their self that they can manage without the other's affirmation for a while. They will need to rely on their own resources without panicking until the conflict can be resolved. In major disagreements, this may take weeks or months. The same principle applies, however, with the common, small irritations that ensue when any two people spend extended periods of time together. As two people in conflict learn to expand their viewpoints to include the other's perspective, they will find that conflict resolution can be based optimally on a win-win approach (Campbell, 1984).

Committing Oneself.   The last quality we will mention that we see as an essential ingredient in healthy relationships is the ability to commit oneself to the ongoing relationship process. Although some of your clients may associate commitment with entrapment, we see commitment less as an eternally binding promise than as a willingness and desire to fully invest oneself. Commitment is not loyalty to the status quo (the name for that phenomenon is often "insecurity"), nor is it a sense of duty to the fulfilling of joyless responsibilities and obligations. Duty may well be virtuous and at times required, but it is usually more closely related to resignation and resentment than to the wholehearted investment in a life-enhancing process. Ideally, people make commitments from a position of strength, not weakness, and they do it because they believe such commitment will allow them an opportunity to nurture and enhance their self.

The clients you work with who are afraid of commitment may need your help in understanding that psychologically healthy people do not make commitments because they feel certain that no one "better" will come along; they make them because the interaction between them and the other person is so enhancing they do not want to live without it. If, after many relationships, clients still insist that the "right person" has just not crossed their path, the problem instead might be that they have not invested enough in any of the interactions to feel challenged and fulfilled (Yalom, 1980).

Therapeutic Considerations

There are several suggestions we offer for your consideration to help you as you work with clients on relationship issues. Some of these have been alluded to previously.

Educate Yourself Regarding Cultural Differences in Relationship Expectations, Values, and Styles.   As indicated in Chapter 10, Multicultural Counseling, research in the last 20 years has confirmed what clinicians have suspected all along—that men and women often approach relationship issues differently (Lawler, 1990), and that cultural norms exercise considerable influence over what individuals feel is appropriate behavior in relationships. To avoid imposing your own biases on your clients, it will be necessary to understand some of these between-group and within-group differences and to learn to work within the clients' worldviews as much as possible.

Become Familiar with the Professional and Popular Literature on Relationships.   Especially in this time of managed care and very brief therapy, there are a number of important areas in which we think you should develop expertise in order to be of maximum benefit to your clients. You need to know about attachment and loss, especially the grief process, nuances of which vary depending upon the relationship. (There are resources available describing parents losing children, young and adult children losing family members, loss of romantic relationship, loss of role through retirement, and the like.) You should be able to understand and know well enough to roleplay for your clients such skills as self-assertiveness, conflict resolution (including fair fighting and listening-during-conflict skills), problem solving, initiating friendships, negotiating in the business setting, and understanding and coping with very difficult people. Your clients need to know how to engage themselves in ways that are likely to be productive, as well as when to back off, relax, and take another perspective (this may include teaching them relaxation skills, self-comforting approaches, etc.) Among the many resources we have found helpful in our work with clients are Manuel Smith's *When I Say No, I Feel Guilty,* Harriet Lerner's *The Dance of Intimacy* and *The Dance of Anger,* Harriet Schift's *The Bereaved Parent,* Dan Kiley's *What To Do When He Won't Change,* Nathaniel Branden's *The Psychology of Romantic Love* and *Six Pillars of Self Esteem,* Sam Keen's *To Love and Be Loved,* Christine Courtois' *Healing the Incest Wound,* John Gottman's *Why Marriages Succeed or Fail,* Lucia Gilbert's *Having It All,* and Judith Viorst's *Imperfect Control.*

Monitor Countertransference. For a further exploration of this topic, refer to the specific chapter, Transference and Countertransference. At this point, we would only underscore two related issues: (a) The client's interactional patterns with you often provide valuable clues regarding his or her style with others, and (b) part of your responsibility to your clients involves your refraining from impulsively acting out your nontherapeutic reactions to them and instead consistently offering them a relationship that to some extent models those skills and qualities described in the previous section. When working with couples, it is especially important to monitor countertransference (Solomon and Siegel, 1997).

Encourage Empathy. Many of your clients will be experiencing relationship difficulties as a result of becoming polarized from their associates. In an attempt to defend their position and protect themselves from hurt or criticism, they may have quit listening to others or considering alternative perceptions. (It is difficult, after all, to prove to someone else that you are right and still listen.) Part of your task may be to simultaneously provide support and empathy for your clients and also help them broaden their understanding of what may be happening in a given situation. Asking occasional *well-timed* questions such as, "How does your wife feel about that?" or "What do you suppose was going on with him when he said that?" or "How did she feel differently after you made your point?" can begin to sensitize them to others' feelings. More dramatically, you may want to set up role plays or use imagery or a modified empty-chair technique to encourage a client to take on the role of someone he or she is in conflict with or does not understand. Similarly, well-timed narratives or self-disclosure, when blended with empathy, can serve to open a client to unexplored alternative perspectives. The timing of such interventions is crucial. Remember that from your clients' perspective, your challenging their point of view may seem as if you have broken the alliance and are now "against" them instead of "for" them. This is particularly likely if you are encouraging them to understand the position of someone with whom they are in a power struggle.

Investigate Overt Behavior.   In much of this book, we have suggested you focus heavily on the client's intra- and interpersonal dynamics. We would like to suggest at this point that you not forget to ask about what and how they communicate with others. Most therapists have been in the position from time to time of "stumbling on" a piece of client behavior that suddenly clarifies many of that client's difficulties (for example, finding out that in arguments the client withdraws and sulks). Accordingly, many of us have trained ourselves to routinely inquire about behavior, even if our orientation is far from behaviorist. We think you will understand your clients' relationships much more fully if you can get an idea of how they express anger, fear, vulnerability, affection, regret, and so forth. Asking specifically, "What did you do when you were feeling that?" is certainly one way to get such information. Other ways include asking related questions such as, "How would an objective observer have described you at that point?" or, with humor, "If I talked to your _____ , what would she tell me you had done?" Again, setting up a role play, either for the client to demonstrate how an event transpired or to rehearse new ways of coping, can give you valuable insights into your client's style. Presumably, you will be able to explain and model all of the relationship-enhancing skills we have listed earlier.

Certainly, the most direct way to learn about clients' interactions with others is to observe them, as in couples, family, or group therapy. One of the authors was astonished to discover, for example, that the reserved, middle-40s male she had been seeing individually for a year, and had understood to be somewhat fearful and subservient with his lover, was quite different when his partner came to the session. The fear and passivity he had alluded to in therapy were cloaked in a heavy veneer of defensiveness, and even when his lover reached out, he tended to respond with suspicion and veiled attacks. Being able to see how the system worked was very enlightening and offered new direction for therapeutic focus.

Discuss Others Discreetly.   In discussing with a client his or her relationship with another, it may be tempting for you to speculate on this absent third person's behavior or motives. We suggest professional restraint. Remember that your clients are not bound by confidentiality, although you are. Remember also that their styles in these outside relationships may be dysfunctional, and in a conflict they may be tempted to quote you. One of our students, for example, received an irate phone call at 1:00 A.M. from the boyfriend of a client, demanding to know if in fact she had called him a "jerk." (As it turned out, it was true that she had said, "He sounds like a real jerk," and she admitted in supervision that she had been tempted originally to use a more colloquial anatomical term than jerk.) The guideline we offer is that you exercise great caution in your speculations and that you never say anything about a third person unless you would be willing to say it if she or he were present.

Know Referral Sources.   Not everything that is helpful or therapeutic for a client takes place during the psychotherapy hour. If you can recommend to clients appropriate outside forms of help, you may be able to help them structure their "nontherapy" hours in ways that support the work the two of you are doing. Often therapists recommend relevant self-help books to clients who enjoy reading. Similarly, referrals are often made to such self-help groups as AA, Al Anon, Emotions Anonymous, Compassionate Friends, Tough Love, and the like, to give clients further support and insight as they struggle with relationship issues. You should become familiar with the groups in your area so that you can make knowledgeable suggestions. Finally, it will be important to become familiar with other community agency policies and procedures, such as psychiatric hospitalization procedures and police interventions, since some of your clients' relationship and personal issues may escalate to crisis proportions.

Never Assume You Have All the Answers.   After you have been practicing therapy for a while, you will learn, if you didn't already know it, that what makes relationships "work" cannot be fully identified. Some families, friends, colleagues, seem to break all the rules and still happily endure with each other; others that seem to do everything right, flounder and disintegrate. There really are no magic answers. We think Grudin (1982) summed it up well:

> Three-dimensional chess is an invitation to insanity. But human relationships, even of the simplest order, are like a kind of four-dimensional chess, a game whose pieces and positions change subtly and inexorably *between* moves, whose players stare dumbly while their powerful positions deteriorate into hopeless predicaments and while improbable combinations suddenly become inevitable. To make matters worse, some games are open to any number of players, and all sides are expected to win. (p. 95)

Summary

Many of your clients will want your help with their relationship difficulties. Some of them may be haunted by past experiences of abuse, neglect, or abandonment; others will be struggling with how to improve or extricate themselves from present relationships. As you attempt to help such individuals, a solid understanding of the interpersonal dynamics that lead to both healthy and dysfunctional relationships will be very important. We encourage you to listen carefully to the patterns your clients describe—and especially to attend to their habitual ways of interacting with you—so that you can help them resolve some of their pain from the past and create more fulfilling relationships in the present. We also encourage you to consider developing a skill level, especially skills needed in conflict, since, as Gottman (1994) discovered, it was less the presence of conflict than the overt behavior that led to happy or disastrous outcomes in relationships.

DISCUSSION QUESTIONS

- What can you identify as developmental precursors to any difficulties you have in relationships?

- As you listen to music in the next week, notice how various song writers depict relationships. What explicit and implicit messages do they carry that may be absorbed by the public?

- Of the concepts and research provided in this chapter, which do you think are relevant across cultures and generations? How universal are they?

BIBLIOGRAPHY

Atkinson, L., & Zucker, K. J. (Eds.). *Attachment and psychopathology.* New York: Guilford.

Bauer, G. P., & Kobos, J. C. (1987). *Brief therapy: Short term psychodynamic intervention.* Northvale, NJ: Aronson.

Bowlby, J. (1973). *Attachment and loss: Vol. 2, Separation: Anxiety and anger.* New York: Basic Books.

Branden, N. (1986). *To see what I see and know what I know.* New York: Bantam Books.

Campbell, S. (1984). *Beyond the power struggle.* San Luis Obispo, CA: Impact.

Davanloo, H. (1990). *Unlocking the unconscious.* Chichester, England: Wiley.

Davenport, D. (1982). Women—And the daimonic. *The Counseling Psychologist, 10,* 76–78.

Fonagy, P., Target, M., Steele, M., Steele, H., Leigh, T., Levinson, H., & Kennedy, R. (1997). Morality, disruptive behavior, borderline personality disorder, crime, and their relationship to security of attachment. In L. Atkinson & K. J. Zucker (Eds.), *Attachment and psychopathology* (pp. 171–195). New York: Guilford.

Freud, S. (1926/1961). Inhibitions, symptoms, and anxiety. *Standard edition.* London: Hogarth Press.

Gilbert, L., & Rachlin, V. (1987). Mental health and psychological functioning of dual-career families. *The Counseling Psychologist, 15,* 7–49.

Gilligan, C. (1982). *In a different voice.* Cambridge, MA: Harvard University Press.

Gottman, J. (1994). *Why marriages succeed or fail.* New York: Simon & Schuster.

Grudin, R. (1982). *Time and the art of living.* New York: Ticknor & Fields.

Guisinger, S., & Blatt, S. J. (1994). Individuality and relatedness. *American Psychologist, 49,* 104–111.

Hamilton, N. G. (1988). *Self and others: Object relations theory in practice.* Northvale, NJ: Aronson.

Holmes, J. (1993). *John Bowlby and attachment theory.* New York: Routledge.

Kaplan, A., Miller, J. B., Stiver, I., & Surrey, J. L. (Eds.). 1991. *Women's growth in connection.* New York: Guilford Press.

Lawler, A. (1990). The healthy self: Variations on a theme. *Journal of Counseling and Development, 68,* 652–654.

Malcolm, J. (1989, March 13). Reflections: The journalist and the murderer. *The New Yorker,* 38–73.

McKay, M., Fanning, P., & Paleg, K. (1994). *Couple skills: Making your relationships work.* Oakland, CA: New Harbinger.

Perls, F. (1969). *Gestalt therapy verbatim.* Lafayette, CA: Real People Press.

Person, E. S. (1988). *Dreams of love and fateful encounters.* New York: W. W. Norton.

Rappaport, A. (1996). The structure of psychotherapy: Control-Mastery theory's diagnostic plan formulation. *Psychotherapy, 33,* 1–10.

Ryan, W. (1971). *Blaming the victim.* New York: Vintage.

Sable, P. (1997a). Attachment, detachment, and borderline personality disorder. *Psychotherapy, 34,* 89–109.

Sable, P. (1997b). Disorders of adult attachment. *Psychotherapy, 34,* 286–296.

Solomon, M. F., & Siegel, J. P. (1997). *Countertransference in couples therapy.* New York: W. W. Norton.

Sperry, L., & Carlson, J. (1991). *Marital therapy: Integrating theory and technique.* Denver: Love Publishing.

Strean, H. (1985). *Resolving resistance in psychotherapy.* New York: Wiley.

Strupp, H., & Binder, J. (1984). *Psychotherapy in a new key.* New York: Basic Books.

Sullivan, H. S. (1954). *The psychiatric interview.* New York: W. W. Norton.

Teyber, E. (1997). *Interpersonal process in psychotherapy: A relational approach.* Pacific Grove, CA: Brooks/Cole.

Viorst, J. (1986). *Necessary losses.* New York: Ballantine.

Viorst, J. (1998). *Imperfect control.* New York: Simon & Schuster.

Yalom, I. (1980). *Existential psychotherapy.* New York: Basic Books.

Young, M. E., & Long, L. L. (1998). *Counseling and therapy for couples.* Pacific Grove, CA: Brooks/Cole.

16 A Final Note: Brief Therapy

In addition to the numerous traditional debates within academia about how best to train therapists, there are a number of debates within the helping professions—partially in response to developments external to those professions—that will likely have a significant impact on how one practices therapy in the twenty-first century. Indeed, some of these issues began to have a significant impact on practicum sites for counselors and psychologists in training during the 1980s. Issues now impacting discussions and/or practice in psychology and counseling include the issue of manualization of psychotherapy and empirically supported treatments (e.g., Nathan & Gorman, 1997; Silverman, 1996), prescription privileges (e.g., Olmedo, 1997), managed care (e.g., Pipal, 1995; Sank, 1997; Shueman, 1997; Steenbarger, Smith, & Budman, 1996), and brief therapy (e.g, Bloom, 1997; Cooper, 1995). Issues of managed care and brief therapy often "intersect" since managed care emphasizes brief therapy (e.g., Budman & Gurman, 1988; Miller, 1997a, 1997b). Each of these areas involves a vast literature and is far beyond the scope of this book; however, we give a very brief summary of one of the issues (brief therapy) because it is directly affecting so many training agencies. We have made several comments throughout the book about the implications of brief therapy for the respective topics under discussion.

Brief Therapy

One of the current "realities" of practicing psychotherapy is that short-term (or brief) therapy is now used in many settings. At times, its use is certainly mandated by a managed care arrangement, but there are also many agencies not directly involved in managed care that have adopted it as a model, perhaps most often for the same reason that managed care emphasizes it—cost savings. Furthermore, for practical reasons, many clients seem to prefer psychotherapy of a relatively brief duration, and some therapists prefer this model for philosophical reasons (Friedman, 1997). Other psychologists are quite opposed to the model (Miller, 1997a, 1997b). In any event, if you have not had a course in brief therapy, you should certainly read one or two books about it prior to being placed in a practicum setting, because more and more agencies are using some variant of it.

What is "brief" therapy? Of course this depends on the type of therapy; but just as a general idea, anything less than approximately 15 sessions can be considered brief therapy; 15 to 25 sessions may also be considered brief, depending on one's theoretical orientation. Brief therapy is a generic group of "therapies" that share some common assumptions and approaches, but which can also differ dramatically in style and process (Bloom, 1997). Some of these models call for screening clients carefully to evaluate their suitability for brief therapy; other models essentially take the position that any client can benefit from a brief format (Bloom, 1997). Although, when compared to our eclectic and integrative orientation, many brief therapy models tend to be more solution-focused (e.g., Miller, Hubble, & Duncan, 1996; Walter & Peller, 1992) and/or draw more heavily from cognitive therapy models, we believe that there is little of "common clinical wisdom" that is not applicable to brief therapy. For example, brief therapy models have often emphasized the importance of the therapeutic relationship (Cooper, 1995). Furthermore, issues concerning ethics, the fears of clients, therapist fears, and the like, obviously also apply to brief therapy. Because many students have not had an introduction to short-term therapy, we briefly describe the basic tenets of more generic models such as that of Cooper (1995).

Although there are many types of brief therapy (they essentially cover the entire theoretical spectrum), the great majority of them have at least seven elements in common.

1. Every session (and every part of each session) is designed to accomplish something. Essentially this means that you do not have the luxury of "wandering around the therapeutic landscape." There is an emphasis on doing something "today" (Walter & Peller, 1992) that makes a difference in the life of the client. For example, reframing the problem so that it is seen as an attempted solution may help clients begin to see themselves as actually wanting positive things to happen; helping the client generate hope about the possibility of change may help lift depression and begin a cycle of focused effort by the client. These two examples, recognizing client strengths and assisting the client in generating hope, are examples we emphasized in Chapter 6, Intake Interviewing; these essentially represent "common clinical wisdom."

2. The treatment is highly focused in terms of problem identification. The problem chosen for treatment should be negotiated with the client and mutually agreed upon. Once a focus has been selected (problem identified), there is emphasis on working to solve that problem rather than being drawn into other areas. This process of identifying and "sticking with" a focus brings with it two challenges: There is a premium on being able to identify a significant problem, and there must be skill on the part of the therapist to continue to focus on that problem to the exclusion of others. One's broad-based training in assessment and diagnosis may be particularly helpful in identifying the problem. Obviously some probing is necessary. For example, one client came to therapy complaining that she was about to move into a university residence hall, but had a fear of the dark and wanted to rid herself of this fear (that is, she was afraid that at a certain time during the night all the lights would be turned off in the building). Only a naive therapist would immediately begin to work on helping her lose her fear of the dark without considering what more fundamental problems (in this case anxiety about leaving home) might be operating.

Especially with some types of clients, this "sticking with" the chosen focus may bring great challenges in that clients may try repeatedly to change the focus from one problem to another. The result of such changes may be a lack of progress on *any* problem. A part of this issue (identifying and continuing to focus on the problem) involves the therapist's being able to tolerate the anxiety that comes from making choices (with the client). To decide on a focus and continue it means that sacrifices must be made. The sacrifice lies in being willing to give up the possibility of solving other problems. This does not mean that one *never* changes the focus. Suppose that in the fourth session the client says, "We've been talking about how to make my marriage better and I've come to the conclusion that I do not want to be married." Again, only a therapist with poor skills would say something to the effect of, "I'm sorry, we can't discuss divorce right now because we need to have a few more sessions about how to make your marriage better." In fact, in this case, perhaps the client has just become anxious about his or her new way of being in the relationship, but unless the therapist knows that or can conclude that, the therapist must pay some attention to this new development in therapy. On the other hand, if the client has committed to working on her relationship with her boyfriend and then suddenly decides that it is her relationship with her father that she really wants to work on, the therapist would perhaps be hesitant about switching the treatment focus until some improvement was noted in the relationship with the boyfriend. The degree of flexibility afforded the therapist in this regard varies somewhat from model to model, but in all of them the therapist clearly makes an effort to continue to deal with the problem that had been identified as the one to focus on in therapy.

In selecting goals for short-term work, one tries not to ignore the focus that might be employed if one had longer to work. That doesn't mean it can always be adhered to, but it should not be contradicted. For example, if a client has long-term authority issues, which leak out all over the place—with his own parents, with bosses, with his wife and kids, with his employees—then if he's in major trouble with his boss, about to get fired, and needs to work on stress reduction, keeping his mouth shut, and so forth, it should be remembered that the messages we give him about how to respond to authority will likely carry over to how he expects others to respond to *his* authority. We may help in one area, but inadvertantly set him up for difficulties in another if we're too simplistic.

3. Therapeutic goals that can be accomplished are selected. There are two implications. First, there is an emphasis on selecting goals, the accomplishment of which can be judged by a specific criterion. The goals, "I would like to feel better," or "I would like to be more assertive," would need to be refined and specified behaviorally. Additionally one must choose goals that can in fact be accomplished.

"Self-actualization" would not be a therapeutic goal. In part, this emphasis on the type and quality of the goal expresses the idea of accountability, which is an assumption that is often implied, but not stated in brief therapies. Of course, behavior therapy has always stressed the quality of the goal for any type of therapy, but this idea of an achievable goal runs very strongly through the brief therapy literature. Friedman (1997) emphasizes that the goal should be stated in positive language (what the client *wants*, rather than what he or she *doesn't want*).

4. Homework is frequently assigned. There are at least three reasons for assigning homework. First, depending on the type of homework, it may help the client generalize the work that is going on in therapy. Second, it may help clients feel that they are taking action on their own behalf. This process may help reduce depression and help give clients a new sense of mastery. Third, homework gives the client a sense of investment in, and commitment to, psychotherapy. Therefore, assuming that the homework is cooperatively endorsed by the client, the process of carrying out the therapeutic plan may be made easier.

5. The therapeutic relationship is very important because resistance, distrust, and lack of involvement by the client may doom the enterprise to failure. With perhaps one or two exceptions, the brief therapy literature emphasizes that the therapist must be able to elicit the cooperation of the client and should be seen by clients as working diligently in their best interests. Sustained negative feelings are seen as a significant threat to the effectiveness of therapy; attempts are made to maintain a good working relationship throughout therapy. Again, this emphasis is clearly seen in the idea of common clinical wisdom.

6. As implied above, the client is highly involved in the treatment, and is consulted repeatedly on goals and progress. Feedback is solicited from the client with a view to empowering the client and ensuring full cooperation.

7. There is a focus on the present rather than the past. This does not mean that the client should not discuss things that have happened in the past, but the general thrust of therapy is forward. In focusing on the present and future, the therapist notes how clients have solved similar problems in the past. Clients are viewed as having previously solved many problems and as capable of addressing new ones effectively. A related assumption is that you should try to identify client strengths. These often are building blocks for solutions to problems.

In addition to the general principles just summarized, there are obviously a number of implications for clinicians. These include being able to write problem-oriented, goal-focused treatment plans with specific interventions. Clients should be encouraged to feel pride at modest gains, reassured that continued growth can occur outside of treatment, and invited to return for additional work as necessary (Schreter, 1997).

As noted, the principles above are common to many forms of brief therapy. In the majority of agencies where psychotherapy is practiced, it is simply not possible to engage in one's favorite type of therapy without regard to length of treatment and accountability. Sadly, many of our training programs have failed to respond adequately to this change. This is not to say that the "old" theories do not apply. It is to say that the *meaning* of the old-fashioned virtue of practicing psychotherapy for the client's welfare is up both for discussion and scrutiny. Furthermore, the question of whether a particular type of therapy or intervention is worth paying for has never been more pressing. To advance psychology as a science, to do well by those whom we seek to serve, and to preserve both our vision and our grasp of the essential ingredients of the art of psychotherapy—these are our goals in an era of brief therapy and managed care.

BIBLIOGRAPHY

Bloom, B. L. (1997). *Planned short-term psychotherapy: A clinical handbook* (2nd ed.). Boston: Allyn and Bacon.

Budman, S. H., & Gurman, A. S. (1988). *The theory and practice of brief therapy.* New York: Guilford.

Cooper, J. F. (1995). *A primer of brief psychotherapy.* New York: W. W. Norton.

de Shazer, S. (1994). *Words were originally magic.* New York: Norton.

Friedman, A. (1997). *Time-effective psychotherapy: Maximizing outcomes in an era of minimized resources.* Boston: Allyn and Bacon.

Hoyt, M. (Ed.). (1994). *Constructive therapies.* New York: Guilford.

Hoyt, M. (Ed.). (1996). *Constructive therapies 2.* New York: Guilford.

Miller, I. J. (1997a). Some "short-term therapy values" are a formula for invisible rationing. *Professional Psychology: Research and Practice, 27,* 577–582.

Miller, I. J. (1997b). Time-limited brief therapy has gone too far: The result is invisible rationing. *Professional Psychology: Research and Practice, 27,* 567–576.

Miller, S. D., Hubble, M. A., Duncan, B. L. (Eds.). (1996). *Handbook of solution-focused brief therapy.* San Francisco: Jossey-Bass.

Nathan, P. E., & Gorman, J. M. (Eds.). (1997). *A guide to treatments that work.* New York: Oxford University Press.

Olmedo, E. L. (Ed.). Psychopharmacology and prescription privileges I (Special Section). *Profes-sional Psychology: Research and Practice, 28,* 101–127.

Pekarik, G., & Wolff, C. B. (1996). Relationship of satisfaction to symptom change, follow-up adjustment, and clinical significance. *Professional Psychology: Research and Practice, 27,* 202–208.

Pipal, J. E. (1995). Managed care: Is it the corpse in the living room: An expose. *Psychotherapy, 32,* 323–332.

Sank, L. I. (1997). Taking on managed care: One reviewer at a time. *Professional Psychology: Research and Practice, 28,* 548–554.

Schreter, R. K. (1997). Essential skills for managed behavioral health care. *Psychiatric Services, 48,* 653–658.

Shueman, S. A. (1997). Confronting health care realities: A reply to Sank (1997). *Professional Psychology: Research and Practice, 28,* 555–558.

Silverman, W. H. (1996). Cookbooks, manuals, and paint-by-numbers: Psychotherapy in the 90's. *Psychotherapy, 33,* 207–215.

Sperry, L., Brill, P. L., Howard, K., & Girssom, G. R. (1996). *Treatment outcomes in psychotherapy and psychiatric interventions.* Philadelphia: Brunner/Mazel.

Steenbarger, B. N., Smith, H. B., & Budman, S. H. (1996). Integrating science and practice in outcomes assessment: A Bolder model for a managed era. *Psychotherapy, 33,* 245–253.

Walter, J. L., & Peller, J. E. (1992). *Becoming solution-focused in brief therapy.* New York: Brunner/Mazel.

NAME INDEX

SUBJECT INDEX